**Praise for Anthony Dias Blue's**
*American Wine: A Comprehensive Guide* (the hardcover book on which this guide is based):

"Bravo for a voluminous, courageous undertaking. A most informative and interesting reference work on American wines for everyone's vinous bookshelf."
—Alexis Lichine

"I doubt there's anyone in this country who knows more about American wines than Anthony Dias Blue. For years I've admired his unique insights on the subject, his ability to simplify a very complex topic . . . and, to be sure, his keen palate."
—James Villas, Food & Wine Editor,
*Town & Country*

"A preliminary investment in *American Wine* could easily save many times the price of the book by avoiding inappropriate choices."
—*The Plain Dealer*, Cleveland

"I doubt if anyone has tasted as many American wines as Andy Blue, and I know no one has assembled so many clean, unpretentious, and pungent tasting notes."
—Harvey Steiman, Managing Editor,
*The Wine Spectator*

"The wine event of the year! . . . the most complete, comprehensive volume currently available . . . entertaining and in-depth report . . . an incomparable star-system rating . . . an invaluable survey. . . . It may be the most important book on American wine ever written."
—*East Side Wine News*

"It's a dandy. . . . Don't go into a wine store again without a copy of *American Wine* under your arm. . . . The first and only book on wine I'd put my money on. Besides being an excellent resource, it makes good reading."
—Kit Snedaker, Food Editor,
Los Angeles *Herald Examiner*

"A lively and very handsome volume."
—Frank Prial, *The New York Times*

"Should be on the shelf of all wine drinkers."
—Larry Walker, *San Francisco Chronicle*

"An impressive work . . . a corker."
—Jack Schreibman, Associated Press

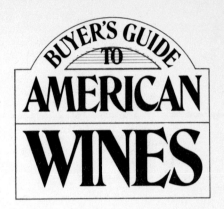

BUYER'S GUIDE
TO
AMERICAN
WINES

# ANTHONY DIAS BLUE

# BUYER'S GUIDE TO AMERICAN WINES

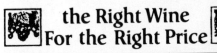

the Right Wine
For the Right Price

Authoritative Ratings Of
More Than 5,000 Currently
Available Wines From
America's Foremost Expert

PERENNIAL LIBRARY

Harper & Row, Publishers, New York
Cambridge, Philadelphia, San Francisco, Washington
London, Mexico City, São Paulo, Singapore, Sydney

BUYER'S GUIDE TO AMERICAN WINES. Copyright © 1988 by Anthony Dias Blue. All rights reserved. Printed in the United States of America. No part of this book may be used or reproduced in any manner whatsoever without written permission except in the case of brief quotations embodied in critical articles and reviews. For information address Harper & Row, Publishers, Inc., 10 East 53rd Street, New York, N.Y. 10022. Published simultaneously in Canada by Fitzhenry & Whiteside Limited, Toronto.

FIRST EDITION

Library of Congress Cataloging-in-Publication Data

Blue, Anthony Dias.
   Buyer's guide to American wines.

   1. Wine and wine making—United States. I. Title.
TP557.D533   1988b      641.2'22'0973      87-46121
ISBN 0-06-09274-7 (pbk.)

88 89 90 91 92 MPC 10 9 8 7 6 5 4 3 2 1

# Contents

# Contents

# Acknowledgments

Juggling thousands of tiny bits of data and keeping everything straight is a difficult job. The coordinator of this project was hardworking assistant editor Jack Weiner, who confirmed every wine fact and figure in the book. His close helpmate was the amazing data management system DBASE III PLUS, which handled and processed all the raw data and turned it into a coherent whole.

Editor Pat Brown shepherded the project through the publishing maze and Pamela Mosher labored long hours making the manuscript readable, supervising the design, and getting it set into type. She also worked closely with computer whiz William B. Smith, who created a space-age program for turning my scribblings and tasting notes into a book.

Thanks also to *Bon Appétit* magazine and *The Wine Spectator*, whose organized tastings have been so important in helping me assemble the judgments contained in this book. Finally, I want to thank my family for cheerfully enduring my ongoing tasting ordeal.

# Introduction

The idea of this book is simple: to help you get as much enjoyment from American wines as possible.

Buying American wines can be a hit-or-miss affair. Although the government requires that certain information appear on each wine label, there still is no sure way for the consumer to know about the quality of the wine inside the bottle. Among European wines, there are certain estates that have established long-standing reputations for making superior wines. Most American wineries, on the other hand, haven't been around long enough to have established such a track record.

The American wine industry is young and still quite volatile; a great Chardonnay from a particular winery one year doesn't guarantee an equally delicious effort the next year. With established French or Italian wines the differences between bottlings from different years are mainly attributable to variations of weather. But in the United States, even if the climate remains the same over the different years, the winery may have changed winemakers, purchased its grapes from a different source, or just made its wine in a different style. In each circumstance the wine will taste different. Consequently, the purpose of this book is to take the unpleasant surprises out of your wine buying.

## Why Trust Me?

Over the past year or two I have tasted and rated more than 5,000 wines. Although I was unable—much as I may have wished otherwise—to taste absolutely everything on the market, I would guess that the wines rated in this book represent more than 90 percent of the American wines you are likely to encounter at your local wine shop.

I tasted the vast majority of the wines "blind"—with the label hidden—and I tasted most of them more than once. Twice every week I meet with a small group of wine professionals to taste between thirty and fifty wines. These intensive exercises, carried out under the aegis of *Bon Appétit* magazine and *The Wine Spectator*, allow me to keep up with the continuous flow of new releases.

In addition, I have judged a host of comprehensive wine events in California and elsewhere. I also attend many industry wine tastings, and I constantly sample wines at home, where my wife is not at all delighted with the half-empty wine bottles cluttering up the kitchen.

So I've tasted many wines—what qualifies me to judge them? I can tell you that I have an excellent, well-trained palate, and I can spot volatile acidity or mercaptans at fifty paces. But that's not enough. I am also extremely consistent. When I hold a wine up to a standard set of criteria, I come away with a judgment that complements all the judgments that have gone before. I have tested myself frequently by tasting the same wine at several different times and comparing the notes recorded at each tasting, and there is almost never a serious disparity in my ratings.

It is these tasting notes that set this book apart from most other wine books that have come before it. They represent my personal opinions, but they are thorough, informed, carefully achieved, and consistent. So if you agree with me on one or two wines, you will probably agree with me on most of them.

## How I Judge Wines

Every professional taster agrees that there are certain characteristics that make some wines unacceptable. Oxidation (spoilage due to excessive exposure to oxygen), volatile acidity (sour, vinegary acid), and dirtiness or bacterial spoilage (the result of sloppy winemaking) are some of the most noticeable problems. Luckily not many wines are so blatantly flawed, so most wines are not so clearly classifiable.

Too many people who taste wine will break a wine down into its various components—clarity, aroma, balance, mouth feel, sweetness, varietal character, finish, aging potential—but will neglect to form an impression of the wine as a whole. Many winemakers and enology professors will criticize a wine that has a minor flaw, despite the fact that it may be delicious and quite enjoyable to drink.

## A Wine Taster's Lexicon

For me, the bottom line in wine judging is "Does it taste good?" I like to think that I have a consumer's palate; I steer clear of technical terminology and pretentious pronouncements. In my tasting notes I haven't tried to reach dizzying literary heights. In fact, you'll find the notes fairly repetitive, because I use the same words to describe the same characteristics. Here are some of the most frequently used descriptives:

*Big*: Robust, intense, full-bodied, usually with high alcohol. Synonym: *fat*.

*Body*: The richness and viscosity of a wine, usually tied closely to the amount of alcohol in the wine.

*Buttery*: Having the taste of butter. Actually, the compound that gives wine a buttery taste is the same that is found in butter.

*Clean*: This is one of the most important characteristics of good wine. Modern technology has made it possible to avoid the dirt and spoilage that used to plague the winemaking process. Well-made wines should always be clean.

*Coarse*: Crude, simple, lacking finesse.

*Complex*: Having depth, intricacy and subtlety of flavor.

*Crisp*: This refers to fresh, fruity acidity which is a highly desirable quality, especially for white wines. Synonyms: *snappy*, *tart*, *brisk*.

*Dull*: Flat, lifeless, lacking crispness.

*Elegant*: Having complexity and finesse without being aggressive or heavy.

*Fruity*: The taste of fresh fruit (apples, pears, cherries, grapefruit and, especially, grapes). This is a characteristic of well-made young wines.

*Grassy*: A herbaceous flavor that is often characteristic of Sauvignon Blanc. Attractive as a part of a whole, but overbearing when too pronounced.

*Herbaceous*: A characteristic which is desirable in small quantity. Subtle herbal flavors are associated with Cabernet Sauvignon and Sauvignon Blanc.

*Long*: This refers to a wine's flavors lasting a prolonged time in the mouth after the wine has been tasted.

*Oaky*: The flavors of wood, toast and vanilla that come from good oak barrels.

*Oxidized*: A spoilage condition caused by excessive exposure to oxygen in air. Oxidation causes a wine to lose its fruitiness and freshness.

*Raisiny*: The dried grape flavor that appears in wines made from overripe fruit.

*Residual sugar*: Unfermented sugar that remains in a finished wine. A small amount of residual sugar rounds the flavor of a wine. More than half a percent of residual sugar (by weight) will begin to make the wine taste sweet.

*Silky*: Smooth and light in texture and mouth feel.

*Soft*: Lacking harshness; smoothly textured.

*Structure*: A very important element of any wine, especially reds. A good Cabernet Sauvignon, for instance, should have a firm backbone of acidity, upon which all of its other characteristics hang. This backbone gives the wine structure and indicates that it will age well. Without structure a wine is flabby, shapeless, lacking in promise, and ultimately flawed.

*Tannic*: Characteristic of young red wines, tannin manifests itself as an astringent, puckery feeling in the mouth. It can be a product of the grape or of the oak in which the wine is stored. Eventually—in the ideal scenario—the tannin softens and allows the fruit and varietal character of the wine to show through.

*Varietal character*: The particular flavor of the grape variety used in making the wine. Definitely a desirable characteristic.

*Velvety*: Soft, thick and smooth on the palate.

*Vegetal*: Smelling and/or tasting of vegetables. This could manifest itself in a number of ways, all of them unattractive. Some of the more common vegetable likenesses that show up are bell peppers, asparagus, and broccoli.

*Vinous*: A heavy, sometimes oily quality that tastes more of leaves and stems than fruit.

*Volatile acidity*: A vinegary taste brought about by the presence of acetic acid and ethyl acetate. Acceptable in small amounts but very undesirable in large quantities.

The rest of my descriptive terms should be easily understandable, but a few technical terms need defining. They are:

*Botrytis*: Short for *botrytis cenera*, the Latin name for a mold that attacks grapes on the vine and dehydrates them, thereby intensifying their sugar content. Wines made from these grapes are sweet and rich. In the United States such wines are usually designated as "late harvest."

*Carbonic Maceration*: The technique used most frequently in France's Beaujolais district, in which whole uncrushed clusters of grapes are put into the fermenting tank. The resulting wine is fruity and ready to drink when quite young.

*Solera*: A stack of barrels that is used in making sherry. The young wine is placed in the top barrels, which are exposed to the heat of the sun, thus giving the wine its nutty flavor. As the wines age, they are transferred to lower barrels in the solera until they reach the bottom level, from which they are bottled.

## Personal Prejudices

I must confess some preferences and prejudices. Everyone can look back at magical moments, crucial events that changed the direction of their lives. I like to think about the summer of 1952, when at age eleven I was dragged kicking and screaming to France. My parents wanted me to get some culture; I wanted to stay home and play baseball with my friends.

One of our stops was Beaune because my father was particularly fond of the wines of the Burgundy region. I remember one morning in particular: We drove to Pommard, where we visited the cellar of a small producer. The place was dark and rank. The farmer, a fellow with wide suspenders and a two-day growth of beard, offered me a taste of wine in a chipped and dirty glass. Before my parents could object I put the glass to my lips and drank.

Then came the thunderclap, the drum roll. This glorious wine from the 1949 vintage jolted me like nothing I had experienced before. In an instant I was transformed from a reluctant traveler into a wine lover. I'll never forget that velvety, rich, explosive flavor; it has stood as a model for all the other wine experiences of my life.

Aside from its dramatic aspects, this event made me a lover of Pinot Noir and an appreciator of French wines. Even

today, thirty-six years later, I am a great fancier of Pinot
Noir, and I also tend to like wines that are French in style—
which means I generally prefer wines with good, firm acidity.

I am very sensitive to the vegetal qualities that show up in
many American Cabernet Sauvignons and Merlots. I like my
wines on the young side—one to three years old for whites,
two to five years old for reds—and I appreciate the judicious
use of oak barrels in the making of wine.

## What About Cellaring?

In my comments about some Cabernets and a few other wines
I have tried to project when the better ones will reach their
optimum drinkability. When I say "drink 1991" I don't mean
1991 is the only year in which the wine should be consumed. If
a good wine reaches its maturity in 1991 it should stay at that
level for at least three or four years, maybe more. If, like me,
you prefer wine on the youthful side, you should probably
shave a year or two off the ready date; if you like them well
aged, hold them for a year or two after the date given.

## Special Designations

I have tried to identify each wine as fully as possible. In most
cases you will find the year, the variety, the vineyard, the ap-
pellation (the geographic place of origin), the price, and any
special designations, such as "Reserve" or "Late Harvest," that
are recorded on the label. These distinctions are important,
because many wineries produce a number of wines of the same
variety in the same year. When you want to pair a wine up
with a rating in the book, be sure to pay attention to all
of these.

## Price

Price is the most inexact of the book's elements. I have tried to
list the suggested retail price, which is usually the price
charged in the winery tasting room. But in the highly competi-
tive wine market, very few retail establishments actually take
the full markup, which means you are likely to find many of
the wines at prices 10 to 25 percent below those listed in the
book. If you live in or near a large metropolitan area, you are
more likely to be able to buy wines at discounted prices. If you
are unfortunate enough to live in a state where wine sales are
still controlled by the state, the prices may very well be higher.

## The Rating System

In this book I have used six different ratings: "✰✰✰✰," "✰✰✰," "✰✰," "✰," no stars, and "○." Let me explain each of these:

✰✰✰✰      This is the top rating, given to only a very few "outstanding" or "extraordinary" wines. Some of these show great aging potential, but most of them are wines that will provide you with a superb, world-class drinking experience right now. For those who are familiar with the twenty-point rating system, these four-star wines would correspond to those rated eighteen points or better. In the 100-point system they would be 90 points or better. (Of 5,534 wines rated, 258 were awarded ✰✰✰✰. This represents 4.7 percent of all wines rated.)

✰✰✰      These are wines I have rated "excellent," among the very best wines in the marketplace. These are wines for special occasions, wines for cellaring. Most three-star wines finished close to the top in their tastings. Three stars corresponds to sixteen or seventeen points on the twenty-point scale, 80 points or better on the 100-point scale. (2,019 wines were awarded ✰✰✰. This represents 36.5 percent of all wines rated.)

✰✰      These are wines that I have judged to be "very good." Two-star wines are appealing, everyday wines with no serious faults. These are luncheon wines, pizza wines, picnic wines, casual wines that are quite pleasant without demanding a great deal of attention. Two stars corresponds to fifteen points on the twenty-point scale, or better than 70 on the 100-point scale. (1,846 wines were awarded ✰✰, which represents 33.4 percent of all wines rated.)

✰      These are wines that I have rated "good." One-star wines are drinkable but lack depth, charm, style, or a combination of these traits. These wines are not repugnant, but they offer little more than liquid refreshment. One star corresponds to fourteen points on the twenty-point scale or 60 points ("acceptable") on the 100-point scale. (847 wines were awarded ✰. This represents 15.3 percent of all wines rated.)

No Stars.      These are wines that I have rated "fair"—marginal wines that suffer from one, two, or a combination of flaws. These wines should be avoided if possible. No stars corresponds to thirteen points on the twenty-point scale, or 50 or better on the 100-point scale. (456 wines were awarded no stars, which represents 8.2 percent of all wines rated.)

○      These are wines that I have judged to be "poor," seriously flawed wines that should be avoided at all costs. They have characteristics that render them undrinkable. This rating corresponds to less than thirteen points on the twenty-point scale, or less than 50 points on the 100-point scale. (107 wines were rated "O," representing 1.9 percent of all wines rated.)

## Good Value Wines

In addition to these ratings, I have occasionally designated a wine as a "good value." Good-value wines are the entries in red. There are no set rules for these wines except that they impressed me as being good or very good wines that were definitely underpriced. For this reason a good-value Chenin Blanc might have to be less than $4 while a good-value Chardonnay could easily cost $8.

Many wines are released without a vintage date. These non-vintage wines are denoted by the letters "NV."

## The American Way

As I worked on this book and got to know the people who make up our domestic wine industry, I was struck by the differences between American winemakers and those I have encountered in Europe. Unlike the vintners of France and Italy, who come out of an agricultural tradition that goes back hundreds of years and many generations, most American winemakers are new to wine and have made a conscious commitment to winemaking as a career. For many, being in the wine business is the fulfillment of a lifelong dream. American vintners are a dedicated band of individualists who are in the business by choice. They do what they do because they love it, not because they have to or because they think they are going to get rich. (One of the favorite quips among winemakers in California is "Do you know how to make a small fortune in the wine business? Start with a big fortune.")

I have been very impressed by the generally high quality of the wines that are being produced in the United States. Fine wines are being made in California, New York, Oregon, and Washington—that we know. But they are also beginning to appear with regularity from such places as Maryland, Virginia, Ohio, New Jersey, Idaho, and Texas.

Although there are a substantial number of "fair" and "poor" ratings in the book, there are also a remarkable number of "very good" and "excellent" wines. I have subjected all these wines to tough, uncompromising scrutiny; there has been no room for chauvinism. In fact, many of the tastings at which these judgments were made were not limited to American wines. Foreign wines were judged along with the products of domestic wineries.

American wines easily hold their own when judged against wines from abroad. And especially now, with the dollar low against European currencies, the best American wines represent a remarkable value by comparison. Among inexpensive wines there is no contest—American jug wines offer considerably more consistency and depth than the ordinary plonk that is exported to the United States from abroad. Among premium wines, America's best bottlings are now just as good (if not better) as the best from abroad, and at current prices they are nothing less than amazing bargains.

The American wine industry has arrived. It offers endless variety as well as excellent quality. I hope this book helps maximize your enjoyment of the many enological delights that await you.

る

BUYER'S GUIDE
TO
AMERICAN
WINES

# The Wines

## *Acacia Winery*                    NAPA COUNTY

### WHITE

☆☆☆ 1982 CHARDONNAY ($12.50) Napa Valley. *Crisp, clean, lovely fruit, good balance.*

☆☆☆ 1982 CHARDONNAY ($16.00) Marina, Napa Valley-Carneros. *Vinous, good oak, rich and clean.*

☆☆☆ 1982 CHARDONNAY ($17.50) Winery Lake, Napa Valley-Carneros. *Lovely, rich oak; great varietal character and ripe fruit.*

☆☆☆ 1983 CHARDONNAY ($12.50) Napa Valley. *Fatter than the others. Ripe, oaky, very nice.*

☆☆☆ 1983 CHARDONNAY ($14.00) Napa Valley-Carneros. *Oaky, fruity, charming.*

☆☆☆ 1983 CHARDONNAY ($15.00) Marina, Napa Valley-Carneros. *Crisp, balanced, slightly vinous, lovely.*

☆☆☆ 1983 CHARDONNAY ($17.50) Winery Lake, Napa Valley-Carneros. *Oaky, rich, firm fruit, deep.*

☆☆ 1984 CHARDONNAY ($12.50) Napa Valley. *Greenish, disjointed, although clean and varietal.*

☆☆☆☆ 1984 CHARDONNAY ($14.00) Napa Valley-Carneros. *Concentrated, intense, lovely oak. Beautiful flavors and length.*

☆☆☆ 1984 CHARDONNAY ($15.00) Marina, Napa Valley-Carneros. *Lovely fruit, clean flavors, good balance.*

☆☆☆ 1985 CHARDONNAY ($9.00) Vin de Lies, Napa Valley. *Ripe, fresh, balanced, clean, quite lovely.*

☆☆ 1985 CHARDONNAY ($14.00) Napa Valley. *Simple, heavy, coarse.*

☆☆☆ 1985 CHARDONNAY ($15.00) Napa Valley-Carneros. *Lean, clean, lovely fruit, elegant oak, rich and delicious.*

1985 CHARDONNAY ($18.00) Marina, Estate, Napa Valley-Carneros. *Heavy, vegetal, unappealing.*

☆☆☆ 1985 CHARDONNAY ($18.00) Winery Lake, Napa Valley-Carneros. *Rich, soft, clean, fresh, charming, with great aging potential.*

☆☆☆ 1986 CHARDONNAY ($14.25) Napa Valley. *Rich, woody, soft pineapple and pear fruit flavors.*

☆☆☆ 1986 CHARDONNAY ($15.00) Napa Valley-Carneros. *Tart, tight, rich, complex, deep and showing great aging potential.*

☆☆☆ 1986 CHARDONNAY ($18.00) Marina, Napa Valley-Carneros. *Crisp, lean, herbal, nicely made; a big improvement for this particular vineyard.*

### RED

☆☆☆ 1983 CABERNET SAUVIGNON ($15.00) Napa Valley. *Lean and beautifully structured. Fruity, varietal, lovely. Drink 1991.*

☆☆☆☆ 1984 CABERNET SAUVIGNON ($15.00) Napa Valley. *Supple, ripe, clean, crisp, great fruit, lovely structure. Drink 1991.*

☆☆ 1984 MERLOT ($15.00) Napa Valley. *Soft, lush, some oiliness and herbaceousness.*

☆☆☆ 1979 PINOT NOIR ($15.00) Iund, Napa Valley-Carneros. *Cherry, spice and snappy fruit. Drink now.*

☆☆☆ 1979 PINOT NOIR ($15.00) Lee, Napa Valley-Carneros. *Fruity and crisp. A little less stuffing than the other two.*

☆☆☆ 1979 PINOT NOIR ($15.00) St. Clair, Napa Valley-Carneros. *Balanced, clean and fruity. Good varietal character.*

☆☆☆ 1980 PINOT NOIR ($15.00) Iund, Napa Valley-Carneros. *Earthy and firmly structured.*

☆☆ 1980 PINOT NOIR ($15.00) Lee, Napa Valley-Carneros. *Dense, rich and fruity but essentially clumsy.*

☆☆☆☆ 1980 PINOT NOIR ($15.00) Madonna, Napa Valley-Carneros. *Earthy, lush, deep, with a hint of cherries. Stunning.*

☆☆☆☆ 1980 PINOT NOIR ($15.00) St. Clair, Napa Valley-Carneros. *Snappy and crisp, graceful, balanced, superb.*

☆☆☆ 1981 PINOT NOIR ($15.00) Iund, Napa Valley-Carneros. *Toasty and fruity but with a touch of tar.*

☆☆☆ 1981 PINOT NOIR ($15.00) Lee, Napa Valley-Carneros. *Perhaps the best Acacia of 1981. Soft, lush and lovely.*

☆☆☆ 1981 PINOT NOIR ($15.00) Madonna, Napa Valley-Carneros. *Crisp, balanced, charming.*

☆☆ 1981 PINOT NOIR ($15.00) St. Clair, Napa Valley-Carneros. *Lush fruit, soft texture.*

☆☆ 1981 PINOT NOIR ($15.00) Winery Lake, Napa Valley-Carneros. *Meaty and well structured. Long aging potential.*

☆☆ 1982 PINOT NOIR ($15.00) Iund, Napa Valley-Carneros. *Peppery, vegetal, lean and crisp.*

☆☆☆ 1982 PINOT NOIR ($15.00) Lee, Napa Valley-Carneros. *Rich, hard, lovely structure. Drink now and beyond.*

☆☆☆ 1982 PINOT NOIR ($15.00) Madonna, Napa Valley-Carneros. *Toasty nose, rich berries, earth and some hardness.*

☆☆☆☆ 1982 PINOT NOIR ($15.00) St. Clair, Napa Valley-Carneros. *Cherry-berry flavors, lush, full, fat, balanced. Drink now.*

☆☆☆☆ 1982 PINOT NOIR ($15.00) Winery Lake, Napa Valley-Carneros. *Deep, brooding, complex, incredible. Drink now.*

☆☆☆ 1983 PINOT NOIR ($15.00) Iund, Napa Valley-Carneros. *Peppery, nice, lush, soft, intense richness.*

☆☆☆ 1983 PINOT NOIR ($15.00) Lee, Napa Valley-Carneros. *A bit softer than the '82; lovely.*

☆☆☆☆ 1983 PINOT NOIR ($15.00) St. Clair, Napa Valley-Carneros. *Rich, fat, with berries and depth of fruit.*

☆☆☆ 1983 PINOT NOIR ($15.00) Winery Lake, Napa Valley-Carneros. *Lush, fruity and remarkably complex.*

☆☆☆☆ 1983 PINOT NOIR ($15.50) Madonna, Napa Valley-Carneros. *Super rich and velvety in texture, deeply colored, gentle earth and lush fruit flavors. Superb.*

☆☆☆☆ 1984 PINOT NOIR ($11.00) Napa Valley. *Smokey, cherry, rich fruit, superb texture and weight. Drink now.*

☆☆☆ 1984 PINOT NOIR ($15.00) Iund, Napa Valley-Carneros. *Rich, leathery, lovely cherry fruit, clean, lush, superb.*

☆☆☆ 1984 PINOT NOIR ($16.00) Madonna, Napa Valley-Carneros. *Crisp, bright, attractive, well made.*

☆☆☆☆ 1984 PINOT NOIR ($16.00) St. Clair, Napa Valley. *Ripe, spicy, deep red cherry flavors, intense, superb. Drink 1988.*

☆ 1985 PINOT NOIR ($11.00) Napa Valley-Carneros. *Decent but a bit on the weedy, stemmy side.*

☆☆☆ 1985 PINOT NOIR ($16.00) St. Clair, Napa Valley-Carneros. *Rich cherry-berry flavors, lovely texture, long finish.*

☆☆☆ 1985 PINOT NOIR ($16.00) Madonna, Napa Valley-Carneros. *Crisp, snappy fruit, lovely silky texture, good finish.*

🙙

## Adams Vineyard Winery       OREGON
### WHITE
☆☆☆ 1982 CHARDONNAY ($11.00) Yamhill. *Rich, lush, deep, fat, oaky, superb.*

☆☆☆ 1983 CHARDONNAY ($13.50) Yamhill. *Rich, deep, luscious, balanced, remarkable.*

☆ 1985 CHARDONNAY ($12.00) Reserve, Yamhill. *Harsh, hard, bitter; decent but not likable.*
### RED
☆☆☆ 1982 PINOT NOIR ($11.00) Yamhill. *Toasty, herbal, rich fruit, Burgundian.*

## Adelaida Cellars       SAN LUIS OBISPO COUNTY
### WHITE
☆☆ 1982 CHARDONNAY ($7.75) Paso Robles. *Clean, rich, good fruit and oak. A nice first effort.*
### SPARKLING
☆☆☆ 1982 TONIO CONTI BLANC DE BLANC ($17.00) Paso Robles. *Crisp, ripe, fresh, well balanced.*
### RED
☆☆ 1981 CABERNET SAUVIGNON ($7.25) Paso Robles. *Herbal, clean, rich, nicely made, short on middle palate.*

## Adelsheim Vineyard       OREGON
### WHITE
☆☆ 1982 CHARDONNAY ($11.00) Yamhill. *Attractive fruit and rich flavors balanced by crisp acidity.*

☆☆ 1983 CHARDONNAY ($11.25) Yamhill. *Oily, vinous, rich, fruity, odd.*

☆☆ 1985 CHARDONNAY ($11.00) Oregon. *Tart, lean, lemony, decent.*

☆☆ 1984 PINOT GRIS ($7.50) Oregon. *Lush, fruity, clean, decent.*
### RED
☆ 1981 MERLOT ($9.00) Sagemoor Farms, Washington. *Vegetal and simple.*

☆☆☆ 1981 MERLOT ($12.00) Limited Bottling, Sagemoor Farms, Washington. *Tart, fruity, clean and lovely.*

☆☆☆ 1982 MERLOT ($9.00) 90% Washington, 10% Oregon. *5% Cabernet. Rich, spicy, clean and well built.*

☆☆☆ 1981 PINOT NOIR ($10.00) Yamhill. *Thin but balanced and elegant.*

☆☆☆ 1983 PINOT NOIR ($12.50) Yamhill. *Crisp, fresh, lush, complex, varietal, lovely.*

☆☆☆ 1985 PINOT NOIR ($15.00) Oregon. *Crisp, good cherry fruit, lovely texture and charm.*

## Adler Fels Winery       SONOMA COUNTY
### WHITE
☆☆ 1982 CHARDONNAY ($8.00) Barra, Mendocino. *Lush, rich, oaky, attractive.*

☆ 1983 CHARDONNAY ($11.00) Nelson, Sonoma Valley. *Dull, heavy, lacking fruit.*

○ 1984 CHARDONNAY ($7.00) Dion Family, Sonoma Valley. *Dull, lacking fruit, no character.*

☆☆☆ 1984 CHARDONNAY ($12.00) Sonoma Valley. *Lush, buttery, soft, lovely.*

○ 1984 CHARDONNAY ($12.00) Nelson, Sonoma Valley. *Oxidized, odd.*

☆☆ 1986 FUME BLANC ($8.75) Sonoma. *Clean and balanced; herbal, with varietal flavors.*

☆ 1985 JOHANNISBERG RIESLING ($15.00) Select Cluster Late Harvest, Sonoma. *9.6% residual sugar. Fruity, decent, some odd flavors.*

### SPARKLING

☆☆ 1984 MELANGE A DEUX ($15.00) Sonoma. *50% Gewürztraminer, 50% Johannisberg Riesling. Yeasty, woody, clean, unusual but interesting.*

☆☆ 1985 MELANGE A DEUX ($15.00) Sonoma. *50% Gewürztraminer, 50% Johannisberg Riesling. Odd but attractive; balanced.*

### RED

☆ 1980 CABERNET SAUVIGNON ($12.00) Napa Valley. *Weedy, decent structure, clean.*

☆ 1982 CABERNET SAUVIGNON ($10.00) Napa Valley. *3% Merlot. Weedy, dense, balanced.*

🍇

## Ahern Winery                LOS ANGELES COUNTY
### WHITE

☆ 1982 CHARDONNAY ($10.00) Edna Valley. *A trifle weedy but pleasant.*

☆ 1982 CHARDONNAY ($12.00) MacGregor, San Luis Obispo. *Snappy, crisp and smooth but with some strong vegetal notes.*

☆☆☆ 1982 CHARDONNAY ($12.00) Paragon, San Luis Obispo. *Rich, full and oaky. Good lemony fruit.*

☆☆☆ 1984 CHARDONNAY ($9.50) Pleasant Valley Ranch, Paso Robles. *Crisp, ripe, good oak and acidity.*

### RED

☆☆☆ 1984 ZINFANDEL ($7.50) Grand Père, Amador. *Lush, ripe, deep, clean fruit flavors.*

🍇

## Ahlgren Vineyard                SANTA CRUZ COUNTY
### WHITE

1982 CHARDONNAY ($13.00) Ventana, Monterey. *Earthy, rich, fat and hot, with a touch of volatile acidity.*

☆☆☆ 1983 CHARDONNAY ($13.00) Ventana, Monterey. *Rich, toasty, clean, lovely.*

☆☆ 1984 CHARDONNAY ($12.50) Ventana, Monterey. *Lush, earthy, lovely oak, with a touch of volatile acidity.*

### RED

☆☆ 1979 CABERNET SAUVIGNON ($10.00) 17% Petite Sirah, 4% Merlot, Ventana, Central Coast. *Inky and intense, rich, fruity and harsh but very good.*

☆ 1980 CABERNET SAUVIGNON ($10.50) Rutherford-Napa Valley. *Intense, dark, tannic, chocolatey, a monster.*

☆☆ 1980 CABERNET SAUVIGNON ($10.50) Bates Ranch, Santa Cruz Mountains. *Herbs and berries. Rich, dense, tannic. Drink now.*

☆☆ 1981 CABERNET SAUVIGNON ($10.00) Cristina, Napa Valley. *Herbal, balanced, clean, lovely structure. Drink now.*

☆☆ 1982 CABERNET SAUVIGNON ($12.50) Bates Ranch, Santa Cruz Mountains. *Soft, clean, attractive.*

☆ 1980 ZINFANDEL ($7.50) California. *Intense, berried, overdone, too concentrated.*

☆ 1981 ZINFANDEL ($6.75) Livermore Valley. *Hard, lacking freshness.*

🍇

## Alba Vineyard                                   *NEW JERSEY*

### WHITE

☆☆  1986 CAYUGA ($4.50) Warren. *Fresh apple flavors, soft, charming, off-dry.*

○  1985 CHARDONNAY ($8.00) Reserve, Warren. *Barnyard aromas and flavors.*

☆☆  1984 RIESLING ($6.50) New Jersey. *Crisp, clean, light fruit, attractive.*

☆  1985 SEYVAL BLANC ($4.75) New Jersey. *Crisp, rich, decent, some bitterness.*

### BLANC DE NOIR

☆☆  1986 BLUSH ($4.00) New Jersey. *Decent, some fruit.*

### RED

☆☆☆  1985 CABERNET SAUVIGNON ($8.00) New Jersey. *Herbal, lush, ripe, clean, snappy. Drink 1988.*

੨੦

## Alderbrook Winery                          *SONOMA COUNTY*

### WHITE

☆☆  1982 CHARDONNAY ($8.25) Sonoma. *Clean, vinous, lovely, with a charming oak sweetness.*

☆☆☆  1983 CHARDONNAY ($8.75) Sonoma. *Crisp, clean, balanced, complex, lovely.*

☆  1984 CHARDONNAY ($8.75) Sonoma. *Overripe, candied.*

☆☆  1985 CHARDONNAY ($8.75) Dry Creek Valley. *Rich, ripe, round, clean, lush, generous.*

☆☆☆  1985 SAUVIGNON BLANC ($7.50) Dry Creek Valley. *Soft, lush, supple, clean, balanced.*

੨੦

## Alexander Valley Fruit
## & Trading Company                          *SONOMA COUNTY*

### WHITE

☆☆☆  1985 CHARDONNAY ($8.00) Alexander Valley. *Big, lush, clean, deep, varietal.*

### RED

☆  1982 CABERNET SAUVIGNON ($7.50) Sommer, Sonoma. *Herbal, green flavors, simple, decent.*

੨੦

## Alexander Valley Vineyards             *SONOMA COUNTY*

### WHITE

☆☆☆  1982 CHARDONNAY ($10.00) Estate, Alexander Valley. *Rich, crisp, clean and lovely.*

☆☆☆  1983 CHARDONNAY ($10.00) Estate, Alexander Valley. *Lush, rich yet more elegant than the '82.*

1984 CHARDONNAY ($10.50) Alexander Valley. *Heavy, unappealing.*

☆☆  1985 CHARDONNAY ($10.50) Alexander Valley. *Lush, earthy, clean, decent.*

### RED

☆☆☆  1978 CABERNET SAUVIGNON ($6.50) Estate, Alexander Valley. *This wine has matured beautifully. Rich, balanced, elegant.*

☆☆  1979 CABERNET SAUVIGNON ($7.00) Estate, Alexander Valley. *Balanced, attractive, well made.*

☆☆  1980 CABERNET SAUVIGNON ($9.00) Estate, Alexander Valley. *Rich, intense, clean and raisiny.*

☆☆☆  1981 CABERNET SAUVIGNON ($9.00) Estate, Alexander Valley. *Rich, intense, balanced. Drink now.*

☆☆  1982 CABERNET SAUVIGNON ($10.00) Estate, Alexander Valley. *Lush, clean, rich, good finish. Drink 1988 and beyond.*

☆☆☆ 1983 CABERNET SAUVIGNON ($10.50) 10th Anniversary, Estate, Alexander Valley. *Dark, rich. Clean, lovely fruit and structure. Drink 1988.*

☆☆☆ 1984 CABERNET SAUVIGNON ($11.00) Wetzel Family Selection, Alexander Valley. *Soft, fresh, herbal, lush, nicely balanced.*

☆ 1985 CABERNET SAUVIGNON ($12.00) Wetzel Family Estate, Alexander Valley. *Herbal, big, intense, ripe, chalky.*

☆☆☆ 1985 MERLOT ($11.00) Wetzel Family Selection, Alexander Valley. *Soft, herbal, velvety, balanced. Drink now.*

☆☆ 1981 PINOT NOIR ($6.00) Estate, Alexander Valley. *Rich and attractive; simple, with a touch of weediness.*

☆☆ 1982 PINOT NOIR ($6.50) Estate, Alexander Valley. *Fresh, clean, simple, quite decent.*

☆☆☆ 1984 PINOT NOIR ($7.00) Estate, Alexander Valley. *Spicy cherry fruit, lush, rich, balanced.*

❧

## *Almaden Vineyards*　　　　　　MADERA COUNTY
### WHITE

☆☆ NV GOLDEN CHABLIS ($2.50) California. *Sappy and heavy but clean and attractive.*

☆☆ NV MONTEREY CHABLIS ($2.50) Monterey. *Clean, herbal, fresh and attractive.*

☆ NV MOUNTAIN WHITE CHABLIS ($2.88) California. *Fruity, off-dry, dull but decent.*

☆ 1985 PREMIUM WHITE ($3.50) California. *Soft, decent but flat and watery.*

☆ 1983 CHARDONNAY ($5.50) San Benito. *Dull, lacking varietal character.*

1984 CHARLES LEFRANC CELLARS CHARDONNAY ($7.50) Monterey. *Sour, off, filter pad flavors.*

☆ 1984 CHARDONNAY ($8.00) Sage Ranch, San Benito. *Oily, heavy, intense, lacking fruit.*

☆☆ 1984 CHARLES LEFRANC CELLARS CHARDONNAY ($10.50) Tepusquet, Santa Barbara. *Lush, vegetal, nicely balanced, pleasant.*

☆☆☆ 1984 CHARLES LEFRANC CELLARS CHARDONNAY ($15.40) Napa. *Heavy, rich, lovely oak and a great deal of varietal character.*

☆ 1985 CHARDONNAY ($5.00) Monterey *Lush, earthy, rich, smoothly textured, attractive but a bit dirty.*

☆☆ 1985 CHARLES LEFRANC CELLARS CHARDONNAY ($8.85) Sage Ranch, San Benito. *Crisp, balanced, decent.*

☆☆ 1985 CHARLES LEFRANC CELLARS CHARDONNAY ($10.50) Tepusquet, Santa Barbara. *Soft, tart, crisp, some herbaceousness.*

☆ 1985 CHARLES LEFRANC CELLARS CHARDONNAY ($12.00) Napa. *Dull, lacking fruit, decent.*

☆☆ 1984 CHARLES LEFRANC CELLARS GEWURZTRA-MINER ($11.00) Selected Harvest, San Benito. *8.9% residual sugar. Soft, simple, clean, balanced.*

○ 1985 CHARLES LEFRANC CELLARS SAUVIGNON BLANC ($7.00) Monterey. *Flat, ugly, oxidized.*

☆☆ 1984 CHARLES LEFRANC CELLARS WHITE TABLE WINE ($3.40) California. *Herbal, fresh, clean, attractive.*

### SPARKLING

☆☆ NV BLUSH CHAMPAGNE ($5.25) California. *Sweet, simple, a bit heavy, pleasant.*

☆☆ NV GOLDEN CHAMPAGNE ($4.00) California. *Lush, deep, round and quite clean. Attractive.*

NV LE DOMAINE ($4.00) California. *Sweet and oily.*

☆☆ NV EXTRA DRY CHAMPAGNE ($5.00) California. *Crisp, fresh, attractive.*

☆ 1984 VINTAGE EXTRA DRY CHAMPAGNE ($8.00) California. *Crisp, clean, vanillin, off-dry, decent.*

1985 CHARLES LEFRANC CELLARS EXTRA DRY ($16.75) California. 100% *White Zinfandel. Oily, heavy.*

☆☆ NV CHARLES LEFRANC CELLARS SPARKLING WHITE ZINFANDEL ($6.35) California. *Sweet, strawberry flavors; simple, pleasant.*

## BLANC DE NOIR

☆☆ 1986 CHARLES LEFRANC CELLARS GAMAY BEAUJOLAIS ($4.00) Nouveau Blanc, Sage Ranch, Paicines. *Soft, clean, fresh, decent.*

☆ 1986 CHARLES LEFRANC CELLARS WHITE ZINFANDEL ($4.25) California. *Fat, sweet, clean, dull, watery.*

## RED

☆☆ NV MONTEREY BURGUNDY ($2.50) Monterey. *Herbal, smooth, attractive.*

☆☆ 1982 CALIFORNIA PREMIUM RED ($7.00) California. *1.5 liters. Good texture, clean, ripe, smooth.*

☆ 1982 CHARLES LEFRANC CELLARS CABERNET PFEFFER ($7.30) San Benito. *Peppery, crisp, thin, decent but odd.*

☆ 1983 CHARLES LEFRANC CELLARS MAISON ROUGE ($3.00) San Benito. *Crisp, clean, snappy, a bit thin.*

☆ 1983 CHARLES LEFRANC CELLARS RED ($3.40) California. *Clean, balanced, decent.*

☆☆ 1978 CABERNET SAUVIGNON ($4.50) Monterey. *Clean, balanced, varietal, herbal, lovely.*

☆☆ 1979 CABERNET SAUVIGNON ($5.00) Monterey. *Slightly vegetal, thick, rich, lacks grace.*

☆☆ 1979 CHARLES LEFRANC CELLARS CABERNET SAUVIGNON ($8.50) Monterey. *Herbal, ripe, rich, well made.*

☆☆☆ 1980 CABERNET SAUVIGNON ($5.50) Monterey. *Ripe, soft and beautifully structured.*

☆☆☆ 1981 CABERNET SAUVIGNON ($4.00) Monterey. *Clean, fruity, varietal, charming. Drink now.*

☆☆☆ 1981 CHARLES LEFRANC CELLARS CABERNET SAUVIGNON ($8.50) Monterey. *Rich, lush, fat, complex, delightful.*

☆☆☆ 1982 CABERNET SAUVIGNON ($5.00) Monterey. *Rich, clean, balanced, lush texture. Lovely.*

☆☆ 1982 CHARLES LEFRANC CELLARS CABERNET SAUVIGNON ($9.85) San Lucas Ranch, Monterey. *Crisp, meaty, clean, attractive. Drink now.*

☆☆ 1983 CABERNET SAUVIGNON ($5.00) Monterey. *Crisp, clean, nice herbal flavors, bright, fruity finish.*

☆☆☆ 1983 CABERNET SAUVIGNON ($9.00) San Lucas Ranch, Monterey. *Soft, lush, fruity, delicious oak and crisp acidity. Lovely. Drink 1989.*

☆☆ 1984 CHARLES LEFRANC CELLARS CABERNET SAUVIGNON ($12.00) Napa. *Earthy, varietal, attractive.*

☆ 1986 CHARLES LEFRANC CELLARS GAMAY BEAUJOLAIS ($4.00) Nouveau, Sage Ranch, Paicines. *Fruity and ripe but with some earthy, dirty overtones.*

☆☆ 1984 MERLOT ($8.50) San Lucas Ranch. *Jammy, ripe, Zinfandel-like.*

☆☆ 1982 PINOT NOIR ($5.00) San Benito. *Green, herbal, nice flavors.*

☆☆ NV ZINFANDEL ($2.50) California. *Rich, clean, with nicely controlled vegetation.*

❧

## Almarla Vineyards and Winery     MISSISSIPPI
### WHITE
NV SCUPPERNONG ($2.50) Sauterne, Mississippi. *Sweet.*
### ROSE
○ NV PINK MUSCADINE ($2.50) Mississippi. *Heavy, sweet, medicinal.*

❧

## Alpine Vineyards     OREGON
### RED
☆☆☆ 1982 PINOT NOIR ($9.00) Estate, Willamette Valley. *Lovely, elegant, light, balanced.*

☆☆☆ 1983 PINOT NOIR ($9.50) Estate, Willamette Valley. *Rich, clean, toasty, varietal.*

❧

## Alta Vineyard Cellar     NAPA COUNTY
### WHITE
○ 1983 CHARDONNAY ($15.00) Napa Valley. *Oily, fat, heavy, oxidized, ugly.*

❧

## Amador Foothill Winery     AMADOR COUNTY
### BLANC DE NOIR
1986 WHITE ZINFANDEL ($5.50) Amador. *Sour, unattractive.*
### RED
☆☆☆ 1980 ZINFANDEL ($8.00) Eschen Vineyard, Fiddletown, Amador. *Super fruit and varietal character.*

☆ 1981 ZINFANDEL ($6.00) Amador. *Raisiny, tannic, intense.*

❧

## Amity Vineyards     OREGON
### WHITE
☆☆ 1982 CHARDONNAY ($15.00) Winemaker's Reserve, Oregon. *Toasty, rich, earthy, smooth.*

1984 CHARDONNAY ($11.00) Willamette Valley. *Dull, flat.*

☆☆ 1984 CHARDONNAY ($11.00) Estate, Willamette Valley. *Crisp, soft, snappy, clean, balanced.*

☆☆☆ 1986 WHITE RIESLING ($7.50) Willamette Valley. *1% residual sugar. Lush, fat, clean, good fruit.*
### RED
☆☆ 1978 PINOT NOIR ($8.00) Oregon. *Burgundian and elegant.*

☆☆☆ 1978 PINOT NOIR ($20.00) Winemaker's Reserve, 76% Windhill, 24% Estate Gamay, Oregon. *Rich, earthy and complex, with some Burgundian style.*

☆☆ 1980 PINOT NOIR ($8.00) Oregon. *Lush fruit in nose but somewhat slim on the palate.*

☆☆ 1980 PINOT NOIR ($15.00) Winemaker's Reserve, Oregon. *Rich, stemmy, earthy and complex.*

☆ 1981 PINOT NOIR ($7.00) Four Vineyards, Oregon. *Thin, dull.*

☆ 1982 PINOT NOIR ($7.00) Four Vineyards, Oregon. *Pale, dull, lacking varietal character.*

☆ 1982 PINOT NOIR ($16.00) Winemaker's Reserve, Oregon. *Varietal, strange.*

☆ 1984 PINOT NOIR ($9.00) Oregon. *Decent flavors but too tart and thin.*

🍂

## Amizetta Vineyards                    NAPA COUNTY
### RED
☆☆☆ 1985 CABERNET SAUVIGNON ($16.00) Estate, Napa. *Rich, minty, well balanced, elegant, spicy. Drink 1989.*

🍂

## S. Anderson Vineyard                    NAPA COUNTY
### WHITE
☆☆☆ 1982 CHARDONNAY ($12.50) Napa Valley. *Fresh, crisp, fruity, with nice oak and balance.*

☆☆ 1983 CHARDONNAY ($12.50) Estate, Napa Valley. *Woody, intense, alcoholic, lacks finesse.*

☆ 1983 CHARDONNAY ($15.00) Proprietor's Selection, Estate, Napa Valley. *Oaky, intense volatile acidity, odd flavors.*

☆☆ 1984 CHARDONNAY ($12.50) Napa Valley. *Soft, decent fruit, nice structure, some earthy qualities.*

☆☆ 1985 CHARDONNAY ($12.00) Napa Valley. *Crisp, clean, decent, lacking depth.*
### SPARKLING
☆☆☆ 1982 BLANC DE NOIR ($12.50) Napa Valley. *Rich, deep, complex, lush, charming.*

☆☆☆ 1982 CUVEE DE LA CAVE ($14.00) Napa Valley. *Yeasty, fresh, lush, lovely.*

☆☆ 1984 TIVOLI BLANC DE NOIR ($11.50) Napa Valley. *Clean, simple, decent.*

☆ 1984 BLANC DE NOIR ($16.00) Napa Valley. *Crisp, hard, simple, okay.*

☆☆☆ 1984 BLANC DE NOIRS ($16.00) Napa Valley. *100% Pinot Noir. Lush, rich, round, complex.*

🍂

ANDRE *see* E. & J. Gallo Winery

## Arbor Crest                    WASHINGTON
### WHITE
☆☆☆ 1982 CHARDONNAY ($10.00) Sagemoor. *Crisp, clean, balanced, citric; a delightful wine.*

☆☆☆ 1983 CHARDONNAY ($9.75) Washington. *Lush, rich, fat, spicy, lovely oak, good balance.*

☆☆ 1983 CHARDONNAY ($15.00) Cameo Reserve, Sagemoor, Columbia Valley. *Tart, hard-edged, clean, decent.*

☆☆ 1984 CHARDONNAY ($9.75) Columbia Valley. *Clean, varietal, hard-edged and a bit high in alcohol.*

1986 JOHANNISBERG RIESLING ($9.50) Select Late Harvest, Washington. *8.9% residual sugar. Botrytis and volatile acidity. Not pleasant.*
### RED
☆☆☆ 1982 CABERNET SAUVIGNON ($17.50) Bacchus, Washington. *Tart fruit, clean, ripe, buttery, lovely oak, stunning. Drink now.*

☆☆☆ 1983 CABERNET SAUVIGNON ($17.50) Bacchus, Columbia Valley. *Soft, ripe, rich, clean flavors and lovely structure. Drink 1989.*

☆☆ 1982 MERLOT ($7.50) Bacchus. *18% Cabernet Sauvignon. Rich, woody, clean and complex.*

1983 MERLOT ($12.00) Bacchus, Columbia. *Skunky, unattractive.*

☆☆ 1985 MERLOT ($8.00) Bacchus, Columbia Valley. *Soft, fruity, herbal, fat, appealing.*

☆☆☆ 1985 MERLOT ($10.00) Cameo Reserve, Winemaker's Selection, Bacchus, Columbia Valley. *Herbs, mint, good oak, supple, with some elegance.*

≈

ARCADIA *see* Stuermer Winery

## Arciero Winery                    PASO ROBLES COUNTY
### WHITE
1984 CHARDONNAY ($8.00) Paso Robles. *Soft, flabby, not clean.*

☆ 1985 CHARDONNAY ($8.00) Paso Robles. *Buttery flavors but dull and simple.*

☆☆ 1985 JOHANNISBERG RIESLING ($9.00) December Harvest, Santa Barbara. *9.9% residual sugar. Rich botrytis, oily texture.*

☆☆ 1986 JOHANNISBERG RIESLING ($9.00) Late Harvest, Paso Robles. *375 ml. 12.9% residual sugar. Tart, crisp, with nice fruit and texture.*

☆ 1986 WHITE TABLE WINE ($3.50) La Venera, Central Coast. *87% Semillon, 13% Chenin Blanc. Clean, decent, spicy, pleasant.*

### RED
☆ NV LA VENERA ($3.50) Central Coast. *35% Cabernet Sauvignon, 28% Petite Sirah, 27% Zinfandel, 10% Sauvignon Blanc. Not worth the effort. Tannic, earthy and dull.*

1984 CABERNET SAUVIGNON ($4.50) Santa Barbara. *Vegetal, earthy, lacking structure, unattractive.*

☆☆ 1985 CABERNET SAUVIGNON ($8.50) Paso Robles. *Crisp, ripe, rich fruit, good structure. Drink now.*

☆☆ 1984 ZINFANDEL ($7.00) Paso Robles. *Dense, heavy, tannic.*

≈

ARIEL *see* J. Lohr Winery
ARROYO SONOMA WINERY *see* Bandiera Winery

## David Arthur Vineyards            NAPA COUNTY
### WHITE
☆☆ 1985 CHARDONNAY ($12.50) Napa Valley. *Crisp, lean, good structure, lacking complexity.*

≈

## Artisan Wines                     NAPA COUNTY
### WHITE
☆☆ 1983 ULTRAVINO CHARDONNAY ($8.00) Napa Valley. *Clean, fresh, attractive.*

☆☆ 1984 CRUVINET CHARDONNAY ($5.50) California. *Clean, fresh, balanced, lovely, a bit oily.*

☆☆ 1984 ULTRAVINO CHARDONNAY ($8.50) Napa Valley. *Woody, crisp, fresh, spicy.*

☆☆☆ 1984 CHARDONNAY ($8.75) Napa Valley. *Toasty, rich, lovely, delicate finish.*

1984 MICHAEL'S CHARDONNAY ($15.00) Napa Valley. *Flat, bitter, dirty, not much.*

☆☆ 1986 CRUVINET SAUVIGNON BLANC ($5.00) 51% Russian River Valley, 49% Alexander Valley. *Soft, lush, rich, deep, attractive.*

### RED
☆☆☆ 1982 MICHAEL'S CABERNET SAUVIGNON ($12.00) Napa Valley. *Herbal, earthy, Bordeaux-like, smooth, elegant. Drink 1988.*

☆☆ 1983 MICHAEL'S CABERNET SAUVIGNON ($15.00) Napa
Valley. *Tart, crisp, lean, some minty flavors. Drink
1989.*

☆☆☆ 1984 MICHAEL'S CABERNET SAUVIGNON ($15.00) Napa
Valley. *Rich, lush, astringent. Drink 1991.*

☆☆ 1984 MICHAEL'S CABERNET SAUVIGNON ($15.00)
Reserve, Summit, Spring Mountain. *Big, rich,
dense, some volatile acidity. Drink 1992.*

ès

## Ashly                      SANTA CLARA COUNTY
### WHITE
☆☆☆ 1984 CHARDONNAY ($18.00) Monterey. *Big, lush, oaky,
good acidity and smooth texture.*

☆☆☆ 1985 CHARDONNAY ($18.00) Monterey. *Toasty, oaky, crisp,
lovely fruit but wood is dominant.*

ès

## Au Bon Climat            SANTA BARBARA COUNTY
### WHITE
☆☆ 1982 CHARDONNAY ($10.00) Santa Barbara. *Toasty, but-
tery, nice.*

☆☆☆ 1983 CHARDONNAY ($10.00) Santa Barbara. *Crisp, tight,
Burgundian, elegant, slightly vinous; superb.*

☆☆☆ 1983 CHARDONNAY ($10.00) Los Alamos, Santa Barbara.
*Toasty, oaky, ripe fruit, complex.*

☆☆☆☆ 1983 CHARDONNAY ($20.00) Babcock, Santa Barbara.
*Soft, rich, balanced, complex, remarkable.*

☆☆☆ 1984 CHARDONNAY ($9.00) Santa Barbara. *Clean, fresh,
balanced, attractive.*

☆☆☆ 1985 CHARDONNAY ($11.00) Los Alamos, Santa Barbara.
*Elegant and well balanced. Clean, varietal and
complex.*

☆☆☆☆ 1985 CHARDONNAY ($20.00) Reserve, Santa Barbara.
*Crisp, elegant, clean, with lovely oak and fresh
fruit; superb.*

### RED
☆☆ 1982 PINOT NOIR ($12.00) Santa Barbara. *Rich, Burgun-
dian, some vegetal overtones, quite good.*

ès

AUGUST SEBASTIANI *see* Sebastiani Vineyards

## Austin Cellars          SANTA BARBARA COUNTY
### WHITE
○ 1985 SAUVIGNON BLANC ($15.00) Botrytis, Sierra Madre,
Santa Barbara. *Intensely vegetal, bitter and
unpleasant.*

### RED
☆☆ 1981 PINOT NOIR ($18.00) Sierra Madre, Santa Barbara.
*Lush, fat, clean.*

☆☆☆ 1982 PINOT NOIR ($10.00) Bien Nacido, Santa Barbara.
*Ripe, clean, smooth, powerful, deep, lovely.*

☆☆☆ 1982 PINOT NOIR ($12.00) Sierra Madre, Santa Barbara.
*Rich, complex, superb, a classic. Drink now.*

ès

## Babcock Vineyards       SANTA BARBARA COUNTY
### WHITE
☆☆☆ 1984 CHARDONNAY ($12.00) Estate, Santa Ynez Valley.
*Snappy fruit, crisp, clean, elegant.*

☆☆☆ 1985 CHARDONNAY ($12.00) Estate, Santa Ynez Valley.
*Lush, ripe, clean, fat, juicy.*

☆☆ 1986 CHARDONNAY ($14.00) Reserve, Estate, Santa Ynez Valley. *Rich, deep, candied, oaky, heavy.*
☆☆☆ 1986 JOHANNISBERG RIESLING ($6.00) Santa Ynez Valley. *2.2% residual sugar. Lush, ripe, clean, lovely, with rich fruit flavors.*

ва

## Estate William Baccala                    SONOMA COUNTY
### WHITE
☆☆ 1982 STEPHEN ZELLERBACH VINEYARD CHARDONNAY ($6.00) Alexander Valley. *Citric, clean, fresh, nice fruit, smooth finish.*
☆☆☆ 1983 STEPHEN ZELLERBACH VINEYARD CHARDONNAY ($10.00) Alexander Valley. *Toasty, clean, fruity.*
☆☆☆☆ 1983 CHARDONNAY ($11.00) Mendocino. *Crisp fruit, fragrant oak, elegance, finesse.*
☆☆☆ 1984 CHARDONNAY ($11.00) Mendocino. *Soft, toasty, rich, elegant and quite lovely.*
☆☆☆ 1985 CHARDONNAY ($10.00) Mendocino. *Fresh apple fruit, clean and delicate.*
☆☆☆ 1986 STEPHEN ZELLERBACH VINEYARD CHARDONNAY ($6.00) California. *Soft, fresh, clean, smooth and beautifully balanced.*
### RED
☆ 1978 STEPHEN ZELLERBACH VINEYARD CABERNET SAUVIGNON ($8.50) Alexander Valley. *Decent, simple, attractive.*
☆☆ 1980 STEPHEN ZELLERBACH VINEYARD CABERNET SAUVIGNON ($8.00) Alexander Valley. *Rich, deep, clean, attractive. Drink now.*
☆☆ 1982 STEPHEN ZELLERBACH VINEYARD CABERNET SAUVIGNON ($6.00) Alexander Valley. *Minty, lush, clean.*
☆☆ 1979 STEPHEN ZELLERBACH VINEYARD MERLOT ($9.00) Alexander Valley. *Herbal, complex, tannic. Drink 1988.*
☆☆ 1980 STEPHEN ZELLERBACH VINEYARD MERLOT ($10.00) Alexander Valley. *5% Cabernet Sauvignon. Fruity, oaky, ripe, attractive.*
☆☆☆ 1982 STEPHEN ZELLERBACH VINEYARD MERLOT ($8.50) Estate, Alexander Valley. *10% Cabernet Sauvignon. A real winner. Fruity, complex, rich, clean, lovely. Ready to drink.*
☆☆☆ 1984 MERLOT ($9.50) Alexander Valley. *Earthy, bright, clean, rich. Drink now.*

ва

BACIGALUPI *see* Belvedere Wine Company

## Alexis Bailly Vineyard                    MINNESOTA
### RED
☆☆ 1979 LEON MILLOT ($8.00) Minnesota. *Earthy, rich, balanced, rather attractive.*
☆☆ 1983 LEON MILLOT ($8.00) Leon Millot, Minnesota. *Crisp, complex, Pinot Noir style, earthy, attractive.*

ва

## Baily Vineyard and Winery              RIVERSIDE COUNTY
### WHITE
○ 1986 CHARDONNAY ($7.50) Temecula. *Odd color, sour, lacking fruit, overripe, extremely weird.*

☆☆☆ 1986 SAUVIGNON BLANC ($6.50) Richards, Temecula. *Lean, crisp, lively fruit.*

☆☆ 1986 WHITE RIESLING ($6.00) Temecula. *Crisp, dry, clean, fresh.*

### BLANC DE NOIR

☆☆☆ 1986 CABERNET BLANC ($5.00) Temecula. *Fresh, clean, varietal, lively, delicious.*

### RED

☆ 1986 CABERNET SAUVIGNON ($5.50) Cabernet-Nouveau, Temecula. *Spicy, light, some odd flavors. An interesting stylistic experiment.*

🎗

## Bainbridge Island Winery                    WASHINGTON
### WHITE
1982 CHARDONNAY ($6.00) Late Harvest, Washington. *375 ml. Grapey, sweet, awkward.*

🎗

## Baldinelli Vineyards                    AMADOR COUNTY
### RED
☆☆☆ 1979 CABERNET SAUVIGNON ($7.00) Estate, Amador. *Soft, clean, intense, spicy.*

☆☆ 1980 CABERNET SAUVIGNON ($7.75) Estate, Amador. *Dense, concentrated, violets in the nose. Drink now.*

☆☆ 1981 CABERNET SAUVIGNON ($7.50) Shenandoah Valley. *Intense, concentrated, fruity. Drink now.*

☆☆☆ 1980 ZINFANDEL ($6.00) Lot 1, Shenandoah Valley, Amador. *Crisp, fruity, delightfully elegant.*

🎗

## Baldwin Vineyards                    NEW YORK
### WHITE
○ 1984 CHARDONNAY ($10.00) Reserve, Barrel Fermented, New York. *Cheesy, sour, bitter, strange.*

1984 RAVAT ($6.00) Select Late Harvest, New York. *8% residual sugar. Oily, ugly, awful, flat, sweaty.*

○ 1985 SEYVAL BLANC ($5.00) New York. *Bitter, sour, unattractive.*

### RED
☆☆☆☆ 1982 LANDOT NOIR ($6.00) New York. *Cherry, berry, rose petal. Superb.*

🎗

## Ballard Canyon Winery    SANTA BARBARA COUNTY
### WHITE
1983 CHARDONNAY ($13.00) Santa Barbara. *Oily, vegetal, heavy, unattractive.*

☆☆ 1984 CHARDONNAY ($12.00) Santa Barbara. *Lush fruit, clean, sweetish, unusual.*

☆ 1985 CHARDONNAY ($9.00) Dr.'s Fun Baby, Santa Barbara. *Simple, dull, not much.*

### RED
○ 1981 CABERNET SAUVIGNON ($9.00) Estate, Santa Ynez Valley. *Intense flavors of asparagus.*

○ 1982 CABERNET SAUVIGNON ($9.00) Santa Ynez Valley. *Volatile acidity, some moldiness, unappealing.*

☆ 1982 CABERNET SAUVIGNON ($12.00) Reserve, Estate, Santa Ynez Valley. *Earthy, rich, good texture.*

🎗

BALLATORE *see* E. & J. Gallo Winery

## *Balverne Winery & Vineyards*　　SONOMA COUNTY
### WHITE
☆☆☆ 1982 CHARDONNAY ($12.00) Deerfield, Sonoma. *Clean, austere, good structure, varietal, very good.*

☆☆☆ 1983 CHARDONNAY ($13.00) Deerfield, Chalk Hill. *Soft, varietal, rich, clean, smooth, lovely.*

☆☆☆ 1984 CHARDONNAY ($11.00) Deerfield, Chalk Hill. *Soft, rich, clean, nicely balanced, mature flavors.*

### RED
☆☆☆ 1981 CABERNET SAUVIGNON ($20.50) Sonoma. *Soft, herbal, lush, complex, great olive and cedar, lovely.*

☆☆☆ 1982 CABERNET SAUVIGNON ($20.00) Sonoma. *Lush, balanced, rich, complex, very elegant and mature. Ready to drink.*

☆ 1980 ZINFANDEL ($10.00) Estate, Sonoma. *Decent but muddy and a bit vegetal.*

☆☆☆ 1982 ZINFANDEL ($10.00) Quartz, Sonoma. *Ripe, balanced, fresh, lovely.*

## *Bandiera Winery*　　SONOMA COUNTY
### WHITE
1983 ARROYO SONOMA WINERY CHARDONNAY ($6.00) California. *Thin, unpleasant.*

☆☆☆ 1984 CHARDONNAY ($6.25) Sonoma. *Soft, clean, lovely flavors, charming.*

☆☆ 1985 CHARDONNAY ($6.00) Sonoma. *Soft, simple, clean, dull.*

### BLANC DE NOIR
☆☆ 1986 WHITE ZINFANDEL ($4.00) North Coast. *2.25% residual sugar. Crisp, clean, simple, not much character.*

### RED
☆ 1981 WILDFLOWER RED ($6.00) North Coast. *Simple, dull, decent.*

☆☆☆ 1981 JOHN B. MERRITT CABERNET SAUVIGNON ($8.00) Sonoma. *A lovely wine—crisp, varietal, delightful. Drink now.*

☆☆ 1982 CABERNET SAUVIGNON ($4.00) North Coast. *Clean, simple, varietal, fruity, attractive. Drink now.*

☆☆☆ 1982 JOHN B. MERRITT CABERNET SAUVIGNON ($6.50) Dry Creek Valley. *Fruity and crisp, charming varietal character and good structure. Drink now.*

☆☆☆ 1983 CABERNET SAUVIGNON ($4.50) North Coast. *Soft, lush, balanced, clean, some complexity. Drink now.*

☆☆☆ 1980 ZINFANDEL ($4.25) North Coast. *Varietal, clean and crisp.*

## *Barboursville Vineyards*　　VIRGINIA
### RED
☆ 1980 CABERNET SAUVIGNON ($6.50) Virginia. *15% Merlot. Soft, herbal and elegant. Simple but clean.*

1982 MERLOT ($7.00) Virginia. *Spicy, leathery, some dirty flavors.*

## *Bargetto Winery*                           SANTA CRUZ COUNTY
### WHITE
☆☆☆ 1984 CHARDONNAY ($10.00) Tepusquet, Santa Maria Val-
ley. *Ripe, lush, fresh, deep.*

☆ 1985 CHARDONNAY ($7.00) Tepusquet, Santa Maria Val-
ley. *Sour, off flavors.*

1986 CHARDONNAY ($7.00) Cypress, Santa Maria Valley.
*Bitter, herbal, heavy.*

☆☆ 1986 GEWURZTRAMINER ($7.00) Santa Maria Valley.
*1.8% residual sugar. Fat, simple, some vegetation.*

☆☆☆ 1984 JOHANNISBERG RIESLING ($9.00) Late Harvest,
Tepusquet, Santa Maria Valley. *9% residual sugar.
Clean, botrytis flavors, lush, fat, charming.*

☆☆ 1986 WHITE RIESLING ($7.00) Central Coast. *1.7% residual
sugar. Snappy, fresh fruit, some softness and nice
balance.*

### SPARKLING
☆☆☆ 1981 BLANC DE NOIR ($12.50) Monterey. *Lovely, lush, bal-
anced, 1% dosage. Méthode champenoise.*

### BLANC DE NOIR
☆☆ 1986 WHITE ZINFANDEL ($6.00) Alexander Valley. *Fresh,
fruity, decent.*

### RED
☆☆☆ 1981 CABERNET SAUVIGNON ($12.00) Dedication, St.
Regis, Napa Valley. *Clean and delicious, with
good fruit and acid. Drink now.*

☆ 1982 CABERNET SAUVIGNON ($12.50) St. Regis, Napa
Valley. *Heavy, vegetal, lacking charm.*

1983 CABERNET SAUVIGNON ($11.00) Napa Valley.
*Metallic, vegetal.*

☆☆ 1985 CABERNET SAUVIGNON ($12.00) Bates Ranch,
Santa Cruz Mountains. *Tart, tannic, subtle fruit,
good spice. Drink 1990.*

☆☆ 1981 ZINFANDEL ($7.00) Napa Valley. *Berried, fruity, clean,
nice.*

☆☆ 1981 ZINFANDEL ($7.00) St. Regis, Napa Valley. *Rich, con-
centrated, good fruit.*

ও

BARON JAQUAB DE HERZOG *see* Royal Kedem Wine Corporation

## *Bay Cellars*                                 ALAMEDA COUNTY
### WHITE
☆☆☆ 1982 CHARDONNAY ($12.00) Tepusquet, Santa Maria.
*Rich, vinous, clean, good fruit, lovely.*

1984 CHARDONNAY ($12.00) Los Carneros. *Heavy, dull.*

### RED
☆☆ 1982 CLARION ($10.50) Napa Valley. *66% Merlot, 24%
Cabernet, 10% Cabernet Franc. Oaky, rich.*

☆☆☆ 1982 PINOT NOIR ($13.50) Buena Vista, Carneros. *Fruity,
rich, varietal, clean and very lovely. Drink now.*

ও

## *Beaulieu Vineyard*                            NAPA COUNTY
### WHITE
☆ 1982 CHARDONNAY ($11.00) Beaufort, Napa Valley. *Clean,
crisp, decent, short and simple.*

☆☆☆ 1982 CHARDONNAY ($14.00) Los Carneros Region, Napa
Valley. *Lovely, sweet oak, rich flavors, intense, balanced—superb.*

☆☆☆ 1984 CHARDONNAY ($14.00) Los Carneros Reserve, Napa Valley. *Crisp, lovely sweet new oak, clean fruit.*

☆☆☆ 1985 CHARDONNAY ($14.00) Los Carneros Reserve, Napa Valley. *Crisp, clean, lovely fruit, sweet new oak. Maybe BV's best ever Chardonnay.*

## RED

☆☆☆ 1978 CABERNET SAUVIGNON ($18.00) Private Reserve, Estate, Napa Valley. *Minty, oaky, ripe, very classy. Drink now.*

☆☆ 1979 CABERNET SAUVIGNON ($20.00) Private Reserve, Estate, Napa Valley. *Big, fruity, complex, balanced but a bit clumsy. Drink now.*

☆☆ 1980 CABERNET SAUVIGNON ($9.00) Rutherford, Estate, Napa Valley. *Coffee nose, herbal flavors, simple and clean. Drink now.*

☆ 1981 CABERNET SAUVIGNON ($7.25) Beau Tour, Estate, Napa Valley. *Decent but lacking finesse and middle range. Drink now.*

☆☆ 1981 CABERNET SAUVIGNON ($8.00) Rutherford, Napa Valley. *Charming, round, oaky, varietal. Drink now.*

1982 CABERNET SAUVIGNON ($7.50) Beau Tour, Estate, Napa Valley. *11% Merlot. Stewed vegetables, sour, thin, unattractive.*

1982 CABERNET SAUVIGNON ($10.00) Claret, Napa Valley. *1.5 liters. Weedy, rough and unattractive.*

☆☆☆ 1982 CABERNET SAUVIGNON ($27.00) Private Reserve, Napa Valley. *Velvety and rich, with complexity and good firm acidity. Drink 1990.*

☆ 1984 CABERNET SAUVIGNON ($6.80) Beau Tour, Estate, Napa Valley. *Simple, metallic, lacking fruit.*

☆☆☆ 1976 PINOT NOIR ($8.00) Los Carneros, Napa Valley. *Elegant and rich, with hints of cherry and violet.*

☆☆ 1977 PINOT NOIR Los Carneros, Napa Valley. *Tannic and richly varietal.*

1979 PINOT NOIR ($9.00) Los Carneros, Napa Valley. *Stemmy, raisiny. This one has not aged gracefully.*

☆☆ 1980 PINOT NOIR ($7.50) Beaumont, Napa Valley. *Vigorous, fruity, firmly structured.*

☆☆☆ 1980 PINOT NOIR ($10.00) Los Carneros. *Rich, deep, balanced, very attractive.*

☆ 1984 PINOT NOIR ($6.60) Beaumont, Napa Valley. *Ripe, heavy, clean, old-style California Pinot. Decent but nothing much.*

☆☆ 1984 PINOT NOIR ($10.00) Los Carneros Reserve, Napa Valley. *Soft, spicy, perfumed, heavy.*

☆☆ 1985 PINOT NOIR ($10.00) Los Carneros Reserve, Napa Valley. *Crisp, clean, good fruit, balanced, attractive.*

ঌ

BEL ARBRES VINEYARDS *see* Fetzer Vineyards

## *Bellerose Vineyard* SONOMA COUNTY

### WHITE

☆☆☆ 1986 SAUVIGNON BLANC ($9.00) Sonoma. *24% Semillon. Rich, lush, deep, clean, lovely.*

### RED

☆☆☆ 1980 CABERNET SAUVIGNON ($12.00) Cuvée Bellerose, Sonoma. *18% Merlot, 10% Cabernet Franc, 2% Malbec. Classic.*

☆☆☆ 1983 CABERNET SAUVIGNON ($12.00) Cuvée Bellerose,
Sonoma. *Lean, clean, balanced, elegant, richly
fruity. Drink 1989.*

☆☆☆ 1984 CABERNET SAUVIGNON ($14.00) Cuvée Bellerose,
Sonoma. *11% Cabernet Franc, 10% Merlot, 3%
Petit Verdot and Malbec. Tangy, tight, complex,
balanced, Bordeaux-structured wine. Drink 1992.*

☆☆☆ 1983 MERLOT ($8.50) Sonoma. *Lean and elegant in struc-
ture, with lovely fruit and varietal flavors. Classic;
built to age well. Drink 1989.*

☆☆ 1984 MERLOT ($12.00) Estate, Sonoma. *Spicy, clean, good
varietal character. Nice.*

&

## Belli and Sauret Vineyards   *SAN LUIS OBISPO COUNTY*

### RED
☆☆☆ 1982 ZINFANDEL ($6.75) Paso Robles. *Lush, rich, fruity,
clean and delicious.*

&

## Belvedere Wine Company            *SONOMA COUNTY*

### WHITE
☆☆☆ 1983 BACIGALUPI CHARDONNAY ($12.00) Sonoma.
*Crisp, complex, elegant, richly fruity, superb.*

☆☆☆ 1983 WINERY LAKE CHARDONNAY ($12.00) Napa Val-
ley. *Clean, balanced, rich, fruity, classic.*

☆ 1984 CHARDONNAY ($4.75) Discovery Series, North
Coast. *Clean, fresh, attractive but tastes more like
Gewürztraminer than Chardonnay.*

☆☆☆ 1984 BACIGALUPI CHARDONNAY ($12.00) Sonoma.
*Crisp, ripe, intense, rich, deep, balanced.*

☆☆ 1985 CHARDONNAY ($4.75) Discovery Series, Napa Valley.
*Snappy, crisp, clean and spicy. Light and fresh.*

☆☆☆ 1985 BACIGALUPI CHARDONNAY ($12.00) Sonoma.
*Crisp, fresh, lean and classically structured. A de-
lightful departure for this wine.*

☆☆☆ 1985 WINERY LAKE CHARDONNAY ($12.00) Napa Val-
ley. *Rich, intense, with some oiliness balanced by
lovely acidity.*

☆☆ 1986 SAUVIGNON BLANC ($4.00) Discovery Series,
Sonoma. *Grassy, crisp, fresh, ripe and charming.*

### RED
☆ 1982 CLASSIC RED ($3.00) Napa Valley. *Flat, dull, decent,
clean.*

☆☆☆☆ 1980 ROBERT YOUNG VINEYARDS CABERNET SAU-
VIGNON ($12.00) Sonoma. *Elegant, rich, superb.
Drink now.*

☆☆ 1982 CABERNET SAUVIGNON ($4.00) Discovery Series,
Lake. *Herbal, lush, clean, simple but attractive.*

☆☆☆ 1982 ROBERT YOUNG VINEYARDS CABERNET SAU-
VIGNON ($10.00) Alexander Valley. *Very crisp,
clean, lovely. Drink 1988.*

☆☆☆ 1982 YORK CREEK CABERNET SAUVIGNON ($12.00)
Napa Valley. *Lush oak and fruit, lovely structure.
Drink 1990.*

☆ 1983 CABERNET SAUVIGNON ($4.00) Discovery Series,
Lake. *Sour, vegetal, decent structure, clean.*

☆☆☆ 1983 ROBERT YOUNG VINEYARDS CABERNET SAU-
VIGNON ($12.00) Alexander Valley. *Firm, lovely
fruit, great structure. Drink 1989.*

☆☆☆ 1983 YORK CREEK CABERNET SAUVIGNON ($12.00) Napa Valley. *Rich, tight, beautifully built. Rich fruit and complexity. Drink 1990.*

☆☆☆☆ 1984 ROBERT YOUNG VINEYARDS CABERNET SAUVIGNON ($12.00) Alexander Valley. *Intense, fruity, superb balance. Drink 1992.*

☆☆☆ 1982 ROBERT YOUNG VINEYARDS MERLOT ($10.00) Alexander Valley. *Soft, herbal, super rich, lovely. Drink now.*

☆☆ 1983 ROBERT YOUNG VINEYARDS MERLOT ($12.00) Alexander Valley. *Herbal, clean, varietal, a bit thin and short on fruit. Drink now.*

☆☆☆ 1979 BACIGALUPI PINOT NOIR ($15.00) Sonoma. *Spicy and fruity. Drink now.*

☆☆☆ 1981 BACIGALUPI PINOT NOIR ($11.00) Sonoma. *Rich, deep, clean, fruity, varietal, lovely.*

☆☆☆☆ 1981 WINERY LAKE PINOT NOIR ($12.00) Estate, Los Carneros. *Rich, varietal, fruity, with sweet oak; very Burgundian. At its peak now.*

☆☆ 1982 PINOT NOIR ($3.50) Discovery Series, Napa Valley. *25% Petite Sirah. Decent, varietal, clean, slightly metallic.*

☆☆☆ 1982 BACIGALUPI PINOT NOIR ($12.00) Sonoma. *Rich, deep, soft, fruity, complex, varietal, and lovely.*

1982 WINERY LAKE PINOT NOIR ($12.00) Napa Valley. *Swampy and vegetal.*

☆☆ 1983 WINERY LAKE PINOT NOIR ($12.00) Los Carneros. *Crisp, clean, fresh, good varietal fruit. Give it time. Drink 1989.*

☆☆☆ 1985 BACIGALUPI PINOT NOIR ($12.00) Sonoma. *Soft, floral, buttery, lovely.*

🙰

## *Benmarl Wine Company, Ltd.*          NEW YORK
### WHITE
☆☆ 1985 SEYVAL BLANC ($8.00) Hudson River Region. *Crisp, fruity, with some interesting oak complexity.*
### RED
☆ 1982 RED ($10.00) Marlboro Village, Hudson River Region. *Crisp, clean, deep. Decent flavor.*

☆☆ 1979 BACO NOIR ($12.00) Estate, Hudson River Region. *Earthy, rich, fruity, clean, rather pleasant.*

🙰

## *Bergfeld Wine Cellars*          NAPA COUNTY
### WHITE
☆☆☆ 1986 SAUVIGNON BLANC ($5.00) Reserve, Estate, Napa Valley. *Crisp, clean, fruity, nice.*

🙰

## *Beringer Vineyards*          NAPA COUNTY
### WHITE
☆☆☆ 1985 SAUVIGNON BLANC ($8.50) Proprietor Grown, Knights Valley. *Snappy and crisp, with interesting oak complexity and lush nut-like flavors. Unusual but nice.*

☆☆☆ 1982 CHARDONNAY ($9.75) Estate, Napa Valley. *Vinous, rich and clean; well made.*

☆☆ 1982 CHARDONNAY ($15.00) Private Reserve, Napa Valley. *Big, rich, deep, fruity.*

☆☆ 1983 CHARDONNAY ($9.50) Napa Valley. *Clean, fresh, attractive.*

☆☆☆ 1983 CHARDONNAY ($12.00) Gamble Ranch, Napa Valley. *Barrel fermented. Toasty, lush, big yet balanced.*

☆ 1983 CHARDONNAY ($14.00) Private Reserve, Estate, Napa Valley. *Heavy, oily, fruity, fat and clumsy.*

☆☆☆ 1984 CHARDONNAY ($10.00) Napa Valley. *Crisp, snappy, clean, varietal, charming.*

☆☆☆ 1984 CHARDONNAY ($13.00) Gamble, Napa Valley. *Rich, deep, barrel-fermented oak, lush fruit. A well-made wine in an assertive style.*

☆☆☆☆ 1984 CHARDONNAY ($15.00) Private Reserve, Estate, Napa Valley. *Rich, lovely fruit, great oak, complex flavors and superb balance.*

☆☆☆ 1985 NAPA RIDGE CHARDONNAY ($5.75) California. *Soft, sweetish new oak, clean, lovely fruit. Quite a value.*

☆☆☆ 1985 CHARDONNAY ($10.00) Napa Valley. *Fresh, soft, nicely balanced, varietal.*

☆☆☆☆ 1985 CHARDONNAY ($14.50) Private Reserve, Estate, Napa Valley. *Crisp, toasty, focused, with exquisite fruit and acidity. Elegant and mouth-filling.*

☆☆ 1986 NAPA RIDGE CHARDONNAY ($5.75) North Coast. *Lush, fruity, soft, attractive.*

☆☆☆ 1986 CHARDONNAY ($10.50) Estate, Napa Valley. *Soft, lush, balanced, clean and mellow.*

☆☆ 1985 FUME BLANC ($7.80) Napa Valley. *Grassy, crisp, fresh, clean, varietal.*

☆ 1986 NAPA RIDGE SAUVIGNON BLANC ($4.75) North Coast. *Meaty, ripe, coarse, decent.*

☆☆☆ 1986 SAUVIGNON BLANC ($8.50) Knights Valley. *24% Semillon. Soft, rich, lush, with lovely wood complexity.*

## BLANC DE NOIR
1986 WHITE ZINFANDEL ($4.25) North Coast. *Sugary, mawkish, watery; a strictly commercial effort.*

## RED
1982 NAPA RIDGE NAPA RANCH RED ($3.60) North Coast. *50% Cabernet Sauvignon. Thin, herbaceous.*

☆☆☆☆ 1978 CABERNET SAUVIGNON ($22.00) Private Reserve, Lemmon Ranch, Napa Valley. *Depth, richness and fruit. A classic. Will last into the next century.*

☆☆ 1979 CABERNET SAUVIGNON ($8.00) Knights Valley, Sonoma. *Elegant, clean, but a little simple. Lovely velvety texture.*

☆☆☆ 1979 CABERNET SAUVIGNON ($9.00) State Lane, Napa Valley. *Their best '79 Cabernet—rich, unctuous, complex and lovely.*

☆☆ 1980 CABERNET SAUVIGNON ($8.00) Knights Valley, Sonoma. *Berried, sweet fruit, clean and attractive. Drink now.*

☆☆☆ 1980 CABERNET SAUVIGNON ($15.00) State Lane, Napa Valley. *Rich, complex, clean, a real beaut'. Drink now.*

☆☆☆☆ 1980 CABERNET SAUVIGNON ($20.00) Private Reserve, Lemmon-Chabot, Napa Valley. *Rich, structured, deep, complex, stunning. Drink 1988.*

☆☆ 1981 CABERNET SAUVIGNON ($7.00) Napa Valley. *Fruity, clean, oaky, appealing. Drink now.*

☆☆ 1981 CABERNET SAUVIGNON ($10.00) Knights Valley, Sonoma. *Clean, varietal, attractive. Drink now.*

☆☆☆ 1981 CABERNET SAUVIGNON ($18.00) Private Reserve, State Lane, Lemmon-Chabot, Napa Valley. *Soft, rich, clean, mellow. Drink 1988.*

☆☆☆☆ 1981 CABERNET SAUVIGNON ($25.00) Lemmon-Chabot, Napa Valley. *Powerful, rich, clean, lovely, fruity, complex. Drink 1992.*

☆☆ 1982 NAPA RIDGE CABERNET SAUVIGNON ($5.50) North Coast. *Fresh, herbal, varietal, attractive.*

☆☆☆ 1982 CABERNET SAUVIGNON ($9.00) Proprietor Grown, Knights Valley. *Fruity and nicely structured. Lush, clean and charming. Drink 1988.*

☆☆ 1982 CABERNET SAUVIGNON ($9.00) Napa Valley. *Herbal, clean, good balance, charming. Drink now.*

☆☆☆☆ 1982 CABERNET SAUVIGNON ($18.00) Private Reserve, Napa Valley. *Soft, lush, crisp, cedary flavors, good structure. Drink 1990.*

☆☆☆ 1983 CABERNET SAUVIGNON ($12.50) Proprietor Grown, Knights Valley. *Tart, woody, with good cherry fruit; clean, straightforward. Not as good as the 1982. Drink 1989.*

☆☆☆ 1983 CABERNET SAUVIGNON ($19.00) Private Reserve, Napa Valley. *Superb. Silky, long, lovely cherry fruit. Drink 1990.*

☆ 1984 NAPA RIDGE MERLOT ($5.75) California. *Simple, slight, decent.*

ঽ৶

## *Bethel Heights Vineyard* OREGON
### WHITE
☆☆ 1984 CHARDONNAY ($10.75) Willamette Valley. *Clean, round, fresh, varietal, attractive.*

☆☆ 1985 CHARDONNAY ($10.75) Oregon. *Ripe, clean, decent.*
### RED
☆ 1984 PINOT NOIR ($10.75) Willamette Valley. *Tannic, volatile acidity, oily, thin.*

ঽ৶

## *Binns Vineyards and Winery* NEW MEXICO
### RED
☆ 1983 VALLE ROJO ($5.00) New Mexico. *Vegetal, crisp, clean, decent.*

☆ 1983 ZINFANDEL ($6.00) New Mexico. *Herbaceous, thin, decent fruit.*

ঽ৶

BLACK MOUNTAIN *see* J. W. Morris Wineries

## *Black Sheep Vintners* CALAVERAS COUNTY
### RED
☆ 1984 ZINFANDEL ($7.00) Amador. *Tart, astringent, low fruit, decent.*

ঽ৶

## *Blackwood Canyon Vintners* WASHINGTON
### WHITE
☆☆ 1984 WHITE RIESLING ($9.00) Late Harvest, Clear, Columbia Valley. *6.2% residual sugar. Crisp, clean, with some herbal qualities; balanced.*

ঽ৶

## *Boeger Winery* EL DORADO COUNTY
### WHITE

☆☆☆ 1982 CHARDONNAY ($9.00) El Dorado. *Nice, fruity, clean, rich, long finish, very good. Showing age.*

☆☆☆ 1984 CHARDONNAY ($9.50) El Dorado. *Crisp, clean, varietal, good oak, fruity finish.*

☆☆☆ 1985 CHARDONNAY ($10.00) El Dorado. *Clean, lean, varietal, complex and neatly balanced.*

☆☆☆ 1986 JOHANNISBERG RIESLING ($6.50) Estate, El Dorado. *2.54% residual sugar. 21% Muscat Canneli. Lush, lovely, clean, soft and charming.*

☆☆☆ 1986 SAUVIGNON BLANC ($7.50) Estate, El Dorado. *Lovely, soft, lush, fruity, clean. A stunning wine.*

### BLANC DE NOIR

☆ 1986 WHITE CABERNET ($5.50) Estate, El Dorado. *Soft, varietal, simple, a bit dull.*

### RED

☆ 1982 HANGTOWN RED ($4.00) California. *Raisiny, spicy, rich, decent.*

☆☆ 1983 HANGTOWN RED ($4.00) California. *Crisp, earthy, lush, good fruit.*

1980 CABERNET SAUVIGNON ($8.50) El Dorado. *Good fruit and earth, clean and fat, simple. Drink now.*

☆☆ 1981 CABERNET SAUVIGNON ($9.00) El Dorado. *Ripe, fat, berried, intense, clean. Drink 1990.*

1982 CABERNET SAUVIGNON ($6.00) El Dorado. *Dull, musty.*

☆☆ 1982 CABERNET SAUVIGNON ($9.00) Estate, El Dorado. *Earthy, smooth, clean, ripe, decent. Drink 1988.*

☆☆☆ 1983 CABERNET SAUVIGNON ($10.00) Estate, El Dorado. *Rich, tight fruit and firm structure. Lovely finish. Drink 1989.*

☆☆☆ 1983 CABERNET SAUVIGNON ($15.00) Reserve, Potter Valley. *Richly fruity, firmly structured, showing balance and finesse. Drink 1989.*

☆☆ 1980 MERLOT ($8.50) 10th Anniversary, Estate, El Dorado. *Soft and delicate, balanced.*

☆☆ 1981 MERLOT ($9.50) Estate, El Dorado. *Soft and appealing, with a nice lushness.*

☆☆ 1982 MERLOT ($10.00) Estate, El Dorado. *Fruity clean, attractive.*

☆☆☆ 1983 MERLOT ($12.50) GBV, Estate, El Dorado. *18% Cabernet Sauvignon. Ripe, sweet oak, good fruit.*

☆ 1984 MERLOT ($12.50) GBV, Estate, El Dorado. *19% Cabernet Sauvignon. Soft, raisiny, lush, lacking freshness.*

☆☆ 1985 MERLOT ($10.00) GBV, Estate, El Dorado. *Soft sweet pea nose, lush texture, some vegetal flavors but good fruit; balanced.*

☆☆ 1981 ZINFANDEL ($6.00) El Dorado. *Leathery, soft textured, clear, decent.*

☆☆ 1984 ZINFANDEL ($6.50) El Dorado. *Herbal, ripe, clean, decent.*

૨ન

## *Bogle Vineyards* YOLO COUNTY
### WHITE

1984 GREY RIESLING ($4.50) Clarksburg. *Heavy, sweet, coarse, unattractive.*

### RED

☆☆ 1983 PETITE SIRAH ($5.00) Clarksburg. *Ripe, fat, berried, clean. Drink now.*

૨ન

## *Bonny Doon Vineyard*       SANTA CRUZ COUNTY
### WHITE

☆☆☆ 1983 VIN DE PAILLE ($12.00) Central Coast. *375 ml. 12.5% residual sugar. Muscat, rich, grapey.*

☆☆☆ 1985 LE SOPHISTE ($20.00) California. *Buttery, lush, complex, ripe like a good white Rhone. 60% Marsanne and 40% Roussanne.*

☆☆☆ 1983 CHARDONNAY ($12.00) La Reina, Monterey. *Rich, complex, deep, attractive.*

☆☆ 1984 CHARDONNAY ($13.00) La Reina, Monterey. *Crisp, balanced, some barrel fermentation flavors, pleasant.*

☆☆☆ 1985 CHARDONNAY ($13.00) La Reina, Monterey. *Lush, juicy, heavy, good oak, intense but tangy. A bit overblown.*

☆☆ 1986 GRAHM CREW CHARDONNAY ($8.50) Sonoma. *Ripe, fat, lush, clean, pleasant.*

☆☆☆ 1986 GRENACHE ($6.50) Clos de Gilroy, California. *Lush, ripe, fresh, spicy, clean.*

☆ 1984 PINOT BLANC ($8.50) Arroyo Seco, Monterey. *Sour, vegetal, smooth.*

1985 PINOT BLANC ($12.50) California. *Flat, dull, vegetal.*

### RED

☆☆ 1982 VIN ROUGE ($6.00) California. *Peppery, rich, interesting. Read the label notes.*

☆☆ 1982 CLARET ($9.00) Mendocino. *Vegetal but nicely made, clean and complex. Drink now.*

☆☆☆ 1983 CLARET ($9.00) Central Coast. *75% Cabernet, 25% Merlot. Rich, clean, lush.*

☆☆☆ 1984 LE CIGARE VOLANT ($10.50) California. *72% Grenache, 25% Syrah, 3% Mourvèdre. Ripe, blackberry fruit; spicy; delicious. A delightful attempt at a Rhône-style wine.*

☆☆☆ 1985 GRAHM CREW VIN ROUGE ($6.50) California. *Lush, round, charming red wine with depth and charm.*

☆☆☆☆ 1985 LE CIGARE VOLANT ($12.50) Calilfornia *77% Grenache. 18% Syrah and 5% Mourvèdre. Rich, lush, concentrated, complex, balanced, delicous. Drink now.*

☆☆☆ 1983 CABERNET SAUVIGNON ($14.00) B.J.Carney, Anderson Valley. *25% Merlot. Crisp, balanced, clean, attractive. Drink 1988.*

☆☆ 1981 PINOT NOIR ($9.00) Arrendell, Sonoma. *Earthy and balanced, soft fruit, a bit underripe.*

☆☆☆ 1983 PINOT NOIR ($18.00) Bethel Heights, Willamette Valley, Oregon. *Rich fruit, elegant, clean, charming.*

☆☆☆ 1983 SYRAH ($10.50) Central Coast. *Crisp, complex, graceful, very Rhone-like.*

☆☆☆ 1984 SYRAH ($12.00) Paso Robles. *Rich, berried, ripe, intense.*

જ⋅

BOONE'S FARM *see* E. & J. Gallo Winery

## *Boordy Vineyards*       MARYLAND
### WHITE

☆☆☆ 1984 VIDAL BLANC ($5.00) Semi-dry, Maryland. *Spicy, crisp, fresh, with lovely fruit and clean acidity.*

જ⋅

## *Bouchaine Vineyards*                    NAPA COUNTY

### WHITE
☆☆☆ NV CHARDONNAY ($7.50) Napa Valley. *Clean, fresh, lively fruit, charming.*

☆☆☆ 1982 CHARDONNAY ($12.50) Alexander Valley. *Clean, fresh, fruity, complex, good acidity.*

☆☆☆ 1982 CHARDONNAY ($14.00) 50% Keith, 50% Black Mountain, Alexander Valley. *Ripe, fruity, classy, very likable.*

☆☆ 1982 CHARDONNAY ($14.50) Napa Valley. *Heavy, decent, a bit coarse.*

☆☆☆ 1983 CHARDONNAY ($14.50) Napa Valley-Los Carneros. *Crisp, clean, balanced, lovely varietal flavors.*

☆☆☆ 1984 CHARDONNAY ($15.00) Napa Valley. *Crisp, lush, clean, with some fruit.*

☆☆☆ 1984 CHARDONNAY ($19.50) Napa Valley-Los Carneros. *Clean, structured, a bit coarse but very nicely built.*

☆ 1984 CHARDONNAY ($22.50) Winery Lake, Napa Valley-Los Carneros. *Heavy, oily, vegetal.*

☆☆☆ 1985 CHARDONNAY ($13.50) Napa Valley. *Soft, rich, lush, deep, well built and delicious.*

### RED
☆☆☆ 1982 CABERNET SAUVIGNON ($15.00) Jerry Luper Reserve, Rutherford. *Rich, elegant, great structure. Drink 1988.*

☆☆ 1981 PINOT NOIR ($15.00) Winery Lake, Napa Valley-Carneros. *Clean, earthy, light, lovely.*

☆☆ 1982 PINOT NOIR ($12.50) Los Carneros, Napa Valley. *Cherry flavors, clean, attractive, short.*

☆☆☆ 1982 PINOT NOIR ($15.00) Winery Lake, Napa Valley-Carneros. *Fruity, complex flavors, a bit fuller than the '81.*

☆☆☆ 1982 PINOT NOIR ($20.00) Napa Valley. *Crisp cherry fruit, spicy, lean, lovely.*

☆☆ 1983 PINOT NOIR ($12.00) Napa Valley-Los Carneros. *Crisp, fresh, nice fruit, attractive.*

☆☆ 1983 PINOT NOIR ($13.25) Winery Lake, Napa Valley. *Eucalyptus flavors, soft, clean, nicely made.*

☆☆ 1985 PINOT NOIR ($7.50) Los Carneros. *Crisp, fruity, clean, varietal.*

❧

## *The Brander Vineyard*        SANTA BARBARA COUNTY

### WHITE
☆☆☆☆ 1984 CHARDONNAY ($11.00) Santa Ynez Valley. *Oaky, ripe, with rich fruit and superb balance.*

☆☆ 1985 CHARDONNAY ($9.00) Santa Ynez Valley. *Varietal, crisp, with some earthy, vegetal flavors.*

☆ 1986 SAUVIGNON BLANC ($8.50) Santa Ynez Valley. *Earthy, lush, lacking freshness. A disappointment.*

### RED
☆☆☆ 1984 BOUCHET ($15.00) Santa Ynez Valley. *65% Cabernet Franc and 35% Merlot. Lush, smooth, well structured, stunning fruit. Drink 1989.*

☆☆☆ 1983 CABERNET SAUVIGNON ($9.50) California. *Crisp, earthy, nicely structured. Drink now.*

❧

## Braren Pauli Winery                    MENDOCINO COUNTY
### RED
☆☆ 1983 CABERNET SAUVIGNON ($8.00) Walt Family, Mendocino. *Rich, oaky, intense, heavy. Drink 1990.*

☆☆☆ 1984 MERLOT ($10.00) Mauritson, Alexander Valley. *Rich, fresh, fruity, clean, lovely balance and texture. Drink now.*

☆☆ 1980 ZINFANDEL ($8.50) Redwood Valley, Mendocino. *Big, fat, lush, intense, old style.*

☆☆ 1982 ZINFANDEL ($7.50) Ricetti, Mendocino. *Crisp, clean, varietal, some volatile acidity.*

## Brenner Cellars                        SONOMA COUNTY
### RED
☆☆ 1981 CABERNET SAUVIGNON ($8.50) San Luis Obispo. *Varietal, fruity, charming. Drink now.*

☆ 1979 ZINFANDEL ($7.50) Sonoma. *Decent, simple, clean and bland.*

## Bridgehampton Winery                   NEW YORK
### WHITE
☆ 1982 CHARDONNAY ($12.00) Long Island. *Clean and fruity.*

☆ 1985 CHARDONNAY ($8.50) Estate, Long Island. *Crisp, varietal, a bit strange.*

1985 CHARDONNAY ($11.00) Estate Reserve, Long Island. *Oily, heavy, odd.*

☆☆☆ 1986 JOHANNISBERG RIESLING ($10.00) Late Harvest, Long Island. *6.5% residual sugar. Apricot botrytis flavors, crisp acidity and long, soft, luscious finish.*

☆ 1984 RIESLING ($7.50) Long Island. *Oily, intense, some varietal character, a bit flat.*

☆☆☆ 1986 SAUVIGNON BLANC ($10.00) Long Island. *Crisp, tart, fruity, with lovely varietal character.*
### RED
☆☆☆ 1984 MERLOT ($11.00) Long Island. *Rich, with fresh fruit and good structure; lovely. Drink 1989.*

☆☆ 1984 PINOT NOIR ($16.00) Long Island. *Fresh, simple, clean and Beaujolais-like.*

## Bronte Champagne & Wine Company        MICHIGAN
### RED
○ NV  BACO NOIR ($4.00) Michigan. *Dirty, unattractive.*

## Brotherhood Winery                     NEW YORK
### FLAVORED
☆ HOLIDAY ($3.75) New York. *Spicy, cinnamon-flavored white wine.*

☆☆ MAY WINE ($3.75) New York. *Sweet, charming rosé, flavored with woodruff and strawberry.*

## David Bruce Winery                     SANTA CRUZ COUNTY
### WHITE
☆☆ 1982 CHARDONNAY ($18.00) Estate, Santa Cruz Mountains. *Heavy, ripe, clean, lush, intense, lovely.*

☆ 1983 CHARDONNAY ($10.00) California. *Vinous, rich, unbalanced, clumsy.*

☆☆☆ 1984 CHARDONNAY ($10.00) California. *Toasty, lush, oaky, rich, lovely.*

1984 CHARDONNAY ($18.00) Estate, Santa Cruz Mountains. *Heavy, oily, not pleasant.*

### RED

☆ 1980 CABERNET SAUVIGNON ($12.50) Vintner's Selection, Santa Clara. *Weedy, some volatile acidity.*

☆☆☆ 1981 CABERNET SAUVIGNON California. *Rich, berried, tannic, dense, good. Drink 1988 and beyond.*

☆☆☆ 1982 CABERNET SAUVIGNON ($12.50) Vintners Select, California. *Lush, structured, classic. Drink now.*

☆☆☆ 1983 CABERNET SAUVIGNON ($10.50) 65% Alexander Valley, 35% Santa Cruz Mountains. *Crisp, clean, elegant, lovely varietal character. Drink 1989.*

☆☆ 1983 CABERNET SAUVIGNON ($12.50) Vintner's Select, California. *Ripe, fruity, rich, some vegetation but attractive. Drink 1989.*

☆☆ 1984 CABERNET SAUVIGNON ($12.50) Vintner's Select, California. *Earthy, lush, deep. Drink now.*

☆ 1975 PINOT NOIR Santa Cruz. *For lovers of old wines. Chocolatey, raisiny, smooth, ripe.*

☆ 1978 PINOT NOIR ($12.00) Estate, Santa Cruz. *Chocolate and walnuts. Decent but past its prime.*

☆ 1979 PINOT NOIR ($12.00) Estate, Santa Cruz Mountains. *Spicy, with some vegetal characteristics. Decent balance, smooth.*

☆☆☆ 1980 PINOT NOIR ($15.00) Estate, Santa Cruz. *High alcohol, cherry flavors; complex and delicious.*

☆☆☆ 1981 PINOT NOIR ($12.50) Estate, Santa Cruz Mountains. *Earthy, rich and loaded with lovely cherry flavors.*

☆☆☆ 1982 PINOT NOIR ($12.50) Estate, Santa Cruz Mountains. *Crisp, soft, lovely fruit and varietal character.*

☆☆☆ 1983 PINOT NOIR ($12.50) Estate, Santa Cruz Mountains. *Tangy, rich, varietal, attractive. Drink now.*

☆☆ 1983 PINOT NOIR ($15.00) Santa Cruz Mountains. *Tea-like flavors, tart, tight, earthy, attractive.*

☆☆☆ 1984 PINOT NOIR ($15.00) Estate, Santa Cruz Mountains. *Fresh, crisp, lovely cherry fruit, clean, balanced.*

1985 PINOT NOIR ($15.00) Silver Anniversary, Estate, Santa Cruz Mountains. *Astringent and lemony.*

☆ 1981 ZINFANDEL ($5.50) Mendocino. *Rich, buttery oak, some odd flavors, decent.*

ᵛᴬ

## Buehler Vineyards                    NAPA COUNTY

### WHITE

☆☆☆ 1984 PINOT BLANC ($8.00) Estate, Napa Valley. *Crisp, clean, lovely structure, varietal, very attractive. Drink 1988.*

☆☆ 1985 PINOT BLANC ($8.00) Napa Valley. *Soft, clean, fruity, attractive but very understated.*

### BLANC DE NOIR

☆☆☆ 1986 WHITE ZINFANDEL ($5.00) Napa Valley. *Crisp, fresh, dry and delicious. Great with food.*

### ROSE

☆☆☆ 1986 ZINFANDEL ROSE ($5.75) Napa Valley. *Crisp, fresh, snappy, dry (only 5% residual sugar); lovely.*

## RED

☆☆☆ 1978 CABERNET SAUVIGNON ($9.00) Estate, Napa Valley. *Soft and lush, with some sugar and good varietal character.*

☆☆ 1980 CABERNET SAUVIGNON ($12.00) Estate, Napa Valley. *Rich, decent, showing its age.*

☆☆ 1981 CABERNET SAUVIGNON ($12.00) Estate, Napa Valley. *Intense, tight and tannic. Drink now.*

☆☆☆ 1982 CABERNET SAUVIGNON ($10.00) Estate, Napa Valley. *Lush, rich, dense, good structure. Drink 1988.*

☆☆☆ 1983 CABERNET SAUVIGNON ($10.00) Estate, Napa Valley. *Deep, concentrated, lush, soft yet beautifully structured. Drink 1989.*

☆☆☆ 1984 CABERNET SAUVIGNON ($11.00) Napa Valley. *Meaty, earthy, rich, complex, nicely structured. Drink 1992.*

☆☆☆ 1980 ZINFANDEL ($8.00) Estate, Napa Valley. *Lush, velvety and rich.*

☆☆ 1981 ZINFANDEL ($7.00) Napa Valley. *Soft, lush and big.*

☆☆ 1982 ZINFANDEL ($6.00) Estate, Napa Valley. *Crisp, clean, tart and attractive.*

☆☆☆ 1983 ZINFANDEL ($6.00) Napa Valley. *Ripe, intense, fleshy, nicely structured, balanced.*

☆☆☆ 1985 ZINFANDEL ($8.00) Napa Valley. *Big, ripe, intense, with plummy fruit and concentrated varietal character. A bruiser with a heart of gold.*

☙

## *Buena Vista Winery*　　　　SONOMA COUNTY
## WHITE

☆☆ 1985 CHAARBLANC ($4.75) Carneros. *Soft, rich, decent white wine with some complexity.*

☆☆☆ 1985 SPICELING ($5.50) Carneros. *1.2% residual sugar. A blend of Riesling and Gewürztraminer. Fresh, spicy, crisp, delightful.*

☆☆ 1982 CHARDONNAY ($9.00) Sonoma Valley. *Crisp, clean, simple, attractive.*

☆☆ 1982 CHARDONNAY ($16.50) Private Reserve, Sonoma Valley-Carneros. *Decent, soft, lacking focus.*

☆☆ 1983 CHARDONNAY ($9.00) Sonoma Valley-Carneros. *Clean, crisp, dense, not much depth.*

☆ 1983 CHARDONNAY ($12.50) Special Selection, Jeanette's, Sonoma Valley-Carneros. *Simple, sour, not likable.*

☆☆☆ 1983 CHARDONNAY ($16.50) Private Reserve, Sonoma Valley-Carneros. *Crisp, clean, fresh, delicious.*

☆☆ 1984 CHARDONNAY ($10.75) Sonoma Valley-Carneros. *Crisp, fresh, apple flavors. Balanced, clean, pleasant.*

☆ 1984 CHARDONNAY ($12.50) Vineyard Selection, Jeanette's, Sonoma Valley-Carneros. *Dull, soft, a bit oily, decent.*

☆☆ 1984 CHARDONNAY ($16.50) Private Reserve, Estate, Sonoma Valley-Carneros. *Fruity, spicy, sweetish.*

☆☆ 1985 CHARDONNAY ($10.75) Sonoma Valley-Carneros. *Clean, fresh, lemony, good balance.*

☆☆ 1985 CHARDONNAY ($13.25) Jeanette's, Sonoma Valley. *Spicy, clean, mature, subtle, decent.*

☆☆ 1985 CHARDONNAY ($14.50) Private Reserve, Estate, Carneros Sonoma Valley. *Crisp and clean, nicely balanced but lacking fruit and charm.*

☆☆ 1985 CHARDONNAY ($16.50) Proprietor's Reserve, Carneros Sonoma Valley. *Ripe and rich, hot, overdone.*

☆☆ 1986 CHARDONNAY ($8.50) Jeanette's, Carneros Sonoma Valley. *Fresh, bright and fruity; a charming, unde-manding wine.*

☆☆ 1986 FUME BLANC ($8.50) Wasson, Alexander Valley. *Crisp, varietal, balanced, decent.*

☆☆ 1986 GEWURZTRAMINER ($7.00) Estate, Carneros Sonoma Valley. *Spicy, crisp, clean, rich, some herbs, decent balance.*

☆☆ 1985 JOHANNISBERG RIESLING ($15.00) Late Harvest, Carneros. *375 ml. 12% residual sugar. Fat, syrupy, sweet and essentially simple.*

☆☆☆ 1986 JOHANNISBERG RIESLING ($7.00) Estate, Carneros. *Crisp, clean, fruity, with good acidity and melon flavors.*

☆☆☆ 1986 SAUVIGNON BLANC ($7.00) Lake. *Fresh, lively vari-etal fruit; clean and appealing.*

## BLANC DE NOIR

☆☆☆ 1986 STEELHEAD RUN ($4.75) Blanc de Pinot Noir, Car-neros. *Crisp, fresh, peachy, lively, delicious.*

## RED

☆☆☆ 1984 L'ANNEE ($30.00) Carneros. *1.5 liters. Cabernet Sauvig-non/Merlot blend. Rich, deep, concentrated flavors, good balance. Drink 1989.*

☆☆☆ 1978 CABERNET SAUVIGNON ($18.00) Special Selection, Estate, Sonoma Valley. *Rich and ripe, great depth and structure, herbal and deep.*

☆☆☆ 1979 CABERNET SAUVIGNON ($18.00) Special Selection, Estate, Sonoma Valley. *Rich, complex, supple, for-ward. Will improve for years.*

☆☆ 1980 CABERNET SAUVIGNON ($9.00) Sonoma. *Soft, well-structured, nice herbal notes. Drink now.*

☆☆☆ 1980 CABERNET SAUVIGNON ($18.00) Special Selection, Estate, Sonoma Valley. *Lush and berried, rich, complex. Needs time.*

☆☆☆ 1981 CABERNET SAUVIGNON ($11.00) Sonoma-Carneros. *Silky, lush, concentrated, attractive. Drink now.*

☆☆☆☆ 1981 CABERNET SAUVIGNON ($18.00) Special Selection, Estate, Sonoma Valley-Carneros. *Crisp, fresh, clean, lovely, complex, balanced. Drink 1988.*

☆☆☆ 1982 CABERNET SAUVIGNON ($11.00) Napa Valley-Carneros. *Crisp, clean, soft, lovely fruit, charming. Drink 1988.*

☆☆☆ 1982 CABERNET SAUVIGNON ($18.00) Proprietor's Re-serve, Sonoma Valley-Carneros. *Rich, smooth, lush, velvety, lovely. Drink 1990.*

☆☆ 1983 CABERNET SAUVIGNON ($9.75) Carneros. *Rich, deep, intense varietal fruit; not greatly complex but quite charming for current drinking.*

☆☆☆ 1983 CABERNET SAUVIGNON ($18.50) Private Reserve, Sonoma Valley-Carneros. *Meaty, crisp, complex flavors; rich, velvety texture; intense fruit and long, lush finish. Drink 1992.*

☆☆☆ 1984 CABERNET SAUVIGNON ($10.00) Estate, Carneros. *Bright, fresh, well balanced, cherry fruit; charming. Drink now.*

☆☆☆ 1986 GAMAY BEAUJOLAIS ($6.00) Sonoma Valley. *Tart, clean, raspberry flavors; lovely.*

☆☆☆ 1982 MERLOT ($14.00) Private Reserve, Carneros. *Crisp, clean, snappy, with lush, ripe fruit.*

☆☆ 1983 MERLOT ($14.00) Private Reserve, Estate, Carneros. *Thin, crisp, clean, lacks depth.*

☆☆☆☆ 1984 MERLOT ($14.50) Private Reserve, Carneros. *Soft, bright, fruity, clean, tangy cherry fruit, delicious. Drink now.*

☆☆ 1976 PINOT NOIR ($8.25) Sonoma Valley. *Lush, soft and attractive. Relatively simple.*

☆☆☆ 1981 PINOT NOIR ($12.00) Special Selection, Sonoma Valley. *Rich, clean, soft yet beautifully structured.*

☆☆ 1983 PINOT NOIR ($14.00) Sonoma Valley-Carneros. *Fresh, clean, good fruit, simple flavors, pleasant.*

☆☆☆ 1984 PINOT NOIR ($14.50) Private Reserve, Carneros. *Soft, fresh, fruity, spicy, attractive.*

☆☆ 1981 ZINFANDEL ($6.00) Sonoma. *Crisp, fresh, spicy, charming.*

☆☆☆ 1981 ZINFANDEL ($12.00) Special Selection, Sonoma Valley. *Spicy, crisp, clean and very elegant.*

☆ 1982 ZINFANDEL ($6.00) Sonoma-Carneros. *Varietal, a bit heavy on the sulfur.*

☆ 1982 ZINFANDEL ($6.00) Sonoma. *Vegetal, smokey, decent.*

☆☆☆ 1982 ZINFANDEL ($10.00) Vineyard Selection, Barricia, Sonoma Valley. *Crisp, fruity, clean, delightful. The way Zinfandel should be made.*

☆☆☆ 1984 ZINFANDEL ($7.00) Estate, North Coast. *Tangy, lean, fresh fruit, crisp finish.*

ᕀ

# Burgess Cellars                     NAPA COUNTY
## WHITE

☆☆☆ 1982 CHARDONNAY ($11.75) Vintage Reserve, Napa Valley. *Crisp, lean, balanced, nicely structured. Very good.*

☆☆☆ 1983 CHARDONNAY ($12.00) Vintage Reserve, Napa Valley. *Fresh, fruity, clean, balanced, showing lovely finesse.*

☆☆☆ 1984 CHARDONNAY ($11.75) Vintage Reserve, Napa Valley. *Crisp, fresh, varietal, balanced.*

☆☆☆ 1985 CHARDONNAY ($13.00) Vintage Reserve, Napa Valley. *Crisp, rich, deep oak and fruit; charming and nicely balanced.*

## RED

☆☆☆☆ 1978 CABERNET SAUVIGNON ($16.00) Vintage Selection, Napa Valley. *Classy, deep, lovely oak and fruit. Drink 1988.*

☆☆☆ 1979 CABERNET SAUVIGNON ($17.00) Vintage Selection, Napa Valley. *Superb, rich, deep, great structure. Drink now.*

☆☆☆ 1980 CABERNET SAUVIGNON ($16.00) Vintage Selection, Napa Valley. *Lean, super crisp, complex and elegant. Drink 1988 and later.*

☆☆☆ 1981 CABERNET SAUVIGNON ($16.00) Vintage Selection, Napa Valley. *12% Merlot. Soft, complex, earthy, cherry fruit, lovely. Drink 1994.*

☆☆☆ 1982 CABERNET SAUVIGNON ($16.00) Vintage Selection, Napa Valley. *Intense, rich, varietal, complex, and fruity. Drink 1995.*

☆☆☆ 1983 CABERNET SAUVIGNON ($17.00) Vintage Selection, Napa Valley. *12% Merlot and 11% Cabernet Franc. Firm and tannic, with deep, concentrated fruit. Should mellow nicely. Drink 1991.*

☆☆ 1976 PINOT NOIR ($8.00) Winery Lake, Napa Valley. *Classy and well made but not Burgundian.*

☆☆ 1979 PINOT NOIR ($9.00) Napa Valley. *Simple, clean and attractive.*

☆☆ 1980 PINOT NOIR ($6.00) Napa Valley. *Crisp, toasty, clean.*

☆☆☆ 1977 ZINFANDEL ($6.75) Napa Valley. *Rich and berried, balanced and clean. Ready to drink.*

☆☆ 1978 ZINFANDEL ($7.00) Napa Valley. *Clean, lush, lovely fruit. Drink now.*

☆☆ 1980 ZINFANDEL ($7.00) Napa Valley. *Spicy, brambly, intense.*

☆☆ 1981 ZINFANDEL ($6.00) Napa Valley. *Varietal, clean, intense but nicely balanced.*

☆☆☆ 1982 ZINFANDEL ($6.50) Napa Valley. *Rich, dark, concentrated, with lovely berry fruit. Drink now.*

☆☆☆ 1983 ZINFANDEL ($7.50) Napa Valley. *Tannic, clean, balanced, lovely varietal character. Drink 1990.*

☆☆☆ 1984 ZINFANDEL ($8.00) Napa Valley. *Ripe berries and luscious fruit, great structure, good aging potential.*

🍇

## Davis Bynum Winery                     SONOMA COUNTY
### WHITE

☆ 1982 CHARDONNAY ($12.50) Reserve, Sonoma. *Clean but vegetal and oily.*

☆☆☆ 1983 CHARDONNAY ($12.50) Allen-Hafner Reserve, Sonoma. *Clean, rich yet delicate, great balance.*

1984 CHARDONNAY ($7.00) Sonoma. *Oily, vegetal, not much.*

☆☆ 1984 CHARDONNAY ($12.50) Reserve, Sonoma. *Oily, vegetal, varietal, decent.*

☆☆ 1985 CHARDONNAY ($8.00) Reserve, Sonoma. *Soft, fresh, rich, clean, good fruit.*

☆☆ 1985 CHARDONNAY ($13.50) Sonoma. *Crisp, clean, open, attractive, decent.*

☆ 1986 GEWURZTRAMINER ($6.50) Reserve, Russian River Valley. *Soft, dull, lacking fruit, decent but not much.*

### RED

☆☆ 1980 CABERNET SAUVIGNON ($8.00) Sonoma. *Intense and overripe, but clean and balanced. Drink now.*

☆☆ 1981 CABERNET SAUVIGNON ($9.00) Sonoma. *15% Merlot. Crisp, clean, quite nice. Drink now.*

☆☆ 1981 CABERNET SAUVIGNON ($25.00) Reserve, Sonoma. *Grapey, nicely structured, clean, moderately appealing. Drink now.*

☆☆☆ 1983 CABERNET SAUVIGNON ($12.00) Reserve, Sonoma. *Fresh, crisp, ripe cherry fruit; good structure and oak. Drink 1990.*

☆ 1980 MERLOT ($10.00) Jack Long, Dry Creek Valley, Sonoma. *Marred by dirty flavors and aromas.*

1980 MERLOT ($12.00) Reserve Bottling, 93% Jasper Long, Sonoma. *Earthy, weedy, not pleasant.*

☆☆ 1980 PINOT NOIR ($8.00) Russian River Valley. *Earthy and intense.*

☆☆☆ 1980 PINOT NOIR ($10.50) Reserve, Sonoma. *Big, lush, rich, soft, lovely. Drink now.*

☆☆☆ 1982 PINOT NOIR ($10.00) Westside Road, Russian River Valley. *Rich, deep, varietal, well made.*

☆☆ 1983 PINOT NOIR ($10.00) Westside Road, Russian River Valley. *Ripe, decent fruit, clean, lacking depth.*

☆☆ 1984 PINOT NOIR ($7.00) Westside, Sonoma. *Clean, varietal, decent.*

☆☆ 1984 PINOT NOIR ($13.00) Reserve, Sonoma. *Soft, clean, decent, lacking complexity.*

☆☆ 1983 ZINFANDEL ($7.00) Russian River Valley. *Ripe, fat, herbal, soft and quite nice.*

1984 ZINFANDEL ($6.50) Reserve, Russian River Valley. *Off flavors, odd.*

ಶಿ

## Byrd Vineyards                    MARYLAND
### WHITE
☆☆ 1983 CHARDONNAY ($7.50) Estate, Catoctin. *Toasty, rich, balanced.*

### RED
☆ 1982 CATOCTIN ($10.00) Estate, Maryland. *Thin, snappy, decent, clean.*

☆☆☆ 1980 CABERNET SAUVIGNON ($12.00) Maryland. *Violets, fruit, oak—all nicely balanced. Superb.*

☆☆☆ 1982 CABERNET SAUVIGNON ($10.00) Estate, Catoctin. *Crisp, clean, elegantly structured, remarkable. Drink 1988.*

ಶಿ

## Byron Vineyard & Winery     SANTA BARBARA COUNTY
### WHITE
☆☆ 1984 CHARDONNAY ($13.00) Reserve, 80% Santa Maria Hills, 20% Sierra Madre, Santa Barbara. *Rich, fat, deep, varietal, lush.*

☆☆ 1985 CHARDONNAY ($9.50) Santa Barbara. *Crisp, snappy, lovely oak, some oiliness.*

### RED
☆ 1984 CABERNET SAUVIGNON ($12.00) Santa Barbara. *Straightforward, herbal, some bitterness.*

☆☆☆ 1984 PINOT NOIR ($12.50) Sierra Madre, Santa Barbara. *Earthy, floral, with fresh cherry flavors and smooth texture.*

☆ 1985 PINOT NOIR ($12.00) Santa Barbara. *Berried, raisiny, snappy, decent.*

ಶಿ

## Caché Cellars                    SOLANO COUNTY
### WHITE
☆☆ 1982 CHARDONNAY ($11.00) La Reina, Monterey. *Crisp, complex, fruity; not as rounded as the '81.*

☆☆☆ 1983 CHARDONNAY ($11.00) La Reina, Monterey. *Great fruit and nice oak plus good finesse.*

### RED
☆☆☆ 1983 CABERNET SAUVIGNON Napa Valley. *Supple, complex, herbs and cherries.*

☆☆ 1979 PINOT NOIR ($7.50) Sonoma. *Pleasant, clean, fruity, nice oak, some tannic hardness.*

☆☆ 1982 PINOT NOIR ($7.50) Vinco, Monterey. *Clean, earthy, light, pleasant.*

☆ 1980 ZINFANDEL ($6.00) Baldinelli, Amador. *Spicy, good balance, lacking charm.*

☆☆☆ 1981 ZINFANDEL ($6.50) Baldinelli, Amador. *Intense but beautifully balanced. Good acid and fresh fruit.*

ಶಿ

## Cain Cellars                    NAPA COUNTY
### WHITE
1983 CHARDONNAY ($10.00) Napa Valley. *Toasty and rich, but marred by spoilage.*

☆☆☆ 1985 CHARDONNAY ($16.00) Carneros. *Rich, lush but firm and intense. Balanced and attractive.*

☆☆ 1985 SAUVIGNON BLANC ($8.00) 56% Napa, 44% Sonoma. *Fresh, decent, balanced, good varietal character.*

### RED

☆☆☆ 1982 CABERNET SAUVIGNON ($11.00) Napa Valley. *7% Merlot. Lean, crisp, tangy fruit, elegant. Drink 1988.*

☆☆☆ 1983 CABERNET SAUVIGNON ($14.00) Napa Valley. *Soft, herbal, with crisp fruit and lovely structure. Drink 1988.*

☆☆ 1984 CABERNET SAUVIGNON ($25.00) Estate, Napa Valley. *Astringent, lean, snappy, intense fruit, bitter, very tart. Drink 1992.*

☆☆☆ 1982 MALBEC ($15.00) Napa Valley. *Tart, clean, crisp, lean, nicely structured. Drink 1987.*

☆☆☆ 1982 MERLOT ($11.00) Napa Valley. *Fruity, crisp, lovely structure. Drink 1988.*

🐚

## Cakebread Cellars                                    NAPA COUNTY
### WHITE

☆☆☆ 1982 CHARDONNAY ($13.75) Napa Valley. *Fresh, clean, some oak complexity.*

☆☆ 1983 CHARDONNAY ($13.50) Napa Valley. *Clean, pleasant but not as good as the '82.*

☆☆ 1984 CHARDONNAY ($13.75) Napa Valley. *Crisp, varietal, clean, balanced.*

### RED

☆☆ 1978 CABERNET SAUVIGNON ($12.00) Jt-L1, Napa Valley. *Minty, woody, fat, chewy. Drink now.*

☆☆☆ 1979 CABERNET SAUVIGNON ($14.00) Napa Valley. *Herbal, ripe, forward, oaky.*

☆ 1980 CABERNET SAUVIGNON ($16.00) Napa Valley. *Herbal, tight, not much.*

☆☆☆ 1980 CABERNET SAUVIGNON ($35.00) Rutherford Reserve, Napa Valley. *Fleshy, rich, dense flavors; complex. Drink now.*

☆☆ 1981 CABERNET SAUVIGNON ($10.50) Napa Valley. *Smokey, deep fruit. Drink now.*

☆☆☆ 1982 CABERNET SAUVIGNON ($14.00) Napa Valley. *Clean, herbal, subtle oak, soft fruit, good structure. Drink 1990.*

☆☆☆ 1983 CABERNET SAUVIGNON ($16.00) Napa Valley. *Ripe, rich, deep cherry flavors. Lovely structure and complexity. Drink 1991.*

☆☆ 1980 ZINFANDEL ($10.75) Beatty Ranch, Howell Mountain, Napa Valley. *Brambly, big and fruity.*

☆☆☆ 1981 ZINFANDEL ($10.75) Napa Valley. *Clean, fresh, balanced, crisp. Cakebread's best and last Zinfandel.*

🐚

## Calafia Cellars                                     NAPA COUNTY
### RED

☆☆☆ 1981 CABERNET SAUVIGNON ($11.00) Kitty Hawk, Napa Valley. *Fruity, crisp, lean and attractive. Drink now.*

☆☆ 1982 CABERNET SAUVIGNON ($18.00) Fourreeminette, Napa Valley. *Big, intense, spicy, persistent fruit. Drink 1990.*

☆☆ 1979 MERLOT ($10.00) Napa Valley. *Fruity, rich, with good, long finish.*

☆☆ 1981 MERLOT ($13.50) Pickle Canyon, Napa Valley. *Rich, velvety, lush and lovely.*

☆☆☆ 1982 MERLOT ($12.00) Pickle Canyon, Napa Valley. *Lovely fruit, rich, clean, nicely structured.*

☆☆☆ 1980 ZINFANDEL ($7.50) Pickle Canyon, Napa Valley. *Lush fruit and rich flavors.*

ॐ

## Calera Wine Company          SAN BENITO COUNTY
### WHITE

☆☆ 1982 CHARDONNAY ($9.75) Santa Barbara. *Toasty, rich, eclectic.*

☆☆ 1983 CHARDONNAY ($10.75) Santa Barbara. *Fat, heavy, decent, but with some off flavors.*

1984 CHARDONNAY ($10.00) Santa Barbara. *Overoaked, sour, lactic.*

### RED

☆☆ NV ROUGE DE ROUGE ($4.00) California. *Zinfandel. Blackberry fruit, crisp, clean, spicy, jammy.*

☆☆☆ 1978 PINOT NOIR ($9.00) Jensen, California. *Only 744 375-ml bottles made. Fragrant, berried, silky, mellow.*

☆☆ 1978 PINOT NOIR ($9.00) Reed, California. *Only 600 375-ml bottles made. Silky, smooth, deep.*

☆☆☆ 1978 PINOT NOIR ($9.00) Selleck, California. *Only 432 375-ml bottles made. Violet, earthy, silky, supple.*

☆☆ 1979 PINOT NOIR ($18.00) Jensen, California. *Somewhat thin and stemmy, but complex and interesting.*

☆☆☆ 1979 PINOT NOIR ($18.00) Reed, California. *Earthy, rich, fruity, very complex and balanced. Will improve for years.*

☆☆☆ 1979 PINOT NOIR ($18.00) Selleck, California. *Firm, rich, varietal, some stems, very complex.*

☆ 1980 PINOT NOIR ($18.00) Jensen, California. *Stemmy, green, clean but harsh.*

☆☆☆ 1981 PINOT NOIR ($18.00) Jensen, California. *Deep, tannic, leathery, chalky. Should age well for twenty years.*

☆☆ 1981 PINOT NOIR ($18.00) Selleck, California. *Green and hard, clean, fresh and spicy. Drink 1988.*

1982 PINOT NOIR ($10.00) Los Alamos, Santa Barbara. *Heavily vegetal.*

☆☆☆ 1982 PINOT NOIR ($23.00) Jensen, California. *Rich, stemmy, angular, intense. Drink 1987.*

☆☆☆ 1982 PINOT NOIR ($23.00) Reed, California. *Herbal, rich, with deep lovely varietal flavors. Drink now.*

☆☆☆ 1983 PINOT NOIR ($23.00) Jensen, California. *Edgy, crisp, beautifully structured, varietal. Drink 1988.*

☆☆☆ 1983 PINOT NOIR ($23.00) Selleck, California. *Fresh, lush, beautifully structured. Drink 1988.*

☆☆☆ 1984 PINOT NOIR ($23.00) Jensen, California. *Complex, tart, cherry flavors, great structure. Drink 1989.*

☆☆☆☆ 1984 PINOT NOIR ($25.00) Selleck, California. *Ripe, soft, great fruit, lively acidity, great structure. Should live for years. Drink 1992.*

☆☆☆ 1985 PINOT NOIR ($14.00) Bien Nacido, Santa Barbara. *Rich earth and varietal fruit, good balance.*

☆☆ 1985 PINOT NOIR ($23.00) Selleck, San Benito. *Green olive, under ripe, well structured.*

☆☆☆ 1976 ZINFANDEL ($6.00) Cienega District. *Crisp, balanced, aging beautifully.*

☆☆ 1979 ZINFANDEL ($7.50) Cienega District. *Big, dark, berried.*

☆☆  1979 ZINFANDEL ($8.50) Reserve, Cienega District. *Big, overdone, ripe and intense.*
☆☆  1980 ZINFANDEL ($7.00) Reserve, Doe Mill. *Big, dark and rich. Lacking finesse.*
☆☆  1981 ZINFANDEL ($7.00) Templeton. *Jammy and clean.*
☆☆  1981 ZINFANDEL ($8.50) Reserve, Cienega Valley. *Round, crisp, full and fresh.*
     1982 ZINFANDEL ($7.00) Cienega Valley. *Vegetal, weird.*
☆☆  1982 ZINFANDEL ($9.00) Reserve, Cienega Valley. *Tart, fruity, intense, a bit rough.*

🍷

## California Cooler                    SAN JOAQUIN COUNTY
### FLAVORED
☆☆  CALIFORNIA COOLER CITRUS ($0.75) California. *12 oz. 6% alcohol. Fresh fruity flavors, with some interesting almond/spice nuances. Tangy and well balanced.*
☆☆  CALIFORNIA COOLER ORANGE ($0.75) California. *12 oz. 6% alcohol. Fresh orange flavors; crisp, clean and attractive.*

🍷

## California Growers Winery                    TULARE COUNTY
### SPARKLING
☆  NV  LEBLANC ($3.00) California. *Sweet, heavy, simple.*
   NV  LEBLANC BLANC DE NOIR ($3.00) California. *Pruny, awful.*

🍷

## California Soleil Vineyards                    NAPA COUNTY
### WHITE
☆☆  1983 JOHANNISBERG RIESLING ($8.00) Special Select Late Harvest, Napa Valley. *375 ml. 18% residual sugar. Soft, lush, sweet, lacking acidity.*
☆☆  1985 JOHANNISBERG RIESLING ($7.95) Late Harvest, California. *375 ml. 18% residual sugar. Fresh, clean, balanced, some vegetal qualities but quite luscious.*
☆☆  1986 WHITE RIESLING ($6.00) Napa Valley. *Fruity, soft, lush, clean, grapey.*

🍷

## Callaway Vineyard and Winery                    RIVERSIDE COUNTY
### WHITE
☆☆  1985 VIN BLANC ($4.75) California. *1.25% residual sugar. Soft, fresh, nicely balanced.*
☆  1982 CHARDONNAY ($8.50) Temecula. *No oak used. Clean, lemony, uncomplicated.*
☆  1983 CHARDONNAY ($8.75) Temecula. *Oily, vegetal, decent.*
☆☆  1983 CHARDONNAY ($18.00) Select Late Harvest, Temecula. *375 ml. 13.6% residual sugar. Lush, clean, soft, balanced, decent.*
☆☆  1984 CHARDONNAY ($9.00) Temecula. *Crisp, clean, balanced, varietal, attractive. Some bottle variation.*
☆☆☆  1985 CHARDONNAY ($9.25) Calla-Lees, California. *Rich, ripe, clean, balanced. Aged without oak. A lovely wine.*
☆☆  1986 CHARDONNAY ($9.50) Calla-Lees, California. *Clean, good varietal character, pineapple fruit; lacking complexity.*

   ☆  1986 CHENIN BLANC ($6.25) Dry, Temecula. *Grassy, lush, crisp, some sweetness and vegetation.*

☆☆  1985 FUME BLANC ($7.50) Temecula. *Clean, fruity, simple, decent.*

   ☆  1984 PINOT BLANC ($7.75) California. *Clean, balanced, simple, earthy.*

☆☆  1985 SAUVIGNON BLANC ($7.75) Temecula. *Crisp, fresh, well balanced.*

☆☆  1986 WHITE RIESLING ($5.50) Temecula. *Snappy, clean, nicely balanced.*

இ

## Camas Winery                *IDAHO*

### RED
1984 CABERNET SAUVIGNON ($6.75) Columbia River Valley. *Vegetal, odd.*

இ

CAMBIASO VINEYARDS *see* Domaine St. Georges

## Canandaigua Wine Company       *NEW YORK*

### SPARKLING
     NV  J. ROGET EXTRA DRY ($4.00) American. *Sweet and caramel flavored. Charmat bulk process.*

   ☆  NV  J. ROGET SPUMANTE ($4.00) American. *Muscat-like and sweet. Bulk process.*

### FLAVORED
   ☆  SUN COUNTRY COOLER CITRUS ($0.75) American. *12 oz. 6% alcohol. Lemony, simple, dull.*

☆☆  SUN COUNTRY COOLER ORANGE ($0.75) American. *12 oz. 6% alcohol. Fresh orange flavors; lovely, with clean fruit and a crisp finish.*

☆☆  SUN COUNTRY COOLER TROPICAL FRUIT ($0.75) American. *12 oz. 6% alcohol. Crisp, clean, tangy, with interesting flavors.*

இ

CANTERBURY *see* Stratford

## Caparone Winery     *SAN LUIS OBISPO COUNTY*

### RED
1981 CABERNET SAUVIGNON ($8.50) Tepusquet, Santa Maria Valley. *Big, lush and weedy.*

1981 MERLOT ($12.00) Tepusquet, Santa Maria Valley. *Weedy, tannic, bitter.*

☆☆  1982 MERLOT ($8.50) Santa Maria. *Earthy, rich, dark, deep, lush, intense.*

இ

## J. Carey Cellars     *SANTA BARBARA COUNTY*

### WHITE
☆☆☆  1982 CHARDONNAY ($9.50) Estate, Santa Ynez Valley. *Lovely oak, crisp fruit, very Burgundian.*

☆☆☆  1983 CHARDONNAY ($10.50) Santa Barbara. *Big, oaky and rich, with lovely crisp fruit and depth.*

☆☆☆  1985 CHARDONNAY ($10.00) Santa Barbara. *Rich and oaky, with lovely fruit and acidity. Beautifully balanced.*

☆☆☆  1985 CHARDONNAY ($12.00) Adobe Canyon, Santa Ynez Valley. *Woody, crisp, complex, rich, intense.*

   ☆  1985 SAUVIGNON BLANC ($7.50) Santa Barbara. *Vegetal, spicy, heavy.*

**BLANC DE NOIR**
☆☆☆ 1986 CABERNET BLANC ($5.50) Estate, Santa Ynez Valley. *Lovely herbal varietal character, crisp acidity, clean, balanced.*

**RED**
☆☆ 1979 CABERNET SAUVIGNON ($10.50) Estate, Santa Ynez Valley. *Brambly, herbal, dense, raisiny; power but no finesse.*
☆ 1981 CABERNET SAUVIGNON ($8.75) Alamo Pintado, Santa Ynez Valley. *Nicely made, very vegetal.*
☆ 1982 CABERNET SAUVIGNON ($9.00) Estate, Santa Ynez Valley. *Vegetal, soft, decent texture, unattractive.*
☆☆ 1982 CABERNET SAUVIGNON ($12.00) La Cuesta, Santa Ynez Valley. *Soft, rich, clean and velvety, with pronounced vegetal qualities.*
☆☆ 1981 MERLOT ($11.50) Santa Ynez Valley. *Richly varietal, tannic and angular.*
🦐

## Carmel Bay Winery                MONTEREY COUNTY
**WHITE**
☆ 1982 CHARDONNAY ($9.00) Monterey. *Dull, unpleasant.*
**RED**
☆☆☆ 1979 ZINFANDEL ($5.00) Shandon Valley, San Luis Obispo. *Berried and appealing, with nice oak and fruit.*
🦐

## Carmenet Vineyard                SONOMA COUNTY
**WHITE**
☆☆☆ 1986 COLOMBARD ($5.00) Cyril Saviez, Napa Valley. *A silk purse from a sow's ear. A rich, complex wine with balance and finesse.*
☆☆ 1985 SAUVIGNON BLANC ($10.00) Edna Valley. *16% Semillon. Smoky, heavy, big, intense.*
☆☆ 1985 SAUVIGNON BLANC ($10.00) Sonoma. *14% Semillon. Crisp, lemony, Sancerre style.*
**RED**
☆☆☆☆ 1982 CARMENET RED ($16.00) Sonoma Valley. *85% Cabernet, 10% Merlot, 5% Cabernet Franc. Great structure, fruit. Drink 1988.*
☆☆☆ 1983 RED TABLE WINE ($16.00) Estate, Sonoma Valley. *100% Cabernet. Tight, complex, deep, lovely. Drink 1989.*
☆☆☆ 1984 RED TABLE WINE ($17.50) Estate, Sonoma. *Crisp, fresh, complex, great, tight fruit and lovely finish. Drink 1989.*
🦐

## Carneros Creek Winery                NAPA COUNTY
**WHITE**
☆☆ 1982 CHARDONNAY ($13.00) Napa Valley. *Rich, heavy, clean, some nice fruit acid. Bottle variation.*
☆☆☆ 1983 CHARDONNAY ($13.00) Napa Valley. *Rich, nicely structured, clean, varietal.*
☆☆ 1984 CHARDONNAY ($11.00) Carneros. *Fresh, crisp, lean, earthy.*
☆☆☆ 1985 CHARDONNAY ($10.50) Napa Valley. *Crisp, lively fruit and good balance.*
**RED**
☆☆ 1980 CABERNET SAUVIGNON ($10.00) Amador. *Atypical. Big, jammy and Zinfandel-like. Starting to mellow.*
☆☆☆ 1980 CABERNET SAUVIGNON ($10.00) Fay, Napa Valley. *12% Merlot. Herbal, fresh and fruity.*

☆☆ 1980 CABERNET SAUVIGNON ($12.00) Napa Valley. *Oaky and jammy but with firm structure. Good aging potential.*

☆☆☆ 1980 CABERNET SAUVIGNON ($13.50) Truchard, Napa Valley. *30% Merlot, 10% Cabernet Franc. Crisp, fresh, lively. Drink now.*

☆ 1980 CABERNET SAUVIGNON ($15.00) Fay-Turnbull, Napa Valley. *Weedy, intense, deep, rough.*

☆☆ 1981 CABERNET SAUVIGNON ($12.00) 91% Fay, 9% Amador, Napa Valley. *Crisp, clean, full, intense.*

☆ 1981 CABERNET SAUVIGNON ($13.50) Fay, Napa Valley. *Dull, dank, tannic, decent.*

1982 CABERNET SAUVIGNON ($12.00) Napa Valley. *Very weedy and unattractive.*

☆ 1982 CABERNET SAUVIGNON ($13.00) Fay, Napa Valley. *Herbaceous, green, thin, dull.*

1982 MERLOT ($9.50) Napa. *Vegetal, sour, unattractive.*

☆☆ 1983 MERLOT ($9.50) Truchard, Napa. *Soft, clean, nice but a bit thin.*

☆☆☆☆ 1977 PINOT NOIR ($12.50) Napa Valley. *Lush, superb, rich, velvety. Wonderful.*

☆☆☆ 1978 PINOT NOIR ($12.00) Napa Valley-Carneros. *Rich, fruited and complex; cherries and oak, lovely.*

☆☆☆ 1980 PINOT NOIR ($15.00) Carneros District, Napa Valley. *Earthy and green, with good aging potential.*

☆☆ 1981 PINOT NOIR ($16.00) Napa Valley. *Cherry-berry, earthy, rich and full.*

☆☆☆ 1983 PINOT NOIR ($12.50) Napa Valley-Carneros. *Lean, lively, cherry and raspberry flavors; elegant and complex.*

☆☆☆☆ 1983 PINOT NOIR ($16.00) Napa Valley. *Soft, rich fruit flavors, delicate, superb. Drink now or hold for a few years.*

☆☆☆ 1984 PINOT NOIR ($15.00) Los Carneros. *Soft, fresh, bright cherry flavors, good finish.*

☆☆☆ 1985 PINOT NOIR ($15.00) Carneros. *Soft, fruity, clean, buttery, very lovely.*

છ

## Maurice Carrie Winery          RIVERSIDE COUNTY
### WHITE
☆☆☆☆ 1986 MOSCATO CANELLI ($7.00) Temecula. *Melony, fresh, spicy, clean, wonderful fruit, great texture, some spritz. Superb.*

☆☆ 1986 CHARDONNAY ($7.00) Temecula. *Crisp, fruity, clean, charming.*

☆ 1986 SAUVIGNON BLANC ($6.00) Estate, Temecula. *Sweet peas, crisp, clean, spritzy, decent but some odd flavors.*

### BLANC DE NOIR
☆☆ 1986 SARA BELLA CABERNET BLANC ($5.00) Temecula. *Green pepper fruit, crisp, fresh, with good varietal character.*

☆☆ 1986 ZINFANDEL BLANC ($5.00) Temecula. *Sweet, crisp, with some unattractive barnyard flavors.*

છ

## Cartlidge & Browne          NAPA COUNTY
### WHITE
☆☆ 1983 CHARDONNAY ($11.50) Napa Valley. *Vinous, rich, varietal.*

☆☆☆  1985 CANTERBURY CHARDONNAY ($6.50) California. *Oaky, fresh, clean, lovely.*

1985 CHARDONNAY ($9.75) Napa Valley. *Cheesy, sour, odd.*

❧

## Casa Larga Vineyards                        NEW YORK
### WHITE
☆☆  1982 CHARDONNAY ($7.50) Finger Lakes. *Lemony, crisp, fresh but lacking varietal character.*

☆  1985 CHARDONNAY ($8.50) Finger Lakes. *Soft, vegetal, decent.*

### SPARKLING
☆☆  NV  BLANC DE BLANCS ($12.00) Finger Lakes. *Crisp, fresh, nicely balanced, clean, attractive.*

☆  NV  BLANC DE BLANC ($12.00) Naturel, Finger Lakes. *Crisp, heavy, coarse, decent.*

### RED
☆  1980 CABERNET SAUVIGNON ($9.00) Finger Lakes. *Herbaceous, odd.*

☆  1984 DECHAUNAC ($5.50) Finger Lakes. *Soft, clean, ripe, decent.*

☆☆  1985 PINOT NOIR ($10.00) Finger Lakes. *Smokey, crisp, earthy, a bit thin but an impressive effort.*

❧

## Cascade Mountain Vineyards                   NEW YORK
### WHITE
NV  A LITTLE WHITE WINE ($3.00) New York. *Simple, oily, dry, odd.*

NV  PARDONNEZ-MOI ($5.00) New York. *Watery, dull.*

☆☆☆  1985 VIGNOLES ($6.00) New York. 375 ml. *Crisp, lush, crisp, balanced, lovely.*

☆☆  1985 SEYVAL BLANC ($6.00) New York. *Floral, crisp, tangy.*

### RED
○  1985 RED TABLE WINE ($7.00) New York. *Sour, vegetal, awful.*

❧

## Castoro Cellars                           SAN LUIS OBISPO
### WHITE
☆☆☆  1984 CHARDONNAY ($6.75) San Luis Obispo. *Smooth, crisp, clean, varietal, very lovely.*

### RED
☆☆  1983 CABERNET SAUVIGNON ($6.75) San Luis Obispo. *Soft, lush, ripe, decent.*

☆☆☆  1984 ZINFANDEL ($5.25) Paso Robles. *Ripe, rich, fat, lovely, buttery oak and clean fruit.*

❧

## Caswell Vineyards                         SONOMA COUNTY
### WHITE
1984 CHARDONNAY ($10.00) Sonoma. *Bitter, unattractive.*

### RED
☆☆☆  1983 CLARET ($8.00) North Coast. *Ripe, rich, fruity, charming.*

❧

## Caymus Vineyards                           NAPA COUNTY
### WHITE
☆☆  1982 CHARDONNAY ($9.00) Estate, Napa Valley. *Toasty, good fruit, solid, medium weight.*

☆  1984 LIBERTY SCHOOL CHARDONNAY ($6.00) Lot 4, Napa Valley. *Decent, drinkable but dirty.*

☆☆ 1985 LIBERTY SCHOOL CHARDONNAY ($6.00) Lot 7, California. *Fresh, soft, decent fruit, clean.*

☆☆ 1986 LIBERTY SCHOOL CHARDONNAY ($6.00) Lot 10, California. *Crisp, lemony, clean, simple. Mâcon-like.*

☆☆☆ 1983 JOHANNISBERG RIESLING ($15.00) Special Selection Late Harvest, Andres Acres, Napa Valley. *11% residual sugar. Crisp acidity, lush, fresh, fruit and honey.*

☆ 1986 LIBERTY SCHOOL SAUVIGNON BLANC ($5.50) Lot 4, Napa Valley. *Crisp, lean, decent, a bit thin.*

☆☆☆ 1986 SAUVIGNON BLANC ($8.50) Napa Valley. *Soft, round, rich, varietal, clean.*

**BLANC DE NOIR**

1986 OEIL DE PERDRIX ($5.00) Napa Valley. *Pinot Noir Blanc. Stinky, flat, unattractive.*

**RED**

☆☆ NV LIBERTY SCHOOL CABERNET SAUVIGNON ($6.00) Lot 16, California. *Soft, smooth, lovely herbal fruit. Balanced and very attractive.*

☆☆☆ 1978 CABERNET SAUVIGNON ($12.50) Napa Valley. *Snappy, oaky, attractive.*

☆☆☆ 1978 CABERNET SAUVIGNON ($30.00) Special Selection, Estate, Napa Valley. *Crisp, balanced, elegant, fruity, lovely structure. Will age.*

☆☆☆ 1979 CABERNET SAUVIGNON ($12.50) Napa Valley. *Fresh, clean, snappy and delightful. Aging nicely.*

☆☆☆☆ 1979 CABERNET SAUVIGNON ($30.00) Special Selection, Estate, Napa Valley. *Superb. Crisp, clean, classic, complex and elegant. Ready to drink now but might be even better in a decade or two.*

☆☆☆☆ 1980 CABERNET SAUVIGNON ($12.50) Estate, Napa Valley. *Lean, elegant, herbal and intense. Good now, better in 1988.*

☆☆☆ 1980 CABERNET SAUVIGNON ($30.00) Special Selection, Napa Valley. *Crisp, lush, tart, clean, great structure. Drink 1990.*

☆☆☆☆ 1981 CABERNET SAUVIGNON ($12.50) Estate, Napa Valley. *Elegant, firm, complex, fruity, great acidity. Drink 1988.*

☆☆☆☆ 1981 CABERNET SAUVIGNON ($35.00) Special Selection, Napa Valley. *Crisp, rich, superb, elegant, complex. Another great one. Drink 1992.*

☆☆ 1982 LIBERTY SCHOOL CABERNET SAUVIGNON ($6.00) Lot 11, Alexander Valley. *Fresh, clean, attractive. Drink now.*

☆☆☆ 1982 LIBERTY SCHOOL CABERNET SAUVIGNON ($6.00) Lot 12, Alexander Valley. *Balanced, attractive, clean, quite lovely. Drink now.*

☆☆☆☆ 1982 CABERNET SAUVIGNON ($35.00) Special Selection, Napa Valley. *Crisp, clean, balanced, wonderfully structured, focused fruit, superb, but not quite as good as the 1981. Drink 1992.*

☆☆☆☆ 1983 CABERNET SAUVIGNON ($15.00) Napa Valley. *Superb, lush, ripe, fruity, lovely, great lean structure. Drink 1990.*

☆☆☆☆ 1984 CABERNET SAUVIGNON ($12.00) Cuvée, Napa Valley. *Rich, balanced, lovely fruit and stunning structure. Delicious now and even better in 1992.*

☆☆☆ 1984 CABERNET SAUVIGNON ($14.00) Estate, Napa Valley. *Crisp, intense berry fruit, leathery flavors and charming new oak. Drink 1990.*

☆ 1980 PINOT NOIR ($6.50) Estate, Napa Valley. *Balanced but a bit underripe. Beginning to show some age.*

☆☆☆ 1981 PINOT NOIR ($7.50) Estate, Napa Valley. *Fresh, clean, balanced, complex.*

☆☆ 1981 PINOT NOIR ($12.50) Special Selection, Napa Valley. *Rich, balanced, nicely structured.*

☆☆☆ 1982 PINOT NOIR ($12.50) Special Selection, Napa Valley. *Clean, soft, fresh cherry fruit, lovely Burgundian character.*

☆☆☆ 1983 PINOT NOIR ($12.50) Special Selection, Napa Valley. *Rich, deep, concentrated, leathery, attractive.*

☆☆☆ 1984 PINOT NOIR ($12.50) Special Selection, Napa Valley. *Lush, ripe, cherry fruit, rich texture, great depth.*

☆☆☆ 1977 ZINFANDEL ($5.50) California. *Spicy, balanced, clean.*

☆☆☆ 1978 ZINFANDEL ($6.50) California. *Complex, rich, balanced, varietal.*

☆☆ 1979 ZINFANDEL ($7.50) California (Amador and Napa). *Big, rich, intense, lacks finesse.*

☆☆☆ 1980 ZINFANDEL ($6.50) Napa Valley. *Firmly structured and well balanced. Drink now or hold.*

☆☆☆ 1981 ZINFANDEL ($6.50) Napa Valley. *Crisp, ripe, lovely, fruity, superb.*

☆☆☆ 1982 ZINFANDEL ($7.50) Napa Valley. *Soft, rich, velvety, beautifully structured. Delightful.*

☆☆☆ 1983 ZINFANDEL ($7.50) Napa Valley. *Great fruit, lovely structure, delightful and nicely balanced.*

☆☆☆ 1984 ZINFANDEL ($8.00) Napa Valley. *10% Petite Sirah. Lush, berried, fleshy, full, balanced.*

☆☆☆ 1985 ZINFANDEL ($8.00) Napa Valley. *Crisp, lively, clean, berry fruit, long flavors. Delicious.*

❧

## *Cecchetti Sebastiani Cellar*          SONOMA COUNTY
### WHITE
☆☆☆ 1986 CHARDONNAY ($9.50) Cask Lot 2, Napa Valley. *Good fruit and balance, well made, good flavors.*
### RED
☆☆ 1983 CABERNET SAUVIGNON ($12.50) Sonoma. *Lean, varietal, crisp, decent. Drink 1988.*

1983 PINOT NOIR ($12.50) Reserve, Santa Maria. *Awful, old, tired, ugly.*

☆☆ 1984 PINOT NOIR ($10.50) San Benito. *Balanced and well made but green and lacking depth of fruit.*

❧

## *Chaddsford Winery*               PENNSYLVANIA
### WHITE
1983 CHARDONNAY ($14.00) Stargazer's, Pennsylvania. *Sour, tart, odd.*

☆☆☆ 1984 CHARDONNAY ($17.00) Phillip Roth, Pennsylvania. *Rich, oaky, clean, toasty, ripe, fruity, well made.*

☆ 1985 CHARDONNAY ($16.00) Philip Roth, Pennsylvania. *Tart, a bit sour, decent.*

☆ 1986 WHITE TABLE WINE ($6.00) Pennsylvania. *Heavy, oily, deep, clean, decent.*
### SPARKLING
○ NV BLANC DE NOIR ($14.00) Pennsylvania. *Oily, oxidized, ugly.*

☆ NV SPARKLING BLUSH ($15.00) Pennsylvania. *Sweet, snappy, decent.*
### RED
☆☆ 1985 COUNTRY ROUGE ($4.50) Pennsylvania. *Crisp, sweet, clean, Beaujolais-like.*

42

1984 CABERNET SAUVIGNON ($8.00) Pennsylvania. *Meaty, sour, not much charm.*

1984 CABERNET SAUVIGNON ($12.00) Long Island, New York. *Vegetal, unattractive.*

☆☆ 1986 RED TABLE WINE ($5.00) Pennsylvania. *Spicy, light, crisp, fresh, attractive.*

❧

## Chalk Hill Winery                SONOMA COUNTY
### WHITE
☆☆ 1983 CHARDONNAY ($7.00) Sonoma. *Crisp, snappy, balanced, very nice.*

☆☆ 1983 CHARDONNAY ($10.00) Proprietor's Reserve, Sonoma. *Clean, varietal, smokey, attractive.*

☆☆ 1984 CHARDONNAY ($8.00) Sonoma. *Rich pear fruit and fresh, new oak. A pleasant, attractive wine.*

☆☆☆ 1985 CHARDONNAY ($8.00) Sonoma. *Crisp, clean, balanced, rich.*

☆ 1986 CHARDONNAY ($8.00) Sonoma. *Balanced but sour and a little bitter.*

1985 SAUVIGNON BLANC ($7.50) Sonoma. *Oxidized, dull, flat.*

### RED
☆☆☆ 1981 CABERNET SAUVIGNON ($8.00) Sonoma. *Rich, beautifully structured, fruity. Drink now.*

☆☆☆ 1982 CABERNET SAUVIGNON ($9.00) Day, Sonoma. *Crisp, tangy, clean, very attractive. Drink now.*

☆☆☆ 1983 CABERNET SAUVIGNON ($9.00) Sonoma. *Lush, fruity, clean, very lovely. Drink now.*

☆☆☆ 1984 CABERNET SAUVIGNON ($8.75) Sonoma. *Rich, berried, lively fruit, great balance. Drink now.*

☆☆ 1981 PINOT NOIR ($6.00) Estate, Chalk Hill, Sonoma. *Pleasant cherry nose, lush fruit, varietal, very nice. Drink now.*

☆ 1982 PINOT NOIR ($6.00) Chalk Hill, Sonoma. *Rich, lush, peppery, some odd flavors, decent.*

❧

## Chalone Vineyard                MONTEREY COUNTY
### WHITE
☆☆☆☆ 1982 CHARDONNAY ($17.00) Estate, Monterey. *More finesse and elegance than the '81, the same depth.*

☆☆☆ 1983 CHARDONNAY ($18.75) Estate, Monterey. *Earthy, rich, deep, big.*

☆☆ 1985 CHARDONNAY ($20.00) Chalone. *Heavy, ripe, oily, oaky. Perhaps time will soften it.*

☆☆☆ 1986 CHARDONNAY ($22.00) Estate, Chalone. *Toasty, intense fruit, rich barrel fermentation flavors. A big, assertive wine with great complexity.*

☆☆ 1984 GAVILAN FRENCH COLOMBARD ($4.00) Cyril Saviez, Monterey. *Barrel fermented, earthy, complex, fruity, very interesting.*

### RED
☆☆ 1983 RED TABLE WINE ($9.00) Chalone. *100% Pinot Noir. Astringent, clean, slim but quite snappy and pleasant.*

☆☆☆ 1976 PINOT NOIR Estate, Monterey. *Rich and Burgundian, complex and fruity. Drink now.*

☆☆ 1979 PINOT NOIR ($15.00) Estate, Monterey. *Complex and stemmy, showing its age.*

☆☆☆ 1980 PINOT NOIR ($20.00) California. *Rich, meaty, earthy, great fruit.*

☆☆☆ 1981 PINOT NOIR ($15.00) Estate, Monterey. *Clean, rich, with oak, earth, fruit and some stems.*

☆☆☆☆ 1981 PINOT NOIR ($28.00) Reserve, Estate, Chalone. *Dark, intense, rich. An amazing wine: complex fruit and oak, deep flavors and remarkable structure. Very Burgundian.*

☆☆ 1982 PINOT NOIR ($15.00) Estate, Monterey. *Earthy, rich, deep. Drink 1988 and beyond.*

☆☆☆ 1983 PINOT NOIR ($18.50) Estate, Chalone. *Spicy, earthy, rich fruit, clean, smooth, Burgundian, elegant, superb.*

☆☆☆ 1984 PINOT NOIR ($18.00) Chalone. *Earthy, crisp, deep, lovely fruit, tart, attractive. Great aging potential. Drink 1991.*

## Chamisal Vineyard            SAN LUIS OBISPO COUNTY
### WHITE
1982 CHARDONNAY ($8.00) Estate, Edna Valley. *Dull, vinous, thin and unappealing.*

☆☆ 1984 CHARDONNAY ($10.00) Estate, Edna Valley. *Very tart and quite clean, a bit low in varietal character but certainly the best yet from Chamisal.*

1985 CHARDONNAY ($10.00) Estate, Edna Valley. *Cheesy, dirty, bitter, ugly.*

## Champs de Brionne Winery               WASHINGTON
### WHITE
1983 CHARDONNAY ($10.00) Reserve, Washington. *Oxidized, unpleasant.*

## Channing Rudd Cellars               LAKE COUNTY
### RED
☆☆ 1979 CABERNET SAUVIGNON ($7.00) Cary Gott, Amador. *15% Zinfandel. Ripe, berried, intense. Showing some age.*

☆☆ 1979 CABERNET SAUVIGNON ($7.00) Guenoc Ranch, Lake. *15% Petite Sirah, 10% Zinfandel. Clean, balanced, very pleasant.*

☆☆☆ 1980 CABERNET SAUVIGNON ($14.00) Bella Oaks, Napa Valley. *Rich, deep, concentrated, oaky, lovely. Drink 1988.*

☆☆ 1979 MERLOT ($9.00) Guenoc Valley. *Lush and velvety.*

## Chanter Winery               NAPA COUNTY
### WHITE
☆☆☆ 1983 CHARDONNAY ($12.00) Napa Valley. *Oaky, rich, varietal, balanced, intense.*

☆☆ 1984 CHARDONNAY ($12.50) Napa Valley. *Oaky, lush, ripe.*

☆☆ 1985 CHARDONNAY ($12.50) Napa Valley. *Tart, lean, crisp, attractive.*

## Chanticleer Vineyards               SONOMA COUNTY
### WHITE
○ 1983 CHARDONNAY ($8.75) Rancho Venido, Santa Maria Valley. *Vegetal, oily, very unpleasant.*

☆ 1984 FRENCH COLOMBARD ($3.75) California. *Leafy, unappealing.*

**RED**

1981 ZINFANDEL ($6.25) Sonoma Valley, Dry Creek Hills. *6% French Colombard. Dirty, unattractive.*

❧

## Chappellet Vineyard NAPA COUNTY

**WHITE**

☆ 1983 CHARDONNAY ($14.00) Napa Valley. *Decent fruit, bitter finish, some odd flavors.*

☆☆☆ 1985 CHENIN BLANC ($7.50) Napa Valley. *Soft, complex, lush, deep, clean, dry.*

**RED**

☆☆ 1978 CABERNET SAUVIGNON ($15.00) Napa Valley. *Cherry nose, vegetal, crisp, clean but not elegant.*

☆☆☆ 1979 CABERNET SAUVIGNON ($12.50) Napa Valley. *Gorgeous depth, fresh, tannic. Great aging potential.*

☆☆☆☆ 1980 CABERNET SAUVIGNON ($18.00) Napa Valley. *Graceful, firm and intense. Earthy, complex and superb.*

☆☆ 1982 CABERNET SAUVIGNON ($10.00) Napa Valley. *Herbal, structured, but not very appealing. Maybe time will help. Drink 1990.*

☆☆ 1983 CABERNET SAUVIGNON ($16.00) Napa Valley. *Soft, tart, clean, decent structure. Drink 1991.*

❧

CHASE CREEK *see* Shafer Vineyards

## Château Benoit Winery OREGON

**WHITE**

○ 1983 CHARDONNAY ($10.00) Champoeg, Oregon. *Overripe, ugly.*

☆☆☆ 1985 MULLER-THURGAU ($6.00) Oregon. *2.8% residual sugar. Sweet, clean, good acidity, lovely. Made with a "sweet reserve."*

**SPARKLING**

☆☆ NV BRUT ($14.00) Oregon. *70% Pinot Noir, 20% Chardonnay, 10% Pinot Blanc. Crisp, clean, lively, balanced.*

**RED**

☆☆ 1983 PINOT NOIR ($12.00) Oregon. *Crisp, clean, fresh, a bit faint.*

☆ 1985 PINOT NOIR ($14.00) Oregon. *Crisp, slim, tart, clean.*

❧

## Château Boswell NAPA COUNTY

**RED**

☆☆ 1979 CABERNET SAUVIGNON ($12.00) Napa Valley. *Dark, lush and raisiny.*

☆☆☆ 1982 CABERNET SAUVIGNON ($15.00) Private Reserve, Napa Valley. *Crisp acidity, lush fruit, superb balance. Drink 1990.*

☆☆☆ 1983 CABERNET SAUVIGNON ($10.00) Private Reserve, Napa Valley. *Crisp, lean, lovely structure. Focused, elegant, excellent. Drink 1988.*

❧

## Château Chevalier Winery NAPA COUNTY

**RED**

☆☆ 1982 CABERNET SAUVIGNON ($12.00) Napa Valley. *15% Merlot. Dense, raisined, tannic.*

☆☆ 1981 MERLOT ($10.50) Napa Valley. *Fruity and varietal, some light herbaceousness.*

○ 1980 PINOT NOIR ($10.50) Stanton's Pinot Patch, Napa Valley. *Asparagus flavors. Lacking in varietal character.*

☆☆☆ 1981 PINOT NOIR ($11.50) Stanton's Pinot Patch, Napa Valley. *Toasty, earthy, with some stems and earth. Very nice.*

&

## Château Chèvre Winery NAPA COUNTY
### RED
☆☆☆ 1979 MERLOT ($10.50) Napa Valley. *Meaty, rich, velvety, clean and oaky.*

☆☆ 1980 MERLOT ($10.50) Napa Valley. *Slightly vegetal, clean, tannic.*

☆☆☆ 1983 MERLOT ($12.50) Napa Valley. *Oaky, crisp, complex, lovely long finish.*

☆☆☆ 1984 MERLOT ($12.50) Estate, Napa Valley. *Fruity, rich, complex, superb. Drink 1989.*

☆☆☆ 1984 MERLOT ($15.00) Reserve, Estate, Napa Valley. *Soft, rich, deep, good.*

&

## Château de Leu Winery SOLANO COUNTY
### WHITE
☆☆ 1982 CHARDONNAY ($10.00) Estate, Green Valley, Solano. *Crisp, fruity, simple, fresh and appealing.*

&

## Château DeBaun SONOMA COUNTY
### WHITE
☆☆☆ 1985 SYMPHONY ($6.50) Theme, Sonoma. *4.3% residual sugar. Rich, clean, lovely, spicy, super.*

☆☆☆ 1985 SYMPHONY ($8.50) Overture, Sonoma. *0.7% residual sugar. Spicy, delicate, fresh, clean, superb.*

☆☆☆ 1985 SYMPHONY ($8.50) Prelude, Sonoma. *3.4% residual sugar. Spicy, clean, rich, complex, delicious.*

☆☆☆ 1986 SYMPHONY ($8.50) Prelude, Sonoma. *2.5% residual sugar. Soft, spicy, lush, fruity, delicious.*

☆☆ 1986 SYMPHONY ($8.50) Overture, Dry, Sonoma. *Spicy, crisp, clean, complex, with intense flavors.*

☆☆☆☆ 1986 SYMPHONY ($10.50) Theme, Sonoma. *5.5% residual sugar. Spicy, crisp, beautiful fruit, silky texture; superb.*

☆☆☆ 1986 SYMPHONY ($12.00) Finale, Sonoma. *3.75 ml. 12% residual sugar. Soft and lush, with great spice and apricot fruit backed with excellent fruity acidity.*

### BLANC DE NOIR
☆☆☆ NV CLASSICAL JAZZ ($6.50) Sonoma. *1.5% residual sugar. 52% Pinot Noir, 32% Symphony, 12% Chardonnay. Crisp, clean and spicy, with some complexity and loads of charm.*

&

## Château Diana SONOMA COUNTY
### WHITE
○ 1984 CHARDONNAY ($6.50) Barrel Fermented, Napa Valley. *Flat, unattractive.*

☆☆☆ 1985 CHARDONNAY ($6.50) Napa Valley. *Crisp, clean, good oak and varietal character. Lovely.*

☆☆ 1984 JOHANNISBERG RIESLING ($7.50) Late Harvest, Private Reserve, Tepusquet, Santa Barbara. *5.52% residual sugar. Decent but lacking excitement.*

**RED**

☆☆☆ 1982 CABERNET SAUVIGNON ($6.00) Dawn Manning Select, Alexander Valley. *Soft, fresh, good structure, nice fruit. Drink 1990.*

☆☆☆ 1983 CABERNET SAUVIGNON ($10.00) Dry Creek Valley. *Lean, elegant, lovely structure. Drink 1991.*

≈●

## Château Georges                                      NEW YORK

**WHITE**

1985 CHARDONNAY ($9.00) New York. *Lush and fat but overcome by oxidation.*

☆☆ 1986 RAVAT ($16.00) Late Harvest, New York. 6.9% residual sugar. .Crisp, with soft apple fruit and a touch of vegetation; ripe, lush finish.*

☆ 1985 RIESLING ($9.00) Special Select, New York. *Lush, apple flavors, heavy.*

≈●

## Château Grand Traverse                               MICHIGAN

**WHITE**

☆☆ 1985 JOHANNISBERG RIESLING ($9.00) Late Harvest, Michigan. *Crisp, fresh, dry, intense.*

☆☆ 1985 JOHANNISBERG RIESLING ($35.00) Ice Wine, Michigan. *Lush, ripe, silky, lush.*

**SPARKLING**

☆ NV ($6.00) Michigan. *Simple, clean, decent, fresh.*

**RED**

☆ 1985 MERLOT ($13.00) Michigan. *Chalky, spicy, some crisp berry flavors, clean, lean.*

≈●

## Château Julien                              MONTEREY COUNTY

**WHITE**

☆☆ 1985 EMERALD BAY MONTONNAY ($3.50) Monterey. *Soft, rich, good balance.*

☆☆☆ 1982 CHARDONNAY ($17.00) Private Reserve, Monterey. *Sweet oak, lovely complexity, rich and loaded with finesse.*

1983 CHARDONNAY ($8.75) Rancho Tierra Rejada, San Luis Obispo. *Heavy and overdone.*

1983 CHARDONNAY ($20.00) Private Reserve, Cobblestone, Monterey. *Strange.*

☆☆ 1984 CHARDONNAY ($12.25) Paraiso Springs, Monterey. *Good fruit and decent balance, with some bitterness.*

☆☆ 1984 JOHANNISBERG RIESLING ($5.75) Bien Nacido, Santa Barbara. *Soft, rich, oily, decent.*

**RED**

☆ 1982 MERLOT ($12.00) Sonoma. *Berried, a bit thin, lacking varietal character.*

1983 MERLOT ($12.00) Bien Nacido, Santa Barbara. *Intensely vegetal, thin, unappealing.*

1984 MERLOT ($12.00) Bien Nacido, Santa Barbara. *Dull, raisiny, unattractive.*

≈●

## *Château Larraine*                                    ALABAMA

### WHITE
1986 SEYVAL BLANC ($89.00) Alabama. *Get serious. This is a clean but fairly flat Seyval, drinkable but not much more. It lacks fruit and depth.*

### SPARKLING
NV   EXTRA DRY ($4.00) New York. *Simple, sweet, dull.*

### RED
☆☆ 1981 CABERNET SAUVIGNON ($9.50) Paso Robles. *Intense, ripe, crisp, not much depth, attractive. Drink now.*

૨ঌ

## *Château Montelena Winery*               NAPA COUNTY

### WHITE
☆☆☆ 1982 CHARDONNAY ($14.00) Alexander Valley. *Ripe, clean, fresh, deep. A lovely and serious wine.*

☆☆☆ 1982 CHARDONNAY ($16.00) Estate, Napa Valley. *Rich, vinous, deep, lush, balanced.*

☆☆☆ 1983 CHARDONNAY ($14.00) Alexander Valley. *Big, lush, balanced, oaky, rich, lovely fruit.*

☆☆☆ 1983 CHARDONNAY ($16.00) Estate, Napa Valley. *Rich, lush yet beautifully balanced and quite charming.*

☆☆☆ 1984 CHARDONNAY ($16.00) Alexander Valley. *Rich, smooth, perfumed and complex. A wine that should age well.*

☆☆☆ 1984 CHARDONNAY ($18.00) Napa Valley. *Rich, fruity, fat, intense, oaky, varietal. A big wine with aging potential.*

☆☆☆ 1985 CHARDONNAY ($18.00) Alexander Valley. *Crisp, clean, balanced, varietal, complex, well built. Drink 1989.*

☆☆☆ 1985 CHARDONNAY ($18.00) Napa Valley. *Rich, soft, intense, ripe, good oak and balance.*

### RED
☆☆☆ 1978 CABERNET SAUVIGNON ($12.00) Sonoma. *Herbal and intense, with nice oak and a long future.*

☆☆ 1978 CABERNET SAUVIGNON ($16.00) Centennial Bottling, Estate, Napa Valley. *Rich, intense, concentrated. Drink now.*

☆☆☆ 1979 CABERNET SAUVIGNON ($14.00) Sonoma. *Rich and balanced, fruity and complex. Will improve further.*

☆☆☆ 1979 CABERNET SAUVIGNON ($16.00) Estate, Napa Valley. *Rich, clean, nicely structured. Drink now and beyond.*

☆☆☆ 1980 CABERNET SAUVIGNON ($16.00) Estate, Napa Valley. *Intense, complex, rich, dark, lovely structure. Drink 1988.*

☆☆☆ 1982 CABERNET SAUVIGNON ($18.00) Estate, Napa Valley. *Intense, dark, rich, earthy, nicely built, some nice currant flavors. Drink 1991.*

☆☆☆☆ 1983 CABERNET SAUVIGNON ($18.00) Estate, Napa Valley. *Crisp, ripe berry flavors, superb structure, long finish. Rich but not heavy. A keeper. Drink 1990 and beyond.*

☆☆ 1977 ZINFANDEL ($6.50) California. *Dense but well bred. Clean and varietal, ready to drink.*

☆☆ 1979 ZINFANDEL ($7.00) California. *Big and rich but with some finesse.*

☆☆ 1981 ZINFANDEL ($8.00) Napa Valley. *Clean, tangy, fruity and rich.*

☆☆☆ 1982 ZINFANDEL ($10.00) Estate, Napa Valley. *Rich, dense, berry flavors. Clean and complex. Drink now.*

☆☆☆ 1983 ZINFANDEL ($10.00) Estate, Napa Valley. *Concentrated, fruity, hard and rich; needs mellowing. Drink 1988.*

☆☆☆ 1984 ZINFANDEL ($10.00) Estate, Napa Valley. *Ripe, smooth, berried, deep, intense. Drink 1988.*

≈●

## Château Montgolfier Vineyard TEXAS
### WHITE
1985 YELLOW ROSE OF TEXAS ($6.00) Parker. *1% residual sugar. Mostly Chenin Blanc. Oxidized, heavy.*

≈●

## Château Morrisette Winery VIRGINIA
### WHITE
☆☆☆☆ 1986 WHITE RIESLING ($6.25) Virginia. *2% residual sugar. Snappy, fresh, lively, intense fruit, elegant structure.*

≈●

CHATEAU RUTHERFORD *see* Rutherford Vintners

## Château St. Jean SONOMA COUNTY
### WHITE
☆☆☆ 1982 SAUVIGNON D'OR ($15.00) Sonoma. *12.8% residual sugar. 59% Sauvignon Blanc, 41% Semillon. Superb.*

☆☆☆ 1984 SEMILLON D'OR ($15.00) St. Jean, Sonoma Valley. *8.2% residual sugar. 62% Semillon, 38% Sauvignon Blanc. Lush, nutty, Sauternes-like. Rich, complex and very charming.*

☆☆☆ 1985 VIN BLANC ($4.00) Sonoma. *32% Sauvignon Blanc, 11% Gewürztraminer, 14% White Riesling, 15% Chardonnay, 1% Semillon, 1% Muscat Canelli. Crisp, tart, good.*

☆ 1985 SEMILLON D'OR ($15.00) Sonoma. *10% residual sugar. 59% Semillon, 41% Sauvignon Blanc. Fresh and fruity, with decent balance and some volatile acidity.*

☆☆☆ 1980 CHARDONNAY ($18.00) Robert Young, Alexander Valley. *Assertive and toasty, with some crisp fruit.*

☆☆☆☆ 1981 CHARDONNAY ($18.00) Robert Young, Alexander Valley. *Exquisite and complex. Rich and deep, yet very elegant. Still St. Jean's best Chardonnay—especially in magnums.*

☆☆ 1982 CHARDONNAY ($11.00) Sonoma. *Earthy, decent, lacks finesse.*

☆☆ 1982 CHARDONNAY ($15.50) Belle Terre, Alexander Valley. *Fresh, clean, attractive. Nicely balanced.*

☆ 1982 CHARDONNAY ($15.50) St. Jean, Sonoma. *Off aromas and off flavors.*

☆☆☆ 1982 CHARDONNAY ($18.00) Robert Young, Alexander Valley. *Lush, clean, big, intense.*

☆☆ 1982 CHARDONNAY ($45.00) Reserve, Robert Young, Alexander Valley. *Magnums only. Rich, earthy, heavy flavors, intense oak, lacking finesse.*

☆ 1983 CHARDONNAY ($12.00) Sonoma. *Dull, lacking finesse.*

☆☆☆ 1983 CHARDONNAY ($14.25) McCrea, Sonoma Valley. *Rich, round, lush, pretty oak, clean, very lovely.*

1983 CHARDONNAY ($14.75) St. Jean, Sonoma Valley. *Dirty, odd flavors, sour, unpleasant. Tasted several times.*

☆☆☆ 1983 CHARDONNAY ($16.00) Jimtown Ranch, Alexander Valley. *Rich, firm, varietal, clean, complex.*

☆☆☆ 1983 CHARDONNAY ($16.75) Belle Terre, Alexander Valley. *Balanced, rich, oaky, elegant, very stylish.*

☆☆☆ 1983 CHARDONNAY ($18.00) Robert Young, Alexander Valley. *Crisp and balanced, good acidity and complexity.*

☆☆ 1984 CHARDONNAY ($12.00) Sonoma. *Crisp, clean, simple, well made.*

☆☆ 1984 CHARDONNAY ($14.00) Frank Johnson, Dry Creek Valley. *Lovely, ripe fruit and clean, new oak. Some vegetal qualities.*

☆☆☆ 1984 CHARDONNAY ($14.00) McCrea, Sonoma Valley. *Big, rich oak and fruit; husky and long, with some obvious alcohol.*

☆☆ 1984 CHARDONNAY ($16.00) Belle Terre, Alexander Valley. *Crisp, clean, lush, ripe, fruity, attractive.*

☆ 1984 CHARDONNAY ($16.00) St. Jean, Sonoma Valley. *Dull, bitter, decent flavors but not attractive.*

☆☆☆ 1984 CHARDONNAY ($18.00) Robert Young, Alexander Valley. *Soft, clean, focused fruit, rich oak.*

☆☆ 1985 CHARDONNAY ($11.00) Sonoma. *Crisp, clean, decent fruit, nicely balanced.*

☆☆ 1985 CHARDONNAY ($14.00) Frank Johnson, Dry Creek Valley. *Big, ripe, intense, mouthfilling, high alcohol. Needs time to mellow out.*

☆☆ 1985 CHARDONNAY ($14.00) McCrea, Sonoma Valley. *Big, aggressive, oily, with power and depth. Some age may smooth it out.*

☆☆☆☆ 1985 CHARDONNAY ($18.00) Robert Young, Alexander Valley. *Pear fruit, subtle oak, vivid; good, crisp fruit on the finish. Drink 1990.*

☆☆☆ 1986 CHARDONNAY ($11.00) Sonoma. *Soft, smooth, bright fruit and gentle oak. The most accessible and drinkable of St. Jean's Chardonnays.*

☆☆☆☆ 1986 CHARDONNAY ($18.00) Robert Young, Alexander Valley. *Crisp and fresh, lovely balance, intense fruit; clean, new oak; great aging potential.*

☆☆☆ 1986 FUME BLANC ($6.00) Sonoma. *Crisp, snappy, clean; quite lovely. Long finish.*

☆☆☆☆ 1986 FUME BLANC ($10.50) La Petite Etoile, Russian River Valley. *Smooth, crisp, fresh, complex, lovely fruit and finish.*

☆☆☆☆ 1984 GEWURZTRAMINER ($14.00) Select Late Harvest, Belle Terre, Anderson Valley. *375 ml. 11.7% residual sugar. Spicy, lush, rich varietal character, soft fruit and lovely flavors.*

1986 GEWURZTRAMINER ($8.00) Frank Johnson, Russian River Valley. *Mushroomy and moldy, with some attractive fruit underneath.*

☆☆ 1986 GEWURZTRAMINER ($8.00) Sonoma. *Dry, crisp, tight, clean, attractive.*

☆ 1983 JOHANNISBERG RIESLING ($11.00) Sonoma. *Vegetal and flabby.*

☆☆ 1985 JOHANNISBERG RIESLING ($12.00) Late Harvest, Russian River Valley. *15.3% residual sugar. Crisp, lovely, botrytized fruit, some herbal qualities; soft, sweet finish.*

☆☆ 1986 JOHANNISBERG RIESLING ($8.50) Sonoma. *Rich, green apple fruit, with some bitter flavors.*

☆☆☆ 1985 PINOT BLANC ($9.00) Robert Young, Alexander Valley. *Soft, fruity, clean, subtly oaked, charming.*

☆☆☆ 1985 WHITE RIESLING ($15.00) Selected Late Harvest, Russian River Valley. *15.3% residual sugar. Rich apricot fruit, lovely botrytis, balanced.*

☆☆☆ 1986 WHITE TABLE WINE ($4.00) Sonoma. *Clean, rich, fresh, complex and lovely.*

### SPARKLING

☆☆ 1982 BRUT ($13.00) Sonoma. *Crisp, snappy, firm and fruity, with a trace of vegetal quality.*

☆☆ 1982 BRUT BLANC DE BLANCS ($13.00) Sonoma. *Crisp, tangy, yeasty, slightly vegetal.*

☆ 1983 BRUT BLANC DE BLANCS ($11.50) Sonoma. *Sweet, oily, heavy, coarse.*

☆ 1983 BRUT ($12.25) Sonoma. *70% Pinot Noir, 23% Chardonnay. Snappy, spicy, tart, clean.*

☆☆☆ 1984 BRUT ($10.50) Sonoma. *Ripe, rich mouthfilling. The best St. Jean sparkling wine in quite a while.*

### BLANC DE NOIR

☆☆☆ 1984 PINOT BLANC ($9.00) Robert Young, Alexander Valley. *Rich, oaky, smooth, balanced.*

### RED

☆☆☆ 1978 CABERNET SAUVIGNON ($17.00) Glen Ellen, Sonoma. *Rich, fruity, clean and lovely. Will continue to improve.*

☆☆☆☆ 1979 CABERNET SAUVIGNON ($17.00) Wildwood, Sonoma Valley. *Rich, deep, fruity, complicated and superb. Drink 1988.*

☆☆ 1981 CABERNET SAUVIGNON ($15.00) Sonoma. *Dense, rich, concentrated, dull. Drink 1990.*

☆☆☆ 1983 PINOT NOIR ($12.00) McCrea, Sonoma Valley. *Crisp, fresh, cherry fruit; clean and nicely balanced.*

❧

## *Château Ste. Michelle* WASHINGTON
### WHITE

☆☆ NV FARRON RIDGE CELLARS WHITE TABLE WINE ($3.10) Washington. *Crisp, clean, fresh, attractive.*

☆☆ 1982 CHARDONNAY ($9.75) Washington. *Fresh, clean, varietal, simple.*

☆☆☆ 1983 CHARDONNAY ($18.00) Château Reserve, River Ridge, Washington. *Tight, hard-edged, firm fruit. Drink 1993.*

☆☆☆ 1984 CHARDONNAY ($9.00) Washington. *Crisp, clean, fresh, Mâcon-style.*

☆☆☆ 1985 CHARDONNAY ($10.00) Washington. *Tart, clean, snappy lemon fruit.*

☆☆☆ 1986 COLUMBIA CREST CHARDONNAY ($8.00) Columbia Valley. *Soft, crisp, clean, balanced, charming.*

☆ 1986 CHENIN BLANC ($5.00) Washington. *Spritzy, decent but lacking freshness.*

☆ 1986 COLUMBIA CREST CHENIN BLANC ($5.00) Columbia Valley. *Crisp, decent fruit, varietal, unexciting.*

☆☆☆ 1986 COLUMBIA CREST GEWURZTRAMINER ($6.00) Columbia Valley. *Crisp, fresh, varietal, fruity.*

☆☆☆ 1986 JOHANNISBERG RIESLING ($5.50) Washington. *Tart, crisp, lively, fresh.*

☆ 1986 COLUMBIA CREST JOHANNISBERG RIESLING ($6.00) Columbia Valley. *Decent flavors but flat and dull.*

☆☆☆  1986 COLUMBIA CREST SAUVIGNON BLANC ($7.00)
        Columbia Valley. *Soft, fresh, clean, rich, lovely.*
☆☆  1985 SEMILLON ($5.50) Washington. *Soft, ripe, herbal,*
        *attractive.*
☆☆  1986 COLUMBIA CREST SEMILLON ($5.00) Columbia
        Valley. *Soft, lush, rounded.*
☆  1984 WHITE RIESLING ($14.00) Hand-Selected Clusters
        Late Harvest, Hahn Hill, Washington. *6.2% re-*
        *sidual sugar. Oily, sappy, low fruit, dull.*

## SPARKLING
☆☆  1980 BLANC DE NOIR ($23.00) Washington. *Crisp, fresh,*
        *smooth, good fruit. Nicely balanced.*

## RED
☆  NV  FARRON RIDGE CELLARS PREMIUM ROSE TABLE
        WINE ($3.50) Washington. *Decent, herbal, clean.*
○  1978 CABERNET SAUVIGNON ($9.00) Washington.
        *Skunky, vegetal.*
☆  1978 CABERNET SAUVIGNON ($17.00) Château Reserve,
        Cold Creek, Benton. *Meaty, clean, decent. Drink*
        *now.*
☆  1979 CABERNET SAUVIGNON ($17.00) Cold Creek, Ben-
        ton. *Raisiny, clean and lacking in fresh fruit.*
☆  1980 CABERNET SAUVIGNON ($9.00) Washington. *Dull,*
        *dreary, lacking fruit.*
☆☆  1980 CABERNET SAUVIGNON ($16.00) Reserve, Cole
        Ranch, Washington. *Minty, intense, clean and very*
        *well made. Attractive.*
☆☆  1980 CABERNET SAUVIGNON ($20.00) Château Reserve,
        Benton, Washington. *Intense. Good cherry fruit*
        *and acidity; attractive.*
☆☆☆  1982 CABERNET SAUVIGNON ($10.50) Washington. *Min-*
        *ty, tight, good fruit and structure, complex. Drink*
        *1992.*
☆☆☆  1983 CABERNET SAUVIGNON ($10.00) Washington. *Lean,*
        *complex, nicely structured. Tart, tight fruit. Drink*
        *1991.*
☆☆  1978 MERLOT ($7.00) Washington. *Light, clean and*
        *pleasant.*
    1980 MERLOT ($7.25) Washington. *Varietal, clean, light but*
        *thin.*
☆  1981 MERLOT ($10.00) Washington. *Lean, green, decent*
        *fruit, clean.*
    1983 PINOT NOIR ($13.30) Limited Bottling, Washington.
        *Simple, dull, some oxidation.*

                      ☙

## *Château Souverain*                    SONOMA COUNTY
### WHITE
☆☆  1982 CHARDONNAY ($9.00) North Coast. *Crisp and*
        *snappy, with a touch of oiliness.*
☆☆  1986 CHARDONNAY ($8.00) Sonoma. *Soft, fresh, clean,*
        *nicely balanced.*
☆☆  1985 SAUVIGNON BLANC ($8.00) Reserve, Wasson, Alex-
        ander Valley. *Lean, varietal, balanced but lacking*
        *fruit and charm.*

### RED
    1982 SOUVIN ROUGE ($4.00) California. *45% Cabernet*
        *Sauvignon, 41% Zinfandel, 8% Pinot Noir, 6%*
        *Merlot. Sweet, ripe, sappy, unexciting.*
☆☆  1978 CABERNET SAUVIGNON ($7.00) North Coast. *Pleas-*
        *ant. Drink now.*

☆☆ 1978 CABERNET SAUVIGNON ($12.00) Vintage Selection, Estate, Sonoma. *Soft and rich, with good fruit and varietal character. Drink now.*

☆☆☆ 1979 CABERNET SAUVIGNON ($7.75) North Coast. *Rich, clean, varietal and charming. Drink now.*

☆☆☆ 1984 CABERNET SAUVIGNON ($8.00) Sonoma. *Lush, ripe, lovely. Super.*

☆☆ 1979 MERLOT ($5.50) North Coast. *Fresh and appealing. Simple but very nice.*

☆ 1981 MERLOT ($6.75) North Coast. *Light, soft, decent.*

☆☆☆ 1984 MERLOT ($8.00) Sonoma. *Soft herbs and lush fruit; charming and lively.*

☆ 1978 PETITE SIRAH ($5.00) North Coast. *Rich, deep, clean, some off qualities in the nose.*

☆☆ 1980 ZINFANDEL ($5.00) North Coast. *Balanced and quite nice.*

෨ᓗ

## Château Woltner                            NAPA
### WHITE
☆☆ 1985 CHARDONNAY ($18.00) Woltner Estates, Napa Valley. *Soft, lush, ripe, smooth, nicely built.*

☆☆☆ 1985 CHARDONNAY ($30.00) St. Thomas, Napa Valley. *Rich, complex, great fruit, lovely acidity, very Burgundian. Drink 1988.*

☆☆☆ 1985 CHARDONNAY ($40.00) Titus, Napa Valley. *Tight, complex, rich, firm acidity, great structure, needs time. Drink 1989.*

෨ᓗ

## Chatom Vineyards              CALAVERAS COUNTY
### WHITE
☆☆☆ 1985 CALAVERAS FUME ($6.00) Calaveras. *Crisp, smooth, charming balance and lovely fruit.*

෨ᓗ

## Chermont Winery                         VIRGINIA
### RED
☆ 1981 CABERNET SAUVIGNON ($7.50) Albemarle. *Toasty nose, rich, complex, clean, varietal, a bit simple.*

෨ᓗ

## Chicama Vineyards            MASSACHUSETTS
### SPARKLING
☆ NV  SEA MIST BRUT ($10.00) Massachusetts. *Clean, spicy, heavy, decent.*
### RED
1980 CABERNET SAUVIGNON ($12.50) Massachusetts. *Grapey, clumsy, tannic, decent.*

෨ᓗ

## Chimney Rock                        NAPA COUNTY
### WHITE
☆☆ 1984 CHARDONNAY ($14.00) Napa Valley. *Dense, heavy, rich, clean, varietal, attractive but clumsy.*

☆☆☆ 1985 CHARDONNAY ($14.00) Napa Valley. *Crisp, clean, lovely fruit, good balance.*

☆☆ 1985 FUME BLANC ($9.00) Napa Valley. *Crisp, varietal, clean, balanced, lacking charm.*

**RED**

☆☆☆ 1984 CABERNET SAUVIGNON ($10.00) Napa Valley. *Rich, smokey, lush, plummy. Drink 1990.*

🍷

## The Christian Brothers                    NAPA COUNTY
**WHITE**

☆☆☆ NV PREMIUM WHITE ($4.00) California. *Soft, clean, fruity.*

☆☆ 1984 CHARDONNAY ($8.50) Napa Valley. *Ripe, oaky, clean, lacking depth but very nice.*

☆ 1985 CHARDONNAY ($8.50) Barrel Fermented, Napa Valley. *Spicy, woody, slim, lacking depth.*

☆☆☆☆ 1985 CHARDONNAY ($8.50) Napa Valley. *Spicy and rich, with lovely toasty oak and great structure.*

**SPARKLING**

NV EXTRA DRY ($7.00) California. *60% Chenin Blanc, 40% French Colombard. Bitter, dense, dull.*

**BLANC DE NOIR**

☆ 1986 WHITE ZINFANDEL ($5.00) Napa Valley. *Tart, sweet, simple, candied.*

**RED**

☆ NV PREMIUM CALIFORNIA RED ($4.00) California. *Blend of Cabernet Sauvignon, Zinfandel and Pinot Noir. Old, faded, lacking fruit.*

☆ 1978 CABERNET SAUVIGNON ($8.00) Napa Valley. *Soft, elegant, ready to drink.*

1982 CABERNET SAUVIGNON ($4.50) Napa Valley. *Bitter, dull, not much charm.*

☆☆☆ 1984 CABERNET SAUVIGNON ($7.50) Napa Valley. *Soft, smooth, good herbs and delicious fruit; balanced and fresh. Drink 1990.*

☆☆ 1982 MERLOT ($6.75) Napa Valley. *Leathery, rich, herbal.*

☆ 1982 ZINFANDEL ($5.00) Napa Valley. *Crisp, thin, decent.*

**FORTIFIED**

☆☆ COCKTAIL SHERRY ($7.00) California. *60% Chenin Blanc, 40% Colombard. Earthy, crisp, fresh, sweet.*

🍷

## Christophe Vineyards                    SAN FRANCISCO COUNTY
**WHITE**

☆☆ 1986 JOLIESSE ($4.75) California. *Soft, crisp, clean, fruity, off-dry, appealing. 58% Sauvignon Blanc, 20% Pinot Blanc, 17% Chenin Blanc, 5% Johannisberg Riesling*

☆☆☆ 1984 CHARDONNAY ($5.50) California. *Elegant, round, fresh flavors, attractive.*

☆ 1985 CHARDONNAY ($6.50) California. *Simple, decent, overripe.*

☆☆☆ 1986 SAUVIGNON BLANC ($5.75) California. *Softly herbal, clean, lush fruit, delicious.*

**RED**

☆☆ 1982 CABERNET SAUVIGNON ($4.50) California. *Green olive, herbal flavors. Good structure, crisp finish. Drink now.*

☆☆☆ 1982 CABERNET SAUVIGNON ($5.50) Napa Valley. *Clean, ripe, snappy, rich, with good flavor.*

🍷

## Cilurzo Vineyard and Winery                    RIVERSIDE COUNTY
**WHITE**

○ 1984 CHARDONNAY ($9.50) Temecula. *Oily, dull, flat, awful.*

### RED

○ 1980 CABERNET SAUVIGNON ($5.00) La Cresta and Long Valley, Temecula. *Vegetal, unattractive.*

☆ 1980 PETITE SIRAH ($7.00) Temecula. *Intense, cooked, dull.*

☆☆ 1984 PINOT NOIR ($9.50) Temecula. *Tart, varietal, lacking depth.*

🐚

## Cimmaron Cellars                    OKLAHOMA

### RED

1983 MARECHAL FOCH ($5.00) Oklahoma. *Green, vegetal, not likable.*

🐚

## Claiborne & Churchill Vintners         SAN LUIS OBISPO COUNTY

### WHITE

☆☆☆ NV EDELZWICKER ($4.75) Paragon, Edna Valley. *Clean, richly fruity, simple.*

🐚

## Cline Cellars                    CONTRA COSTA COUNTY

### BLANC DE NOIR

1985 WHITE ZINFANDEL ($3.85) Dragon, Contra Costa. *Flat, dull, unattractive.*

### RED

○ NV ZINFANDEL ($6.00) Contra Costa. *Big, inky, sweet, some volatile acidity.*

1984 ZINFANDEL ($5.00) Late Harvest, Contra Costa. *4% residual sugar. Lush, earthy, sweet, clumsy.*

☆☆ 1984 ZINFANDEL ($16.00) Late Harvest, Mazzoni, Contra Costa. *5% residual sugar. Rich, varietal flavors, crisp, sweet, Port-like.*

🐚

## Clos du Bois Winery                SONOMA COUNTY

### WHITE

☆☆☆ 1982 CHARDONNAY ($9.00) Barrel Fermented, Alexander Valley. *Rich, toasty, intense, with good, crisp fruit.*

☆☆ 1982 CHARDONNAY ($11.25) Calcaire, Alexander Valley. *Crisp, clean, tangy, very good.*

☆☆ 1982 CHARDONNAY ($11.25) Flintwood, Dry Creek Valley. *Toasty, earthy, nice fruit.*

☆☆ 1983 RIVER OAKS VINEYARDS CHARDONNAY ($6.00) Sonoma. *Fresh, clean, varietal, low-key, attractive.*

☆☆ 1984 CHARDONNAY ($6.00) Alexander Valley. *Woody, clean, appealing.*

☆☆ 1984 RIVER OAKS VINEYARDS CHARDONNAY ($6.00) Alexander Valley. *Fresh, fruity, simple but quite attractive.*

☆☆☆ 1984 CHARDONNAY ($9.00) Barrel Fermented, Alexander Valley. *Toasty and rich without being heavy, this wine is charming and very accessible.*

☆☆☆ 1984 CHARDONNAY ($11.25) Flintwood, Dry Creek Valley. *Rich, oaky, lush, varietal, ripe.*

☆☆☆☆ 1984 CHARDONNAY ($15.00) Calcaire, Alexander Valley. *Soft, complex and spectacular. Beautiful, with sweet new oak and elegant fruit. Very Montrachet-like.*

☆☆☆☆ 1984 CHARDONNAY ($18.00) Proprietor's Reserve, Alexander Valley. *Stunning oak, lush fruit, crisp and delicious.*

☆☆☆ 1985 RIVER OAKS VINEYARDS CHARDONNAY ($6.25) Sonoma. *Crisp, clean, snappy, great fruit.*

☆☆ 1985 CHARDONNAY ($9.00) Barrel Fermented, Alexander Valley. *Snappy, fresh, clean, varietal, simple, appealing.*

☆☆☆ 1985 CHARDONNAY ($15.00) Calcaire, Alexander Valley. *Rich, lush, balanced, great fruit.*

☆☆ 1985 CHARDONNAY ($15.00) Flintwood, Dry Creek Valley. *Crisp apple fruit, clean finish.*

☆☆☆ 1985 CHARDONNAY ($18.00) Proprietor's Reserve, Alexander Valley. *Fresh, clean, lovely balance, great blend of fruit and oak.*

☆☆☆ 1986 CHARDONNAY ($9.00) Barrel Fermented, Alexander Valley. *Crisp, lean, toasty, lively fruit, lovely balance.*

☆☆☆ 1986 JOHANNISBERG RIESLING ($8.50) Early Harvest, Alexander Valley. *1.7% residual sugar. Crisp, fresh fruit, lovely long finish.*

☆☆☆ 1985 SAUVIGNON BLANC ($10.50) Proprietor's Reserve, Dry Creek Valley. *Soft, delicate, simple charms but very attractive.*

☆☆☆☆ 1986 SAUVIGNON BLANC ($7.50) Alexander Valley. *13% Semillon. Lean, elegant, lush fruit.*

### RED

NV RIVER OAKS VINEYARDS PREMIUM RED ($3.21) Sonoma. *Metallic.*

☆☆☆☆ 1981 MARLSTONE ($16.00) Alexander Valley. *55% Cabernet Sauvignon, 40% Merlot, 5% Cabernet Franc. Rich, clean, sweet oak, ripe fruit, superb. Drink now.*

☆☆ 1982 MARLSTONE ($15.00) Alexander Valley. *55% Cabernet Sauvignon, 40% Merlot, 5% Cabernet Franc. Deep, rich, earthy, balanced, lovely. Drink 1990.*

☆☆ 1983 VIN ROUGE ($4.50) Alexander Valley. *Mostly Cabernet Sauvignon. Soft, herbal, decent fruit, simple but nice.*

☆☆ 1978 CABERNET SAUVIGNON ($12.00) Briarcrest, Alexander Valley. *Soft, herbal, lovely.*

☆☆☆ 1979 RIVER OAKS VINEYARDS CABERNET SAUVIGNON ($5.95) Alexander Valley. *Simple, herbal, clean and fruity. Drink now.*

☆☆ 1979 CABERNET SAUVIGNON ($9.00) Dry Creek Valley. *Simple and very nice.*

1980 CABERNET SAUVIGNON ($9.50) Sonoma. *Weedy and dull, lacking fruit.*

☆☆ 1980 CABERNET SAUVIGNON ($12.75) Briarcrest, Alexander Valley. *Ripe, herbaceous, rich, balanced. Drink now.*

☆☆☆ 1980 CABERNET SAUVIGNON ($15.00) Marlstone, Alexander Valley. *55% Cabernet, 45% Merlot. Rich and herbal, velvety and super.*

☆☆☆ 1980 CABERNET SAUVIGNON ($15.00) Proprietor's Reserve, Dry Creek Valley. *Soft, herbal, clean, lovely complexity, rich fruit. Drink 1988.*

☆☆☆ 1981 RIVER OAKS VINEYARDS CABERNET SAUVIGNON ($6.25) Healdsburg, Sonoma. *Rich, deep, great fruit, lovely balance. Drink now.*

☆☆☆☆ 1981 CABERNET SAUVIGNON ($9.00) Alexander Valley. *Rich, sweet oak, lush, complex, great structure. Drink 1988.*

☆☆☆ 1981 CABERNET SAUVIGNON ($13.00) Briarcrest, Alexander Valley. *Earthy, clean, balanced, toasty and delicious.*

1982 RIVER OAKS VINEYARDS CABERNET SAUVIG-
NON ($6.00) Sonoma. *Skunky.*

☆☆☆ 1982 CABERNET SAUVIGNON ($9.00) Alexander Valley.
*Herbs and fruit. Good texture, soft, fleshy, rich,
generous. Drink now.*

☆☆☆ 1982 CABERNET SAUVIGNON ($13.00) Briarcrest, Alex-
ander Valley. *Crisp, ripe, clean, complex, great oak
and fruit. Drink 1990.*

☆☆☆ 1982 CABERNET SAUVIGNON ($19.50) Proprietor's
Reserve, Dry Creek Valley. *Smokey, rich, clean,
tangy, good.*

☆ 1983 RIVER OAKS VINEYARDS CABERNET SAUVIG-
NON ($6.00) Sonoma. *Simple, chalky, herbal,
some good jammy fruit.*

☆☆ 1983 CABERNET SAUVIGNON ($17.00) Briarcrest, Alex-
ander Valley. *Big, oily, rich, vegetal, intense.*

☆☆ 1984 RIVER OAKS VINEYARDS CABERNET SAUVIG-
NON ($6.00) North Coast. *Simple, clean,
attractive.*

☆☆☆ 1984 CABERNET SAUVIGNON ($12.00) Alexander Valley.
*10% Cabernet Franc. Rich, toasty, heavy, balanced.*

☆☆ 1979 MERLOT ($8.00) Napa Valley. *25% Cabernet. Bal-
anced, clean and decent.*

☆☆☆ 1981 MERLOT ($8.50) Alexander Valley. *Fragrant, firm, rich
and balanced.*

☆☆ 1982 MERLOT ($8.50) Alexander Valley. *20% Cabernet.
Ripe, lush, balanced. Drink now.*

☆☆☆ 1983 MERLOT ($9.00) Sonoma. *Soft, smooth, rich berry fruit.
Drink now.*

☆☆ 1985 MERLOT ($10.00) Sonoma. *20% Cabernet Sauvignon.
Herbal, rich, with lush texture and good fruit.*

☆☆☆ NV PINOT NOIR ($8.00) Sonoma. *Rich, earthy, lush, good
fruit; lovely.*

☆☆☆ 1979 PINOT NOIR ($8.50) Cherry Hill, Dry Creek Valley.
*Richly varietal, crisp and tangy.*

☆☆ 1980 PINOT NOIR ($6.50) Alexander Valley. *Crisp, clean,
fresh, modestly attractive.*

☆☆☆ 1980 PINOT NOIR ($11.25) Proprietor's Reserve, Dry Creek
Valley. *Snappy, fresh, clean, attractive.*

☆☆ 1981 PINOT NOIR ($7.00) Dry Creek Valley. *Crisp, clean,
attractive, simple but nice. Drink now.*

☆☆☆ 1984 PINOT NOIR ($10.00) Sonoma. *Soft, lush cherry fruit,
complex, nice oak.*

☆☆☆ 1980 RIVER OAKS VINEYARDS ZINFANDEL ($7.00)
Private Reserve, Alexander Valley. *Rich and balanced, with lovely varietal character. Drink now.*

❧

## *Clos du Val*                                    NAPA COUNTY
### WHITE

☆☆ NV WHITE TABLE WINE ($5.00) California. *Simple, clean,
nice fruit, a bit short.*

☆☆ 1982 CHARDONNAY ($12.50) Napa Valley. *Lemony, fresh
and appealing.*

☆ 1983 GRAN VAL CHARDONNAY ($8.00) California.
*Snappy, clean, simple.*

☆☆ 1983 CHARDONNAY ($11.50) Napa Valley. *Spicy, nice oak,
decent.*

☆☆ 1984 GRAN VAL CHARDONNAY ($8.00) California.
*Clean, fresh, lovely fruit, attractive.*

☆☆☆ 1984 CHARDONNAY ($11.50) California. *Lovely fruit, rich
flavors yet elegant structure. CdV's best yet.*

        1985 GRAN VAL CHARDONNAY ($8.00) California. *Clammy, odd flavors.*

☆☆☆ 1985 CHARDONNAY ($12.50) Napa Valley. *Crisp, fruity, varietal, good structure. One of the better Clos du Val Chardonnays.*

☆☆ 1986 GRAN VAL CHARDONNAY ($8.50) California. *Crisp, clean, decent, a bit coarse.*

☆☆☆ 1986 SAUVIGNON BLANC ($8.50) Napa Valley. *Crisp, tangy, good varietal character; clean, nice finish.*

☆☆☆ 1985 SEMILLON ($8.50) Napa Valley. *Soft, round, herbal fruit, clean and balanced.*

☆☆☆ 1986 SEMILLON ($8.50) Napa Valley. *Soft, round, lush, spicy, clean and elegant.*

## RED

☆☆ NV   RED TABLE WINE ($7.50) Napa Valley. *Clean, fresh, herbal, nicely balanced, charming.*

☆☆☆ 1978 CABERNET SAUVIGNON ($12.00) Napa Valley. *Varietal, ripe, crisp and aristocratic. Drink now.*

☆☆☆ 1978 CABERNET SAUVIGNON ($25.00) Reserve, Napa Valley. *Silky and elegant, fruity and complex. Drink 1986 and beyond.*

☆☆☆ 1979 CABERNET SAUVIGNON ($12.50) Napa Valley. *Elegant, varietal, long finish. Drink 1989 and beyond.*

☆☆☆ 1979 CABERNET SAUVIGNON ($25.00) Reserve, Napa Valley. *Fat and rich, with lovely structure and depth.*

☆☆☆☆ 1980 CABERNET SAUVIGNON ($12.50) Napa Valley. *Stunning, rich, deep, velvety. Will age beautifully.*

☆☆☆☆ 1981 CABERNET SAUVIGNON ($12.50) Napa Valley. *Soft, rich, complex, elegant, superb. Drink 1988 and beyond.*

☆☆ 1982 GRAN VAL CABERNET SAUVIGNON ($7.50) Napa Valley. *Fresh, fruity, clean, delightful for present drinking.*

☆☆☆ 1982 CABERNET SAUVIGNON ($13.50) Napa Valley. *Clean, smooth, fresh, varietal, balanced. Drink 1992. Some bottle variation.*

☆☆☆ 1982 CABERNET SAUVIGNON ($28.00) Reserve, Napa Valley. *Lush and velvety, with gentle herbs and oak. Elegant, nicely structured and quite complex. Drink 1992.*

☆☆☆ 1984 GRAN VAL CABERNET SAUVIGNON ($8.50) Napa Valley. *Intense, soft texture, rich, deep, nice. Drink now.*

☆☆☆ 1984 CABERNET SAUVIGNON ($15.50) Napa Valley. *Tight, nicely structured, clean and balanced. This one needs some time to open up. Drink 1991.*

☆☆ 1985 GRAN VAL CABERNET SAUVIGNON ($8.50) Napa Valley. *Cedar and olive nose; soft, rich, smooth flavors, nice finish. Drink now.*

☆☆☆ 1978 MERLOT ($10.00) Napa Valley. *Structured and attractive. Drink now.*

☆☆ 1979 MERLOT ($12.00) Napa Valley. *Snappy, fruity, tannic. Drink 1986 and beyond.*

☆☆☆ 1980 MERLOT ($12.50) Napa Valley. *Dense, rich, complex and stylish. Aging gracefully.*

☆☆☆ 1981 MERLOT ($13.50) Napa Valley. *Soft and herbal; clean, rich and lovely. Great structure.*

☆☆☆ 1982 MERLOT ($12.50) Napa Valley. *Deeply colored, plummy, ripe, structured.*

☆☆☆☆ 1983 MERLOT ($14.00) Napa Valley. *Superb fruit, intense varietal character, great texture. Drink now.*

☆☆☆ 1984 MERLOT ($14.00) Napa Valley. *Crisp, fruity, fresh cherry flavors, great structure. Drink 1989.*

☆☆☆ 1985 MERLOT ($15.50) Napa Valley. *Lush, balanced, with soft texture, bright fruit and lovely herbs. Drink now.*

☆☆☆ 1980 PINOT NOIR ($10.00) Napa Valley. *From the Madonna Vineyard used by Acacia. Rich and superb.*

☆ 1981 PINOT NOIR ($9.75) Napa Valley. *O.K. structure and stemmy flavors.*

☆☆ 1981 PINOT NOIR ($10.75) Proprietor's Reserve, Sonoma. *Spicy, varietal, decent, some green flavors.*

☆ 1982 PINOT NOIR ($10.75) Napa Valley. *Odd, off aromas, meaty, decent acid, good balance.*

☆ 1983 PINOT NOIR ($11.50) Napa Valley. *Odd, menthol taste, decent fruit, thin flavors. Disappointing.*

☆☆ 1984 PINOT NOIR ($11.50) Napa Valley. *Soft, fresh, fruity, clean, and attractive. Balanced but somewhat simple.*

☆☆☆ 1985 PINOT NOIR ($12.00) Napa Valley. *Crisp, rich, complex; lean structure but plenty of flavor nuance; cherry fruit and lovely Burgundian character.*

☆☆ 1973 ZINFANDEL Napa Valley. *Rich, elegant, clean, nice.*

☆☆☆ 1977 ZINFANDEL ($7.50) Napa Valley. *Peppery, rich, berried. Drink now.*

☆☆☆ 1979 ZINFANDEL ($10.00) Napa Valley. *Elegant, well bred, delightful.*

☆☆☆ 1980 ZINFANDEL ($9.00) Napa Valley. *Berried but beautifully structured, clean and snappy.*

☆☆ 1981 ZINFANDEL ($9.00) Napa Valley. *Elegant and well built but lacking fruit.*

☆☆☆ 1983 ZINFANDEL ($10.00) Napa Valley. *Crisp, buttery, nicely balanced. Drink 1988.*

☆☆ 1984 ZINFANDEL ($12.00) Napa Valley. *Herbal, lean, pale, hard. Drink 1990.*

☆☆☆☆ 1985 ZINFANDEL ($12.00) Napa Valley. *Tangy, fresh, superb structure, rich, claret-style, great. Drink now or in the next two to three years.*

🍃

## Clos Pegase                    NAPA COUNTY
### WHITE
☆☆☆ 1985 CHARDONNAY ($12.00) Alexander Valley. *Soft, balanced, varietal, attractive.*

☆☆ 1985 FUME BLANC ($9.00) Napa Valley. *Crisp, fruity and intensely varietal. Grassy and tart.*

☆☆☆ 1986 SAUVIGNON BLANC ($8.50) Napa Valley. *Fresh, soft, clean, balanced, varietal.*

🍃

COASTAL WINE COMPANY *see* J. Patrick Doré

## B.R. Cohn Winery                SONOMA COUNTY
### WHITE
☆☆ 1985 CHARDONNAY ($10.00) Sonoma Valley. *Crisp, fresh, clean, attractive.*

☆☆☆☆ 1985 CHARDONNAY ($20.75) Olive Hill, Sonoma Valley. *The oak is dominant, but the wine is graceful and balanced. Lovely, lean structure.*

🍃

## Colony                          SONOMA COUNTY
### WHITE
☆☆☆ 1983 CHARDONNAY ($6.00) Sonoma. *Lush, oaky, rich, complex, buttery, really lovely.*

&#9734;&#9734; 1985 NORTH COAST CELLARS SAUVIGNON BLANC ($5.00) North Coast. *Clean, good fruit, nice balance.*

&#9734; 1985 SBARBARO CHARDONNAY ($11.00) Gauer Ranch, Alexander Valley. *Snappy, herbal, decent.*

&#9734;&#9734;&#9734; 1984 CHARDONNAY ($6.00) Gauer Ranch, Alexander Valley. *A stunning wine. Elegant, great oak and fruit, lovely varietal character.*

&#9734;&#9734;&#9734; 1985 JOHANNISBERG RIESLING ($8.00) Select Late Harvest, Alexander Valley. *375 ml. 18.6% residual sugar. Lush, fat, clean, lovely balance, honey flavors.*

&#9734;&#9734; 1986 NORTH COAST CELLARS CHARDONNAY ($6.00) North Coast. *Crisp, clean, lean and nicely structured. Fruity and attractive.*

### SPARKLING

&#9734; NV ROYAL KNIGHTS BRUT ($4.50) California. *Sweet and sappy.*

NV LEJON CHAMPAGNE CELLARS ($5.00) California. *Medicinal, herbal.*

NV LEJON CHAMPAGNE CELLARS BRUT ($5.00) California. *Soapy, fat, sweet.*

### BLANC DE NOIR

&#9734; 1986 WHITE ZINFANDEL ($4.50) North Coast. *Clean, simple, devoid of character.*

1986 NORTH COAST CELLARS WHITE ZINFANDEL ($5.00) North Coast. *Dull, awful.*

### RED

&#9734; 1983 LEJON BURGUNDY ($3.00) North Coast. *Soft, sweet, simple.*

&#9734;&#9734;&#9734; 1982 CABERNET SAUVIGNON ($7.00) Sonoma. *Crisp, ripe, lush, oaky, delicious. Drink now.*

&#9734;&#9734;&#9734; 1983 SBARBARO CABERNET SAUVIGNON ($10.00) Sonoma. *Toasty, fresh cherries, with excellent structure and delicious fruit finish. Drink 1989.*

&#9734;&#9734; 1985 NORTH COAST CELLARS CABERNET SAUVIGNON ($5.00) North Coast. *Soft, clean, fresh, simple but attractive.*

&#9734; NV NORTH COAST CELLARS RED TABLE WINE ($4.00) North Coast. *Tart, tangy, fresh, decent, clean, thin, simple.*

NV ZINFANDEL ($2.75) California. *Vegetal, soft, sweet.*

&#9734;&#9734; 1982 ZINFANDEL ($5.00) Sonoma. *Balanced, clean, rounded and quite attractive.*

&#9734;&#9734;&#9734; 1983 ZINFANDEL ($2.50) Sonoma Valley. *Crisp, fruity, clean, lovely. An incredible value.*

&#9734;&#9734; 1984 SBARBARO ZINFANDEL ($9.00) Sonoma. *Deep, rich, intense, good balance.*

&#8766;

## Colorado Mountain Vineyards     COLORADO
### WHITE

&#9734;&#9734; 1982 CHARDONNAY ($8.00) Colorado. *Soft and nutty, with good oak and nice varietal character.*

&#8766;

COLUMBIA CREST *see* Château Ste. Michelle

## Columbia Winery     WASHINGTON
### WHITE

1983 CHARDONNAY ($8.50) Washington. *Simple, chalky, odd.*

&#9734; 1983 CHARDONNAY ($15.00) Wyckoff, Yakima Valley. *Simple, floral, slight oxidation.*

☆☆☆ 1984 CHARDONNAY ($8.50) Washington. *Tart, crisp, fresh fruit, lovely.*

☆☆ 1985 CHARDONNAY ($8.00) Washington. *Oaky, earthy, soft, decent.*

☆☆☆ 1986 JOHANNISBERG RIESLING ($6.00) Washington. *Soft, luscious, delicate, great finesse. Charming.*

☆☆ 1986 JOHANNISBERG RIESLING ($6.00) Yakima and Columbia Valleys. *Soft, lush, clean, attractive.*

☆☆ 1986 JOHANNISBERG RIESLING ($7.00) Cellarmaster's Reserve, Washington. *7% residual sugar. Crisp, fruity, clean, attractive.*

### RED

☆☆ 1980 ASSOCIATED VINTNERS (AV) CABERNET SAUVIGNON ($9.00) Yakima Valley. *Dusty, varietal, nicely structured, appealing.*

☆ 1981 CABERNET SAUVIGNON ($8.00) Yakima Valley. *Deep, berried, fat. This one just misses.*

☆☆☆ 1982 CABERNET SAUVIGNON ($12.00) Red Willow, Yakima Valley. *Crisp, varietal, lush fruit, velvety texture, lovely.*

☆☆ 1982 CABERNET SAUVIGNON ($13.00) Otis, Yakima Valley. *Ripe, raspberry flavors, fruity, balanced, smooth texture. Drink 1988.*

1983 CABERNET SAUVIGNON ($9.00) Washington. *Metallic, dull.*

☆☆☆ 1981 MERLOT ($8.50) 76% Bacchus, 24% Cabernet Sauvignon, Otis. *Lush and elegant, with complexity and grace. Drink now.*

☆☆☆ 1983 MERLOT ($8.50) Sagemoor, Washington. *Herbal, clean, lovely structure, elegant.*

☆☆☆ 1984 MERLOT ($9.00) Washington. *Crisp, clean, snappy, lean, lovely fruit. Drink 1988.*

☆☆☆ 1979 ASSOCIATED VINTNERS (AV) PINOT NOIR ($9.00) Yakima Valley. *Great color, intense and angular, splendid fruit and acid.*

☆☆☆ 1984 WOODBURNE PINOT NOIR ($13.00) Washington. *Fruity, crisp, complex, charming.*

🎗

## Commonwealth Winery          MASSACHUSETTS

### WHITE

☆ 1983 CHARDONNAY ($7.95) Dana. *Clean, decent, soft.*

☆ 1985 CHARDONNAY ($10.00) Reserve, Massachusetts. *Oily, heavy, decent.*

### RED

NV DECHAUNAC ($6.45) Massachusetts. *"Bottled in 1981." Vegetal, deep, rich, ripe.*

☆ NV DECHAUNAC ($8.00) Massachusetts. *"Bottled in 1980." Snappy, decent fruit, vegetal.*

🎗

## Concannon Vineyard          ALAMEDA COUNTY

### WHITE

☆☆ 1983 CHARDONNAY ($8.00) 62% Tepusquet, Santa Maria; 38% Santa Clara, California. *Decent varietal character, dense, clean.*

☆☆☆ 1983 CHARDONNAY ($8.00) Selected Vineyards, 38% Mistral, 62% Tepusquet, California. *Rich, fruity, clean, beautifully balanced.*

☆☆ 1984 CHARDONNAY ($9.50) Mistral, Tepusquet, 26% Santa Clara, 74% Santa Maria Valley. *Crisp, clean, apple fruit.*

&#9734;  1985 CHARDONNAY ($10.50) Mistral, Tepusquet, 52% Santa Clara, 48% Santa Maria Valley. *Earthy, heavy, decent.*

&#9734;&#9734;&#9734;  1985 SAUVIGNON BLANC ($9.00) Estate, Livermore. *Barrel fermented, earthy, rich, snappy, clean.*

## RED

&#9734;  1978 CABERNET SAUVIGNON ($9.00) Estate, Livermore Valley. *Raisiny and earthy.*

1978 CABERNET SAUVIGNON ($9.75) 100 Year Anniversary, Livermore Valley. *Lacking fruit, rich, complex, not delicious.*

&#9734;  1979 CABERNET SAUVIGNON ($7.25) Livermore Valley. *Vegetal, lacking depth.*

&#9734;  1981 CABERNET SAUVIGNON ($9.00) Estate, Livermore Valley. *Thin, vegetal.*

&#9734;&#9734;&#9734;  1982 CABERNET SAUVIGNON ($10.25) Estate, Livermore Valley. *Clean, elegant, with lovely fruit and oak; charming. Drink 1988.*

&#9734;&#9734;&#9734;  1985 CABERNET SAUVIGNON ($10.50) Livermore Valley. *Lush, deep, rich, clean, concentrated. Drink 1989.*

&#9734;&#9734;  1974 PETITE SIRAH ($20.00) Limited Bottling, Estate, Livermore Valley. *Jammy and intense but nicely balanced. Drink now.*

&#9734;  1977 PETITE SIRAH ($13.50) Estate, Livermore Valley. *Berries and oak, nicely balanced but limited appeal.*

&#9734;  1978 PETITE SIRAH ($8.00) Estate, Livermore Valley. *Bigger and more aggressive than usual. Chewy, intense, mature.*

&#9734;&#9734;&#9734;  1979 PETITE SIRAH ($6.50) California. *Clean, balanced and rich, with nice complexity. Drink now.*

&#9734;&#9734;  1979 PETITE SIRAH ($15.00) Centennial, Estate, Livermore Valley. *Grapey, rich, intense but short.*

&#9734;&#9734;&#9734;  1980 PETITE SIRAH ($5.75) 54% Wilson, Clarksburg; 46% Estate, California. *Rich, clean, balanced, well made. Drink now or hold.*

&#9734;&#9734;&#9734;  1981 PETITE SIRAH ($6.50) Estate, Livermore. *Clean, well made, rich, attractive. Drink now or hold.*

&#10086;

## *Congress Springs Vineyard*     SANTA CLARA COUNTY

### WHITE

&#9734;&#9734;&#9734;  1982 CHARDONNAY ($10.00) Santa Clara. *Balanced, attractive, good fruit, low alcohol.*

&#9734;&#9734;&#9734;  1983 CHARDONNAY ($11.50) Santa Clara. *Barrel fermented. Clean, fresh, oaky, crisp fruit.*

&#9734;&#9734;&#9734;  1984 CHARDONNAY ($13.50) Santa Clara. *Oaky, lush, ripe, nicely rounded, very attractive.*

&#9734;&#9734;&#9734;  1985 CHARDONNAY ($12.00) Santa Clara. *Barrel fermented. Crisp, rich, lovely varietal fruit and good oak.*

&#9734;&#9734;&#9734;&#9734;  1985 CHARDONNAY ($20.00) Estate, Santa Cruz Mountains. *Rich, lush fruit, lovely soft flavors, clean oak and good balance.*

&#9734;&#9734;&#9734;  1986 CHARDONNAY ($16.50) Reserve, Barrel Fermented, San Ysidro, Santa Clara. *Lush, deep, smokey, intensely fruity.*

&#9734;&#9734;  1986 JOHANNISBERG RIESLING ($7.50) Santa Clara. *Lush, juicy fruit, intense, some unusual flavors.*

&#9734;&#9734;&#9734;  1984 PINOT BLANC ($8.00) St. Charles, Santa Cruz Mountains. *Lovely, rich, buttery, nicely oaked.*

&#9734;&#9734;  1985 PINOT BLANC ($8.25) Santa Clara. *Meaty, toasty, rich, clean fruit, decent.*

☆ 1985 PINOT BLANC ($9.25) 70% St. Charles, 30% San Ysidro, Santa Clara. *Dull, flabby, intense, lacking structure.*

☆☆☆ 1985 SEMILLON ($8.00) 22% St. Charles, 78% San Ysidro, Santa Clara. *Round, soft, crisp, fresh, lovely fruit.*

## SPARKLING

☆ 1985 BRUT ($7.50) Santa Cruz. 80% *Chenin Blanc,* 20% *Pinot Blanc. Decent but sour and a bit odd.*

## RED

☆☆ 1984 CABERNET FRANC ($12.00) Santa Cruz Mountains. *Grapey, intense, fat, dense. Drink now.*

☆ 1979 CABERNET SAUVIGNON ($7.00) Santa Clara Valley. *Crisp, light and without much varietal character.*

☆ 1980 CABERNET SAUVIGNON ($10.00) Santa Cruz. 10% *Merlot. Oaky, earthy, decent.*

1981 CABERNET SAUVIGNON ($8.50) California. *Thin, tart, unattractive.*

☆ 1982 CABERNET SAUVIGNON ($8.00) Santa Cruz Mountains. *Lean, fresh, simple, tart, balanced.*

☆☆ 1983 CABERNET SAUVIGNON ($8.00) 80% Santa Clara, 20% San Luis Obispo. *Soft, clean, crisp, fresh, simple. Drink now.*

☆☆☆ 1981 PINOT NOIR ($15.00) Private Reserve, Santa Cruz Mountains. *Varietal, fruity, lovely, crisp.*

☆☆☆ 1982 PINOT NOIR ($15.00) Private Reserve, Santa Cruz Mountains. *Intense, tannic, ripe, complex, woody.*

☆ 1985 PINOT NOIR ($12.00) Santa Clara. *Rich, ripe, a bit coarse.*

☆☆☆ 1981 ZINFANDEL ($9.00) Santa Cruz Mountains. *Lush, soft, fruity.*

☆ 1983 ZINFANDEL ($9.00) Montmartre, Estate, Santa Cruz Mountains. *Tart, some volatile acidity.*

☙

# Conn Creek Winery                    NAPA COUNTY

## WHITE

☆☆ 1982 CHARDONNAY ($12.50) Napa Valley. *Deep, rich, vinous, ripe.*

## RED

☆☆☆ 1978 CABERNET SAUVIGNON ($12.50) Lot 1, Napa Valley. *Rich, herbal, velvety, aristocratic. Drink now.*

☆☆☆ 1978 CABERNET SAUVIGNON ($12.50) Lot 2, Napa Valley. *Lush and deep, smooth and complex.*

☆☆☆ 1979 CABERNET SAUVIGNON ($13.00) Napa Valley. *Rich and plummy, with excellent depth. Drink 1987.*

☆☆☆ 1980 CABERNET SAUVIGNON ($13.00) Napa Valley. *Herbed, fat, classic. Drink 1988.*

☆☆☆ 1981 CABERNET SAUVIGNON ($13.50) Napa Valley. *Rich, crisp, hard, with a lovely future. Drink 1989.*

☆☆☆ 1982 CABERNET SAUVIGNON ($15.00) Napa Valley. *Rich, deep, ripe, lush and nicely structured. Drink 1989.*

☆☆ 1982 CABERNET SAUVIGNON ($16.75) Barrel Select, Napa Valley. *Soft, earthy, rich, nicely structured. Drink 1990.*

☆☆☆ 1982 CABERNET SAUVIGNON ($18.00) Colinas and Silverado, Napa Valley. 11% *Merlot. Rich, deep, clean and nicely proportioned; complex fruit. Drink 1991.*

☆☆☆☆  1984 CABERNET SAUVIGNON ($25.00) Private Reserve, Collins, Napa Valley. *10% Merlot, 5% Cabernet Franc. Lush, elegant, complex, great structure. Drink 1995.*

☆☆☆  1978 ZINFANDEL ($7.50) Napa Valley. *Big but well under control. Complex, clean and good fruit.*

☆☆☆  1979 ZINFANDEL ($7.50) Napa Valley. *Clean, rich, balanced, lovely.*

☆☆  1980 ZINFANDEL ($7.50) Estate, Napa Valley. *Tannic and intense. Drink now.*

☆☆  1981 ZINFANDEL ($8.50) Collins, Napa Valley. *Rich, ripe, intense, spicy.*

૨ક

COOK'S CHAMPAGNE CELLAR *see* Guild Wineries

## Copenhagen Cellars          SANTA BARBARA COUNTY
### WHITE
1984 STEARNS WHARF CHARDONNAY ($9.00) La Presa, Santa Ynez Valley. *Odd and slightly fishy.*

૨ક

## Corbett Canyon Vineyards          SAN LUIS OBISPO COUNTY
### WHITE
☆  1983 CHARDONNAY ($8.00) Central Coast. *Earthy, clean, crisp, some oiliness.*

☆☆  1984 CHARDONNAY ($6.00) Coastal Classic, Central Coast. *1 liter. Round, lush, clean, attractive.*

☆☆  1984 CHARDONNAY ($8.00) Central Coast. *Clean, nice varietal character, charming.*

☆☆☆  1984 CHARDONNAY ($10.00) Winemaker's Reserve, Edna Valley. *Lush, balanced, beautiful oak and fruit. A splendid wine.*

☆☆  1985 CHARDONNAY ($6.00) Coastal Classic, California. *1 liter. Soft, simple, clean, balanced.*

☆☆☆  1985 CHARDONNAY ($9.00) Select, Central Coast. *Clean, fresh, good oak and fruit, fairly elegant.*

1985 CHARDONNAY ($12.00) Reserve, Edna Valley. *Heavy, clumsy, unappealing.*

☆  1985 SAUVIGNON BLANC ($6.00) Select, Central Coast. *Sweet pea flavors, crisp, simple.*

☆☆  1986 SAUVIGNON BLANC ($6.00) Coastal Classic, California. *1 liter. Crisp, balanced, a trifle weedy but attractive.*

### BLANC DE NOIR
☆  1986 WHITE ZINFANDEL ($5.00) Coastal Classic, Central Coast. *1 liter. Soft, fresh, clean, simple, short.*

### RED
☆☆  1983 CABERNET SAUVIGNON ($7.00) Central Coast. *Herbal, crisp, clean, very attractive. Drink now.*

☆  1984 CABERNET SAUVIGNON ($7.00) Coastal Classic, Central Coast. *1 liter. Herbaceous, soft, decent.*

☆☆☆  1984 CABERNET SAUVIGNON ($8.00) Select, Central Coast. *Soft, lush, clean, ripe, charming. Drink now.*

☆☆☆  1983 ZINFANDEL ($6.25) Massoni, Amador. *Round, ripe, woody, nice complexity.*

૨ક

## Cosentino Wine Company          STANISLAUS COUNTY
### WHITE
☆☆  1984 CRYSTAL VALLEY CELLARS CHARDONNAY ($8.50) Napa Valley. *Earthy, decent fruit, interesting.*

☆☆ 1986 CHARDONNAY ($10.00) North Coast. *Lush, ripe, smooth and cleanly varietal.*

☆☆☆ 1986 CHARDONNAY ($17.00) Select, The Sculptor, Napa Valley. *Soft, ripe, charming, oak and rich fruit.*

### SPARKLING

☆ NV ROBIN'S GLOW BLANC DE NOIR ($9.00) California. *Simple, lush, heavy.*

☆☆ NV CRYSTAL VALLEY CELLARS SPUMANTE ($5.75) California. *Muscat. Sweet, lush, very appealing.*

☆☆ NV CRYSTAL VALLEY CELLARS EXTRA DRY ($6.50) California. *Snappy, fresh, crisp and simple.*

### RED

☆ 1984 CRYSTAL VALLEY CELLARS GRAND VIN ROUGE ($4.25) Santa Barbara. *Decent fruit, some oxidation, acceptable.*

☆☆☆ 1982 CRYSTAL VALLEY CELLARS CABERNET SAUVIGNON ($8.00) North Coast. *20% Merlot. Clean, soft, lovely fruit, ripe and complex. Drink 1988.*

☆☆☆☆ 1982 CRYSTAL VALLEY CELLARS CABERNET SAUVIGNON ($9.50) Reserve Edition, North Coast. *10% Merlot. Toasty, rich, firmly fruity, buttery, superb. Drink 1989.*

☆☆☆ 1983 CRYSTAL VALLEY CELLARS CABERNET SAUVIGNON ($8.50) North Coast. *Lush, rich, great structure. Drink 1988.*

☆☆☆ 1983 CRYSTAL VALLEY CELLARS CABERNET SAUVIGNON ($12.50) The Winemaster, Napa Valley. *10% Merlot. Grapey, tart, berried, forward, attractive. Drink 1988.*

☆☆☆ 1984 CRYSTAL VALLEY CELLARS CABERNET SAUVIGNON ($9.00) North Coast. *5% Merlot, 3% Cabernet Franc. Berried, intense, soft, attractive. Drink now.*

☆☆☆ 1984 CABERNET SAUVIGNON ($14.00) Reserve, North Coast. *Lush, ripe fruit, subtle oak, forward and supple, with a long finish. Drink 1990.*

☆☆☆ 1985 CABERNET SAUVIGNON ($14.00) North Coast. *15% Cabernet Sauvignon and 5% Merlot. Bright, tangy, tight, with balance and complexity. Drink 1990.*

1978 CYRSTAL VALLEY CELLARS MERLOT ($7.00) Napa Valley. *Nicely made but a bit tired.*

1980 CRYSTAL VALLEY CELLARS MERLOT ($7.00) California. *15% Cabernet Merlot. Dull and tired.*

☆☆ 1982 CRYSTAL VALLEY CELLARS MERLOT ($12.50) The Poet, Select, Sonoma. *18% Cabernet Sauvignon. Earthy, tannic, clean, balanced. Drink 1989.*

☆☆☆ 1983 CRYSTAL VALLEY CELLARS MERLOT ($9.50) Reserve Edition, Napa Valley. *23% Cabernet Sauvignon. Rich, deep, clean, lush, complex, super. Drink now.*

☆☆☆ 1985 MERLOT ($12.50) Napa *Herbal, ripe, clean, assertive and deep; powerful.*

☆☆☆ 1986 PINOT NOIR ($10.00) Reserve Edition, North Coast. *Crisp, fresh; lovely cherry fruit; clean and balanced.*

৵

## Costello Vineyards                    NAPA COUNTY

### WHITE

☆☆ 1982 CHARDONNAY ($9.00) Estate, Napa Valley. *Charming, crisp, well made. An impressive first wine.*

☆☆ 1983 CHARDONNAY ($9.75) Estate, Napa Valley. *Quite dark. Big, balanced, clean and intense.*

☆☆☆ 1984 CHARDONNAY ($10.50) Estate, Napa Valley. *Oaky, rich, clean, good fruit and balance.*

☆☆ 1985 CHARDONNAY ($10.50) Estate, Napa Valley. *Soft, lush, oaky, varietal, good fruit.*

❧

## *H. Coturri and Sons*                    SONOMA COUNTY

### WHITE

○ 1982 CHARDONNAY ($9.00) Gordon, Sonoma Valley. *Oxidized, hazy, horrible.*

○ 1982 CHARDONNAY ($12.50) Freiberg, Sonoma Valley. *"Burnt match" nose, overdone. Process flavors spoil good fruit.*

### RED

NV RED TABLE WINE ($5.00) Sonoma Valley. *Acidic, weird.*

1979 CABERNET SAUVIGNON ($20.00) Sonoma. *Raisiny, concentrated, overpowering—lacks finesse.*

1980 CABERNET SAUVIGNON ($13.00) Sonoma Valley. *Raisiny, hot, no varietal character.*

☆☆ 1980 CABERNET SAUVIGNON ($25.00) Old Vines, Glen Ellen, Sonoma Valley. *Intense, dark, concentrated, complex. Drink 1990.*

☆☆ 1981 CABERNET SAUVIGNON ($11.25) Horne, Sonoma Valley. *Lush, complex, fruity, some dirty flavors.*

1979 PINOT NOIR ($15.75) Glen Ellen, Sonoma Valley. *Weird, sweet, not clean.*

☆☆☆ 1980 PINOT NOIR ($15.00) Sonoma Valley. *Lush, rich, earthy, aggressive.*

☆ 1981 PINOT NOIR ($10.00) Sangiacoma, Sonoma Valley. *Smokey, intense, earthy, heavy, a bit overdone.*

☆☆☆ 1981 PINOT NOIR ($10.00) Miller Ranch, Sonoma. *Soft, fruity, clean and quite lovely.*

☆ 1980 ZINFANDEL ($10.00) Les Vignerons, Sonoma Valley. *Berries and jam, intense, no finesse.*

☆☆ 1980 ZINFANDEL ($13.00) Glen Ellen, Sonoma Valley. *Big, rich, berried, late harvest style.*

☆☆ 1981 ZINFANDEL ($8.50) Sonoma Valley. *Dark, dense, crisp acidity, earthy and a bit heavy.*

❧

## *Covey Run Vintners*                    WASHINGTON

### WHITE

☆☆ 1985 WHITE TABLE WINE ($5.00) Washington. *1.5% residual sugar. Spicy, clean, nicely made.*

☆☆ 1983 QUAIL RUN VINTNERS CHARDONNAY ($8.00) Yakima Valley. *Ripe, fresh, oaky, clean.*

1984 CHARDONNAY ($8.00) Yakima Valley. *Sour, off nose, bitter.*

☆☆☆ 1984 QUAIL RUN VINTNERS CHARDONNAY ($9.00) Washington. *Crisp, clean, lean, dry, quite lovely.*

1985 CHARDONNAY ($9.50) Yakima. *Bitter, flat, oily, unattractive.*

☆☆ 1986 JOHANNISBERG RIESLING ($6.00) Yakima Valley. *Ripe, rich, decent, balanced.*

☆☆ 1985 SEMILLON ($8.00) La Caille de Fumé, Yakima Valley. *Herbal, rich, fruity, soft, intense.*

☆☆☆ 1985 WHITE RIESLING ($7.00) Botrytized, Mahre, Yakima Valley. *7.5% residual sugar. Lush botrytis, apricot fruit, good balance.*

**RED**

☆☆☆ 1982 QUAIL RUN VINTNERS CABERNET SAUVIGNON ($15.00) Yakima Valley. *Lovely fruit, great oak, a charmer. Drink 1989.*

☆☆☆ 1983 QUAIL RUN VINTNERS CABERNET SAUVIGNON ($12.00) Yakima Valley. *Soft, round, balanced, good fruit, complexity. Drink 1989.*

1984 CABERNET SAUVIGNON ($11.00) Yakima Valley. *Astringent, harsh, earthy, with low fruit.*

☆☆ 1983 QUAIL RUN VINTNERS MERLOT ($8.00) Yakima Valley. *Fragrant, floral, nicely structured.*

☆☆☆ 1984 MERLOT ($8.50) Yakima Valley. *Rich, firm, clean, nice structure, good firm fruit.*

🙖

## Crescini Wines                    SANTA CRUZ COUNTY

**RED**

☆☆☆ 1981 CABERNET SAUVIGNON ($7.50) Napa Valley. *Minty, berried, deep, very good. Drink now.*

☆☆ 1981 MERLOT ($6.50) Napa Valley. *Ripe, fruity, oaky, charming.*

🙖

CRESTA BLANCA *see* Guild Wineries

## Creston Manor
## Vineyards & Winery          SAN LUIS OBISPO COUNTY

**WHITE**

☆☆☆ 1984 CHARDONNAY ($13.75) Edna Valley. *Clean, soft, fruity, lovely.*

☆☆ 1985 CHARDONNAY ($12.00) San Luis Obispo. *Snappy, clean, ripe, round, nice.*

☆ 1985 CHARDONNAY ($13.00) Central Coast. *Sour, vegetal, oily; decent fruit.*

☆☆☆ 1986 SAUVIGNON BLANC ($10.75) San Luis Obispo. *Assertive herbal fruit, good crisp acidity and varietal flavors.*

**BLANC DE NOIR**

☆ 1986 WHITE ZINFANDEL ($5.50) San Luis Obispo. *Tart, crisp, clean, dry, slightly bitter.*

**RED**

1982 CABERNET SAUVIGNON ($10.25) Central Coast. *Vegetal, dirty.*

☆☆☆ 1983 CABERNET SAUVIGNON ($12.00) Edna Valley. *Lean, silky, elegant and nicely balanced. Drink 1988.*

☆☆ 1984 CABERNET SAUVIGNON ($10.00) Edna Valley. *Lush, weedy, velvety. Drink 1991.*

☆☆☆ 1985 CABERNET SAUVIGNON ($10.00) Central Coast. *Lush, spicy, herbal, complex. Drink 1992.*

1985 PINOT NOIR ($7.00) Petit d' Noir, Central Coast. *Prickly texture, asparagus flavors.*

🙖

CRIBARI & SONS *see* Guild Wineries

## Crichton Hall Vineyard          NAPA COUNTY

**WHITE**

☆☆☆ 1985 CHARDONNAY ($13.50) Napa Valley. *Soft, elegant, rich fruit, clean varietal flavors.*

🙖

## *Cronin Vineyards*                    SAN MATEO COUNTY

### WHITE

☆☆☆ 1982 CHARDONNAY ($12.00) Ventana, Monterey. *Deep, lush, lovely depth and balance.*

☆☆☆ 1982 CHARDONNAY ($12.00) Alexander Valley, Sonoma. *Deep, lush, rich, balanced.*

☆☆☆ 1982 CHARDONNAY ($14.00) Napa Valley. *Lush, deep, clean, lovely.*

☆☆ 1983 CHARDONNAY ($13.50) Napa Valley. *Earthy, rich, intense, ripe.*

☆☆☆☆ 1984 CHARDONNAY ($13.50) Alexander Valley. *Crisp, clean, sweet oakiness, rich, balanced, very impressive.*

☆☆☆☆ 1984 CHARDONNAY ($13.50) Ventana, Monterey. *Super rich, intense, with lovely balance between fruit and oak.*

☆☆☆☆ 1984 CHARDONNAY ($14.00) Napa Valley. *Oaky, rich, intense fruit, ripe, beautifully balanced.*

☆☆☆☆ 1985 CHARDONNAY ($12.00) Vanumanutagi, Santa Cruz Mountains. *Super oak and vanilla, great toast; deep, lush fruit.*

☆☆☆ 1985 CHARDONNAY ($14.00) Alexander Valley. *Crisp, complex, intense, ripe, balanced.*

☆☆☆☆ 1985 CHARDONNAY ($14.00) Ventana, Monterey. *Lush, soft, rich, complex flavors, great acidity.*

☆☆☆ 1985 CHARDONNAY ($14.00) Napa Valley. *Big, rich, heavy, oily, intense.*

### RED

☆☆ 1980 CABERNET SAUVIGNON ($14.00) Napa Valley. *Earthy and intense but with a lovely fruitiness.*

☆☆ 1981 CABERNET SAUVIGNON ($12.00) Napa Valley. *Berry fruit, balanced, tangy, attractive. Drink now.*

☆☆ 1983 CABERNET SAUVIGNON ($12.00) Napa Valley. *Tart, oaky, intense, nice but lacking fruit.*

1980 PINOT NOIR ($15.00) Ventana, Monterey. *Overly stemmy.*

☆☆ 1981 PINOT NOIR ($8.50) Ventana, Monterey. *Crisp, clean, complex, nicely made.*

☆ 1981 PINOT NOIR ($10.00) Winery Lake, Napa Valley. *Pale, thin but nice. Good flavors.*

1982 PINOT NOIR ($9.00) Ventana, Monterey. *Soapy, vegetal, unpleasant.*

☆ 1983 PINOT NOIR ($10.50) Ventana, Monterey. *Stemmy, thin.*

ॐ

## *Cross Canyon Vineyards*    SAN LUIS OBISPO COUNTY

### RED

1979 CABERNET SAUVIGNON ($8.50) Estate, San Luis Obispo. *Dull, lifeless.*

☆ 1979 PETITE SIRAH San Luis Obispo. *Rich, earthy, lacking finesse.*

1980 ZINFANDEL ($6.50) San Luis Obispo. *Vegetal, earthy, clumsy.*

ॐ

## *Crosswoods Vineyards*                    CONNECTICUT

### WHITE

1984 CHARDONNAY ($13.50) Estate, Southeastern New England. *Oily, vegetal, dull.*

ॐ

## *Crown Regal Wine Cellars*      NEW YORK
### ROSE
☆☆ NV KESSER KOSHER CONCORD ($3.00) New York. *Fruity, sweet, clean and attractive.*

₹&

CRUVINET *see* Artisan Wines
CRYSTAL CREEK *see* San Martín Winery
CRYSTAL VALLEY CELLARS *see* Cosentino Wine Company

## *John Culbertson Winery*      SAN DIEGO COUNTY
### SPARKLING
☆ NV BLANC DE NOIR CUVEE ROUGE ($12.00) California. *Heavy, dark, decent.*
☆☆ NV DEMI-SEC ($12.00) California. *Heavy, dense, clean, balanced, good.*
☆☆ NV CUVEE DE FRONTIGNAN ($14.00) Demi-Sec, California. *Spicy, crisp, decent, heavy.*
☆☆☆ 1981 NATURAL, RECENT DISGORGE ($19.50) California. *Austere, toasty, clean, attractive.*
☆☆☆ 1984 BRUT ($14.00) California. *Balanced, clean, rich, snappy, ripe.*
☆☆☆ 1984 BLANC DE NOIR BRUT ROSE ($16.50) California. *Crisp, clean, fresh, nice fruit, classy.*
☆☆ 1984 BLANC DE NOIR ($19.00) California. *Crisp, clean, fresh, nice.*
☆☆ 1985 BLANC DE NOIR ($14.00) California. *Clean, crisp, decent, simple.*

₹&

RICHARD CUNEO *see* Sebastiani Vineyards

## *Cuvaison Vineyard*      NAPA COUNTY
### WHITE
☆☆☆ 1982 CHARDONNAY ($12.50) Napa Valley. *Youthful, hard, partly from new Carneros vines, nice.*
☆☆ 1983 CHARDONNAY ($14.00) Napa Valley. *Clean, lush, unfocused, decent. Young Carneros fruit is a big part of this.*
☆☆☆☆ 1986 CHARDONNAY ($13.50) Napa Valley. *Lovely crisp acidity, rich varietal fruit, smooth and complex.*
### RED
☆☆☆ 1978 CABERNET SAUVIGNON ($12.00) Napa Valley. *Tannic, clean, intense, balanced.*
1979 CABERNET SAUVIGNON ($10.00) Napa Valley. *Very disappointing—off flavors, odd aromas.*
☆☆☆ 1980 CABERNET SAUVIGNON ($10.00) Napa Valley. *Lush, rich, clean and well made. Drink now.*
☆☆☆ 1981 CABERNET SAUVIGNON ($9.00) Napa Valley. *Crisp, clean, ripe, good acidity and fruit, plummy. Drink 1992.*
☆☆☆ 1982 CABERNET SAUVIGNON ($14.50) Napa Valley. *Firm, rich, deep plum and cassis flavors, good wood, with a lovely long finish. Drink 1989.*
☆☆ 1983 CABERNET SAUVIGNON ($14.00) Napa Valley. *Intense, tight, powerful but low on fruit. Drink 1991.*
☆☆☆☆ 1984 MERLOT ($13.50) Anniversary Reserve, Napa Valley. *Lovely fruit and elegant structure. Superb. Drink now.*

☆☆☆ 1978 ZINFANDEL ($8.50) Napa Valley. *Peppery, rich and complex. Aging nicely.*

☆☆☆ 1983 ZINFANDEL ($7.50) Napa Valley. *Spicy, clean, rich, intense, good fruit.*

કે

CYPRESS LANE *see* Landmark Vineyards

## D'Agostini Winery                    AMADOR COUNTY

### WHITE

1983 CHARDONNAY ($6.00) Reserve, Sonoma. *Dull, flat, not much here.*

### RED

1980 CABERNET SAUVIGNON ($9.50) Reserve, Amador. *Old, tired, and unattractive.*

☆ NV ZINFANDEL ($6.00) Reserve, Bin 32, Amador. *Clean, nice flavors, but thin and lacking fruit.*

કે

## The Daume Winery                    VENTURA COUNTY

### WHITE

☆☆ 1982 CHARDONNAY ($10.00) Central Coast. *Rich, fat, clean, spicy.*

કે

## De Loach Vineyards                    SONOMA COUNTY

### WHITE

☆☆☆ 1982 CHARDONNAY ($12.00) Russian River Valley. *Ripe, sweetish, rich and fruity.*

☆☆☆ 1983 CHARDONNAY ($12.50) Sonoma. *Big, ripe, rich, clean and crisp.*

☆☆☆☆ 1984 CHARDONNAY ($12.50) Russian River Valley. *Ripe, sweet fruit, new oak, deep, balanced, lovely.*

☆☆☆ 1985 CHARDONNAY ($12.50) Russian River Valley. *Big, heavy, butterscotch, oaky, intense, clean.*

☆☆ 1985 CHARDONNAY ($18.00) O.F.C., Russian River Valley. *Big, lush, oily and slightly vegetal. Rich, fruity, clean.*

☆☆ 1986 CHARDONNAY ($12.00) Russian River Valley. *Oily, rich, heavy.*

### BLANC DE NOIR

☆☆ 1986 WHITE ZINFANDEL ($6.00) Russian River Valley. *Crisp, snappy, clean, intense. Good, but not as attractive as previous years.*

### RED

☆☆ 1981 CABERNET SAUVIGNON ($11.00) Dry Creek Valley. *Rich, lush, fruity, balanced, structured. Drink 1987.*

☆☆☆ 1982 CABERNET SAUVIGNON ($11.00) Dry Creek Valley. *Richly fruity, with soft, clean flavors; well structured, charming. Drink now.*

☆☆☆ 1983 CABERNET SAUVIGNON ($11.00) Dry Creek Valley. *Fresh, ripe, berried, varietal, nicely balanced. Drink 1988.*

☆☆☆ 1981 PINOT NOIR ($9.00) Estate, Sonoma. *Velvety and lush, with great fruit. A stunner.*

☆☆☆ 1981 PINOT NOIR ($12.00) Reserve, Estate, Sonoma. *Rich, clean, cherry fruit, sturdy, complex.*

☆☆ 1982 PINOT NOIR ($10.00) Estate, Russian River Valley. *Some depth and youthful tannin.*

☆☆ 1982 PINOT NOIR ($10.00) Russian River Valley. *Ripe, raisiny, coarse, fleshy, charming.*

☆☆☆ 1983 PINOT NOIR ($10.00) Estate, Russian River Valley. *Velvety rich, deep fruit, lovely structure, charming.*

☆☆☆ 1981 ZINFANDEL ($7.50) Estate, Russian River Valley. *Rich, velvety, complex, balanced, fruity, varietal, super.*

☆☆☆ 1982 ZINFANDEL ($8.00) Estate, Russian River Valley. *Rich, intense, deep, great fruit, lovely texture.*

☆☆ 1983 ZINFANDEL ($8.00) Estate, Russian River Valley. *Concentrated, clean, ripe, attractive.*

☆☆☆ 1984 ZINFANDEL ($8.50) Estate, Russian River Valley. *Rich, smooth, fresh, fruity, charming.*

🦌

## De Lorimier                    SONOMA COUNTY
### WHITE
☆☆☆ 1986 SPECTRUM ($8.50) Alexander Valley. *65% Sauvignon Blanc and 35% Semillon. Rich, lush, ripe, lively.*

☆☆ 1986 SAUVIGNON BLANC ($11.00) Late Harvest, Estate, Alexander Valley. *375 ml. 15% residual sugar. Soft, lush, smooth, simple.*

🦌

## DeMoor Winery                   NAPA COUNTY
### WHITE
1982 CHARDONNAY ($11.50) Black Mountain, Alexander Valley. *Oily, vegetal, bitter.*

☆☆ 1983 NAPA CELLARS CHARDONNAY ($11.50) Alexander Valley. *85% barrel fermented. Fresh, oily, earthy, clean.*

### RED
☆☆☆ 1978 CABERNET SAUVIGNON ($12.00) Napa Valley. *Lush, intense, herbal. Ready to drink.*

☆☆☆ 1979 CABERNET SAUVIGNON ($12.00) Napa Valley. *Chocolatey nose; well bred and delicate.*

☆☆ 1980 CABERNET SAUVIGNON ($12.00) Napa Valley. *Fat, good, with nice rich fruitiness but some weediness.*

☆☆☆ 1980 CABERNET SAUVIGNON ($16.00) Alexander Valley. *Big, rich and earthy. Drink now.*

☆☆ 1981 CABERNET SAUVIGNON ($12.00) Napa Valley. *Big, fat, lush, well made. Drink 1988 and beyond.*

☆☆☆ 1982 CABERNET SAUVIGNON ($14.50) Napa Valley. *Rich, round, intense fruit, oaky. Drink 1994.*

☆☆☆ 1982 NAPA CELLARS ZINFANDEL ($7.00) Alexander Valley. *Tart, clean, Claret-style, tight, nicely structured.*

☆☆☆ 1984 ZINFANDEL ($8.00) Napa Valley. *Tart, spicy, bright fruit, delicious.*

🦌

## Deer Park Winery                 NAPA COUNTY
### WHITE
☆☆☆ 1982 CHARDONNAY ($9.50) Napa Valley. *Big, intense, with fresh fruit acidity and elegant bearing.*

☆☆ 1983 CHARDONNAY ($12.00) Summit Lake, Howell Mountain, Napa Valley. *Rich, intense.*

1984 CHARDONNAY ($10.00) Napa Valley. *Oxidized, dull, no fruit.*

### RED
☆☆ 1979 ZINFANDEL ($6.75) Napa Valley. *Soft, grapey, intense.*

☆☆ 1980 ZINFANDEL ($6.75) Napa. *Varietal and fresh, with good fruit.*

☆☆☆ 1981 ZINFANDEL ($6.50) Napa Valley. *Woody, rich, intense, deep, wonderful fruit, very good.*

☆☆☆ 1982 ZINFANDEL ($10.00) Beatty Ranch, Howell Mountain. *Black currants and rich earth, spicy and ripe. A lovely, big wine.*

🦌

DEER VALLEY *see* Smith & Hook Vineyard

## *Dehlinger Winery*                    SONOMA COUNTY
### WHITE
☆☆ 1982 CHARDONNAY ($9.00) Russian River Valley. *Earthy, deep, oily, vegetal.*

☆☆ 1984 CHARDONNAY ($10.00) Estate, Russian River Valley. *Rich, fat, intense, oily but snappy and crisp.*

☆☆☆ 1986 CHARDONNAY ($11.00) Estate, Russian River Valley *Fresh apple fruit, clean and lively.*

☆☆ 1985 JOHANNISBERG RIESLING ($8.00) Special Select, Estate, Santa Ynez. *10% residual sugar. Soft, fruity, clean, simple.*
### RED
☆☆ 1979 CABERNET SAUVIGNON ($8.75) Sonoma. *Assertive and Zinfandel-like. Should mellow with age.*

☆☆☆ 1980 CABERNET SAUVIGNON ($9.00) Sonoma. *Rich, full, berry-style with plummy, lush flavors. Drink now.*

☆☆ 1981 CABERNET SAUVIGNON ($10.00) Sonoma. *Peppers, rich, lush, clean.*

☆ 1982 CABERNET SAUVIGNON ($11.00) Russian River Valley. *13% Merlot. Vegetal, simple, clean, decent.*

☆☆ 1986 CABERNET SAUVIGNON ($12.00) Russian River Valley. *Ripe, lush, herbal, green bean flavors.*

☆☆☆☆ 1984 MERLOT ($12.00) Sonoma. *Rich raspberry and plum fruit, soft texture, lovely long finish.*

☆☆ NV PINOT NOIR ($8.00) Russian River Valley. *Earthy, rich, intense, heavy.*

☆ 1979 PINOT NOIR ($7.50) Sonoma. *Varietal, earthy. Some good fruit but lacking richness.*

☆☆ 1980 PINOT NOIR ($10.00) Sonoma. *Varietal, rich, earthy and lean. Nice structure.*

☆ 1981 PINOT NOIR ($10.00) Sonoma. *Earthy, raisiny, varietal.*

☆☆☆ 1982 PINOT NOIR ($10.00) Sonoma. *Lush, oaky but delicate, varietal, charming.*

☆☆☆ 1983 PINOT NOIR ($10.00) Russian River Valley. *Spicy, silky texture, long finish, lean, delicate, lovely.*

☆☆☆ 1984 PINOT NOIR ($11.00) Russian River Valley. *Snappy, clean, cherry-berry fruit; charming.*

☆☆☆ 1979 ZINFANDEL ($7.00) Sonoma. *13% Petite Sirah. Ripe, fruity, balanced.*

☆☆ 1980 ZINFANDEL ($7.50) Sonoma. *21% Petite Sirah. Jammy, peppery, ripe and fruity.*

☆☆ 1981 ZINFANDEL ($7.50) Sonoma. *14% Petite Sirah. Snappy fruit, rich, varietal.*

☆☆ 1982 ZINFANDEL ($8.75) Sonoma. *24% Petite Sirah. Fat, lush, round, intense, herbal.*

☆☆ 1983 ZINFANDEL ($8.00) Sonoma. *13% Petite Sirah. Soft, rich, deep, clean, decent.*

🍷

## *Delicato Vineyards*                    SAN JOAQUIN COUNTY
### WHITE
1984 CHARDONNAY ($6.00) California. *Oily, fat, vinous.*

1984 CHARDONNAY ($10.00) Oak Knoll, Napa Valley. *Dull, some spoilage.*

○ 1984 CHARDONNAY ($12.50) 50th Anniversary, Barrel Fermented, Napa Valley. *Dull, flabby, unattractive.*

☆ 1985 SAUVIGNON BLANC ($5.50) California. *Crisp, fruity, simple.*

## BLANC DE NOIR

✫ 1986 WHITE CABERNET ($3.50) California. *Soft, clean, dull, flat.*

✫ 1986 WHITE ZINFANDEL ($3.50) California. *Clean, soft, simple, dull, flat.*

## RED

✫✫ NV BURGUNDY ($2.40) Northern California. *Brambly, decent fruit, rich and soft.*

1982 CABERNET SAUVIGNON ($3.75) California. *Clean and decent but a bit sweet and very strange.*

✫✫ 1983 CABERNET SAUVIGNON ($8.50) California. *Light, simple, clean, varietal, quite pleasant.*

○ 1984 PETITE SIRAH ($5.00) California. *Pruney, medicinal, unattractive.*

✫ 1983 ZINFANDEL ($4.75) California. *Thin, simple, clean, decent.*

✫✫ 1985 ZINFANDEL ($5.30) California. *Spicy, soft, berry fruit, clean and charming.*

🦞

# *Devlin Wine Cellars*          SANTA CRUZ COUNTY

## WHITE

1982 CHARDONNAY ($8.00) Sonoma. *Some oxidation, lacks varietal character and fruit.*

## RED

✫✫ 1980 CABERNET SAUVIGNON ($6.00) Sonoma. *Herbal, balanced, clean and attractive. Drink now.*

✫✫✫ 1982 CABERNET SAUVIGNON ($7.00) Sonoma. *Lovely herbs and fruit, clean, fresh, balanced. Drink 1989.*

✫✫ 1983 CABERNET SAUVIGNON ($7.00) Sonoma. *Earthy, clean, decent fruit. Drink now.*

✫✫ 1981 MERLOT ($9.00) Sonoma. *Lush, rich, clean; a very nice wine.*

✫✫ 1982 MERLOT ($8.00) Central Coast. *Lush, varietal, clean and attractive.*

🦞

# *Diamond Creek Vineyards*          NAPA COUNTY

## RED

✫✫✫ 1978 CABERNET SAUVIGNON ($12.50) Gravelly Meadow, Napa Valley. *Deep, complex and aristocratic. Great potential.*

✫✫✫ 1978 CABERNET SAUVIGNON ($12.50) Red Rock Terrace, Napa Valley. *Tight, rich and showing great aging potential. Drink 1988.*

✫✫✫ 1978 CABERNET SAUVIGNON ($12.50) Volcanic Hill, Napa Valley. *Perhaps the best of the three—firm yet very supple. Superb.*

✫✫✫ 1979 CABERNET SAUVIGNON ($15.00) Gravelly Meadow, Napa Valley. *Concentrated, complex and gracefully structured.*

✫✫✫ 1979 CABERNET SAUVIGNON ($15.00) Red Rock Terrace, Napa Valley. *Slightly lighter and more delicate. Complex. Drink now.*

✫✫✫ 1979 CABERNET SAUVIGNON ($15.00) Volcanic Hill, Napa Valley. *Austere, hard-edged, rich and complex. Needs time. Drink 1988.*

✫✫✫ 1980 CABERNET SAUVIGNON ($20.00) Gravelly Meadow, Napa Valley. *Softer, richer, more herbal than Red Rock.*

✫✫✫ 1980 CABERNET SAUVIGNON ($20.00) Red Rock Terrace, Napa Valley. *Tight and austere but showing great promise. Drink 1990.*

☆☆☆ 1980 CABERNET SAUVIGNON ($20.00) Volcanic Hill, Napa Valley. *Austerely structured but deep and rich. Drink 1989 or beyond.*

☆☆☆ 1982 CABERNET SAUVIGNON ($18.75) Special Selection, Volcanic Hill, Napa Valley. *Clean, crisp, lovely, but not as complex as the regular Volcanic Hill below.*

☆☆☆ 1982 CABERNET SAUVIGNON ($20.00) Gravelly Meadow, Napa Valley. *Rich, complex, lovely structure. Drink 1988.*

☆☆☆ 1982 CABERNET SAUVIGNON ($20.00) Red Rock Terrace, Napa Valley. *Dark, intense, rich, a bit coarse. Drink 1989.*

☆☆☆☆ 1982 CABERNET SAUVIGNON ($20.00) Volcanic Hill, Napa Valley. *Rich, clean, soft, lovely, balanced. Drink 1988.*

☆☆☆☆ 1983 CABERNET SAUVIGNON ($20.00) Red Rock Terrace, Napa Valley. *Lush, ripe, great structure, deep fruit, complex. Drink 1988.*

☆☆☆ 1983 CABERNET SAUVIGNON ($20.00) Gravelly Meadow, Napa Valley. *Tart, lean, firmly structured, complex. Drink 1990.*

☆☆☆☆ 1983 CABERNET SAUVIGNON ($20.00) Volcanic Hill, Napa Valley. *Minty, lush, lovely oak and fruit, superb. Drink 1989.*

☆☆☆☆ 1984 CABERNET SAUVIGNON ($25.00) Red Rock Terrace, Napa Valley. *Ripe, lush, lovely fruit, supple and very complex. Quite superb. Very drinkable now; should peak in 1990.*

☆☆☆☆ 1985 CABERNET SAUVIGNON ($30.00) Red Rock Terrace, Napa Valley. *Olive and cedar flavors, rich cherry fruit and lush oak. Drink 1990.*

☆☆☆ 1985 CABERNET SAUVIGNON ($30.00) Volcanic Hill, Napa Valley. *Crisp, fresh, ripe and smooth, with charming varietal character and lush texture. Drink 1993.*

☆☆☆ 1985 CABERNET SAUVIGNON ($30.00) Gravelly Meadow, Napa Valley. *Meaty, rich, with suppleness and smooth texture. Herbs, oak and a hint of bell peppers. Drink 1993.*

ße

## Dolan Vineyards                    MENDOCINO COUNTY
### WHITE
☆☆ 1982 CHARDONNAY ($13.00) Lolonis, Mendocino. *Fresh, crisp, attractive.*
### RED
☆☆ 1981 CABERNET SAUVIGNON ($12.00) Mendocino. *Herbal, big, fat, deep.*

ße

## Domaine Chandon                    NAPA COUNTY
### SPARKLING
☆☆☆ NV BRUT ($13.80) Napa Valley. *Ripe, fresh, clean, complex, yeasty, delicious.*

☆☆ NV BLANC DE NOIR ($14.00) Napa Valley. *100% Pinot Noir. Heavy, rich, complex.*

☆☆☆ NV 10TH ANNIVERSARY RESERVE ($17.00) Napa Valley. *16% Pinot Blanc gives this wine complexity and roundness.*

☆☆☆ NV BRUT ($37.50) Reserve, Napa Valley. *1.5 liters. Rich, complex, balanced, charming.*

☆☆☆ NV BRUT SPECIAL RESERVE ($40.00) Napa Valley. *Magnums only. 1979 vintage. Pinot Noir, Chardonnay and Pinot Blanc. Rich but delicate, clean and beautifully balanced.*

≈♠

## Domaine Cheurlin                    NEW MEXICO
### SPARKLING
NV BRUT ($10.00) New Mexico. *Bitter, unattractive.*

○ NV EXTRA DRY ($10.00) New Mexico. *Awful, bitter.*

≈♠

## Domaine Karakash                    NAPA COUNTY
### WHITE
☆ 1983 CHARDONNAY ($11.75) Mendocino. *Rich, intense, lacking fruit, lacking definition.*

☆☆ 1984 CHARDONNAY ($10.00) Mendocino. *Rich, heavy, decent.*

≈♠

## Domaine Laurier                    SONOMA COUNTY
### WHITE
☆☆☆ 1982 CHARDONNAY ($15.00) Sonoma. *Soft, carefully constructed, a lovely wine.*

☆☆☆ 1983 CHARDONNAY ($13.00) Sonoma. *Oaky, austere, crisp and lovely structure; delightful.*

☆☆☆ 1984 CHARDONNAY ($13.00) Sonoma. *Rich, crisp, lovely ripe fruit.*

☆☆☆ 1985 CHARDONNAY ($13.00) Sonoma. *Crisp and clean, with bright apple fruit.*

☆☆ 1985 SAUVIGNON BLANC ($9.00) Sonoma. *Earthy, vegetal, intense, clean, good balance.*

### BLANC DE NOIR
☆☆ 1986 PALOMA VINEYARDS BLANC DE NOIR ($7.50) Estate, Sonoma Green Valley. *Clean, crisp, off-dry, with lively fruit and acid.*

### RED
☆ 1978 CABERNET SAUVIGNON ($10.00) Estate, Sonoma. *Weedy, crisp and balanced. Drink now.*

☆☆☆ 1979 CABERNET SAUVIGNON ($12.50) Sonoma. *Elegant, varietal, fruity.*

1980 CABERNET SAUVIGNON ($12.00) Green Valley. *Intense, raisiny and marred by off odors.*

☆☆ 1982 CABERNET SAUVIGNON ($12.00) Estate, Sonoma, Green Valley. *Minty, good structure, a bit on the thin side.*

☆☆☆ 1983 CABERNET SAUVIGNON ($13.50) Estate, Sonoma, Green Valley. *Crisp, lean, lovely fruit, elegant. Drink 1989.*

☆☆☆ 1984 CABERNET SAUVIGNON ($13.00) Green Valley, Sonoma. *Rich, deep, berried and youthful, with crisp acidity. Drink 1990.*

☆☆ 1978 PINOT NOIR ($10.00) Estate, Russian River Valley, Sonoma. *Good fruit and varietal character.*

☆ 1979 PINOT NOIR ($10.00) Estate, Russian River Valley, Sonoma. *Meaty, balanced, decent.*

☆ 1981 PINOT NOIR ($10.00) Estate, Sonoma Green Valley. *Thin, pale, vegetal, earthy.*

1982 PINOT NOIR ($10.00) Estate, Green Valley. *Astringent, stemmy.*

≈♠

## Domaine Michel                    SONOMA COUNTY
### WHITE
☆ 1984 LA MARJOLAINE CHARDONNAY ($9.00) Sonoma. *Tart, heavy flavors, lacking fruit.*

☆☆☆ 1986 CHARDONNAY ($15.00) Sonoma. *Crisp, lean, lovely fruit and good structure.*

### RED
· ☆☆ 1983 LA MARJOLAINE CABERNET SAUVIGNON ($10.00) Sonoma. *Crisp, balanced, clean and decent. Drink now.*

☆☆☆ 1984 CABERNET SAUVIGNON ($16.00) Sonoma. *Soft, rich, smooth, good fruit, attractive. Drink 1990.*

☆☆☆ 1985 CABERNET SAUVIGNON ($16.00) Sonoma. *Rich, herbal, good structure. Drink 1993.*

☆☆☆ 1986 CABERNET SAUVIGNON ($16.00) Sonoma. *Ripe, lush, spicy, cherry fruit, lovely oak. Drink 1994.*

## Domaine Mum                    NAPA COUNTY
### SPARKLING
☆☆☆☆ NV BRUT ($14.50) Cuvée Napa, Napa Valley. *Snappy, crisp, tangy, rich fruit, delicious.*

## Domaine St. Georges                    SONOMA COUNTY
### WHITE
☆☆ 1982 CHARDONNAY ($6.50) Sonoma. *Simple, clean, fruity, fresh.*

○ 1984 CAMBIASO VINEYARDS CHARDONNAY ($6.00) Sonoma. *Dank, dull, oxidized.*

1985 CHARDONNAY ($5.00) Sonoma. *Overripe, flat, unpleasant.*

☆☆ 1986 CHARDONNAY ($4.50) Sonoma. *Crisp, lean, clean and attractive.*

### RED
☆☆ 1981 CAMBIASO VINEYARDS CABERNET SAUVIGNON ($4.75) Dry Creek Valley. *Decent, clean, simple, lacking character.*

1982 CABERNET SAUVIGNON ($6.00) Mendocino. *Floral, thin, dull.*

☆☆ 1981 CAMBIASO VINEYARDS ZINFANDEL ($5.00) Chalk Hill, Sonoma. *Fruity, clean, simple.*

## Dominus                    NAPA COUNTY
### RED
☆☆☆ 1983 DOMINUS ($35.00) Estate, Napa Valley. *75% Cabernet Sauvignon, 12% Merlot, 12% Cabernet Franc. Lean and hard but great structure and depth of fruit; a beauty. Drink 1994.*

☆☆☆ 1984 DOMINUS ($35.00) Estate, Napa Valley. *Lovely ripe fruit, clean flavors, great structure, gentle oak. Drink 1994.*

☆☆☆☆ 1985 DOMINUS ($35.00) Estate, Napa Valley. *25% Merlot, Cabernet Franc field blend. Rich fruit, lovely oak and focused flavor. Elegant and superb. 1988 release. Drink 1992.*

## Donatoni Winery                    LOS ANGELES COUNTY
### RED
☆ 1979 CABERNET SAUVIGNON ($8.50) Lot 2, Nepenthe, California (San Luis Obispo). *A bit overdone— vegetal, earthy and lush.*

## *J. Patrick Doré*                    MARIN COUNTY
### WHITE
☆☆ 1982 CHARDONNAY ($6.50) Napa Valley. *Dense, rich, earthy, varietal.*

☆ 1983 CHARDONNAY ($4.75) California. *Simple, clean, varietal, decent but dull.*

☆☆ 1984 CHARDONNAY ($4.00) Santa Maria Valley. *Crisp, fruity, decent.*

☆☆☆ 1984 CHARDONNAY ($5.50) Signature Selection, Santa Maria Valley. *Butterscotch, fresh, clean varietal fruit, nicely balanced.*

☆ 1983 SAUVIGNON BLANC ($5.00) Rancho Tierra Rejada, San Luis Obispo. *Decent but somewhat flat and bitter.*

☆☆ 1985 SAUVIGNON BLANC ($4.00) California Florals, California. *Decent, clean, a bit dull.*
### SPARKLING
NV BRUT ($5.50) Signature Selection, Special Cuvée, Sonoma. *Fat, lush, sweet, coarse.*
### RED
NV COASTAL WINE COMPANY CABERNET SAUVIGNON ($4.00) California Florals, California. *Bitter, dull, vegetal.*

○ 1981 CABERNET SAUVIGNON ($4.00) Napa Valley. *Dead meat.*

☆☆☆ 1981 CABERNET SAUVIGNON ($4.25) Signature Selections, Napa Valley. *Plums, cherries and lovely herbs. Nice structure. Drink 1988.*

☆☆ 1982 CABERNET SAUVIGNON ($4.00) Signature Selections, Sonoma. *Earthy, rich, smooth, attractive.*

☆ 1983 CABERNET SAUVIGNON ($4.00) Signature Selection, Pacini, Mendocino. *Decent flavors but thin and simple.*

☆ 1984 COASTAL WINE COMPANY CABERNET SAUVIGNON ($7.00) California Florals, California. *1.5 liters. Peppery, spicy, simple, decent.*

☆ 1980 MERLOT ($4.00) Napa Valley. *Smokey, light, nice flavors.*

☆ 1983 MERLOT ($5.00) Collector Series, Mendocino. *Snappy, tart, thin.*

☆☆ 1983 ZINFANDEL ($4.00) Signature Selection, Mendocino. *Lush, raisiny, hearty, good fruit and rich texture.*

❧

## *Dover Vineyards*                    OHIO
### WHITE
☆ NV CREAM NIAGARA ($2.50) New York. *Lush, Labrusca flavor, good balance.*
### RED
☆ NV LABRUSCA Ohio. *Labrusca character, crisp, sweet, fresh, some volatile acid.*

❧

## *Dry Creek Vineyard*                    SONOMA COUNTY
### WHITE
☆☆ 1982 CHARDONNAY ($10.00) 62% Estate, 30% Robert Young, 8% others, Sonoma. *Crisp and clean but lacking varietal character and depth.*

☆☆ 1982 DAVID S. STARE CHARDONNAY ($15.00) Dry Creek Valley. *Snappy, green apple, oak, decent balance and flavor.*

☆☆☆ 1983 CHARDONNAY ($10.00) Sonoma. *Crisp, fruity, clean, nicely made.*

☆☆☆ 1984 CHARDONNAY ($10.00) Sonoma. *Elegant, clean, complex, charming.*

☆☆ 1984 CHARDONNAY ($15.00) Dry Creek Valley. *Clean, some pickle flavors, decent.*

☆☆☆ 1985 CHARDONNAY ($10.00) Sonoma. *Fresh, clean, crisp, nicely structured, medium-weight, easy to like.*

☆☆☆ 1986 CHENIN BLANC ($6.25) 63% Sonoma, 37% Calaveras. *Crisp, soft, lovely fruit and charming flavors.*

☆☆ 1986 SAUVIGNON BLANC ($8.75) Sonoma. *Spicy, hard, peppery, herbal.*

### RED

☆ 1983 DAVID S. STARE DRY CREEK RESERVE ($17.00) 68% Home, 21% West Dry Creek Road, Dry Creek Valley. *51.1% Cabernet Sauvignon, 48.9% Merlot. Dense, rich, a bit muddy. Drink 1992.*

☆☆ 1978 CABERNET SAUVIGNON ($8.00) Sonoma. *Clean, well structured, nice acidity. Drink now.*

☆ 1979 CABERNET SAUVIGNON ($8.00) Sonoma. *Weedy, dense, raisiny.*

☆☆ 1980 CABERNET SAUVIGNON ($9.50) Sonoma. *40% Merlot. Herbal, rich, smooth textured. Drink now or hold.*

☆ 1981 CABERNET SAUVIGNON ($8.00) Sonoma. *15% Merlot, 9% Petite Sirah. Vegetal and soft.*

☆☆ 1982 CABERNET SAUVIGNON ($9.50) Sonoma. *24% Merlot. Herbal, nicely structured, clean, attractive. Drink 1988.*

☆ 1983 DAVID S. STARE CABERNET SAUVIGNON ($15.00) Sonoma. *51% Cabernet Sauvignon, 49% Merlot. Vegetal, unattractive.*

☆☆ 1984 CABERNET SAUVIGNON ($10.00) Sonoma. *8% Merlot, 3% Cabernet Franc. Clean, crisp, lively, clean, a bit thin. Drink 1990.*

☆☆ 1980 MERLOT ($12.00) Estate, Dry Creek Valley. *18% Cabernet Sauvignon. Spicy, clean and rich.*

☆ 1981 MERLOT ($12.00) Sonoma. *Nice velvety texture, a bit weedy.*

☆☆ 1982 DAVID S. STARE MERLOT ($15.00) Dry Creek Reserve, Estate, Dry Creek Valley. *29% Cabernet Sauvignon. Herbal, earthy, soft, decent. Drink now.*

☆☆ 1982 PETITE SIRAH ($9.00) Dry Creek Valley. *Dark, intense, raisiny, clean, attractive.*

☆☆ 1977 ZINFANDEL ($7.50) Sonoma. *Rich, powerful but the fruit is fading fast.*

☆ 1978 ZINFANDEL ($6.00) Late Harvest Style, Sonoma. *Vegetal, slightly sweet, a silly style.*

☆☆☆ 1978 ZINFANDEL ($6.50) Sonoma. *Rich, berried, earthy and well structured. Drink now.*

☆☆ 1980 ZINFANDEL ($7.00) Sonoma. *Clean and fresh, with appealing flavors and fruit. Drink now.*

☆☆☆ 1981 ZINFANDEL ($7.50) Dry Creek Valley. *Fragrant, snappy, attractively varietal.*

☆☆☆ 1984 ZINFANDEL ($8.00) Dry Creek Valley. *Lush, blackberry fruit, rich, delicious.*

☙

## Duckhorn Vineyards NAPA COUNTY

### WHITE

☆☆☆ 1986 SAUVIGNON BLANC ($9.00) Napa Valley. *23% Semillon. Crisp, bright, tangy, fruity.*

**RED**

☆☆☆ 1978 CABERNET SAUVIGNON ($10.50) Napa Valley. *Rich, firmly structured, complex. Drink now.*

☆☆☆ 1980 CABERNET SAUVIGNON ($14.00) Napa Valley. *Austere and angular, with great depth. Drink now.*

☆☆☆ 1981 CABERNET SAUVIGNON ($15.00) Napa Valley. *Rich and structured, lovely. Drink now and for the next six years.*

☆☆☆☆ 1982 CABERNET SAUVIGNON ($15.00) Napa Valley. *5% Merlot, 5% Cabernet Franc. Crisp, tangy, firm, berry fruit, complex flavors. Drink 1990.*

☆☆☆☆ 1983 CABERNET SAUVIGNON ($16.00) Napa Valley. *Ripe, complex, intense, lovely structure and fruit. Drink 1992.*

☆☆☆ 1984 CABERNET SAUVIGNON ($17.00) Napa Valley. *Lean, well built, lovely cherry fruit, great aging potential. Drink 1992.*

☆☆☆ 1978 MERLOT ($12.50) Three Palms, Napa Valley. *Crisp and fruity, complex, intense, balanced. Drink 1989.*

☆☆☆ 1979 MERLOT ($12.50) Napa Valley. *Meaty, open, clean and rich. Drink 1988.*

☆☆☆ 1980 MERLOT ($12.50) Napa Valley. *Deep, cherry flavor, supple, exquisite. Will age many more years. Drink 1990.*

☆☆☆☆ 1981 MERLOT ($12.50) Three Palms, Napa Valley. *Tart and deep, with great fruit. Drink now and over the next decade.*

☆☆☆☆ 1981 MERLOT ($13.00) Napa Valley. *11% Cabernet Franc. Rich, lush, remarkably complex and deep. Drink 1992.*

☆☆☆☆ 1982 MERLOT ($13.00) Napa Valley. *Deep, lush, balanced, structured, berried. Drink 1989.*

☆☆☆☆ 1983 MERLOT ($15.00) Napa Valley. *Cassis and tart fruit, complex, rich, beautifully balanced. Drink 1988.*

☆☆☆☆ 1983 MERLOT ($18.00) Three Palms, Napa Valley. *Ripe, rich, intense, supple, beautifully structured, focused. Drink 1990.*

☆☆☆☆ 1984 MERLOT ($15.00) Napa Valley. *Great fruit, crisp acidity, lovely structure. Drink 1989.*

☆☆☆☆ 1984 MERLOT ($18.00) Three Palms, Napa Valley. *Lush, lean, lovely fruit, charming berry flavors, complex, superb. Drink 1992.*

☆☆☆ 1985 MERLOT ($16.00) Napa Valley. *15% Cabernet Sauvignon, 7% Cabernet Franc. Lush, soft, clean, ripe, intense. Drink 1989.*

☆☆☆☆ 1985 MERLOT ($18.00) Three Palms, Napa Valley. *Perhaps the best of all. Clean, focused, complex, lush, superb. To be released in 1988. Drink 1994.*

❧

## *Dunn Vineyards*  NAPA COUNTY

**RED**

☆☆☆☆ 1979 CABERNET SAUVIGNON ($12.00) Napa Valley. *Elegant, complex, refined, lovely. Drink now.*

☆☆☆☆ 1980 CABERNET SAUVIGNON ($12.50) Napa Valley. *Lovely, crisp, tannic, elegant. Great structure. Drink 1988.*

☆☆☆☆ 1981 CABERNET SAUVIGNON ($12.50) Howell Mountain-Napa Valley. *Deep, rich, structured, very complex. Drink 1988.*

☆☆☆☆ 1982 CABERNET SAUVIGNON ($12.50) Napa Valley. *Crisp, fruity, elegant, deep cherry fruit, superb. Drink 1989.*

☆☆☆☆ 1982 CABERNET SAUVIGNON ($14.00) Howell Mountain. *Supple, elegant, remarkable structure, concentrated fruit. Drink 1989.*

☆☆☆☆ 1983 CABERNET SAUVIGNON ($18.00) Napa Valley. *Crisp, lush, deep, intense, complex. Drink 1992.*

ᕤ

## Durney Vineyard                    MONTEREY COUNTY

### WHITE

☆☆☆ 1984 CHARDONNAY ($12.00) Carmel Valley. *Lush, round, soft, elegant, beautifully made.*

### RED

☆☆☆ 1978 CABERNET SAUVIGNON ($12.00) Estate, Carmel Valley. *Lovely fruit, clean, delightful. Drink now or age up to five years.*

☆☆☆ 1978 CABERNET SAUVIGNON ($15.00) Private Reserve, Estate, Carmel Valley. *Rich, dense but nicely structured. Drink now.*

☆ 1980 CABERNET SAUVIGNON ($12.50) Estate, Carmel Valley, Monterey. *Grapey and berried like a Zinfandel.*

☆☆☆ 1981 CABERNET SAUVIGNON ($12.50) Carmel Valley, Monterey. *Rich and tannic, lush and beautifully balanced.*

☆☆☆ 1982 CABERNET SAUVIGNON ($12.00) Estate, Carmel Valley. *Oaky, crisp fruit, clean flavors, complex. Drink 1989.*

ᕤ

## Duxoup Wine Works                    SONOMA COUNTY

### RED

☆☆☆ 1984 NAPA GAMAY ($6.50) Dry Creek Valley. *20% Gamay Beaujolais. Lush, grapey, rich, deep, fruity. Delicious.*

☆☆☆ 1985 NAPA GAMAY ($6.50) Dry Creek Valley. *Rich, velvety, complex, dark, fruity, nicely balanced. Delicious.*

☆☆ 1985 CHARBONO ($10.00) Napa Valley. *Smooth, rich, complex, dense.*

☆☆☆ 1980 SYRAH ($9.00) Preston, Sonoma. *Splendid. Rich, berried, very Rhône-like.*

☆☆☆ 1981 SYRAH ($9.00) Preston, Sonoma. *California's best Syrah—rich, firm and complex.*

☆☆ 1982 SYRAH ($9.00) Sonoma. *Rich, structured, some off-quality in nose, aging potential.*

☆☆☆ 1983 SYRAH ($10.00) Sonoma. *Rich, deep, lush, peppery, clean, superb. Drink now or hold.*

☆☆ 1984 SYRAH ($10.00) Dry Creek Valley. *Dense, fruity, lush.*

☆☆☆ 1985 SYRAH ($10.00) Dry Creek Valley. *Rich, intense, fruity, clean, velvety.*

☆☆☆ 1980 ZINFANDEL ($7.50) Sonoma. *Lush but elegant and well structured.*

☆☆ 1984 ZINFANDEL ($8.50) Teldeschi, Dry Creek Valley. *Rich, balanced, clean, austere, lovely.*

☆☆ 1985 ZINFANDEL ($8.50) Dry Creek Valley. *Clean, varietal, balanced.*

ᕤ

## Eagle Ridge Winery                    SONOMA COUNTY

### WHITE

☆☆ NV FUME BLANC ($8.50) Sonoma. *Grassy, crisp, clean, balanced. Ugly label.*

☆☆☆ 1986 SAUVIGNON BLANC ($7.75) Giusso, Alexander Valley. *Varietal fruit, crisp acidity, good balance.*

ᕤ

EAGLEPOINT *see* Scharffenberger Cellars

## Eberle Winery SAN LUIS OBISPO COUNTY

### WHITE

☆☆ 1982 CHARDONNAY ($10.00) Paso Robles. *Woody, herbal. Rich and balanced, but a bit short in the finish.*

☆☆ 1984 CHARDONNAY ($12.00) Paso Robles. *Lush, ripe, lacking fruit, decent balance, clean.*

☆☆ 1985 MUSCAT ($7.00) Paso Robles. *5.1% residual sugar. Snappy, fresh, lacking fruit.*

1986 MUSCAT ($7.00) Paso Robles. *5.4% residual sugar. Spicy, crisp, fresh, rich flavors.*

### RED

☆☆☆ 1979 CABERNET SAUVIGNON ($10.00) San Luis Obispo. *Crisply fruity and lean in structure. Will age well.*

☆☆☆ 1980 CABERNET SAUVIGNON ($10.00) Paso Robles. *Rich, meaty, ripe, intense, with great depth. Drink 1987.*

☆☆☆ 1981 CABERNET SAUVIGNON ($10.00) Paso Robles. *Earthy but nicely structured, clean, attractive. Drink 1986.*

☆☆☆ 1981 CABERNET SAUVIGNON ($18.00) Reserve, Paso Robles. *Rich, crisp, fresh, lovely texture, lively acidity. Drink 1990.*

☆☆☆ 1982 CABERNET SAUVIGNON ($10.00) Paso Robles. *Ripe, rich, deep, lush texture, crisp fruit. Lovely. Drink 1988.*

☆☆☆ 1983 CABERNET SAUVIGNON ($10.00) Paso Robles. *Rich, clean, lush, long, deep, complex and balanced. Drink 1990.*

☆☆☆ 1984 CABERNET SAUVIGNON ($18.00) Paso Robles. *Velvety, lush, fruity, superb. Drink 1992.*

ਏ&

## Edna Valley Vineyard SAN LUIS OBISPO COUNTY

### WHITE

☆☆ 1982 CHARDONNAY ($12.00) Edna Valley. *Toasty, rich, oaky, earthy, with a touch of vegetation.*

☆ 1983 CHARDONNAY ($12.00) Edna Valley. *Heavy, oily, barrel fermented, vinous.*

☆☆☆ 1984 CHARDONNAY ($12.75) Edna Valley. *Fruity, rich, deep, complex, spicy, balanced.*

☆☆☆ 1985 CHARDONNAY ($13.00) Edna Valley. *Oaky, rich, toasty, butterscotch flavors. Should age nicely.*

☆☆☆ 1986 CHARDONNAY ($13.50) Estate, Edna Valley. *Rich, toasty, balanced, complex, lovely.*

### BLANC DE NOIR

☆ 1984 VIN GRIS ($5.00) Edna Valley. *Heavy, bitter; past its prime.*

### RED

○ 1980 PINOT NOIR ($14.00) San Luis Obispo. *Overpoweringly weedy, plus volatile acidity.*

☆☆ 1981 PINOT NOIR ($14.00) Estate, Edna Valley. *Less weedy than the '80; rich, fruited, with nice structure.*

☆☆ 1982 PINOT NOIR ($12.50) Edna Valley. *Earthy, some veggies, well built, should age well.*

1983 PINOT NOIR ($10.00) Estate, Edna Valley. *Earthy, thin, lacking fruit and depth, cooked asparagus flavor.*

☆ 1984 PINOT NOIR ($10.00) Edna Valley. *Weedy and crisp, with some volatile acidity. Disappointing.*

☆☆ 1984 PINOT NOIR ($16.00) Estate, Edna Valley. *Herbal, rich, earthy, some volatile acidity.*

ਏ&

## Ehlers Lane Winery                    NAPA COUNTY
### WHITE
☆☆ 1983 CHARDONNAY ($13.75) Napa Valley. *Woody, ripe, decent fruit, nice but lacking finesse.*

☆☆☆ 1984 CHARDONNAY ($13.00) Napa Valley. *Toasty, clean, varietal, well balanced.*

☆☆☆ 1985 CHARDONNAY ($12.50) Napa Valley. *Crisp, lovely fruit, balanced, fresh, attractive.*

### RED
☆☆☆ 1983 CABERNET SAUVIGNON ($12.00) Napa Valley. *Crisp, fruity, clean, beautifully structured. Drink 1987.*

☆☆ 1984 CABERNET SAUVIGNON ($12.00) Napa Valley. *Fruity, earthy, ripe, charming. Drink 1988.*

❧

## El Paso de Robles Winery    SAN LUIS OBISPO COUNTY
### RED
1983 CABERNET SAUVIGNON ($8.25) Nepenthe, Paso Robles. *Raisiny, vegetal, dense, unappealing.*

☆☆ 1982 MERLOT ($7.50) Radike, Paso Robles. *Fat, lush, rich, fruity.*

☆ 1984 MERLOT ($7.50) Bien Nacido, Santa Maria Valley. *Herbal, short, lacking fruit, decent.*

☆☆ 1984 PETITE SIRAH ($7.00) Shell Creek, Paso Robles. *Meaty, tannic, raisiny, varietal, decent.*

☆☆ 1984 PINOT NOIR ($6.50) Bien Nacido, Santa Maria Valley. *Earthy, composty flavors, some nice fruit and varietal character.*

☆☆ 1984 ZINFANDEL ($7.50) Paso Robles. *Intense, heavy, blackberry fruit, earthy.*

❧

## Elk Cove Vineyards                    OREGON
### WHITE
1982 CHARDONNAY ($12.00) Dundee Hills, Willamette Valley. *Dull, with a touch of oxidation.*

☆☆ 1983 CHARDONNAY ($12.50) Willamette Valley. *Clean, fresh, varietal, likable.*

☆☆ 1985 CHARDONNAY ($9.75) Oregon. *Crisp, clean, fresh, good oak, decent.*

1985 JOHANNISBERG RIESLING ($12.00) Late Harvest, Willamette Valley. *Dull, flat, thin.*

### RED
☆ 1979 PINOT NOIR ($9.00) Wind Hill, Willamette Valley. *Peppery, berried, fruity and appealing.*

☆☆ 1979 PINOT NOIR ($12.00) Reserve, Estate, Willamette Valley. *Soft, varietal, violets and earth. Very nice.*

☆ 1981 PINOT NOIR ($6.00) Oregon. *Simple, thin.*

☆☆ 1982 PINOT NOIR ($9.25) Estate, Willamette Valley. *Spicy, decent, green and a bit flat.*

☆☆ 1982 PINOT NOIR ($12.00) Reserve, 50% Dundee Hills, 50% Estate, Willamette Valley, Oregon. *Earthy, firm, good fruit, nice structure.*

☆ 1983 PINOT NOIR ($15.00) Reserve, Estate, Willamette Valley. *Strongly vegetal, drinkable.*

❧

## Enz Vineyards                    SAN BENITO COUNTY
### RED
☆ 1979 ZINFANDEL ($6.50) Estate, San Benito. *Intense, tannic, decent.*

❧

ESTANCIA *see* Franciscan Vineyards

## *Estrella River Winery*  SAN LUIS OBISPO COUNTY
### WHITE
☆☆ 1982 CHARDONNAY ($9.00) Estate, Paso Robles. *Simple, clean, decent.*

☆☆☆ 1984 CHARDONNAY ($9.00) Estate, Paso Robles. *Crisp, fruity, lovely, clean, super.*

☆☆☆ 1985 MUSCAT ($7.50) Paso Robles. 4.8% residual sugar. *Spicy, clean, fresh, delightful.*

☆ 1985 SAUVIGNON BLANC ($6.50) Estate, Paso Robles. *Simple, lemony and tart.*
### SPARKLING
☆ 1982 BLANC DE BLANC ($15.00) Star Cuvée, Paso Robles. *Oily, minty, decent.*
### RED
☆☆ 1978 CABERNET SAUVIGNON ($10.00) Estate, San Luis Obispo. *Fat, rich, concentrated. Drink now.*

☆ 1979 CABERNET SAUVIGNON ($8.50) Estate, San Luis Obispo. *Nice, lighter weight, attractive.*

☆☆ 1980 CABERNET SAUVIGNON ($10.00) Paso Robles. *Rich, lush, fruity. Drink now.*

☆ 1981 CABERNET SAUVIGNON ($9.00) Paso Robles. *Big and clumsy.*

☆☆ 1981 CABERNET SAUVIGNON ($10.00) Estate, Paso Robles. *Rich, good fruit, nice acidity, clean. Drink now.*

☆☆ 1982 CABERNET SAUVIGNON ($10.00) Estate, Paso Robles. *Tart, simple, decent, pleasant.*

☆☆ 1983 CABERNET SAUVIGNON ($8.00) Estate, Paso Robles. *Tart, decent, clean.*

☆☆ 1979 ZINFANDEL ($4.70) Estate, San Luis Obispo. *Soft and raisiny.*

☆☆ 1980 ZINFANDEL ($5.00) San Luis Obispo. *Lush, deep, heavy, decent.*

☆☆ 1984 ZINFANDEL ($6.00) Paso Robles. *Rich, good fruit, a bit of volatile acidity and some herbs.*

## *The Eyrie Vineyards*  OREGON
### WHITE
☆☆ 1984 CHARDONNAY ($11.00) Willamette Valley. *Fresh, lean, clean, snappy.*

☆☆☆ 1985 CHARDONNAY ($11.00) Oregon. *Fresh, clean, nice fruit and oak, balanced, lovely.*
### RED
☆☆ 1982 PINOT NOIR ($12.50) Willamette Valley, Yamhill. *Smokey, toasty, a bit green, pretty fruit.*

☆☆☆ 1983 PINOT NOIR ($15.00) Oregon. *Rich, clean, complex, lovely varietal character.*

☆☆☆ 1984 PINOT NOIR ($13.00) Willamette Valley. *Gentle, clean, richly flavored, soft and complex.*

☆☆☆ 1984 PINOT NOIR ($16.00) Reserve, Willamette Valley. *Richly flavored, light in color but intensely varietal, complex.*

☆☆☆ 1985 PINOT NOIR ($13.00) Willamette Valley. *Soft, lush, cherry fruit; clean and focused.*

## *Fairmont Cellars*  NAPA COUNTY
### WHITE
☆☆☆ 1984 CHARDONNAY ($9.00) Private Selection, Napa Valley. *Fresh, clean, crisp acidity, charming fruit.*

**RED**
☆ 1982 CABERNET SAUVIGNON ($9.50) Private Selection, Napa Valley. *Herbal, varietal, decent.*

৯৯

## *Fall Creek Vineyards*                    TEXAS
**WHITE**
☆☆ 1985 BLANC DE BLANCS ($5.75) Texas. *Crisp, snappy, some Sauvignon Blanc varietal character.*
☆ 1985 CHARDONNAY ($11.25) Llano. *Hard, crisp, snappy, decent.*
☆☆ 1985 EMERALD RIESLING ($6.00) Llano. *Fresh, soft, clean, quite decent.*
☆☆ 1986 SAUVIGNON BLANC ($9.00) Texas. *Crisp, snappy, lemony, some varietal herbs, attractive.*
**RED**
☆☆ 1985 PROPRIETOR'S RED ($7.00) Llano. *77% Cabernet Sauvignon, 17% Ruby Cabernet, 5% Merlot, 1% Carnelian. Soft, clean, fresh, lively, attractive.*
☆☆ 1985 CABERNET SAUVIGNON ($15.00) Texas. *Rich, soft, fruity, clean, meaty, nicely textured. Drink 1989.*
☆☆ 1985 CARNELIAN ($11.25) Texas. *Clean, fruity, quite decent.*

৯৯

## *Far Niente Winery*                    NAPA COUNTY
**WHITE**
☆☆ 1980 CHARDONNAY ($16.50) Napa Valley. *Toasty oak and crisp fruit. Good, but not as good as the '81.*
☆☆☆ 1981 CHARDONNAY ($18.00) Estate, Napa Valley. *Rich and well balanced, lovely ripe fruit.*
☆☆ 1982 CHARDONNAY ($18.00) Napa Valley. *Rich, full, forward, well made, with lovely ripe qualities.*
☆☆☆ 1982 CHARDONNAY ($20.00) Estate, Napa Valley. *Outstanding—rich, oaky, lush, fruity, complex.*
☆☆☆☆ 1983 CHARDONNAY ($18.00) Napa Valley. *Toasty, rich, heavy, oaky.*
☆☆☆ 1983 CHARDONNAY ($20.00) Estate, Napa Valley. *Toasty, rich, earthy, ripe, balanced.*
☆☆☆ 1984 CHARDONNAY ($20.00) Napa Valley. *Balanced, clean, with lovely fruit and acidity.*
☆☆☆ 1985 CHARDONNAY ($22.00) Napa Valley. *Big, juicy, lush, rich, round and powerful.*
☆☆ 1986 CHARDONNAY ($24.00) Napa Valley. *Decent, some complexity, lacking power. Quite a disappointment.*
**RED**
☆☆☆ 1982 CABERNET SAUVIGNON ($25.00) Estate, Napa Valley. *Tart, lean, rich flavors, wonderful structure. Drink 1989.*
☆☆☆☆ 1983 CABERNET SAUVIGNON ($25.00) Estate, Napa Valley. *Deep, dark color; rich, smooth fruit; stunning acidity and balance. A lovely wine with great potential. Drink 1992.*
☆☆☆ 1984 CABERNET SAUVIGNON ($25.00) Napa Valley. *12% Cabernet Franc, 3% Merlot. Lush, deep, dark, intense. Great structure. Drink 1992.*

৯৯

## *Gary Farrell Wines*                    SONOMA COUNTY
**WHITE**
☆☆☆ 1985 CHARDONNAY ($12.00) Sonoma. *Ripe, crisp, good oak, firm, lean.*

## RED
☆☆☆ 1985 PINOT NOIR ($13.50) Russian River Valley. *Soft, lush, deep, elegantly structured, charming.*

🍂

FARRON RIDGE CELLARS *see* Château Ste. Michelle

# Farview Farm Vineyard    SAN LUIS OBISPO COUNTY
## RED
1980 MERLOT ($7.25) Templeton. *Weedy.*

🍂

FELTA SPRINGS *see* Mill Creek Vineyards

# Felton Empire Vineyards    SANTA CRUZ COUNTY
## WHITE
☆ 1983 CHARDONNAY ($11.00) Santa Barbara. *Crisp, earthy, odd.*

☆☆ 1983 CHARDONNAY ($11.00) Tonneaux Francais, Tepusquet, Santa Barbara. *Rich, woody, fat, lush; lacks finesse.*

☆☆☆ 1985 CHARDONNAY ($11.00) Talmage Town, Mendocino. *Lush, rich, oily, fat but quite attractive.*

☆☆☆ 1984 WHITE RIESLING ($12.00) Select Late Harvest, Tepusquet, Santa Barbara. *375 ml. 16.5% residual sugar. Crisp, soft, lush, smooth, with lovely honey and apricot flavors.*

## RED
1979 CABERNET SAUVIGNON ($12.00) Beauregard Ranch, Santa Cruz Mountains. *Big and crude, lacking fruit.*

1980 CABERNET SAUVIGNON ($12.00) Napa Valley. *Herbal and simple, without much appeal.*

☆☆ 1980 CABERNET SAUVIGNON ($12.00) Santa Cruz Mountains. *Cherry-berry fruit, clean, snappy.*

1980 CABERNET SAUVIGNON ($20.00) Hallcrest, Santa Cruz Mountains. *Medium-weight, skunky.*

☆☆ 1981 CABERNET SAUVIGNON ($20.00) Hallcrest, Santa Cruz Mountains. *Lovely, subtle flavors; extremely tannic. Will it mellow out with time? It's anybody's guess.*

☆☆ 1982 CABERNET SAUVIGNON ($11.00) Bates Ranch, Santa Cruz Mountains. *Youthful, bitter but crisp and fruity. Drink 1992.*

☆☆ 1980 PETITE SIRAH ($7.00) Bergstrom Ranch, San Miguel, Santa Cruz. *Big, dense, with some late harvest character.*

☆ 1980 PETITE SIRAH ($7.38) Maritime Series, Santa Cruz. *Jammy, intense, chocolatey, late harvest style.*

☆ 1981 PETITE SIRAH ($7.50) Bergstrom Ranch, San Miguel, Santa Cruz. *Decent, clean, intense.*

☆☆☆ 1979 PINOT NOIR ($7.50) Maritime Series, Reserve, Chaparral, San Luis Obispo. *Lovely, rich, Burgundian, fleshy and showing great promise.*

○ 1980 PINOT NOIR ($10.00) Maritime Series, Sonoma Mountain, Sonoma. *Weedy and unappealing.*

☆☆ 1981 PINOT NOIR ($7.50) Fort Ross, Sonoma. *Firm, varietal, attractive.*

1981 PINOT NOIR ($10.00) Maritime Series, California. *Chocolate, intensely leathery, vegetal.*

☆☆ 1981 PINOT NOIR ($10.00) Tonneaux Americains, California. *Dense, fruity, fresh flavors, attractive.*

☆☆ 1981 PINOT NOIR ($11.00) Tonneaux Francais, California. *Nicely structured, French oak, Burgundian.*

☆☆☆ 1982 PINOT NOIR ($11.00) Tonneaux Francais, California.
        *Super varietal and balanced. Rich, complex,*
        *charming.*
 ☆☆  1984 PINOT NOIR ($12.00) Tonneaux Francis, California.
        *Rich, deep, complex oak and fruit flavors, some*
        *weediness.*

                            🙣

## Fenestra Winery                          ALAMEDA COUNTY
### WHITE
 ☆☆  1982 CHARDONNAY ($9.50) La Reina, Monterey. *Crisp,*
        *oaky, varietal, pleasant.*
  ☆  1985 MALVASIA ($7.50) Alameda. *5% residual sugar. Dull,*
        *bitter.*
  ☆  1986 SAUVIGNON BLANC ($7.50) Livermore. *Tart, sour,*
        *decent.*
### RED
  ☆  1979 CABERNET SAUVIGNON ($6.25) Monterey. *A bit*
        *weedy, with dense, big flavors and low fruit.*
 ☆☆  1982 MERLOT ($11.00) Napa Valley. *Herbal, clean, well*
        *made.*
  ○  1983 MERLOT ($11.00) Napa Valley. *Thin, dull, volatile*
        *acidity.*
  ☆  1980 ZINFANDEL ($5.25) Livermore Valley. *16.5% alcohol.*
        *Port-like late harvest.*

                            🙣

## Ferrara Winery                          SAN DIEGO COUNTY
### WHITE
☆☆☆ 1985 MUSCAT OF ALEXANDRIA ($6.35) San Diego. *Spicy,*
        *fresh, delicate, floral, charming, very elegant.*
### SPARKLING
  ☆  NV  BRUT ($12.00) Sonoma. *Coarse, dull.*
☆☆☆ NV  BRUT ($15.00) Reserve Cuvée, Sonoma. *Snappy, fresh,*
        *clean, fruity.*

                            🙣

## Gloria Ferrer                           SONOMA COUNTY
### SPARKLING
☆☆☆ NV  BRUT NATURAL ($12.00) Sonoma. *Yeasty, rich, ele-*
        *gant, lovely fruit, complex. Very impressive.*
☆☆☆ NV  BRUT ($13.00) Sonoma. *90% Pinot Noir, 10% Chardon-*
        *nay. Clean, balanced, yeasty, charming.*

                            🙣

## Fetzer Vineyards                        MENDOCINO COUNTY
### WHITE
 ☆☆  1982 CHARDONNAY ($10.00) Special Reserve, California
        (Monterey-Mendocino). *Toasty, rich, smooth and*
        *intensely varietal.*
     1982 CHARDONNAY ($12.00) Tasting Room Select, Men-
        docino. *Rather unpleasant.*
 ☆☆  1983 CHARDONNAY ($6.50) Sundial, Mendocino. *Apple*
        *nose; crisp and fruity, very pleasant.*
  ☆  1983 CHARDONNAY ($8.50) Barrel Select, California. *Sim-*
        *ple, clean, not much.*
☆☆☆ 1983 CHARDONNAY ($10.00) Special Reserve, California.
        *Rich, silky, smooth, fruity, delightful.*
 ☆☆  1984 CHARDONNAY ($6.50) Sundial, Mendocino. *Fresh,*
        *simple, attractive.*
☆☆☆ 1984 CHARDONNAY ($8.00) Barrel Select, California.
        *Clean, lovely oak, crisp fruit, great structure.*
 ☆☆  1984 CHARDONNAY ($13.00) Special Reserve, California.
        *Soft, earthy, oaky, complex but a bit clumsy.*

☆☆ 1985 CHARDONNAY ($6.50) Sundial, Mendocino. *Clean, varietal, fresh, very appealing.*

☆☆☆ 1985 CHARDONNAY ($9.00) Barrel Select, California. *Lush, fruity, clean, lovely.*

1985 CHARDONNAY ($12.00) Special Reserve, California. *Dull, heavy, lacking depth.*

☆☆ 1986 CHARDONNAY ($6.50) Sundial, Mendocino. *Clean, decent, simple, a bit oily.*

☆☆☆ 1986 CHENIN BLANC ($6.00) Mendocino. 2.2% *residual sugar. Fresh, soft, fruity, snappy, delicious.*

☆☆ 1986 FUME BLANC ($6.50) Valley Oaks, California. *Herbal, crisp, varietal, ripe, medium weight, clean, nice fruity finish.*

☆☆☆ 1987 GEWURZTRAMINER ($6.50) California 0.3% *residual sugar. Soft, lush, varietal fruit, clean, rose petal flavors; a very charming wine.*

☆☆ 1985 JOHANNISBERG RIESLING ($9.00) Late Harvest, Mendocino. *375 ml. 21% residual sugar. Rich, ripe, syrupy, intense.*

☆☆ 1986 JOHANNISBERG RIESLING ($6.00) California. *Spritzy, crisp, clean and softly varietal.*

☆☆☆ 1985 MUSCAT ($6.00) Lake. *Peachy, snappy, lovely fruit.*

## BLANC DE NOIR

☆☆☆ 1986 BEL ARBRES WHITE MERLOT ($5.00) California. *Crisp, charming, fruity, lovely, floral, clean.*

☆☆☆ 1986 BEL ARBRES WHITE PINOT NOIR ($5.00) Mendocino. *Crisp, clean, varietal, lively, delicious.*

☆ 1986 BEL ARBRES WHITE ZINFANDEL ($5.00) California. *Clean but quite flabby, lacking balance.*

☆☆☆ 1987 BEL ARBES WHITE ZINFANDEL ($5.00) California. *Spritzy, crisp, bright fruit, lovely color.*

## RED

☆☆ 1979 CABERNET SAUVIGNON ($8.50) Home, Mendocino. *Crisp and fruity, good varietal character.*

☆☆ 1979 CABERNET SAUVIGNON ($10.00) Cole Ranch, Mendocino. *Fragrant, clean, herbal. Good structure but a trifle simple.*

☆ 1980 CABERNET SAUVIGNON ($5.50) Lake. *Fresh, fruity, some weediness, nicely balanced.*

☆☆ 1980 CABERNET SAUVIGNON ($7.00) Mendocino. *Rich, velvety, nice.*

☆☆ 1981 CABERNET SAUVIGNON ($5.50) Lake. *Simple but fresh, soft and appealing.*

☆ 1981 CABERNET SAUVIGNON ($7.00) Mendocino. *Soft, fruity, clean and simple.*

☆ 1982 CABERNET SAUVIGNON ($5.50) Lake. *Simple, clean, a bit dull.*

☆ 1982 CABERNET SAUVIGNON ($8.00) Barrel Select, Mendocino. *Grapey, intense, overdone, some off flavors.*

☆☆ 1983 CABERNET SAUVIGNON ($5.50) Lake. *Clean, simple, quite decent. Drink now.*

☆☆☆ 1983 CABERNET SAUVIGNON ($8.50) Barrel Select, California. *Rich, deep, complex, lovely oak and fruit. Drink now.*

☆☆☆ 1984 CABERNET SAUVIGNON ($6.50) Lake. *Rich, deep, charming, simple but lush and very attractive. Drink now.*

☆☆ 1984 CABERNET SAUVIGNON ($9.00) Barrel Select, Mendocino. *Crisp, fresh, lively berry fruit; clean and well balanced.*

☆☆☆ 1984 CABERNET SAUVIGNON ($10.50) Reserve, Mendocino. *Lush, balanced, spicy, loaded with fruit. Drink 1988.*

☆☆☆ 1985 CABERNET SAUVIGNON ($6.50) California. *Crisp, lean, tight; clean, tart fruit, fine structure. Drink now.*

☆ 1981 BEL ARBRES MERLOT ($7.00) Sonoma. *Intense, lacking finesse.*

☆☆ 1980 PETITE SIRAH ($5.50) Mendocino. *Decent, clean, a bit off target.*

☆☆☆ 1980 PETITE SIRAH ($8.50) Special Reserve, Redwood Valley, Mendocino. *Peppery, dark, rich, clean and tannic.*

☆☆ 1981 PETITE SIRAH ($5.50) Mendocino. *Fresh, attractive and relatively light.*

☆☆ 1982 PETITE SIRAH ($5.50) Mendocino. *Fresh, dense, spicy, pleasant, forward, nice.*

1980 PINOT NOIR ($13.00) Special Reserve, California. *Ripe, raisiny, vegetal, no fruit, coarse.*

☆☆ 1981 PINOT NOIR ($5.50) Mendocino. *Beaujolais-like, snappy, clean, simple; good red wine.*

☆☆ 1979 ZINFANDEL ($5.50) Mendocino. *Rich and raisiny.*

☆☆☆ 1979 ZINFANDEL ($7.50) Lolonis, Mendocino. *Snappy, clean and peppery.*

1979 ZINFANDEL ($8.50) Ricetti, Mendocino. *Hard and raisiny. May benefit from aging.*

☆☆☆ 1980 ZINFANDEL ($3.00) Lake. *Crisp, clean and lovely, with great balance.*

☆ 1980 ZINFANDEL ($5.50) Mendocino. *Vegetal, heavy, not appealing.*

☆ 1980 ZINFANDEL ($5.50) Redwood Valley and Talmage, Mendocino. *Decent but dull and vegetal.*

☆☆ 1980 ZINFANDEL ($8.00) Scharffenberger, Mendocino. *Good structure, snappy fruit.*

☆☆ 1980 ZINFANDEL ($9.00) Ricetti, Mendocino. *15.7% alcohol. Intense; may never cool down.*

☆☆ 1981 ZINFANDEL ($8.00) Lolonis, Mendocino. *Balanced, Bordeaux-style.*

☆ 1982 ZINFANDEL ($4.50) Lake. *Vegetal nose, tart, crisp, some muddiness, decent.*

☆☆ 1982 ZINFANDEL ($5.50) Mendocino. *Light, balanced, clean, varietal, charming.*

☆☆☆ 1982 ZINFANDEL ($8.00) Home, Mendocino. *Fruity, soft, clean, rich, balanced. Drink now.*

☆☆☆ 1982 ZINFANDEL ($8.00) Lolonis, Mendocino. *Soft, rich, velvety, clean and balanced. Drink now.*

☆☆☆ 1982 ZINFANDEL ($8.00) Ricetti, Mendocino. *Rich, deep, balanced.*

☆☆ 1982 ZINFANDEL ($8.00) Scharffenberger, Mendocino. *Soft, brambly, clean, tart.*

☆☆ 1983 ZINFANDEL ($4.50) Lake. *Good, clean fruit, heavy texture, tannic. Drink 1988.*

☆☆ 1983 ZINFANDEL ($8.50) Special Reserve, 75% Home, 25% Ricetti, Mendocino. *Rich, big, deep, complex, intense. Drink 1988.*

☆☆☆ 1983 ZINFANDEL ($8.50) Ricetti, Mendocino. *Lush, rich, black pepper, smooth texture, attractive.*

☆☆ 1984 ZINFANDEL ($5.00) Lake. *Snappy, crisp, clean, varietal, easy to like.*

☆☆☆ 1984 ZINFANDEL ($8.50) Special Reserve, Home, Lolonis, Middleridge., Mendocino. *Big, lush, ripe, lovely. Drink 1988.*

☆☆☆☆ 1985 ZINFANDEL ($5.00) Lake. *Bright berry fruit, deep, complex and simply delicious. Drink now.*

☆☆ 1986 ZINFANDEL ($5.00) Lake. *Spicy, smooth, crisp, with good clean fruit.*

ॐ

## Field Stone Winery                    SONOMA COUNTY

### WHITE

☆☆☆ 1984 GEWURZTRAMINER ($12.00) Late Harvest, Individual Bunch Selected, Alexander Valley. *15% residual sugar. Soft, varietal, rich, balanced, clean and charming.*

### ROSE

☆☆☆ 1985 ROSE OF PETITE SIRAH ($6.50) Estate, Alexander Valley. *1.3% residual sugar. Crisp, cherry flavors, lovely fruit; excellent balance, remarkable complexity.*

### RED

☆ 1978 CABERNET SAUVIGNON ($7.50) Alexander Valley. *Dense and earthy; soft and lacking structure.*

1979 CABERNET SAUVIGNON ($10.00) Estate, Alexander Valley. *Weedy and clumsy.*

☆☆ 1980 CABERNET SAUVIGNON ($10.00) Estate, Alexander Valley. *Berried, clean, tannic, soft and mellow.*

☆☆ 1982 CABERNET SAUVIGNON ($12.00) Turkey Hill, Alexander Valley. *Big, rich, heavy, soft and a little simple. Drink now.*

☆☆☆ 1982 CABERNET SAUVIGNON ($16.00) Hoot Owl Creek, Alexander Valley. *Herbal, rich, complex, clean, lovely fruit. Drink 1989.*

☆☆☆ 1979 PETITE SIRAH ($7.50) Estate, Alexander Valley. *Rich, fruity and clean. Very good.*

☆☆☆ 1981 PETITE SIRAH ($8.50) Alexander Valley. *Rich, fruity, graceful, lovely.*

☆☆ 1982 PETITE SIRAH ($8.50) Estate, Alexander Valley. *Soft, berry fruit, some volatile acidity.*

ॐ

## Fieldbrook Valley Winery          HUMBOLDT COUNTY

### RED

☆ 1981 MERLOT ($7.25) Humboldt. *Dense, berried, Zinfandel-like.*

☆☆ 1980 PETITE SIRAH ($7.00) Special Reserve, Humboldt. *Rich, deep, clean, attractive.*

ॐ

## Firelands Winery                              OHIO

### WHITE

☆ 1985 SEYVAL BLANC ($5.00) Lake Erie. *Soft, ripe, decent.*

### RED

☆ 1983 CABERNET SAUVIGNON ($6.00) Lake Erie. *Soft, smooth, lacking fruit.*

ॐ

## The Firestone Vineyard        SANTA BARBARA COUNTY

### WHITE

☆ 1982 CHARDONNAY ($10.00) Santa Ynez Valley. *Pineapple and oak; good fruit but lacking finesse.*

1983 CHARDONNAY ($10.00) Santa Ynez Valley. *Tart, sour, oily, varietal.*

1984 CHARDONNAY ($10.00) Santa Ynez Valley. *Oily, heavy, herbaceous.*

1985 CHARDONNAY ($10.00) Tenth Anniversary, Santa Ynez Valley. *Flat, heavy, not particularly varietal.*

1985 JOHANNISBERG RIESLING ($9.50) Selected Harvest, Ambassador's, Santa Ynez Valley. *375 ml. 22.5% residual sugar. Intense botrytis, syrupy fruit, a strong dose of volatile acidity.*

☆☆☆ 1986 JOHANNISBERG RIESLING ($6.50) Santa Ynez Valley. *Lush, sweet, soft, fruity, clean and very likable. Good acidity; delicious.*

1985 SAUVIGNON BLANC ($7.50) Santa Ynez Valley. *Dull, soft, some vegetation.*

## ROSE

☆☆ 1984 ROSE OF CABERNET SAUVIGNON ($4.50) Santa Ynez Valley. *Herbal, rich, fruity, clean.*

## RED

☆☆ 1978 CABERNET SAUVIGNON ($9.75) Arroyo Perdido, Santa Ynez Valley. *Rich, velvety and perfumy, with a hint of mushrooms. Drink now.*

☆☆☆ 1978 CABERNET SAUVIGNON ($12.00) Vintage Reserve, Estate, Santa Ynez Valley. *Rich, full and appealing. Should age gracefully.*

☆☆ 1979 CABERNET SAUVIGNON ($8.00) Arroyo Perdido, Santa Ynez Valley. *Rich, full, clean and velvety.*

☆ 1981 CABERNET SAUVIGNON ($8.00) Estate, Santa Ynez Valley. *Fat, dull, earthy, vegetal.*

☆☆ 1982 CABERNET SAUVIGNON ($8.00) Estate, Santa Ynez Valley. *14% Merlot. Clean, medium weight, varietal, herbal. Drink now.*

☆☆☆ 1983 CABERNET SAUVIGNON ($9.00) Santa Ynez Valley. *Herbal, rich, ripe, lush, lovely.*

☆☆ 1979 MERLOT ($7.50) Ambassador's, Santa Ynez Valley. *Stylish, with good wood and varietal richness; elegant.*

○ 1981 MERLOT ($6.50) Santa Ynez Valley. *Aggressively vegetal. Heavy, coarse and very unattractive.*

☆ 1982 MERLOT ($7.50) Ambassador's and Arroyo Perdido, Santa Ynez Valley. *Herbal, dense, inky, tannic. Drink 1990.*

☆☆ 1983 MERLOT ($7.00) Santa Ynez Valley. *Crisp, fresh, lush, complex fruit.*

☆☆ 1984 MERLOT ($9.00) Santa Ynez Valley. *Crisp, bright, good fruit, attractive. Drink now.*

☆☆ 1981 PINOT NOIR ($8.50) Santa Ynez Valley. *Spicy, lush, clean, attractive.*

❧

## *Fisher Vineyards*                    SONOMA COUNTY

### WHITE

☆☆☆ 1982 CHARDONNAY ($14.00) Sonoma. *Soft, rich, clean, holding up nicely.*

☆☆ 1983 EVERYDAY CHARDONNAY ($8.50) Sonoma. *Varietal, clean, some volatile acidity—a decent everyday wine.*

☆☆☆ 1983 CHARDONNAY ($14.00) 65% Sonoma, 35% Napa. *Elegant, balanced, lovely oak, charming varietal character, a classic.*

☆☆☆ 1984 EVERYDAY CHARDONNAY ($8.50) Sonoma. *Simple, clean, oaky, charming.*

☆☆ 1984 CHARDONNAY ($15.00) Coach Insignia, Sonoma. *Soft, rich, deep, balanced, clean, nice oak. Some excessive sulfur in a few samples.*

1985 CHARDONNAY ($11.00) Napa-Sonoma. *Dirty, oxidized.*

☆☆☆ 1985 CHARDONNAY ($16.00) Coach Insignia, Sonoma. *Elegant, lush, fresh and spicy.*

**RED**

☆☆☆ 1983 EVERYDAY CABERNET ($8.00) Sonoma. *Ripe, rich, deep, charming, lacking depth. Drink now.*

☆☆☆ 1979 CABERNET SAUVIGNON ($12.00) Sonoma. *Lovely fruit, varietal intensity and balance.*

☆☆☆ 1980 CABERNET SAUVIGNON ($12.00) Sonoma. *Balanced, soft and quite Bordeaux-like.*

☆☆☆ 1981 CABERNET SAUVIGNON ($12.00) Sonoma. *Tart, clean, varietal, lean.*

☆☆☆ 1982 CABERNET SAUVIGNON ($12.50) Wedding, Sonoma. *7% Merlot. Deep, tart, tangy, lovely structure. Drink 1988.*

☆☆☆ 1983 CABERNET SAUVIGNON ($12.50) Wedding, Sonoma. *Lush, deep, rich, velvety, generous. Drink 1989.*

☆☆☆ 1984 CABERNET SAUVIGNON ($16.00) Coach Insignia, 76% Sonoma, 24% Napa. *Lush, bright fruit, clean, balanced. Drink 1990.*

કે.

## Fitch Mountain Cellars          SONOMA COUNTY

**WHITE**

☆ 1984 CHARDONNAY ($7.00) Sonoma. *Soft, fresh, clean, dull.*

**RED**

☆☆ 1983 CABERNET SAUVIGNON ($5.00) Mendocino. *Lush, crisp fruit, lovely. Drink now.*

☆☆☆ 1985 MERLOT ($9.00) Napa Valley. *Soft, lush, cherry fruit, cinnamon and spice flavors, pretty oak and lovely bright acidity. Drink now.*

☆☆ 1984 ZINFANDEL ($5.00) 76% Sonoma, 24% Napa Valley. *Earthy, herbal, balanced, clean, attractive.*

કે.

## Fitzpatrick Winery          EL DORADO COUNTY

**WHITE**

☆☆☆ 1983 CHARDONNAY ($9.00) El Dorado. *Fruity, clean, fresh, lovely.*

☆☆ 1984 CHARDONNAY ($9.00) El Dorado. *Fat, lush, ripe, a bit dull.*

**RED**

☆ 1980 CABERNET SAUVIGNON ($7.00) El Dorado. *Earthy and big without much finesse. Not typically varietal.*

☆☆ 1981 CABERNET SAUVIGNON ($7.50) Mount Lassen, Tehama. *Dense, rich, tannic, fruity. Drink 1988 and beyond.*

☆☆☆ 1982 CABERNET SAUVIGNON ($9.00) Stonebarn, El Dorado. *Fruity, clean, complex, long, lean, lovely. Drink 1991.*

☆☆ 1981 ZINFANDEL ($6.50) Clockspring, Shenandoah Valley. *Tangy, rich, clean.*

☆☆ 1982 ZINFANDEL ($5.50) Jehling, Shenandoah Valley. *Crisp, fruity, clean, good.*

કે.

## Five Palms Winery          NAPA

**WHITE**

☆☆☆ 1985 CHARDONNAY ($8.00) Napa Valley. *Lush, oaky, complex, charming.*

☆☆ 1986 CHARDONNAY ($8.00) Napa Valley. *Snappy, crisp, clean, tart, decent.*
### RED
☆☆☆ 1984 CABERNET SAUVIGNON ($6.00) Napa Valley. *Soft, clean, ripe, balanced, lovely. Drink now.*
☆☆ 1985 CABERNET SAUVIGNON ($6.00) Napa Valley. *9% Cabernet Franc, 9% Merlot, 2% Petite Verdot. Meaty, lush, rich fruit, good structure. Drink 1989.*

🍒

## Flax Vineyards                        SONOMA COUNTY
### WHITE
☆☆☆ 1984 CHARDONNAY ($14.00) Sonoma. *Crisp, fresh, attractive and nicely balanced.*

🍒

## Flora Springs Wine Company            NAPA COUNTY
### WHITE
☆☆☆ 1982 CHARDONNAY ($12.00) Napa Valley. *Rich, fruity, clean and lush.*
☆☆ 1983 CHARDONNAY ($13.50) Barrel Fermented, Napa Valley. *Rich, deep, soft, fruity, lush.*
☆☆☆ 1984 CHARDONNAY ($14.00) Napa Valley. *Soft, fresh, clean, fruity, with pretty flavors and charming varietal character.*
☆☆☆ 1984 CHARDONNAY ($18.00) Barrel Fermented, Napa Valley. *Rich, earthy, fresh, clean, delicious.*
☆☆☆ 1985 CHARDONNAY ($14.00) Estate, Napa Valley. *Crisp, fresh, lovely fruit, delicate structure.*
☆☆☆ 1985 CHARDONNAY ($20.00) Barrel Fermented, Napa Valley. *Earthy, rich, woody, with a good, crisp backbone of fruit.*
### RED
☆☆ 1984 TRILOGY ($30.00) Napa Valley. *33% Cabernet Sauvignon, 33% Merlot, 33% Cabernet Franc. Rich, intense, lovely structure, some bitterness. Drink 1992.*
☆☆☆☆ 1985 TRILOGY ($20.00) Napa Valley. *33% Cabernet Sauvignon, 33% Cabernet Franc, 33% Merlot. Ripe, supple, velvety, cassis and plum flavors. Drink 1991.*
☆☆ 1980 CABERNET SAUVIGNON ($12.00) Napa Valley. *Oaky and forward, nice complexity. Drink now.*
☆☆ 1981 CABERNET SAUVIGNON ($12.00) Napa Valley. *12% Merlot, 3% Cabernet Franc. Oaky, ripe and clean. Drink now.*
☆☆ 1982 CABERNET SAUVIGNON ($10.00) Napa Valley. *Vegetal but balanced and nicely structured. Drink 1989.*
☆ 1983 CABERNET SAUVIGNON ($13.00) Napa Valley. *Heavy eucalyptus, crisp, bitter.*
☆ 1984 CABERNET SAUVIGNON ($13.00) Napa Valley. *Stinky, tart, bitter. Needs time. Drink 1992.*
☆☆☆ 1984 MERLOT ($18.00) Napa Valley. *Ripe, berried, lush, intense. Drink 1989.*

🍒

## Thomas Fogarty Winery            SAN MATEO COUNTY
### WHITE
☆ 1982 CHARDONNAY ($10.50) Portola Springs, Napa Valley. *Decent, somewhat sour, lacking depth.*
☆☆ 1982 CHARDONNAY ($14.50) Ventana, Monterey. *Crisp, well made, lacking finesse.*

&#9734; 1983 CHARDONNAY ($15.00) Winery Lake, Napa Valley. *Very oaky, big, earthy, a bit unbalanced.*

&#9734;&#9734;&#9734; 1984 CHARDONNAY ($15.00) Ventana, Monterey. *Buttery, soft, lush, oaky and crisp. Very lovely.*

1984 CHARDONNAY ($15.00) Winery Lake, Napa Valley-Carneros. *Oily, lush, deep, vegetal.*

&#9734;&#9734; 1985 CHARDONNAY ($15.00) Winery Lake, Carneros. *Woody, rich, oily, intense.*

&#9734;&#9734; 1985 CHARDONNAY ($16.50) Santa Cruz Mountains. *Big, intense, oily, powerful, clumsy, massive.*

### RED

&#9734;&#9734;&#9734; 1981 CABERNET SAUVIGNON ($17.50) Napa Valley. *Elegant, clean, lovely oak and varietal character. Drink 1987.*

&#9734; 1982 CABERNET SAUVIGNON ($18.00) Steltzner, Napa Valley. *Floral, simple, clean, decent.*

&#9734;&#9734;&#9734; 1981 PINOT NOIR ($15.00) Winery Lake, Napa Valley. *Rich, soft, complex—a dazzling first effort.*

&#9734;&#9734; 1982 PINOT NOIR ($12.00) Ventana, Monterey. *Herbal, clean, nice fruit.*

&#9734;&#9734; 1982 PINOT NOIR ($15.00) Winery Lake, Napa Valley. *Lovely varietal character, deep and complex, with slightly thin fruit.*

&#9734;&#9734;&#9734; 1983 PINOT NOIR ($15.00) Winery Lake, Napa Valley. *Great cherry fruit, rich texture, complex, superbly balanced.*

&#9734;&#9734;&#9734;&#9734; 1984 PINOT NOIR ($15.00) Winery Lake, Napa Valley. *Cherry fruit, lush texture, great balance; complex and superb.*

&#10086;

## Folie à Deux Winery      NAPA COUNTY

### WHITE

&#9734;&#9734; 1982 CHARDONNAY ($12.00) Napa Valley. *Lovely, crisp and fruity but lacks depth in middle.*

&#9734;&#9734;&#9734; 1984 CHARDONNAY ($13.00) Napa Valley. *Lovely fruit and oak. Crisp, fresh, nicely made.*

&#9734;&#9734;&#9734; 1985 CHARDONNAY ($13.00) Napa Valley. *Crisp, clean, varietal, snappy, attractive.*

### RED

&#9734;&#9734; 1982 CABERNET SAUVIGNON ($10.00) Robert Egan, State Lane, Napa Valley. *Leafy, dense, good structure, balanced.*

&#9734;&#9734;&#9734; 1983 CABERNET SAUVIGNON ($13.00) Napa Valley. *Lovely fruit, fresh acidity, great varietal character. Drink 1989.*

&#10086;

## Louis Foppiano Wine Company    SONOMA COUNTY

### WHITE

&#9734;&#9734; 1982 CHARDONNAY ($9.25) Sonoma. *Fresh, lemony fruit, decent varietal character.*

&#9734;&#9734; 1983 CHARDONNAY ($10.00) Sonoma. *Balanced, fruity, decent.*

&#9734; 1984 CHARDONNAY ($8.50) Sonoma. *Tart, some odd flavors.*

### RED

&#9734;&#9734; NV RIVERSIDE FARM PREMIUM RED ($2.75) California. *Open, soft, fruity and good.*

&#9734; 1978 CABERNET SAUVIGNON ($6.00) Sonoma. *Simple and direct, somewhat heavy-handed.*

&#9734; 1979 CABERNET SAUVIGNON ($6.00) Sonoma. *Another very drinkable and simple Cabernet; pleasant, decent.*

&#9734;&#9734; 1980 CABERNET SAUVIGNON ($6.50) Sonoma. *Some vegetal quality, nice fruit, clean. Drink now.*

&#9734;&#9734;&#9734; 1981 CABERNET SAUVIGNON ($7.75) Russian River Valley. *15% Merlot, 5% Cabernet Franc. Lush, lovely. Drink now.*

&#9734;&#9734;&#9734; 1981 FOX MOUNTAIN CABERNET SAUVIGNON ($16.00) Russian River Valley. *Ripe, clean, dry, crisp, lush, beginning to show its age. Drink now.*

&#9734;&#9734; 1982 CABERNET SAUVIGNON ($7.50) Sonoma. *Lush, clean, balanced, simple, charming. Drink now.*

&#9734;&#9734; 1982 CABERNET SAUVIGNON ($7.75) Russian River Valley. *Soft, clean varietal flavors; slight but charming.*

&#9734;&#9734; 1983 RIVERSIDE FARM CABERNET SAUVIGNON ($4.00) North Coast. *Herbal, supple, varietal, very drinkable.*

&#9734;&#9734;&#9734; 1984 CABERNET SAUVIGNON ($8.00) Sonoma. *Soft, lush, deep, snappy, complex. Drink now.*

&#9734;&#9734; 1979 PETITE SIRAH ($5.50) Sonoma. *Balanced and fresh tasting.*

&#9734;&#9734; 1980 PETITE SIRAH ($6.25) Sonoma. *Berries, well structured, clean and rich. Drink now.*

&#9734;&#9734; 1981 PETITE SIRAH ($7.00) Estate, Russian River Valley. *Rich, deep, tannic, clean, attractive. Drink 1990.*

&#9734;&#9734; 1982 RIVERSIDE FARM ZINFANDEL ($4.00) Sonoma. *Rich, soft, good balance, clean.*

‘&#128;&#128;

## Forgeron Vineyard                                      OREGON

**RED**

&#9734;&#9734; 1980 PINOT NOIR ($7.50) Lane County, Oregon. *Perfumy, with a candied nose; earthy, thin, nice flavors.*

‘&#128;&#128;

## Forman Vineyard                                   NAPA COUNTY

**WHITE**

&#9734;&#9734;&#9734; 1984 CHARDONNAY ($15.00) Napa Valley. *Crisp, balanced, lovely fruit and soft, new oak.*

&#9734;&#9734;&#9734;&#9734; 1985 CHARDONNAY ($18.00) Napa Valley. *Clean, fresh fruit, sweet new oak, great acidity; superb.*

&#9734;&#9734;&#9734; 1986 CHARDONNAY ($16.50) Napa Valley. *Lush fruit and lovely, sweet oak, with great subtlety and finesse.*

**RED**

&#9734;&#9734;&#9734; 1983 CABERNET SAUVIGNON ($15.00) Napa Valley. *Lush, ripe, fruity, with great structure. Drink 1990.*

&#9734;&#9734;&#9734;&#9734; 1984 CABERNET SAUVIGNON ($16.50) Napa Valley. *Lush, soft, rich, deep, beautifully structured. Like a great Margaux. Drink 1989.*

‘&#128;&#128;

## Fortino Winery                            SANTA CLARA COUNTY

**WHITE**

1985 MALVASIA ($5.50) Santa Clara. *Dry, bitter, unappealing.*

**RED**

&#9734;&#9734; 1980 CABERNET SAUVIGNON ($7.50) San Benito. *Good, clean and attractive; simple but decent.*

&#9734; 1981 CABERNET SAUVIGNON ($10.50) Central Coast. *Grapey, raisiny, woody, dried out.*

&#9734; 1978 PETITE SIRAH ($6.50) San Benito. *Intense and somewhat overdone.*

‘&#128;&#128;

## Four Chimneys Farm Winery            NEW YORK
### WHITE
1984 CHARDONNAY ($15.00) Finger Lakes. *Heavy, ox-idized, odd.*

☆☆ 1982 DELAWARE ($8.25) Late Harvest-Organic, Estate, Finger Lakes. *Labrusca nose, rich, thick, fruity, clean, nice.*

### RED
☆☆ 1981 CABERNET SAUVIGNON ($12.00) Finger Lakes. *Chocolate nose, smooth, varietal, good acidity.*

○ 1984 CABERNET SAUVIGNON ($17.00) New York. *Candy, skunky.*

❧

FOX MOUNTAIN *see* Louis Foppiano Wine Company

## Franciscan Vineyards            NAPA COUNTY
### WHITE
☆☆☆ 1982 CHARDONNAY ($10.50) Vintner Grown, Alexander Valley. *A stunner. Delicate, balanced, with lush fruit and oak—superb.*

☆☆☆ 1982 CHARDONNAY ($12.00) Carneros Reserve, Napa Valley. *Crisp, snappy, very lovely.*

☆ 1982 CHARDONNAY ($12.00) Reserve, Oakville Estate, Napa Valley. *A once great wine that has become oily and heavy. Past its prime.*

1983 CHARDONNAY ($10.00) Estate, Oakville, Napa Valley. *Mousey, off flavors, unattractive.*

☆☆ 1983 CHARDONNAY ($10.50) Alexander Valley. *Toasty, oaky, crisp, fruity and lush.*

☆☆ 1984 CHARDONNAY ($8.00) Oakville Estate, Napa Valley. *Crisp, clean, lean, very attractive.*

☆☆ 1984 CHARDONNAY ($10.00) Reserve, Oakville Estate, Napa Valley. *Rich, ripe, bright, attractive.*

☆☆ 1985 ESTANCIA CHARDONNAY ($6.00) Alexander Valley. *Clean, fresh, simple, attractive.*

☆☆ 1985 CHARDONNAY ($8.50) Oakville Estate, Napa Valley. *Lemony, crisp, snappy, simple.*

☆☆ 1986 ESTANCIA CHARDONNAY ($6.50) Alexander Valley. *Crisp, clean, simple, good fruit.*

☆☆ 1982 JOHANNISBERG RIESLING ($25.00) Select Late Harvest, Estate, Napa Valley. *375 ml. 19% residual sugar. Rich, lush, a bit musty.*

☆☆☆ 1983 JOHANNISBERG RIESLING ($10.00) Select, Estate, Napa Valley. *375 ml. 20% residual sugar. Deep, golden, syrupy, thick and rich.*

☆☆☆ 1983 JOHANNISBERG RIESLING ($12.00) Select Late Harvest, Estate, Napa Valley. *375 ml. 20% residual sugar. Rich, deeply colored, softly balanced, with smooth, caramel flavors.*

☆ 1984 JOHANNISBERG RIESLING ($6.50) Oakville Estate, Napa Valley. *Clean, oily, heavy and lush.*

☆ 1985 SAUVIGNON BLANC ($6.00) Alexander Valley. *Flat, dull, lacking freshness.*

### RED
☆ 1978 CABERNET SAUVIGNON ($12.50) Private Reserve, Napa. *A well-made wine that is spoiled by excessive weediness.*

☆☆☆ 1980 CABERNET SAUVIGNON ($7.50) Alexander Valley. *Round, fresh, deep, charming. Drink now and beyond.*

☆ 1980 CABERNET SAUVIGNON ($8.50) Oakville, Napa Valley. *Rich, nice texture, very vegetal.*

☆ 1980 CABERNET SAUVIGNON ($11.00) Private Reserve, Napa Valley. *Smokey, earthy, mature flavors; balanced but low on fruit and depth.*

☆ 1982 ESTANCIA CABERNET SAUVIGNON ($6.00) Alexander Valley. *Soft, earthy, vegetal, decent. Drink now.*

☆☆☆ 1983 ESTANCIA CABERNET SAUVIGNON ($6.00) Alexander Valley. *Intense, balanced, with classic fruit and olive flavors. Drink 1989.*

☆☆☆ 1983 CABERNET SAUVIGNON ($8.50) Oakville Estate, Napa Valley. *Crisp, balanced, ripe, clean and quite lovely. Drink 1990.*

☆☆ 1984 ESTANCIA CABERNET SAUVIGNON ($6.50) Alexander Valley. *Soft, crisp, clean, with good olive and cedar flavors.*

☆☆ 1978 MERLOT ($7.00) Napa Valley. *20% Cabernet. Soft, lovely and rich; finishes short.*

☆☆ 1979 MERLOT ($8.50) Oakville, Napa Valley. *25% Cabernet. Lightly vegetal and nicely oaked.*

☆☆☆ 1981 MERLOT ($8.50) Napa Valley. *Lush, deep, beautiful flavors. Drink now.*

☆☆ 1983 MERLOT ($8.50) Oakville Estate, Napa Valley. *Silky, rich fruit, ripe, earthy, ripe currants.*

☆☆☆ 1984 MERLOT ($6.00) Oakville Estate, Napa Valley. *Ripe, rich, smooth texture, good structure. Drink now.*

☆☆ 1985 MERLOT ($9.25) Oakville Estate, Napa Valley. *22% Cabernet Sauvignon. Lush, ripe, crisp, fruity.*

≥⋅

## Freemark Abbey Winery                    NAPA COUNTY
### WHITE

☆☆ 1982 CHARDONNAY ($12.00) Napa Valley. *Initial off aromas give way to a richly oaked, good wine.*

☆☆☆ 1983 CHARDONNAY ($14.00) Napa Valley. *Lovely fruit and acid, good oak.*

☆☆☆ 1984 CHARDONNAY ($14.00) Napa Valley. *Rich, soft, lovely fruit, a bit overripe.*

☆☆ 1982 EDELWEIN GOLD JOHANNISBERG RIESLING ($17.50) Napa Valley. *375 ml. 21.9% residual sugar. Rich, nutty, syrupy, rich.*

☆☆☆ 1986 JOHANNISBERG RIESLING ($7.75) Napa Valley. *1.4% residual sugar. Spicy, crisp, balanced, charming, melony.*

☆☆☆☆ 1986 EDELWEIN GOLD JOHANNISBERG RIESLING ($18.50) Napa Valley. *375 ml. 20.2% residual sugar. Soft, lovely botrytis, rich texture, great subtlety and balance.*

### RED

☆ 1979 CABERNET BOSCHE ($12.50) Napa Valley. *Nicely structured, but some off flavors intrude.*

☆☆☆ 1980 CABERNET BOSCHE ($14.50) Napa Valley. *Crisp, balanced, clean, complex, lovely. Ready to drink.*

☆☆☆ 1981 CABERNET BOSCHE ($14.00) Napa Valley. *Lovely fruit and structure. Earthy, complex. Drink 1988.*

☆☆☆ 1982 CABERNET BOSCHE ($15.00) Napa Valley. *Rich, balanced, lovely fruit and structure. Firm and showing great aging potential. Drink 1989.*

☆☆☆☆ 1983 CABERNET BOSCHE ($18.00) Napa Valley. *Crisp, balanced, clean, complex, tangy fruit and firm structure. Drink 1990.*

☆☆☆ 1978 CABERNET SAUVIGNON ($11.50) Napa Valley. *Intense, rich fruit, lovely structure, deep. Drink now.*

☆☆ 1979 CABERNET SAUVIGNON ($11.50) Napa Valley. *Herbal and a bit muddy but firm, with good aging potential.*

☆ 1980 CABERNET SAUVIGNON ($14.00) Napa Valley. *Intense, chocolatey, vegetal, deep, composty, oily.*

☆ 1982 CABERNET SAUVIGNON ($12.00) Napa Valley. *Vegetal nose mars lovely fruit and great structure.*

☆☆☆ 1980 PETITE SIRAH ($8.50) Yale Creek Vineyards, Napa Valley. *Peppery, fresh, soft and very attractive. Drink now.*

ॐ

## French Creek Cellars WASHINGTON

### WHITE
☆☆ 1985 CHARDONNAY ($11.35) Reserve Bottling, Washington. *Lush, ripe, clean, fresh.*

### RED
○ 1983 CABERNET SAUVIGNON ($14.00) Reserve, Otis, Washington. *20% Merlot. Spicy and peppery but stinky and lacking varietal character.*

ॐ

## Fretter Wine Cellars ALAMEDA COUNTY

### RED
☆☆☆ 1980 LEAKY LAKE CABERNET SAUVIGNON ($12.00) Napa Valley. *Berried, oaky, clean, balanced. Drink now and beyond.*

1981 LEAKY LAKE CABERNET SAUVIGNON ($9.00) Napa Valley. *Raisiny, dense, bitter, not much fruit.*

☆☆☆ 1983 CABERNET SAUVIGNON ($11.00) Leaky Lake, Napa Valley. *Crisp, clean, with lovely oak and fruit. Drink 1989.*

☆☆☆ 1980 MERLOT ($10.00) Narsai David, Napa Valley. *Snappy, rich, tannic, oaky and big. Aging nicely.*

☆☆ 1981 MERLOT ($10.00) Narsai David, Napa Valley. *Clean, appealing but some off characteristics.*

☆☆☆ 1982 MERLOT ($10.00) Narsai David, Napa Valley. *Oaky and big, with rich, deep fruit. Drink 1989.*

☆☆ 1984 MERLOT ($10.00) Lot 4, Narsai David, Napa Valley. *Ripe and tannic, intense, lacking finesse. Drink 1991.*

ॐ

## Frey Vineyards MENDOCINO COUNTY

### RED
☆ 1980 CABERNET SAUVIGNON ($6.00) Mendocino. *Light, herbal, decent.*

☆ 1980 CABERNET SAUVIGNON ($9.00) Special Reserve, Mendocino. *Rich, intense but lacking in fruit.*

ॐ

## Frick Winery SANTA CRUZ COUNTY

### WHITE
☆ 1982 CHARDONNAY ($11.00) Monterey. *Off flavors, ripe, heavy, oaky.*

1984 CHARDONNAY ($12.00) Santa Maria Valley. *Sour, bitter.*

☆☆ 1985 CHARDONNAY ($13.00) Central Coast. *Simple, balanced, decent.*

### RED
☆☆ NV CAFE RED ($4.00) California. *Clean, tart, decent Pinot Noir character.*

1980 PINOT NOIR ($10.00) Monterey. *Earthy, peppery; overdone and lacking freshness but decent.*

☆☆☆ 1981 ZINFANDEL ($6.00) Santa Clara. *Sweet oak, rich vari-etal fruit, buttery, nice. Drink now.*

☆☆ 1983 ZINFANDEL ($6.50) Santa Clara. *Berried, jammy, crisp, some volatile acidity.*

≈●

## Fritz Cellars                                    SONOMA COUNTY
### WHITE

☆☆ 1982 CHARDONNAY ($9.00) Sonoma. *Rich, clean, hard-edged, complex and woody.*

☆☆☆ 1983 CHARDONNAY ($8.00) Dry Creek Valley. *Rich, deep, oily fruit, lovely oak and balance.*

☆☆☆ 1984 CHARDONNAY ($8.00) Dry Creek Valley. *Crisp, clean, lovely acidity, lean yet softly textured.*

☆☆ 1985 CHARDONNAY ($8.50) Russian River Valley. *Oily, rich, clean, simple, bright, attractive.*

☆☆☆ 1985 FUME BLANC ($7.00) Dry Creek Valley. *Crisp, fresh, varietal, lovely, soft fruit.*

### BLANC DE NOIR

☆☆☆ 1986 PINOT NOIR BLANC ($4.75) Russian River Valley. *Crisp, slightly spritzy, tart, fruity, balanced and charming.*

### RED

☆☆☆ 1981 CABERNET SAUVIGNON ($7.00) North Coast. *Com-plex, rich, fruity and very attractive.*

☆☆☆ 1979 PINOT NOIR ($6.50) Sonoma. *Delicate but complex and very a ttractive.*

1984 ZINFANDEL ($7.00) Dry Creek Valley. *Jammy, concen-trated, deep, nice berry flavors. Simpler and lighter than the "Reserve."*

☆☆☆ 1984 ZINFANDEL ($8.50) Private Reserve, Dry Creek Valley. *Deep, rich, concentrated, lovely berry flavors, firm structure, super.*

≈●

## Frog's Leap Winery                               NAPA COUNTY
### WHITE

☆☆☆ 1982 CHARDONNAY ($11.00) Napa Valley. *Delightfully crisp and fruity, angular and graceful.*

1983 CHARDONNAY ($11.00) Napa Valley. *Dull, flabby.*

☆☆☆ 1984 CHARDONNAY ($12.00) Napa Valley. *Lush, ripe, crisp, balanced, lovely.*

☆☆☆ 1985 CHARDONNAY ($12.00) Napa Valley. *Crisp, oaky, lovely fruit, clean, delightful.*

☆☆☆ 1986 SAUVIGNON BLANC ($8.50) Napa Valley. *Crisp, vari-etal, lovely fruit.*

### RED

☆☆ 1982 CABERNET SAUVIGNON ($9.00) Napa Valley. *Bal-anced, oaky and fruity, with good lean structure. Drink 1988.*

☆☆☆ 1983 CABERNET SAUVIGNON ($9.00) Napa Valley. *Clean, ripe, fruity, lovely, balanced, nicely made. Drink 1988.*

☆☆☆☆ 1984 CABERNET SAUVIGNON ($12.00) Napa Valley. *Big, lush, rich, earthy, complex, charming. Drink 1989.*

☆☆☆ 1981 ZINFANDEL ($6.50) Spottswoode, Napa Valley. *15% Cabernet. Fruity, crisp, spicy and charming.*

≈●

## Fruit Wines of Florida                           FLORIDA
### RED

☆ 1983 MIDULLA JEAN DE NOIR ($4.00) Florida. *Sweet, tart, clean; odd but attractive.*

≈●

## Fulton Valley Winery SONOMA COUNTY
### WHITE
☆☆☆ 1985 CHARDONNAY ($9.50) Alexander Valley. *Fresh, clean, ripe, soft, charming.*

☆ 1985 WOLFSPIERRE CHARDONNAY ($10.00) Sonoma Mountain. *Soft, lush, spicy, bitter, intense.*

☆☆ 1985 BERLIN SEMILLON ($14.00) Berlin, Sonoma Mountain. *Rich, lush, ripe, complex.*

### RED
1982 CABERNET SAUVIGNON ($15.00) Steiner, Sonoma Mountain. *Overcome by vegetation, unattractive.*

☆☆☆☆ 1984 STEINER CABERNET SAUVIGNON ($15.00) Wolfspierre Vineyards, Steiner, Sonoma Mountain. *Buttery, fresh, cherry fruit, delicate oak and lovely, clean flavors. Drink now.*

☆☆☆ 1984 PINOT NOIR ($7.50) Russian River Valley. *Fresh, ripe, soft, clean cherry fruit, delightful.*

ε**λ**

## The Gainey Vineyard SANTA BARBARA COUNTY
### WHITE
☆ 1984 CHARDONNAY ($9.50) Santa Barbara. *Oily, rich, decent.*

☆☆☆ 1985 CHARDONNAY ($15.00) Limited Selection, Santa Barbara. *Rich, complex, with lovely oak and intense fruit.*

☆☆ 1985 JOHANNISBERG RIESLING ($17.50) Special Selection Late Harvest, Santa Barbara. *375 ml. 23.3% residual sugar. Crisp, clean, fresh, good acidity.*

☆ 1985 SAUVIGNON BLANC ($8.00) Santa Barbara. *Fat, vegetal, oily.*

### RED
☆ 1982 CABERNET SAUVIGNON ($9.00) 77% Alamo Pintada, 23% Cuesta, Santa Ynez Valley. *Vegetal, clean, decent.*

ε**λ**

## E. & J. Gallo Winery STANISLAUS COUNTY
### WHITE
☆☆ NV RHINE WINE ($1.75) California. *Clean, spritzy, sweet, great acidity, balanced.*

☆☆ NV CHABLIS BLANC ($2.00) California. *1.4% residual sugar. Spicy, grassy, crisp, charming.*

☆ NV CARLO ROSSI CHABLIS ($2.30) California. *1.5 liters. Sweet, fresh, fruity, decent.*

NV CARLO ROSSI RHINE ($2.30) California. *1.5 liters. Vegetal, sweet, clean.*

☆☆☆ NV RESERVE CHABLIS ($2.60) California. *Dry, clean, fruity and very attractive.*

☆ 1983 CHARDONNAY ($8.50) California. *Clumsy, overdone, ripe, varietal.*

○ 1986 CHARDONNAY ($4.00) Reserve, California. *Flat, miserable.*

☆☆ NV FRENCH COLOMBARD ($2.30) California. *Crisp, off-dry, not varietal but attractive.*

☆☆ 1984 SAUVIGNON BLANC ($3.50) California. *Grassy and varietal, off-dry, pleasant.*

### SPARKLING
☆ NV ANDRE COLD DUCK ($4.00) California. *Clean, sweet, strawberry flavors, simple.*

☆☆☆ NV ANDRE PINK CHAMPAGNE ($4.00) California. *Lush, ripe, fruity, clean, very nice.*

☆☆ NV ANDRE BRUT ($4.20) California. *Soft, fresh, clean, simple but quite lovely.*

☆☆☆ NV BALLATORE SPUMANTE ($4.50) California. *Spicy, sweet, fruity, clean, delightful.*

### ROSE

☆ NV CARLO ROSSI PINK CHABLIS ($2.30) California. *1.5 liters. Off-dry, lively, fresh, attractive.*

☆ NV ROSE OF CALIFORNIA ($2.30) California. *Crisp, somewhat sweet, clean, decent.*

☆☆ NV CARLO ROSSI VIN ROSE ($2.30) California. *1.5 liters. Fresh, clean, pleasant.*

☆ NV VIN ROSE ($1.75) California. *Crisp, simple, decent.*

### RED

☆ NV BOONE'S FARM WILD MOUNTAIN ($1.30) California. *Concord grape. Fresh, sweet, fruity.*

☆ NV BURGUNDY ($1.75) California. *Clean, balanced, pleasant.*

☆☆ NV HEARTY BURGUNDY ($1.75) California. *A classic— herbal, clean, fresh and deep. Amazing.*

NV CARLO ROSSI BURGUNDY ($2.30) California. *1.5 liters. Sweet and vegetal.*

☆ NV CARLO ROSSI PAISANO ($2.30) California. *1.5 liters. Crisp, sweet, decent.*

☆ NV RESERVE BURGUNDY ($2.60) California. *Good fruit, clean but heavy; lacking depth.*

☆ NV ZINFANDEL ($2.60) California. *Husky, raisiny, intense, low varietal character.*

☆☆ 1978 CABERNET SAUVIGNON ($8.00) Limited Release, California. *Gallo's first vintage wine. Soft, ripe and still quite lovely.*

☆☆ 1980 CABERNET SAUVIGNON ($4.50) Limited Release, California. *Earthy, herbal, complex, balanced. Drink 1988.*

☆ 1981 ZINFANDEL ($5.50) California. *Snappy, fresh, decent balance, lacking fresh fruitiness.*

### FLAVORED

☆☆ TYROLIA ($1.50) California. *Spicy, fresh, sweet.*

CARLO ROSSI SANGRIA ($2.30) California. *1.5 liters. Vegetal, clean, fruit flavors, sweet.*

୬ଈ

## *Gan Eden Winery*      SONOMA COUNTY

### WHITE

☆☆☆ 1986 CHARDONNAY ($7.50) Alexander Valley. *Kosher. Soft, rich, complex, fruity, charming.*

☆☆ 1986 GEWURZTRAMINER ($6.50) Alexander Valley. *Kosher. Sweet, lush, clean, with nice spicy fruit.*

### RED

☆☆ 1986 GAMAY BEAUJOLAIS ($6.35) Sonoma. *Kosher. Fresh, crisp, spicy, balanced.*

୬ଈ

GAVILAN *see* Chalone Vineyard

## *Gemello Winery*      SANTA CLARA COUNTY

### RED

☆ 1982 CABERNET SAUVIGNON ($10.00) Alexander Valley. *Lush texture, vegetal.*

☆☆ 1977 PETITE SIRAH ($7.00) California. *Complex, fruity and showing its age well.*

☆☆☆ NV ZINFANDEL ($6.25) Reminiscence, Lot 75A, Amador. *Lush, rich, deep, intense, lovely.*

୬ଈ

## J. H. Gentili Wines          SAN MATEO COUNTY
### WHITE
1982 CHARDONNAY ($12.00) Napa Valley. *Good varietal character but flabby.*

ა

## Geyser Peak Winery          SONOMA COUNTY
### WHITE
☆ NV OPULENCE ($7.50) California. *9% residual sugar. Mostly Gewürztraminer. Heavy, thick, sweet.*

☆ 1982 CHARDONNAY ($7.00) Sonoma. *Crisp, clean, uncomplicated.*

☆☆ 1982 CHARDONNAY ($8.00) Kiser Ranch, Los Carneros-Sonoma. *Decent, clean, attractive.*

○ 1983 TRIONE CHARDONNAY ($8.00) Alexander Valley. *Flabby, unattractive.*

☆☆☆ 1984 CHARDONNAY ($7.00) Sonoma Valley-Carneros. *Clean, crisp, fresh, balanced, charming.*

☆☆☆ 1985 CHARDONNAY ($7.00) Sonoma Valley-Carneros. *Floral, fresh, clean, earthy, charming.*

☆ 1985 CHARDONNAY ($9.00) Vintner Grown, Sonoma. *Decent but dull and flat.*

☆ 1985 TRIONE CHARDONNAY ($10.00) Owner's Reserve, Alexander Valley. *Decent but quite simple and showing very little finish.*

☆☆ 1986 CHENIN BLANC ($5.00) Alexander Valley. *Spicy, crisp, clean, soft, decent.*

☆☆ 1986 GEWURZTRAMINER ($5.50) Sonoma. *Spicy, balanced, attractive.*

☆ 1986 JOHANNISBERG RIESLING ($6.00) Soft, Carneros Sonoma. *Soft, clean, a bit faint.*

☆ 1986 SAUVIGNON BLANC ($5.00) Sonoma. *Soft, off-dry, grassy, sweet pea flavors.*

### SPARKLING
☆☆ 1984 BLANC DE NOIR ($10.00) Trione Family Vineyards, Sonoma. *Crisp, clean, fresh, simple, attractive.*

### BLANC DE NOIR
☆☆ 1986 WHITE ZINFANDEL ($4.50) Sonoma. *Crisp, decent, fresh, appealing.*

### RED
1982 SONOMA VINTAGE RED ($3.25) Sonoma. *Dull, bitter.*

☆☆☆ 1983 RESERVE ALEXANDRE ($15.00) Alexander Valley. *48% Cabernet Sauvignon, 48% Merlot, 4% Cabernet Franc. Buttery, velvety texture, earthy and rich, with great depth. Drink 1988.*

☆ 1978 CABERNET SAUVIGNON ($7.25) California. *Herbaceous but decent.*

☆ 1979 CABERNET SAUVIGNON ($7.25) Estate, Hoffman Ranch, Alexander Valley. *Lush and weedy, balanced, decent.*

☆☆☆ 1981 CABERNET SAUVIGNON ($7.00) Sonoma. *Rich, round, berried, attractive.*

☆ 1982 CABERNET SAUVIGNON ($8.00) Estate, Alexander Valley. *Murky, dense, no structure, overripe, clumsy.*

☆☆☆ 1983 CABERNET SAUVIGNON ($7.00) Sonoma. *Lush, olives, fruit, cedar, soft texture. A lovely wine. Drink now.*

☆ 1983 CABERNET SAUVIGNON ($7.50) Alexander Valley, Sonoma. *Hard, simple, bitter.*

✩ 1984 TRIONE CABERNET SAUVIGNON ($10.00) Owners Reserve, Alexander Valley. *18% Merlot. Crisp, clean, modest, well balanced.*

✩✩✩ 1982 MERLOT ($5.50) Trione Family, Alexander Valley. *Velvety, clean, herbal, lovely.*

✩✩ 1983 MERLOT ($6.95) Estate, Alexander Valley. *Buttery, oaky, rich, dense.*

✩✩ 1984 MERLOT ($7.50) Alexander Valley, Sonoma. *Well structured and varietal.*

1981 PINOT NOIR ($10.00) Sonoma Valley-Carneros. *Tannic, dull, unappealing.*

1984 PINOT NOIR ($6.00) Carneros, Sonoma. *Simple, astringent, decent.*

☙

## Girard Winery                    NAPA COUNTY
### WHITE

✩✩✩ 1982 CHARDONNAY ($12.50) Estate, Napa Valley. *Snappy, clean, lean.*

✩✩ 1983 CHARDONNAY ($12.50) Estate, Napa Valley. *Lean, austere, buttery, attractive.*

✩✩✩ 1984 CHARDONNAY ($13.50) Estate, Napa Valley. *Ripe, fruity, intense, heavy, rich oak, big.*

✩✩✩ 1985 CHARDONNAY ($13.00) Estate, Napa Valley. *Crisp acidity, ripe fruit, smooth oak. A well-balanced wine.*

✩✩✩ 1986 CHENIN BLANC ($6.50) Dry, Napa Valley. *Crisp, rich, varietal, clean, attractive.*

1984 SAUVIGNON BLANC ($8.00) North Coast. *Leafy, herbaceous, heavy.*

### RED

✩✩ 1980 CABERNET SAUVIGNON ($12.00) Napa. *Dark, raisiny and big.*

✩✩✩ 1981 CABERNET SAUVIGNON ($14.00) Estate, Napa Valley. *Lush, velvety, firm, complex, superb. Aging well.*

✩✩✩ 1982 CABERNET SAUVIGNON ($14.00) Napa Valley. *Concentrated, dark, with cassis and violet flavors. A stunning wine. Drink 1989.*

✩ 1982 CABERNET SAUVIGNON ($18.00) Estate, Napa Valley. *Heavy, rich, decent.*

✩ 1983 CABERNET SAUVIGNON ($12.00) Napa Valley. *Overripe, simple, vegetal, lacking structure.*

✩✩✩ 1983 CABERNET SAUVIGNON ($20.00) Reserve, Estate, Napa Valley. *Crisp, lean, tight fruit and firm structure. This one needs time, but the potential is there. Drink 1991.*

✩✩✩ 1984 CABERNET SAUVIGNON ($11.00) Napa Valley. *Tart, crisp, earthy, with nice olive and oak flavors. Drink 1990.*

☙

## Giumarra Vineyards                KERN COUNTY
### WHITE

✩ 1983 CHARDONNAY ($6.00) California. *0.3% residual sugar. Lush, fat, clean, but lacking fruit.*

✩ 1985 CHARDONNAY ($6.00) Proprietor's Reserve, Central Coast. *Crisp, simple, decent, lacking varietal character.*

### RED

✩✩ 1981 PETITE SIRAH ($6.00) California. *Berried, lush, late-harvest style.*

☙

## Glen Ellen Winery                    SONOMA COUNTY
### WHITE
☆☆ **1982 CHARDONNAY** ($10.00) Les Pierres, Sonoma Valley. *Fruity, clean and attractive.*

☆☆ **1983 CHARDONNAY** ($12.00) Sonoma Valley. *Fat, intense, heavy, pleasant, clean.*

☆☆☆ **1984 CHARDONNAY** ($7.00) Lot II, Sonoma Valley. *Lush, complex, lovely fruit, rich texture.*

☆☆ **1984 CHARDONNAY** ($9.00) Sonoma Valley. *Fresh, fruity, clean, nicely balanced, attractive.*

☆ **1985 CHARDONNAY** ($5.00) Proprietor's Reserve, California. *Soft, dull, clean, lacks structure.*

☆☆ **1986 SAUVIGNON BLANC** ($9.00) Proprietor's Reserve, California. *Soft, fruity, simple, clean.*

### RED
☆☆☆ **NV PROPRIETOR'S RESERVE RED** ($3.00) California. *Zinfandel and Syrah. Buttery rich, lush and delicious.*

☆☆ **1979 CABERNET SAUVIGNON** ($8.00) Sonoma. *Big, rich, uncomplicated.*

☆☆ **1981 CABERNET SAUVIGNON** ($9.75) Sonoma Valley. *Rich, intense. Aging nicely.*

☆☆ **1982 CABERNET SAUVIGNON** ($4.00) Proprietor's Reserve, Sonoma. *15% Zinfandel. Lush and charming. Drink now.*

☆☆☆ **1982 CABERNET SAUVIGNON** ($10.00) Estate, Sonoma Valley. *Peppery, lush, deep and beautifully structured.*

☆☆ **1984 CABERNET SAUVIGNON** ($8.00) Sonoma. *Some soft bell pepper flavors, with nice fruit and a soft finish. Drink now.*

☆☆ **1984 CABERNET SAUVIGNON** ($12.00) Estate, Sonoma. *Decent, clean, balanced.*

☆☆ **1983 MERLOT** ($8.50) Sonoma. *Soft, earthy, attractive.*

☆☆☆ **1982 BENZIGER FAMILY WINERY & VINEYARDS ZIN-FANDEL** ($4.50) Geyserville, Sonoma. *Rich, lush, deep, complex, balanced.*

🔊

## Glenora Wine Cellars                    NEW YORK
### WHITE
☆☆ **1985 JOHAN BLANC** ($5.50) Hazlett/Ancher Acres, Finger Lakes. *Tart, crisp, dry (0.5% residual sugar), pleasant.*

☆☆ **1984 CAYUGA** ($5.25) Spring Ledge Farms, Finger Lakes. *Crisp, clean, fresh, complex.*

☆☆ **1985 CAYUGA** ($4.75) Spring Ledge Farms, Finger Lakes. *Crisp, soft, clean.*

☆ **1982 CHARDONNAY** ($10.00) Finger Lakes. *Light, in the French Chablis style.*

☆☆☆ **1984 CHARDONNAY** ($9.00) Finger Lakes. *Crisp, clean, steely, very attractive.*

☆ **1986 CHARDONNAY** ($8.00) 10th Anniversary Edition, Finger Lakes. *Vegetal, oily, heavy.*

☆☆☆ **1986 CHARDONNAY** ($10.00) Finger Lakes. *Crisp, fresh, brightly fruity, balanced.*

☆☆☆ **1982 JOHANNISBERG RIESLING** ($9.00) Select Late Harvest, Finger Lakes. *9.6% residual sugar. Toasty, botrytized, nutty, lovely.*

☆☆ **1986 JOHANNISBERG RIESLING** ($8.00) Finger Lakes. *Crisp, fruity but a bit heavy.*

☆ 1984 RAVAT ($7.00) Select Late Harvest, Finger Lakes. *375 ml. 7.5% residual sugar. Big, vegetal, intense.*

☆☆☆ 1985 SEYVAL BLANC ($6.00) Finger Lakes. *Fresh, snappy, clean, charming.*

**SPARKLING**

☆ 1981 BLANC DE BLANCS ($15.00) Finger Lakes. *Clean, fresh, some vegetal qualities.*

❧

## Gold Seal Vineyards                    NEW YORK

**WHITE**

☆ NV CHABLIS SUPERIEUR ($4.00) American. *Slightly foxy, pleasant, balanced, off-dry, dull finish.*

**SPARKLING**

NV BRUT ($7.75) American. *Sweet, low fruit.*

○ NV EXTRA DRY ($7.75) New York. *Sweet, fat, awful.*

○ NV PINK CHAMPAGNE ($7.75) New York. *Oily and sweet.*

NV BLANC DE BLANCS ($10.50) Fournier, New York. *Sweet, dull, lacking fruit.*

☆☆ NV BLANC DE NOIRS ($10.50) Fournier, American. *Nice, crisp, sweet, clean and likable.*

**RED**

○ NV BURGUNDY SUPERIEUR ($4.00) American. *Foxy, sweet nose, thin, unattractive.*

❧

## Golden Creek Vineyard               SONOMA COUNTY

**RED**

☆☆☆ NV CABERLOT ($4.50) Sonoma. *50% Cabernet Sauvignon, 50% Merlot. Tart, rich, balanced, lovely.*

☆☆ 1986 CABERNET SAUVIGNON ($6.00) California. *Clean, fruity, ripe, good balance.*

❧

## Good Harbor Vineyards                    MICHIGAN

**WHITE**

☆ NV TRILLIUM WHITE TABLE WINE ($5.50) Michigan. *Tart, fresh, a bit heavy. Decent.*

☆☆ 1985 VIGNOLES ($6.00) Leelanau Peninsula, Michigan. *Crisp, lemony, earthy. Charming.*

**SPARKLING**

NV TRILLIUM BRUT ($8.50) Michigan. *Heavy, fat, sweet.*

**RED**

☆ NV BACO NOIR ($4.50) Leelanau Peninsula, Michigan. *Pale, some fruit, lacking oomph.*

❧

## Goosecross Cellars                       NAPA COUNTY

**WHITE**

☆☆ 1985 CHARDONNAY ($13.75) Napa Valley. *Decent, varietal, lacking depth of fruit.*

❧

GRAN VAL *see* Clos du Val

## Grand Cru Vineyards                  SONOMA COUNTY

**WHITE**

☆☆ 1986 SAUVIGNON BLANC ($9.00) Sonoma. *Crisp, balanced, vegetal.*

**RED**

☆☆☆ 1979 CABERNET SAUVIGNON ($14.50) Collector Series, Garden Creek Ranch, Alexander Valley. *Earthy and lush, with wonderful structure.*

☆☆ 1980 CABERNET SAUVIGNON ($14.00) Collector Series, Alexander Valley. *Raisiny, fat, lush. Drink now.*

☆☆ 1981 CABERNET SAUVIGNON ($8.50) California. *Simple, herbed, clean and decent. Drink now.*

☆ 1982 CABERNET SAUVIGNON ($4.50) Vin Maison, California. *Decent, weedy, fruity.*

☆☆ 1982 CABERNET SAUVIGNON ($14.50) Collector's Reserve, Alexander Valley. *Sweet pea flavors, some nice oak, good fruit.*

☆☆ 1983 CABERNET SAUVIGNON ($4.50) Vin Maison, California. *Deep, lush, dense, clean.*

☆☆ 1983 CABERNET SAUVIGNON ($8.50) Sonoma. *Herbal, soft, fresh, balanced, charming. Drink now.*

○ 1984 CABERNET SAUVIGNON ($8.50) Sonoma. *Cheesy, decadent, metallic.*

☆☆ 1981 ZINFANDEL ($8.50) Sonoma Valley. *Snappy, crisp and light.*

❧

## *Granite Springs Winery*     EL DORADO COUNTY
### WHITE
☆☆☆ 1986 CHENIN BLANC ($5.00) El Dorado. *Crisp, off-dry, fresh, fruity, varietal, charming.*
### RED
☆☆ 1983 ZINFANDEL ($6.00) El Dorado. *Tart, earthy, clean, varietal.*

❧

GREAT WESTERN *see* Taylor Wine Company

## *Green and Red Vineyards*     NAPA COUNTY
### WHITE
☆☆ 1982 CHARDONNAY ($9.50) Napa Valley. *Rich, vinous, deep, varietal. Lacks finesse.*

☆☆ 1985 CHARDONNAY ($10.25) Estate, Napa Valley. *Clean, varietal, simple.*
### BLANC DE NOIR
☆ 1985 WHITE ZINFANDEL ($5.25) Napa Valley. *Tart, simple, not much.*
### RED
☆ 1977 ZINFANDEL ($7.00) Napa Valley. *Rich, full and complex but lacking finesse.*

1978 ZINFANDEL ($6.50) Napa Valley. *Hard-edged and lacking fruit.*

1979 ZINFANDEL ($6.00) Chiles Canyon, Napa. *Lacking fruit and depth.*

☆☆ 1980 ZINFANDEL ($7.00) Chiles Canyon, Napa. *Vegetal and earthy, with brambly, peppery flavors.*

☆☆☆ 1981 ZINFANDEL ($5.75) Estate, Napa Valley. *Elegant, balanced, fruity, very attractive.*

☆☆ 1982 ZINFANDEL ($7.50) Napa Valley. *Peppery, green, elegant, Claret-like. Clean and serious.*

☆ 1983 ZINFANDEL ($7.25) Napa Valley. *Thin, dull, simple, watery.*

❧

## *Greenwood Ridge Vineyards*     MENDOCINO COUNTY
### WHITE
☆☆☆ 1986 JOHANNISBERG RIESLING ($7.00) Mendocino. *1.6% residual sugar. Crisp, snappy, floral, superb.*

☆☆☆ 1986 SAUVIGNON BLANC ($6.50) Anderson Valley. *Clean, fresh, varietal, attractive.*

☆☆☆ 1986 WHITE RIESLING ($7.00) Mendocino. *1.6% residual sugar. Crisp, fresh, balanced, varietal, charming.*

### RED

☆☆ 1981 CABERNET SAUVIGNON ($9.75) Mendocino. *Herbal, toasty, some interesting bottle flavors. Drink now.*

☆☆☆ 1982 CABERNET SAUVIGNON ($9.75) Estate, Mendocino. *20% Merlot. Lush, elegant, clean, complex.*

‽

## *Grgich Hills Cellar* NAPA COUNTY

### WHITE

☆☆☆ 1980 CHARDONNAY ($17.00) Napa Valley. *Full, round, oaky, fresh fruit. A stunning wine.*

☆☆ 1981 CHARDONNAY ($17.00) Napa Valley. *A bit more two-dimensional than previous efforts; should age.*

☆☆☆ 1982 CHARDONNAY ($17.00) Napa Valley. *Rich, oaky, clean, lush.*

☆☆☆ 1982 CHARDONNAY ($18.00) Napa Valley. *A later release. Rich, oaky, intense, balanced, clean, handsome.*

☆☆☆ 1983 CHARDONNAY ($17.00) Napa Valley. *Rich and fruity, with lovely oak and varietal character. One of the best Grgich Chardonnays.*

☆☆☆☆ 1984 CHARDONNAY ($18.00) Napa Valley. *One of the nicest Grgich Chardonnays yet! Rich fruit, deep oak, round, balanced, quite special. Drink 1988.*

☆☆☆☆ 1985 CHARDONNAY ($18.00) Napa Valley. *Crisp, lush, deep, complex, lovely oak, great fruit.*

### RED

☆☆☆ 1980 CABERNET SAUVIGNON ($16.00) 34% Napa, 66% Sonoma. *Rich, ripe, complex, velvety and lovely. Drink now.*

☆☆ 1981 CABERNET SAUVIGNON ($16.00) Napa Valley. *10% Merlot. Varietal but lacking depth and charm.*

☆☆ 1982 CABERNET SAUVIGNON ($16.00) Napa Valley. *Earthy nose, crisp, fruity, balanced. Drink 1988.*

☆☆☆ 1978 ZINFANDEL ($9.00) Alexander Valley. *Velvety, rich, complex, deep.*

☆☆☆ 1979 ZINFANDEL ($10.00) Alexander Valley. *Tart, fruity, deep and rich.*

☆☆☆ 1980 ZINFANDEL ($10.00) Alexander Valley. *Rich, deep, brambly and supple, with great aging potential.*

☆☆☆ 1981 ZINFANDEL ($10.00) Sonoma. *Rich, fresh, deeply fruity and balanced. Delicious.*

☆☆☆☆ 1982 ZINFANDEL ($10.00) Alexander Valley. *Lush, clean flavors, rich fruit, complex, superb, classic.*

☆☆ 1983 ZINFANDEL ($10.00) Alexander Valley. *Jammy, dense, ripe, complex. Good but not up to the 1982.*

☆☆☆☆ 1984 ZINFANDEL ($10.00) Alexander Valley. *Lush, concentrated berry flavors, lovely oak and good structure; elegant and delicious.*

‽

## *Groth Vineyards and Winery* NAPA COUNTY

### WHITE

☆☆☆ 1982 CHARDONNAY ($12.50) Napa Valley. *Exquisite acidity, great oak and fruit.*

☆☆ 1984 CHARDONNAY ($13.00) Napa Valley. *Simple, crisp, fresh, attractive.*

☆☆☆☆ 1985 CHARDONNAY ($12.00) Napa Valley. *Bright fruit and lush oak; quite lively and delicious.*

**RED**

☆☆☆☆ 1982 CABERNET SAUVIGNON ($13.00) Napa Valley. *Stunning. Lovely, delicate fruit and great acidity. Drink 1988.*

☆☆☆ 1983 CABERNET SAUVIGNON ($13.00) Napa Valley. *Dark, lush, berried, buttery, very lovely. Drink 1989.*

🍂

## Grover Gulch Winery                    SANTA CRUZ COUNTY
**RED**

☆☆☆ 1981 CABERNET SAUVIGNON ($9.50) Santa Cruz Mountains. *Nice, rich, good depth and fruit. Drink now.*

☆☆ 1980 CARIGNANE ($6.50) Santa Cruz Mountains. *Rich, deep, balanced—a fine example of a little-made wine.*

☆☆ 1980 PETITE SIRAH ($8.50) Santa Cruz Mountains. *Spicy, clean, good fruit.*

🍂

## Guenoc Winery                          LAKE COUNTY
**WHITE**

☆ 1982 CHARDONNAY ($9.25) 67% Lake, 33% Mendocino. *Earthy, dull, lacking fruit.*

☆ 1983 CHARDONNAY ($9.25) North Coast. *Heavy, sappy, vegetal.*

☆☆ 1984 CHARDONNAY ($9.15) North Coast. *Soft, clean, pleasant, simple.*

☆☆☆ 1984 CHARDONNAY ($15.00) Vintner's Selection, Guenoc Valley. *Lush, fat, round, deep, lovely.*

☆☆☆ 1985 CHARDONNAY ($9.75) North Coast. *Oaky, crisp, fruity, clean, with lovely rich spices.*

**RED**

☆☆☆ 1980 CABERNET SAUVIGNON ($8.00) 70% Lake, 30% Napa. *Snappy, clean and balanced. Complex and lovely. Drink now.*

☆☆☆ 1981 CABERNET SAUVIGNON ($8.00) Lake. *Lovely fruit and balance, nice oak. Drink now.*

☆☆ 1982 CABERNET SAUVIGNON ($8.25) Guenoc Valley. *Herbaceous, soft, fresh, clean. Drink now.*

☆☆☆ 1983 CABERNET SAUVIGNON ($9.25) Lake. *Fruity, lush, ripe, charming. Drink 1988.*

1981 PETITE SIRAH ($6.50) Lake. *Meaty, rubbery, past its prime.*

☆☆ 1983 PETITE SIRAH ($7.00) Lake. *Peppery, soft, balanced, lovely fruit.*

☆☆ 1981 ZINFANDEL ($5.50) Lake. *Crisp fruit, clean.*

☆☆☆ 1983 ZINFANDEL ($5.00) Lake. *Crisp, clean, lovely fruit, simple but charming.*

☆☆☆ 1984 ZINFANDEL ($5.00) Guenoc Valley. *Ripe, rich, fat, with lovely fruit.*

🍂

## Guild Wineries                         SAN JOAQUIN COUNTY
**WHITE**

○ 1983 CRIBARI & SONS CHARDONNAY ($2.50) Albert B. Cribari Selection, California. *Rotting vegetation, awful.*

○ 1983 CRESTA BLANCA CHARDONNAY ($6.25) Estate, Mendocino. *Sour, oxidized, ugly.*

## SPARKLING

NV COOK'S CHAMPAGNE CELLARS BLANC DE NOIR ($6.00) Imperial, American. *Oily, heavy.*

☆☆ NV COOK'S CHAMPAGNE CELLARS AMERICAN CHAMPAGNE, IMPERIAL ($5.00) California. *Sweet, strawberry fruit, crisp.*

NV J. ROGET CHAMPAGNE CELLARS AMERICAN CHAMPAGNE ($3.50) New York. *Bitter, petroleum flavors.*

NV CRESTA BLANCA CHARDONNAY CHAMPAGNE ($9.50) California. *Oily, dull, heavy.*

☆ NV CRIBARI & SONS EXTRA DRY ($3.50) California. *Rich, heavy, decent.*

☆ NV CRIBARI & SONS SPUMANTE ($2.50) California. *Sappy, dull, decent.*

☆☆ NV COOK'S CHAMPAGNE CELLAR AMERICAN WHITE ZINFANDEL ($5.75) California. *Crisp, lush, snappy, quite attractive.*

## RED

☆☆ 1978 CRESTA BLANCA CABERNET SAUVIGNON ($5.00) Mendocino. *Herbal, clean, light and lovely.*

☆ 1980 CRESTA BLANCA ZINFANDEL ($4.00) Mendocino. *Smokey, nice varietal character, light, good.*

∂⋑

# Gundlach-Bundschu Winery          SONOMA COUNTY

## WHITE

☆☆ NV SONOMA WHITE WINE ($4.00) Sonoma Valley. *Fresh, crisp, clean, appealing.*

☆☆ 1985 KLEINBERGER ($7.00) Estate, Sonoma Valley. *0.9% residual sugar. Crisp, lemony, clean, fresh.*

1983 CHARDONNAY ($9.75) Sonoma Valley. *Bitter, dirty.*

☆☆ 1984 CHARDONNAY ($8.50) Special Selection, Sangiacomo, Sonoma. *Rich, deep, intense fruit, lemony finish.*

☆☆ 1984 CHARDONNAY ($9.75) Sonoma Valley. *Oily, vegetal, some nice acidity, decent.*

☆☆ 1984 CHARDONNAY ($11.00) Sangiacomo, Sonoma Valley. *Clean fruit, nice oak, some oiliness, charming.*

☆☆ 1985 CHARDONNAY ($9.75) Sonoma Valley. *Soft, rich, clean, varietal, pleasant.*

☆ 1986 GEWURZTRAMINER ($5.50) Rhinefarm, Sonoma Valley. *Dry, crisp, clean, decent.*

☆☆ 1986 RIESLING ($5.00) Sonoma Riesling, Dresel's, Sonoma Valley. *Clean, crisp, bright, a bit heavy.*

## RED

☆☆☆ NV SONOMA RED WINE ($3.50) Sonoma Valley. *Lush, clean, fruity, lovely balance, delicious.*

☆☆☆ 1979 CABERNET SAUVIGNON ($8.00) Gregory, Sonoma Valley. *Rich, berried and round; good structure and aging potential.*

☆☆☆ 1979 CABERNET SAUVIGNON ($9.00) Batto Ranch, Sonoma Valley. *Lovely. Fruity, with firm structure. Great aging potential. Drink 1988.*

☆☆ 1979 CABERNET SAUVIGNON ($9.00) Olive Hill, Sonoma Valley. *Fruity, oaky and attractive. Drink now.*

☆☆ 1979 CABERNET SAUVIGNON ($12.00) 125th Anniversary, Rhinefarm, Sonoma. *It's all here and it is coming together. Drink 1988.*

☆☆☆ 1979 CABERNET SAUVIGNON ($12.50) Special Selection, Rhinefarm, Sonoma Valley. *Earthy, rich and showing great aging potential.*

☆☆ 1980 CABERNET SAUVIGNON ($9.50) Rhinefarm, Estate, Sonoma Valley. *Spicy, herbal, toasty, earthy, attractive. Drink now.*

☆☆☆ 1980 CABERNET SAUVIGNON ($13.50) Batto Ranch, Sonoma Valley. *Complex and nicely structured.*

☆☆☆ 1981 CABERNET SAUVIGNON ($9.95) Sonoma Valley. *Deep, rich, fat, lush. Drink now.*

☆☆☆☆ 1981 CABERNET SAUVIGNON ($12.00) Batto Ranch, Sonoma Valley. *Complex, elegant, rich, magnificently structured. Drink now or hold a few more years.*

☆☆ 1981 CABERNET SAUVIGNON ($12.00) Rhinefarm, Sonoma Valley. *Soft, rich, elegant and fruity. Drink now.*

☆☆☆ 1981 CABERNET SAUVIGNON ($20.00) Vintage Reserve, Rhinefarm, Sonoma Valley. *Rich, elegant, herbal, fruity, superb structure, lovely oak. Drink 1991.*

☆☆ 1982 CABERNET SAUVIGNON ($10.00) Rhinefarm, Sonoma Valley. *Dense, tannic, earthy, unfocused at present. Drink 1990.*

☆☆☆ 1982 CABERNET SAUVIGNON ($12.00) Batto Ranch, Sonoma Valley. *Clean, fruity, stiff, angular. Drink 1988.*

☆ 1983 CABERNET SAUVIGNON ($10.50) Rhinefarm, Sonoma Valley. *Odd, minty, woody flavors; lacking fruit.*

☆☆☆ 1983 CABERNET SAUVIGNON ($14.00) Batto Ranch, Sonoma Valley. *Clean, fresh, lush, complex, great fruit and oak. Drink 1990.*

☆☆☆ 1977 MERLOT Rhinefarm, Sonoma Valley. *Soft, well structured, lovely, clean, mature.*

☆☆☆ 1978 MERLOT ($7.50) Rhinefarm, Sonoma Valley. *Soft, clean, lovely. Drink up.*

☆☆☆ 1979 MERLOT ($9.50) Rhinefarm, Sonoma Valley. *Lovely, clean, complex and rich. Drink now and over the next three years.*

☆☆☆ 1980 MERLOT ($10.00) 125th Anniversary, Rhinefarm, Sonoma Valley. *Big, rich and raisiny.*

☆☆ 1980 MERLOT ($10.15) Rhinefarm, Sonoma Valley. *Tarry, dense and tannic when young, this has smoothed nicely. Drink now.*

☆☆ 1981 MERLOT ($10.00) Rhinefarm, Sonoma Valley. *Soft, lush, clean.*

☆☆☆☆ 1983 MERLOT ($12.00) Estate, Sonoma Valley. *Rich, deep, ripe, lush, firmly structured, exceptional. Drink now.*

☆☆☆ 1984 MERLOT ($12.00) Rhinefarm Estate, Sonoma Valley. *Lush, ripe, berry flavors, good balance and structure. Drink 1989.*

☆☆☆☆ 1985 MERLOT ($12.00) Rhinefarm, Estate, Sonoma Valley. *Rich black currant and cherry fruit, lovely oak, excellent structure. Drink 1989.*

☆☆☆ 1982 PINOT NOIR ($9.95) Estate-Rhinefarm, Sonoma Valley. *Medium weight, good fruit and varietal character.*

☆☆ 1983 PINOT NOIR ($10.00) Rhinefarm Estate, Sonoma Valley. *Soft, light, tart, clean, simple.*

☆☆☆ 1984 PINOT NOIR ($10.00) Rhinefarm Estate, Sonoma Valley. *Crisp, varietal, clean, balanced, charming.*

☆ 1980 ZINFANDEL ($8.00) Rhinefarm, Sonoma Valley. *Deep, berried and oaky but lacking structure and integrity.*

☆☆  1980 ZINFANDEL ($9.00) Late Harvest, Barricia, Sonoma
Valley. *0.6% residual sugar. Peppery, fruity and
intense.*

☆☆  1981 ZINFANDEL ($7.00) Rhinefarm, Sonoma Valley. *Spicy,
fresh, clean.*

❧

## *Habersham Vintners*                           GEORGIA
### WHITE
☆☆  1985 SEYVAL BLANC ($6.50) Select Harvest, Georgia. *Soft,
balanced, dry, nicely made.*
### RED
☆   NV   ZINFANDEL ($9.00) Georgia. *Earthy, tart, tangy, fresh.*

❧

HACIENDA DEL RIO WINERY *see* Williams Selyem Winery

## *Hacienda Winery*                    SONOMA COUNTY
### WHITE
1982 CHARDONNAY ($9.00) Selected Reserve, Sonoma Val-
ley. *Lacks fruit and depth. Bitter.*

☆☆☆  1983 CHARDONNAY ($9.00) Clair de Lune, Sonoma. *Crisp,
rich, good fruit and oak.*

☆☆☆☆  1984 CHARDONNAY ($10.00) Clair de Lune, Sonoma. *Rich,
oaky, snappy, clean, complex, focused.*

☆☆☆  1985 CHARDONNAY ($11.00) Clair de Lune, Sonoma.
*Crisp, clean, snappy varietal fruit, lovely texture.*

☆☆☆  1986 CHENIN BLANC ($6.00) Clarksburg. *Crisp, tangy,
lovely fruit, good structure, charming.*

☆☆  1985 JOHANNISBERG RIESLING ($12.00) Select Late Har-
vest, Sonoma Valley. *375 ml. 11.4% residual sugar.
Fresh, soft, nice fruit, some volatility.*
### RED
☆☆☆  1978 CABERNET SAUVIGNON ($10.00) Sonoma Valley.
*Rich but nicely structured. Drink now.*

☆☆☆  1979 CABERNET SAUVIGNON ($11.00) Sonoma. *Balanced,
graceful, attractive. Drink now.*

☆☆☆  1980 CABERNET SAUVIGNON ($11.00) Sonoma. *Lush and
rich; great depth and complexity. Drink 1988 and
later.*

☆☆☆  1981 CABERNET SAUVIGNON ($11.00) 76% Jansen, 24%
Buena Vista, Sonoma Valley. *Minty, clean and
velvety.*

☆☆☆  1982 CABERNET SAUVIGNON ($11.00) Sonoma Valley.
*Rich, fruity, clean, balanced, varietal, delicious.
Drink now.*

☆☆☆  1982 CABERNET SAUVIGNON ($18.00) Selected Reserve,
Sonoma Valley. *Lush, ripe, clean, intense, good
oak. Drink 1989.*

☆☆  1981 PINOT NOIR ($12.00) Sonoma Valley. *Leathery, with
some stem character but well made.*

☆☆  1982 PINOT NOIR ($12.00) Sonoma. *Crisp, jammy, decent.*

☆☆  1983 PINOT NOIR ($12.00) Estate, Sonoma Valley. *Decent
balance, dried-out fruit. Acceptable.*

☆☆  1984 PINOT NOIR ($15.00) Reserve, Estate, Sonoma Valley.
*Minty, fruity, clean, attractive.*

1984 ZINFANDEL ($7.50) Alexander Valley. *Good balance
but extremely vegetal.*

❧

## *Hafner Vineyard*                     SONOMA COUNTY
### WHITE
☆☆☆  1982 CHARDONNAY ($12.00) Estate, Alexander Valley.
*Rich, intense, balanced and oaky. A stunner.*

☆☆☆ 1983 CHARDONNAY ($11.00) Estate, Alexander Valley. *Rich, oaky and varietal, balanced, attractive.*

☆☆☆ 1984 CHARDONNAY ($12.00) Estate, Alexander Valley. *Complex, crisp, good oak, lovely varietal fruit.*

☆☆☆☆ 1985 JOHANNISBERG RIESLING ($15.00) Special Selection Late Harvest, Estate, Alexander Valley. *375 ml. 19.2% residual sugar. Superb, lush, with apricot and honey flavors, deep fruit and tangy acidity.*

### RED

☆☆☆ 1982 CABERNET SAUVIGNON ($15.00) Estate, Alexander Valley. *Crisp, structured, rich and complex, with loads of finesse. Drink 1988.*

☆☆☆ 1983 CABERNET SAUVIGNON ($15.00) Estate, Alexander Valley. *Crisp, complex, good fruit, lovely structure. Drink 1989.*

෨

## Hagafen Cellars                    NAPA COUNTY

### WHITE

☆☆ 1982 CHARDONNAY ($13.50) Winery Lake, Napa Valley. *Kosher. Lush, fruity, varietal.*

☆☆ 1983 CHARDONNAY ($13.50) Napa Valley. *Kosher. Crisp, decent, clean.*

### RED

☆☆☆ 1982 CABERNET SAUVIGNON ($12.00) Yountville Selection, Napa Valley. *Kosher. Rich, clean, complex, charming, excellent. Drink now.*

☆☆☆ 1983 CABERNET SAUVIGNON ($12.00) Napa Valley. *Kosher. Soft, rich fruit, snappy acidity, good oak. Drink 1989.*

☆☆☆ 1984 CABERNET SAUVIGNON ($13.50) Napa Valley. *Kosher. Lovely, lean, with great fruit and good structure. A small dose of Cabernet Franc adds complexity. Drink 1988.*

෨

## Haight Vineyard                    CONNECTICUT

### WHITE

☆ NV COVERSIDE ($5.00) Connecticut. *Overripe, heavy, oily, intense.*

### RED

☆ NV MARECHAL FOCH ($4.98) Connecticut. *Oak nose, rich, slightly sweet and heavy.*

෨

## Hallmark Cellars                    NAPA COUNTY

### RED

☆ 1983 ZINFANDEL ($4.50) Napa Valley. *Good structure, lacking fruit.*

☆☆☆ 1983 ZINFANDEL ($7.50) Whitfield, Napa Valley. *Fresh, clean, snappy, graceful, very lovely.*

෨

## Hamlet Hill Wines Company            CONNECTICUT

### WHITE

☆☆☆ 1985 SEYVAL BLANC ($7.75) Connecticut. *Soft, fresh, lovely fruit, clean and attractive.*

### BLANC DE NOIR

1986 AUTUMN BLUSH ($7.80) Connecticut. *Dull, flat, lifeless.*

෨

## Handley Cellars                    MENDOCINO COUNTY
### WHITE
☆☆ 1982 CHARDONNAY ($12.00) 55% Handley, 45% Carney, North Coast. *Oaky and ripe, with good, firm acidity.*
☆☆☆☆ 1983 CHARDONNAY ($12.50) Dry Creek Valley. *Elegant, balanced and clean; richly varietal with good oak. Lovely.*
☆☆☆ 1984 CHARDONNAY ($12.50) Dry Creek Valley. *Buttery, rich, oaky, lovely, intense.*
☆☆☆ 1985 CHARDONNAY ($12.50) Dry Creek Valley. *Buttery, lush, deep, lovely.*
☆☆ 1985 SAUVIGNON BLANC ($7.00) Dry Creek Valley. *Crisp, fresh, grassy, decent.*

ु

## Hanna Winery                         SONOMA COUNTY
### WHITE
☆☆☆ 1985 CHARDONNAY ($13.50) Sonoma. *Soft, rich, balanced, lovely.*
☆☆☆ 1986 SAUVIGNON BLANC ($8.75) Sonoma. *Crisp, round flavors, ripe fruit, good balance.*

ु

## Hanzell Vineyards                    SONOMA COUNTY
### WHITE
☆☆ 1982 CHARDONNAY ($19.00) Sonoma Valley. *Rich oak, vinous, lacking fruit.*
☆ 1984 CHARDONNAY ($20.00) Sonoma. *Grapefruity, oily, vegetal, unappealing.*
### RED
☆☆ 1982 CABERNET SAUVIGNON ($20.00) Sonoma Valley. *Vegetal, hard, good structure but not much charm.*
☆☆ 1977 PINOT NOIR ($14.00) Sonoma Valley. *Rich and complex but just not very likable. Maybe age will help, but it hasn't so far.*
☆☆ 1978 PINOT NOIR ($15.00) Sonoma Valley. *Clean, varietal and nicely structured.*
☆☆☆ 1979 PINOT NOIR ($15.00) Sonoma Valley. *Lush, ripe, rounded, complex, superb.*
☆☆ 1980 PINOT NOIR ($16.00) Sonoma Valley. *Hard, austere and dense. Drink 1988.*
☆☆ 1982 PINOT NOIR ($20.00) Sonoma Valley. *Big, complex, intense, earthy and a bit vegetal.*
☆☆☆ 1983 PINOT NOIR ($17.50) Sonoma Valley. *Soft, lush, fruity, clean, attractive but not perfect.*

ु

## Harbor Winery                          YOLO COUNTY
### RED
☆ 1979 CABERNET SAUVIGNON ($9.00) Napa Valley. *Ripe, soft and pleasant.*

ु

## Hargrave Vineyard                        NEW YORK
### WHITE
☆☆☆ 1982 CHARDONNAY ($12.00) Collector Series, Estate, Long Island. *Rich fruit and buttery complexity.*
### RED
☆ 1980 CABERNET SAUVIGNON ($5.50) North Fork, New York. *Vegetal but decently structured.*
☆☆ 1980 CABERNET SAUVIGNON ($10.00) North Fork, Long Island. *Peppery and deep but a bit overoaked.*

☆ 1981 CABERNET SAUVIGNON ($11.00) Estate, North Fork, Long Island. *Lush, green, weedy, rich and heavy. Drink 1988.*

☆☆☆ 1983 CABERNET SAUVIGNON ($12.00) Vintner's Signature, North Fork. *Herbal, ripe, deep, complex, soft. Drink 1988.*

&

## Hart Winery                                    RIVERSIDE COUNTY
### RED
☆☆ 1981 CABERNET SAUVIGNON ($8.00) Temecula. *6% Merlot. Rich, balanced and intense, with good varietal character.*

&

## Haviland Vinyards                                    WASHINGTON
### WHITE
☆☆ 1982 CHARDONNAY ($9.00) Dionysis, Columbia Valley. *Soft and complex.*

☆ 1983 CHARDONNAY ($12.00) Barrel Fermented, Columbia Valley. *Rich, heavy, earthy, some bitterness.*

☆ 1984 CHARDONNAY ($12.95) Dionysus, Columbia Valley. *Earthy, ripe, odd.*

### RED
☆☆☆ 1983 CABERNET SAUVIGNON ($12.95) Estate, Yakima Valley. *Ripe, lush, superb oak and fruit, lovely texture.*

☆ 1982 MERLOT ($6.00) Washington. *Vegetal nose and grapey flavors. Decent.*

☆☆ 1982 MERLOT ($6.00) Manor Reserve, Washington. *12% Cabernet Sauvignon. Grapey, ripe, fruity.*

☆☆ 1983 MERLOT ($11.00) Columbia Valley. *Chalky, rich, deep fruit, tannic. Drink 1990.*

☆☆☆ 1983 MERLOT ($15.00) Manor Reserve, Columbia Valley. *Grapey, rich, dense, berried, super. Drink 1988.*

☆☆ 1985 MERLOT ($11.00) Washington. *Crisp, lean, snappy, lovely varietal flavors. Drink 1989.*

&

HAWK CREST *see* Stag's Leap Wine Cellars

## Haywood Winery                                    SONOMA COUNTY
### WHITE
☆☆☆ NV LINGUINI WHITE ($4.50) Sonoma. *Spicy, peachy, snappy and fresh. A charming picnic wine.*

☆☆☆ 1983 CHARDONNAY ($11.00) Sonoma Valley. *Fresh, fruity, crisp; very attractive.*

☆☆☆ 1984 CHARDONNAY ($9.50) Sonoma Valley. *Clean, varietal, crisp, with charming, toasty oak.*

☆☆☆ 1984 CHARDONNAY ($12.50) Reserve, Estate, Sonoma Valley. *Fresh, clean, lush, oaky, complex, charming.*

☆☆ 1985 CHARDONNAY ($9.50) Sonoma Valley. *Crisp, clean, with decent fruit and varietal character.*

☆☆ 1985 CHARDONNAY ($14.50) Reserve, Estate, Sonoma. *Crisp, clean, snappy, decent but lacking depth.*

☆☆☆ 1986 FUME BLANC ($8.50) Sonoma Valley. *Fragrant, soft, ripe, rich, clean, very attractive.*

☆☆ 1986 WHITE RIESLING ($7.50) Estate, Sonoma Valley. *1.6% residual sugar. Heavy, oily texture, lacking finesse.*

### RED
☆☆ NV SPAGHETTI RED ($4.50) Sonoma. *Clean, complex, decent.*

☆ 1980 CABERNET SAUVIGNON ($9.75) Sonoma Valley. *Dark, intense, lacking fruit.*

☆☆☆ 1982 CABERNET SAUVIGNON ($11.00) Estate, Sonoma Valley. *Dark, rich, concentrated, balanced. Drink 1988.*

☆☆☆ 1983 CABERNET SAUVIGNON ($12.50) Estate, Sonoma Valley. *18% Merlot. Crisp, clean, fresh, classy. Drink 1990.*

☆☆☆ 1984 CABERNET SAUVIGNON ($12.50) Estate, Sonoma. *18% Merlot. Lush, deep, clean, lovely, delicious. Drink 1989.*

1980 MERLOT ($25.00) Late Harvest, Chamizal, Sonoma Valley. *17.8% alcohol. Raisiny and Port-like. A bad idea all around.*

☆☆ 1982 ZINFANDEL ($7.50) Estate, Sonoma Valley. *Clean, fresh, snappy.*

☆☆☆ 1983 ZINFANDEL ($8.00) Estate, Sonoma Valley. *Elegant, clean, fruity, delightful.*

☆☆☆ 1984 ZINFANDEL ($9.00) Estate, Sonoma Valley. *Lovely, ripe, clean, fruity.*

☆☆☆ 1985 ZINFANDEL ($9.50) Estate, Sonoma Valley. *Crisp, snappy, clean, fresh, nicely balanced. A lovely modern Zin.*

🐚

## *Hecker Pass Winery*      SANTA CLARA COUNTY
### ROSE
☆ 1981 CARIGNANE ROSE ($4.00) Santa Clara. *Sweet, heavy, grapey, decent.*
### RED
☆☆ 1984 CARIGNANE ($9.00) Estate, Santa Clara Valley. *Rich, intense, ripe, mouth filling.*

☆☆ 1984 GRENACHE ($6.00) Santa Clara. *Ripe, fruity, grapey, tart.*

☆ 1981 PETITE SIRAH ($6.00) Select, Santa Clara Valley. *Tangy, soft, berry-flavored, tart.*

☆☆ 1984 PETITE SIRAH ($8.00) Estate, Santa Clara. *Dark, ripe, berried, crisp fruit, smooth texture, intense.*

☆☆☆ 1984 ZINFANDEL ($10.00) Santa Clara Valley. *Intense, ripe, fat, lush, smokey, good fruit and balance.*

🐚

## *Heitz Wine Cellars*      NAPA COUNTY
### WHITE
1983 CHARDONNAY ($12.75) Napa Valley. *Moldy, maderized, unattractive.*

☆☆☆ 1984 CHARDONNAY ($11.00) Napa Valley. *Ripe, deep, sweet new oak, lovely fruit, superb. The best Heitz Chardonnay in years.*
### RED
☆☆☆ NV RYAN'S RED ($5.75) Napa Valley. *Plummy, rich, lovely, delightful.*

☆☆☆☆ 1978 CABERNET SAUVIGNON ($20.00) Bella Oaks, Napa Valley. *Rich, smooth, nicely structured.*

☆ 1978 CABERNET SAUVIGNON ($27.00) Martha's, Napa Valley. *Very disappointing. Gluey, dull and lacking structure.*

☆☆☆☆ 1979 CABERNET SAUVIGNON ($30.00) Martha's, Napa Valley. *Mint and eucalyptus in nose, with fruit, oak, depth and richness. Drink now or hold for another decade.*

☆☆ 1980 CABERNET SAUVIGNON ($11.75) Napa Valley. *Lean, herbal, clean, with good structure. Ready now.*

☆☆ 1980 CABERNET SAUVIGNON ($25.00) Bella Oaks, Napa Valley. *Soft, ripe, lush, good earth and fruit flavors. Ready to drink.*

☆☆ 1980 CABERNET SAUVIGNON ($35.00) Martha's, Napa Valley. *Minty, rich, complex, with wonderful structure and intensity. Drink 1988.*

☆☆ 1981 CABERNET SAUVIGNON ($35.00) Martha's, Napa Valley. *Minty, rich, concentrated, woody, lots of lush, currant fruit. Drink 1990.*

☆☆ 1982 CABERNET SAUVIGNON ($21.00) Bella Oaks, Napa Valley. *Lovely fruit and crisp acidity, focused, attractive.*

☆☆☆ 1982 CABERNET SAUVIGNON ($35.00) Martha's, Napa Valley. *Minty, lush, rich, powerful but balanced and complex. Lovely. Drink 1992.*

☆ 1979 PINOT NOIR ($7.50) Napa Valley. *Tart, simple and clean.*

☆ 1981 ZINFANDEL ($6.25) Napa Valley. *Clean, decent.*

🍂

## Henry Winery                                   OREGON
### RED
☆☆ 1979 PINOT NOIR ($9.00) Oregon. *Soft and complex, with good fruit and firm structure.*

🍂

## Herbert Vineyards            EL DORADO COUNTY
### WHITE
☆☆ 1985 SAUVIGNON BLANC ($5.00) El Dorado. *Tight, crisp, fruity, decent.*
### RED
☆☆ 1982 ZINFANDEL ($6.00) Herbert, El Dorado. *Rich, deep, clean, intense, quite nice.*

☆☆☆ 1983 ZINFANDEL ($5.75) El Dorado. *Lush, fruity, clean, really a ttractive.*

☆☆ 1984 ZINFANDEL ($6.00) El Dorado. *Decent fruit, intense, rich, a trifle muddy.*

🍂

## Heron Hill Vineyards                    NEW YORK
### WHITE
☆☆ 1984 CHARDONNAY ($8.00) Estate, Finger Lakes. *Simple but clean and fresh. Good balance.*

☆☆☆ 1985 SEYVAL BLANC ($5.00) Ingle, Finger Lakes. *Crisp, snappy, fruity, clean. Super.*

🍂

## Hess Collection Winery            NAPA COUNTY
### RED
☆☆☆ 1983 HESS ESTATE VINEYARDS CABERNET SAUVIGNON ($12.75) Napa Valley. *Crisp, snappy, rich, clean, charming. Drink 1989.*

☆☆☆ 1983 CABERNET SAUVIGNON ($25.00) Napa Valley. *Soft, lush, rich, elegant, complex, lovely. Drink 1990.*

☆☆ 1985 CABERNET SAUVIGNON ($13.00) Napa Valley. *Heavy, ripe, intense, tannic. Drink 1990.*

🍂

## Hidden Cellars            MENDOCINO COUNTY
### WHITE
☆☆ 1985 BON FUME ($5.00) Mendocino. *Mostly Sauvignon Blanc. Soft, fruity, clean and quite charming.*

☆☆ 1985 CHEVRIGNON D'OR ($10.00) Bailey J. Lovin, Mendocino. *375 ml. 15.6% residual sugar. Oily, vegetal, syrupy, rich, intense. Made from Sauvignon Blanc and Semillon.*

☆☆ 1983 CHARDONNAY ($10.00) Matheu, Mendocino. *Fruity, crisp, varietal, complex, attractive.*

☆☆ 1984 CHARDONNAY ($9.75) Grasso, Mendocino. *Oaky, rich, deep, a bit heavy.*

☆☆ 1985 CHARDONNAY ($9.75) Grasso, Mendocino. *Ripe, crisp, clean, decent.*

☆☆☆ 1985 GEWURZTRAMINER ($7.00) North Coast. *A good attempt at an almost dry (0.65% residual sugar) Gewürz. Crisp, clean and attractive, with subtle varietal flavors.*

☆☆☆☆ 1982 JOHANNISBERG RIESLING ($10.00) Late Harvest, Bailey J. Lovin, Mendocino. *375 ml. Botrytized, rich, sweet (8.1% residual sugar) and balanced.*

☆☆☆ 1984 JOHANNISBERG RIESLING ($10.00) Botrytized Late Harvest, Bailey J. Lovin, Mendocino. *11.6% residual sugar. Rich, fat, botrytis honey flavors, crisp acid, good balance.*

☆☆☆ 1986 JOHANNISBERG RIESLING ($17.50) Botrytized Late Harvest, Bailey J. Lovin, Mendocino. *375 ml. 25.5% residual sugar. Rich, syrupy, with intense botrytis, good fruit and complex finish.*

☆☆ 1985 SAUVIGNON BLANC ($8.00) Sonoma. *Crisp, earthy, varietal, fresh, pleasant.*

**RED**

☆☆ 1983 CABERNET SAUVIGNON ($8.50) Mountanos, Mendocino. *Buttery, ripe, clean, decent.*

☆☆ 1981 ZINFANDEL ($7.75) Mendocino. *Rich but not overbearing.*

☆☆ 1982 ZINFANDEL ($7.50) Mendocino. *Tangy, clean, decent.*

☆☆☆ 1984 ZINFANDEL ($7.50) Pacini, Mendocino. *Rich, dense, berried, ripe, long and lovely.*

☆☆ 1985 ZINFANDEL ($7.50) Pacini, Mendocino. *Big, lush, jammy, grapey, fat.*

🍷

## *Hidden Springs Winery*      OREGON
**RED**

1982 PINOT NOIR ($10.00) Oregon. *Thin, not much depth.*

☆ 1983 PINOT NOIR ($14.00) Eola Hills, La Grande, Cambus Bellas, Oregon. *Thin, green flavors, not much.*

🍷

## *Highland Manor Winery*      TENNESSEE
**WHITE**

☆ 1985 CHARDONNAY ($7.00) Tennessee. *Crisp, clean, good acidity.*

☆ 1986 CHARDONNAY ($7.00) Tennessee. *Crisp, snappy, lively, with good fruit and some odd flavors.*

🍷

## *William Hill Winery*      NAPA COUNTY
**WHITE**

☆☆ 1982 CHARDONNAY ($10.50) Silver Label, California. *Clean, crisp and varietal.*

☆☆ 1982 CHARDONNAY ($16.50) Gold Label, Napa Valley. *Rich, varietal, vinous, oaky; very good.*

☆☆☆ 1982 CHARDONNAY ($25.00) Reserve, Napa Valley. *Rich and oaky yet crisp and fruity. Should age well. Drink 1988.*

☆☆ 1983 CHARDONNAY ($10.50) Silver Label, Napa Valley. *Crisp, fresh, clean, balanced.*

☆☆☆ 1983 CHARDONNAY ($12.00) Gold Label, Napa Valley. *Clean, rich, complex, varietal, lush, oaky.*

☆☆ 1984 CHARDONNAY ($6.00) Silver Label, Napa Valley. *Crisp, clean, snappy, varietal, very nice.*

☆☆☆ 1984 CHARDONNAY ($16.00) Gold Label, Napa Valley. *Crisp, clean, supple, lovely fruit, good structure.*

**RED**

☆☆☆ 1978 CABERNET SAUVIGNON ($15.00) Mount Veeder-Napa Valley. *Great fruit in a classy package—intense, firm and beautiful. Ready to drink.*

☆☆☆ 1979 CABERNET SAUVIGNON ($17.00) Mount Veeder-Napa Valley. *Rich, firmly structured and elegant. Will improve for 10 years or more.*

☆☆☆☆ 1980 CABERNET SAUVIGNON ($18.00) Napa Valley. *Rich, smooth, lean and elegant. Superb. Drink now or hold.*

☆☆☆ 1981 CABERNET SAUVIGNON ($16.00) Mount Veeder-Napa Valley. *Rich, angular, deep and stunning. Drink 1988.*

☆☆ 1982 CABERNET SAUVIGNON ($10.50) Silver Label, California. *50% Monterey. Fruity, simple, soft, earthy. Drink now.*

☆☆☆☆ 1982 CABERNET SAUVIGNON ($15.00) Gold Label, Napa Valley. *Lean, focused, great fruit, toasty, varietal, elegant and beautifully structured. Drink 1990.*

☆☆☆ 1983 CABERNET SAUVIGNON ($16.50) Reserve, Napa Valley. *Crisp, clean, snappy, beautifully structured. Drink 1993.*

❧

## Hillcrest Vineyard                                   OREGON
**RED**

☆ 1979 CABERNET SAUVIGNON ($12.00) Oregon. *Rich, woody, decent.*

1980 CABERNET SAUVIGNON ($8.00) Oregon. *Peppery and crisp, with some volatile acidity. Odd.*

1979 PINOT NOIR ($15.00) Oregon. *Earthy, dirty, green.*

❧

## Hinzerling Vineyards                          WASHINGTON
**RED**

☆☆ 1978 CABERNET SAUVIGNON ($11.00) Yakima Valley. *Tart, crisp and cherry flavored.*

☆☆☆ 1979 CABERNET SAUVIGNON ($13.00) Yakima Valley. *Rich, tart and tannic. Lovely fruit. Drink now.*

☆☆ 1980 CABERNET SAUVIGNON ($12.00) Yakima Valley. *Lush and raisiny; attractive but on the heavy side.*

☆☆ 1981 CABERNET SAUVIGNON ($8.00) Yakima Valley. *16% Merlot, 2% Malbec. Grassy, unusual, decent. Drink now.*

☆☆ 1981 CABERNET SAUVIGNON ($15.00) Estate, Yakima Valley. *Rich, tight, tannic, clean, earthy, ripe, lush. Drink 1990.*

☆☆ 1982 CABERNET SAUVIGNON ($10.00) Estate, Yakima Valley. *Rich, deep, dark, well structured, clean. Drink 1990.*

❧

## The Hogue Cellars                              WASHINGTON
**WHITE**

☆☆ 1984 CHARDONNAY ($8.00) Yakima Valley. *Tangy, clean, crisp, attractive.*

☆☆ 1985 CHARDONNAY ($8.00) Washington. *Tart, crisp, snappy, lean.*

1986 CHARDONNAY ($8.00) Washington. *Flat, dull, simple, unappealing.*

☆☆☆ 1986 FUME BLANC ($7.00) Washington. *Crisp fruit, herbal, round, fresh, attractive.*

☆☆ 1986 JOHANNISBERG RIESLING ($6.00) Washington. *Crisp, clean, with decent fruit; a bit heavy.*

☆☆ 1985 SEMILLON ($8.50) Reserve, Washington. *Tart, clean, rich, good balance, lacking fruit.*

1985 WHITE RIESLING ($8.00) Late Harvest, Yakima Valley. *375 ml. 9.37% residual sugar. Geranium flavors; unattractive.*

### RED

☆☆ 1983 CABERNET SAUVIGNON ($18.00) Reserve, Washington. *Intense, dense, rich, well made but slightly bitter. Drink 1989.*

1984 CABERNET SAUVIGNON ($18.00) Reserve, Washington. *24% Merlot. Chalky, herbs, coffee flavors, not attractive.*

☆☆☆ 1985 MERLOT ($12.00) Washington. *Black cherries, lush, rich, deep, clean.*

❧

## Hood River Vineyards                OREGON
### RED

☆☆ 1981 ZINFANDEL ($5.95) Washington. *Beaujolais-style. Pale, snappy, fruity, crisp.*

❧

## Hoodsport Winery                WASHINGTON
### RED

☆☆ 1984 MERLOT ($10.00) Washington. *Crisp, lean, good structure, a bit thin. Drink 1989.*

❧

## Hop Kiln Winery                SONOMA COUNTY
### WHITE

1983 CHARDONNAY ($10.00) Alexander Valley. *Fat, dirty.*

☆☆☆ 1986 SAUVIGNON BLANC ($7.00) Bien Neider, Russian River Valley. *Fresh, clean, crisp and varietal.*

### RED

☆☆☆ NV BIG RED ($6.50) Russian River Valley. *Ripe, rich, intense, deep.*

☆☆☆ 1981 CABERNET SAUVIGNON ($9.00) Alexander Valley. *Earthy, big, concentrated. Aging nicely.*

☆☆☆ 1984 CABERNET SAUVIGNON ($10.00) Alexander Valley. *Jammy, ripe, good, rich fruit and fine balance. Drink 1989.*

☆☆☆ 1976 PETITE SIRAH ($8.00) Russian River Valley. *Lovely balance, great fruit, intense without being heavy.*

☆☆☆ 1981 PETITE SIRAH ($8.50) Russian River Valley. *Dark, lush and plummy, with great fruit. Drink now through 1988.*

☆☆ 1982 PETITE SIRAH ($10.00) Russian River Valley. *Clean, vinous, complex, fruity.*

☆☆☆ 1984 PETITE SIRAH ($10.00) Estate, Russian River Valley. *Dark, boysenberry fruit, cassis, intense, lovely. Drink 1988.*

1983 PINOT NOIR ($10.00) Russian River Valley. *Sour, old, ugly.*

☆ 1978 ZINFANDEL ($8.00) Russian River Valley. *This award-winning wine hasn't aged well.*

☆☆☆ 1981 ZINFANDEL ($8.50) Russian River Valley. *Crisp, clean, great fruit.*

☆☆☆ 1982 ZINFANDEL ($8.50) Russian River Valley. *Rich, deep, lush, berry fruit, super. Drink now.*

☆☆ 1983 ZINFANDEL ($8.50) Russian River Valley. *Spicy, rich, lush fruit, brambly.*

☆☆ 1984 ZINFANDEL ($8.50) Russian River Valley. *Decent, crisp, thin.*

ه‌

## Hopkins Vineyard CONNECTICUT
### RED
☆☆ NV BARN RED ($5.00) American. *Rich nose, crisp, fruity and tart flavors.*

☆☆ NV SACHEM'S PICNIC RED ($5.00) American. *Semisweet but clean, fresh and attractive.*

ه‌

## Houtz Vineyards SANTA BARBARA COUNTY
### WHITE
☆ 1985 CHARDONNAY ($9.00) Santa Ynez Valley. *Tart, sour, crisp, clean but no depth.*

ه‌

## Huber Orchard Winery INDIANA
### RED
☆ NV DECHAUNAC ($8.00) Indiana. *Odd, earthy, some nice cherry fruit.*

ه‌

## Hudson Valley Winery NEW YORK
### WHITE
○ NV DELAWARE ($5.25) New York. *Dull, flat, heavy sulfur, unattractive.*

ه‌

## Robert Hunter SONOMA COUNTY
### SPARKLING
☆☆ 1981 BRUT DE NOIRS ($14.00) Sonoma Valley. *Fresh, clean, balanced, somewhat coarse.*

☆☆☆☆ 1982 BRUT DE NOIRS ($13.50) Sonoma. *Rich, yeasty, deep, superb, great Pinot Noir varietal character.*

☆ 1983 BRUT DE NOIRS ($14.00) California. *Simple, clean, dull, decent.*

ه‌

HUNTER ASHBY *see* Jaeger Family Wine Company

## Husch Vineyards MENDOCINO COUNTY
### WHITE
☆☆ 1985 LA RIBERA BLANC ($5.00) Estate, Mendocino. *Fresh, tangy, clean, balanced and lively.*

☆☆ 1986 LA RIBERA BLANC ($7.50) Estate, Mendocino. *83% Sauvignon Blanc, 17% Chardonnay. Soft, ripe, decent fruit, good finish.*

☆☆☆ 1982 CHARDONNAY ($9.00) La Ribera Ranch, Mendocino. *Crisp and bright, with good structure and great fruit acidity.*

☆☆ 1983 CHARDONNAY ($10.00) Mendocino. *Crisp, fresh, not much depth.*

☆☆☆ 1984 CHARDONNAY ($9.75) Estate, Mendocino. *Lush, deep, clean, varietal, delicious.*

☆☆☆ 1985 CHARDONNAY ($9.75) Mendocino. *Elegant, focused, compact, lovely, clean, tart, lemony finish.*

☆☆☆ 1985 CHARDONNAY ($15.00) Special Reserve, Mendocino. *Fresh, crisp, fruit and oak; delicious.*

☆☆☆ 1986 CHARDONNAY ($9.75) Mendocino. *Fresh, spicy, oaky, honey and melon. Lovely, rich but elegant.*

☆☆☆ 1986 CHENIN BLANC ($6.00) Mendocino. *Crisp, delicate, with good varietal fruit.*

☆☆☆ 1986 GEWURZTRAMINER ($6.25) Estate, Anderson Valley. *1.2% residual sugar. Gentle, crisp varietal fruit, rose petals and lovely spritz.*

☆☆☆ 1985 SAUVIGNON BLANC ($7.00) La Ribera, Mendocino. *Snappy, bright, elegant.*

☆☆☆ 1986 SAUVIGNON BLANC ($7.00) Mendocino. *Fresh, elegant, fruity, clean, good varietal character.*

**RED**

☆☆☆ 1981 CABERNET SAUVIGNON ($10.00) La Ribera, Mendocino. *Fruity, oaky, balanced, structured. Drink 1988 and beyond.*

☆☆ 1982 CABERNET SAUVIGNON ($10.00) La Ribera Ranch, Estate, Mendocino. *Heavy, varietal, decent. Drink now.*

☆☆ 1983 CABERNET SAUVIGNON ($10.00) La Ribera, Estate, Mendocino. *Eucalyptus, clean and lush, velvety texture. Drink 1988.*

☆☆ 1984 CABERNET SAUVIGNON ($10.00) La Ribera, Mendocino. *Crisp, clean, soft, fruity; an undemanding and attractive wine. Drink now.*

☆☆ 1982 PINOT NOIR ($9.00) Estate, Anderson Valley. *Balanced, clean, attractive, fairly simple.*

ॐ

## *Inglenook Napa Valley*                     NAPA COUNTY

**WHITE**

☆☆ 1982 CHARDONNAY ($9.00) Estate, Napa Valley. *Simple, crisp, clean, fruity.*

☆ 1982 CHARDONNAY ($14.00) Special Reserve, Estate, Napa Valley. *Small lot. Overdone, vinous and oaky.*

☆☆ 1983 CHARDONNAY ($9.50) Estate, Napa Valley. *Crisp, fresh, varietal and well balanced.*

☆☆ 1983 CHARDONNAY ($16.00) Limited Reserve Select, Napa Valley. *Heavy flavors, low fruit, not altogether pleasant.*

☆☆☆ 1984 CHARDONNAY ($13.50) Reserve, Estate, Napa Valley. *Soft, lush, clean, with lovely oak and rich fruit. 72% Carneros fruit.*

☆☆ 1985 CHARDONNAY ($5.00) Napa Valley. *Crisp, simple, clean and quite drinkable.*

☆☆☆ 1985 CHARDONNAY ($15.00) Reserve Cask, Napa Valley. *Crisp, lean, nicely structured, complex and correct.*

☆☆ 1986 CHARDONNAY ($9.50) Estate, Napa Valley. *Crisp, clean, lean, varietal, attractive.*

☆☆ 1985 GEWURZTRAMINER ($9.50) Late Harvest, Estate, Napa Valley 375 ml. 11.4% residual sugar. *Soft, rich, smooth; lacking varietal character and depth.*

☆ 1985 GEWURZTRAMINER ($9.50) Estate, Napa Valley. *Tart, crisp, low varietal character, bland.*

☆☆ 1985 JOHANNISBERG RIESLING ($6.50) Estate, Napa Valley. *Crisp, clean, dry, lemony, thin; an attractive food wine.*

☆☆ 1986 MUSCAT ($8.50) Estate, Napa Valley. *Heavy, sweet, spicy.*

☆☆☆ 1985 SAUVIGNON BLANC ($7.50) Reserve, Estate, Napa Valley. *Crisp, clean, grassy varietal flavors.*

☆☆☆ 1986 SAUVIGNON BLANC ($9.50) Estate, Napa Valley. *Crisp, lean, fruity, elegant and beautifully balanced.*

## BLANC DE NOIR

☆☆ 1986 WHITE CABERNET ($5.50) Estate, Napa Valley. *Crisp, lean, herbal, varietal.*

## RED

☆☆☆ 1982 NAPA VALLEY RED ($4.00) Napa Valley. *Rich, lush, clean, charming.*

☆☆☆ 1983 NIEBAUM CLARET ($12.00) Napa Valley. 47% Cabernet Sauvignon, 29% Merlot, 24% Cabernet Franc. *Cedary, plummy, good crisp acidity, lovely finish. Drink 1989.*

☆☆ 1978 CABERNET SAUVIGNON ($6.00) Napa Valley. *Simple but charming and easy-going.*

☆☆ 1978 CABERNET SAUVIGNON ($8.50) Cask 14, Estate, Napa Valley. *Soft, earthy, leathery, attractive.*

☆☆☆ 1978 CABERNET SAUVIGNON ($14.00) Limited Cask, Estate, Napa Valley. *Soft, elegant, clean and firm. Good aging potential.*

☆☆☆ 1979 CABERNET SAUVIGNON ($7.00) Centennial, Napa. *Clean and nice; herbal and delightful. Drink now.*

☆☆ 1979 CABERNET SAUVIGNON ($14.00) Limited Cask, Centennial, Napa Valley. *Herbal, clean and attractive but slight. Drink now.*

☆ 1980 CABERNET SAUVIGNON ($5.00) Cabinet Selection, Napa Valley. *Herbal, dense, clean, a bit short.*

☆☆ 1980 CABERNET SAUVIGNON ($8.00) Estate, Napa Valley. 12% Merlot. *Soft, clean, simple but nice. Drink now.*

☆☆☆ 1980 CABERNET SAUVIGNON ($9.00) Lot 2, Estate, Napa Valley. *Bright, lush, clean, fruity. Drink now and for the next eight years.*

☆☆☆ 1980 CABERNET SAUVIGNON ($19.00) Limited Cask Reserve, Napa Valley. *Stunning. Crisp, clean, elegant, complex.*

☆ 1981 CABERNET SAUVIGNON ($5.00) Cabinet, Napa Valley. *Lacking varietal definition and depth.*

☆☆☆ 1981 CABERNET SAUVIGNON ($15.50) Limited Cask Reserve, Estate, Napa Valley. *Rich, beautifully structured, clean and complex. A dazzler. Drink 1990 and beyond.*

☆☆☆ 1982 CABERNET SAUVIGNON ($9.00) Estate, Napa Valley. 8% Merlot. *Crisp, lean, herbal, clean and lovely. Drink 1989.*

☆☆☆☆ 1982 CABERNET SAUVIGNON ($18.50) Reserve Cask, Estate, Napa Valley. *Mint and eucalyptus, great structure, superb fruit. Drink 1992.*

☆☆☆ 1983 CABERNET SAUVIGNON ($5.00) Cabinet Selection, Napa Valley. *Lush, deep, ripe, lovely.*

☆☆ 1983 CABERNET SAUVIGNON ($9.50) Estate, Napa Valley. *Herbal, tight, crisp, good structure, clean varietal fruit. Drink now.*

☆☆☆ 1983 CABERNET SAUVIGNON ($30.00) Reunion, Reserve Cask, Estate, Napa Valley. *Crisp, lean, rich, complex, tight. Drink 1994.*

☆☆☆ 1981 CHARBONO ($7.00) Napa Valley. *Crisp, fresh, fruity, delightful.*

☆☆☆ 1982 CHARBONO ($8.00) Estate, Napa Valley. *Rich, fruity, clean, very appealing. Drink now.*

☆ 1983 CHARBONO ($8.00) Estate, Napa Valley. *Tart, lean, earthy, decent, but lacking the richness of previous vintages.*

☆☆ 1980 MERLOT ($10.00) Limited Bottling, Napa Valley. *Soft, lush, clean, well made.*

☆☆ 1981 MERLOT ($12.00) Limited Cask, Estate, Napa Valley. *Rich, deep, clean and varietal.*

☆☆ 1982 MERLOT ($8.50) Limited Bottling, Napa Valley. *Lean, well made, clean, herbal. Drink now.*

☆☆☆ 1983 MERLOT ($11.50) Reserve, Estate, Napa Valley. *Rich herbs, fresh fruit and great acidity. Balanced and nicely structured. Drink now or hold until 1988.*

☆☆☆ 1980 PETITE SIRAH ($6.90) Estate, Napa Valley. *Rich, fruity and very lovely.*

☆☆☆ 1981 PETITE SIRAH ($6.00) Napa Valley. *Varietal, lush, balanced.*

☆☆☆ 1982 PETITE SIRAH ($5.50) Napa Valley. *Crisp, clean, balanced, super.*

☆☆ 1980 PINOT NOIR ($6.00) Napa Valley. *Soft, complex and well balanced.*

☆☆ 1981 PINOT NOIR ($7.50) Napa Valley. *Clean, simple.*

☆ 1982 PINOT NOIR ($7.50) Napa. *Good texture but lacking fruit.*

☆☆☆ 1983 PINOT NOIR ($10.00) Reserve, Napa Valley. *Crisp, snappy, varietal, charming.*

☆☆☆ 1985 PINOT NOIR ($10.00) Napa Valley. *Fruity, crisp, lush, sweet oak, great structure.*

☆ 1980 ZINFANDEL ($5.50) Napa Valley. *Tannic; decent but low in fruit.*

☆☆ 1981 ZINFANDEL ($7.00) Napa Valley. *Claret-style. Clean and balanced.*

☆☆ 1983 ZINFANDEL ($7.50) Napa Valley. *Tart, decent, mature and a bit tired.*

ॐ

## Ingleside Plantation Winery    VIRGINIA
### WHITE

☆☆ NV CHARDONNAY ($8.50) Virginia. *Dense, deep, rich, complex.*

☆ 1983 CHARDONNAY ($10.00) Virginia. *Soft, simple.*

☆☆☆ 1984 CHARDONNAY ($9.00) Virginia. *Lush, clean, lovely, complex, quite remarkable.*

1985 CHARDONNAY ($8.00) Virginia. *Cheesy, sour, unappealing.*

### SPARKLING

☆ NV CHAMPAGNE ($10.00) Virginia. *Yeasty nose; crisp, clean and nice. Méthode champenoise.*

### RED

☆☆ 1983 CABERNET SAUVIGNON ($9.00) Virginia. *Crisp, clean, thin, fresh acidity. Drink 1988.*

☆☆☆ 1984 CABERNET SAUVIGNON ($12.00) Virginia. *15% Merlot. Toasty, rich, balanced, clean. Drink 1989.*

ॐ

INNISFREE *see* Joseph Phelps Vineyards

## Iron Horse Vineyards    SONOMA COUNTY
### WHITE

☆☆ 1982 CHARDONNAY ($13.00) Estate, Green Valley, Sonoma. *Tight and hard at first but softening now.*

☆☆ 1983 CHARDONNAY ($12.00) Estate, Green Valley, Sonoma. *Clean, fresh, tangy, nice oak, pleasant but lacking varietal intensity.*

☆☆☆ 1984 CHARDONNAY ($12.00) Estate, Green Valley, Sonoma. *Lush, clean, rich, fruity, firm.*

☆☆☆ 1984 CHARDONNAY ($13.50) Sonoma. *Big, fruity, elegant and quite lively.*

☆☆☆ 1985 CHARDONNAY ($12.50) Estate, Green Valley, Sonoma. *Crisp, snappy, varietal, with good fruit and firm acidity.*

☆☆☆ 1986 FUME BLANC ($9.25) Alexander Valley. *Snappy fruit and sweet oak, complex but not highly varietal.*

## SPARKLING

☆☆☆ 1981 BLANC DE NOIR ($16.50) Green Valley, Sonoma. *Rich, deep, complex, clean and lovely.*

☆☆ 1981 BLANC DE BLANCS ($18.00) Green Valley, Sonoma. *Dense, lush, clean, charming.*

☆☆ 1981 BRUT ($19.00) Green Valley, Sonoma. *Crisp, lush, good fruit, lovely yeastiness.*

☆☆☆ 1982 BLANC DE BLANCS ($16.50) Green Valley, Sonoma. *Crisp, angular, tangy, with Chardonnay varietal character.*

☆☆☆ 1982 BLANC DE NOIR ($16.50) Estate, Green Valley, Sonoma. *Deep, round, good Pinot Noir character, charming.*

☆☆☆ 1982 BRUT ($16.50) Green Valley, Sonoma. *Lush, round, rich, fruity and clean.*

☆☆☆ 1984 BLANC DE NOIRS ($16.50) Wedding Cuvée, Green Valley, Sonoma. *Smokey, intensely fruity, good finish, elegant.*

☆☆☆ 1984 BRUT ($20.00) Late Disgorged, Estate, Green Valley, Sonoma. *Ripe, fresh, clean, snappy, elegant.*

## RED

☆☆☆ 1978 CABERNET SAUVIGNON ($12.00) Sonoma. *Herbal and elegant, with plenty of time left.*

☆☆☆ 1979 CABERNET SAUVIGNON ($12.00) Alexander Valley. *Soft, balanced, lovely fruit, delightful.*

☆☆☆ 1980 CABERNET SAUVIGNON ($12.00) Estate, Alexander Valley. *Sleek, clean and richly flavored. Drink now.*

☆☆☆☆ 1981 CABERNET SAUVIGNON ($13.50) Estate, Green Valley, Sonoma. *Crisp, beautifully structured, clean and elegant. Drink now.*

☆☆☆ 1982 CABERNET SAUVIGNON ($15.00) Proprietor Grown, Alexander Valley. *Rich fruit, berry flavors, good structure; lovely. Drink 1988.*

☆☆☆ 1983 CABERNET SAUVIGNON ($15.00) Estate, Green Valley, Sonoma. *Lush, lovely, ripe, fruity. Drink 1988.*

☆☆ 1982 PINOT NOIR ($13.50) Estate, Green Valley, Sonoma. *Clean, elegant, varietal.*

☆☆ 1981 ZINFANDEL ($6.50) Alexander Valley. *Varietal and clean; fruity and attractive.*

☆☆ 1982 ZINFANDEL ($7.00) Alexander Valley. *Spicy, rich, hard, intense. Aging nicely.*

☆☆☆ 1983 ZINFANDEL ($7.00) Proprietor Grown, Alexander Valley. *Dark, rich, lush, berried and quite delicious. Drink now.*

એ

## *Jaeger Family Wine Company*  NAPA COUNTY
### WHITE

☆☆ 1985 HUNTER ASHBY CHARDONNAY ($6.00) Napa Valley. *Lush, rich, deep, attractive.*

☆☆ 1985 HUNTER ASHBY FUME BLANC ($4.00) Napa. *Ripe, fat, soft, decent fruit and varietal flavors.*

## RED

☆☆ 1979 MERLOT ($12.00) Inglewood, Napa Valley. *Mellow, complex, rich. Drink now.*

☆☆ 1980 MERLOT ($12.00) Inglewood, Napa Valley. *Rich, berried, clean, good. Drink now.*

☆☆☆ 1981 MERLOT ($12.00) Inglewood, Napa Valley. *Fruity, varietal, attractive. Ready.*

☆ 1982 HUNTER ASHBY MERLOT ($6.50) Napa Valley. *Thin, simple, some earthy flavors, restrained fruit.*

☆☆☆ 1982 MERLOT ($12.75) Inglewood, Napa Valley. *Rich, lush, balanced, clean, complex. Drink 1989.*

☆☆ 1983 MERLOT ($12.75) Inglewood, Napa Valley. *Clean, bright acidity, good fruit and balance. Drink 1989.*

☆ 1985 HUNTER ASHBY MERLOT ($6.50) Napa Valley. *Vegetal, herbal, soft and lushly textured.*

☆☆ 1982 HUNTER ASHBY PINOT NOIR ($7.00) Napa Valley. *Green, vegetal, soft, fruity, clean. Drink now.*

☆☆ 1984 HUNTER ASHBY PINOT NOIR ($7.00) Napa Valley. *Spicy, jammy, varietal, complex, decent.*

≥∂

## *Jekel Vineyard*                    MONTEREY COUNTY

## WHITE

☆☆ 1984 ARROYO BLANC ($6.50) Monterey. *Pinot Blanc. Crisp, earthy, fruity, attractive. Should improve over the next few years. Drink 1988 and beyond.*

☆☆☆ 1981 CHARDONNAY ($16.00) Private Reserve, Home, Monterey. *Toasty, crisp, soft, lush, complex and delicious. Holding up beautifully. A re-release.*

1982 CHARDONNAY ($10.00) Home, Estate, Arroyo Seco. *Oily, heavy, no finesse, unappealing.*

1982 CHARDONNAY ($10.00) Monterey. *Nice fruit and oak but marred by volatile acidity.*

☆☆ 1982 CHARDONNAY ($14.50) Private Reserve, Estate, Monterey. *Clean, fresh, simple at first but now developing complexity.*

1983 CHARDONNAY ($10.50) Monterey. *Heavy, dull, lacking interest.*

○ 1984 CHARDONNAY ($10.50) Arroyo Seco. *Bitter, sour, oily, unappealing.*

☆☆ 1984 CHARDONNAY ($14.50) Estate, Arroyo Seco. *Oily, vegetal, rich, with good balance and structure.*

1984 CHARDONNAY ($16.00) Home, Arroyo Seco. *Flabby, earthy, dull.*

☆☆ 1986 JOHANNISBERG RIESLING ($6.75) Arroyo Seco. *Snappy, tart, fresh, lively, good.*

☆☆ 1986 JOHANNISBERG RIESLING ($10.00) Estate, Arroyo Seco. *Spicy, fresh, some herbs, clean and balanced.*

## RED

1978 CABERNET SAUVIGNON ($12.00) Private Reserve, Estate, Monterey. *Overwhelmed by weediness.*

☆☆☆ 1979 CABERNET SAUVIGNON ($10.00) Estate, Monterey. *Nice fruit, clean, good depth.*

☆ 1979 CABERNET SAUVIGNON ($16.50) Private Reserve, Estate, Monterey. *Weedy, raisiny, oaky, heavy.*

☆ 1981 CABERNET SAUVIGNON ($10.00) 65% Monterey, 35% San Luis Obispo. *Ponderous, heavy, vegetal, with decent varietal character underneath.*

1981 CABERNET SAUVIGNON ($18.00) Private Reserve, Home, Estate, Monterey. *Heavy, vegetal, composty. Maybe it will smooth out in 4 years.*

1982 CABERNET SAUVIGNON ($11.00) Monterey. *Chalky, heavy, concentrated, vegetal.*

☆ 1982 CABERNET SAUVIGNON ($18.00) Private Reserve, Home, Estate, Monterey. *Vegetal, soft, lush, intense, complex, ripe.*

☆☆ 1979 PINOT NOIR ($8.50) Estate, Monterey. *Toasty and clean.*

☆☆ 1980 PINOT NOIR ($9.00) Home, Monterey. *Stemmy but nicely made. Good fruit.*

☆☆ 1981 PINOT NOIR ($9.00) Home, Monterey. *Burgundian but a bit underripe.*

☆ 1982 PINOT NOIR ($9.00) Estate, Arroyo Seco. *Crisp, fruity, clean, with some earth and herbs.*

## Jepson Vineyards                    MENDOCINO
### WHITE
☆☆☆☆ 1985 CHARDONNAY ($12.00) Mendocino. *Round and smooth, great fruit and delicious wood, tangy finish; superb.*

☆☆ 1986 SAUVIGNON BLANC ($7.00) Estate, Mendocino. *Soft, herbal, delicate, clean, attractive.*

## Johnson Turnbull Vineyards        NAPA COUNTY
### RED
☆☆ 1979 CABERNET SAUVIGNON ($10.50) Estate, Napa Valley. *Good structure and fruit. Underripe but pleasant. Drink now.*

☆☆☆ 1980 CABERNET SAUVIGNON ($12.00) Napa Valley. *Balanced and charming now, will improve for years.*

☆☆☆ 1981 CABERNET SAUVIGNON ($12.00) Napa Valley. *Lovely nose, lush, fruity. Not as elegant as the '80. Drink 1988.*

☆☆☆ 1982 CABERNET SAUVIGNON ($12.50) Estate, Napa Valley. *Minty, clean, nicely structured, firm fruit. Drink 1989.*

☆☆☆ 1983 CABERNET SAUVIGNON ($15.00) Estate, Napa Valley. *Very stylish; minty, eucalyptus flavors, ripe currants, intense. Drink 1990.*

☆☆ 1984 CABERNET SAUVIGNON ($14.50) Napa Valley. *Extremely minty, fruity and intense; very rich. Maybe this one will tone down by 1990.*

## Johnson's Alexander Valley Wines    SONOMA COUNTY
### WHITE
☆☆☆ 1985 CHARDONNAY ($6.50) Alexander Valley. *Crisp, clean, fresh, tight fruit and soft oak. A lovely wine.*
### RED
☆☆ 1979 PINOT NOIR ($6.00) Alexander Valley. *Rich, deep, balanced, attractive.*

☆ 1981 PINOT NOIR ($12.00) Alexander Valley. *Lush, overripe, hot, berried.*

☆ 1979 ZINFANDEL ($6.50) Alexander Valley. *Thick, jammy, overdone.*

☆ 1980 ZINFANDEL ($12.00) Late Harvest, Sauers, Alexander Valley. *2.85% residual sugar.*

## Jordan Vineyard and Winery        SONOMA COUNTY
### WHITE
☆☆☆ 1982 CHARDONNAY ($15.75) Alexander Valley. *Crisp, balanced, stylish, elegant.*

○ 1983 CHARDONNAY ($16.00) Estate, Alexander Valley. *Overripe, honeyed, oxidized. Something really went wrong here. Tasted several times.*

☆☆☆ 1984 CHARDONNAY ($15.00) Alexander Valley. *Lush, ripe, intense, oaky, attractive.*

** 1985 CHARDONNAY ($16.00) Alexander Valley. *Thin, tart, decent but minor.*

## RED

☆☆ 1978 CABERNET SAUVIGNON ($16.00) Estate, Alexander Valley. *Rich, earthy, lush and complex.*

☆☆☆ 1979 CABERNET SAUVIGNON ($16.00) Alexander Valley. *8% Merlot. Earthy, well structured, elegant. Ready to drink.*

☆☆☆ 1980 CABERNET SAUVIGNON ($18.00) Estate, Alexander Valley. *Sweet oak and clean flavors, earthy, rich. Drink now.*

☆☆ 1981 CABERNET SAUVIGNON ($18.00) Estate, Alexander Valley. *Elegant, silky, lovely structure, herbaceous. Drink 1988.*

☆☆☆ 1982 CABERNET SAUVIGNON ($18.00) Estate, Alexander Valley. *Soft, lush, herbal, balanced, delicious. Drink 1988.*

☆☆☆ 1983 CABERNET SAUVIGNON ($18.00) Estate, Alexander Valley. *10% Merlot. Crisp, snappy, lively, complex, great fruit, lovely structure. Drink 1989.*

🙚

## Kalin Cellars                    MARIN COUNTY
### WHITE

☆☆☆ 1982 CHARDONNAY ($15.00) Cuvée D, Dutton Ranch, Sonoma. *Unfiltered, rich, lush, heavy, intense; old style.*

☆☆☆ 1982 CHARDONNAY ($16.00) Cuvée L, Sonoma. *Toasty, rich, good fruit.*

☆☆☆☆ 1985 CHARDONNAY ($17.50) Cuvée BL, Potter Valley. *Lush, intense, ripe, balanced, lovely oak and structure.*

☆☆☆ 1985 CHARDONNAY ($17.50) Cuvée L, Sonoma. *Intense without being heavy-handed, richly fruity yet elegant.*

☆☆☆ 1985 CHARDONNAY ($17.50) Cuvée LV, Sonoma. *Hard-edged; closed in but showing great potential. Drink 1990.*

☆☆☆ 1986 CHARDONNAY ($18.00) Sonoma. *Soft, earthy, lush, smooth, complex.*

### RED

☆ 1979 CABERNET SAUVIGNON ($15.00) Santa Barbara. *Clean and well made but very weedy.*

1980 CABERNET SAUVIGNON ($17.95) Tepusquet, Santa Barbara. *Vegetal, asparagus flavor, rich fruit, balanced.*

☆☆ 1979 PINOT NOIR ($12.50) Santa Barbara. *Varietal and rich, with some vegetal notes.*

☆☆ 1981 PINOT NOIR ($15.00) Cuvée WD, Dutton Ranch, Sonoma. *Rich, intense, deep, earthy; quite lovely.*

☆☆☆ 1983 PINOT NOIR ($16.00) Sonoma Valley. *Rich, cherry fruit, ripe, intense flavors, good oak.*

🙚

## Karly                    AMADOR COUNTY
### WHITE

☆☆☆ 1983 CHARDONNAY ($12.00) Tepusquet, Santa Maria Valley. *Lovely, rich, deep, clean.*

☆☆☆ 1984 CHARDONNAY ($12.00) Tepusquet, Santa Maria Valley. *Clean, oaky, lush, lovely.*

○ 1985 CHARDONNAY ($12.00) Santa Maria Valley. *Sour, intensely vegetal, extremely unpleasant.*

## BLANC DE NOIR

☆☆☆ 1986 WHITE ZINFANDEL ($5.25) Amador. *Fresh, lovely fruit, good varietal character, delicious.*

## RED

☆☆ 1980 ZINFANDEL ($7.50) Amador. *Big, spicy, brambly.*

☆☆ 1981 ZINFANDEL ($7.50) Amador. *Berried, rich and clean.*

☆☆ 1982 ZINFANDEL ($7.50) Amador. *Raisiny, intense, with some sweetness.*

☆ 1983 ZINFANDEL ($7.50) Amador. *Decent, clean, lacking fruit.*

1984 ZINFANDEL ($7.50) Amador. *Sour, washed out, awful.*

☆☆☆ 1985 ZINFANDEL ($9.00) Amador. *Lush, concentrated, berry fruit, lovely.*

❧

# Robert Keenan Winery                    NAPA COUNTY

## WHITE

☆☆ 1982 CHARDONNAY ($14.50) Napa Valley. *Clean, crisp, attractive but lacking complexity.*

☆☆☆ 1983 CHARDONNAY ($12.50) Napa Valley. *Soft, ripe, toasty, clean, balanced and quite good.*

☆☆ 1984 CHARDONNAY ($10.75) Napa Valley. *Fresh, clean, balanced, decent flavors and good complexity.*

☆☆☆ 1984 CHARDONNAY ($12.00) Estate, Napa Valley *Full, rich, balanced, clean and quite charming. Lovely oak and round, lush flavors.*

☆☆☆ 1985 CHARDONNAY ($13.00) Estate, Napa Valley *Rich, crisp, clean and well made; need's more fruit intensity.*

## RED

☆☆☆ 1979 CABERNET SAUVIGNON ($12.00) Napa Valley. *Big and lumbering but complex, structured and promising.*

☆☆☆ 1980 CABERNET SAUVIGNON ($12.00) Napa Valley. *Dark, dense, berried, with good acidity. Lovely. Drink now.*

☆☆☆ 1981 CABERNET SAUVIGNON ($12.00) Napa Valley. *Lovely, crisp, clean, varietal, balanced. Drink 1988.*

☆☆☆ 1982 CABERNET SAUVIGNON ($12.50) 90% Estate, 5% Carneros, 5% Napa Valley, Napa Valley. 10% Merlot. *Tart and fruity, with firm structure and rich flavors. Drink 1988.*

☆☆☆ 1983 CABERNET SAUVIGNON ($10.75) Napa Valley. *Crisp, firm, intensely fruity, beautifully built. A classic Spring Mountain Cabernet. Drink 1990.*

☆☆☆ 1985 CABERNET SAUVIGNON ($12.00) Napa Valley. *Lush, soft, smooth, clean, lovely balance. Drink 1989.*

☆☆ 1978 MERLOT ($9.00) Napa Valley. *Peppery, clean and rich. Drink now or hold.*

☆☆☆ 1979 MERLOT ($11.00) Napa Valley. *Rich, fruity, lush, cherry-flavored. Lovely. Drink now or hold.*

☆☆☆☆ 1982 MERLOT ($12.50) Napa Valley. *Lush, fresh, complex, with beautiful fruit flavors. Drink 1988.*

☆☆☆☆ 1983 MERLOT ($15.00) Napa Valley. 4% Cabernet Sauvignon. *Crisp, tart, richly varietal, quite superb. Drink 1988.*

☆☆☆☆ 1984 MERLOT ($16.00) Napa Valley. *Big berry flavors, smooth, complex, great structure. Good now, better in 1989.*

❧

## *Kendall-Jackson Vineyards & Winery*   LAKE COUNTY

### WHITE

☆☆ 1983 CHARDONNAY ($9.50) Reserve, Santa Barbara 23%, Napa 21%, Monterey 20%, California. *Simple, fruity, lacking varietal definition, decent.*

☆☆☆ 1983 CHARDONNAY ($9.50) Vintner's Reserve, California. *Charming, ripe, balanced, clean and fruity.*

☆☆ 1983 CHARDONNAY ($11.00) Royale, California. *Fruity, lush, clean, attractive.*

☆☆ 1984 CHARDONNAY ($9.50) Vintner's Reserve, California. *Same regional blend as the '82. 0.65% residual sugar. Soft, ripe, clean, easy and pleasant. Better than the '82.*

☆☆ 1984 CHARDONNAY ($13.00) Royale, California. *Clean, fresh, balanced, a bit simple.*

☆☆ 1984 CHARDONNAY ($13.50) Proprietor's Reserve, California. *Crisp, clean, fruity, overripe, decent.*

☆☆☆ 1985 CHARDONNAY ($9.50) Vintner's Reserve, California. *Clean, fruity, dense, ripe, delicious.*

☆☆☆ 1985 CHARDONNAY ($18.00) Proprietor's Reserve, California. *Oaky and lush, with intense flavors; powerful, but lacking finesse.*

☆☆☆ 1986 CHARDONNAY ($10.00) Vintner's Reserve, California. *Ripe, lush, rich, deep, intense, good balance.*

☆☆ 1983 JOHANNISBERG RIESLING ($15.00) Late Harvest, Anderson Valley. *375 ml. 20.6% residual sugar. Grapey, lush, balanced, attractive.*

☆☆☆ 1985 MUSCAT ($7.50) Lake. *4% residual sugar. Spicy, crisp, clean, lively.*

☆☆☆ 1985 SAUVIGNON BLANC ($8.00) Chevriot, Lake. *22% Semillon. Crisp, fresh, spicy, with great fruit and balance.*

☆☆☆ 1986 SAUVIGNON BLANC ($8.00) Clear Lake. *Fresh, smokey, ripe, spritzy, with lovely fig flavors.*

☆☆☆☆ 1986 SAUVIGNON BLANC ($11.00) Jackson, Lake. *Rich, fruity, lush, lovely oak and luxurious complexity. Remarkable.*

### RED

☆☆ 1982 CABERNET SAUVIGNON ($7.00) Clear Lake. *Ripe, balanced, some weediness, pleasant, clean. Drink now.*

☆☆ 1983 CABERNET SAUVIGNON ($9.00) Cardinale, California. *Fruity, lush, fat, sweet oak. Drink now.*

☆☆☆ 1984 CABERNET SAUVIGNON ($7.50) Lake. *Lush, soft, clean, lovely ripe fruit; charming. Drink now.*

☆☆ 1984 CABERNET SAUVIGNON ($8.50) Anderson Valley. *Clean, fruity, appealing.*

☆☆☆ 1984 CABERNET SAUVIGNON ($12.00) Cardinale, California. *Fresh, rich, ripe, smokey, supple, fruity; lovely stuff. Drink now.*

☆☆☆ 1983 ZINFANDEL ($7.00) Viña-Las Lomas, Clear Lake. *Light, fruity, fresh, Beaujolais-style.*

☆☆☆ 1983 ZINFANDEL ($7.00) Zeni, Mendocino. *Stunning, rich, lovely fruit, balanced, new oak, wonderful.*

☆☆☆ 1983 ZINFANDEL ($10.00) DuPratt-DePatie, Mendocino. *Rich, rounded, complex, loaded with fruit. Drink now.*

☆☆☆☆ 1984 ZINFANDEL ($8.00) Mariah, Mendocino. *Rich and buttery, with lush fruit and charming spiciness.*

☆☆ 1984 ZINFANDEL ($9.00) Zeni, Mendocino. *A dense, rich wine with plenty of berry and oak flavors. Should mellow out nicely. Drink 1988.*

☆☆☆ 1984 ZINFANDEL ($10.00) Ciapusci, Mendocino. *Ripe, spicy, tart, fruity, crisp, clean.*

☆☆☆ 1984 ZINFANDEL ($12.00) DuPratt-DePatie, Mendocino. *Snappy, cherry fruit, lovely structure, long, crisp finish.*

☆☆ 1985 ZINFANDEL ($10.00) Ciapusci, Mendocino. *Tart, with some brambly, bitter flavors; rich but lean structure.*

☆☆☆ 1986 ZINFANDEL ($8.00) Mendocino. *Lean, balanced, spicy, crisp, brambly fruit.*

☆☆ 1986 ZINFANDEL ($10.00) Ciapusci, Mendocino. *Tart, crisp, ripe flavors; intense and astringent. Drink 1989.*

ॐ

## Kathryn Kennedy Winery　　SANTA CLARA COUNTY
### RED

☆ 1979 CABERNET SAUVIGNON ($12.00) Estate, Santa Cruz Mountains. *Spicy, intense, lacking structure, with plum and tobacco flavors.*

☆ 1981 CABERNET SAUVIGNON ($12.00) Estate, Santa Cruz Mountains. *Aging quickly, losing its freshness. Drink now.*

☆☆ 1983 CABERNET SAUVIGNON ($18.00) Santa Cruz Mountains. *Ripe, berried, lush, fat, raisiny, intense. Drink 1990.*

ॐ

## Kenwood Vineyards　　SONOMA COUNTY
### WHITE

☆ 1985 VINTAGE TABLE WHITE ($4.50) California. *64% Sauvignon Blanc, 36% Chenin Blanc. Sappy, sweet, some odd flavors.*

☆☆ 1982 CHARDONNAY ($14.00) Beltane Ranch, Sonoma Valley. *Balanced, fruity and rich, with lovely oak and depth.*

☆☆ 1983 CHARDONNAY ($9.50) Sonoma Valley. *Clean, decent, fresh, a bit flabby.*

☆☆☆ 1983 CHARDONNAY ($12.50) Yulupa, Sonoma Valley. *Crisp, fruity, balanced, forward yet well proportioned.*

☆☆☆ 1983 CHARDONNAY ($14.00) Beltane, Sonoma Valley. *Rich, oaky, deep, complex, balanced.*

☆☆☆ 1984 CHARDONNAY ($9.50) Sonoma Valley. *Crisp, round, snappy, nice fruit and finish.*

☆☆☆ 1984 CHARDONNAY ($12.50) Yulupa, Sonoma Valley. *Soft, lush, deep, round, fresh.*

☆☆☆ 1984 CHARDONNAY ($14.00) Beltane Ranch, Sonoma Valley. *Rich, deep, crisp, lovely, balanced.*

☆☆ 1985 CHARDONNAY ($12.50) Yulupa, Sonoma Valley. *Crisp, balanced, tight fruit, lacking depth.*

☆☆☆ 1984 JOHANNISBERG RIESLING ($10.00) Late Harvest, Sonoma. *375 ml. 8.64% residual sugar. Fruity, balanced, luscious, lovely.*

☆☆☆☆ 1985 JOHANNISBERG RIESLING ($10.00) Late Harvest, Estate, Sonoma. *11.35% residual sugar. Lush, exquisitely balanced, crisp acidity; stunning.*

☆☆☆☆ 1986 SAUVIGNON BLANC ($8.75) Sonoma Valley. *Crisp, snappy, lively melon fruit, varietal, lovely. Great finish.*

## BLANC DE NOIR

☆☆☆ 1986 WHITE ZINFANDEL ($5.75) Sonoma Valley. *Rich, lovely fruit, good varietal character, clean and tangy.*

## RED

☆ 1982 VINTAGE TABLE RED ($4.50) California. *47% Cabernet Sauvignon. Herbal, rich, clean.*

☆☆ 1983 VINTAGE TABLE RED ($4.50) California. *Decent, clean, simple.*

☆☆ 1978 CABERNET SAUVIGNON ($8.50) Sonoma Valley. *37% Merlot. Deep and lush. Drink 1988 and beyond.*

☆ 1978 CABERNET SAUVIGNON ($10.00) Jack London, Sonoma Valley. *Supple, ripe but short and lacking depth. Drink now.*

☆☆☆ 1978 CABERNET SAUVIGNON ($20.00) Artist Series, Laurel Glen & Steiner, Sonoma Valley. *Intense fruit and rich flavors. Drink now or hold for a few more years.*

☆☆☆ 1979 CABERNET SAUVIGNON ($20.00) Artist Series, Sonoma Valley. *Rich, rounded and fruity. Drink now.*

1980 CABERNET SAUVIGNON ($12.00) Jack London, Sonoma Valley. *Dense and vegetal, tannic, clean but unattractive.*

☆ 1980 CABERNET SAUVIGNON ($12.00) Sonoma Valley. *Heavy, vegetal, clean but unpleasant.*

☆☆ 1980 CABERNET SAUVIGNON ($25.00) Artist Series, Sonoma Valley. *Some weeds, some depth, good fruit and structure. Drink 1988.*

☆ 1981 CABERNET SAUVIGNON ($8.50) Sonoma. *16% Merlot. Earthy, simple, decent.*

☆☆☆ 1981 CABERNET SAUVIGNON ($12.50) Jack London, Sonoma Valley. *Lush, deep, charming, ripe, fruity, attractive.*

☆☆ 1981 CABERNET SAUVIGNON ($25.00) Artist Series, Sonoma Valley. *Herbed, rich, dense, big, lush. Drink 1988.*

☆☆☆ 1982 CABERNET SAUVIGNON ($10.00) Sonoma. *Clean, intense, lush, complex, heavy. Drink 1990.*

☆☆ 1982 CABERNET SAUVIGNON ($12.50) Jack London, Sonoma Valley. *Clean, herbal, fruity, decent. Drink 1987.*

☆☆☆ 1982 CABERNET SAUVIGNON ($25.00) Artist Series, Sonoma Valley. *Herbs and blackberries, deep, beautifully structured. Drink 1990.*

☆☆ 1983 CABERNET SAUVIGNON ($10.00) Sonoma Valley. *Clean, tight fruit, good balance, tannic.*

☆☆☆ 1983 CABERNET SAUVIGNON ($12.50) Jack London, Sonoma Valley. *Lush, ripe, earthy, clean, bright fruit flavors. Drink 1989.*

☆☆☆☆ 1983 CABERNET SAUVIGNON ($30.00) Artist Series, Sonoma Valley. *Lush, rich, deep, ripe, complex, superb. Drink 1993.*

☆☆☆☆ 1984 CABERNET SAUVIGNON ($16.00) Jack London, Sonoma Valley. *Velvety, lush plums and chocolate, very lovely. Drink 1989.*

☆☆☆☆ 1984 CABERNET SAUVIGNON ($30.00) Artist Series, Sonoma Valley. *Lively, cherry and plum flavors; elegant and rich, with great aging potential. Drink 1992.*

☆☆ 1981 PINOT NOIR ($10.00) Jack London, Sonoma. *Fruity, clean, varietal, lacking depth but quite charming.*

☆☆☆ 1982 ZINFANDEL ($7.50) Sonoma Valley. *Lovely, intense, rich fruit, fresh raspberry flavors.*

☆☆☆ 1983 ZINFANDEL ($7.50) Sonoma Valley. *Clean, fresh, lovely, varietal. Good oak and persistent fruit.*

☆☆☆ 1984 ZINFANDEL ($8.50) Sonoma Valley. *Lively, crisp, assertive, good balance, attractive.*

❧

## Kenworthy Vineyards                    AMADOR COUNTY
### WHITE
☆☆ 1985 CHARDONNAY ($7.00) Stonebarn, El Dorado. *Clean, crisp, decent, good oak.*

### RED
☆☆ 1982 CABERNET SAUVIGNON ($6.00) Stonebarn, El Dorado. *Rich, meaty, crisp, snappy, nice varietal fruit. Drink 1988.*

☆ 1982 ZINFANDEL ($5.00) Potter-Cowan, Amador. *Grapey, rich, simple, earthy, decent.*

❧

## Kiona Vineyards and Winery          WASHINGTON
### WHITE
☆☆ 1985 CHARDONNAY ($9.00) Barrel Fermented, Estate, Yakima Valley. *Lush, earthy, ripe, fat, decent.*

☆☆ 1985 WHITE RIESLING ($6.25) Late Harvest, Estate, Yakima Valley. *6% residual sugar. Soft, fresh, fruity, attractive.*

### ROSE
☆☆ 1985 MERLOT ROSE ($5.25) Washington. *Herbal, crisp, rich, very attractive.*

### RED
☆☆☆ 1983 CABERNET SAUVIGNON ($12.00) Estate, Yakima Valley. *Lush fruit, crisp acidity, lovely varietal flavors. Drink 1988.*

❧

## Kistler Vineyards                    SONOMA COUNTY
### WHITE
☆☆☆ 1982 CHARDONNAY ($12.50) Sonoma-Cutrer, California. *Rich and toasty yet exquisitely balanced. A classic.*

☆☆☆ 1982 CHARDONNAY ($15.00) Dutton Ranch, Sonoma. *Rich and vinous, with good acid and fruit; high alcohol.*

☆ 1983 CHARDONNAY ($10.50) Sonoma Valley. *Oaky but short on fruit.*

☆☆☆ 1983 CHARDONNAY ($12.00) Napa Valley. *Crisp, clean, balanced, lovely oak.*

☆☆☆ 1983 CHARDONNAY ($14.00) Winery Lake, California. *Big, rich, toasty, fruity, intense.*

☆☆☆ 1983 CHARDONNAY ($15.00) Dutton Ranch, Sonoma. *Clean, crisp, balanced, oaky.*

☆☆☆ 1984 CHARDONNAY ($12.50) Sonoma. *Fruity, lush, clean, lovely, soft fruit. A charmer.*

☆☆☆☆ 1984 CHARDONNAY ($15.00) Dutton Ranch, Sonoma. *Lush, fruity, round, balanced, sweet oakiness and elegance.*

☆☆☆ 1985 CHARDONNAY ($15.00) Dutton Ranch, Winery Lake, California. *Crisp, lean, nicely built, good fruit and varietal character.*

☆☆☆ 1985 CHARDONNAY ($15.00) Sonoma. *Rich, balanced, fruity and smooth.*

☆☆☆ 1986 CHARDONNAY ($14.50) Durell, Sonoma Valley. *Snappy, bright, clean and balanced, with lively fruit and delicate oak.*

☆☆☆ 1986 CHARDONNAY ($16.50) Dutton Ranch, Russian River Valley *Bright, crisp fruit; clean, rich, somewhat oily flavors.*

☆☆☆☆ 1986 CHARDONNAY ($18.00) Kistler, Sonoma Valley. *Smooth, balanced, elegant fruit, sweet new oak; complex and superbly structured.*

### RED

☆☆ 1979 CABERNET SAUVIGNON ($18.00) Glen Ellen, California. *Big and somewhat awkward; obviously good but not likable.*

☆ 1979 CABERNET SAUVIGNON ($20.00) Veeder Hills-Veeder Peak, California. *Complex but essentially strange.*

☆☆☆ 1980 CABERNET SAUVIGNON ($16.00) Veeder Hills-Veeder Peak, Napa. *Herbal, rich and snappy; clean. Drink 1988 and beyond.*

☆☆☆ 1980 CABERNET SAUVIGNON ($20.00) Glen Ellen, California. *Big, rich, complex, with delicacy and finesse.*

☆☆☆ 1981 CABERNET SAUVIGNON ($12.00) Veeder Hills-Veeder Peak, California. *Rich and dense, with excellent structure and aging potential.*

☆☆☆ 1982 CABERNET SAUVIGNON ($11.00) Veeder Hills-Napa Valley. *Lush, deep, dense, with good fruit and oak.*

☆☆☆ 1983 CABERNET SAUVIGNON ($13.50) Veeder Hills. *Tart, lovely varietal fruit, complex. Drink 1989.*

☆☆ 1979 PINOT NOIR ($16.00) Winery Lake, California. *Powerful but still awkward. Further aging may help.*

☆☆ 1983 PINOT NOIR ($10.00) 90% Winery Lake, 10% Dutton Ranch, California. *Spicy, clean, lean, lacking some depth but quite attractive.*

🍃

## Klingshirn Winery OHIO
### WHITE
1985 SEYVAL BLANC ($4.50) Ohio. *Sour, simple.*

🍃

## Knapp Farms NEW YORK
### WHITE
☆☆ NV WINDMILL CHABLIS ($4.00) Finger Lakes. *Seyal Blanc. Sweet, clean, fresh, charming.*

NV WINDMILL WHITE TABLE WINE ($4.00) New York. *47.5% Cayuga, 47.5% Seyval, 5% Chardonnay. Sour, odd, unattractive.*

○ 1983 CHARDONNAY ($8.00) Finger Lakes. *Rotting wood and grapes; dirty, unpleasant.*

### RED
○ 1982 CABERNET SAUVIGNON ($16.00) New York. *Bitter, composty, medicinal.*

🍃

## Knudsen-Erath Winery OREGON
### WHITE
1985 CHARDONNAY ($10.00) Vintage Select, Estate, Willamette Valley. *Heavy, overdone, coarse, lacking fruit and finesse. Some oxidation.*

○ 1986 CHARDONNAY ($8.00) Estate, Willamette Valley. *Dank, heavy, oxidized, ugly.*

## RED

☆☆☆ NV CABERNET SAUVIGNON ($8.00) Oregon. *Tart, crisp, fresh berry flavors. Good structure and charming finish. Drink now.*

☆☆ NV PINOT NOIR ($6.00) Willamette Valley. *Crisp, varietal, some volatile acidity, attractive.*

☆☆☆ 1982 PINOT NOIR ($12.25) Vintage Select, Yamhill. *Lush, rich, deep, clean, lovely, complex.*

☆☆☆ 1983 PINOT NOIR ($12.50) Vintage Select, Yamhill. *Crisp, fruity, balanced, clean, complex, elegant.*

☆☆☆ 1986 PINOT NOIR ($10.00) Willamette Valley. *Peppery, bright, crisp, tart, cherry finish; a bit thin, but quite attractive.*

🙚

## *Konocti Winery*      LAKE COUNTY

### WHITE

☆☆ 1985 CHARDONNAY ($6.50) Lake. *Soft, fresh, clean, simple but at tractive.*

☆☆☆ 1986 CHARDONNAY ($6.50) Lake. *Bright, fresh, clean, focused, with lovely fruit and balance.*

☆☆☆ 1986 FUME BLANC ($5.50) Lake. *Lively, crisp, herbal, clean.*

☆☆☆ 1986 WHITE RIESLING ($5.50) Lake. *Crisp, fresh, tangy, peachy fruit, clean finish.*

### RED

☆☆ 1979 CABERNET SAUVIGNON ($6.00) Estate, Lake. *Herbaceous, balanced, well made. Drink now.*

☆☆ 1979 CABERNET SAUVIGNON ($6.00) Lot II, Lake. *Earthy, varietal, clean and appealing. Drink now.*

☆☆ 1980 CABERNET SAUVIGNON ($6.50) Lake. *5% Cabernet Franc. Fruity, oaky, attractive. Drink now.*

☆ 1982 CABERNET SAUVIGNON ($5.50) Lake. *14.5% Merlot, 8.8% Cabernet Franc. Simple, slight, herbal, nice.*

☆☆ 1983 CABERNET SAUVIGNON ($5.75) Lake. *Herbs, tobacco, soft fruit. Drink now.*

1980 ZINFANDEL ($5.00) Primitivo, Late Harvest, Lake. *375 ml. 8.5% residual sugar. Peppery, odd, decent.*

☆☆ 1981 ZINFANDEL ($4.75) Lake. *Fruity, clean and attractive in a simple style.*

🙚

## *F. Korbel and Brothers*      SONOMA COUNTY

### SPARKLING

☆ NV ROSE-PINK CHAMPAGNE ($9.00) California. *Fresh berry flavors.*

☆ NV BRUT ($10.00) California. *Dull, sweet, decent.*

☆☆ NV BLANC DE BLANC ($12.50) California. *100% Chardonnay. Fresh, fruity, coarse, decent.*

☆ NV BLANC DE NOIR ($12.50) California. *Heavy, grapey, decent.*

☆ NV EXTRA DRY ($12.85) California. *Clean and balanced but heavy and a bit coarse.*

☆☆ NV BRUT NATURAL ($13.50) California. *Fruity, clean, fresh, pleasant.*

🙚

## *Hanns Kornell Champagne Cellars*    NAPA COUNTY

### SPARKLING

○ NV ROSE ($9.75) Dry, California. *Off odors and flavors.*

○ NV BRUT ($10.75) California. *Méthode champenoise. Heavy, oily flavors.*

NV MUSCAT ALEXANDRIA ($11.00) California. *Bitter, unpleasant.*

   NV  SEHR TROCKEN ($14.00) California. *Strange, off fla-
         vors, clean.*
☆☆☆  1982 BLANC DE BLANCS ($14.75) California. *100% Char-
         donnay. Rich, fruity, clean, balanced, complex.
         Easily the best Kornell wine ever.*
   ○  1984 BLANC DE NOIR ($14.75) California. *Bitter, flat, metal-
         lic, awful.*

                              ⋙

## Charles Krug Winery                          NAPA COUNTY
### WHITE
   ☆  1983 CHARDONNAY ($10.00) Napa Valley. *Fresh, fruity,
         clean, simple, with some modest apppeal.*
  ☆☆  1984 CHARDONNAY ($10.00) Napa Valley. *Clean, fresh, va-
         rietal, simple but attractive.*
   ○  1984 CHARDONNAY ($15.00) Brown Ranch, Los Carneros.
         *Sour, oxidized, unattractive.*
      1984 CHARDONNAY ($15.00) Cabral Ranch, Los Carneros.
         *Fat and lush, with some off flavors.*
      1986 C.K. MONDAVI CHARDONNAY ($4.50) California.
         *Flat, simple, not varietal.*
   ☆  1986 CHARDONNAY ($10.00) Carneros. *Flat, decent, clean
         but dull.*
   ☆  1986 JOHANNISBERG RIESLING ($7.00) Napa Valley.
         *Ripe, heavy, oily.*
☆☆☆  1986 SAUVIGNON BLANC ($6.75) Napa Valley. *Tart, herbal,
         clean, good fruit.*
### BLANC DE NOIR
   ☆  1986 WHITE ZINFANDEL ($4.00) Sonoma-Green Valley.
         *Soft, sweet, dull, watery.*
   ☆  1986 WHITE ZINFANDEL ($5.50) North Coast. *Dull, flat,
         lacking fruit.*
### RED
  ☆☆  1978 CABERNET SAUVIGNON ($12.50) Vintage Selection,
         Napa Valley. *Rich, oaky and beginning to show
         some age.*
  ☆☆  1979 CABERNET SAUVIGNON ($6.50) Napa Valley. *Earthy,
         grapey, pleasant. Drink now.*
      1981 CABERNET SAUVIGNON ($7.00) Napa Valley. *Chal-
         ky, some berry fruit, intense, not together.*
☆☆☆  1982 CABERNET SAUVIGNON ($7.00) Napa Valley. *Soft,
         herbal, richly fruity, good balance. Drink 1990.*
  ☆☆  1982 C. K. MONDAVI CABERNET SAUVIGNON ($7.00)
         California. *1.5 liters. Snappy, clean, fruity, attrac-
         tive. Drink now.*
   ☆  1983 C.K.MONDAVI CABERNET SAUVIGNON ($4.50)
         Napa Valley. *Simple, decent, marginal.*
  ☆☆  1978 MERLOT ($7.00) Napa Valley. *Leathery and older in
         style.*
  ☆☆  1979 PINOT NOIR ($5.50) Napa Valley. *Clean, balanced,
         pleasant.*
   ☆  1984 PINOT NOIR ($6.00) Napa Valley. *Tangy, tart, simple.*
  ☆☆  1979 ZINFANDEL ($4.80) Napa. *Jammy and intense.*

                              ⋙

## Thomas Kruse Winery              SANTA CLARA COUNTY
### SPARKLING
   ☆  NV  BLANC DE BLANCS ($10.00) San Benito. *Méthode
         champenoise. Clean, simple and attractive.*
### RED
   NV  GILROY RED ($4.50) Santa Clara. *100% Cabernet Sau-
         vignon. Quite vegetal.*

☆ 1982 GRIGNOLINO ($5.00) Santa Clara. *Floral, astringent, snappy.*

☆ 1981 CABERNET SAUVIGNON ($7.00) Santa Clara. *Grapey, simple, decent.*

🍃

L'ANNÉE *see* Buena Vista Winery

LA BELLE *see* Raymond Vineyard & Cellar

## *La Buena Vida Vineyards*                    TEXAS
### WHITE
○ 1985 RAYON D'OR ($8.00) Parker. *1.8% residual sugar. Brown, oxidized, awful.*
### SPARKLING
NV BLANC DE BLANC ($11.00) Texas. *Dull, simple, oxidized.*
### BLANC DE NOIR
☆☆ 1986 SPRINGTOWN MIST ($4.00) Parker. *2.8% residual sugar. Crisp, fresh, cherry flavors, lovely.*
### RED
☆ 1986 ESPRIT ($4.00) Parker. *1.2% residual sugar. Crisp, fresh, clean, thin.*

🍃

## *La Chiripada Winery*              NEW MEXICO
### RED
☆ 1983 MARECHAL FOCH ($6.75) New Mexico. *Deep, clean, decent.*

🍃

## *La Crema*                    SONOMA COUNTY
### WHITE
1982 CHARDONNAY ($13.50) Winery Lake, Napa Valley. *Lush, intense, oxidized, very oaky.*

☆ 1982 CHARDONNAY ($16.00) Ventana, Monterey. *Very oaky and big, awkward and heavy.*

1983 CHARDONNAY ($9.00) Green Valley. *Overwhelmed by oak. Bitter, unpleasant.*

☆☆☆ 1984 CHARDONNAY ($11.00) California. *Rich barrel-fermented flavors, oaky, deep, delicious.*

☆☆☆☆ 1985 CHARDONNAY ($11.00) California. *Lovely structure, toasty oak, delicious fruit. Complex but restrained.*

☆☆☆☆ 1985 CHARDONNAY ($18.00) Reserve, California. *Butter and oak, lush fruit, long Burgundian toast. Elegant; superb.*

☆☆ 1985 CHARDONNAY ($18.00) Reserve, Napa Valley. *Smokey, intense, butterscotch flavors, good balance.*

### RED
☆☆☆ 1979 PINOT NOIR ($14.50) Winery Lake, Carneros District. *Earthy and fresh, with good fruit and considerable complexity.*

☆☆ 1980 PINOT NOIR ($15.00) Ventana, Monterey. *Rich, appealingly varietal, needs age. Lots of sediment.*

☆☆ 1982 PINOT NOIR ($9.00) Vineburg, Carneros District, Sonoma. *Big and earthy, with great depth.*

☆☆ 1982 PINOT NOIR ($10.00) Winery Lake, Napa Valley-Carneros. *Thin, acidic but quite Burgundian.*

☆☆☆☆ 1982 PINOT NOIR ($10.00) Porter Creek, Russian River Valley. *Violets, rich, lovely, complex, elegant, superb.*

☆☆☆☆ 1984 PINOT NOIR ($14.00) California. *Complex, elegant, mature, remarkable structure and balance.*

🍃

## La Jota Vineyard Company                    NAPA COUNTY
### WHITE
☆☆☆ 1986 VIOGNIER ($16.00) Howell Mountain. *Crisp but rich;
soft and quite complex. A splendid non-
Chardonnay.*
### RED
☆☆☆ 1983 CABERNET SAUVIGNON ($15.00) Howell Mountain-
Napa Valley. *Tight, crisp, good structure, good
fruit. Drink 1990.*
☆☆☆ 1984 CABERNET SAUVIGNON ($15.00) Howell Mountain.
*Long, lovely, lush, wonderfully structured and
deep. Drink 1992.*
☆☆ 1984 ZINFANDEL ($10.00) Howell Mountain. *Intense,
earthy, concentrated, nicely structured but hot and
bitter from high alcohol.*

&.

LA MARJOLAINE *see* Domaine Michel
LAMONT *see* Perelli–Minetti Winery

## La Reina                    MONTEREY COUNTY
### WHITE
☆☆☆ 1984 CHARDONNAY ($12.00) Monterey. *Soft, fruity, clean,
lovely oak.*

&.

## La Vieille Montagne                    SONOMA COUNTY
### RED
☆☆ 1981 CABERNET SAUVIGNON ($9.00) Sonoma. *Extremely
tart and astringent, with good, deep, clean varietal
flavors. I wonder if it will ever soften up. Drink
1991.*

&.

## Lafayette Vineyards                    FLORIDA
### WHITE
☆ NV STOVER ($9.00) Special Reserve, Florida. *Grapey,
sweet, strange but clean and balanced.*

&.

## Laird Vineyards                    NAPA COUNTY
### WHITE
☆ 1983 CHARDONNAY ($11.00) Napa Valley. *Lean, earthy,
oily, lacking fruit, decent.*
### RED
☆☆☆ 1980 CABERNET SAUVIGNON ($11.00) Napa Valley. *Clean,
balanced, elegant. Drink now.*
☆☆ 1982 CABERNET SAUVIGNON ($11.00) Napa Valley. *Tart,
firm, snappy fruit, herbal flavors. Drink 1989.*

&.

## Lake Sonoma Winery                    SONOMA COUNTY
### RED
☆☆ 1978 CABERNET SAUVIGNON North Coast. *Soft, dense,
earthy, decent. Drink now.*
☆☆☆ 1978 DIABLO VISTA CABERNET SAUVIGNON ($9.00)
North Coast. *3% Merlot. Earthy, rich, delightful
for current drinking.*
1981 CABERNET SAUVIGNON ($9.50) Dry Creek Valley.
*Berried, sweetish, some volatility.*
☆☆ 1980 DIABLO VISTA MERLOT ($8.50) Polson, Dry Creek
Valley. *Grapey and simple; good texture, rich and
forward.*

☆☆ 1981 DIABLO VISTA MERLOT ($7.50) Sonoma. *Big, berried, Zinfandel-like. Not varietal but still interesting.*

○ 1982 MERLOT ($9.00) Dry Creek Valley. *Sour, volatile acidity, unappealing.*

☆☆☆ 1980 DIABLO VISTA ZINFANDEL ($6.90) Polson, Dry Creek Valley, Sonoma. *Earthy, complex, big.*

☆☆ 1981 ZINFANDEL ($6.90) Dry Creek Valley. *Grapey, rich, clean, attractive.*

☆☆☆ 1981 DIABLO VISTA ZINFANDEL ($6.90) Dry Creek Valley. *Grapey, rich, fruity, clean, with great acidity. Super.*

1982 ZINFANDEL ($6.50) Dry Creek Valley. *Sour, unattractive.*

ॐ

## Lakespring Winery                    NAPA COUNTY
### WHITE

☆☆ 1983 CHARDONNAY ($11.50) Napa Valley. *Heavy, rich, oaky.*

☆☆☆ 1984 CHARDONNAY ($11.00) Napa Valley. *Fresh, balanced, crisp and fruity. A lovely wine.*

☆☆☆ 1985 CHARDONNAY ($11.00) Napa Valley. *Lean, firmly structured, with good fruit and oak flavors.*

### RED

☆☆ 1980 CABERNET SAUVIGNON ($11.00) Napa Valley. *Ripe, clean, raisiny, with some vegetal qualities.*

☆☆☆☆ 1981 CABERNET SAUVIGNON ($11.00) Napa Valley. *Rich, fat, lush, superbly complex and beautifully structured. Drink now.*

☆☆☆ 1982 CABERNET SAUVIGNON ($14.00) Napa Valley. *Ripe, velvety, soft, intense, balanced, superb. Drink 1989.*

☆☆ 1983 CABERNET SAUVIGNON ($11.00) Napa Valley. *Smokey, oaky, lacking fruit, some bitterness. Drink 1989.*

☆☆ 1980 MERLOT ($9.00) Napa Valley. *Lush and well structured but just a bit vegetal.*

☆☆☆ 1981 MERLOT ($10.00) Napa Valley. *Rich, varietal, attractive. Drink now.*

☆☆☆ 1983 MERLOT ($11.00) Napa Valley. *Rich, balanced, complex, clean, lovely fruit. Drink now.*

☆☆☆ 1984 MERLOT ($12.00) Napa Valley. *Tart, crisp, good firm fruit, balanced. Drink 1989.*

ॐ

## Ronald Lamb Winery          SANTA CLARA COUNTY
### RED

☆ 1979 ZINFANDEL ($6.50) Upton Ranch, Amador. *Clumsy and harsh.*

ॐ

## Lambert Bridge                    SONOMA COUNTY
### WHITE

☆☆☆ 1982 CHARDONNAY ($13.00) Sonoma. *Crisp, balanced, clean, complex, lovely, vinous.*

☆☆☆ 1983 CHARDONNAY ($13.50) Sonoma. *Clean, crisp, apple fruit.*

☆ 1984 CHARDONNAY ($11.00) Sonoma. *Clean, simple, fruity.*

☆☆ 1985 CHARDONNAY ($11.25) Sonoma. *Earthy, soft, clean, ripe.*

### RED

1980 CABERNET SAUVIGNON ($8.00) Sonoma. *Simple, weedy.*

☆ 1981 CABERNET SAUVIGNON ($11.00) Sonoma. *Clean, snappy, balanced but very vegetal. Drink now.*

☆☆ 1984 CABERNET SAUVIGNON ($11.75) Sonoma. *Lush, ripe, herbal, attractive. Drink 1989.*

☆ 1981 MERLOT ($11.50) Sonoma. *Weedy, lush and complex. Drink now.*

☆☆ 1982 MERLOT ($11.50) Sonoma. *Soft and rich but vegetal.*

☆ 1983 MERLOT ($11.50) Sonoma. *25% Cabernet Sauvignon. Herbaceous, lean, unappealing.*

☆☆ 1985 MERLOT ($10.00) Sonoma. *Weedy, lush, deep, overdone, decent.*

❧

## Landmark Vineyards                    SONOMA COUNTY
### WHITE
☆☆☆ 1982 CHARDONNAY ($9.50) Sonoma. *Fresh and clean, with crisp acid and good balance.*

☆☆ 1982 CHARDONNAY ($10.00) Proprietor Grown, Alexander Valley. *Vinous, intense, lacking finesse.*

☆☆☆ 1983 CHARDONNAY ($9.00) Proprietor Grown, Sonoma Valley. *Rich, clean, with great fruit.*

☆☆ 1984 CHARDONNAY ($9.00) Sonoma. *Fresh, fruity, varietal, pleasant.*

☆☆ 1985 CYPRESS LANE VINEYARDS CHARDONNAY ($6.00) California. *Clean, rich, spicy, simple, attractive.*

☆☆ 1985 CHARDONNAY ($9.50) Sonoma. *Oily, heavy, intense, rich, clean and balanced.*

☆☆ 1985 CHARDONNAY ($14.00) Reserve, Estate, Sonoma. *Rich, smokey, soft, ripe and varietal, with good fruit.*

☆ 1986 CYPRESS LANE VINEYARDS CHARDONNAY ($6.00) California. *Sweaty, not very varietal, clean.*

☆☆ 1986 CYPRESS LANE VINEYARDS SAUVIGNON BLANC ($4.50) California. *Soft, sweet peas and herbs, clean, balanced.*

### BLANC DE NOIR
☆ 1986 CYPRESS LANE WHITE ZINFANDEL ($4.50) Clarksburg. *Crisp, balanced, vegetal.*

### RED
☆☆☆ 1978 CABERNET SAUVIGNON ($7.00) 75% Sonoma, 25% Napa. *Fragrant, soft and deep; delicious. Drink now.*

☆☆☆ 1980 CABERNET SAUVIGNON ($8.50) Estate, Alexander Valley. *Lovely, crisp and complex, with wonderful fruit and earth.*

☆ 1981 CABERNET SAUVIGNON ($8.50) Robert Young, Alexander Valley. *Decent but a trifle bitter.*

❧

F.W. LANGGUTH *see* Snoqualmie Winery

## Las Montañas Winery                    SONOMA COUNTY
### RED
1983 ZINFANDEL ($8.00) Naturel, Sonoma. *Strange nose, not much varietal character.*

❧

## Laurel Glen Vineyard                    SONOMA COUNTY
### RED
☆☆☆☆ 1981 CABERNET SAUVIGNON ($12.50) Estate, Sonoma Mountain. *Firm, rich, deep, beautifully made. Still improving. Drink 1989.*

☆☆☆ 1982 CABERNET SAUVIGNON ($12.50) Estate, Sonoma Mountain. *Rich, deep, intense, concentrated, clean, varietal. Quite lovely. Drink 1990.*

☆☆ 1983 CABERNET SAUVIGNON ($12.50) Estate, Sonoma Mountain. *Earthy, rich, herbal, softly textured. Good structure. Drink 1990.*

☆☆☆ 1984 CABERNET SAUVIGNON ($14.25) Estate, Sonoma Mountain. *Soft, elegant, rich, clean.*

☆☆☆☆ 1985 CABERNET SAUVIGNON ($18.00) Estate, Sonoma Mountain. *Rich, spicy, lush, deep, varietal character. Superb. Drink 1992.*

☆☆☆ 1986 CABERNET SAUVIGNON ($18.00) Estate, Sonoma Mountain. *Firm, rich, deep, elegant. Drink 1993.*

☆☆☆ 1982 MERLOT ($9.00) Estate, Sonoma. *Cherry fruit, good clean oak, fresh flavors. Drink now.*

≥∙

## Lazy Creek Winery          MENDOCINO COUNTY
### WHITE
☆☆☆ 1985 CHARDONNAY ($8.75) Estate, Anderson Valley. *Lush, soft, varietal fruit, delightful.*

☆☆☆ 1985 GEWURZTRAMINER ($6.50) Estate, Anderson Valley. *0.6% residual sugar. Lush, varietal, intense, rich.*

☆☆☆ 1986 GEWURZTRAMINER ($6.50) Estate, Anderson Valley. *Lush, deep, ripe, varietal, lovely.*

### RED
☆☆ 1985 PINOT NOIR ($8.75) Estate, Anderson Valley. *Rich, deep, lush fruit and firm structure.*

☆☆☆ 1986 PINOT NOIR ($8.75) Estate, Anderson Valley. *Crisp, fresh, peppery, with lovely cherry flavors.*

≥∙

LEAKY LAKE *see* Fretter Wine Cellars
LEBLANC *see* California Growers Winery
LE DOMAINE *see* Almaden Vineyards

## Leeward Winery          VENTURA COUNTY
### WHITE
☆☆☆ 1982 CHARDONNAY ($12.00) Bien Nacido, Santa Maria Valley. *Lush and oaky; fragrant and nicely balanced. The best of the '82s.*

☆☆☆ 1982 CHARDONNAY ($14.00) Central Coast. *Toasty nose and crisp, lemony flavor.*

☆☆ 1982 CHARDONNAY ($14.00) MacGregor, Edna Valley. *Buttery nose and crisp, tangy fruit. Complex and delicious.*

☆ 1982 CHARDONNAY ($14.00) Ventana, Monterey. *Earthy nose, crisp, snappy fruit but unbalanced.*

☆ 1983 CHARDONNAY ($8.00) 54% Edna Valley, 46% Santa Maria Valley, Central Coast. *Heavy, clumsy, oaky, intense.*

☆☆☆ 1983 CHARDONNAY ($14.00) MacGregor, Edna Valley. *Crisp and angular, with nice oak and plenty of fruit.*

☆☆ 1983 CHARDONNAY ($15.00) Ventana, Monterey. *Lush, clean, fruity, a bit heavy.*

☆☆ 1984 CHARDONNAY ($8.00) Central Coast. *Clean, lush, fruity, attractive.*

1984 CHARDONNAY ($10.00) Bien Nacido, Santa Maria Valley. *Fat, lush, heavy, candied, oxidized, unattractive.*

☆☆☆ 1984 CHARDONNAY ($12.00) MacGregor, Edna Valley. *Rich, ripe, with great oak, complexity and fruit. Excellent.*

☆ 1985 CHARDONNAY ($14.00) MacGregor, Edna Valley. *Oily, heavy, herbaceous, lacking fruit.*

**RED**

☆ 1980 CABERNET SAUVIGNON ($9.50) Jensen, San Luis Obispo. *Clumsy and unbalanced.*

☆☆☆ 1985 CABERNET SAUVIGNON ($12.00) Alexander Valley. *Lush, ripe, soft, smooth, clean, herbal, lovely. Drink 1989.*

☆☆☆ 1985 MERLOT ($10.00) Napa Valley. *Soft, varietal, clean, elegant, charming.*

☆☆☆ 1981 ZINFANDEL ($7.50) Shenandoah Valley, Amador. *Lovely oak and fruit; elegant and superb.*

❧

CHARLES LEFRANC CELLARS *see* Almaden Vineyards

LEJON *see* Colony

## Lenz Vineyards                              NEW YORK

**WHITE**

☆☆ 1983 CHARDONNAY ($9.00) North Fork, Long Island. *Crisp, firm, varietal, clean, attractive.*

☆☆ 1986 CHARDONNAY ($16.00) North Fork, Long Island. *Crisp, clean, varietal, lacking richness of fruit but quite nice.*

☆☆☆ 1986 GEWÜRZTRAMINER ($11.00) North Fork, Long Island. *Crisp, balanced, clean, spicy fruit; a well-made, serious wine.*

**RED**

☆☆☆ 1983 RESERVE ($12.00) North Fork, Long Island. *Cabernet Sauvignon, Merlot and Cabernet Franc. Rich and complex. Drink now.*

☆☆☆ 1983 MERLOT ($8.00) North Fork, Long Island. *Herbal, rich, soft, balanced, charming. Drink now.*

❧

## Leonetti Cellars                          WASHINGTON

**RED**

☆ 1981 MERLOT ($10.00) Washington. *Crisp and clean, with some vegetal qualities.*

❧

LIBERTY SCHOOL *see* Caymus Vineyards

## Livingston Vineyards                      NAPA COUNTY

**RED**

☆☆☆☆ 1984 CABERNET SAUVIGNON ($18.00) Moffett, Napa Valley. *Lush, rich, cherry fruit, crisp acidity; deep, complex flavors; long, clean, focused finish. Drink 1991.*

❧

## Llano Estacado Winery                          TEXAS

**WHITE**

☆☆ 1985 LLANO WHITE ($4.50) Texas. *Soft, fresh, clean, decent, mainly Chenin Blanc.*

☆☆☆ 1984 CHARDONNAY ($10.00) Leftwich-Slaughter, Lubbock. *A remarkable wine. Crisp, clean, fresh, varietal, balanced.*

☆☆☆ 1984 CHARDONNAY ($10.00) Lubbock. *Crisp, clean, lovely fruit, varietal character.*

&#9734;&#9734;&#9734; 1985 CHARDONNAY ($12.00) Leftwich-Slaughter, Lubbock. *Fresh, clean, super fruit, crisp, lovely.*

&#9734; 1986 FUME BLANC ($9.00) Cellar Select, Texas. *Crisp, dense, clean, decent.*

&#9734;&#9734;&#9734; 1986 JOHANNISBERG RIESLING ($8.00) Texas. *Spicy, crisp and clean, with bright, persistent fruit.*

1986 SAUVIGNON BLANC ($7.00) Crosnoe, Lubbock. *Flat, simple, not much.*

**ROSE**

&#9734; 1985 ROSE OF CABERNET ($6.00) Lubbock. *2.5% residual sugar. Herbal, clean, heavy, decent.*

**RED**

&#9734;&#9734; 1985 LLANO RED ($4.50) Texas. *Crisp, fresh, thin, decent.*

O 1983 CABERNET SAUVIGNON ($12.00) Leftwich-Slaughter, Lubbock. *Musty, herbal, weedy.*

&#9734;&#9734;&#9734; 1985 CABERNET SAUVIGNON ($12.00) Slaughter Leftwich, Lubbock. *Rich, lush, deep, ripe fruit, with lovely balance and structure. Drink 1989.*

&#10086;

LLORDS & ELWOOD WINERY *see* Monticello Cellars

## *J. Lohr Winery*     SANTA CLARA COUNTY
**WHITE**

&#9734; 1982 CHARDONNAY ($9.00) Greenfield, Monterey. *Fruity and clean but without much depth.*

1983 CHARDONNAY ($9.00) Greenfield, Monterey. *Oily, vegetal, unpleasant.*

1983 CHARDONNAY ($12.00) Reserve, Monterey. *Minty and quite bizarre.*

&#9734; 1984 CHARDONNAY ($9.00) Greenfield, Monterey. *Clean, oily, decent.*

&#9734;&#9734; 1985 CHARDONNAY ($9.00) Greenfield, Monterey. *Soft, smooth, earthy, some heavy flavors, decent.*

**BLANC DE NOIR**

&#9734;&#9734;&#9734; 1986 WHITE ZINFANDEL ($4.50) California. *2.6% residual sugar. Fruity, fresh, great acidity, balanced.*

1986 ARIEL WHITE ZINFANDEL ($4.50) California. *No alcohol. Sour, simple, unappealing.*

**RED**

&#9734;&#9734;&#9734; 1981 CABERNET SAUVIGNON ($9.00) St. Regis, Napa. *Crisp, clean and lively, with attractive floral notes.*

&#9734; 1983 CABERNET SAUVIGNON ($9.00) Napa Valley. *Simple, decent, not much.*

&#9734;&#9734;&#9734; 1984 CABERNET SAUVIGNON ($5.00) California. *Fresh, soft, charming, delicious. Drink now.*

O 1985 ARIEL CABERNET SAUVIGNON ($4.25) California. *No alcohol. Tea-like, dull, unappealing.*

&#9734;&#9734;&#9734; 1985 GAMAY ($4.50) Greenfields, Monterey. *Fruity, spicy, fresh, absolutely delightful.*

&#9734;&#9734;&#9734; 1986 GAMAY ($4.50) Monterey Gamay, Greenfield, Monterey. *Spicy, peppery, lush, delicious.*

&#10086;

## *Lolonis Winery*     MENDOCINO COUNTY
**WHITE**

&#9734;&#9734; 1982 CHARDONNAY ($12.50) Estate, Mendocino. *Crisp, intense, vinous, lacking finesse and depth.*

&#9734;&#9734; 1984 CHARDONNAY ($13.00) Mendocino. *Simple, clean, decent fruit, lacks depth.*

&#9734; 1985 FUME BLANC ($9.00) Lolonis, Mendocino. *Lush, fat, some oxidation; low varietal character.*

&#10086;

## Long Vineyards                                    NAPA COUNTY
### WHITE
✩✩✩  1982 CHARDONNAY ($24.00) Napa Valley. *Barrel fermented. Rich, deep, toasty, complex.*

✩✩  1985 CHARDONNAY ($4.50) California. *Clean, lemony, crisp, balanced.*

૨⬤

## Lonz Winery                                        OHIO
### SPARKLING
NV  EXTRA DRY ($5.50) Lake Erie, Ohio. *Odd nose, intense flavors, not attractive.*

NV  BRUT ($7.50) Ile de Fleurs, American. *Bitter, coarse.*

૨⬤

## Lost Hills Vineyards                  SAN JOAQUIN COUNTY
### SPARKLING
✩  NV  MY ZIN ($5.00) California. *Oily, dense, decent.*
### RED
NV  ZINFANDEL ($2.00) California. *Tart, thin, decent.*

૨⬤

LOWER LAKE WINERY *see* Stuermer Winery

## Lucas Vineyards                                  NEW YORK
### WHITE
✩✩  1985 SEYVAL BLANC ($4.75) Finger Lakes. *Crisp, fresh, spritzy, charming.*

૨⬤

## The Lucas Winery                     SAN JOAQUIN COUNTY
### RED
✩✩  1983 ZINFANDEL ($6.25) Estate, Lodi. *Earthy, clean, elegant structure, decent fruit.*

✩✩  1984 ZINFANDEL ($6.25) Estate, Lodi. *Rich, soft, clean, nicely balanced.*

૨⬤

## Lyeth Vineyard and Winery            SONOMA COUNTY
### WHITE
✩✩✩  1982 WHITE TABLE WINE ($9.00) Alexander Valley. *75% Sauvignon Blanc, 20% Semillon, 5% Muscat. Rich, clean, fruity, soft.*

✩✩  1984 WHITE TABLE WINE ($10.00) Alexander Valley. *Mostly Sauvignon Blanc. Crisp, complex, austere, a bit hard.*

✩✩✩  1985 WHITE TABLE WINE ($10.00) Alexander Valley. *74% Sauvignon Blanc, 20% Semillon, 6% Muscadelle du Bordelaise. Soft, spicy, rich, complex, oaky, smokey, lush and unusual.*
### RED
✩✩✩  1981 RED TABLE WINE ($15.00) Alexander Valley. *65% Cabernet Sauvignon, 30% Cabernet Franc, 5% Merlot. Clean, rich, structured. Drink now.*

✩✩✩  1982 RED TABLE WINE ($15.00) Alexander Valley. *Same blend as the '81. Rich and deep, with a lovely violet flavor. Drink 1988.*

✩✩✩  1983 RED TABLE WINE ($15.00) Alexander Valley. *Crisp, lean, lovely Cabernet character, elegant, complex. Drink 1989.*

૨⬤

142

## Lytton Springs Winery          SONOMA COUNTY
### WHITE
☆  1984 CHARDONNAY ($7.50) Sonoma. *Dull, fat, not much.*
### RED
☆☆☆  1977 ZINFANDEL ($6.50) Sonoma. *Lush, smooth, complex, superb. Aging nicely.*
☆☆  1978 ZINFANDEL ($7.50) Sonoma. *Rich, clean and mellow. A classic aged Zinfandel.*
☆☆  1979 ZINFANDEL ($7.50) Sonoma. *Intense, big, rich, berried. Holding well.*
1980 ZINFANDEL ($7.50) Special Select, Sonoma. *Low on fruit and musty to boot!*
☆☆☆  1980 ZINFANDEL ($8.00) Sonoma. *Rich, briary, velvety, concentrated but likable.*
☆☆☆  1981 ZINFANDEL ($8.00) Sonoma. *Rich, intense and balanced, with nice, fresh berry flavors. Aging nicely.*
☆☆☆  1983 ZINFANDEL ($12.00) Private Reserve, Valley Vista, Sonoma. *Peppery, spicy, fat, lush, delicious.*
☆☆☆☆  1984 ZINFANDEL ($8.00) Sonoma. *Superb. Lush, berry flavors, crisp acidity, delicious.*
☆☆☆☆  1985 ZINFANDEL ($8.00) Sonoma. *Intense and rich but with lovely structure and surprising finesse. A superb wine.*

MADDALENA *see* San Antonio Winery
MADELINE ANGEVINE *see* Mount Baker Vineyards

## Madrona Vineyards          EL DORADO COUNTY
### WHITE
☆☆☆  1982 CHARDONNAY ($8.50) El Dorado. *Crisp, snappy and fresh, with good oak and fruit flavors.*
☆☆  1985 JOHANNISBERG RIESLING ($12.50) Select Late Harvest, El Dorado. *375 ml. 21% residual sugar. Fresh, crisp, clean, charming.*
### RED
☆☆☆  1979 CABERNET SAUVIGNON ($6.50) El Dorado. *5% Merlot. Beautiful structure, nice fruit, complex.*
☆☆☆  1980 CABERNET SAUVIGNON ($8.75) El Dorado. *Structured and richly varietal, with good oak and fruit. Drink now.*
☆  NV  ZINFANDEL ($4.50) Lot 24, El Dorado. *Tart, simple, uninteresting.*
☆☆☆  1980 ZINFANDEL ($6.00) Estate, El Dorado. *Elegant and nicely structured.*
☆☆  1981 ZINFANDEL ($6.00) Estate, El Dorado. *Raisiny, intense, tannic, rich. Ready to drink.*
☆  1983 ZINFANDEL ($6.50) El Dorado. *Intense, rich, a bit dried out.*

## Maison Deutz          SAN LUIS OBISPO COUNTY
### SPARKLING
☆☆☆  NV  BRUT CUVEE ($15.00) Santa Barbara. *Soft, fresh, complex, lovely.*

## Manzanita          NAPA COUNTY
### WHITE
☆☆☆  1982 CHARDONNAY ($14.00) Napa Valley. *Nice fruit and oak, well made and nicely balanced.*

☆☆☆ 1983 CHARDONNAY ($12.50) Napa Valley. *Balanced, richly varietal, complex and very lovely.*

☆☆☆ 1984 CHARDONNAY ($12.50) Napa Valley. *Rich, rounded, clean, oaky, intense, quite lovely.*

### RED
☆☆☆ 1982 CABERNET SAUVIGNON ($14.00) Napa Valley. *Dark, rich, intense, plummy, varietal, superb. Drink 1990.*

🦪

## Marietta Cellars                    SONOMA COUNTY
### BLANC DE NOIR
☆☆ 1986 WHITE ZINFANDEL ($4.75) Geyserville. *Simple, decent, a bit flat.*

### RED
☆☆ 1981 CABERNET SAUVIGNON ($9.75) Sonoma. *Ripe, forward, attractive fruit. Drink 1988 and beyond.*

☆☆☆ NV ZINFANDEL ($5.00) Old Vine Red, Lot Number 4, Sonoma. *Soft, lush, currant fruit, balanced, lovely.*

☆☆☆ 1984 ZINFANDEL ($7.00) Sonoma. *Rich, dense, berries, plums and lots of other fruit. Long, lush finish. Superb.*

🦪

## M. Marion & Company          SANTA CLARA COUNTY
### WHITE
☆ NV WHITE TABLE WINE ($3.25) California. *Fat, soft, dull, decent.*

☆ 1982 CHARDONNAY ($4.50) California. *Soft, herbal, clean.*

1983 CHARDONNAY ($4.50) California. *Dull, flabby.*

☆ 1985 DOMAINE M. MARION CHARDONNAY ($8.00) Reserve, Mendocino. *Minty, spicy, lush, heavy, a bit odd.*

☆☆ 1986 CHARDONNAY ($6.00) California. *Crisp, lean, balanced, varietal.*

1986 FUME BLANC ($6.00) California. *Chalky, bitter, herbaceous.*

☆ 1986 WHITE RIESLING ($4.50) California. *Decent, clean, lacking charm.*

### SPARKLING
☆☆☆ NV DOMAINE M. MARION FAIRLY DRY ($13.50) Mendocino. *Clean and balanced, lovely fruit and attractive flavors.*

### BLANC DE NOIR
☆ NV SABRINA'S CUVEE ($4.50) California. *Heavy, syrupy, candied, fat and dull.*

### RED
1982 CABERNET SAUVIGNON ($5.00) California. *Odd, off aromas. Decent fruit.*

☆☆☆ 1984 CABERNET SAUVIGNON ($4.50) Napa Valley, Sonoma Valley. *Soft, clean, varietal, charming. Drink now.*

☆ 1984 CABERNET SAUVIGNON ($8.00) Reserve, Arroyo Seco. *Dark, earthy, meaty, with some raisiny fruit. Drink now.*

☆ 1985 CABERNET SAUVIGNON ($6.00) California. *Crisp, simple, clean, thin, sour.*

🦪

## Mariposa Wines              SAN FRANCISCO COUNTY
### WHITE
☆ 1984 CHARDONNAY ($5.00) Sonoma. *Simple, clean, coarse, some vegetal qualities.*

☆☆☆ 1986 SAUVIGNON BLANC ($5.00) Lake. *Soft, round fruit, crisp acidity, lovely clean finish.*

### RED
☆☆ 1984 CABERNET SAUVIGNON ($7.00) Napa. *Black raspberry flavors, soft texture, charming. Drink now.*

🦋

## Mark West Vineyards                    SONOMA COUNTY
### WHITE
☆ 1982 CHARDONNAY ($11.50) Russian River Valley. *Vinous, heavy, oily, lacking fruit.*

☆ 1983 CHARDONNAY ($10.00) Estate, Russian River Valley. *Vegetal, heavy, lacking grace and appeal.*

1985 CHARDONNAY ($10.00) Russian River Valley. *Oily, herbaceous, dull, fat.*

☆☆☆ 1985 CHARDONNAY ($16.00) Reserve, Russian River Valley. *Peach and honey, dark color, oily, dense, old-fashioned, really ripe.*

☆☆☆ 1982 JOHANNISBERG RIESLING ($12.50) Late Harvest, Sonoma. *375 ml. 9.4% residual sugar. Crisp, fruity and lovely.*

☆☆ 1983 JOHANNISBERG RIESLING ($10.00) Late Harvest, Estate, Russian River Valley. *375ml. 10.1% residual sugar. Heavy, fat, lacking finesse.*

☆☆ 1986 JOHANNISBERG RIESLING ($7.00) Estate, Russian River Valley. *0.9% residual sugar. Melony nose; crisp, tart, intense, with a touch of bitterness.*

### SPARKLING
☆☆ 1981 BLANC DE NOIRS ($12.00) Russian River Valley. *Clean, fresh, balanced. Mostly Pinot Noir.*

### BLANC DE NOIR
☆☆ 1985 PINOT NOIR BLANC ($5.75) Estate, Russian River Valley. *0.5% residual sugar. Crisp, clean, decent.*

### RED
☆☆ 1979 PINOT NOIR ($8.50) Estate, Russian River Valley. *Tart, crisp, clean and snappy.*

☆ 1983 PINOT NOIR ($10.00) Estate, Russian River Valley. *Simple, tart, lacking charm.*

☆☆☆ 1984 PINOT NOIR ($10.00) Russian River Valley. *Soft, lush, berried, clean, simple but lovely.*

☆☆ 1984 PINOT NOIR ($12.00) Estate, Russian River Valley. *Soft, spicy, berried, decent.*

☆☆☆ 1980 ZINFANDEL ($8.50) Sonoma. *Big berry nose and snappy fruit flavors; crisp.*

☆☆☆ 1983 ZINFANDEL ($11.00) Sonoma. *Rich, intense, lovely. The grapes were from 77-year-old vines.*

☆☆☆ 1984 ZINFANDEL ($12.00) Robert Rue, Sonoma. *Lush, berried, clean, lovely.*

🦋

## Markham Winery                         NAPA COUNTY
### WHITE
☆☆☆ 1985 MUSCAT DE FRONTIGNAN ($9.00) Markham, Napa Valley. *8.9% residual sugar. Rich, clean, lively spice, charming.*

☆☆☆ 1982 CHARDONNAY ($10.35) Napa Valley. *Crisp, clean, toasty, superb.*

☆☆☆ 1982 CHARDONNAY ($12.00) Markham Estate, Napa Valley. *Soft, round, clean and fresh, with lush fruitiness.*

☆☆ 1983 CHARDONNAY ($12.00) Estate, Napa. *Heavy, rich, oily, balanced.*
1984 CHARDONNAY ($12.00) Napa Valley. *Sour, thin, unattractive.*

### RED

☆☆☆ 1978 CABERNET SAUVIGNON ($12.00) Estate, Yountville, Napa Valley. *Lovely, well balanced, nicely structured.*
☆☆☆ 1979 CABERNET SAUVIGNON ($12.85) Yountville, Napa. *Austere, tannic, fruity. Drink now or hold for a few years.*
☆ 1980 CABERNET SAUVIGNON ($13.00) Markham, Napa Valley. *Crisp, toasty, well structured, mature, some odd flavors.*
☆☆☆ 1981 CABERNET SAUVIGNON ($13.00) Markham, Napa Valley. *Crisp, lean, supple, oaky, very fresh. Drink 1989.*
☆☆☆ 1982 CABERNET SAUVIGNON ($13.00) Markham, Yountville. *Crisp, snappy, balanced, complex and long. Drink 1990.*
☆☆☆ 1980 MERLOT ($8.75) Stag's Leap District, Napa Valley. *Crisp and snappy, with nice cherry fruit.*
☆☆☆ 1981 MERLOT ($8.75) Napa Valley. *Rich, fruity, velvety. Drink now.*
☆☆☆ 1983 MERLOT ($9.50) Napa Valley. *Crisp fruit, clean, fresh, very lovely. Drink now.*
☆☆☆ 1984 MERLOT ($9.50) Napa Valley. *Lush, rich earthy flavors; good structure and long finish. Drink 1990.*

※

## Markko Vineyard                    OHIO

### WHITE

☆☆ 1982 CHARDONNAY ($9.00) Ohio. *Lush, ripe and fruity. Beginning to show its age.*

### RED

☆ 1980 CABERNET SAUVIGNON ($9.00) Ohio. *10% Chambourcin. Crisp, tart, attractive.*

※

## Marston Vineyard                    NAPA COUNTY

### WHITE

1984 CHARDONNAY ($12.00) Estate, Napa Valley. *Sour, vegetal, unattractive.*

※

## Martin Brothers Winery          SAN LUIS OBISPO COUNTY

### WHITE

☆☆☆ 1982 CHARDONNAY ($10.00) Edna Valley. *Crisp, clean, fresh and snappy.*
○ 1983 CHARDONNAY ($10.00) 20% Paragon, 80% Los Alamos, Central Coast. *Sour, vegetal, very unattractive.*
○ 1984 CHARDONNAY ($10.00) Central Coast. *Sour, dirty, awful.*
☆☆☆ 1985 SAUVIGNON BLANC ($7.50) Paso Robles. *Crisp, lean, clean, tangy, balanced.*

### BLANC DE NOIR

☆☆☆ 1986 WHITE ZINFANDEL ($5.50) Paso Robles. *Fairly dry, crisp, tangy, lively.*

### RED

☆☆ 1982 NEBBIOLO ($7.00) California. *Fresh, intense and youthful. Developing nicely.*

☆☆☆ 1983 NEBBIOLO ($7.00) California. *Spicy, fruity, fresh, clean, very nice.*

☆☆ 1985 NEBBIOLO ($7.50) California. *Sweet pea, pepper, snappy, clean, interesting.*

☆☆ 1981 ZINFANDEL ($5.50) Paso Robles. *Tart, fruity, somewhat simple.*

☆☆☆ 1983 ZINFANDEL ($6.00) Paso Robles. *Light, tangy, fruity, fresh, charming.*

☆☆ 1983 ZINFANDEL ($7.50) 49% Venturini, 26% Obermeyer, 25% Sauret, Paso Robles. *Lush, clean, varietal, nice.*

☆ 1984 ZINFANDEL ($6.00) 34% Venturini, 55% Sauret, 11% Obermeyer, Paso Robles. *Simple, decent but dull.*

❧

# Louis M. Martini                          NAPA COUNTY

## WHITE

☆ 1982 CHARDONNAY ($7.00) Napa Valley. *Snappy, crisp, decent but not completely clean.*

1982 CHARDONNAY ($10.00) Vineyard Selection, Los Vinedos del Rio, Russian River Valley. *Lacking fruit, dull.*

1982 CHARDONNAY ($12.00) Vineyard Selection, Napa Valley. *Musty wood, lacking fruit, thin flavors.*

1983 CHARDONNAY ($7.85) North Coast. *Thin, cardboard flavors.*

○ 1983 CHARDONNAY ($12.00) Napa Valley-Los Carneros. *Botrytis-affected, unattractive, dull.*

1984 CHARDONNAY ($8.00) North Coast. *Dull, very little fruit, unattractive.*

## BLANC DE NOIR

☆☆ 1986 WHITE MERLOT ($4.75) Alexander Valley. *1.2% residual sugar. Sour, herbal, clean, decent.*

☆☆ 1986 WHITE PETITE SIRAH ($4.75) Napa Valley. *Crisp, fresh, varietal, lovely fruit.*

☆☆ 1986 WHITE ZINFANDEL ($4.75) California. *Crisp, snappy, clean, attractive.*

## RED

☆☆ 1981 BARBERA ($4.50) California. *Clean, crisp, varietal; showing some age but lively and complex. Drink now.*

☆ 1978 CABERNET SAUVIGNON ($9.00) Special Selection, California. *Clean, lacking fruit.*

☆☆ 1978 CABERNET SAUVIGNON ($10.00) Vineyard Selection Series, California. *Sold only as part of a series. The blend of the other six. Soft, round, complex, quite appealing.*

☆☆ 1978 CABERNET SAUVIGNON ($10.00) Vineyard Selection Series, International, Monterey. *Sold only as part of a series. Green pepper nose; clean, green pepper flavors, good firm fruit; balanced.*

☆☆☆ 1978 CABERNET SAUVIGNON ($10.00) Vineyard Selection Series, La Loma, Napa Valley. *Sold only as part of a series. Crisp, clean, earthy, balanced; showing bottle complexity and depth.*

☆ 1978 CABERNET SAUVIGNON ($10.00) Vineyard Selection Series, Rancho Tierra Rejada, Paso Robles, San Luis Obispo. *Sold only as part of a series. Thin, with flavors of earth and wood.*

1978 CABERNET SAUVIGNON ($10.00) Vineyard Selection Series, Tepesquet, Santa Maria, Santa Barbara. *Sold only as part of a series. Sweet pea vegetation, odd flavors, unappealing.*

☆☆ 1978 CABERNET SAUVIGNON ($10.00) Vineyard Selection Series, Foxen Canyon, Santa Ynez Valley, Santa Barbara. *Sold only as part of a series. Balanced, earthy, tight fruit and good structure.*

1979 CABERNET SAUVIGNON ($4.75) North Coast. *Thin, dull, lacking varietal character.*

☆☆☆ 1979 CABERNET SAUVIGNON ($12.00) Vineyard Selection, Lot 2, Monte Rosso, Sonoma. *Rich fruit, mint and varietal character. Complex. Drink now.*

☆☆☆ 1979 CABERNET SAUVIGNON ($15.00) Vineyard Selection, Lot 1, Monte Rosso, Sonoma. *Classic structure, richly varietal, fruity. Ready to drink.*

1980 CABERNET SAUVIGNON ($6.00) North Coast. *Dull, lacking fruit, tired.*

1980 CABERNET SAUVIGNON ($6.50) Monte Rosso, Sonoma. *A pleasant wine that is overridden by dirty, moldy flavors.*

☆ 1980 CABERNET SAUVIGNON ($12.00) Special Selection, North Coast. *Tea-like, thin, clean, lacking fruit. Drink now.*

☆☆ 1981 CABERNET SAUVIGNON ($15.00) La Loma, Napa Valley. *Clean, lithe, lovely, a bit short.*

☆☆☆ 1981 CABERNET SAUVIGNON ($15.00) Monte Rosso, Sonoma Valley. *Crisp, clean, fresh, good structure, snappy finish. Drink 1988.*

☆☆ 1982 CABERNET SAUVIGNON ($7.00) North Coast. *Soft, elegant, clean, complex. Drink now.*

☆ 1982 CABERNET SAUVIGNON ($18.00) Vineyard Selection, Monte Rosso, Sonoma Valley. *Oily, heavy, overdone.*

☆☆ 1982 CABERNET SAUVIGNON ($25.00) Los Ninos, Sonoma Valley. *Clean, complex, mature. Drink now.*

☆ 1983 CABERNET SAUVIGNON ($7.00) North Coast. *Thin, earthy, drinkable.*

☆ 1980 MERLOT ($5.00) North Coast. *Earthy and dull.*

☆ 1981 MERLOT ($5.50) Napa. *Musty, decent fruit.*

☆☆☆ 1981 MERLOT ($10.00) Russian River Valley. *Elegant, balanced, lovely, a very graceful wine.*

☆☆ 1981 MERLOT ($10.00) Vineyard Selection, Los Vinedos del Rio, Russian River Valley. *Light and pleasant, with attractive fruit and some oak.*

☆☆☆ 1981 MERLOT ($15.00) Monte Rosso, Sonoma Valley. *Rich, clean, leathery, superb. Drink 1989.*

☆☆ 1982 MERLOT ($6.00) Napa Valley. *Soft, crisp, clean, lacking depth. Drink now.*

☆☆☆ 1982 MERLOT ($10.00) Vineyard Selection, Los Vinedos del Rio, Russian River Valley. *Clean, fresh, balanced, crisp fruit, lovely. Drink 1988.*

☆ 1983 MERLOT ($5.85) North Coast. *Pleasant spice, oak, fruit. Lean structure.*

☆ 1984 MERLOT ($6.70) North Coast. *Astringent, slightly vegetal, decent.*

☆☆ 1984 MERLOT ($12.00) Los Vinedos del Rio, Russian River Valley. *Soft, clean, elegant, nicely balanced. Drink 1989.*

1981 PETITE SIRAH ($4.90) Napa Valley. *Moldy flavors mar the potential appeal here.*

☆☆ 1982 PETITE SIRAH ($5.00) Napa Valley. *1% Barbera. Clean, balanced, fruity and attractive.*

☆☆ 1983 PETITE SIRAH ($5.00) Napa Valley. *Soft, rich, jammy, earthy but nicely structured. Drink now.*

☆☆ 1975 PINOT NOIR ($8.50) Special Selection, California. *Earthy, varietal, very appealing.*

☆☆☆ 1976 PINOT NOIR ($4.00) California. *Smokey, balanced, smooth and Burgundian.*

☆☆☆ 1976 PINOT NOIR ($11.00) Special Selection, California. *Smokey, fresh, crisp, clean and varietal, with fresh fruitiness.*

☆ 1977 PINOT NOIR ($9.00) Special Selection, La Loma, Napa Valley. *Good structure but very earthy, with dirty flavors.*

☆☆☆ 1978 PINOT NOIR ($8.00) Special Selection, California. *Earthy, toasty, fresh, soft, lovely.*

☆☆ 1979 PINOT NOIR ($3.40) Napa Valley. *Nice structure; clean, simple and pleasant.*

○ 1979 PINOT NOIR ($10.00) Vineyard Selection, La Loma, Napa Valley. *Oxidized.*

☆☆ 1979 PINOT NOIR ($10.00) Vineyard Selection, Las Amigas, Napa Valley. *Soft, rich and earthy. Aging nicely.*

☆☆ 1980 PINOT NOIR ($10.00) Vineyard Selection, Las Amigas, Napa Valley. *Thin, earthy, good fruit, clean.*

☆☆ 1982 PINOT NOIR ($6.00) Napa Valley. *Spicy, clean, varietal.*

☆ 1982 PINOT NOIR ($8.00) Los Carneros. *Fat, overripe.*

☆☆ 1983 PINOT NOIR ($5.85) Napa Valley. *Crisp, fruity, spicy, clean, balanced.*

☆☆☆ 1968 ZINFANDEL Monte Rosso, Sonoma. *Lush, smooth, complex, mellow.*

☆☆ 1974 ZINFANDEL ($10.00) Special Selection, California. *Nice, rich, clean and decent.*

○ 1977 ZINFANDEL ($10.00) Special Selection, Monte Rosso (Sonoma), California. *Dried fruit, bitter, unpleasant.*

☆☆ 1978 ZINFANDEL ($8.00) Special Selection, California. *Ripe, plummy, intense but showing its age.*

☆☆ 1978 ZINFANDEL ($10.00) Special Selection, Monte Rosso (Sonoma), California. *15.3% alcohol. Bramble and fruit; earthy and hot.*

☆☆ 1980 ZINFANDEL ($4.45) North Coast. *Clean, with nice, snappy fruit.*

☆☆ 1981 ZINFANDEL ($4.90) North Coast. *Fresh, clean, snappy, charming.*

☆☆☆ 1983 ZINFANDEL ($7.75) North Coast. *Lush, ripe, soft, clean, lovely.*

☆☆☆ 1984 ZINFANDEL ($5.85) Napa. *Rich, clean, good fruit, easy to like.*

☆☆ 1984 ZINFANDEL ($5.85) North Coast. *Balanced, ripe, soft, attractive fruit flavors, charming.*

❧

## Paul Masson Vineyards          SANTA CLARA COUNTY
### WHITE
☆ NV RHINE California. *Fresh, sweet, crisp; fruity, clean and nice.*

☆ NV ST. REGIS BLANC ($3.00) California. *Nonalcoholic. Strange but drinkable; off-dry and fruity.*

1983 CHARDONNAY ($6.50) Monterey. *Soft, limp, lacking character and charm.*

### SPARKLING
☆ NV CRACKLING CHABLIS ($5.15) California. *Crisp, clean, Muscat nose, not bad.*

NV CRACKLING ROSE ($5.15) California. *Sweet.*

☆ NV BLANC DE NOIR ($8.00) California. *Tart, crisp, decent, oaky, simple.*

☆    1982 BRUT ($8.00) California. *Sweet, heavy, decent but not very interesting.*

☆    1982 EXTRA DRY CHAMPAGNE ($8.00) California. *Simple, lush, fat, fruity.*

☆☆   1984 BLANC DE NOIR ($9.00) Centennial Cuvée, Monterey. *80% Pinot Noir, 20% Pinot Blanc. Decent, clean, snappy, okay.*

### RED

☆☆   NV   PREMIUM BURGUNDY ($3.25) California. *Rich, lush, good balance.*

☆☆   1982 CABERNET SAUVIGNON ($6.20) Sonoma. *Simple and a bit thin, but pleasant.*

☆☆☆  1983 CABERNET SAUVIGNON ($6.25) Sonoma. *Ripe, clean, lovely. Drink now.*

☆☆   1982 PINOT NOIR ($5.40) Sonoma. *Decent fruit, clean but simple.*

☆☆☆  1979 ZINFANDEL ($3.75) California. *Fruity, clean and appealing.*

☆    1982 ZINFANDEL ($3.25) California. *Crisp and vegetal; decent.*

☆☆   1984 ZINFANDEL ($3.35) California. *Decent, clean, varietal, simple.*

28.

## Mastantuono Winery          SAN LUIS OBISPO COUNTY
### RED

☆☆   1982 PINOT NOIR ($15.00) Paso Robles. *Earthy, clean, rich, intense.*

☆☆   1980 ZINFANDEL ($8.25) Dusi, Templeton, San Luis Obispo. *Lush, big, peppery, berried.*

☆    1981 ZINFANDEL ($9.25) Dusi, Templeton, San Luis Obispo. *Heavy and simple; decent but not lovable.*

○    1981 ZINFANDEL ($20.00) Centennial, San Luis Obispo. *Raisiny, late harvest, grotesque.*

28.

## Matanzas Creek Winery          SONOMA COUNTY
### WHITE

☆☆   1982 CHARDONNAY ($15.00) Sonoma. *Toasty, soft, clean, lacking depth of fruit.*

☆☆☆☆ 1982 CHARDONNAY ($18.00) Estate, Sonoma Valley. *Rich and oaky, with lovely balance and finesse. A classic.*

☆☆☆☆ 1983 CHARDONNAY ($18.00) Estate, Sonoma Valley. *Crisp, clean, angular, elegant.*

☆☆☆☆ 1984 CHARDONNAY ($15.00) Sonoma Valley. *Exquisite fruit, oak and balance. Complex and delicious.*

☆☆☆  1984 CHARDONNAY ($18.00) Estate, Sonoma Valley. *Spicy, richly fruity, vinous, intense.*

☆☆☆  1985 CHARDONNAY ($16.00) Sonoma Valley. *Lush, fruity, lovely oak, delicious.*

☆☆☆  1985 CHARDONNAY ($18.00) Estate, Sonoma Valley. *Rich, lush, fat, fruity, balanced.*

☆☆☆  1986 CHARDONNAY ($16.00) Sonoma. *Lush fruit, subtle oak, rich, mouthfilling flavors, crisp acidity. Splendid.*

☆☆☆  1986 SAUVIGNON BLANC ($11.00) Sonoma. *Lush, ripe, rich flavors, intense herbs and fruit.*

### RED

☆☆☆  1979 CABERNET SAUVIGNON ($16.00) Sonoma. *Velvety and rich, with lovely complexity. Ready to drink.*

1980 CABERNET SAUVIGNON ($16.00) Sonoma. *Hard and weedy. Maybe time will help, but I'm not optimistic.*

☆☆☆ 1982 CABERNET SAUVIGNON ($14.00) Sonoma. *Lovely balance, rich fruit, nice wood. Drink 1988.*

☆☆☆ 1983 CABERNET SAUVIGNON ($14.00) Sonoma Valley. *Ripe, rich, berried, intense. Drink 1992.*

☆ 1978 MERLOT ($18.00) Estate, Sonoma. *Big, concentrated, lacking finesse.*

☆☆ 1979 MERLOT ($12.00) Sonoma. *Intense and complicated but basically unsatisfying. Still needs time.*

☆☆☆ 1980 MERLOT ($12.50) Sonoma Valley. *Lush, lovely, ripe and earthy.*

☆☆☆ 1981 MERLOT ($14.00) Sonoma. *Earthy, clean, complex, lovely. Drink 1988.*

☆☆ 1982 MERLOT ($12.50) Sonoma. 20% Cabernet Sauvignon. *Tight, soft, earthy, clean, solid.*

☆☆☆ 1983 MERLOT ($10.50) Sonoma Valley. *Berry fruit and crisp acidity, lush and balanced. Drink 1988.*

☆☆ 1984 MERLOT ($10.50) Sonoma Valley. *Soft, lush, cherry-berry flavors, lovely structure. Drink now and into the mid-1990s.*

☆☆☆☆ 1985 MERLOT ($12.50) Sonoma. 23% Cabernet Franc. *Incredible depth and lush fruit. Ripe and beautifully structured, complex and superb. Drink 1990.*

☆☆☆ 1986 MERLOT ($12.00) Sonoma Valley. 24% Cabernet Sauvignon. *Lush fruit, ripe, clean flavors, lovely cherry, good structure. Drink 1991.*

☆☆ NV PINOT NOIR ($10.50) Assemblage de Deux Vins, Quail Hill Ranch, Sonoma. *Lithe, clean and a bit stemmy.*

≥≥

## Joseph Mathews Winery                    NAPA COUNTY
### WHITE
☆☆ 1985 CHARDONNAY ($12.00) Napa Valley. *Crisp, earthy, varietal, oaky, decent.*
### RED
☆☆☆ 1982 CABERNET SAUVIGNON ($8.95) Napa Valley. *Crisp cherry flavors, clean, lively, excellent structure. Drink 1989.*

☆☆ 1983 CABERNET SAUVIGNON ($13.75) Napa Valley. *Earthy, crisp, charming fruit and good balance. Drink 1988.*

≥≥

## Matrose Wines                    SONOMA COUNTY
### WHITE
☆☆☆ 1985 SYMPHONY ($6.00) Sonoma. 375 ml. 6.12% residual sugar. *Rich, soft, lovely fruit and spice.*

≥≥

## L. Mawby Vineyards                    MICHIGAN
### WHITE
1984 VIGNOLES ($10.50) Leelanau Peninsula. *Big, intense, oily flavors, heavy, overdone.*

☆☆ 1985 VIGNOLES ($6.00) Elm Valley. *Lush, rich, balanced, off-dry, lovely flavors.*

☆☆ 1985 VIGNOLES ($7.50) Leelanau Peninsula. *Rich, lemony, balanced, clean, complex.*

≥≥

## Mayacamas Vineyards                    NAPA COUNTY
### WHITE
☆ 1983 CHARDONNAY ($16.00) Napa Valley. *Earthy, intense, vinous, chalky.*

☆☆☆ 1984 CHARDONNAY ($18.00) Napa Valley. *Rich, intense, well structured; serious but smooth and appealing.*

☆☆☆ 1985 SAUVIGNON BLANC ($10.00) Napa Valley. *Crisp, snappy, ripe, fresh, good balance and charming finish.*

### RED

☆☆ 1978 CABERNET SAUVIGNON ($18.00) Napa Valley. *Big and hulking, lacking the fruit needed to carry it through.*

☆☆ 1980 CABERNET SAUVIGNON ($18.00) California. *Herbaceous, big, heavy—maybe time will help. Drink 1990.*

☆☆ 1982 CABERNET SAUVIGNON ($18.00) Napa Valley. *Earthy, composty, great structure, lively fruit. Drink 1994.*

☆☆☆ 1979 PINOT NOIR ($18.00) Napa Valley. *Rich, earthy, leathery, intense, with fine oak and mature fruit.*

☆☆ 1984 PINOT NOIR ($12.00) Napa Valley. *Soft, clean, balanced, essentially simple now but with great aging potential. Drink 1992.*

≈•

## Mazza Vineyards                                    PENNSYLVANIA
### WHITE
☆ 1984 CAYUGA ($7.00) Pennsylvania. *Fresh, decent.*

≈•

## Mazzocco Vineyards                              SONOMA COUNTY
### WHITE
☆☆ 1985 CHARDONNAY ($10.50) Winemaster's Cuvée, Sonoma. *Soft, clean and quite pleasant. Simple but true flavors.*

☆☆☆ 1985 CHARDONNAY ($16.00) River Lane, Alexander Valley. *Crisp and beautifully structured. New oak and clean, complex flavors. Balanced and substantial.*

≈•

## Peter McCoy Vineyards                            NAPA COUNTY
### WHITE
☆☆☆ 1984 CHARDONNAY ($10.00) Clos des Pierres, Knights Valley. *Toasty oak, lush fruit, a really lovely first effort.*

☆☆☆ 1986 CHARDONNAY ($11.00) Clos des Pierres, Knights Valley. *Soft, lush, barrel fermentation flavors, rich oak and fruit.*

### RED
☆☆ 1983 CABERNET SAUVIGNON ($7.00) Clos des Pierres, Alexander Valley. *Herbal, lean, soft, slight. Bordeaux-like. Drink 1988.*

≈•

## McDowell Valley Vineyards          MENDOCINO COUNTY
### WHITE
☆☆ 1982 CHARDONNAY ($9.50) Estate, McDowell Valley. *Soft, round, oaky, pleasant.*

☆☆ 1983 CHARDONNAY ($11.00) Estate, McDowell Valley. *Fat, buttery, oily, rich, good.*

1983 CHARDONNAY ($12.00) Reserve, Estate, McDowell Valley. *Oily, vegetal, unappealing.*

☆☆☆ 1984 CHARDONNAY ($11.00) Estate, Mendocino. *Soft, fresh, clean, attractive.*

### BLANC DE NOIR
1986 WHITE ZINFANDEL ($5.00) Estate, McDowell Valley. *Sweaty, sour, unattractive.*

## RED

☆☆ 1979 CABERNET SAUVIGNON ($8.50) Estate, McDowell Valley. *A pleasant, well-made wine, with modest charms.*

☆☆☆ 1980 CABERNET SAUVIGNON ($9.00) Estate, McDowell Valley. *Crisp, tart, nice varietal character, delightful. Drink now.*

☆☆ 1981 CABERNET SAUVIGNON ($10.75) Estate, McDowell Valley. *Decent, clean, pleasant.*

☆☆☆ 1982 CABERNET SAUVIGNON ($10.85) Estate, McDowell Valley. *Soft, fresh, rich, complex. Drink 1988.*

☆☆☆ 1982 CABERNET SAUVIGNON ($14.95) Reserve, Estate, McDowell Valley. *Cherry fruit, lovely balance, rich, complex. Drink 1990.*

○ 1982 GRENACHE ($8.75) Estate, McDowell Valley. *13% Syrah blend. Thin, pale, fruity, slightly sweet, strange.*

☆☆☆ 1979 PETITE SIRAH ($7.50) Estate, McDowell Valley. *Elegant, restrained, attractive.*

☆ 1980 PETITE SIRAH ($9.00) Estate, McDowell Valley, Mendocino. *Heavy and rich.*

☆☆☆ 1980 SYRAH ($7.50) Estate, McDowell Valley. *Soft and rich, with great charm and balance.*

☆☆ 1981 SYRAH ($9.50) Estate, McDowell Valley. *Tart and clean, with great fruit and good balance. Ready to drink.*

☆☆ 1982 SYRAH ($10.00) Estate, McDowell Valley. *Cassis fruit, earthy, clean, nice balance.*

☆☆☆ 1983 SYRAH ($8.50) Estate, McDowell Valley. *Soft, lush, clean, lovely.*

જ્જ

## McGregor Vineyard Winery — NEW YORK

### WHITE

1984 CHARDONNAY ($8.00) Finger Lakes. *Vegetal, heavy, not varietal or pleasant.*

### RED

☆☆ 1982 PINOT NOIR ($11.95) Finger Lakes, New York. *Simple but clean, varietal and attractive.*

☆ 1983 PINOT NOIR ($14.00) Reserve, Finger Lakes. *Varietal, clean, admirable but not quite together.*

☆ 1984 PINOT NOIR ($12.00) Finger Lakes. *Tart, crisp, some varietal character, clean, astringent.*

જ્જ

## McHenry Vineyard — SANTA CRUZ COUNTY

### WHITE

☆ 1983 CHARDONNAY ($12.00) Estate, Santa Cruz Mountains. *Ripe, oily, with some serious volatile acidity.*

### RED

☆☆☆ 1980 PINOT NOIR ($17.50) Santa Cruz Mountains. *Lush, deep, graceful, complex, superb. Only 42 cases made.*

☆☆☆ 1981 PINOT NOIR ($14.50) Santa Cruz Mountains. *Rich, deep, complex, lovely.*

☆☆ 1982 PINOT NOIR ($12.50) Santa Cruz Mountains. *Lush, fruity, clean, some herbaceousness.*

☆☆☆ 1983 PINOT NOIR ($14.50) Estate, Santa Cruz Mountains. *Tart, spicy, fresh, clean, simple, quite nice.*

☆☆☆ 1984 PINOT NOIR ($12.50) Estate, Santa Cruz Mountains. *Soft, elegant, cherry fruit, toasty oak, lovely finesse.*

જ્જ

## McLester Winery                 LOS ANGELES COUNTY
### WHITE
NV  RUNWAY WHITE ($2.75) California. *Bitter celery and oil. Unattractive.*

☆☆  NV  MUSCAT ($7.50) Suite 13, California. *13% residual sugar. Lush, syrupy, honeyed, alcoholic (13%), rich.*

### RED
☆☆  1982 CABERNET SAUVIGNON ($9.00) Lot 1, Nepenthe, San Luis Obispo. *French-oak aged. Heavy, fat, intense, meaty.*

☆  1982 CABERNET SAUVIGNON ($9.00) Lot 2, Nepenthe, San Luis Obispo. *American-oak aged. Intense, simple, decent.*

☆☆☆  1980 ZINFANDEL ($7.50) Cowan, Shenandoah Valley, Amador. *A bit crude but balanced and appealing. Aging nicely. Ready to drink.*

☆  1981 ZINFANDEL ($6.50) Radike, San Luis Obispo. *Dull, heavy, lacking finesse.*

☆☆  1983 ZINFANDEL ($6.50) Baldinelli, Amador. *Earthy, leathery, complex, but the fruit is tired.*

ॐ

## The Meeker Vineyard                    SONOMA COUNTY
### WHITE
☆☆  1983 CHARDONNAY ($11.00) Dry Creek Valley. *Fresh, clean, soft, good varietal fruit.*

☆☆☆  1984 CHARDONNAY ($11.00) Dry Creek Valley. *Fresh, varietal, well structured, clean and nicely oaked.*

☆☆☆☆  1985 CHARDONNAY ($11.00) Dry Creek Valley. *Lean, crisply structured, tangy fruit, lovely new oak; stunning.*

### RED
☆☆☆  1984 ZINFANDEL ($7.00) Dry Creek Valley. *Soft, lush, ripe, lovely.*

☆☆☆  1985 ZINFANDEL ($8.00) Dry Creek Valley. *Spicy, fresh, snappy, cherry fruit flavors; well bred and tasty.*

☆☆☆  1985 ZINFANDEL ($8.00) Napa Valley. *Spicy, black currant, clean, rich, tart.*

ॐ

## Meier's Wine Cellars                         OHIO
### WHITE
NV  RHINE ($3.50) American. *Sweet but sappy and odd.*

NV  WALLEYE WHITE ($5.00) Ohio. *Sappy, heavy, off-dry.*

☆☆  1985 CHARDONNAY ($5.00) Isle St. George. *Soft, simple, clean, a ttractive.*

☆  1985 SEYVAL BLANC ($4.50) Ohio. *Soft, clean, heavy.*

☆  1985 VIDAL BLANC ($4.50) Lake Erie. *Off-dry, heavy, decent.*

ॐ

MENDOCINO ESTATE *see* Tyland Vineyards

## Meredyth Vineyard                        VIRGINIA
### WHITE
☆☆  1982 CHARDONNAY ($9.50) Virginia. *Crisp, clean and European in style.*

☆☆  1983 CHARDONNAY ($9.00) Virginia. *Balanced, clean, varietal.*

☆  1985 SEYVAL BLANC ($6.00) Virginia. *Herbal, soft, pleasant.*

☆  1984 VILLIARD BLANC ($6.00) Virginia. *Oily, heavy flavors. Decent.*

**RED**

☆☆ 1980 CABERNET SAUVIGNON ($8.00) Virginia. *Herbal and elegant. Very French in style. Only 95 cases made.*

☆☆ 1981 CABERNET SAUVIGNON ($8.00) Virginia. *Balanced and attractive. Drink now.*

☆☆☆ 1983 CABERNET SAUVIGNON ($8.50) Virginia. *Tart, crisp, good fruit, structure and varietal character. Drink 1992.*

☆☆☆ 1980 MERLOT ($9.00) Virginia. *25% Cabernet Sauvignon. Soft, clean and elegant. Only 30 cases made.*

❧

## Meridian Wine Cellars NAPA COUNTY
**WHITE**

☆☆☆ 1984 CHARDONNAY ($11.00) Napa Valley. *Fresh, delicate, round and very lovely.*

☆☆☆ 1985 CHARDONNAY ($11.00) Napa Valley. *Soft, luscious, with great oak and soft fruit. Charming.*

❧

## Merlion Winery NAPA COUNTY
**WHITE**

☆☆☆ NV SAUVRIER ($9.50) Napa Valley. *50% Sauvignon Blanc, 50% Semillon. Crisp, snappy, varietal, clean, very nice.*

1985 PICCOLO PAMINA ($4.00) Napa Valley. *Sour, salty, harsh.*

1985 PICCOLO CHARDONNAY ($7.50) Carneros. *Dull, low fruit, oily.*

☆☆ 1985 CHARDONNAY ($15.00) Napa Valley. *Snappy, oaky, ripe flavors.*

☆☆☆ 1985 MELON ($9.50) Coeur de Melon, Napa Valley. *The Muscadet grape makes a crisp, soft, round, fruity wine.*

❧

JOHN B. MERRITT *see* Bandiera Winery

## The Merry Vintners SONOMA COUNTY
**WHITE**

☆☆ 1983 CHARDONNAY ($11.00) Sonoma. *Clean, herbal, fresh, balanced, but lacking charm and finesse.*

☆☆☆ 1984 CHARDONNAY ($13.75) Sonoma. *Clean, elegant, fruity, crisp acidity, lovely.*

☆☆ 1985 CHARDONNAY ($9.75) Vintage Preview, Sonoma. *Clean, crisp, fresh, light, attractive.*

☆☆☆ 1985 CHARDONNAY ($14.75) Sonoma. *Crisp, clean, subtle, elegant; charming fruit and light oak.*

❧

## Merryvale Vineyards NAPA COUNTY
**WHITE**

☆☆☆ 1985 CHARDONNAY ($15.00) Napa Valley. *Crisp, fresh, lovely structure, good oak; complex and charming.*

1986 SUNNY ST. HELENA CHARDONNAY ($9.00) Napa Valley. *Bitter, brackish, metalic, odd.*

☆ 1986 SUNNY ST. HELENA CHENIN BLANC ($4.85) Napa Valley. *Sweaty, tart, odd.*

☆ 1986 SUNNY ST. HELENA SAUVIGNON BLANC ($6.00) Napa Valley. *Intensely varietal, hard and unrelenting. Lacks charm.*

## RED

☆☆☆☆  1983 RED TABLE WINE ($19.50) Napa Valley. *An exquisite blend of fruit and oak. Delicious now, will be better in 1991. Round, smooth, superb.*

☆☆☆☆  1984 RED TABLE WINE ($18.00) Napa Valley. *Soft, crisp, cherry flavors, complex, elegant. Drink 1991.*

෨

## *Messina Hof Wine Cellars*                TEXAS

### WHITE

☆☆  1986 CHARDONNAY ($9.00) Bell Brothers, Texas. *Crisp, lean, clean, balanced.*

☆☆  1986 CHENIN BLANC ($5.50) Texas. *Crisp, fresh, grapey, attractive.*

☆☆☆  1986 JOHANNISBERG RIESLING ($8.00) Red Oak, Hale. *1.9% residual sugar. Soft, fruity, fresh, decent.*

### BLANC DE NOIR

☆  1986 BLUSH ($5.75) Texas. *Dull, lacking fruit.*

### RED

☆☆  1984 CABERNET SAUVIGNON ($9.00) Private Reserve, Texas. *Lush, fat, clean.*

෨

MEV *see* Mount Eden Vineyards

MICHAEL'S *see* Artisan Wines

## *Michtom Vineyards*                SONOMA COUNTY

### WHITE

☆☆  1983 CHARDONNAY ($7.00) Alexander Valley. *Rich, oaky, fruity, a bit heavy but attractive.*

☆☆  1984 CHARDONNAY ($8.00) Estate, Alexander Valley. *Decent, clean, oaky, attractive.*

### RED

☆☆  1978 CABERNET SAUVIGNON ($6.00) Alexander Valley. *Lush, earthy and well structured.*

☆☆  1981 CABERNET SAUVIGNON ($6.00) Vintner Grown, Alexander Valley, Sonoma. *Berried, ripe, heavy, a bit muddy. Drink now.*

෨

## *Louis K. Mihaly*                NAPA COUNTY

### WHITE

☆☆  1982 CHARDONNAY ($19.00) Napa Valley. *Crisp, clean, attractive, simple.*

○  1983 CHARDONNAY ($18.00) Special Reserve, Estate, Napa Valley. *Chalky, vegetal, oxidized, horrible.*

### RED

☆☆  1982 PINOT NOIR ($18.00) Special Release, Estate, Napa Valley. *Spicy, clean, decent.*

෨

## *Milano Winery*                MENDOCINO COUNTY

### WHITE

☆☆  1982 CHARDONNAY ($10.00) 29% San Luis Obispo, 71% Mendocino, California. *Clean, attractive, fruity, yet soft.*

☆☆☆  1982 CHARDONNAY ($12.00) Oakgrove, Sonoma. *Clean, lush, balanced.*

☆☆  1982 CHARDONNAY ($14.00) Lolonis, Mendocino. *Rich, clean, soft, very lush.*

☆  1983 CHARDONNAY ($7.50) Sonoma-Mendocino. *Heavy, oily, oaky.*

☆☆  1983 CHARDONNAY ($10.00) Sonoma. *10% residual sugar. Soft, vanillin, good fruit.*

☆☆ 1984 CHARDONNAY ($8.50) Sonoma. *Decent fruit and varietal character. Lacks depth and charm.*

☆☆☆☆ 1982 JOHANNISBERG RIESLING ($25.00) Individual Bunch Select Late Harvet, Ordway's Valley Foothills, Mendocino. *375 ml. 17.2% residual sugar. Apples and botrytis; superb.*

## RED

☆☆ 1978 CABERNET SAUVIGNON ($15.00) Sanel, Mendocino. *Plummy, intense, unusual but attractive. Ready to drink.*

☆ 1980 CABERNET SAUVIGNON ($18.00) Sanel Valley, Mendocino. *Intense, overdone.*

☆☆ 1981 CABERNET SAUVIGNON ($18.00) Sanel Valley, Mendocino. *Soft, good balance, clean fruit, attractive. Drink now.*

☆ 1982 CABERNET SAUVIGNON ($5.00) California Reserve, California. *Minty, metallic, not much.*

☆☆ 1984 MERLOT ($5.00) California Reserve, California. *Herbal, clean, fresh.*

☆☆ 1981 ZINFANDEL ($6.00) Mendocino. *Lush, soft, clean.*

৯৯

# *Mill Creek Vineyards*        SONOMA COUNTY

## WHITE

☆☆☆ 1984 CHARDONNAY ($10.00) Estate, Dry Creek Valley. *Clean; lovely fruit, good balance.*

☆ 1985 FELTA SPRINGS CHARDONNAY ($5.50) Sonoma. *Simple, decent, lacking varietal character. Strange nose.*

## ROSE

1984 CABERNET BLUSH ($5.00) Estate, Dry Creek Valley. *Vegetal, sappy, sweet, unappealing.*

☆☆ 1985 CABERNET BLUSH ($5.00) Dry Creek Valley. *1.0% residual sugar. Earthy, herbal, leafy, crisp, varietal, intense, rich.*

## RED

☆ 1978 CABERNET SAUVIGNON ($8.50) Estate, Sonoma. *Simple and a bit weedy.*

☆☆☆ 1979 CABERNET SAUVIGNON ($8.50) Estate, Sonoma. *10% Merlot. Earthy and herbal. Complex and balanced. Drink now.*

☆ 1980 CABERNET SAUVIGNON ($9.00) Sonoma. *Vegetal.*

☆ 1981 CABERNET SAUVIGNON ($9.00) Estate, Dry Creek Valley. *Dirty, intense, overdone, too old.*

☆ 1982 FELTA SPRINGS CABERNET SAUVIGNON ($5.00) Sonoma. *Balanced, vegetal, rich, clean.*

☆☆☆ 1983 FELTA SPRINGS CABERNET SAUVIGNON ($5.00) Sonoma. *7% Merlot. Soft, clean, rich, deep, nice fruit. Drink now.*

☆☆☆ 1980 MERLOT ($8.50) Estate, Sonoma. *Raisiny and intense; good acid and aging potential.*

☆☆ 1981 MERLOT ($9.00) Sonoma. *Lush, simple and a bit vegetal.*

☆☆ 1982 MERLOT ($8.50) Estate, Dry Creek Valley. *Good texture, some vegetal off notes.*

☆☆ 1983 MERLOT ($9.00) Estate, Dry Creek Valley. *Meaty, herbal, softly textured, blackberry flavors.*

1984 MERLOT ($8.50) Estate, Dry Creek Valley. *Thin, vegetal, cooked, no fruit.*

☆☆ 1981 PINOT NOIR ($7.00) Dry Creek Valley, Sonoma. *Pleasant, clean, smokey.*

৯৯

## *Mirassou Vineyards*      SANTA CLARA COUNTY

### WHITE

☆ 1985 DRY WHITE ($4.00) California. *Soft, clean, a bit oily.*

☆☆ 1985 MONTEREY RIESLING ($5.50) Monterey. *Crisp, neutral, charming, simple.*

☆☆☆ 1983 CHARDONNAY ($8.00) Monterey. *Clean, fresh, lovely food wine, simple.*

☆☆ 1983 CHARDONNAY ($11.00) Harvest Reserve, Monterey. *Fresh, clean, good varietal character.*

☆☆ 1984 CHARDONNAY ($8.00) Monterey. *Crisp, lean, green apple flavors, simple.*

1984 CHARDONNAY ($12.00) Harvest Reserve, Monterey. *Sour, volatile.*

☆☆☆ 1985 CHARDONNAY ($8.00) Monterey. *Soft, clean, oaky, pretty, appealing.*

☆☆ 1986 CHARDONNAY ($8.00) Monterey. *Ripe, lush, fat, earthy, some good varietal flavors.*

1986 FUME BLANC ($7.00) California. *Heavy sweet pea nose; herbaceous, sour, bitter flavors.*

○ 1985 JOHANNISBERG RIESLING ($8.50) Monterey. *Oily, sour, frightening.*

☆ 1986 JOHANNISBERG RIESLING ($8.50) Monterey. *Spicy, fresh, decent.*

☆☆ 1985 RIESLING ($5.50) Monterey Riesling, Late Harvest, Monterey. *2.12% residual sugar. Soft, fresh, simple but nice.*

### SPARKLING

☆☆ NV BRUT ROSE ($12.00) Monterey. *Rich, deep, herbal, dry, pink.*

☆☆ 1982 AU NATUREL ($10.00) Monterey. *Snappy, clean, fresh, simple.*

1981 BLANC DE NOIR ($10.00) Monterey. *Heavy, oxidized, unattractive.*

☆☆☆ 1982 BLANC DE NOIR ($10.00) Monterey. *100% Pinot Noir. Lush, fruity, clean, fresh, nice.*

☆ 1980 BRUT ($15.00) Reserve, Monterey. *Simple, clean, decent.*

☆ 1982 BRUT ($10.00) Monterey. *Sour, dull, not much.*

☆ 1983 BRUT AU NATURAL ($10.00) Monterey. *66% Pinot Noir, 22% Chardonnay, 12% Pinot Blanc. Tart, decent, clean.*

1979 LATE DISGORGED ($16.00) Monterey. *Decent fruit but essentially dull and a bit flat.*

### BLANC DE NOIR

☆☆☆ 1986 PASTEL ($5.00) California. *Crisp, bright, fruity, grapey. A combination of wine and fresh grape juice.*

☆☆ 1986 WHITE ZINFANDEL ($5.50) Monterey. *Crisp, fresh, pleasant.*

### ROSE

☆☆☆ 1985 PETITE ROSE ($4.00) California. *Crisp, fresh, fruity, lovely.*

### RED

○ 1978 CABERNET SAUVIGNON ($9.00) Harvest Reserve, Monterey. *Intense and vegetal; good texture but overwhelmed by weeds.*

☆ 1979 CABERNET SAUVIGNON ($6.50) Monterey. *Vegetal but crisp and quite presentable.*

☆ 1979 CABERNET SAUVIGNON ($9.00) Harvest Reserve, Monterey. *Raisiny and lacking structure.*

☆☆ 1982 CABERNET SAUVIGNON ($8.50) North Coast. *Clean, pleasant, balanced, charming. Drink now.*

☆☆ 1982 CABERNET SAUVIGNON ($12.00) Napa Valley. *Rich, deep, soft, velvety, cherry fruit. Drink now.*

☆☆ 1983 CABERNET SAUVIGNON ($7.00) California. *Decent, clean, round, soft, some herbaceousness. Drink now.*

☆ 1983 CABERNET SAUVIGNON ($12.00) Harvest Reserve, Napa Valley. *Clean, oaky, ripe, coarse, lacks depth.*

☆☆ 1985 GAMAY BEAUJOLAIS ($5.50) Monterey. *Crisp, fruity, grapey, delightful.*

1979 PETITE SIRAH ($7.45) Monterey. *Showing too much age and not enough fruit.*

☆ 1981 PINOT NOIR ($7.00) Monterey. *Green, thin, decent.*

1981 PINOT NOIR ($12.00) Harvest Reserve, Monterey. *Sour, bitter, unattractive.*

☆ NV ZINFANDEL ($5.50) Lot 81-4, Monterey. *Decent, varietal, a bit muddy.*

☆☆ 1980 ZINFANDEL ($5.00) Monterey. *Fruity, clean and berried.*

☆ 1981 ZINFANDEL ($8.00) Harvest Reserve, Monterey. *Lush, rich texture, soft, decent.*

ва

## Moceri Winery                    SAN MATEO COUNTY
**WHITE**

☆☆☆ 1984 CHARDONNAY ($5.00) San Bernabe, Monterey. *Clean, fruity, fresh, tangy, very attractive.*

☆☆ 1985 CHARDONNAY ($5.00) Monterey. *Crisp, clean, decent varietal fruit, pleasant.*

**RED**

☆ 1983 CABERNET SAUVIGNON ($4.50) Central Coast. *Thin, decent flavors, tea-like.*

ва

## Mon Ami Wine Company                    OHIO
**SPARKLING**

NV BLANC DE NOIR ($6.00) Lake Erie, Ohio. *Awful nose, decent flavor.*

NV BRUT ($6.00) Lake Erie, Ohio. *Oily, minty, awful.*

ва

## Robert Mondavi Winery                    NAPA COUNTY
**WHITE**

☆☆ 1984 MUSCATO D'ORO ($8.75) Napa Valley. *Nectarine flavors, crisp, spicy, lively.*

☆☆ 1986 ROBERT MONDAVI WHITE ($4.00) California. *Crisp, soft, light, clean; strong Sauvignon Blanc varietal character.*

☆☆☆☆ 1981 CHARDONNAY ($20.00) Reserve, Napa Valley. *Crisp, delicate, elegant. A classic wine, aging well.*

☆☆☆ 1982 CHARDONNAY ($14.00) Napa Valley. *Balanced, clean, varietal, rich.*

☆☆☆ 1982 CHARDONNAY ($20.00) Reserve, Napa Valley. *Lush, rich, oaky, intense, complex.*

☆☆ 1983 CHARDONNAY ($10.00) Napa Valley. *Fresh, decent, clean, somewhat simple.*

☆☆ 1984 CHARDONNAY ($10.00) Napa Valley. *Rich, fat, lush, heavy.*

☆☆☆ 1984 CHARDONNAY ($23.00) Reserve, Napa Valley. *Toasty, rich, woody; an extreme style but attractive.*

☆☆ 1985 CHARDONNAY ($11.75) Napa Valley. *Heavy, overripe, decent flavors, lacking fruit.*

☆☆☆☆ 1985 CHARDONNAY ($22.50) Reserve, Napa Valley. *Toasty oak, intense fruit, great balance and structure; complex, elegant and dazzling; Mondavi's best Chardonnay yet.*

☆☆ 1986 CHENIN BLANC ($6.25) California. *Crisp, clean, decent, unexciting.*

☆☆ 1985 JOHANNISBERG RIESLING ($8.00) Napa Valley. *Sweet, soft, lush, fruity, sappy.*

☆☆ 1985 JOHANNISBERG RIESLING ($9.50) Special Selection, Napa Valley. *Thin, fruity, some candied flavors.*

### BLANC DE NOIR

☆☆ 1986 WHITE ZINFANDEL ($4.50) California. *Crisp, simple, decent.*

### ROSE

☆☆ 1986 ZINFANDEL ROSE ($5.00) California. *Crisp, clean, balanced, varietal, nearly dry.*

### RED

☆☆ 1983 RED TABLE WINE ($3.75) California. *83.5% Cabernet. Lush, round, fruity, very attractive.*

☆☆ 1984 ROBERT MONDAVI RED ($5.00) California. *Herbal, simple, clean, attractive.*

☆☆ 1985 ROBERT MONDAVI RED ($3.75) California. *Crisp, fresh, varietal, decent.*

☆☆☆☆ 1978 CABERNET SAUVIGNON ($40.00) Reserve, Napa Valley. *Lush, elegant, deep; a great wine with pinpoint balance.*

☆☆ 1979 CABERNET SAUVIGNON ($12.00) Napa Valley. *Soft and fruity, with a subdued spiciness. Clean and appealing.*

☆☆☆ 1979 CABERNET SAUVIGNON ($25.00) Reserve, Napa Valley. *Balanced, rich, deep, fuller than the '78 Reserve. Ready to drink.*

☆☆☆ 1979 OPUS ONE CABERNET SAUVIGNON ($50.00) Napa Valley. *Complex, rich, balanced. Ready now but would benefit from aging a year or two more.*

☆☆ 1980 CABERNET SAUVIGNON ($12.00) Napa Valley. *Angular and herbal, complex. Ready to drink.*

☆☆ 1980 CABERNET SAUVIGNON ($30.00) Reserve, Napa Valley. *Crisp, thin, attractive, lacking the depth of the '79. Ready to drink.*

☆☆☆☆ 1980 OPUS ONE CABERNET SAUVIGNON ($50.00) Napa Valley. *Sweet oak and fruit; elegance, structure and intensity. Super. Ready now but a few more years would make it even better.*

☆☆ 1981 CABERNET SAUVIGNON ($12.00) Napa Valley. *Herbal, balanced, clean, attractive. Drink now.*

☆☆☆ 1981 CABERNET SAUVIGNON ($30.00) Reserve, Napa Valley. *Crisp, firm and beautifully built. Good fruit and oak. Drink 1988.*

☆☆☆☆ 1981 OPUS ONE CABERNET SAUVIGNON ($50.00) Napa Valley. *Dense, complicated, superb flavors, stunning. Drink 1988.*

☆☆☆ 1982 CABERNET SAUVIGNON ($9.50) Napa Valley. *Rich, velvety, plummy, oaky—the best in years. Drink now.*

☆☆☆☆ 1982 CABERNET SAUVIGNON ($35.00) Reserve, Napa Valley. *Rich, deep fruit, buttery oak and lovely structure. One of the best reserves yet. Drink 1989.*

☆☆☆☆ 1982 OPUS ONE CABERNET SAUVIGNON ($50.00) Napa Valley. *Rich, complex, elegant, remarkable fruit, great finesse. Drink 1992.*

☆☆☆☆ 1983 CABERNET SAUVIGNON ($11.75) Napa Valley. *Earthy, smooth, rich herbs and fruit. The nicest "regular" Mondavi Cabernet yet. Drink now.*

☆☆☆☆ 1983 CABERNET SAUVIGNON ($30.00) Reserve, Napa Valley. *14% Cabernet Franc, 7% Merlot. Rich, elegant, with lush fruit and lovely oak; complex and delicious. Drink 1989.*

☆☆☆☆ 1983 OPUS ONE CABERNET SAUVIGNON ($50.00) Napa Valley. *Lovely cherry fruit, crisp acidity, rich oak flavors. Maybe the best Opus yet. Very accessible now; drink in 1990 and beyond.*

☆☆ 1978 PINOT NOIR ($7.50) Napa Valley. *Soft and lush; very appealing.*

☆☆☆ 1978 PINOT NOIR ($15.00) Reserve, Napa Valley. *Lush, clean and complex. Very Burgundian.*

☆☆ 1979 PINOT NOIR ($8.00) Napa Valley. *Spicy and fruity.*

☆☆☆ 1979 PINOT NOIR ($15.00) Reserve, Napa Valley. *Earthy and lush, with rich flavors.*

☆ 1980 PINOT NOIR ($7.50) Napa Valley. *Thin, underripe, decent, clean but essentially dull.*

☆☆☆ 1980 PINOT NOIR ($15.00) Reserve, Napa Valley. *Dark, lush, complex, toasty, superb; delightful cherry tones.*

☆☆ 1981 PINOT NOIR ($8.00) Napa Valley. *Varietal, balanced; nice texture and structure.*

☆☆☆ 1981 PINOT NOIR ($14.00) Reserve, Napa Valley. *The best Mondavi Pinot yet. Delicate, complex, rich, lovely.*

☆☆☆ 1982 PINOT NOIR ($15.00) Reserve, Napa Valley. *Toasty oak, rich, earthy flavors. Really lovely.*

☆☆☆ 1983 PINOT NOIR ($15.75) Reserve, Napa Valley. *Rich and complex, with some stemminess; spicy and varietal.*

☆☆☆ 1984 PINOT NOIR ($7.50) Napa Valley. *Soft, fresh varietal flavors, appealing but not very complex.*

☆☆☆☆ 1985 PINOT NOIR ($18.00) Reserve, Napa Valley. *Cherry fruit, lovely oak, great depth and complexity. Superb.*

❧

## Mont St. John Cellars                    NAPA COUNTY

**WHITE**

☆☆ 1983 CHARDONNAY ($11.00) Napa Valley-Carneros. *Round, varietal, oaky, pleasant.*

☆☆☆ 1984 CHARDONNAY ($11.00) Carneros. *Lush, oaky, rich and smooth.*

**RED**

☆☆ 1981 PINOT NOIR ($10.00) Napa Valley-Carneros. *Rich, clean, deep.*

☆☆ 1983 ZINFANDEL ($7.00) Proprietor's Reserve, Napa Valley. *Crisp, fruity, some volatile acidity.*

❧

## Montali Winery                    ALAMEDA COUNTY

**WHITE**

○ 1982 CHARDONNAY ($9.00) Santa Maria Valley. *Oily, fat, vegetal.*

☆☆ 1984 CHARDONNAY ($9.50) Proprietor's Series, Bien Nacido, Santa Maria Valley. *Rich, deep, clean, ripe.*

☆☆ 1984 CHARDONNAY ($10.00) Audubon Collection, Sonoma Valley. *Simple, clean, fresh, pleasant.*

☆☆☆ 1984 CHARDONNAY ($10.00) Hopkins River, Sonoma. *Rich, varietal, with lovely oak and clean fruit; balanced.*

☆☆ 1986 CHARDONNAY ($12.00) Audubon Collection I, Wilson, Carneros Sonoma Valley. *Crisp, clean, fresh, varietal, charming but lacking depth.*

**RED**

☆☆ 1983 CABERNET SAUVIGNON ($8.50) Napa Valley. *Herbal, rich, smooth.*

☆ 1983 CABERNET SAUVIGNON ($10.00) Audubon Collection, Napa Valley. *Soft, earthy, vegetal, rich, nice texture.*

☆☆ 1984 CABERNET SAUVIGNON ($11.00) Audubon Collection I, Napa Valley. *Soft, simple, clean and quite drinkable.*

☆ 1982 PINOT NOIR ($7.50) Proprietor's Series, Santa Maria Valley. *Vegetal.*

☆ 1983 PINOT NOIR ($7.00) Napa Valley. *Soft and rich, with a hard vegetal edge.*

☆ 1980 ZINFANDEL ($7.50) Shenandoah Valley, Amador. *Tannic, rich, hot, earthy.*

☆ 1982 ZINFANDEL ($4.50) Bowman, Amador. *Varietal, harsh.*

☆☆ 1982 ZINFANDEL ($7.50) Alexander Valley. *Rich, complex, varietal. Drink now.*

ﺬ

## Montdomaine Cellars                VIRGINIA
**WHITE**

☆ 1984 CHARDONNAY ($7.00) Classic, Albemarle. *Oily, vegetal, rich, lemony.*

☆ 1984 CHARDONNAY ($8.00) Albemarle. *Fat, lush, heavy but decent.*

**RED**

☆ 1984 CABERNET SAUVIGNON ($14.00) Private Reserve, Virginia. *Earthy, herbaceous, some good fruit. Drink 1989.*

☆ 1985 CABERNET SAUVIGNON ($10.00) Virginia. *Pale, decent, clean, decent.*

☆☆ 1983 MERLOT ($8.00) Cuvée Bernard Chamberlain, Albemarle. *Lush, soft, balanced, fruity, charming.*

☆☆ 1983 MONTICELLO WINE COMPANY MERLOT ($8.00) Cuvée Bernard Chamberlain, Albemarle, Virginia. *Lush, soft, balanced, fruity and charming.*

1984 MERLOT ($10.00) Virginia. *Chalky, earthy, bitter.*

☆☆☆ 1985 MERLOT ($12.00) Virginia. *Rich new oak, ripe fruit, superb. Drink now.*

1984 PINOT NOIR ($7.00) Albemarle. *Bitter, dull, unattractive.*

ﺬ

## Montelle Vineyards                MISSOURI
**WHITE**

☆ 1985 SEYVAL BLANC ($5.00) Missouri. *Soft, simple, clean, decent.*

ﺬ

## Monterey Peninsula Winery        MONTEREY COUNTY
**WHITE**

☆ NV  BIG SUR WHITE ($3.75) California. *Botrytis, oily, crisp, decent.*

1982 CHARDONNAY ($11.50) Monterey. *Earthy, vegetal, soft, dull.*

☆☆ 1982 CHARDONNAY ($15.00) Cobblestone, Monterey. *Big, fat, rich, oily, balanced.*

☆☆ 1983 CHARDONNAY ($11.00) 50% Cobblestone, 50% Arroyo Seco, Monterey. *Very oaky, rich, some fruit, decent.*

☆ 1984 CHARDONNAY ($8.00) Lot 1, Tank Fermented, Sleepy Hollow, Monterey. *Decent balance but some odd flavors.*

☆☆☆ 1984 CHARDONNAY ($14.00) Lot II, Barrel Fermented, Sleepy Hollow, Monterey. *Toasty, rich, woody, ripe, lush, with good fruit.*

☆ 1985 CHARDONNAY ($14.00) Sleepy Hollow, Monterey. *Woody, heavy, intense, coarse and lacking charm.*

☆☆☆ 1986 PINOT BLANC ($9.00) Cobblestone, Arroyo Seco. *Rich, barrel fermented, toasty, earthy, good fruit and complexity.*

## RED

NV DIEGO RED ($2.75) California. *Vegetal, volatile acidity.*

NV BIG SUR RED ($3.75) California. *Zinfandel and Carnelian. Sappy, heavy, overdone.*

NV BLACK BURGUNDY ($5.00) Monterey. *Alcoholic, intense, some oxidation, harsh and agressive. A blend of Petite Sirah and Pinot St. George.*

☆☆ 1978 CABERNET SAUVIGNON ($9.00) Shell Creek, San Luis Obispo. *Rich, intensely fruity. Deeply colored. Drink now.*

☆☆ 1979 CABERNET SAUVIGNON ($13.00) Santa Lucia Mountains-Monterey. *Lovely, complex, a bit vegetal.*

☆☆☆ 1979 CABERNET SAUVIGNON ($18.00) Arroyo Seco, Monterey. *Herbal, fruity, fresh and attractive, with crisp acid. Drink now.*

☆☆☆☆ 1980 CABERNET SAUVIGNON ($25.00) Monterey. *Lush, beautifully structured, complex, superb.*

☆☆ 1981 CABERNET SAUVIGNON ($12.00) Smith & Hook, Monterey. *Lush, balanced, clean, rich, round. Ready to drink.*

☆☆☆ 1981 CABERNET SAUVIGNON ($14.00) Doctor's Reserve, Monterey. *Rich, deep, lush and lovely.*

1982 CABERNET SAUVIGNON ($11.20) Doctor's Reserve Lot II, Monterey. *Vegetal, bitter, some decent fruit.*

☆☆☆ 1981 MERLOT ($12.00) Monterey. *20% Cabernet. Rich, deep, clean and complex. Aging nicely.*

☆☆ 1983 MERLOT ($9.50) Monterey. *Crisp, fat, lush, ripe. Drink now.*

☆☆☆ 1984 MERLOT ($9.50) Doctor's Reserve, Monterey. *24% Cabernet Sauvignon. Clean, rich, varietal fruit, good balance, long finish. Drink now.*

☆☆ 1981 PINOT NOIR ($12.00) Junction, Monterey. *Tart, crisp, varietal.*

○ 1982 PINOT NOIR ($7.50) Sleepy Hollow, Monterey. *Sour, heavy, overripe, unattractive.*

☆ 1983 PINOT NOIR ($7.00) Vinco, Monterey. *Slim, pale, decent.*

☆ 1977 ZINFANDEL ($12.00) Late Harvest, Amador. *Intense, dark, tannic, deep.*

☆☆☆ 1978 ZINFANDEL ($6.50) 29% Amador, 45% Templeton, 20% Paso Robles, California. *Clean, rich and fruity.*

☆ 1978 ZINFANDEL ($6.50) Late Harvest, Hilltop, Monterey. *Decent—lush and clean, with some volatile acidity.*

☆☆ 1978 ZINFANDEL ($9.00) Late Harvest, Oak Flat, San Luis Obispo. *6.5% residual sugar. Big, lush, berried, clean and good.*

☆☆ 1978 ZINFANDEL ($9.00) Late Harvest, Willow Creek, San Luis Obispo. *6% residual sugar. Intense, coffee-like, rich, good fruit.*

☆☆ 1978 ZINFANDEL ($13.50) Late Harvest, Ferrero Old Ranch, Amador. *3.5% residual sugar. Port-like, rich, lush.*

☆☆ 1978 ZINFANDEL ($15.00) Late Harvest, Dusi, Templeton. *18% residual sugar. Port-like, lush and lovely. A bizarre style.*

☆ 1978 ZINFANDEL ($18.00) Sweet, Late Harvest, Amador. *16% residual sugar. Crisp acid and syrupy sweetness; jammy.*

☆☆☆ 1979 ZINFANDEL ($7.50) California. *Clean, fresh, fruity, fairly simple but very attractive.*

☆☆ 1979 ZINFANDEL ($7.50) Wilpete Farms, Willow Creek, San Luis Obispo. *Jammy and big.*

☆ 1979 ZINFANDEL ($8.00) Ferrero Ranch, Amador. *Soft, dull, lacking fruit.*

☆ 1979 ZINFANDEL ($8.00) Petite Sirah, Shell Creek Vineyard. *Fat, lush, berried, heavy.*

☆ 1979 ZINFANDEL ($8.50) Dusi, San Luis Obispo. *Raisiny, intense, deep.*

☆☆ 1980 ZINFANDEL ($6.00) Ferrero Ranch, Amador. *Simple, clean, decent, lacking fruit, good balance.*

🦃

## *The Monterey Vineyards*   MONTEREY COUNTY
### WHITE

☆☆ 1985 CLASSIC WHITE ($4.00) Monterey. *0.5% residual sugar. Blend of Chardonnay, Chenin Blanc, Sylvaner, Pinot Blanc, Riesling and French Colombard. Ripe, lush, charming.*

☆☆ 1986 CLASSIC WHITE ($4.00) Monterey. *Spicy, clean, some Chenin Blanc varietal character. Balanced and quite drinkable.*

☆ 1983 CHARDONNAY ($6.00) Monterey. *Fresh, clean, lacking varietal character.*

☆☆☆ 1984 CHARDONNAY ($7.00) Monterey. *Crisp, complex, lovely fruit, delicious.*

☆☆☆ 1985 CHARDONNAY ($7.00) Monterey. *Elegant, balanced, lovely oak and complex fruit.*

1984 PINOT BLANC ($9.50) Monterey. *Flat, thin, dull.*
### SPARKLING
☆ 1984 BRUT ($11.00) Monterey. *Simple, clean, fresh.*
### BLANC DE NOIR
☆☆ 1986 WHITE ZINFANDEL ($4.50) Monterey. *Crisp, snappy, with a hint of citrus.*
### RED
☆☆ 1982 CLASSIC RED ($4.25) California. *Herbs and chocolate, lush, good structure.*

☆☆ 1983 CLASSIC RED ($4.00) Monterey. *81% Cabernet, 15% Zinfandel, 4% Petite Sirah. Fresh, simple, clean, attractive.*

1984 CLASSIC RED ($4.75) Monterey. *Heavy vegetation, earthy.*

☆☆ 1979 CABERNET SAUVIGNON ($8.00) French Camp, San Luis Obispo. *Clean, slight and pleasant.*

🦃

## Monteviña Wines                          AMADOR COUNTY

### WHITE

1982 CHARDONNAY ($9.00) 83% Tepusquet, 17% Robert Young, California. *Simple, oily texture, herbaceous.*

☆☆ 1983 CHARDONNAY ($9.00) California. *Crisp, balanced, clean, complex, attractive.*

### BLANC DE NOIR

☆☆ 1986 WHITE ZINFANDEL ($4.50) California. *Soft, fruity, with decent varietal character and acidity.*

### RED

☆ 1981 PREMIUM RED ($3.75) Shenadoah Valley, California. *82% Zinfandel, 18% Cabernet Sauvignon. Ripe, fat, heavy.*

☆ 1981 BARBERA ($6.00) Estate, Shenandoah Valley, California. *Raisiny, berried, overdone.*

☆☆ 1983 BARBERA ($6.00) Estate, Shenandoah Valley, California. *Tart, crisp, clean, fruity, nice.*

☆☆ 1981 CABERNET SAUVIGNON ($7.50) Shenandoah Valley, California. *Lush, round, clean, varietal, charming. Drink now.*

☆☆☆ 1983 CABERNET SAUVIGNON ($7.50) Shenandoah Valley, California. *Crisp, berry flavors, nice structure, charming. Drink 1990.*

☆☆ 1979 ZINFANDEL ($6.50) Shenandoah Valley, Amador. *Berried, oaky, balanced, a bit coarse.*

○ 1980 ZINFANDEL ($5.00) Montino, Amador. *Unattractive, off flavors mar this one.*

☆☆ 1980 ZINFANDEL ($6.50) Amador. *Big, thick, overpowering.*

☆ 1980 ZINFANDEL ($9.00) Winemaker's Choice, Estate, Shenandoah Valley, California. *Big, syrupy, late-harvest style; awkward and overdone.*

☆☆☆ 1981 ZINFANDEL ($5.00) Montino, Estate, Shenandoah Valley, California. *Fruity and pleasant.*

☆☆☆ 1981 ZINFANDEL ($6.50) Estate, Shenandoah Valley, California. *Fruity, lush, berried but not overbearing. Very nice.*

☆☆ 1982 ZINFANDEL ($6.50) Estate, Shenandoah Valley, California. *Spicy, clean, smooth.*

☆☆ 1983 ZINFANDEL ($5.00) Montino, Estate, Shenandoah Valley. *Crisp, fresh, spicy, medium weight; simple but quite attractive.*

☆☆☆ 1984 ZINFANDEL ($9.00) Winemaker's Choice, Shenandoah Valley, California. *Spicy, dense, grapey, intense, ripe, massive.*

🙠

## Monticello Cellars                        NAPA COUNTY

### WHITE

☆☆☆ 1985 CHEVRIER BLANC ($7.50) Estate, Napa Valley. *80% Semillon, 20% Sauvignon Blanc. Crisp, fresh, fruity, herbal, very attractive.*

☆☆☆ 1982 CHARDONNAY ($13.50) Napa Valley. *Crisp, clean, snappy, fresh, lovely.*

☆☆☆ 1982 CHARDONNAY ($14.00) Barrel Fermented, Estate, Napa Valley. *Toasty, rich, varietal, fruity.*

☆☆ 1983 CHARDONNAY ($10.00) Jefferson Ranch, Estate, Napa Valley. *Crisp, clean, balanced, with apple fruit and a touch of oak.*

☆☆☆ 1983 CHARDONNAY ($12.50) Barrel Fermented, Estate, Napa Valley. *Crisp fruit, rich oak, lovely depth and structure.*

☆☆☆ 1984 LLORDS AND ELWOOD WINE CELLARS CHAR-
DONNAY ($8.00) The Rare, Napa Valley. *Lush,
fat, ripe, very lovely.*

☆☆☆ 1984 CHARDONNAY ($10.00) Jefferson Ranch, Napa Val-
ley. *Toasty, rich, complex, elegant, beautifully
balanced.*

☆☆☆ 1984 CHARDONNAY ($12.50) Napa Valley. *Superb fruit,
lovely balance, clean, delicious.*

☆☆☆☆ 1984 CHARDONNAY ($12.50) Corley, Napa. *Lush, soft,
round, with lovely fruit and delicate oak.*

☆☆ 1985 LLORDS & ELWOOD WINE CELLARS CHARDON-
NAY ($8.50) The Rare, Napa Valley. *Soft, fruity,
balanced, attractive.*

☆☆☆ 1985 CHARDONNAY ($10.00) Jefferson Ranch, Napa Val-
ley. *Soft, fresh, fruity, balanced, nicely structured.*

☆☆☆ 1986 LLORDS & ELWOOD WINE CELLARS CHARDON-
NAY ($9.00) The Rare, Napa Valley. *Fresh, apple
fruit, soft texture, pleasant.*

1985 LLORD'S & ELWOOD WINE CELLARS JOHAN-
NISBERG RIESLING ($6.25) Castle Magic, Cal-
ifornia. *Oily, heavy; lacking fruit and finesse.*

☆☆ 1985 SAUVIGNON BLANC ($7.50) Estate, Napa Valley.
*Earthy, lush, rich, pleasant.*

### RED

☆☆☆☆ 1980 CABERNET SAUVIGNON ($9.75) Napa Valley. *22%
Merlot. Fruity, structured, superb. Drink now or
hold.*

☆☆ 1981 CABERNET SAUVIGNON ($10.00) Napa Valley. *Nice
structure, complex, a bit weedy. Drink now.*

☆☆ 1982 LLORDS & ELWOOD WINE CELLARS CABERNET
SAUVIGNON ($9.00) Napa Valley. *Crisp, clean,
fruity, balanced. Drink now.*

☆☆☆ 1982 CABERNET SAUVIGNON ($9.75) Jefferson Ranch,
Estate, Napa Valley. *Lush, deep, concentrated,
balanced, lovely fruit. Drink 1987.*

☆☆☆☆ 1982 CABERNET SAUVIGNON ($14.50) Corley Reserve,
Cope, Napa Valley. *Lush, dark, with wonderful
fruit and structure. Drink 1988.*

☆☆☆ 1983 CABERNET SAUVIGNON ($10.00) Jefferson Cuvée,
Napa Valley. *Soft, herbal, velvety, rich, fresh and
appealing. Drink now.*

☆☆☆ 1984 CABERNET SAUVIGNON ($10.75) Jefferson Cuvée,
Napa Valley. *Rich blackcurrant fruit, velvety texture, complex, intense. Drink 1989.*

☆☆☆☆ 1984 CABERNET SAUVIGNON ($18.50) Corley Reserve,
Napa Valley. *Rich, ripe, velvety cassis fruit, intense,
great structure. Drink 1991.*

☆☆☆ 1984 PINOT NOIR ($12.00) Estate, Napa Valley. *Elegant,
clean, Burgundian, nicely structured.*

☆☆☆ 1985 PINOT NOIR ($12.00) Napa Valley. *Pale but richly fla-
vored, complex, lovely cherry fruit.*

🍇

## Moon Vineyards                    NAPA COUNTY

### WHITE

☆☆☆ 1984 CHARDONNAY ($10.50) Napa Valley-Carneros. *Crisp,
lean, firm fruit, lively acidity. Attractive. Made at
Bouchaine.*

### RED

☆☆☆ 1982 ZINFANDEL ($4.00) Estate, Napa Valley-Carneros.
*Crisp, fruity and superb. Fresh and charming.
Made at Acacia.*

🍇

## Morgan Winery                    MONTEREY COUNTY
### WHITE
☆☆☆☆ 1982 CHARDONNAY ($12.00) Cobblestone, Hillside, Monterey. *Extraordinary Burgundian effort: balanced, elegant, delicious.*

☆☆☆ 1983 CHARDONNAY ($12.50) Monterey. *Rich and balanced. Lovely.*

☆☆☆ 1984 CHARDONNAY ($12.50) 55% Hillside, 30% Cobblestone, 15% Vicente, Monterey. *Rich, toasty, tart, varietal, complex.*

☆☆☆☆ 1985 CHARDONNAY ($13.00) Monterey. *Crisp and elegant, with plenty of lush Monterey fruit and lovely, new oak.*

☆☆☆ 1986 CHARDONNAY ($13.00) Monterey. *Clean, balanced, fresh, good complexity.*

## J. W. Morris Wineries          SONOMA COUNTY
### WHITE
1983 CHARDONNAY ($5.00) Alexander Valley. *Sweaty, heavy, oily.*

1984 CHARDONNAY ($6.00) Alexander Valley. *Lacking freshness, candied fruit, decent.*

☆☆ 1985 BLACK MOUNTAIN CHARDONNAY ($10.00) Douglass Hill, Alexander Valley. *Rich, soft, lush, ripe, good.*

### RED
1981 RED PRIVATE RESERVE ($2.50) California. 50% Pinot Noir, 50% Zinfandel. *Volatile acidity mars this one.*

☆☆☆ 1981 CABERNET SAUVIGNON ($7.50) Alexander Valley. 22% Merlot. *Lovely balance; clean, lean. Ready to drink.*

☆☆☆ 1981 CABERNET SAUVIGNON ($8.00) California Selection. *Lovely fruit, deep oak; smooth and clean. Drink now.*

○ 1983 CABERNET SAUVIGNON ($5.00) Alexander Valley., Sonoma. *Vegetal, awkward, extremely unattractive.*

☆ 1984 CABERNET SAUVIGNON ($3.00) Alexander Valley, Sonoma. *Lush, ripe, a bit short on fruit.*

☆☆☆ 1984 RED TABLE WINE ($3.00) California. *Soft, lush, rich and velvety.*

☆☆☆ 1984 ZINFANDEL ($9.00) Alexander Valley. *Cinnamon, cedar flavors, snappy, fruity, appealing.*

## Mount Baker Vineyards          WASHINGTON
### WHITE
1985 ISLAND CLASSIC ($6.00) Washington. *Dry, dull, heavy.*

☆ 1985 ISLAND SELECT ($6.00) Washington. *Crisp, tart, off-dry, tangy fruit.*

☆☆ 1985 MADELINE ANGEVINE ($6.00) Washington. *Fresh, crisp, tart, lively.*

☆☆ 1986 MADELINE ANGEVINE ($5.00) Noonsack, Washington. 375 ml. *Crisp, tangy, simple.*

☆ 1983 CHARDONNAY ($9.00) Washington. *Vinous, oily, with some fruit and nice oak.*

1984 CHARDONNAY ($9.00) Washington. *Sharp, green, odd flavors, unpleasant.*

☆☆☆ 1985 MULLER-THURGAU ($6.00) Washington. *Ripe, fresh, round, fruity. Delightful.*

🍂

## Mount Eden Vineyards          *SANTA CLARA COUNTY*
### WHITE

☆☆☆ 1982 CHARDONNAY ($18.00) Santa Cruz Mountains. *Rich, big, yet elegant and beautifully structured.*

☆☆ 1985 MEV CHARDONNAY ($14.00) California. *Rich, deep, oily, heavy, well made but a bit clumsy.*

☆☆☆☆ 1985 CHARDONNAY ($25.00) Santa Cruz Mountains. *Toasty, rich, spicy fruit, intense flavors, great balance and finesse. A blockbuster but also quite well-proportioned.*

### RED

☆☆ 1978 CABERNET SAUVIGNON ($25.00) Estate, Santa Cruz Mountains. *Big, simple, earthy, dense.*

☆☆ 1979 CABERNET SAUVIGNON ($25.00) Estate, Santa Cruz Mountains. *Rich, deep, tastes like Zinfandel. Clean and jammy.*

☆ 1980 CABERNET SAUVIGNON ($30.00) Estate, Santa Cruz Mountains. *Weedy, green beans, balanced but a bit weak.*

☆☆ 1981 CABERNET SAUVIGNON ($30.00) Estate, Santa Cruz Mountains. *Big, rich, dense, with lovely earth and chocolate.*

1983 CABERNET SAUVIGNON ($15.00) Santa Cruz Mountains. *Dense, rich, intensely vegetal.*

☆☆ 1976 PINOT NOIR ($10.00) Estate, Santa Cruz Mountains. *Leathery and a bit tired, with some hotness.*

☆☆☆ 1977 PINOT NOIR ($18.00) Estate, Santa Cruz Mountains. *Earthy, rich, clean and super.*

☆☆ 1978 PINOT NOIR ($10.00) Estate, Santa Cruz Mountains. *Fat, lush, meaty, with good fruit acid.*

☆☆☆ 1979 PINOT NOIR ($15.00) Estate, Santa Cruz Mountains. *Peppery, elegant, lovely.*

☆☆☆ 1980 PINOT NOIR ($15.00) Estate, Santa Cruz Mountains. *Superb, rich and complex, with cherry flavors and some stems.*

☆☆☆ 1981 PINOT NOIR ($15.00) Estate, Santa Cruz Mountains. *Cherry, clean, complex, with fruit and floral aromas.*

☆☆ 1983 PINOT NOIR ($18.00) Estate, Santa Cruz Mountains. *Crisp, herbal, clean, nicely structured.*

🍂

## Mount Palomar Winery          *RIVERSIDE COUNTY*
### WHITE

☆ 1983 CHARDONNAY ($6.95) Temecula. *Simple, decent.*

☆☆ 1984 CHARDONNAY ($7.50) Estate, Temecula. *Clean, balanced, fresh, pleasant.*

☆ 1985 CHARDONNAY ($8.50) Estate, Temecula. *Pineapple flavors, decent, sour.*

☆ 1984 JOHANNISBERG RIESLING ($15.00) Select Late Harvest, Temecula. *375 ml. 10.8% residual sugar. Amber, lush, soft, fruity, simple.*

### RED

☆☆☆ 1983 CABERNET SAUVIGNON ($7.50) Napa Valley. *Rich, intense, deep, fat, lovely. Drink 1990.*

☆ 1984 CABERNET SAUVIGNON ($8.50) Napa Valley. *Rich, intense but vegetal.*

○ 1985 GAMAY BEAUJOLAIS ($5.50) Nouveau, Estate, Temecula. *Cement, chalk, unattractive flavors.*

😎

## Mount Veeder Winery        NAPA COUNTY

### WHITE

☆☆☆ 1983 CHARDONNAY ($13.50) Napa. *Rich oak, crisp, lemony fruit, good depth, long finish.*

☆☆ 1984 CHARDONNAY ($13.50) Napa. *Intensely oaky and austere. Stiff but interesting.*

☆☆ 1985 CHARDONNAY ($13.50) Napa. *Toasty, crisp, fresh, good acidity, decent.*

☆☆☆ 1986 CHARDONNAY ($14.00) Napa County. *Tangy, bright, good fruit, lovely oak.*

### RED

☆☆☆ 1979 CABERNET SAUVIGNON ($13.50) Bernstein, Napa. *Rich, fat, with a nice eucalyptus note.*

☆☆ 1980 CABERNET SAUVIGNON ($13.50) Bernstein, Napa. *Big and nicely structured. Ready.*

☆☆ 1981 CABERNET SAUVIGNON ($12.50) Mt. Veeder, Napa. *Lean, herbal, hard-edged. Drink 1988.*

☆ 1982 CABERNET SAUVIGNON ($12.50) Napa Valley. *Vegetal, thin, clean, decent. Drink 1991.*

☆☆☆ 1983 CABERNET SAUVIGNON ($14.00) Mount Veeder, Napa. *Big, heavy, rich and deep. Drink 1990.*

☆☆ 1980 ZINFANDEL ($8.00) Late Harvest, Napa Valley. *0.5% residual sugar.*

☆☆☆ 1981 ZINFANDEL ($8.50) Napa Valley. *Spicy, rich, clean and concentrated.*

☆☆☆ 1982 ZINFANDEL ($8.50) Napa Valley. *Balanced, clean, complex, elegant, lovely.*

😎

## Mountain House Winery        SONOMA COUNTY

### WHITE

☆☆ 1983 CHARDONNAY ($8.00) Sonoma. *Heavy, rich, oaky, intense.*

☆☆ 1984 CHARDONNAY ($11.00) Sonoma. *Clean, simple, a bit dull.*

### RED

☆☆ 1982 CABERNET SAUVIGNON ($12.00) Sonoma. *8% Merlot. Crisp, snappy, ripe, rich, attractive. Drink 1990.*

1982 ZINFANDEL ($6.00) Shenandoah Valley, Amador. *Odd and unattractive.*

😎

## The Mountain View Winery        SANTA CLARA COUNTY

### WHITE

☆☆☆ 1983 CHARDONNAY ($13.00) Dutton Ranch, Sonoma. *Rich, oaky, intense, ripe; a lovely wine in a big style.*

1984 CHARDONNAY ($12.00) Dutton Ranch, Sonoma. *Sour, tart, bitter.*

☆☆ 1985 CHARDONNAY ($12.00) Dutton Ranch, Sonoma. *Rich, ripe, oily, intense, tart.*

☆☆☆ 1986 SAUVIGNON BLANC ($5.00) Mendocino. *Crisp, fresh, lush fruit, round flavors; lovely.*

### RED

☆☆☆ 1982 CABERNET SAUVIGNON ($9.00) Alexander Valley. *Earthy, ripe, fresh, clean, lush cherry fruit. Drink 1989.*

☆ NV ZINFANDEL ($6.00) Amador. *Clean, decent, uninteresting.*

☆☆ 1983 ZINFANDEL ($7.50) Dutton Ranch, Sonoma. *Berried, dense but attractive.*

𐫱

## Moyer Champagne Company                 TEXAS
### SPARKLING

☆☆ NV BRUT ESPECIAL ($10.00) Texas. *Decent fruit, attractive.*

☆ NV BRUT NATURAL ($12.00) Texas. *Clean, fresh, simple.*

𐫱

## Moyer Vineyards                          OHIO
### WHITE

☆ NV VIDAL BLANC ($4.30) Ohio River Valley. *Spicy, fresh, clean, decent fruit.*

𐫱

## Mulhausen Vineyards                    OREGON
### RED

1982 PINOT NOIR ($9.00) Maresh, Oregon. *Flabby, dull, lacking structure.*

𐫱

## Murphy-Goode                    SONOMA COUNTY
### WHITE

1985 CHARDONNAY ($9.00) Alexander Valley. *Cardboard, sulfur, unpleasant.*

☆☆ 1986 CHARDONNAY ($9.00) Alexander Valley. *Tart, crisp, decent, lacks a middle, some oxidation.*

𐫱

## Naked Mountain Vineyard               VIRGINIA
### WHITE

☆☆ 1983 CHARDONNAY ($8.00) Virginia. *Rich, balanced and charming.*

𐫱

## Nalle                           SONOMA COUNTY
### RED

☆☆☆☆ 1984 ZINFANDEL ($8.00) Dry Creek Valley. *Rich, bright, charming oak and berry flavors. Auspicious first release.*

☆☆☆☆ 1985 ZINFANDEL ($8.00) Dry Creek Valley. *Cherries and berries, lovely oak; completely charming.*

𐫱

NAPA CELLARS *see* DeMoor Winery

## Napa Creek Winery                  NAPA COUNTY
### WHITE

☆☆ 1984 CHARDONNAY ($9.00) Napa Valley. *Bitter but nice oak and varietal character.*

### RED

☆ 1981 CABERNET SAUVIGNON ($12.00) Napa Valley. *Dense, herbal, lacking fruit. Drink now.*

☆☆ 1982 CABERNET SAUVIGNON ($9.00) Napa Valley. *Crisp, lean, tight, good varietal flavors. Drink 1989.*

☆☆ 1984 MERLOT ($9.00) Napa Valley. *Good structure, short, clean, lacking depth of fruit.*

𐫱

NAPA RIDGE *see* Beringer Vineyards

## Navarro Vineyards and Winery
MENDOCINO COUNTY

### WHITE

☆☆ 1983 CHARDONNAY ($8.75) Mendocino. *Rich, balanced, attractive.*

☆☆ 1984 CHARDONNAY ($5.50) Vin Blanc, Mendocino. *Soft, pleasant, simple fruit, good balance.*

☆ 1984 CHARDONNAY ($8.75) Mendocino. *Coarse and earthy, lacking clean fruit and finesse.*

☆☆ 1984 CHARDONNAY ($12.00) Premiere Reserve, Anderson Valley, Mendocino. *Earthy, rich, woody, lush, alcoholic. Not for everyone, but those who like theirs "big" will like this one.*

☆☆☆ 1985 CHARDONNAY ($8.75) Mendocino. *Lush, rich, elegant, fruity, neatly structured.*

☆☆☆ 1985 CHARDONNAY ($12.00) Premier Reserve, Anderson Valley. *Toasty, crisp, snappy, fresh, complex, delicious.*

☆☆☆ 1986 GEWURZTRAMINER ($6.50) Estate, Anderson Valley. *0.5% residual sugar. Lovely spice and varietal fruit.*

☆☆☆ 1983 JOHANNISBERG RIESLING ($18.50) Cluster Selected Late Harvest, Anderson Valley. *375 ml. 19.2% residual sugar. Crisp, soft, oily, lovely.*

☆☆☆ 1986 MUSCAT ($6.50) Anderson Valley. *Crisp, snappy, fresh varietal fruit. Complex, delicious.*

☆☆ 1984 WHITE RIESLING ($10.00) Cluster Selected Late Harvest, Anderson Valley. *10.4% residual sugar. Soft, crisp, clean, balanced.*

☆☆☆ 1985 WHITE RIESLING ($18.50) Cluster Select, Anderson Valley. *24.8% residual sugar. Remarkably crisp and lively, with lovely sweetness and depth.*

☆☆☆ 1986 WHITE RIESLING ($7.50) Anderson Valley. *Ripe, fruity, bright, varietal.*

### SPARKLING

☆☆☆ NV BRUT ($14.50) Anderson Valley. *Crisp, balanced, elegant fruit; quite lovely.*

### RED

☆☆☆ NV CABERNET SAUVIGNON TABLE WINE ($7.00) Mendocino. *15% Merlot. Soft, herbal, tangy, balanced and charmingly fresh. Drink now.*

1978 CABERNET SAUVIGNON ($9.50) Mendocino. *Disjointed and a bit off.*

☆☆☆ 1981 CABERNET SAUVIGNON ($12.50) Mendocino. *Tight, beautifully structured, clean, berried. Drink 1989.*

☆ 1982 CABERNET SAUVIGNON ($11.50) Mendocino. *Dull, muddy, not much.*

☆ 1980 PINOT NOIR ($8.75) Estate, Anderson Valley, Mendocino. *Decent but lacking depth.*

☆ 1981 PINOT NOIR ($8.00) Estate, Anderson Valley, Mendocino. *Dense, lacking character.*

☆☆ 1982 PINOT NOIR ($9.75) Estate, Anderson Valley, Mendocino. *Crisp, simple, clean, tart, nice varietal flavors.*

☆☆ 1983 PINOT NOIR ($8.75) Estate, Anderson Valley, Mendocino. *Varietal, balanced, clean, earthy, attractive.*

☆☆☆ 1984 PINOT NOIR ($9.75) Estate, Mendocino. *Lush, soft, clean, delicious.*

☆☆☆ 1984 PINOT NOIR ($12.00) Estate, Anderson Valley. *Spicy, clean, ripe and crisp. Nicely balanced and ready to drink.*

1986 PINOT NOIR ($7.50) Estate, Anderson Valley, Mendocino. *Heavy, oily, vegetal.*

☆☆ 1983 ZINFANDEL ($6.00) Mendocino. *Fresh, simple, berried, attractive.*

ঽ৯

## Naylor Wine Cellars                    PENNSYLVANIA
### RED
☆☆☆ 1982 CHAMBOURCIN ($7.00) York. *Ripe, lush, clean, stunning complexity, earthy and rich.*

ঽ৯

## Nevada City Winery                    NEVADA COUNTY
### WHITE
☆ NV BICYCLE WHITE ($5.00) California. *A fairly pedestrian blend of Riesling and Sauvignon Blanc. Dull and uninteresting.*

☆☆ 1982 CHARDONNAY ($9.00) California. *Earthy, rich, pleasant.*

1984 CHARDONNAY ($9.00) Nevada County. *Oily, vegetal, dull.*

☆☆☆ 1986 CHARDONNAY ($12.00) Napa Valley. *Lush, soft; complex oak and smooth fruit.*

1986 CHENIN BLANC ($5.00) Nevada County. *Oily, heavy, not fresh.*

☆ 1986 GEWURZTRAMINER ($6.00) 73% Sonoma, 27% Placer. *Spritzy, varietal, too heavy.*

### BLANC DE NOIR
☆☆ 1986 ALPENGLOW ($5.00) Nevada County. *Clean, rich, nicely balanced, off-dry.*

### RED
☆☆ 1982 ZINFANDEL-MERLOT ($5.00) California. *Rich, clean, lush, deep, with lovely fruit.*

☆ 1984 DOUCE NOIR ($7.50) Nevada County. *Made from Charbono. Ripe, tart, simple, clean and decent.*

☆☆☆ 1981 CABERNET SAUVIGNON ($6.50) California. *Soft, herbal, supple, appealing. Ready to drink.*

☆☆☆ 1982 CABERNET SAUVIGNON ($6.00) 72% Mt. Lassen, 28% Quail Glen, Shasta. *Toasty, earthy, rich, heavy, very good. Drink 1989.*

☆☆ 1981 CHARBONO ($8.00) Nevada County. *Rich, deep, clean.*

☆☆☆ 1980 PETITE SIRAH ($7.00) Nevada County. *Tart, fruity, clean, snappy and superb.*

☆☆ 1981 PINOT NOIR ($12.00) Nevada County. *Rich, deep, a bit overdone, with good fruit flavors.*

☆☆☆ 1983 PINOT NOIR ($12.00) Cobden, Nevada County. *Lovely cherry-berry flavors and delicate varietal character; clean and impressive.*

1984 PINOT NOIR ($14.00) Nevada County. *Harsh, odd.*

☆☆ NV SIERRA MOUNTAIN ZINFANDEL ($3.75) Nevada County. *Soft, clean, simple, lovely.*

☆☆ 1982 ZINFANDEL ($7.00) Nevada County. *Rich, fruity, dark, clean.*

☆☆ 1984 ZINFANDEL ($7.00) Nevada County. *Lush, ripe, velvety, intense, big.*

ঽ৯

## Newlan Vineyards and Winery NAPA COUNTY
### WHITE
☆☆☆ 1984 CHARDONNAY ($9.50) Napa Valley. *Rich, clean, fruity, toasty oak, lovely balance.*

☆☆ 1982 JOHANNISBERG RIESLING ($13.00) Late Harvest Bunch Selected, Napa Valley. *375 ml. Rich, deep, lush, soft, clean.*

### RED
☆☆☆ 1981 CABERNET SAUVIGNON ($15.00) Reserve, York Creek, Napa Valley. *Lean, lovely fruit, superb structure. Drink 1990.*

☆☆ 1982 CABERNET SAUVIGNON ($12.00) Estate, Napa Valley. *Clean, attractive flavors, somewhat slight. Drink 1988.*

☆☆ 1980 PINOT NOIR ($7.50) Estate, Napa Valley. *Ripe, clean, simple, attractive.*

☆ 1981 PINOT NOIR ($8.00) Second Release, Estate, Napa Valley. *Soft, lush, leathery, some herbs and vegetation.*

☆☆ 1983 PINOT NOIR ($12.00) Estate, Napa Valley. *Crisp, fruity, tart, balanced.*

☆ 1986 PINOT NOIR ($5.00) Beau Nouveau, Napa Valley. *Pale, tangy, tart, some odd flavors.*

૨•

## Newton Vineyard NAPA COUNTY
### WHITE
☆☆☆ 1982 CHARDONNAY ($16.00) Napa Valley. *Toasty oak, lush, clean fruit. A magnificent wine.*

☆☆☆ 1983 CHARDONNAY ($14.00) Napa Valley. *Elegant and crisp, with lovely oak and great varietal fruit.*

☆☆☆ 1984 CHARDONNAY ($14.00) Napa Valley. *Lush, ripe, clean, quite lovely.*

### RED
☆☆☆ 1980 CABERNET SAUVIGNON ($12.50) Estate, Napa Valley. *Tart, firm, assertive, with lovely fruit. Ready to drink.*

☆☆☆☆ 1981 CABERNET SAUVIGNON ($12.50) Estate, Napa Valley. *Super—crisp, deep, elegant, with great potential. Drink 1988.*

☆☆ 1982 CABERNET SAUVIGNON ($12.50) Napa Valley. *Lush, round, clean, decent. Drink 1989.*

☆☆☆☆ 1983 CABERNET SAUVIGNON ($9.00) Napa Valley. *Clean, black currant, luscious, complex, superb. Drink 1989.*

☆☆☆ 1984 CABERNET SAUVIGNON ($12.50) Napa Valley. *15% Merlot, 8% Cabernet Franc, 2% Petite Verdot. Ripe, fruity, clean and complex. Drink 1991.*

☆☆☆ 1980 MERLOT ($10.50) Napa Valley. *Snappy, high acid, clean, beautifully structured.*

☆☆☆ 1982 MERLOT ($12.50) Napa Valley. *Deep, rich, clean flavors. Lovely fruit and oak. Drink 1988.*

☆☆☆ 1983 MERLOT ($11.50) Napa Valley. *Lush, clean, great acid balance, fresh, lovely, complex.*

☆☆☆☆ 1985 MERLOT ($12.00) Napa Valley. *25% Cabernet Franc. Deep, lively, great new oak, lovely balance. Stunning. Drink 1994.*

૨•

## Neyers Winery NAPA COUNTY
### WHITE
☆☆ 1982 CHARDONNAY ($11.00) Napa Valley. *Oaky, buttery, rich, clean, attractive.*

☆☆☆ 1984 CHARDONNAY ($11.75) Napa Valley. *Ripe, earthy, toasty, rich, nice fruit.*

☆☆☆ 1985 CHARDONNAY ($11.75) Napa Valley. *Rich, balanced, clean, attractive.*

**RED**

☆☆☆ 1982 CABERNET SAUVIGNON ($11.00) Napa Valley. *Herbal, toasty, rich and beautifully structured. Drink 1988.*

☆☆☆ 1983 CABERNET SAUVIGNON ($11.75) Napa Valley. *Soft, lush and richly varietal. Charming now and over the short term. Drink now.*

☆☆☆ 1984 CABERNET SAUVIGNON ($11.00) Napa Valley. *Snappy fruit, lush texture, fresh, clean, rich oak.*

🦋

## Nichelini Vineyard                    NAPA COUNTY
**RED**

☆☆ 1982 CABERNET SAUVIGNON ($10.00) Private Reserve, Napa Valley. *Earthy, balanced, attractive, old-style.*

🦋

## Niebaum-Coppola Estate                    NAPA COUNTY
**RED**

☆☆☆ 1978 RUBICON ($25.00) Napa Valley. *60% Cabernet Sauvignon, 38% Cabernet Franc, 2% Merlot. Rich and deep.*

☆☆☆ 1979 RUBICON ($25.00) Napa Valley. *80% Cabernet Sauvignon, 20% Cabernet Franc. Lovely but with less depth than the '78.*

☆☆☆ 1980 RUBICON ($35.00) Napa Valley. *Lovely, rich fruit, clean, intense, balanced, well structured. 73% Cabernet Sauvignon, 23% Cabernet Franc, 4% Merlot. Drink 1992.*

🦋

## Noble Hill Vineyards                    SONOMA COUNTY
**WHITE**

☆ 1986 SAUVIGNON BLANC ($8.75) Noble Hill Vineyards, Sonoma. *Vinous, heavy, herbal, lacking fruit.*

🦋

NORTH COAST CELLARS *see* Colony

## Oak Knoll Winery                    OREGON
**WHITE**

☆ 1985 CHARDONNAY ($12.00) Oregon. *Pine and lemon flavors, clean, decent.*

**BLANC DE NOIR**

☆☆ 1986 PINOT NOIR BLANC ($6.00) Oregon. *Crisp, lean, strawberry fruit, varietal.*

**RED**

☆☆☆ 1980 PINOT NOIR ($20.00) Dion, Oregon. *Great color, fruit harmony and complexity. Burgundian and superb.*

1982 PINOT NOIR ($14.00) Vintage Select, Dion, Oregon. *Composty, dank.*

☆ 1983 PINOT NOIR ($9.10) 70% Dion, 30% Casper, Oregon. *Intense, berried, Zinfandel-like, decent.*

☆ 1983 PINOT NOIR ($9.50) 66% Cooper Mountain, 34% Dion, Oregon. *Stemmy, green, simple, decent balance.*

☆☆☆ 1983 PINOT NOIR ($15.00) Vintner's Selection, Dion, Oregon. *Spicy, clean, lush, lovely fruit; a stunning wine.*

🦋

## Oak Ridge Vineyards                    SAN JOAQUIN COUNTY
### WHITE
☆☆  1985 WHITE BURGUNDY ($5.00) California. *75% Chardonnay. Lush, rich, varietal.*

☆☆☆ 1986 CHENIN BLANC ($3.75) Ryer Island, California. *0.9% residual sugar. Clean, rich, lush, balanced, charming.*
### BLANC DE NOIR
☆  1986 WHITE ZINFANDEL ($4.00) White Tail, Lodi. *Soft, sappy, some decent fruit.*
### RED
NV  BARREL RED ($2.85) California. *75% Cabernet, 15% Zinfandel, 10% Petite Sirah. Thin, sweet, no varietal fruit.*

NV  COUNTRY CLASSIC ($4.00) California. *Lush, fat, sweet, awful.*

☆  1985 GRAN SIRAH ($5.50) California. *Rich, fat, sweetish, smooth.*

ᐤ

## Oakencroft Vineyard and Winery                    VIRGINIA
### WHITE
☆☆  1985 CHARDONNAY ($8.00) Virginia. *Clean, varietal, decent fruit, some bitterness on the finish.*

☆☆  1986 CHARDONNAY ($8.00) Virginia. *Crisp, tangy, lean and nicely made.*

☆☆☆ 1985 SEYVAL BLANC ($6.50) Virginia. *Crisp, fruity, clean, fresh, charming.*

☆☆☆ 1986 SEYVAL BLANC ($6.00) Virginia. *Crisp, tangy, round, fresh and delicious.*
### RED
☆☆  1984 CABERNET SAUVIGNON ($9.50) Virginia. *Crisp, tart, lean, clean, varietal. Drink 1990.*

ᐤ

## Oberhellmann Vineyards                    TEXAS
### WHITE
1985 CHARDONNAY ($9.50) Gillespie. *Oxidized, earthy, unpleasant.*

☆  1985 SEMILLON ($6.50) Gillespie. *Fresh, soft, crisp, decent.*
### RED
1984 EDELBLUME ($6.75) Gillespie. *Carmine and Merlot. Bitter and unattractive.*

☆☆  1984 CABERNET SAUVIGNON ($12.50) Gillespie. *Crisp, ripe, decent, good.*

ᐤ

## Obester Winery                    SAN MATEO COUNTY
### WHITE
☆☆☆ 1985 CHARDONNAY ($12.00) Mendocino. *Crisp and clean, with some rich barrel fermentation flavors.*
### RED
☆☆☆ 1977 PETITE SIRAH ($12.00) John Gemello Tribute, Sonoma. *Rich and full but with grace and complexity. Stunning.*

ᐤ

## The Ojai Vineyard                    VENTURA COUNTY
### RED
☆☆  1985 SYRAH ($10.00) California. *Tart, lean, earthy, herbaceous, rich.*

ᐤ

## The Old Creek Ranch Winery    VENTURA COUNTY
### RED
☆ 1983 MERLOT ($8.00) Rancho Sisquoc, Santa Maria Valley. *Thin, tart, decent but lacking fruit.*

🦢

## Old South Winery    MISSISSIPPI
### WHITE
☆ NV MUSCADINE ($4.50) Carlos, Mississippi. *Intense varietal nose, soft, off-dry, clean, pleasant.*

🦢

## Oliver Winery    INDIANA
### WHITE
☆☆☆ 1986 CHENIN BLANC ($7.50) Indiana. *Crisp, fruit, charming, balanced, delightful.*
NV VIDAL BLANC ($6.50) Swiss Reserve, Indiana. *Vegetative, chalky, off-dry, heavy.*

🦢

## Olson Vineyards Winery    MENDOCINO COUNTY
### WHITE
☆☆ 1985 GLACIER WHITE ($4.50) California. *Crisp, fresh, fruity, clean, appealing.*
☆☆ 1983 CHARDONNAY ($8.75) Mendocino. *Soft, lush, decent.*
☆☆ 1984 CHARDONNAY ($9.00) Mendocino. *Clean, crisp, decent, attractive.*
☆☆ 1985 CHARDONNAY ($8.50) Mendocino. *Spicy, crisp, fresh, clean, attractive.*
### RED
☆☆☆ 1984 VIKING RED ($6.00) Mendocino. *Crisp, clean, ripe, intense.*
☆☆ 1984 PETITE SIRAH ($8.50) Mendocino. *Dark, inky, powerful, rich.*
☆ 1982 ZINFANDEL ($8.00) Special Reserve, Mendocino. *0.8% residual sugar. 16% alcohol. Intense, chocolatey, heavy.*
☆☆ 1983 ZINFANDEL ($8.00) Special Reserve, Mendocino. *Intense, complex, varietal. Drink 1989.*
☆☆ 1984 ZINFANDEL ($6.00) Viking, Mendocino. *Herbal, tart, fruity, decent.*

🦢

OPUS ONE *see* Robert Mondavi Winery

## Orleans Hill Vinicultural Corporation    YOLO COUNTY
### WHITE
☆☆ NV CAJUN WHITE ($4.50) California. *A blend of Chenin Blanc, French Colombard and Muscat. Fresh, clean simple, decent.*
☆ 1984 CHARDONNAY ($5.00) California. *Pineapple flavors, tart, decent.*
☆☆ 1984 CHARDONNAY ($6.75) Clarksburg. *Soft, fruity, clean. A charming everyday white wine.*
### RED
NV CAJUN RED ($4.50) California. *A blend of Cabernet, Zinfandel and Petite Sirah. Hot, heavy and unappealing.*
☆☆ 1984 RED TABLE WINE ($4.00) California. *60% Zinfandel, 40% Cabernet Sauvignon. Spicy, soft, attractive.*
1984 ZINFANDEL ($5.00) Clockspring, Amador. *Herbal, cooked, lacking fruit, muddy.*

🦢

## *Pacheco Ranch Winery*                    MARIN COUNTY
### WHITE
☆☆ 1983 CHARDONNAY ($8.50) Marin. *Earthy, rich, varietal, oaky, quite decent.*
☆ 1984 CHARDONNAY ($9.50) Sonoma. *Soft, dull, lacking fruit.*
### RED
☆☆☆ 1979 CABERNET SAUVIGNON ($9.00) Marin. *Full and cherry-toned; rich and herbal. Drink now.*
☆☆ 1980 CABERNET SAUVIGNON ($9.50) Marin. *Lush, varietal, earthy, big. Ready to drink.*
1982 CABERNET SAUVIGNON ($9.50) Marin. *Flat, dull, lacking fruit.*

❧

## *Page Mill Winery*                    SANTA CLARA COUNTY
### WHITE
☆☆ 1983 CHARDONNAY ($12.50) Keene Dimick, Napa Valley. *Rich, heavy.*
☆☆ 1983 CHARDONNAY ($12.50) Elizabeth Garbett, Santa Clara. *Oaky, rich, smooth.*
1984 CHARDONNAY ($12.50) Keene Dimick, Napa Valley. *Dirty, oxidized.*
### RED
☆☆ 1980 CABERNET SAUVIGNON ($11.50) Volker Eisele, Napa Valley. *Herbal, soft, attractive.*
☆☆ 1982 CABERNET SAUVIGNON ($12.50) Volker Eisele, Napa Valley. *Simple, clean, charming fruit and aroma.*
☆☆ 1980 ZINFANDEL ($8.00) Eisele, Chiles Valley, Napa. *Intense and raisiny.*

❧

## *Palisades Vineyards*                    SAN FRANCISCO COUNTY
### RED
☆☆☆ 1984 CABERNET SAUVIGNON ($12.00) Hewitt, Napa Valley. *Dark, lush, fruity, intense berry flavors, quite attractive. Drink 1991.*
☆☆ 1984 PETITE SIRAH ($9.00) Napa Valley. *Dark, rich, tannic, clean and intense. Drink 1990.*

❧

## *Palmer Vineyards*                    NEW YORK
### WHITE
☆☆☆ 1986 CHARDONNAY ($8.00) North Fork, Long Island. *Crisp, lean, well built, nicely balanced.*
☆☆☆ 1986 GEWURZTRAMINER ($8.00) North Fork. *Elegant, spicy, fresh, balanced, lovely.*
### RED
☆ 1985 MERLOT ($8.00) Aquebogue, North Fork. *Varietal, balanced, thin.*

❧

PALOMA VINEYARDS *see* Domaine Laurier

## *Papagni Vineyards*                    MADERA COUNTY
### SPARKLING
☆☆ NV SPUMANTE D'ANGELO ($7.00) Madera. *Muscat. Fresh, spicy, sweet and appealing.*
1984 SPARKLING WHITE ZINFANDEL ($9.00) California. *Sweet, heavy, dull flavors, unappealing.*
### RED
☆ 1981 CABERNET SAUVIGNON ($7.00) California. *Decent fruit but stinky.*

❧

## Paradise Vintners BUTTE COUNTY
### RED
○ 1983 CLARET, NECTAR OF THE GODS ($5.00) California. *Oxidized, shallow, dull.*
○ 1982 BARBERA ($5.00) California. *Thin, clean, decent.*
☆ 1982 CABERNET SAUVIGNON ($7.00) California. *Lush, dull, lacking acidity.*
    1983 PETITE SIRAH ($5.00) California. *Bitter, muddy.*
☆ 1983 RUBY CABERNET ($5.00) California. *Crisp, thin, vegetal.*

**&**

## Parducci Wine Cellars MENDOCINO COUNTY
### WHITE
☆ 1982 CHARDONNAY ($7.75) Mendocino. *Vinous, herbal, dull.*
☆☆ 1983 CHARDONNAY ($7.50) Mendocino. *Lovely. Clean, balanced and attractive.*
☆☆ 1986 CHARDONNAY ($8.00) Mendocino *Crisp, apple fruit, charming but simple.*
☆☆ 1986 SAUVIGNON BLANC ($6.50) Mendocino. *Fresh, spritzy, varietal, fruity, attractive.*
### RED
☆☆ 1978 CABERNET SAUVIGNON ($12.00) Cellarmaster's Selection, Mendocino. *Cabernet-Merlot. Lush, tannic, attractive. Ready to drink.*
☆ 1979 CABERNET SAUVIGNON ($7.50) Mendocino. *Simple, with very little varietal character.*
☆☆ 1979 CABERNET SAUVIGNON ($10.00) Vintage Selection, Mendocino. *Earthy, clean and ripe.*
☆☆ 1980 CABERNET SAUVIGNON ($8.50) 50th Anniversary, Estate, Mendocino. *Rich, grapey, intense, tannic.*
☆ 1980 CABERNET SAUVIGNON ($8.50) Olympic Bottling, Mendocino. *Vegetal, nicely structured, a bit thin.*
☆ 1982 CABERNET SAUVIGNON ($10.00) Mendocino. *Herbal, simple, dull.*
☆☆☆ 1983 CABERNET SAUVIGNON ($8.00) Mendocino. *12% Merlot. Crisp, snappy, good structure, clean and charming. Drink 1989.*
☆☆ 1978 MERLOT Special Cellar Selection, Mendocino. *Rich and deep, with good varietal character. A bit short.*
☆☆ 1983 MERLOT ($8.00) Mendocino. *Earthy, herbal, varietal, good texture and finish. Drink now.*
☆☆ 1978 PETITE SIRAH ($7.50) Cellarmaster's Selection, Mendocino. *Rich, clean and varietal but a bit short on the finish.*
☆☆ 1979 PETITE SIRAH ($5.75) Mendocino. *Dense, clean, tannic, nicely made.*
☆ 1980 PINOT NOIR ($5.00) Mendocino. *Toasty, light, simple.*
☆☆☆ 1985 PINOT NOIR ($5.50) Mendocino. *Crisp, fresh, clean, simple but very charming.*
☆☆ 1985 ZINFANDEL ($5.60) Mendocino. *Light, clean, decent structure.*

**&**

## Parsons Creek Winery MENDOCINO COUNTY
### WHITE
☆☆ 1983 CHARDONNAY ($9.50) Mendocino. *Crisp yet lush and somewhat deep.*
☆☆ 1984 CHARDONNAY ($8.50) Mendocino. *Soft, lush, deep, attractive.*
### SPARKLING
☆☆☆ NV BRUT ($13.50) Mendocino. *Rich, balanced, impressive.*

## RED
☆ 1981 ZINFANDEL ($6.00) Mendocino. *Earthy. Good structure but not lovable.*

৯

## *Pat Paulsen Vineyards*                SONOMA COUNTY
### WHITE
☆☆ 1985 REFRIGERATOR WHITE ($4.25) Sonoma. *Crisp, fruity, fresh and clean.*

☆☆☆ 1986 REFRIGERATOR WHITE ($4.00) Sonoma. *Crisp, fresh, lovely structure.*

☆☆☆ 1986 MUSCAT CANELLI ($7.50) Alexander Valley. *2.5% residual sugar. Spicy, fresh, fruity and very lovely.*

☆ 1982 CHARDONNAY ($11.00) Sonoma. *Dull, simple.*

☆ 1983 CHARDONNAY ($11.00) Sonoma. *Tight, lean, hard, some off qualities.*

☆☆☆ 1984 CHARDONNAY ($11.00) Sonoma. *Crisp, lush, clean fruit; lovely.*

☆☆☆ 1984 CHARDONNAY ($12.50) Select, Sonoma. *Crisp, fresh, clean, with nice fruit.*

1986 GEWURZTRAMINER ($6.50) Alexander Valley. *Bitter, off flavors, flabby, candied.*

☆☆☆ 1985 MUSCAT ($7.50) Sonoma. *1.2% residual. Spicy, clean, with lovely fruit.*

### RED
☆☆ 1984 AMERICAN GOTHIC RED ($6.50) Sonoma. *1.5 liters. 100% Gamay. Great color, lovely spice and fruit. $1 donated to Farm Aid from the proceeds of each bottle.*

1980 CABERNET SAUVIGNON ($8.00) Sonoma. *Heavy, weedy, unappealing.*

☆☆ 1981 CABERNET SAUVIGNON ($8.00) Sonoma. *Herbal, soft, attractive. Nicely structured.*

☆☆☆ 1982 CABERNET SAUVIGNON ($10.00) Estate, Sonoma. *Lush, soft, herbal, balanced, complex, varietal. Drink now.*

☆☆☆ 1983 CABERNET SAUVIGNON ($11.00) Alexander Valley. *Earthy, lush, fat, soft, lovely, supple. Drink 1988.*

☆☆ 1984 CABERNET SAUVIGNON ($11.00) Alexander Valley. *Smokey, spicy, clean, nicely balanced. Drink now.*

☆☆ 1985 CABERNET SAUVIGNON ($11.00) Sonoma. *4% Cabernet Franc.Herbal, lush, smooth, balanced. Drink now.*

৯

## *Robert Pecota Winery*                NAPA COUNTY
### WHITE
☆ 1985 MUSCATO DI ANDREA ($8.50) California. *10.3% residual sugar. Fat, spicy, heavy.*

☆☆ 1985 SWEET ANDREA MUSCAT BLANC ($16.00) California. *375 ml. 22.5% residual sugar. Crisp, fresh, syrupy, intense fruit, floral.*

☆☆☆☆ 1986 MUSCAT BLANC ($8.50) California. *8.5% residual sugar. Spicy, crisp, charming varietal character, delicious fruit and charming sweetness.*

☆☆☆ 1983 CHARDONNAY ($13.50) Canepa, Alexander Valley. *Rich, heavy, toasty, ripe, dominated by oak.*

☆☆☆☆ 1984 CHARDONNAY ($13.50) Canepa, Alexander Valley. *Lush, oaky, complex, crisp, loaded with depth and finesse.*

☆☆☆ 1985 CHARDONNAY ($16.00) Canepa, Alexander Valley. *Toasty oak, crisp acidity, complex varietal flavors. Serious and quite lovely.*

☆☆☆ 1986 SAUVIGNON BLANC ($9.25) Napa Valley. *Woody, soft, clean, quite lovely.*

### RED

☆☆☆ 1982 CABERNET SAUVIGNON ($12.00) Napa Valley. *Rich, deep, lush, structured, lovely.*

☆☆ 1983 CABERNET SAUVIGNON ($10.00) Estate, Napa Valley. *Rich, soft, lush, attractive.*

☆☆☆ 1983 CABERNET SAUVIGNON ($12.00) 60% Pecota, 40% Williamson, Napa Valley. *Crisp, lean, clean, attractive. Drink 1990.*

☆☆ 1985 GAMAY BEAUJOLAIS ($5.00) Napa Valley. *Fresh, crisp, clean, fruity and simple.*

ðø

## J. Pedroncelli Winery          SONOMA COUNTY

### WHITE

☆ NV SONOMA WHITE WINE ($3.00) Sonoma. *Crisp, herbal, simple but nice.*

☆☆ 1982 CHARDONNAY ($7.75) Sonoma. *Crisp, clean, simple but attractive.*

1983 CHARDONNAY ($7.75) Sonoma. *Off flavors, unattractive.*

☆☆☆ 1984 CHARDONNAY ($7.75) Dry Creek Valley. *Crisp, clean, fresh, lovely.*

☆☆ 1985 CHARDONNAY ($7.75) Sonoma. *Soft, fruity, clean, simple.*

1985 JOHANNISBERG RIESLING ($5.50) Sonoma. *Bitter, soapy, metallic.*

☆☆ 1986 JOHANNISBERG RIESLING ($9.00) Late Harvest, Sonoma. *11.1% residual sugar. Lush, clean, varietal, slightly herbaceous.*

☆ 1986 SAUVIGNON BLANC ($6.00) Dry Creek Valley. *Flat, simple, decent.*

### BLANC DE NOIR

☆☆☆ 1986 WHITE ZINFANDEL ($4.50) Sonoma. *Juicy, luscious, fruity, quite lovely.*

### RED

NV SONOMA RED WINE ($3.00) Sonoma. *Stinky, vegetal.*

☆ 1979 CABERNET SAUVIGNON ($5.50) Sonoma. *Decent, simple and clean.*

☆ 1980 CABERNET SAUVIGNON ($6.00) Sonoma. *Berried, rich and decent.*

○ 1982 CABERNET SAUVIGNON ($6.50) Sonoma. *Muddy, unattractive.*

☆☆☆ 1982 CABERNET SAUVIGNON ($12.00) Reserve, Sonoma. *Soft, clean, lush, rich, good fruit. Drink now.*

1983 CABERNET SAUVIGNON ($6.50) Sonoma. *Dull, simple, tired, not much.*

☆ 1980 PINOT NOIR ($7.50) Sonoma. *10% Petite Sirah. Vegetal nose, earthy, rich, no depth.*

☆☆ 1981 PINOT NOIR ($5.00) Sonoma. *Dark, intense, woody, with decent fruit.*

☆☆ 1982 PINOT NOIR ($5.50) Dry Creek Valley, Sonoma. *Simple but clean and quite drinkable.*

☆ 1983 PINOT NOIR ($5.50) Sonoma. *Simple, clean, lacking varietal character.*

☆☆ 1977 ZINFANDEL ($6.50) Vintage Select, Sonoma. *Rich, fruity and fresh.*

☆☆ 1978 ZINFANDEL ($6.50) Vintage Select, Sonoma. *Nice, soft, complex and mature.*

☆☆ 1979 ZINFANDEL ($4.50) Sonoma. *Simple and decent.*

☆☆ 1980 ZINFANDEL ($4.50) Sonoma. *Spicy and clean, with great fruit.*

☆ 1981 ZINFANDEL ($4.50) Dry Creek Valley, Sonoma. *Clean, tangy, decent.*

☆ 1981 ZINFANDEL ($8.00) Reserve, Sonoma. *Thin, dull, decent.*

☆ 1982 ZINFANDEL ($4.50) Sonoma. *Clean, decent, sour.*

☆☆ 1983 ZINFANDEL ($4.50) Sonoma. *Fruity, clean, appealing.*

🍷

## Peju Province    NAPA COUNTY
### WHITE
☆☆ 1986 SAUVIGNON BLANC ($7.50) Napa Valley. *Balanced, crisp, tart, some odd flavors.*
### RED
☆☆ 1982 CABERNET SAUVIGNON ($10.00) Napa Valley. *Toasty, clean, decent fruit and varietal character.*

🍷

## Pellegrini Brothers Winery    SONOMA COUNTY
### WHITE
☆☆ 1983 CHARDONNAY ($8.50) Russian River Valley. *Varietal, crisp, clean, attractive.*
### RED
☆☆ 1980 CABERNET SAUVIGNON ($7.50) Russian River Valley. *Big berry style; soft and rich.*

🍷

## Pendleton Winery    SANTA CLARA COUNTY
### RED
☆☆☆ 1979 CABERNET SAUVIGNON ($11.00) Adamson-Tupper, Napa Valley. *Clean and bright; lean and very attractive. Aging nicely.*

☆☆ 1980 CABERNET SAUVIGNON ($12.00) Napa Valley. *Big, dense, fruity. Ready to drink.*

🍷

## Robert Pepi Winery    NAPA COUNTY
### WHITE
☆☆ 1983 CHARDONNAY ($11.00) Napa Valley. *Earthy, heavy, deep, rich.*

1984 CHARDONNAY ($11.00) Napa Valley. *Dull, off flavors.*

☆☆ 1985 SAUVIGNON BLANC ($8.00) Napa Valley. *24% Semillon. Clean, ripe, balanced, unexciting.*
### RED
☆☆☆☆ 1981 CABERNET SAUVIGNON ($14.00) Vine Hill Ranch, Napa Valley. *Deep, resonant, oaky, complex, enormous length and richness. Nice flavor of currants. Drink 1989.*

☆☆☆ 1982 CABERNET SAUVIGNON ($14.00) Vine Hill Ranch, Napa Valley. *Buttery, ripe, crisp, soft, clean, nicely structured. Drink 1990.*

🍷

## Pepperwood Springs Vineyards    MENDOCINO COUNTY
### WHITE
☆ 1982 CHARDONNAY ($9.00) Potter Valley, Mendocino. *Dull, simple, decent.*

🍷

## *Perelli–Minetti Winery*      SAN LUIS OBISPO COUNTY
### WHITE
☆ 1984 PERELLI MINETTI CHARDONNAY ($10.50) Napa
     Valley. *Meaty, earthy, flat.*
### RED
☆ 1982 LAMONT WINERY CABERNET SAUVIGNON
     ($10.50) Napa Valley. *Lush, rich, a bit muddy.*

🍷

## *Perret Vineyards*                    NAPA COUNTY
### WHITE
☆☆☆ 1982 CHARDONNAY ($14.50) Estate, Napa Valley-
     Carneros. *Toasty, rich, lush, fruity, lovely.*
☆☆☆ 1983 CHARDONNAY ($13.50) Estate, Napa Valley-
     Carneros. *Lush, tangy, fresh, clean oak, superb.
     Made at Acacia.*
☆☆☆ 1984 CHARDONNAY ($14.00) Perret, Napa Valley-
     Carneros. *Oaky, lean, good structure.*

🍷

## *Pheasant Ridge Winery*                    TEXAS
### WHITE
☆☆ 1983 CHARDONNAY ($10.00) Lubbock, Texas. *Varietal,
     heavy oak, clean.*
☆☆ 1984 CHARDONNAY ($15.00) Lubbock. *Crisp, rich, lovely
     new oak, attractive.*
☆☆ 1985 CHARDONNAY ($8.00) Texas. *Soft, rich, fat, some
     sweetness, attractive.*
☆☆ 1985 SEMILLON ($8.00) Lubbock. *Rich, oaky, pleasant.*
### RED
☆☆☆ 1985 PROPRIETOR'S RESERVE RED ($8.00) Lubbock.
     *Lush, deep, clean, delicious.*

🍷

## *Joseph Phelps Vineyards*                    NAPA COUNTY
### WHITE
☆☆☆ 1983 DELICE DU SEMILLON ($15.00) Napa Valley. *Lush,
     vegetal, clean, honeyed and fruity.*
☆☆☆ 1985 DELICE DU SEMILLON ($7.75) Napa Valley. *375 ml.
     10.3% residual sugar. Rich, spicy, lush, lovely
     botrytis.*
☆ 1982 CHARDONNAY ($14.00) Schellville, Sonoma Valley.
     *Oily, heavy, vinous, overdone.*
☆☆☆ 1982 CHARDONNAY ($14.00) Sangiacomo, Sonoma. *Rich,
     oaky, barrel fermented, complex.*
☆☆☆ 1983 CHARDONNAY ($12.50) Napa Valley. *Lush, rich,
     lovely balance; complex and very attractive.*
☆☆☆ 1983 CHARDONNAY ($14.00) Sangiacomo, Carneros. *Rich
     fruit, round, intense, oaky, nicely balanced.*
☆☆ 1984 INNISFREE CHARDONNAY ($9.00) Napa Valley.
     *Lush, fruity, sweet oak, quite attractive.*
☆☆☆ 1984 CHARDONNAY ($12.75) Napa Valley. *Clean, soft, lush,
     delicate.*
☆☆☆ 1985 INNISFREE CHARDONNAY ($9.00) Napa Valley.
     *Crisp, fresh, tangy, varietal, balanced, spicy, very
     attractive.*
☆☆☆ 1985 CHARDONNAY ($14.00) Sangiacomo, Carneros. *Rich,
     smooth, balanced. Ripe but showing good, crisp
     acidity.*
☆☆☆ 1986 INNISFREE CHARDONNAY ($9.00) Napa Valley.
     *Soft, smooth, clean and nicely balanced.*

☆☆☆ 1982 JOHANNISBERG RIESLING ($11.25) Late Harvest, Napa Valley. *10.5% residual sugar. Lovely, elegant and rich, with great fruit.*

☆☆☆ 1982 JOHANNISBERG RIESLING ($25.00) Special Select Late Harvest, Napa Valley. *375 ml. 25.4% residual sugar. Big, fruity, balanced.*

☆☆☆☆ 1985 JOHANNISBERG RIESLING ($11.75) Late Harvest, Napa Valley. *11.2% residual sugar. Superb fruit and ripe, clean flavors. Botrytis complexity.*

☆☆ 1986 JOHANNISBERG RIESLING ($8.00) Early Harvest, Napa Valley. *1.1% residual sugar. Snappy, dry, clean and tangy.*

☆ 1986 JOHANNISBERG RIESLING ($8.50) Napa Valley. *2.4% residual sugar. Fat, flabby, decent fruit, not great.*

☆☆☆ 1986 JOHANNISBERG RIESLING ($11.75) Late Harvest, Napa Valley. *11% residual sugar. Crisp, snappy, lush fruit, bright finish.*

1986 SAUVIGNON BLANC ($9.00) Napa Valley. *7% Semillon. Tart, mean, unappealing.*

☆☆☆ 1979 SCHEUREBE ($15.00) Late Harvest, Napa Valley. *7.9% residual sugar. Perfumed, lushly fruited, lovely.*

☆☆☆ 1981 SCHEUREBE ($15.00) Late Harvest, Napa Valley. *7.9% residual sugar. Soft, fruity and lush. Lovely and delicate.*

☆☆☆☆ 1982 SCHEUREBE ($15.00) Special Select Late Harvest, Napa Valley. *375 ml. 18% residual sugar. Lush, floral, complex, super.*

☆☆☆☆ 1985 SCHEUREBE ($15.00) Select Late Harvest, Napa Valley. *12.5% residual sugar. Exquisite perfume and lush fruit. Complex flavors and silky texture.*

**RED**

☆☆☆ 1978 INSIGNIA ($25.00) Napa Valley. *50% Cabernet Sauvignon, 30% Merlot, 20% Cabernet Franc. Minty, elegant, lovely.*

☆☆☆ 1979 INSIGNIA ($25.00) Napa Valley. *70% Cabernet Sauvignon, 30% Merlot. Deep, assertive, complex, minty. Drink now and for the next five years.*

☆☆☆ 1980 INSIGNIA ($25.00) Napa Valley. *85% Cabernet Sauvignon, 15% Merlot. Balanced, rich, intense, lovely. Drink 1988.*

☆☆☆ 1981 INSIGNIA ($25.00) Napa Valley. *60% Cabernet Sauvignon, 28% Merlot, 12% Cabernet Franc. Minty, complex, firmly structured, with lovely oak flavors. Drink 1989.*

☆☆ 1982 CLARET ($6.00) Napa Valley. *92% Cabernet Sauvignon, 8% Cabernet Franc. Lush, clean, attractive.*

☆☆☆ 1982 INSIGNIA ($25.00) Napa Valley. *50% Cabernet Sauvignon, 30% Cabernet Franc, 20% Merlot. Smokey, ripe, herbal, cassis flavors, spice, great structure. Drink 1992.*

☆☆☆☆ 1983 INSIGNIA ($25.00) Napa Valley. *60% Cabernet Sauvignon, 20% Merlot, 20% Cabernet Franc. Rich minty nose, velvety texture; intense, complex, ripe flavors. Drink 1990.*

☆☆☆ 1977 CABERNET SAUVIGNON ($35.00) Napa Valley. *Minty, earthy, mature but still lively. Complex and well made. Drink now.*

☆☆ 1978 CABERNET SAUVIGNON ($10.75) Napa Valley. *Pleasant, medium weight; nice herbs and fruit.*

☆☆☆ 1978 CABERNET SAUVIGNON ($16.50) Backus, Napa Valley. *Dark, ripe, concentrated and powerful.*

☆☆☆ 1978 CABERNET SAUVIGNON ($30.00) Eisele, Napa Valley. *Spicy, rich and complex; mature and attractive.*

☆☆☆ 1979 CABERNET SAUVIGNON ($30.00) Eisele, Napa Valley. *Dark, rich and delicious—now and for years. Drink now.*

1980 CABERNET SAUVIGNON ($10.75) Napa Valley. *Herbaceous. Well made but too vegetal.*

☆☆ 1981 CABERNET SAUVIGNON ($11.00) Napa Valley. *Herbal, clean, soft, attractive. Drink now.*

☆☆☆ 1981 CABERNET SAUVIGNON ($15.00) Backus, Napa Valley. *Lush, rich, deep, structured. Drink 1988 and beyond.*

☆☆☆ 1981 CABERNET SAUVIGNON ($30.00) Eisele, Napa Valley. *5% Merlot. Lush, rich, clean, complex, lovely. Drink 1989.*

☆☆ 1982 INNISFREE CABERNET SAUVIGNON ($9.00) Napa Valley. *Lean and tight, with some herbs and soft fruit. Drink 1987*

☆☆☆ 1982 CABERNET SAUVIGNON ($12.00) Napa Valley. *Tart, clean, nicely structured, eucalyptus flavors. Drink 1988.*

☆☆☆ 1982 CABERNET SAUVIGNON ($30.00) Eisele, Napa Valley. *Jammy, intense, ripe, clean, straightforward. Drink 1990.*

☆☆☆ 1983 CABERNET SAUVIGNON ($12.75) Napa Valley. *Herbal, rich, crisply fruity, clean and well built. Drink now.*

☆☆☆ 1983 CABERNET SAUVIGNON ($16.50) Backus, Napa Valley. *Spicy, minty, lush, velvety, complicated. Drink 1990.*

☆☆☆☆ 1983 CABERNET SAUVIGNON ($25.00) Eisele, Napa Valley. *Intense, concentrated fruit, excellent structure and good acidity. Drink 1992.*

☆☆☆ 1975 MERLOT ($35.00) Insignia, Napa Valley. *86% Merlot, 14% Cabernet. Minty, complex and rich.*

☆☆ 1979 SYRAH ($10.50) Napa Valley. *Spicy, clean, complex, very Rhône-like.*

☆☆ 1982 SYRAH ($7.50) Napa Valley. *Meaty, light, attractive. Not Rhône-like.*

☆☆ 1983 SYRAH ($8.50) Napa Valley. *Fruity, rich, deep, clean, attractive.*

☆☆ 1980 ZINFANDEL ($6.75) Alexander Valley. *Lush, deep, attractive.*

☆ 1980 ZINFANDEL ($6.75) Napa Valley. *Old, tired, very little fruit.*

☆☆☆ 1981 ZINFANDEL ($6.75) Alexander Valley. *Rich, balanced, fruity, charming, with some finesse.*

☆☆ 1984 ZINFANDEL ($5.75) Napa Valley. *Crisp, tangy and fresh. Beaujolais-style. Charming.*

☆☆ 1985 ZINFANDEL ($6.00) Napa Valley. *Fresh, Beaujolais-style, spicy and attractive. Serve slightly chilled.*

☆☆ 1985 ZINFANDEL ($10.00) Alexander Valley. *Crisp, fresh, fruity, nicely structured.*

☆☆ 1986 ZINFANDEL ($6.00) Nuovo, Napa Valley. *Spicy, carbonic maceration, fruity, fresh.*

❧

## The R. H. Phillips Vineyards            YOLO COUNTY
### WHITE
☆☆ 1985 NIGHT HARVEST CUVEE ($3.75) Dunnigan Hills, Yolo. *80% Sauvignon Blanc, 20% Semillon. Clean, fresh, very attractive.*

1984 CHARDONNAY ($9.00) Reserve, Yolo. *Soft, vegetal, dull.*

☆ 1985 CHARDONNAY ($6.00) California. *Thin, dull, lacking intensity.*

☆☆ 1986 CHARDONNAY ($6.00) California. *Simple, clean, varietal, at tractive.*

☆☆☆ 1986 SAUVIGNON BLANC ($4.25) Night Harvest, Dunnigan Hills, Yolo. *Crisp, herbal, sweet pea flavors, ripe, clean, appealing.*

○ 1984 SEMILLON ($4.00) Reserve, Dunnigan Hills, Yolo. *Heavy, dirty, unpleasant.*

☆☆☆ 1985 SEMILLON ($6.75) Reserve, Yolo. *Crisp, elegant, clean and charming.*

**RED**

☆☆☆ 1983 CABERNET SAUVIGNON ($6.00) California. *Soft, elegant, rich, deep flavors. Drink 1988.*

1984 ZINFANDEL ($4.75) Yolo. *Intense, berried, heavy, sweet.*

❧

PICCOLO *see* Merlion Winery

## *Piedmont Vineyards & Winery* — *VIRGINIA*

**WHITE**

NV LITTLE RIVER WHITE ($5.25) Virginia. *Tart, skunky.*

1983 CHARDONNAY ($10.00) Virginia. *Oxidized, dull.*

☆☆ 1984 CHARDONNAY ($10.00) Virginia. *Soft, lush, austere, firm, lovely.*

❧

## *Pindar Vineyards* — *NEW YORK*

**WHITE**

☆☆ NV PROPRIETOR'S BLEND ($6.00) Long Island. *Clean, soft, crisp, nice fruit.*

☆☆ NV WINTER WHITE ($6.00) North Fork, Long Island. *Soft, ripe, off-dry, nice fruit.*

1984 CHARDONNAY ($11.00) Long Island. *Odd cereal flavor. Bitter, unattractive.*

☆☆ 1985 CHARDONNAY ($9.00) Long Island. *Ripe, crisp, clean flavors, lean and elegant, subdued fruit.*

☆☆☆ 1984 JOHANNISBERG RIESLING ($30.00) Poetry Edition, Select Berry, Late Harvest, Long Island. *375 ml. Crisp, clean, fruity and smooth, with honey and apricot flavors.*

☆ 1986 JOHANNISBERG RIESLING ($9.00) North Fork, Long Island. *Fat, soft, overripe fruit, heavy texture.*

**RED**

☆ NV LONG ISLAND CLARET ($9.00) New York. *Earthy, rough.*

☆☆ 1984 CABERNET SAUVIGNON ($9.00) Long Island. *Buttery, oak. Decent fruit. Nice varietal character.*

☆ 1985 CABERNET SAUVIGNON ($11.00) Long Island. *Earthy nose, raisiny, concentrated flavors.*

❧

## *Pine Ridge Winery* — *NAPA COUNTY*

**WHITE**

☆☆☆ 1982 CHARDONNAY ($15.00) Oak Knoll District-Napa Valley. *Soft and lush; complex and snappy. Aging nicely.*

☆☆☆ 1982 CHARDONNAY ($16.00) Stag's Leap Cuvée, Napa Valley. *Ripe, fresh, complex, with great fruit.*

☆☆☆ 1983 CHARDONNAY ($13.00) Oak Knoll Cuvée, Napa Valley. *Big, rich, vinous, oaky and fruity.*

☆ 1984 CHARDONNAY ($13.00) Oak Knoll Cuvée, Oak Knoll, Napa Valley. *Heavy, oily, decent.*

☆☆☆ 1984 CHARDONNAY ($16.50) Stag's Leap, Estate, Napa Valley. *Crisp and well built, with great fruit and oak. An exquisite wine.*

☆☆ 1985 CHARDONNAY ($13.00) Jeunesse, Napa Valley. *Fresh, simple.*

### RED

☆☆ 1978 CABERNET SAUVIGNON ($7.50) Rutherford District, Napa Valley. *Balanced and well made. Clean, fruity, complex. Drink now.*

☆☆ 1979 CABERNET SAUVIGNON ($9.00) Rutherford District, Napa Valley. *Attractive, with a touch of weediness. Drink now.*

☆☆ 1980 CABERNET SAUVIGNON ($12.00) Rutherford District, Napa Valley. *Meaty, varietal, decent.*

☆☆☆ 1980 CABERNET SAUVIGNON ($17.00) Stag's Leap District, Napa. *Crisp yet remarkably deep, with complexity and style.*

☆☆☆ 1981 CABERNET SAUVIGNON ($13.00) Rutherford, Napa. *Elegant, deep, crisp, beautifully built. Drink now and beyond.*

☆☆☆ 1981 CABERNET SAUVIGNON ($20.00) Stag's Leap Cuvée, Napa Valley. *Dense, rich, soft, complex, concentrated. Drink 1988.*

☆☆☆ 1982 CABERNET SAUVIGNON ($13.00) Rutherford Cuvée, Napa Valley. *10% Merlot, 5% Cabernet Franc. Clean, rich, structured, lovely. Drink 1988.*

☆☆☆ 1982 CABERNET SAUVIGNON ($14.50) Stag's Leap, Estate, Napa Valley. *Crisp, clean, balanced, complex, elegant. Drink 1989.*

☆☆☆ 1983 CABERNET SAUVIGNON ($14.00) Rutherford Cuvée, Napa Valley. *7% Merlot, 4% Cabernet Franc. Clean, focused, balanced, lovely. Drink 1989.*

☆☆ 1983 CABERNET SAUVIGNON ($20.00) Stag's Leap, Napa Valley. *Tight, tart, intense acidity; needs time to loosen up. Drink 1992.*

1984 CABERNET SAUVIGNON ($14.50) Napa Valley. *8% Merlot. Sour, smokey, watery.*

☆☆ 1980 MERLOT ($10.00) Napa Valley. *15% Cabernet, 9% Malbec. Complex, clean, vegetal, well made.*

☆☆☆ 1981 MERLOT ($12.50) Napa Valley. *9% Cabernet, 5% Malbec. Fruity, clean, superb. Aging nicely.*

☆☆☆ 1982 MERLOT ($12.50) Napa Valley. *Lush, varietal, elegant.*

☆☆☆ 1982 MERLOT ($13.00) Selected Cuvée, Napa Valley. *Richly varietal, great structure. Drink now.*

☆☆☆ 1983 MERLOT ($13.00) Selected Cuvée, Napa Valley. *Dark, rich and velvety, with complex flavors. Drink 1987.*

☆☆ 1984 MERLOT ($13.00) Napa Valley. *5% Cabernet Sauvigon, 4% Cabernet Franc, 2% Malbec. Good structure and acidity, lacking charm.*

☆☆ 1984 MERLOT ($13.00) Selected Cuvée, Napa Valley. *Good structure, varietal, a bit thin.*

🦋

## *Piper-Sonoma*                          SONOMA COUNTY

### SPARKLING

☆☆ 1981 BLANC DE NOIR ($15.25) Sonoma. *Fresh, fruity, clean, attractive.*

☆☆☆ 1982 BLANC DE NOIR ($15.00) Sonoma. *Crisp, round, fruity, charming.*

☆☆☆ 1983 BLANC DE NOIR ($15.00) Sonoma. *Crisp, fresh, clean, snappy, lovely.*

☆☆☆ 1980 BRUT ($14.00) Sonoma. *Crisp, elegant and rounded. Good fruit and finesse.*

☆☆☆ 1981 BRUT ($14.00) Sonoma. *Lovely, crisp and well balanced; elegant and well bred.*

☆ 1982 BRUT ($13.00) Sonoma. *A disappointment. Vegetal and difficult to like. Dirty flavors.*

☆☆☆ 1982 BRUT RESERVE ($20.00) Sonoma. *Rich, earthy, complex, intense.*

☆☆☆ 1983 BRUT ($20.00) Reserve, Sonoma. *60% Chardonnay, 40% Pinot Noir. Lush, fruity, clean, snappy, rich.*

☆☆☆ 1984 BRUT ($15.00) Sonoma. *74% Pinot Noir, 14% Chardonnay, 12% Pinot Blanc. Simple, crisp, fresh, snappy, lovely.*

☆☆☆ 1981 TETE DE CUVEE ($30.00) Sonoma. *Rich, toasty, complex, deep, lovely.*

❧

## Plam Vineyards & Winery       NAPA COUNTY
### WHITE

☆☆☆ 1984 CHARDONNAY ($12.00) Napa Valley. *Ripe, rich, deep, complex, lovely texture and roundness.*

☆☆☆ 1985 CHARDONNAY ($12.00) Napa Valley. *Crisp, lean, fruity, nicely structured, complex and long.*

☆☆☆ 1986 SAUVIGNON BLANC ($8.00) Sacrashé, Napa Valley. *Rich, varietal fruit, round and balanced.*

### RED

☆☆☆☆ 1985 CABERNET SAUVIGNON ($12.00) Napa Valley. *18% Merlot. Crisp, bright, deep; plummy fruit, lovely oak complexity, silky texture. Drink 1991.*

❧

## Plane's Cayuga Vineyard       NEW YORK
### WHITE

☆☆☆ 1982 CHARDONNAY ($9.50) Finger Lakes. *Fragrant, varietal, subtle, clean, balanced.*

1984 CHARDONNAY ($10.00) Finger Lakes. *Sulfur and cheese on nose, odd flavors. Unpleasant.*

### RED

1982 CHANCELLOR ($4.00) Estate, Finger Lakes. *Muddy and weedy but dry, decent, balanced.*

☆☆☆ 1983 CHANCELLOR ($5.00) Finger Lakes. *Clean, rich, deep, lovely color and flavors.*

1984 CHANCELLOR ($5.00) Finger Lakes. *Sappy, heavy, vegetal.*

❧

## Ponzi Vineyards       OREGON
### RED

1981 PINOT NOIR ($10.00) Willamette Valley, Oregon. *Simple, thin.*

☆ 1982 PINOT NOIR ($9.00) Willamette Valley. *Clean, varietal, a trifle thin.*

1982 PINOT NOIR ($12.00) Reserve, Oregon. *Odd flavors, dense.*

❧

## Poplar Ridge Vineyards       NEW YORK
### WHITE

☆ 1984 CAYUGA ($5.00) Finger Lakes. *Soft, fruity, clean.*

☆ 1984 CHARDONNAY ($9.50) Finger Lakes. *Very acidic, decent flavor.*

1985 SEYVAL BLANC ($5.50) Finger Lakes. *Crisp, lemony, lacking dimension, some odd flavors.*

**RED**

○   1981 MARECHAL FOCH ($7.50) New York. *Cooked spinach, awful.*

🍂

## Bernard Pradel Cellars                    NAPA COUNTY
**WHITE**

☆☆☆   1985 CHARDONNAY ($10.00) Napa Valley. *Crisp, tart, lean structure, very Burgundian in style.*

☆☆☆   1986 CHARDONNAY ($9.00) Napa Valley. *Ripe, lush, clean, with good, firm structure; fruity and balanced.*

○   NV   SAUVIGNON BLANC ($9.50) Botrytis, Late Harvest, Allais, Napa Valley. *375 ml. 11% residual sugar. Bitter, ugly.*

**RED**

☆☆☆   1984 CABERNET SAUVIGNON ($11.75) Barrel Select, Napa Valley. *Soft, lush, deep, lovely. Elegant.*

☆☆☆   1984 CABERNET SAUVIGNON ($14.00) Napa Valley. *Lush, smooth, lovely cherry flavors, charming. Drink 1990.*

🍂

## Prager Winery and Port Works                    NAPA COUNTY
**WHITE**

○   1984 CHARDONNAY ($15.00) Napa Valley. *Dark, oxidized, volatile, maderized. So far off, it might pass for sherry.*

**RED**

1981 CABERNET SAUVIGNON ($18.00) Knights Valley. *Decent flavors, excessive volatile acidity.*

🍂

## Presque Isle Wine Cellars                    PENNSYLVANIA
**RED**

☆   1980 CABERNET SAUVIGNON ($6.60) Pennsylvania. *15% Merlot, 10% Cabernet Franc. Light, vegetal, nicely structured.*

🍂

## Preston Vineyards                    SONOMA COUNTY
**WHITE**

☆☆☆   1985 CUVEE DE FUME ($6.75) Estate, Sonoma. *18% Chenin Blanc, 7% Semillon. Lean, crisp, balanced, varietal, lovely.*

☆☆   1985 CHENIN BLANC ($20.00) Citrine, Late Harvest, Estate, Dry Creek Valley. *375 ml. 17.4% residual sugar. Soft, rich, herbal, intense, smooth, syrupy, pleasant.*

☆☆☆   1986 SAUVIGNON BLANC ($6.75) Cuvée de Fumé, Dry Creek Valley. *75% Sauvignon Blanc, 19% Chenin Blanc, 6% Semillon. Elegant, varietal, lovely, complex.*

☆☆☆   1986 SAUVIGNON BLANC ($9.50) Estate, Dry Creek Valley. *Crisp, fresh, lean and delicious. A very nicely proportioned wine.*

**RED**

☆☆☆☆   1985 SIRAH SYRAH ($9.50) Estate, Dry Creek Valley. *54% Petit Sirah, 46% Syrah. Gorgeous, rich, intense berried fruit, mouthfilling, focused acidity; explosive flavors; a stunning wine.*

☆☆☆   1985 BARBERA ($8.00) Estate, Dry Creek Valley. *Tangy, bright, apple-fruit, lively acidity, assertive and charming.*

☆☆☆ 1983 CABERNET SAUVIGNON ($11.00) Estate, Dry Creek Valley. *Lush, rich, clean, ripe, appealing. Drink 1988.*

☆☆ 1984 CABERNET SAUVIGNON ($11.00) Estate, Dry Creek Valley, Sonoma. *Clean, rich, intense, rather brash from lack of finesse. Drink now.*

☆☆ 1985 GAMAY BEAUJOLAIS ($5.00) Dry Creek Valley. *Crisp, fruity, fresh, attractive.*

☆☆ 1987 GAMAY BEAUJOLAIS ($6.25) Estate, Dry Creek Valley. *Bright, fruity, simple.*

☆☆☆ 1986 GAMAY ($6.25) Primeur, Estate, Dry Creek Valley. *Crisp and tart, fresh, fruity. Drink now, chilled.*

☆☆ 1981 PETITE SIRAH ($9.50) Estate, Petite Sirah-Syrah, Dry Creek Valley. *Spicy, lush and Rhône-like.*

☆☆☆ 1980 ZINFANDEL ($7.50) Estate, Dry Creek Valley, Sonoma. *Jammy, with great fruit.*

☆☆ 1980 ZINFANDEL ($8.00) Late Harvest, Dry Creek Valley. *2% residual sugar. Sweet, grapey and snappy. Interesting.*

☆☆ 1981 ZINFANDEL ($6.50) Dry Creek Valley. *Rich and berried, with good, firm acidity.*

☆☆ 1982 ZINFANDEL ($7.00) Dry Creek Valley. *Rich, berried, robust, balanced, attractive.*

☆☆☆ 1983 ZINFANDEL ($7.00) Sonoma. *Rich, full, berried, fruity, dense. Ready to drink.*

☆☆ 1983 ZINFANDEL ($7.50) Dry Creek Valley. *10% Barbera. Clean, nicely balanced, varietal.*

☆☆ 1984 ZINFANDEL ($5.75) Zin II, Sonoma. *Soft, rich, clean, fruity, lacking crispness, attractive.*

☆☆☆ 1984 ZINFANDEL ($8.00) Estate, Dry Creek Valley. *Ripe, fruity, clean, berried, charming.*

☆☆☆ 1985 ZINFANDEL ($8.50) Estate, Dry Creek Valley. *Crisp, fresh, peppery, spicy, nicely balanced.*

❧

## *Preston Wine Cellars*   WASHINGTON
### WHITE

☆☆☆ 1982 WHITE RIESLING ($13.00) Late Harvest, Preston, Washington. *375 ml. 5.1% residual sugar. Complex, fruity, crisp and luscious.*

☆☆☆ 1984 WHITE RIESLING ($5.75) Late Harvest, Collector Series, Preston, Washington. *3.2% residual sugar. Soft and luscious, crisp and b alanced.*

☆☆ 1984 WHITE RIESLING ($13.00) Late Harvest, Collector Series, Preston, Washington. *375 ml. 7.1% residual sugar. Lush, fresh, snappy, clean.*

☆☆ 1986 WHITE RIESLING ($7.00) Select Late Harvest, Washington. *4.5% residual sugar. Crisp, soft, lively, clean, lovely.*

### BLANC DE NOIR

☆ 1985 PINOT NOIR BLANC ($5.50) Washington. *Crisp, clean, decent.*

### RED

☆ 1978 CABERNET SAUVIGNON ($7.50) Washington. *Clumsy and simple.*

☆☆ 1980 CABERNET SAUVIGNON ($7.95) Washington. *Earthy, lean, mature, decent.*

☆☆ 1980 MERLOT ($7.00) Washington. *Clean, elegant, good structure, showing maturity.*
☆ 1981 MERLOT ($7.00) Washington. *Bell pepper flavors, decent balance.*

è&

## Prince Michel Vineyards                              VIRGINIA
### WHITE
☆☆ 1986 WHITE BURGUNDY ($6.00) Virgina. *Rich, complex. Made from Pinot Noir and Chardonnay. Crisp, clean and nicely balanced.*
☆☆☆ 1986 WHITE RIESLING ($8.00) Virginia. *Lean, spicy, elegant, good fruit, excellent finesse.*

è&

## Private Stock Winery                                 IOWA
### ROSE
☆☆ NV   CACO ROSE ($4.85) Iowa. *Sweet, fruity, attractive.*
### RED
☆ NV   VAN BURAN ($4.85) Iowa. *Clean, fruity, grapey, foxy.*

è&

## Prudence Island Vineyards                  RHODE ISLAND
### WHITE
☆☆ 1982 CHARDONNAY ($9.75) Rhode Island. *Clean, fresh, lively.*

è&

## Quady Winery                                MADERA COUNTY
### FORTIFIED
☆☆☆☆ 1984 ELYSIUM ($11.00) California. *Spicy red fortified wine, with lots of fruit and richness.*
☆☆☆ 1985 ELYSIUM ($11.00) California. *Made from Black Muscat grapes. Rich, ripe, clean, blackberry flavors. Lovely.*
☆☆☆ 1984 ESSENCIA ($11.00) California. *White aperitif fortified wine. Orange and apricot; fresh, clean, very attractive.*
☆☆ 1985 ESSENCIA ($11.00) California. *Made from Orange Muscat grapes. Ripe, rich, orange marmalade flavors.*
☆☆☆ 1978 LOT 1 PORT ($9.00) Shenandoah School Road, Amador. *Zinfandel. Varietal, creamy, lovely flavors.*
☆☆☆ 1978 LOT 2 PORT ($9.00) Shenandoah School Road, Amador. *Zinfandel. Crisp, ripe, complex, lush.*
☆☆ 1979 PORT ($9.00) California. *Rich, intense, smooth.*
☆☆☆ 1979 PORT ($9.00) Shenandoah School Road, Amador. *Zinfandel. Lush, complex, spicy, lovely.*
☆☆☆ 1981 PORT ($9.00) Clockspring, Amador. *Zinfandel. Lush, ripe, fat, great fruit, lovely.*
☆☆ 1982 PORT ($9.00) California. *Lush, smooth, attractive.*
☆☆ 1982 PORT ($9.00) Shenandoah Valley, Amador. *Zinfandel. Spicy, rich, deep, a bit simple.*

è&

QUAFF *see* ZMoore

## Quail Ridge          NAPA COUNTY

### WHITE

☆☆☆ 1982 CHARDONNAY ($9.00) Sonoma. *Lemony, lush, clean, quite attractive.*

☆☆ 1982 CHARDONNAY ($14.00) Napa Valley. *Toasty, clean, pleasant.*

☆☆ 1983 CHARDONNAY ($15.00) Napa Valley. *Decent, oily, clean.*

☆☆ 1984 CHARDONNAY ($14.00) Winemaker's Selection, Napa Valley. *Heavy, intense, good varietal character but lacking finesse.*

☆ 1985 CHARDONNAY ($15.00) Napa Valley. *Decent fruit and acceptable structure; a bit dull.*

### RED

☆☆☆ 1982 CABERNET SAUVIGNON ($13.00) Napa Valley. *Richly textured, ripe, well structured, lovely. Ready to drink now but would benefit from a few more cellar years.*

☆ 1983 CABERNET SAUVIGNON ($15.00) Napa Valley. *Muddy, lacking definition.* 🍸

QUAIL RUN VINTNERS *see* Covey Run Vintners

## Quilceda Creek Vintners          WASHINGTON

### RED

☆☆☆ 1979 CABERNET SAUVIGNON ($12.50) Washington. *Fresh and crisp, with new oak and good fruit.*

☆ 1980 CABERNET SAUVIGNON ($12.50) Washington. *Somewhat weedy but lush and quite decent.*

☆☆☆ 1981 CABERNET SAUVIGNON ($13.50) Washington. *Fresh, lively fruit, good structure, meaty, attractive. Drink 1988.*

☆☆☆ 1982 CABERNET SAUVIGNON ($15.50) Washington. *Ripe, lively, green olive, good structure. Drink 1988.* 🍸

## Quivera          SONOMA COUNTY

### WHITE

☆☆ 1986 SAUVIGNON BLANC ($8.00) Dry Creek Valley. *Crisp, lean, good balance, nice fruit and fine finish.*

### RED

☆☆☆ 1983 ZINFANDEL ($7.00) Dry Creek Valley. *15% Petite Sirah. Crisp, lush, lovely fruit, wonderful balance.*

☆☆☆ 1984 ZINFANDEL ($7.00) Dry Creek Valley. *Deep, berried, intense, powerful and very likable. Drink 1989.*

☆☆☆☆ 1985 ZINFANDEL ($7.00) Dry Creek Valley. *Rich, deep, complex, concentrated, balanced, classically proportioned.* 🍸

## Qupé          SANTA BARBARA COUNTY

### WHITE

☆☆ 1983 CHARDONNAY ($10.00) Sierra Madre, Santa Barbara. *Crisp, clean, lush, richly balanced but heavy.*

☆☆☆☆ 1984 CHARDONNAY ($9.00) Sierra Madre, San Luis Obispo. *Crisp, clean, complex, beautiful oak, Burgundian, charming, lovely.*

☆☆☆ 1985 CHARDONNAY ($10.00) Sierra Madre, Santa Barbara. *Fresh, crisp, lovely, good oak. Nice but not as good as the 1984.*

**RED**

☆   1982 SYRAH ($7.00) Paso Robles. *Spicy; balanced but vegetal.*

☆☆☆  1983 SYRAH ($7.50) Central Coast. *Crisp, clean, fresh, Rhône-like, fruity and very charming.*

☆☆☆  1984 SYRAH ($8.50) Central Coast. *Lush, rich, earthy, charming.*

🙚

## A. Rafanelli Winery                    SONOMA COUNTY
**RED**

☆   1983 CABERNET SAUVIGNON ($7.25) Dry Creek Valley. *Tart, decent, lacking depth.*

☆☆☆  1980 ZINFANDEL ($6.25) Dry Creek Valley, Sonoma. *Clean and crisply fruity.*

☆   1984 ZINFANDEL ($6.25) Dry Creek Valley. *Lacking fruit.*

🙚

## Rancho Sisquoc Winery        SANTA BARBARA COUNTY
**WHITE**

☆☆  1983 CHARDONNAY ($7.00) Estate, Santa Maria. *Clean, varietal, quite nice.*

🙚

## Rapazzini Winery                SANTA CLARA COUNTY
**WHITE**

☆☆  1982 CHARDONNAY ($8.00) Special Reserve, Santa Clara. *Decent. Good fruit, clean and attractive.*

**RED**

☆☆  1980 CABERNET SAUVIGNON ($8.00) Special Reserve, Sonoma. *Coarse and raisiny but attractive.*

**FLAVORED**

☆   GARLIC WINE ($4.25) Santa Clara. *Fresh garlic flavor mixed with Chenin Blanc. Weird.*

🙚

## Kent Rasmussen Winery                NAPA COUNTY
**RED**

☆☆☆  1986 PINOT NOIR ($12.00) Estate, Carneros. *Cherry-berry, luscious, great fruit and varietal character.*

🙚

## Ravenswood                        SONOMA COUNTY
**WHITE**

☆☆☆  1985 CHARDONNAY ($15.00) Sangiacomo, Sonoma Valley. *Intensely oaky, rich, ripe and mouthfilling; extreme but likable.*

☆☆☆  1986 CHARDONNAY ($15.00) Sangiacomo, Sonoma Valley. *Rich, smooth, balanced, clean and lovely.*

**RED**

☆☆☆  1978 CABERNET SAUVIGNON ($9.00) California. *Rich, varietal, clean, intense, lovely. Drink now and beyond.*

☆☆  1978 CABERNET SAUVIGNON ($10.50) Madrona, El Dorado. *Spicy, sweet oak, varietal flavors. Growing up nicely.*

☆   1979 CABERNET SAUVIGNON ($8.50) California. *Coarse and disjointed. Aging hasn't helped.*

1980 CABERNET SAUVIGNON ($10.00) Sonoma. *Awkward, vegetal, heavy and unattractive.*

☆☆  1982 CABERNET SAUVIGNON ($11.00) Sonoma. *Balanced, varietal, pleasant.*

☆   1983 MERLOT ($11.00) Sonoma. *Extremely tannic, earthy, lacking in fruit.*

☆☆  1984 MERLOT ($12.00) Sonoma. *Meaty, clean, lush, appealing.*

☆ 1978 ZINFANDEL ($8.00) Madrona, El Dorado. *Intense, sweet, late harvest style.*

1978 ZINFANDEL ($8.50) California. *Late harvest style. Woody, hot, overbearing.*

☆☆ 1979 ZINFANDEL ($6.75) Sonoma. *Aggressive, big and intense. Clean but powerful. Mellowed a bit with age.*

☆☆ 1979 ZINFANDEL ($8.00) California. *Intense, rich, berried, late harvest style.*

☆☆ 1980 ZINFANDEL ($9.00) Sonoma. *Intense, high extract, tannic, heavy. Smoothing out with age.*

☆☆☆ 1981 ZINFANDEL ($6.50) Dry Creek Benchland, Sonoma. *Rich raspberry, deep, woody. Intense but very likable.*

☆☆ 1981 ZINFANDEL ($8.50) Bogensen Vineyard, Sonoma. *Concentrated, berried, dark and rich. Ready to drink.*

☆☆☆ 1982 ZINFANDEL ($11.00) Etched Bottle, Dickerson, Napa Valley. *Lush, rich, complex and lovely.*

○ 1983 ZINFANDEL ($12.00) Sonoma. *Heavy sulfur problems.*

☆ 1984 ZINFANDEL ($6.00) Vintner's Blend, Sonoma Valley. *Overripe, heavy, full bodied, intense.*

☆☆☆ 1985 ZINFANDEL ($8.50) Sonoma. *Rich, berry fruit, lush texture and lovely oak.*

☆☆☆☆ 1985 ZINFANDEL ($10.00) Dickerson, Napa Valley. *Complex, spicy; intense fruit, bright flavors and great finesse. Drink 1990.*

☆☆☆ 1985 ZINFANDEL ($12.00) Old Hill, Sonoma. *Big, fat and powerful; deep berry fruit, good structure and long finish. Drink 1992.*

❧

## *Raymond Vineyard & Cellar*  NAPA COUNTY
### WHITE

☆☆ 1986 VINTAGE SELECT WHITE ($5.00) California. *61% Sauvignon Blanc, 39% Chenin Blanc. Smooth and rounded, with attractive herbal flavors and a soft, clean finish.*

☆☆ 1983 CHARDONNAY ($8.50) California. *Clean, simple, fresh, decent.*

☆☆☆ 1983 CHARDONNAY ($12.00) Napa Valley. *Lush and soft, clean and richly varietal.*

☆☆ 1984 LA BELLE CHARDONNAY ($6.00) California. *Soft, clean, oaky, balanced, attractive.*

☆☆☆ 1984 CHARDONNAY ($8.50) California Selection, California. *Balanced, lovely oak, clean, fruity.*

☆☆ 1984 CHARDONNAY ($12.00) Napa Valley. *Lush, ripe, intense, rich varietal flavors.*

☆☆ 1985 LA BELLE CHARDONNAY ($5.00) California. *Lush, rich, soft varietal flavors.*

☆☆☆ 1985 CHARDONNAY ($8.50) California Selection, California. *Soft, lush, clean, buttery, nice oak.*

☆☆ 1985 CHARDONNAY ($12.00) Napa Valley. *Crisp, clean, fresh, balanced, attractive.*

☆☆☆ 1985 CHARDONNAY ($16.00) Proprietor's Reserve, Napa Valley. *Ripe flavors of nutmeg, butter and pear, soft texture, good balance.*

☆ 1986 LA BELLE CHARDONNAY ($5.25) California. *Clean, herbal, oily, decent.*

☆☆ 1986 CHARDONNAY ($8.50) California Selection, California. *Rich, varietal, clean and nicely balanced.*

☆☆☆ 1986 CHARDONNAY ($13.00) Napa Valley. *Lush fruit and varietal character. Perhaps the best Raymond Chardonnay yet.*

☆☆ 1985 LA BELLE CHENIN BLANC ($3.00) Napa Valley. *0.75% residual sugar. Soft, clean, lush and attractively fruity. Fresh and appealing.*

☆☆ 1985 LA BELLE SAUVIGNON BLANC ($4.75) California. *Rounded and balanced; decent flavors, with a nice clean finish.*

☆☆☆ 1986 SAUVIGNON BLANC ($7.50) Napa Valley. *Round, fruity flavors, great acidity, nicely made.*

### BLANC DE NOIR

☆ 1986 LA BELLE WHITE ZINFANDEL ($4.50) California. *1.75% residual sugar. Simple, clean, decent but dull.*

### RED

☆ 1982 VINTAGE SELECT RED ($4.25) North Coast. 82% *Cabernet Sauvignon. Herbal, decent.*

☆☆ 1983 VINTAGE SELECT RED ($5.00) California. *45% Zinfandel, 55% Cabernet Sauvignon. Soft, smooth, clean; a nice all-purpose red.*

☆☆ 1978 CABERNET SAUVIGNON ($19.00) Estate, Napa Valley. *20% Merlot. Balanced, attractive, big. Drink now or hold a year or two.*

☆☆ 1979 CABERNET SAUVIGNON ($17.00) Estate, Napa Valley. *Rich and berried; raisiny and ripe. Lush and very drinkable.*

☆☆ 1980 CABERNET SAUVIGNON ($15.00) Estate, Napa Valley. *Herbal, soft, charming. A delightful wine which should be at its peak in 1990.*

☆☆ 1981 CABERNET SAUVIGNON ($8.25) Napa Valley. *Clean, attractive. Drink now.*

☆☆☆ 1981 CABERNET SAUVIGNON ($13.00) Estate, Napa Valley. *18% Merlot. Soft, rich, balanced—Raymond's best yet. Very drinkable now but patience over the next five years might pay off.*

☆☆ 1982 LA BELLE CABERNET SAUVIGNON ($6.00) California. *Herbal, soft, clean, balanced, well made. Drink now.*

☆☆☆ 1982 CABERNET SAUVIGNON ($12.00) Napa Valley. *Ripe, rich, velvety, soft and luscious. Charming and nicely structured. Drink now.*

☆☆☆ 1982 CABERNET SAUVIGNON ($16.00) Private Reserve, Estate, Napa Valley. *Lovely oak, rich texture, smooth, fresh flavors, clean, long finish. Drink 1989.*

☆☆ 1983 LA BELLE CABERNET SAUVIGNON ($5.00) California. *Soft, lush, good herbs and fruit, delicate flavors, with some nice finesse.*

☆☆ 1979 ZINFANDEL ($6.00) Napa Valley. *Good structure, clean fruit, aging possibilities. Ready to drink now.*

🍂

## *Martin Ray Vineyards*          SANTA CLARA COUNTY

### WHITE

☆☆☆☆ 1982 CHARDONNAY ($14.00) Dutton Ranch, Sonoma. *Big yet elegant, balanced, aristocratic, stunning.*

☆☆☆ 1982 CHARDONNAY ($15.00) Santa Cruz Mountains. *Fat, rich fruit and oak, with a lovely firm acidity.*

☆ 1983 CHARDONNAY ($14.50) Dutton Ranch, Sonoma. *Earthy, austere, lacking fruit. A big disappointment after the '82.*

### RED

☆ 1979 CABERNET SAUVIGNON ($14.00) Saratoga District, Santa Cruz Mountains. *Intense, dark and deep, with several off flavors. Not much future.*

☆☆ 1980 CABERNET SAUVIGNON ($18.00) Stelzner, Napa Valley. *Jammy, grapey and rich, with nice fruit.*

☆☆☆☆ 1981 CABERNET SAUVIGNON ($16.50) Stelzner, Napa Valley. *5% Merlot. Rich, clean flavors; extraordinary.*

☆☆☆ 1979 MERLOT ($16.50) Winery Lake, Napa Valley. *Earthy, toasty, intense, big. Aging nicely.*

☆ 1980 MERLOT ($10.00) Winery Lake, Napa Valley. *Odd, weedy, overbearing.*

☆☆☆ 1981 MERLOT ($16.00) Winery Lake, Napa Valley. *Rich, deep, clean and complex. Aging gracefully.*

☆☆☆ 1982 MERLOT ($18.00) Winery Lake, Napa Valley. *Rich, minty, clean, complex, lovely. Drink 1988.*

☆☆☆ 1976 PINOT NOIR ($35.00) Winery Lake, Napa Valley. *Heavy and raisiny; deep and balanced.*

☆ 1979 PINOT NOIR ($9.00) Winery Lake, Napa Valley. *Meaty, decent but lacking finesse.*

☆☆ 1980 PINOT NOIR ($9.00) Winery Lake, Napa Valley. *Lush, deep, complex, super.*

☆☆☆ 1981 PINOT NOIR ($14.00) Winery Lake, Carneros-Napa. *Rich, intense, toasty and good. Fine aging potential.*

&

## Revere Winery    NAPA COUNTY
### WHITE

☆☆☆☆ 1985 CHARDONNAY ($15.00) Napa Valley. *Crisp, tangy acidity, lush new oak, lovely fruit, remarkable.*

&

## Richardson Vineyards    SONOMA COUNTY
### RED

☆ 1980 CABERNET SAUVIGNON ($10.00) Sonoma Valley. *Dull, lacking fruit.*

☆☆☆ 1981 CABERNET SAUVIGNON ($7.50) Sonoma Valley. *Crisp, attractive, clean, well made. Drink now through 1988.*

☆☆ 1982 CABERNET SAUVIGNON ($10.00) Sonoma Valley. *Intense, fruity, attractive. Drink now.*

☆☆ 1981 PINOT NOIR ($10.00) Sonoma Valley, Carneros. *Crisp, clean, varietal, attractive.*

☆☆ 1983 PINOT NOIR ($11.75) Sonoma Valley Los Carneros. *Pleasant, clean, attractive.*

☆☆☆ 1981 ZINFANDEL ($8.50) Sonoma Valley. *Solid, clean and dense. Drink now.*

☆☆ 1982 ZINFANDEL ($6.75) Napa Valley. *Snappy, clean, varietal, attractive. Drink now.*

&

## Ridge Vineyards    SANTA CLARA COUNTY
### RED

☆☆ 1980 CLARET ($8.50) Spring Mountain, Napa Valley, California. *57% Zinfandel, 33% Petite Sirah, 10% Carignane. Brambly, interesting.*

☆☆☆ 1978 CABERNET SAUVIGNON ($30.00) Monte Bello, Santa Cruz Mountains. *Smooth, intense yet soft and earthy, very complex. Drink 1988.*

☆☆ 1979 CABERNET SAUVIGNON ($15.00) York Creek, Spring Mountain, Napa Valley. *12% Merlot. Full, herbal, oaky and rich. Drink 1988.*

☆☆ 1980 CABERNET SAUVIGNON ($12.00) York Creek, Napa. *15% Merlot. Rich, lush, tannic. Drink now and beyond.*

☆☆ 1980 CABERNET SAUVIGNON ($27.50) Monte Bello, Santa Cruz Mountains. *Great fruit and structure. Stunning but muddy. Drink 1988.*

☆☆ 1981 CABERNET SAUVIGNON ($7.50) Mendocino. *Decent, clean but nothing special. Drink now.*

☆ 1981 CABERNET SAUVIGNON ($10.50) Tepusquet, Santa Maria Valley. *Earthy, vegetal, a bit dirty.*

☆☆☆ 1981 CABERNET SAUVIGNON ($12.00) York Creek, Napa Valley. *Crisp, clean, lovely structure. Drink 1988.*

☆☆ 1981 CABERNET SAUVIGNON ($12.00) Spring House, Napa. *8% Merlot. Toasty, crisp, lovely fruit. Drink now through 1988.*

☆☆ 1981 CABERNET SAUVIGNON ($12.00) 28% Monte Bello, 72% Jimsomare, Santa Cruz Mountains. *Clean, rich, decent.*

☆☆☆ 1981 CABERNET SAUVIGNON ($27.50) Monte Bello, Santa Cruz Mountains. *Rich, complex and lush, with enormous aging potential.*

☆ 1982 CABERNET SAUVIGNON ($12.00) Jimsomare, California. *Heavy, herbal, vegetal, dense.*

☆☆☆ 1982 CABERNET SAUVIGNON ($12.00) Beatty, Howell Mountain. *Earthy, rich, tangy, structured. Drink 1988.*

☆☆☆ 1982 CABERNET SAUVIGNON ($18.00) Monte Bello, California. *4% Merlot. Nice fruit, clean, varietal, nicely structured. Drink 1989. This is the "second" version of Monte Bello for 1982.*

☆☆ 1983 CABERNET SAUVIGNON ($10.00) Jimsomare, Santa Cruz Mountains. *Clean, oaky, soft, tart, dry. Drink 1989.*

☆☆ 1983 CABERNET SAUVIGNON ($12.00) Beatty, Howell Mountain. *Crisp, lean, nicely structured, attractive. Drink 1988.*

☆☆☆ 1983 CABERNET SAUVIGNON ($30.00) Monte Bello, Santa Cruz Mountains. *Firm and rich, with years to go before it sleeps. Be patient and drink in 1990.*

☆☆☆ 1984 CABERNET SAUVIGNON ($12.00) Santa Cruz Mountains. *Fresh, tangy, great fruit and nice texture. Drink now.*

☆☆ 1984 CABERNET SAUVIGNON ($14.00) York Creek, California. *9% Merlot, 2% Cabernet Franc. Crisp yet complex, with intensity and persistent fruit. Drink 1989.*

☆☆☆ 1984 CABERNET SAUVIGNON ($16.00) Jimsomare, California. *Rich, earthy, intense, big, concentrated. Drink 1989.*

☆☆☆☆ 1984 CABERNET SAUVIGNON ($40.00) Monte Bello, California. *7% Merlot. Intense, concentrated, rich but delicately balanced; a blockbuster; drink 1994 and into the next century.*

☆☆☆☆ 1985 CABERNET SAUVIGNON ($30.00) Monte Bello, California. *Lush, earthy, deep, remarkable. Drink 1994.*

☆☆ 1979 PETITE SIRAH ($9.00) Devil's Hill, York Creek, Napa Valley. *Deep, dark, rich and tannic. Drink now.*

☆☆ 1980 PETITE SIRAH ($7.50) Devil's Hill, York Creek, Napa. *Astringent, clean, fruity. Charming now.*

☆☆☆ 1980 PETITE SIRAH ($9.00) California. *Peppery, crisp, astringent, clean and rich. Drink 1988.*

☆☆ 1981 PETITE SIRAH ($8.50) York Creek, California. *15% Zinfandel. Dark, round, fruity, attractive.*

☆☆☆ 1982 PETITE SIRAH ($9.50) York Creek, California. *Rich, intensely tannic, complex, dark, spicy. Drink 1988.*

☆☆☆ 1983 PETITE SIRAH ($9.00) York Creek, California. *Crisp, ripe, fruity, not too heavy. Really attractive and spicy.*

☆☆☆ 1984 PETITE SIRAH ($9.50) York Creek, California. *Ripe and lush, with bright cherry fruit and considerable finesse; a splendid wine that will only get better.*

☆ 1978 ZINFANDEL ($8.50) York Creek, Napa County. *15% Petite Sirah. Intense, jammy, ripe.*

☆ 1978 ZINFANDEL ($12.00) Late Harvest, Paso Robles, San Luis Obispo. *Acceptable if you like this style. Overripe, heavy, high alcohol.*

☆ 1978 ZINFANDEL ($15.00) Late Picked, Fiddletown, Eschen, Amador. *Overdone, awkward, raisiny.*

☆☆ 1979 ZINFANDEL ($6.00) Early Bottling, Esola, Amador. *Pleasant, clean, attractive. Drink now.*

☆☆ 1979 ZINFANDEL ($6.00) Dusi, San Luis Obispo. *Berried, rich, intense, a bit hot.*

☆ 1979 ZINFANDEL ($7.50) Fiddletown, Eschen, Amador. *A bit disjointed. Drink now.*

1979 ZINFANDEL ($7.50) Jimsomare, Santa Cruz Mountains. *Definite off qualities.*

☆☆ 1979 ZINFANDEL ($9.00) York Creek, Napa Valley. *12% Petite Sirah. Rich, clean, intense, balanced. Drink now.*

☆☆☆ 1979 ZINFANDEL ($9.00) Geyserville, Trentadue Ranch, Sonoma. *5% Petite Sirah. Ripe, berried, oaky, deep.*

☆ 1979 ZINFANDEL ($9.00) Glen Ellen, Sonoma. *Thin and disjointed; oaky and lacking fruit.*

☆☆ 1980 ZINFANDEL ($6.00) Amador Foothills, Amador. *Berried, fresh-faced and charming. Drink now.*

☆☆☆ 1980 ZINFANDEL ($7.50) Esola, Shenandoah Valley, Amador. *5% Petite Sirah. Crisp fruit and varietal character.*

☆☆☆ 1980 ZINFANDEL ($7.50) Fiddletown, Amador. *Richly varietal yet snappy and fresh.*

☆☆☆ 1980 ZINFANDEL ($9.00) Geyserville, Trentadue Ranch, California. *Intense, concentrated, rich, mouthfilling.*

☆ 1980 ZINFANDEL ($9.00) York Creek, Napa. *10% Petite Sirah. Big but lacking depth.*

☆☆ 1980 ZINFANDEL ($9.00) Jimsomare, Santa Cruz Mountains. *Big and berried. 15.9% alcohol.*

☆☆ 1981 ZINFANDEL ($6.00) Hillside, California. *20% Petite Sirah. Fresh, simple, direct, attractive.*

☆☆ 1981 ZINFANDEL ($8.00) Dry Late Picked, Angeli, Alexander Valley. *A monster; big, tannic and hot but not bad. Should smooth out by 1988.*

☆☆☆ 1981 ZINFANDEL ($9.00) 85% Trentadue, 15% Angeli, Geyserville, Alexander Valley. *Crisp and snappy, with good varietal character. Deep, rich.*

☆☆ 1982 ZINFANDEL ($6.75) California. *Lush, berried, rich.*

☆☆☆ 1982 ZINFANDEL ($8.00) Dusi, Paso Robles. *5% Petite Sirah. Balanced, round, fruity, delicious.*

☆☆☆ 1982 ZINFANDEL ($9.00) Beatty, Howell Mountain. *Jammy, peppery, intense, rich, superb. Drink 1988.*

☆☆☆ 1982 ZINFANDEL ($9.50) 20th Anniversary, Geyserville, California. *Fruity, clean and nicely structured. Shows restraint and depth.*

☆☆☆ 1982 ZINFANDEL ($10.50) York Creek, California. *14% Petite Sirah. Structured, rich, clean, balanced, superb. Drink now.*

☆☆☆ 1983 ZINFANDEL ($7.50) Estate, Howell Mountain. *Crisp, balanced, clean, hard-edged. Drink 1988.*

☆☆☆ 1983 ZINFANDEL ($9.00) 73% Beatty, 16% Park-Muscatine, 11% Stout, Howell Mountain. *Peppery, spicy, intense, good balance.*

☆☆ 1983 ZINFANDEL ($9.50) Geyserville, California. *5% Petite Sirah. Varietal, well balanced, restrained.*

☆☆☆ 1983 ZINFANDEL ($10.50) York Creek, California. *12% Petite Sirah. Deep and luscious, with good acidity and ripe fruitiness.*

☆☆ 1984 ZINFANDEL ($9.00) California. *Balanced, clean, fruity, decent but ordinary.*

☆☆☆ 1984 ZINFANDEL ($9.00) Howell Mountain. *Crisp and fruity, lovely varietal flavor and smooth texture.*

☆☆☆ 1984 ZINFANDEL ($9.00) Lytton Springs. *10% Carignane, 5% Grenache. Fruity, fresh, lush, lovely.*

☆☆☆ 1984 ZINFANDEL ($10.50) York Creek, California. *10% Petite Sirah. Blackberry, ginger flavors. Ripe, fresh, fruity, excellent balance.*

☆☆☆ 1984 ZINFANDEL ($13.00) Geyserville, California. *10% Petite Sirah. Meaty, fresh, rich, intense, really lovely.*

☆☆ 1985 ZINFANDEL ($9.00) Lytton Springs, California. *11% Carignane, 9% Grenache. Concentrated, intense, ripe fruit, big spicy flavors.*

☆☆☆ 1985 ZINFANDEL ($10.50) Geyserville, California. *Snappy, crisp, clean, varietal, delicious.*

☆☆ 1985 ZINFANDEL ($10.50) York Creek, California. *10% Petite Sirah. Ripe, intense, brambly berry flavors, hard and somewhat bitter tannins. Drink 1991.*

&

## *Ritchie Creek Vineyards*                    NAPA COUNTY
### WHITE
☆☆☆ 1985 CHARDONNAY ($11.00) Napa Valley. *Lush, crisp fruit, nicely balanced.*
### RED
☆☆☆ 1980 CABERNET SAUVIGNON ($12.50) Napa Valley. *Herbal, very Bordeaux-like, classy.*

☆☆☆ 1981 CABERNET SAUVIGNON ($12.50) Napa Valley. *Herbal, attractive, clean, rich.*

☆☆ 1983 CABERNET SAUVIGNON ($12.50) Napa Valley. *Crisp, tangy, tart, decent, intense, earthy.*

&

RIVER OAKS VINEYARDS *see* Clos du Bois Winery

## *River Road Vineyards*                    SONOMA COUNTY
### RED
☆ 1979 ZINFANDEL ($4.50) Sonoma Valley. *Soft, smooth, decent.*

1979 ZINFANDEL ($5.00) Lot 2, Shandon Valley, California. *Big, fat and very weedy. Essentially unappealing.*

1984 ZINFANDEL ($5.00) Late Harvest, Cienega Valley. *375 ml. 5.5% residual sugar. Crisp, fresh, intense, tannic.*

❧

## *River Run Vintners*          SANTA CRUZ COUNTY

### WHITE
☆☆ 1985 CHARDONNAY ($10.00) Monterey. *Soft, lush, ripe, attractive.*

### RED
☆☆ 1984 CABERNET SAUVIGNON ($8.00) Mountanos, Mendocino. *Rich, tangy, crisp, lovely berry fruit, some earthy qualities. Drink 1989.*

❧

RIVERSIDE FARM *see* Louis Foppiano Wine Company

## *J. Rochioli Vineyards*          SONOMA COUNTY

### WHITE
☆☆ 1983 CHARDONNAY ($10.00) Sonoma. *Soft, ripe, with good, lean fruit; clean and short.*

☆☆ 1984 CHARDONNAY ($9.50) Russian River Valley. *Varietal, clean, tangy, nicely balanced.*

☆☆☆ 1986 CHARDONNAY ($12.00) Estate, Russian River Valley. *Rich, intense, good fruit and lovely varietal character.*

### RED
☆☆ 1982 PINOT NOIR ($13.50) Russian River Valley, Sonoma. *Balanced, varietal, very nice.*

☆ 1983 PINOT NOIR ($12.50) Russian River Valley. *Varietal and fruity, pleasant but somewhat stemmy and bitter.*

☆ 1984 PINOT NOIR ($12.00) Russian River Valley. *Decent but heavy and weedy.*

❧

J. ROGET *see* Canandaigua Wine Company

## *Rolling Hills Vineyard*          VENTURA COUNTY

### WHITE
☆☆ 1983 CHARDONNAY ($11.00) Santa Maria Valley. *Ripe, rich, fat, fruity.*

### RED
☆☆ 1981 CABERNET SAUVIGNON ($8.00) Temescal. *Lush, rich, attractive. Drink now.*

☆☆☆ 1981 MERLOT ($8.00) San Luis Obispo. *Lush, open and fat, with lovely, buttery oak. Splendid.*

1982 MERLOT ($9.00) San Luis Obispo. *Dull.*

❧

## *Rombauer Vineyards*          NAPA COUNTY

### WHITE
☆☆☆ 1982 CHARDONNAY ($12.50) St. Andrews, Napa Valley. *Crisp, clean, intense, balanced.*

☆☆☆ 1983 CHARDONNAY ($13.50) Napa Valley. *Lush, rich, smooth, complex, clean and very lovely.*

☆☆ 1984 CHARDONNAY ($13.50) French, Napa Valley. *Crisp, fresh, tangy, a bit simple.*

☆☆ 1985 CHARDONNAY ($13.50) French, Napa Valley. *Rich, heavy, intense fruit, well made.*

☆☆☆ 1985 CHARDONNAY ($14.50) Napa Valley. *Soft, lush, subtle oak and smooth fruit. Charming.*

**RED**

☆☆☆ 1983 RED TABLE WINE ($12.50) Napa Valley. *61% Cabernet, 31% Cabernet Franc, 8% Merlot. Rich, hard, lovely. Drink 1990.*

☆☆ 1980 CABERNET SAUVIGNON ($12.50) Napa Valley. *Intense, complex and lush; some raisiny notes, well built.*

☆☆ 1981 CABERNET SAUVIGNON ($12.50) Napa Valley. *Rich, elegant, clean, complex. Ready to drink.*

☆☆☆ 1982 CABERNET SAUVIGNON ($12.50) Napa Valley. *Rich, balanced, nicely structured, lovely fruit. Drink 1988.*

☆☆☆ 1983 CABERNET SAUVIGNON ($13.50) Napa Valley. *Soft, smooth, nice fruit and lively acidity. Drink 1989.*

☆☆☆ 1983 MERLOT ($13.50) Napa Valley. *Lush, soft fruit and excellent structure. Drink 1988.*

≥●

## Rose Family Winery                    SONOMA COUNTY

**WHITE**

☆ 1982 CHARDONNAY ($9.25) Cameron, Sonoma. *Vinous and intense; lacks grace and charm.*

☆☆ 1983 CHARDONNAY ($9.75) Western Russian River, Sonoma. *Oily, ripe, oaky, intense.*

☆ 1984 CHARDONNAY ($9.75) Cameron, Russian River Valley. *Vegetal, oily, heavy.*

**RED**

☆☆ 1981 PINOT NOIR ($8.00) Sonoma. *A bit stemmy but some nice varietal character too.*

☆☆ 1982 PINOT NOIR ($8.00) Cameron, Sonoma. *Varietal, clean, simple.*

≥●

## Rosenblum Cellars                    ALAMEDA COUNTY

**WHITE**

1983 CHARDONNAY ($10.00) Los Carneros-Napa. *Oily, dull, bitter.*

☆ 1984 CHARDONNAY ($8.50) Sargent, Napa Valley. *Tart, crisp, decent.*

**RED**

☆☆☆ 1982 ROSENBLUM RED ($4.00) Napa Valley. *58% Pinot Noir. Fruity, structured, superb.*

☆☆ 1978 CABERNET SAUVIGNON ($4.50) Hoffman Ranch, Geyserville, Sonoma. *Round and balanced; quite attractive. Drink now.*

☆☆☆ 1981 CABERNET SAUVIGNON ($10.00) Cohn, Napa Valley. *Rich, fruity, clean, lovely.*

☆☆☆ 1982 CABERNET SAUVIGNON ($10.00) 62% Napa Valley, 38% Sonoma. *Spicy, rich, intense, complex, superb. Drink 1988.*

☆☆ 1982 CABERNET SAUVIGNON ($12.00) Vintner's Reserve, McGilvery Vineyard, Sonoma. *Big, earthy and rich; herbal and fruity. Ready to drink.*

☆ 1983 CABERNET SAUVIGNON ($9.50) Sonoma. *Skunky, vegetal.*

1983 CABERNET SAUVIGNON ($11.00) Napa Valley. *Fat, ripe, volatile acidity.*

☆☆☆ 1980 PETITE SIRAH ($5.50) St. George & Rich Vineyards, Napa Valley. *Lovely, elegant, richly fruity, great balance.*

☆☆☆ 1981 PETITE SIRAH ($6.50) Napa Valley. *Rich, fruity, purple, clean, intense, terrific.*

☆☆☆ 1982 PETITE SIRAH ($7.00) Napa Valley. *Fresh, rich, dark and fruity. Drink now and beyond.*

☆☆☆ 1978 ZINFANDEL ($5.50) Napa Valley. *Lush, fruity, peppery, big, round and lovely. Drink now.*

☆☆ 1980 ZINFANDEL ($8.00) Napa-Sonoma. *20% Petite Sirah. Berried, rich, fruity, nicely balanced.*

☆☆☆ 1981 ZINFANDEL ($6.00) Napa Valley. *Berries and oak; clean fruit and depth. Drink now.*

☆☆☆ 1981 ZINFANDEL ($6.00) Mauritson, Sonoma Valley. *Lovely, berried wine with depth and charm. Drink now.*

☆☆☆ 1983 ZINFANDEL ($7.50) Napa Valley. *11% Petite Sirah. Lush, spicy, rich, very attractive.*

☆☆ 1983 ZINFANDEL ($7.50) Cullinan, Sonoma. *Fresh, fruity, clean, attractive.*

☆☆☆ 1983 ZINFANDEL ($7.50) Sonoma. *Rich, clean, fruity, balanced, charming.*

☆☆☆☆ 1984 ZINFANDEL ($9.00) Reserve, Napa Valley. *Ripe berry fruit, intense color and flavors, velvety texture. A great wine.*

❧

CARLO ROSSI *see* E. & J. Gallo Winery

## *Roudon-Smith Vineyards*     SANTA CRUZ COUNTY

### WHITE

☆☆ 1982 CHARDONNAY ($6.00) Sequoia Coast, California. *Fruity and fresh, with some oak complexity.*

☆ 1982 CHARDONNAY ($11.00) Nelson Ranch, Mendocino. *Overdone, too much oak.*

☆☆☆ 1984 CHARDONNAY ($9.50) Santa Maria Valley. *Lush, clean, balanced, lovely varietal character, soft fruit.*

☆☆☆ 1984 CHARDONNAY ($12.50) Nelson Ranch, Mendocino. *Crisp, snappy, clean, lovely oak.*

☆ 1985 CHARDONNAY ($11.00) Nelson Ranch, Mendocino. *Fat, lush, dull, oxidized.*

☆☆☆ 1986 JOHANNISBERG RIESLING ($7.50) Monterey. *2% residual sugar. Spicy, bright varietal fruit, with tangy acidity.*

☆☆☆ 1984 PINOT BLANC ($6.50) Santa Maria Valley. *11% Chardonnay. Lush and tangy, fruity, clean. Quite lovely.*

### RED

☆☆☆ 1978 CABERNET SAUVIGNON ($25.00) 10th Anniversary, Steiner, Sonoma. *Ripe, intense and attractively complex. Ready to drink.*

☆☆ 1979 CABERNET SAUVIGNON ($13.00) Steiner, Sonoma. *Dark, lush, berried, ripe. Ready to drink.*

1980 CABERNET SAUVIGNON ($8.50) Alexander Valley, Sonoma. *Quite weedy. Simple and clumsy.*

☆☆☆ 1981 CABERNET SAUVIGNON ($12.00) Steiner, Sonoma. *Herbal, rich, balanced, super. Drink 1988 and beyond.*

☆☆☆ 1982 CABERNET SAUVIGNON ($7.50) Nelson Ranch, Mendocino. *Buttery oak, crisp, clean, delightful. Drink 1988 and beyond.*

☆ 1981 PETITE SIRAH ($6.50) San Luis Obispo. *5% Chardonnay. Jammy, clean, intense. Ready to drink.*

☆☆ 1982 PETITE SIRAH ($6.50) San Luis Obispo. *Deep, clean, attractive. Drink now or forget it.*

☆☆ 1983 PETITE SIRAH ($7.50) San Luis Obispo. *Ripe, fat, good fruit, decent.*

☆☆ 1984 PETITE SIRAH ($6.50) San Luis Obispo. *Tart, tannic, concentrated.*

☆ 1981 PINOT NOIR ($14.00) Edna Valley. *Earthy and a bit green; vegetal.*

☆ 1982 PINOT NOIR ($13.00) Edna Valley. *Clean, balanced but vegetal.*

☆ 1978 ZINFANDEL ($6.00) Late Harvest Dry, Central Coast. *Intense, overripe, berried, raisiny.*

☆☆ 1979 ZINFANDEL ($10.00) Old Hill Ranch, Sonoma, California. *Berries and sweet oak; tannic. Drink now.*

☆☆ 1979 ZINFANDEL ($10.00) 10th Anniversary, Chauvet, Sonoma. *Rich, jammy and intense.*

☆☆☆ 1980 ZINFANDEL ($7.50) 10th Anniversary, Chauvet, Sonoma. *Snappy, clean, fresh, delightful. Drink now.*

☆☆☆ 1980 ZINFANDEL ($9.00) 10th Anniversary, Old Hill Ranch, Sonoma. *Spicy nose and rich varietal character; crisp and snappy. Drink now.*

☆☆ 1982 ZINFANDEL ($7.50) Chauvet, Sonoma. *Berried, balanced, intensely varietal, tannic. Drink now.*

## *Round Hill Cellars*                                    NAPA COUNTY

### WHITE

☆☆☆ 1982 CHARDONNAY ($9.00) Napa Valley. *Lovely, varietal, clean, very nice.*

☆☆ 1984 CHARDONNAY ($4.75) California. *Crisp, fresh, clean, attractive.*

☆☆☆ 1984 HOUSE CHARDONNAY ($5.00) California *Rich, fruity, oaky, complex, a real value.*

☆☆ 1984 CHARDONNAY ($7.50) Napa Valley Reserve, Napa Valley. *Rich, deep, clean, attractive.*

☆☆☆ 1984 RUTHERFORD RANCH BRAND CHARDONNAY ($10.00) Reese, Napa Valley. *Rich, lush, clean, beautifully balanced.*

☆☆ 1985 HOUSE CHARDONNAY ($5.00) California. *Lovely, crisp, easy to drink.*

☆☆ 1985 CHARDONNAY ($9.50) Reserve, Napa Valley. *Crisp, fresh, clean, balanced, well made.*

☆☆ 1986 CHARDONNAY ($6.75) North Coast. *Fruity, bright, clean, with a lovely crisp acidity.*

☆☆ 1986 HOUSE FUME BLANC ($5.00) Napa Valley. *Crisp, varietal, intense, quite decent.*

### RED

☆☆ 1978 RUTHERFORD RANCH BRAND CABERNET SAUVIGNON ($8.50) Napa Valley. *Big, ripe, fruity. Ready to drink.*

☆☆☆ 1979 RUTHERFORD RANCH BRAND CABERNET SAUVIGNON ($9.00) Napa Valley. *Big and fleshy; full and rich. Drink now.*

☆ 1980 CABERNET SAUVIGNON ($7.50) Napa Valley. *Nice, varietal, clean but a bit heavy and lacking structure.*

☆☆ 1980 RUTHERFORD RANCH BRAND CABERNET SAUVIGNON ($9.00) Napa Valley. *Intense and varietal; clean and complex. Drink 1988.*

☆☆ 1981 CABERNET SAUVIGNON ($9.00) Napa Valley. *Lush, soft, attractive, clean, varietal. Drink now.*

☆☆☆ 1982 CABERNET SAUVIGNON ($9.00) Napa Valley. *Dark, minty, cassis and vanilla flavors, berried, ripe, balanced. Drink 1990.*

☆☆☆ 1982 RUTHERFORD RANCH BRAND CABERNET SAUVIGNON ($12.00) Napa Valley. *Lush, deep, great fruit, ripe and lovely. Drink 1988.*

☆☆☆ 1983 CABERNET SAUVIGNON ($9.50) Reserve, Napa Valley. *Ripe, rich, round, balanced, fat and lush, lovely. Drink now.*

☆☆☆ 1984 CABERNET SAUVIGNON ($10.00) Reserve, Napa Valley. *Silky, tannic but soft and very pretty. Drink now.*

☆☆ 1982 MERLOT ($7.50) Napa Valley. *Decent, ripe, clean, intense. Drink now.*

☆☆☆ 1983 MERLOT ($7.50) Napa Valley. *Soft, elegant, fruity, rich, superb.*

☆☆☆ 1984 MERLOT ($9.00) Napa Valley. *Soft, fruity, clean, earthy, fleshy, attractive.*

☆☆ 1984 RUTHERFORD RANCH BRAND MERLOT ($10.00) Napa Valley. *Rich, clean, herbal.*

☆☆☆ 1980 PETITE SIRAH ($6.00) Napa Valley. *Spicy, clean, crisp, tangy, delightful.*

☆☆☆ 1981 RUTHERFORD RANCH BRAND PETITE SIRAH ($7.50) Napa Valley. *Lush, clean, spicy, tannic.*

☆☆ 1979 PINOT NOIR ($6.00) Gamay Acres, Napa Valley. *Fruity, clean and berried.*

☆ 1981 PINOT NOIR ($6.00) Gamay Acres, Napa Valley. *Clean, fruity, simple.*

☆ 1978 RUTHERFORD RANCH BRAND ZINFANDEL ($7.50) Late Harvest, Napa Valley. *Clean and fruity but with 16.3% alcohol. Sweet, strange.*

☆☆ 1979 ZINFANDEL ($5.00) Napa Valley. *Harsh and awkward but showing aging potential. Drink 1988.*

☆☆☆ 1979 RUTHERFORD RANCH BRAND ZINFANDEL ($5.00) Napa. *Peppery and fresh, with lovely aging potential. Drink now.*

☆☆ 1980 ZINFANDEL ($4.50) Napa. *Crisp and bright.*

☆☆ 1980 RUTHERFORD RANCH BRAND ZINFANDEL ($6.00) Napa Valley. *Tart, fruity, good.*

☆☆ 1981 ZINFANDEL ($5.00) Napa Valley. *Underripe but nicely structured. A pleasant wine.*

☆ 1981 RUTHERFORD RANCH BRAND ZINFANDEL ($6.00) Napa Valley. *Clean, decent, a bit dull.*

☆☆☆ 1982 ZINFANDEL ($5.00) Napa Valley. *Tart, crisp, clean, fruity, elegant, charming.*

☆☆ 1982 RUTHERFORD RANCH BRAND ZINFANDEL ($6.00) Napa Valley. *Spicy, lush, richly tannic. Ready to drink.*

☆ 1984 ZINFANDEL ($4.75) Napa Valley. *Intense, heavy, some bitterness.*

☆☆☆ 1984 RUTHERFORD RANCH BRAND ZINFANDEL ($6.50) Napa Valley. *Rich, raisin fruit, lush texture, good structure; delicious.*

❧

## Royal Kedem Wine Corporation　　　NEW YORK
### WHITE

☆☆ 1986 BARON JAQUAB DE HERZOG CHARDONNAY ($10.00) California Selection, Sonoma. *Kosher. Crisp, clean and simple.*

☆ 1986 BARON JAQUAB DE HERZOG SAUVIGNON BLANC ($5.50) Sonoma. *Kosher. Tart, simple, decent.*

## SPARKLING
NV BRUT ($5.50) New York. *Kosher. Foxy, odd but drinkable.*

## BLANC DE NOIR
☆☆☆ 1986 WHITE ZINFANDEL ($5.00) Sonoma. *Crisp, bright, fruity, balanced.*

## RED
☆☆ 1985 BARON JAQUAB DE HERZOG CABERNET SAUVIGNON ($11.00) Sonoma. *Kosher. Lush, ripe, fresh, soft, charming. Drink now.*

ROYAL KNIGHTS *see* Colony

# Russian River Wine Cellars          SONOMA COUNTY
## WHITE
1984 CHARDONNAY ($6.00) Alexander Valley. *Bitter, unattractive.*

# Rustridge Winery                      NAPA COUNTY
## RED
☆ 1981 ZINFANDEL ($9.00) Napa Valley. *Balanced, varietal, some odd flavors.*

# Rutherford Hill Winery               NAPA COUNTY
## WHITE
☆☆☆ 1982 CHARDONNAY ($10.00) Jaeger, Napa Valley. *Fruity, crisp, charming, with lovely oak.*

☆☆☆ 1983 CHARDONNAY ($10.75) Jaeger, Napa Valley. *Fresh, fruity, clean, balanced.*

☆☆☆ 1986 CHARDONNAY ($11.00) Special Cuvée, Rutherford Knoll, Napa Valley. *Fresh, clean, balanced, with bright fruit and gentle oak.*

☆☆ 1986 GEWURZTRAMINER ($6.25) Dry, Napa Valley. *Crisp, spicy, some bitterness, nice tight finish.*

☆ 1985 SAUVIGNON BLANC ($7.00) Napa Valley. *Soft, decent flavors, composty and a bit dull.*

## RED
☆☆ 1978 CABERNET SAUVIGNON ($10.50) Napa Valley. *Good fruit, varietal, a nice wine. Drink now.*

☆☆☆ 1979 CABERNET SAUVIGNON ($10.50) Napa Valley. *Subtle, balanced, lush, superb. Drink now.*

☆☆ 1980 CABERNET SAUVIGNON ($12.00) Napa Valley. *24% Merlot. Rich, clean, herbal. Ready.*

☆☆☆ 1980 CABERNET SAUVIGNON ($18.00) Lot 2, Napa Valley. *Soft, ripe, mature but still lively. Drink now.*

☆☆☆ 1981 CABERNET SAUVIGNON ($12.00) Napa Valley. *Rich, graceful, with lovely oak and soft fruit. Drink now.*

☆☆☆ 1982 CABERNET SAUVIGNON ($11.00) Napa Valley. *15% Merlot. Lush, structured, lovely. Drink now and over the next three years.*

☆☆☆ 1983 CABERNET SAUVIGNON ($11.00) Napa Valley. *Earthy but clean, lovely olive and cedar flavors, crisp fruit and good depth. Drink 1989.*

☆☆☆☆ 1979 MERLOT ($9.25) Napa Valley. *Toasty, rich, supple, structured and classic. Drink now.*

☆☆ 1980 MERLOT ($10.00) Napa Valley. *Good fruit and varietal aroma but lacking the depth of the '79.*

☆☆ 1981 MERLOT ($10.00) Napa Valley. *Weedy, heavy, with earthy flavors and decent fruit.*

☆☆☆ 1982 MERLOT ($10.00) Napa Valley. *Soft, rich, varietal, excellent.*

☆☆☆ 1983 MERLOT ($10.00) Napa Valley. *6% Cabernet Sauvig-non, 4% Cabernet Franc. Soft, fresh, good structure, tangy fruit; lovely. Drink now.*

☆☆ 1979 PINOT NOIR ($7.50) Napa Valley. *Toasty, earthy and attractive.*

☆☆ 1977 ZINFANDEL ($7.00) Mead Ranch, Atlas Peak, Napa Valley. *Marred by high alcohol. Drink now.*

**FORTIFIED**

☆ 1983 PORT ($18.00) Napa Valley. *Awkward, crude; too much alcohol. Made from Cabernet Sauvignon.*

≀▲

RUTHERFORD RANCH BRAND *see* Round Hill Cellars

## Rutherford Vintners                    NAPA COUNTY

**WHITE**

☆☆ 1983 CHARDONNAY ($12.00) Napa Valley. *Pineapple, oak, varietal character. Nicely made.*

☆☆☆ 1984 CHARDONNAY ($12.00) Napa Valley. *Soft, lush, clean, lovely varietal character.*

**RED**

☆☆ 1978 CHATEAU RUTHERFORD CABERNET SAUVIG-NON ($13.50) Napa Valley. *Balanced, herbal, a bit low in fruit but attractive. Still hanging in there.*

☆ 1980 MERLOT ($9.00) Napa Valley. *Herbal, stinky, thin, not much.*

≀▲

SADDLE MOUNTAIN *see* Snoqualmie Winery

## St. Andrews Winery                    NAPA COUNTY

**WHITE**

☆☆☆ 1982 CHARDONNAY ($12.50) Napa Valley. *Crisp, clean, fresh, lush, lovely.*

☆☆☆ 1983 CHARDONNAY ($12.50) Napa Valley. *Lovely, elegant, balanced.*

☆☆☆ 1985 CHARDONNAY ($7.50) Napa Valley. *Crisp acidity, lovely, subtle, rich.*

☆☆☆ 1985 CHARDONNAY ($13.00) Estate, Napa Valley. *Crisp and snappy, with good oak and lovely varietal fruit.*

☆☆ 1986 CHARDONNAY ($8.00) Napa Valley. *Rich, intense, soft, fat.*

**RED**

☆☆☆ 1981 CABERNET SAUVIGNON ($9.00) Napa Valley. *Rich, deep, great structure, elegant. Drink now.*

☆☆☆☆ 1983 CABERNET SAUVIGNON ($7.50) Glendale Ranch, Napa Valley. *A remarkable wine. Balanced, soft, lush, plummy, deep, superb. Drink 1988.*

≀▲

## Ste. Chapelle Winery                    IDAHO

**WHITE**

☆ 1983 CHARDONNAY ($7.00) Vin de Maison, 45% Idaho, 55% Washington. *Oily, heavy, not much.*

○ 1984 CHARDONNAY ($10.00) 10th Anniversary, Idaho. *Oxidized, dull, awful.*

☆☆☆ 1986 CHARDONNAY ($10.00) Idaho. *Crisp, balanced, varietal, charming fruit.*

☆ 1986 CHENIN BLANC ($6.00) Washington. *Decent but dull.*

☆☆☆ 1986 SOFT CHENIN BLANC ($6.00) Washington. *7.6% residual sugar. Crisp, spritzy, clean, lively.*

☆☆ 1986 GEWURZTRAMINER ($4.50) Idaho. *Spicy, crisp, fruity, charming.*

☆☆☆ 1985 JOHANNISBERG RIESLING ($15.00) Late Harvest, Ellenburg, Idaho. *6.6% residual sugar. Peachy flavors, crisp, clean, attractive.*

☆☆ 1986 JOHANNISBERG RIESLING ($6.75) Idaho. *2.6% residual sugar. Fresh, clean, varietal fruit, smooth finish.*

☆☆☆ 1986 JOHANNISBERG RIESLING ($10.00) Special Harvest, Winery Block, Idaho. *8.8% residual sugar. Floral, crisp, clean, attractive.*

☆ 1986 JOHANNISBERG RIESLING ($14.00) Late Harvest, Idaho. *9.9% residual sugar. Fruit, decent but lacking intensity.*

☆☆☆ 1986 JOHANNISBERG RIESLING ($15.00) Botrytis, Late Harvest, Idaho. *10.6% residual sugar. Soft, fresh, snappy, clean, peachy fruit.*

### SPARKLING

☆ NV BRUT ($2.00) Washington. *187 ml. 100% Riesling. Charmat method. Crisp, fresh, spicy.*

NV BLANC DE NOIR ($7.50) Washington. *Flat, dull, bitter.*

### BLANC DE NOIR

☆☆☆ 1986 BLANC DE NOIR ($5.00) Idaho. *2.6% residual sugar. Sweet, soft, crisp, lively, attractive.*

### ROSE

☆☆☆ 1986 ROSE OF CABERNET SAUVIGNON ($6.00) Washington. *2.7% residual sugar. Soft, crisp, strawberry fruit, charming.*

### RED

☆ 1981 CABERNET SAUVIGNON ($9.00) Washington. *Herbal, bell pepper flavors, crisp and lean.*

☆☆ 1983 CABERNET SAUVIGNON ($9.50) Washington. *Lush, rich, deep, intense, decent.*

❧

## St. Clement Vineyards                    NAPA COUNTY

### WHITE

☆☆☆ 1982 CHARDONNAY ($14.50) Napa Valley. *Crisp, fruity, delicate and lovely.*

☆☆☆ 1983 CHARDONNAY ($14.50) Napa Valley. *Fragrant, clean, crisp, tangy, complex.*

☆☆☆ 1984 CHARDONNAY ($14.50) Napa Valley. *Something of a departure: delicate, elegant, clean, varietal. Not the usual full, fruity style.*

☆☆☆ 1985 CHARDONNAY ($15.50) Napa Valley. *Lush, soft, richly fruity; lovely oak and excellent balance.*

### RED

☆☆☆☆ 1980 CABERNET SAUVIGNON ($12.50) Napa Valley. *Perfectly built, richly structured, fruity. Aging nicely.*

☆☆☆☆ 1981 CABERNET SAUVIGNON ($12.50) Napa Valley. *Wow! Crisp fruit matched with depth and style. Aging beautifully.*

☆☆☆ 1982 CABERNET SAUVIGNON ($13.50) Napa Valley. *Clean, structured, elegant, varietal, stunning. Ready to drink.*

☆☆☆ 1983 CABERNET SAUVIGNON ($13.50) Napa Valley. *Rich, structured, deep, lively oak and fruit. Drink 1989.*

☆☆☆ 1982 GARRISON FOREST MERLOT ($7.75) Napa Valley. *Big, oaky, intense, good fruit. Ready.*

❧

## *St. Francis Vineyards*  SONOMA COUNTY

### WHITE

☆ 1982 CHARDONNAY ($9.00) Potter Valley, Mendocino and Estate, North Coast. *Heavy, rich and over-oaky. Clumsy and coarse.*

☆☆☆☆ 1982 CHARDONNAY ($14.00) Jacobs, Carneros District, Napa. *Stunningly elegant blend of oak and crisp fruit. Superb.*

☆☆☆ 1983 CHARDONNAY ($10.75) Estate, Sonoma Valley. *Crisp and bright, with beautifully balanced fruit and oak.*

☆☆☆☆ 1984 CHARDONNAY ($12.00) Barrel Select, Estate, Sonoma Valley. *Soft, ripe, rich, sweet oak, lovely fruit.*

☆☆☆ 1985 CHARDONNAY ($9.00) Estate, Sonoma Valley. *Melons and ripe fruit, lovely oak, intense varietal character.*

☆☆☆☆ 1986 CHARDONNAY ($14.00) Barrel Select, Estate, Sonoma Valley. *Superb oak; snappy, luscious fruit; great balance.*

1985 MUSCAT ($7.00) Estate, Sonoma Valley. *3.95% residual sugar. Sour, unattractive.*

### RED

☆ NV POVERELLO RED ($4.75) Estate, Sonoma Valley. *Minty, crisp, clean, decent.*

☆☆☆ 1981 MERLOT ($10.75) Estate, Sonoma Valley. *Dark, herbal, intense, complex, superb.*

☆☆☆ 1982 MERLOT ($10.75) Estate, Sonoma Valley. *Earthy, fruity, balanced, lovely. Drink now or hold.*

☆☆☆ 1983 MERLOT ($10.75) Sonoma Valley. *Lush, soft, supple, deep cherry fruit, great finesse.*

☆☆☆ 1984 MERLOT ($16.00) Reserve, Sonoma Valley., *Lush, soft, herbal, rich, with plummy fruit. A trifle earthy. Drink now.*

☆☆ 1981 PINOT NOIR ($10.75) Estate, Sonoma Valley. *Nice berry ripeness; some stems but attractive and light.*

≈◦

## *Ste. Genevieve Vineyards and Winery*  TEXAS

### RED

☆☆☆ 1984 CHAMBOURCIN ($6.50) Parker. *Lush, lovely, charming, Pinot Noir-like.*

≈◦

## *St. Julian Wine Company*  MICHIGAN

### WHITE

☆☆ 1985 VIGNOLES ($8.50) Michigan. *Tangy, rich, oily, lush, interesting.*

### SPARKLING

☆☆ NV CHATEAU ST. JULIEN BRUT ($7.50) Michigan. *Fresh, simple, sweet, syrupy, good.*

### RED

1982 CHAMBOURCIN ($5.00) Lawton Ridge, Michigan. *Tart, slim, lemony.*

1983 CHAMBOURCIN ($7.00) Michigan. *Pale, dull, simple.*

☆☆☆ 1985 CHAMBOURCIN ($8.50) Lake Michigan Shore. *Soft, ripe, clean, fruity, balanced and quite charming.*

○ 1981 CHANCELLOR ($4.00) Michigan. *Earthy, thin, tart.*

☆☆ 1981 CHANCELLOR ($8.50) Lake Michigan Shore. *Deep, complex, woody. Ready.*

☆   1983 CHANCELLOR ($8.50) Lake Michigan Shore. *Big,
        berry fruit; overripe and grapey.*
☆☆☆  1984 CHANCELLOR ($8.50) Lake Michigan Shore. *Big, ripe,
        rich, deep and luscious.*

᪐

## St. Wendel Cellars                              INDIANA
### RED
☆☆  NV   CRITERION RED ($5.00) Indiana. *Crisp, snappy, fresh,
        attractive.*

᪐

## Saintsbury Winery                          NAPA COUNTY
### WHITE
☆☆  1982 CHARDONNAY ($11.00) Sonoma. *Crisp and earthy,
        with nice varietal flavors. Decent.*
☆☆☆ 1983 CHARDONNAY ($11.00) Napa Valley. *Fresh, balanced,
        lovely.*
☆☆☆ 1984 CHARDONNAY ($11.00) Carneros. *Spicy, vanillin,
        crisp, superb oak and fruit.*
☆☆☆ 1985 CHARDONNAY ($11.50) Carneros. *Rich, herbal, good
        acidity.*
☆☆☆ 1986 CHARDONNAY ($12.50) Carneros. *Butterscotch,
        toasty; lush, sweet oak yet elegant and not too
        heavy.*
### RED
☆☆  1982 PINOT NOIR ($8.00) Sonoma. *Nicely structured, good
        fruit and aging potential.*
☆☆☆ 1982 PINOT NOIR ($11.00) Carneros, Napa Valley. *Lush,
        fruity, clean, with great depth. Drink now.*
☆☆  1983 PINOT NOIR ($8.00) Garnet, Carneros. *Varietal, clean,
        fresh, attractive.*
☆☆☆ 1983 PINOT NOIR ($12.00) Carneros, Napa Valley. *Spicy,
        cherry flavored, clean. Drink now and for the next
        few years.*
☆☆☆ 1984 PINOT NOIR ($8.00) Garnet, Carneros. *Cherry-berry
        flavors and fresh, crisp acidity. Intense and very
        attractive. Coarse but a real winner.*
☆☆☆ 1984 PINOT NOIR ($12.00) 60% Lee, 20% St. Clair, 20%
        Rancho Carneros, Carneros. *Rich, ripe, lush, great
        texture, lovely fruit, complex and charming.*
☆☆☆ 1985 PINOT NOIR ($9.00) Garnet, Carneros. *Fresh, fruity,
        soft and remarkably complex. A charming wine.*
☆☆☆ 1985 PINOT NOIR ($13.00) Carneros. *Superb cherry fruit
        and lovely fresh flavors.*
☆☆☆ 1986 PINOT NOIR ($8.00) Garnet, Santa Barbara. *Crisp,
        bright, lovely soft texture, balanced and delicious.*

᪐

## Sakonnet Vineyards                          RHODE ISLAND
### WHITE
☆   1983 CHARDONNAY ($8.50) Rhode Island. *Clean,
        attractive.*
### RED
☆   NV   PINOT NOIR ($9.00) Estate, Southeast New England.
        *Vegetal, decent.*

᪐

## Salishan Vineyards                          WASHINGTON
### RED
☆☆  1985 PINOT NOIR ($11.00) Vintner's Reserve, Washington.
        *Good varietal flavors although a bit tart and thin.*

᪐

### San Antonio Winery　　　　LOS ANGELES COUNTY
#### WHITE
　　NV　VELVET CHABLIS ($2.75) San Antonio. *1% residual sugar. Dull, flat, not much interest here.*

☆☆　1984 MADDALENA CHARDONNAY ($9.00) Vintner's Reserve, Napa Valley. *Earthy, oily, heavy, overripe.*

☆　1985 MADDALENA CHARDONNAY ($6.00) Napa Valley. *Simple, decent, clean but lacking varietal character and depth.*

☆　1985 CHARDONNAY ($7.00) Napa Cuvée, Napa Valley. *Crisp, lean, simple, decent.*

☆　1986 CHENIN BLANC ($4.75) Napa Valley. *Crisp, fresh, some off flavors.*

#### RED
☆☆　1983 MADDALENA CABERNET SAUVIGNON ($5.00) Sonoma. *Clean, fruity, rich, balanced, nice. Drink now.*

☆☆　1984 MADDALENA CABERNET SAUVIGNON ($8.00) Sonoma. *Lush, clean, fat, good balance.*

☆☆　1984 MADDALENA CABERNET SAUVIGNON ($9.00) Vintner's Reserve, Sonoma. *Soft, spicy, clean, balanced, lovely. Drink now.*

### San Martín Winery　　　　SANTA CLARA COUNTY
#### WHITE
☆☆　1983 CHARDONNAY ($7.25) San Luis Obispo. *Decent, clean, buttery oak; attractive.*

☆☆　1984 CHARDONNAY ($7.00) Central Coast. *Round, fruity, good oak, attractive.*

☆☆　1985 CHARDONNAY ($7.25) Domaine, Central Coast. *Decent fruit, simple, pleasant.*

☆☆　1986 CRYSTAL CREEK CHARDONNAY ($4.00) Monterey. *Soft, good varietal fruit, clean and quite charming.*

☆☆☆　1986 CRYSTAL CREEK SAUVIGNON BLANC ($3.50) Mendocino. *Clean and lean, crisp and appealing.*

#### BLANC DE NOIR
☆☆　1986 CRYSTAL CREEK WHITE ZINFANDEL ($3.00) Central Coast. *Clean, fresh, simple.*

☆　1986 WHITE ZINFANDEL ($5.00) Central Coast. *Soft, clean, balanced but flat and lacking flavor.*

#### RED
☆　1978 CABERNET SAUVIGNON ($12.25) Special Reserve, San Luis Obispo. *Big and fat; grapey, intense. Lacks finesse.*

☆　1979 CABERNET SAUVIGNON ($6.80) San Luis Obispo. *Soft, sweetish, simple.*

☆☆　1982 CABERNET SAUVIGNON ($7.75) Central Coast. *Soft, vegetal, clean, decent. Drink now.*

☆☆　1984 CRYSTAL CREEK CABERNET SAUVIGNON ($4.00) Santa Barbara. *Herbal, soft, clean, quite attractive.*

☆　1982 ZINFANDEL ($6.00) Amador. *Fruity, crisp, clean but lacking varietal character.*

### San Pasqual Vineyards　　　　SAN DIEGO COUNTY
#### SPARKLING
　　NV　ROSE ($14.00) California. *1.5% residual sugar. Lush, fat, decent, lacking finesse.*

#### RED
☆　1984 PINOT NOIR ($10.75) Sierra Madre, Santa Maria Valley. *Rich, complex, composty, earthy.*

## San Saba Vineyard                MONTEREY COUNTY
### RED
☆☆ 1982 CABERNET SAUVIGNON ($15.00) Monterey. *Smooth, elegant, rich, a bit vegetal. Drink 1989.*
☆☆ 1983 CABERNET SAUVIGNON ($15.00) Monterey. *Ripe, rich, flavors of olives and leather. The most interesting of San Saba's first three vintages.*
☆☆ 1984 CABERNET SAUVIGNON ($15.00) Monterey. *Crisp, lean, lovely cherry fruit, some volatility.*

ðŸŒ¿

## Sanford Winery              SANTA BARBARA COUNTY
### WHITE
☆☆☆ 1982 CHARDONNAY ($12.00) Santa Maria Valley. *Very toasty, with ripe, tart fruitiness.*
☆☆ 1983 CHARDONNAY ($12.50) Central Coast. *Toasty, fat, big, luscious but lacking structure.*
☆☆☆ 1984 CHARDONNAY ($12.00) Paragon, Central Coast. *Rich, soft, oaky, fruity, clean, lovely texture.*
☆☆☆ 1985 CHARDONNAY ($12.00) Central Coast. *Toasty, lush, elegant, lovely wood, rich fruit.*
☆☆☆☆ 1985 CHARDONNAY ($19.00) Barrel Select, Santa Barbara. *Rich, toasty oak, ripe, spicy varietal fruit, exquisite balance and finesse.*
### BLANC DE NOIR
☆☆☆ 1984 VIN GRIS ($6.00) Central Coast. *Lush, soft, oaky, clean, lively, complex.*
☆☆☆ 1986 VIN GRIS DE PINOT NOIR ($6.00) Central Coast. *Crisp, clean, with lovely fruit and oak. Balanced and complex.*
### RED
☆☆ 1984 MERLOT ($10.50) Santa Barbara. *Composty, ripe herbs, intense, lush.*
☆☆☆ 1985 MERLOT ($12.00) Santa Barbara. *Earthy, soft, rich, lovely fruit. Drink 1988.*
☆☆ 1981 PINOT NOIR ($10.50) Santa Maria Valley. *Earthy, rich, intense. Still attractive.*
☆☆☆ 1984 PINOT NOIR ($12.00) Central Coast. *Tarry, spicy, earthy, with lovely fruit and great structure.*
☆☆☆ 1985 PINOT NOIR ($12.00) Central Coast. *Lush raspberry fruit, spicy, clean, lovely balance and complexity.*
☆☆☆ 1986 PINOT NOIR ($12.50) Central Coast. *Clean, spicy, lush, intense fruit, lovely balance.*

ðŸŒ¿

## Sangre de Cristo Wines              NEW MEXICO
### WHITE
1985 VIDAL BLANC ($5.00) Demi-Sec, Gailard, Bernalillo. *Meaty, fat, off-dry. Some volatile acidity.*
### RED
☆☆ 1985 LUCIE KUHLMANN ($10.00) Lilley, New Mexico. *Smokey, fruity, rich, decent.*

ðŸŒ¿

## Santa Barbara Winery          SANTA BARBARA COUNTY
### WHITE
1985 CHARDONNAY ($8.50) Santa Ynez Valley. *Vegetal, thin.*
1985 CHARDONNAY ($13.50) Reserve, Santa Ynez Valley. *Lush, green, bitter, vegetal.*

☆☆ 1986 CHARDONNAY ($9.00) Santa Ynez Valley. *Clean, crisp, firm, good fruit and structure.*

☆☆ 1986 JOHANNISBERG RIESLING ($7.00) Santa Ynez Valley. *Clean, decent, some nice fruit.*

## BLANC DE NOIR

☆ 1986 CABERNET SAUVIGNON BLANC ($6.00) Santa Barbara. *1% residual sugar. Balanced and clean but strongly vegetal.*

☆☆ 1986 WHITE ZINFANDEL ($5.50) Central Coast. *1.5% residual sugar. Spicy, crisp, nicely balanced.*

☆☆☆ 1987 WHITE ZINFANDEL ($6.00) Central Coast. *1.5% residual sugar. Fresh, crisp, lively; a charming wine with a lovely color.*

## RED

☆ 1982 CABERNET SAUVIGNON ($12.00) Santa Ynez Valley. *Ripe, earthy, vegetal, fat.*

☆☆ 1981 ZINFANDEL ($7.00) Santa Ynez Valley. *Clean and varietal but lacking charm and grace.*

☆ 1985 ZINFANDEL ($6.50) Santa Ynez Valley. *Sweet peas, vegetables, lush, deep, decent.*

☆☆ 1986 ZINFANDEL ($5.50) Nouveau, Santa Ynez Valley. *Partial carbonic maceration. Snappy, clean, fresh and appealing.*

☆☆ 1987 ZINFANDEL ($6.00) Beaujour, Santa Ynez Valley. *Purple, spicy, fresh and fruity. Charming.*

ॐ

## Santa Cruz Mountain Vineyard

SANTA CRUZ COUNTY

## RED

☆☆ NV 1978/1979 PINOT NOIR ($15.00) Sleepy Hollow, 70% Santa Cruz Mountains, 30% Monterey. *Big, leathery, tart, tannic.*

☆☆ 1978 CABERNET SAUVIGNON ($12.00) Bates Ranch, Santa Cruz Mountains. *Rich, berried, tannic. Drink now.*

☆☆☆ 1979 CABERNET SAUVIGNON ($14.00) Bates Ranch, Santa Cruz Mountains. *Balanced, clean, oaky, varietal, lovely. Ready.*

1980 CABERNET SAUVIGNON ($14.00) Gamble Ranch, Napa Valley. *Weird; rich, sweet and chocolatey.*

☆☆ 1981 CABERNET SAUVIGNON ($12.50) Bates Ranch, Santa Cruz Mountains. *Rough, rich, varietal. Beginning to mellow.*

☆ 1982 CABERNET SAUVIGNON ($12.00) Bates Ranch, Santa Cruz Mountains. *Ripe, intense, good fruit, unfocused.*

☆☆ 1978 DURIF ($7.50) Jones Ranch, California. *Big, fat, lush, tannic.*

☆☆ 1982 DURIF ($9.00) Santa Cruz Mountains. *Smokey, fruity, clean.*

☆☆☆ 1977 PINOT NOIR ($8.00) Estate, Rider Ridge, Santa Cruz. *Deep, rich and complex. Smooth and lovely.*

☆☆ 1979 PINOT NOIR ($15.00) Estate, Rider Ridge, Santa Cruz. *Toasty, clean, with long aging potential. Ready to drink now.*

☆☆☆ 1981 PINOT NOIR ($15.00) Santa Cruz Mountains. *Rich, balanced, deep; delightful.*

☆☆☆ 1984 PINOT NOIR ($15.00) Santa Cruz Mountains. *Rich, lush, deep, soft, velvety, powerful.*

ॐ

## Santa Lucia Winery          SANTA BARBARA COUNTY
### RED
☆☆ 1984 WILD HORSE MERLOT ($10.50) Rancho Sisquoc, Santa Maria Valley. *Deep, lush, herbaceous, attractive.*

1983 WILD HORSE PINOT NOIR ($11.75) Sierra Madre, Santa Maria. *Strange flavors; balanced but flawed.*

☆ 1984 WILD HORSE PINOT NOIR ($11.75) Santa Maria Valley. *Vegetal, spicy, strange.*

વ્ય

## Santa Ynez Valley Winery    SANTA BARBARA COUNTY
### WHITE
○ 1983 CHARDONNAY ($8.50) Santa Ynez Valley. *Sour, bitter, unappealing.*

☆☆ 1984 CHARDONNAY ($9.00) Santa Ynez Valley. *Rich, oily, tart, decent.*

### RED
☆ 1983 MERLOT ($4.25) L'Enfant, Santa Ynez Valley. *Vegetal but fresh; fruity and nicely made.*

વ્ય

## Santino Wines               AMADOR COUNTY
### WHITE
1985 JOHANNISBERG RIESLING ($14.00) Dry Berry Select Harvest, TBA, El Dorado. *375 ml. 30.1% residual sugar. Candied, lacking freshness, out of balance.*

### RED
☆ 1982 ZIN-SIRAH ($4.00) Amador-Sonoma. *88% Amador Zinfandel, 12% Sonoma Valley Petite Sirah. Clean but very thin and dull.*

☆☆ 1980 CABERNET SAUVIGNON ($8.00) Stone Barn, El Dorado. *Tart, oaky, astringent but quite likable.*

☆ 1983 CABERNET SAUVIGNON ($7.50) Shenandoah Valley. *Tart, clean, decent but slight.*

☆☆ 1980 ZINFANDEL ($7.50) Special Selection, Eschen, Amador. *Simple, clean, decent, lacking fruitiness.*

☆☆ 1981 ZINFANDEL ($5.75) Shenandoah Valley. *Tannic, crisp, fruity.*

☆☆ 1981 ZINFANDEL ($7.50) Special Selection, Eschen, Fiddletown, Amador. *Rich, berried, varietal.*

☆☆☆ 1983 ZINFANDEL ($7.50) Eschen, Fiddletown. *Tangy, crisp, clean, some barrel flavors, nice fruit, complex.*

☆☆☆ 1985 ZINFANDEL ($8.50) Dry Berry Select White Harvest, Amador. *375 ml. 31.5% residual sugar. Crisp, fruity, intense, balanced, lovely.*

વ્ય

## Sarah's Vineyard            SANTA CLARA COUNTY
### WHITE
☆☆☆ 1982 CHARDONNAY ($14.00) Monterey. *Crisp, clean and lovely. Great varietal character.*

☆☆☆ 1982 CHARDONNAY ($16.00) Ventana, Monterey. *Crisp, clean and varietal. Lovely.*

☆☆☆ 1983 CHARDONNAY ($16.00) Ventana, Monterey. *Snappy, clean, lively.*

☆☆☆ 1983 CHARDONNAY ($17.00) Estate, Santa Clara. *Crisp, deep, rich, clean, super.*

☆☆☆ 1984 CHARDONNAY ($17.00) Ventana, Monterey. *Soft, lush, rich, complex, lovely fruit and oak.*

☆☆☆ 1984 CHARDONNAY ($18.00) Estate, Santa Clara. *Crisp, snappy, fruity, lovely and fresh varietal flavors.*

**RED**

☆☆ NV RED TABLE WINE ($12.00) San Luis Obispo. *60% Merlot, 40% Cabernet Sauvignon.*

☆☆ 1980 CABERNET SAUVIGNON ($12.00) San Luis Obispo. *Mellow and fruity. Drink now.*

☆☆ 1980 ZINFANDEL ($9.00) Lime Kiln Valley, San Benito. *Big and somewhat harsh. Clean and powerful.*

☆☆ 1980 ZINFANDEL ($10.00) Les Vignerons Vignoble, Sonoma. *Big, late harvest style. Clean, rich and concentrated.*

☆☆ 1981 ZINFANDEL ($9.00) Dry Creek Valley. *Rich, ripe and fruity, with great balance.*

☆☆ 1981 ZINFANDEL ($9.00) Peterson, Sonoma. *Lush, rich, fruity and very appealing.*

ða.

## V. Sattui Winery                    NAPA COUNTY
**WHITE**

☆☆ 1982 CHARDONNAY ($9.75) Napa Valley. *Simple, clean, with nice varietal character.*

**RED**

☆☆☆ 1980 CABERNET SAUVIGNON ($9.75) Preston, Napa Valley. *Rich and chocolatey; complex and forceful. Mellowing out.*

☆☆☆ 1982 CABERNET SAUVIGNON ($25.00) Reserve Stock, Preston, Napa Valley. *Lovely fruit, crisp acidity, complex, superb. Drink 1990.*

☆☆☆ 1983 CABERNET SAUVIGNON ($9.75) Napa Valley. *Crisp, snappy, with good oak and fresh fruit. Drink 1988.*

1983 CABERNET SAUVIGNON ($13.75) Preston, Napa Valley. *Stinky, vegetal.*

☆☆☆ 1980 ZINFANDEL ($9.75) Reserve Stock, Napa Valley. *Crisp, lush, fresh, fat, very lovely.*

☆☆ 1981 ZINFANDEL ($7.25) Napa Valley. *Clean, tangy, attractive.*

☆☆☆ 1984 ZINFANDEL ($9.00) Howell Mountain. *Big, ripe fruit, crisp acidity, lush texture. Drink 1989.*

☆☆ 1984 ZINFANDEL ($9.25) Alexander Valley. *Clean, decent, fruity, some volatility.*

ða.

## Saucelito Canyon
## Vineyard                  SAN LUIS OBISPO COUNTY
**RED**

☆☆ 1982 CABERNET SAUVIGNON ($10.00) San Luis Obispo. *Soft, pleasant, attractive. Drink now.*

ða.

## Sausal Winery                   SONOMA COUNTY
**WHITE**

○ 1984 CHARDONNAY ($8.50) Alexander Valley. *Sour, dirty, awful.*

**RED**

☆☆ 1978 CABERNET SAUVIGNON ($7.50) Alexander Valley. *Fruity, varietal, snappy.*

☆ 1979 CABERNET SAUVIGNON ($7.50) Alexander Valley. *Simple, velvety. Drink now.*

☆☆ 1983 CABERNET SAUVIGNON ($10.00) Alexander Valley. *Fresh, clean, balanced. Drink now.*

☆ 1978 ZINFANDEL ($5.60) Sonoma. *Overdone: ripe, jammy, almost sweet.*

☆☆ 1979 ZINFANDEL ($5.60) Sonoma. *Grapey and lush.*

☆    1980 ZINFANDEL ($10.00) Private Reserve, Alexander Val-
              ley. *Complex, rich, slightly metallic flavors. From
              90-year-old vines.*
☆☆  1981 ZINFANDEL ($5.60) Alexander Valley. *Rich, varietal,
              good fruit, a bit heavy.*
☆☆  1981 ZINFANDEL ($10.00) Private Reserve, Alexander Val-
              ley. *Heavy, berried, late harvest style. Softening
              nicely.*
☆☆☆ 1982 ZINFANDEL ($5.60) Alexander Valley. *Rich, deep, ripe,
              round, soft, quite lovely.*

                                    ❧

SBARBARO *see* Colony

## Scharffenberger Cellars          MENDOCINO COUNTY
### WHITE
☆    1984 EAGLEPOINT CHARDONNAY ($9.50) Mendocino.
              *Tart, crisp, simple.*
☆    1985 EAGLEPOINT SAUVIGNON BLANC ($6.50) Men-
              docino. *Decent flavors but dull.*
### SPARKLING
☆☆☆ 1982 BLANC DE BLANC ($13.00) Mendocino. *Crisp, fresh,
              snappy, yeasty, attractive.*
☆☆☆ 1984 BLANC DE BLANC ($17.50) Mendocino. *Fresh, nice.*
☆☆☆ 1982 BRUT ($12.50) Mendocino. *Clean, balanced, fresh and
              attractive, with considerable finesse.*
☆☆☆ 1984 BRUT ($15.00) Mendocino. *Crisp, nicely balanced, lush
              fruit, complex.*

                                    ❧

## Schramsberg Vineyards             NAPA COUNTY
### SPARKLING
NV   CUVEE DE PINOT ($17.50) Napa Valley. *Oxidized, very
              unpleasant.*
☆☆  1981 RESERVE ($27.00) Napa Valley. *Heavy, with some
              oxidation; complex but lacking finesse.*
☆    1982 CUVEE DE PINOT ($15.40) Napa Valley. *Some bottle
              variation.*
☆☆☆ 1982 BLANC DE NOIRS ($20.00) Napa Valley. *70% Pinot
              Noir, 30% Chardonnay. Balanced, clean, complex,
              lovely.*

                                    ❧

## Schug Cellars                      NAPA COUNTY
### WHITE
        1983 CHARDONNAY ($11.75) Beckstoffer "Los Amigos,"
              Napa Valley-Carneros. *Herbal, intense, oaky, lack-
              ing charm.*
☆☆☆ 1984 CHARDONNAY ($11.75) Beckstoffer, Napa Valley-
              Carneros. *Ripe, earthy, lush, round, fruity, good
              structure. An extreme style.*
☆☆☆ 1985 CHARDONNAY ($9.75) Ahollinger, Napa Valley-
              Carneros. *Earthy, crisp, good fruit, lean acidity.*
### RED
☆☆  1980 PINOT NOIR ($12.00) Heinemann, Napa Valley. *Rich,
              minty, and intense, with some bitterness.*
☆☆  1981 PINOT NOIR ($12.00) Heinemann, Sonoma. *Earthy,
              raisiny, intense and rich.*
☆    1982 PINOT NOIR ($10.75) Heinemann, Napa Valley.
              *Earthy, astringent, leathery.*
☆    1983 PINOT NOIR ($9.75) Beckstoffer, Napa Valley-
              Carneros. *Earthy, bitter, unpleasant. Some varietal
              character and balance.*

214

☆☆☆ 1984 PINOT NOIR ($9.75) Beckstoffer, Napa Valley. *Crisp, fruity, snappy, clean, very attractive.*

1984 PINOT NOIR ($9.75) Los Amigos, Napa Valley Carneros. *Thin, dull, not much.*

ès

## Sea Ridge Winery                    SONOMA COUNTY
### WHITE
○ 1982 CHARDONNAY ($10.00) Sonoma. *Dominated by mercaptans and other off smells and tastes.*

☆☆☆ 1983 CHARDONNAY ($9.00) Green Valley, Sonoma. *Toasty, lush, sweet oak, ripe fruit, complex.*

☆☆☆ 1983 CHARDONNAY ($10.00) Mill Station, Sonoma. *Lush and oaky, with considerable depth.*

☆☆☆ 1984 CHARDONNAY ($10.50) Mill Station, Sonoma. *Soft, earthy, rich, complex.*

○ 1984 CHARDONNAY ($11.50) Hillcrest, Sonoma. *Bitter, some oxidation.*
### RED
☆☆☆ 1981 PINOT NOIR ($10.50) Bohan, Sonoma. *Rich, toasty, sweet oak, lush, clean, mature.*

☆☆ 1983 PINOT NOIR ($11.50) Sonoma. *Toasty, rich, some volatile flavors, earthy.*

☆☆ 1984 PINOT NOIR ($10.50) Sonoma. *Spicy, jammy, rich earthy flavors.*

☆☆ 1981 ZINFANDEL ($8.00) Porter-Bass, Sonoma. *Rich, oaky, good.*

○ 1982 ZINFANDEL ($8.00) Porter-Bass, Sonoma. *Thin, ugly, awful.*

1983 ZINFANDEL ($9.75) Porter-Bass, Sonoma. *Tart, berried, rich, volatile acidity.*

ès

## Sebastiani Vineyards                SONOMA COUNTY
### WHITE
☆☆ 1982 CHARDONNAY ($6.25) Sonoma Valley. *Rich, earthy, clean, quite nice.*

☆☆ 1982 CHARDONNAY ($10.00) Proprietor's Reserve, Sonoma Valley. *Crisp and clean, with lovely fresh fruit. Delightful.*

☆☆ 1983 CHARDONNAY ($10.00) Proprietor's Reserve, Sonoma Valley. *Spicy, clean, fresh, simple.*

☆ 1984 VENDANGE CHARDONNAY ($4.50) California. *Soft, earthy, decent, some vegetal flavors. Drink now.*

☆☆ 1984 CHARDONNAY ($8.00) Sonoma. *Soft, ripe, intense, clumsy.*

☆☆☆ 1984 CHARDONNAY ($12.00) Proprietor's Reserve, Sonoma Valley. *Soft, delicate, charming varietal character, with sweet new oak.*

1985 COUNTRY CHARDONNAY ($7.00) California. *1.5 liters. Dull, very unattractive.*

☆☆☆ 1985 CHARDONNAY ($10.00) Reserve, Sonoma Valley. *Rich, balanced, lovely fruit and structure.*

☆ 1986 VENDANGE CHARDONNAY ($4.00) Reserve, California. *Big, soft, ripe, a bit flabby and showing some oxidation.*

☆☆☆ 1986 CHARDONNAY ($15.00) Clark Ranch, Sonoma Valley. *Ripe, lush, good citrus fruit and nice, sweet oak.*

☆☆ 1986 CHARDONNAY ($15.00) Niles, Sonoma Valley. *Crisp, bright, fruity, clean and decent.*

☆ 1985 SAUVIGNON BLANC ($7.00) Sonoma. *Decent flavors, simple, clean.*

☆☆ 1986 SAUVIGNON BLANC ($7.00) Reserve, Sonoma. *Herbal, intense, clean, balanced.*

## SPARKLING

☆☆☆ NV BRUT THREE STAR ($12.00) Sonoma. *Crisp and tart, with good fruit and depth.*

☆☆☆ NV SPARKLING WINE ($12.00) Sonoma. *Toasty, rich, deep, clean, lovely.*

☆☆ 1983 RICHARD CUNEO BLANC DE BLANC ($14.00) Estate, California. *100% Chardonnay. Crisp, toasty, rich and decent.*

## BLANC DE NOIR

1985 EYE OF THE SWAN ($6.00) Sonoma. *Dry. Dull, flat, boring.*

## RED

☆ 1978 CABERNET SAUVIGNON ($12.00) Proprietor's Reserve, Sonoma. *Earthy, oaky, pleasant but not showing much varietal style.*

☆☆ 1979 CABERNET SAUVIGNON ($5.00) North Coast. *Decent, balanced, clean, unexciting. Drink now.*

☆☆ 1980 CABERNET SAUVIGNON ($10.00) Proprietor's Reserve, Sonoma Valley. *Tangy, rich, deep, clean, earthy, fruity, attractive.*

☆ 1980 CABERNET SAUVIGNON ($20.00) Eagle, Sonoma. *Thick and rich; vegetal, dense, somewhat dull. Drink now.*

☆☆ 1981 CABERNET SAUVIGNON ($5.00) Sonoma. *Simple but attractive.*

☆☆☆ 1981 CABERNET SAUVIGNON ($20.00) Eagle, Sonoma Valley. *Lush, deep, well made, oaky, super. Ready to drink.*

☆ 1982 CABERNET SAUVIGNON ($8.00) Sonoma. *Dull, showing its age.*

☆☆ 1982 CABERNET SAUVIGNON ($10.00) Reserve, Sonoma Valley. *Soft, lush, ripe herbal fruit, excellent aging potential. Drink 1990.*

☆☆ 1982 CABERNET SAUVIGNON ($26.50) Eagle Estate, Sonoma Valley. *Berry fruit, lush, velvety, decent but not brilliant.*

☆☆☆ 1983 CABERNET SAUVIGNON ($20.00) Eagle, Sonoma Valley. *Rich, deep, well structured, complex. Drink 1989.*

☆☆ 1985 VENDANGE CABERNET SAUVIGNON ($4.00) Reserve, California. *Soft, simple, clean, and charming.*

☆☆☆ 1985 CABERNET SAUVIGNON ($15.00) Cherry Block, Sonoma Valley. *Black berry and pepper flavors, rich and silky texture. Drink 1991.*

☆☆ 1984 MERLOT ($7.50) 67% Mendocino, 33% Sonoma. *Thin, simple, clean, attractive.*

☆☆ NV AUGUST SEBASTIANI PINOT NOIR ($5.75) Country, California. *1.5 liters. Spicy, clean, simple but attractive.*

☆☆ NV AUGUST SEBASTIANI ZINFANDEL ($5.75) California. *1.5 liters. Rich, deep fruit, clean and charming.*

☆☆ 1976 ZINFANDEL Propietor's Reserve, Sonoma. *Rich, aging nicely, clean, good.*

☆☆ 1978 ZINFANDEL ($8.00) Proprietor's Reserve, Sonoma Valley. *Lush, deep, rich, clean, attractive.*

☆☆ 1979 ZINFANDEL ($4.00) California. *Clean, varietal, berried, quite decent.*

☆ 1979 ZINFANDEL ($7.75) Proprietor's Reserve, California. *Earthy, metallic flavors.*

1980 ZINFANDEL ($5.00) California. *Sour, bitter, unappealing.*

☆☆ 1980 ZINFANDEL ($10.00) Proprietor's Reserve, Sonoma Valley. *Intense, dark and balanced.*

☆☆ 1982 ZINFANDEL ($5.00) Sonoma Valley. *Crisp, snappy, clean, varietal, appealing.*

## Sam J. Sebastiani Wines  SONOMA COUNTY

### WHITE

☆☆ 1985 CHARDONNAY ($12.50) 67% Napa Valley, 33% Sonoma. *Decent fruit and varietal character but hard and intense. Lacking charm.*

### RED

☆☆☆ 1983 CABERNET SAUVIGNON ($15.00) 67% Napa, 33% Sonoma. *Ripe, deep, rich oak, lovely structure. Drink 1990.*

☆ 1984 CABERNET SAUVIGNON ($15.00) 56% Napa, 42% Sonoma. *Vegetal, lush, deep, and heavy.*

## Seghesio Winery  SONOMA COUNTY

### WHITE

☆☆ 1985 CHARDONNAY ($5.50) California. *Soft, fruity, green.*

### RED

1982 CABERNET SAUVIGNON ($5.00) Northern Sonoma. *Tart, lacking fruit.*

1983 PINOT NOIR ($5.00) Northern Sonoma. *Hard, vegetal, nice texture, some bitterness at the finish.*

☆ 1983 PINOT NOIR ($5.00) Estate, Russian River Valley. *Tart, varietal, decent.*

☆☆ 1983 ZINFANDEL ($4.00) Sonoma. *Berry nose, fresh fruit, spicy flavors.*

## Thomas Sellards Winery  SONOMA COUNTY

### WHITE

☆☆☆ 1982 CHARDONNAY ($10.50) Sonoma. *Fresh, snappy, with good oak and fruit richness.*

☆ 1984 CHARDONNAY ($10.50) Alexander Valley. *Soft, rich, decent, clean, dull.*

### RED

☆☆☆ 1982 CABERNET SAUVIGNON ($9.50) Alexander Valley. *Crisp, fresh, clean, simple but attractive. Drink 1989.*

☆☆ 1984 CABERNET SAUVIGNON ($12.50) Alexander Valley. *Crisp, deep, lush, clean, medium fruit.*

## Sequoia Grove Vineyards  NAPA COUNTY

### WHITE

☆☆ 1982 CHARDONNAY ($10.50) Sonoma. *Fresh, clean, attractive, balanced.*

☆☆☆ 1982 CHARDONNAY ($12.00) Estate, Napa Valley. *Lovely—deep, complex, fruity, balanced.*

☆☆☆ 1983 CHARDONNAY ($12.00) Napa Valley. *Crisp, attractive, clean, nicely balanced, lovely fruit.*

☆☆ 1983 CHARDONNAY ($12.00) Sonoma. *Oily, vegetal, heavy, rich.*

☆☆ 1984 CHARDONNAY ($10.00) Napa Valley. *Rich, coarse, heavy, needs more fruit.*

☆☆ 1984 CHARDONNAY ($12.00) Sonoma. *Rich, intense, ripe, round, good fruit.*

☆☆☆☆ 1984 CHARDONNAY ($14.00) Estate, Napa Valley. *Crisp, varietal, lovely new oak, generous fruit. Superb.*

☆☆ 1985 CHARDONNAY ($12.00) Estate, Carneros Napa Valley. *Clean, soft, rich, nicely textured.*

☆☆☆ 1985 CHARDONNAY ($14.00) Allen Family, Napa Valley. *Crisp, bright, clean, firm fruit, good balance.*

### RED

☆☆ 1980 CABERNET SAUVIGNON ($12.00) Cask One, Napa Valley. *Jammy, ripe but lacking structure.*

☆☆☆ 1980 CABERNET SAUVIGNON ($12.00) Cask Two, 90% Fay, Napa Valley. *Rich, intense, ripe, herbal. Good aging potential.*

☆☆☆ 1981 CABERNET SAUVIGNON ($12.00) Napa Valley. *Lush, clean, balanced, lovely. Aging nicely and ready to drink.*

☆☆ 1981 CABERNET SAUVIGNON ($12.00) Terra Rosa, Alexander Valley, Sonoma. *Varietal, clean, pleasant but fat and clumsy.*

☆☆☆ 1982 CABERNET SAUVIGNON ($12.00) 67% Napa, 33% Alexander Valley. *Lush, complex, clean, structured, varietal. Maturing beautifully.*

☆☆☆ 1982 CABERNET SAUVIGNON ($16.00) Estate, Napa Valley. *Crisp, lean, wonderfully structured, focused and delicious. Drink 1990.*

☆☆☆ 1983 CABERNET SAUVIGNON ($12.00) 75% Napa Valley, 25% Sonoma Valley. *Soft, lush, rich, clean, nicely structured, lovely. Drink 1988.*

☆☆☆ 1984 CABERNET SAUVIGNON ($14.00) Napa Valley. *Rich, deep, intense, luscious, and smooth. Drink 1989.*

৯৯

## Shadow Creek
## Champagne Cellars          SAN LUIS OBISPO COUNTY

### SPARKLING

☆☆ NV ($15.00) California. *100% Chardonnay. Decent, clean, simple.*

☆☆☆ 1984 BLANC DE NOIR ($12.50) California. *Crisp, tangy, fresh, strawberry flavors; clean, yeasty finish.*

৯৯

## Shafer Vineyard Cellars              OREGON

### WHITE

☆☆☆ 1982 CHARDONNAY ($10.50) Willamette Valley, Oregon. *Light, charming, and delicate, with lovely fruit.*

☆☆ 1984 CHARDONNAY ($10.50) Willamette Valley. *Snappy, herbal, thin, decent.*

### BLANC DE NOIR

☆☆ 1984 PINOT NOIR BLANC ($6.00) Willamette Valley. *Lush, deep, juicy, attractive.*

### RED

☆ 1979 PINOT NOIR ($9.00) Willamette Valley, Oregon. *Berry nose, spicy, clean; decent but lacking charm.*

1983 PINOT NOIR ($13.50) Estate, Oregon. *Herbal, thin, unattractive.*

৯৯

## Shafer Vineyards              NAPA COUNTY

### WHITE

☆☆ 1982 CHARDONNAY ($11.00) Napa Valley. *Soft, lush, fruity.*

☆☆ 1983 CHARDONNAY ($12.00) Napa Valley. *Clean, angular, well made, attractive.*

☆☆ 1984 CHASE CREEK CHARDONNAY ($8.50) Napa Valley. *Woody, crisp, decent.*

☆☆ 1984 CHARDONNAY ($12.00) Napa Valley. *Clean, fresh, simple.*

☆☆☆ 1985 CHASE CREEK CHARDONNAY ($7.00) Napa Valley. *Lovely, well bred, clean and civilized.*

☆☆ 1985 CHARDONNAY ($11.50) Napa Valley. *Lean, crisp, tight, well structured, lacks charm.*

### RED

☆☆ 1982 RED TABLE WINE ($8.50) Napa Valley. *Fresh, crisp, light, clean and attractive.*

☆☆☆ 1978 CABERNET SAUVIGNON ($11.00) Estate, Napa Valley. *Deep, lush, Stag's Leap style. Well structured and supple. Drink now.*

☆☆☆ 1979 CABERNET SAUVIGNON ($13.00) Napa Valley. *Crisp and fruity, with a lovely, velvety texture. Drink now.*

☆☆ 1980 CABERNET SAUVIGNON ($11.00) Napa Valley. *Meaty, soft, very nice.*

☆☆☆ 1982 CABERNET SAUVIGNON ($12.00) Napa Valley. *Lush, big, rich, very nicely balanced. Drink now.*

☆☆☆ 1982 CABERNET SAUVIGNON ($16.00) Reserve, Napa Valley. *Deep, rich, mature. Ready to drink.*

☆☆ 1983 CABERNET SAUVIGNON ($13.00) Napa Valley. *3% Cabernet Franc. Ripe, cassis, soft, crisp, decent.*

☆☆☆ 1984 CABERNET SAUVIGNON ($14.00) Napa Valley. *5% Merlot and 2% Cabernet Franc. Lush, smokey, well structured, rich, herbal fruit, good oak. A keeper. Drink 1990.*

☆☆☆☆ 1983 MERLOT ($10.00) Napa Valley. *Lovely, deep color, superb, lush fruit, lemony finish.*

☆☆☆ 1984 MERLOT ($12.50) Napa Valley. *10% Cabernet Sauvignon. Tart, crisp, supple, rich fruit. Drink now.*

☆☆☆ 1985 MERLOT ($12.50) Napa Valley. *11% Cabernet Franc. Lush, deep, ripe, balanced. Drink 1989.*

☆☆☆ 1983 ZINFANDEL ($7.00) Last Chance, Napa Valley. *Tart, fruity, clean, quite lovely. Shafer's last Zin. Too bad.*

≥₳

## Charles F. Shaw Vineyard NAPA COUNTY

### WHITE

☆☆☆ 1983 CHARDONNAY ($12.50) Napa Valley. *Toasty, clean, smooth, well balanced, medium weight.*

☆☆☆ 1984 CHARDONNAY ($12.50) Napa Valley. *Crisp, clean, elegant, delicious, very attractive.*

☆☆☆ 1985 CHARDONNAY ($13.50) Napa Valley. *Crisp, fresh, firm fruit, lovely oak, complex, delicious.*

### BLANC DE NOIR

☆☆ 1986 GAMAY BLANC ($5.50) Napa Valley. *Soft, fresh, ripe, decent.*

### RED

☆☆ 1986 GAMAY NOUVEAU ($5.50) Napa Valley. *Tangy, spicy, crisp, attractive.*

☆☆☆ 1986 NAPA GAMAY ($6.00) Napa Valley. *Peppery, crisp, spicy, delicious.*

☆☆☆ 1985 GAMAY ($5.50) Napa Valley. *Fresh, clean, snappy, raspberry and cassis flavors.*

≥₳

## *Shenandoah Vineyards*        AMADOR COUNTY

### WHITE

☆ 1985 JOHANNISBERG RIESLING ($15.00) Late Harvest, Gold Hill, El Dorado. *375 ml. 24% residual sugar. Soft, a bit dull, decent.*

☆☆ NV RIESLING ($16.00) T.B.A., El Dorado. *375 ml. Dark amber, rich, smooth, clean, intense honey and fruit.*

☆☆ 1986 SAUVIGNON BLANC ($7.00) Amador. *Crisp, sweet pea fruit, clean, spritzy, pleasant.*

### BLANC DE NOIR

☆☆ 1987 WHITE RIESLING ($5.00) Amador. *1.8% residual sugar. Crisp, fruity, fresh, charmingly varietal.*

☆☆☆ 1986 WHITE ZINFANDEL ($5.00) Amador. *1.8% residual sugar. Crisp, wonderful tangy fruit, clean, spritzy, varietal, delicious.*

### RED

☆☆ 1981 CABERNET SAUVIGNON ($12.00) Amador. *Earthy, fresh, fruity, oaky, attractive.*

☆☆ 1982 CABERNET SAUVIGNON ($8.00) Amador. *Dark, intense, tannic, strong. Drink now.*

☆☆ 1984 CABERNET SAUVIGNON ($9.00) Amador. *Lush, rich, intense, berried, attractive.*

☆ 1980 ZINFANDEL ($6.50) Dal Porto, Amador. *Big, hard, intense. Might come around by 1988.*

☆☆ 1980 ZINFANDEL ($8.00) Special Reserve, Eschen, Fiddletown, Amador. *A monster. Heavy, concentrated, tannic. Drink 1990.*

☆ 1982 ZINFANDEL ($6.00) Dal Porto, Amador. *Heavy, clumsy.*

☆☆☆ 1982 ZINFANDEL ($7.50) Special Reserve, Eschen, Amador. *Rich, spicy, velvety, super.*

☆☆ 1983 ZINFANDEL ($7.00) Special Reserve, Fiddletown. *Good fruit, crisp, clean, a bit simple.*

☆☆☆ 1984 ZINFANDEL ($7.00) Special Reserve, Amador. *Lush, fat, spicy, clean, balanced, super.*

☆☆☆☆ 1985 ZINFANDEL ($7.50) Special Reserve, Amador. *Crisp, berried, lively, delicious.*

### FORTIFIED

☆☆☆ 1984 BLACK MUSCAT ($8.75) California. *10% residual sugar. Spicy, clean, round, lovely.*

☆☆☆ 1985 BLACK MUSCAT ($9.00) California. *90% Muscat Hamburg, 6% Muscat Canelli, 4% Cabernet Sauvignon. 9.8% residual sugar. Lush, toasty, spicy, lovely.*

☆☆☆ 1985 ORANGE MUSCAT ($9.00) Amador. *Lush, lovely, clean, delicious.*

1986 ORANGE MUSCAT ($9.00) California. *12% residual sugar. Sour, unattractive.*

○ 1982 PORT ($10.00) Amador. *Sour, bitter, ugly.*

1984 PORT ($10.00) Amador. *64% Zinfandel, 29% Cabernet Sauvignon, 8% Muscat Hamburg. Tart, bitter, decent.*

☆☆ ZINFANDEL PORT ($6.75) Lot 5, Amador. *Spicy, varietal, intense, disjointed, somewhat raw.*

❧

## Shenandoah Vineyards                                    VIRGINIA
### WHITE
☆☆ 1985 SEYVAL BLANC ($5.25) Virginia. *Crisp, dry, snappy, good balance.*

☆ 1985 VIDAL BLANC ($6.50) Medium Sweet, Virginia. *Soft, fruity, off-dry, decent.*

### RED
☆☆ 1982 CABERNET SAUVIGNON ($12.00) Virginia. *Structured, clean; pleasantly complex.*

☆☆ 1983 CABERNET SAUVIGNON ($12.30) Virginia. *Elegant, crisp, clean, lovely. Drink 1989.*

1984 CHAMBOURCIN ($5.25) Virginia. *Decent fruit but too much volatile acidity.*

೭ଈ

## Sherrill Cellars                              SANTA CLARA COUNTY
### RED
☆ 1979 CABERNET SAUVIGNON ($9.50) Shell Creek, California. *Tart, fruity, decent. Drink now and beyond.*

☆☆ 1980 ZINFANDEL ($7.00) Vineyard Hill. *Rich, intense and nicely complex.*

೭ଈ

## Shown and Sons Vineyards                          NAPA COUNTY
### WHITE
☆☆ 1983 CHARDONNAY ($13.50) Napa Valley. *Lush, oaky, big, with good fruit.*

೭ଈ

SIERRA MOUNTAIN *see* Nevada City Winery

## Sierra Vista Winery                          EL DORADO COUNTY
### WHITE
1985 FUME BLANC ($6.25) El Dorado. *10% Semillon. Dull, flat.*

### BLANC DE NOIR
1986 WHITE CABERNET ($5.50) El Dorado. *Flat, dull, lifeless.*

1986 WHITE ZINFANDEL ($5.00) El Dorado. *Flat, dull, no fruit.*

### RED
☆☆ 1979 CABERNET SAUVIGNON ($6.75) El Dorado. *Forward, fruity, tannic. Drink 1988 and beyond.*

☆ 1980 CABERNET SAUVIGNON ($8.50) Estate, El Dorado. *Ripe, intense, Zinfandel-like. Drink 1988 and beyond.*

☆☆ 1981 CABERNET SAUVIGNON ($7.75) Estate, El Dorado. *Fruity, fresh, clean and very lovely.*

☆☆☆ 1982 CABERNET SAUVIGNON ($8.50) Estate, El Dorado. *Rich fruit, soft oak, clean and well built. Drink 1988.*

☆☆☆ 1983 CABERNET SAUVIGNON ($8.50) Estate, El Dorado. *Crisp, clean, rich, fruity, lovely. Drink 1988.*

☆☆ 1980 ZINFANDEL ($6.00) El Dorado. *10% Petite Sirah. Soft, raisiny, lush. Drink now.*

☆☆ 1981 ZINFANDEL ($6.00) El Dorado. *Big, ripe, fruity, appealing.*

☆☆ 1982 ZINFANDEL ($6.00) Estate, El Dorado. *Rich, deep, fruity, attractive.*

☆☆  1984 ZINFANDEL ($8.00) Estate, El Dorado. *Soft and lush,
with fresh fruit flavors and a touch of volatility.*

ॐ

## Silver Mountain Vineyards     SANTA CRUZ COUNTY
### WHITE
☆☆☆  1982 CHARDONNAY ($11.00) Ventana, Monterey. *Rich,
clean, snappy, very well made.*
○  1984 CHARDONNAY ($12.00) Ventana, Monterey. *Ox-
idized, awful.*
### RED
☆☆☆  1980 ZINFANDEL ($6.50) Paso Robles. *Chocolatey, fruity,
clean and fresh. Drink now.*
☆☆  1982 ZINFANDEL ($6.50) El Dorado. *Fruity, clean, quite
attractive.*
☆  1983 ZINFANDEL ($6.50) Sonoma. *Decent, varietal, clean.*

ॐ

## Silver Oak Wine Cellars        NAPA COUNTY
### RED
☆☆☆  1978 CABERNET SAUVIGNON ($16.00) Alexander Valley.
*Elegant but rich and intensely fruity; oaky and
earthy.*
☆☆☆  1979 CABERNET SAUVIGNON ($16.00) Alexander Valley.
*Nice, rich, deep and earthy, with some light vegeta-
tion. Drink now.*
☆☆☆  1979 CABERNET SAUVIGNON ($16.00) Napa Valley. *Rich,
ripe, clean and classic. Gorgeous.*
☆☆☆  1979 CABERNET SAUVIGNON ($32.00) Bonny's, Napa
Valley. *Complex and extraordinary, with French
oak sweetness.*
☆☆☆  1980 CABERNET SAUVIGNON ($18.00) Alexander Valley.
*Big, earthy, fat, berried, clean.*
☆  1980 CABERNET SAUVIGNON ($18.00) Napa Valley. *Rai-
siny, berried, overdone.*
☆☆  1981 CABERNET SAUVIGNON ($20.00) Napa Valley. *Dark,
dull fruit, tarry, jammy, powerful. Drink 1990.*
☆☆☆☆  1982 CABERNET SAUVIGNON ($19.00) Alexander Valley.
*Rich, black current, vanillin, rich texture, superb.
Drink 1990.*
☆☆☆☆  1982 CABERNET SAUVIGNON ($19.00) Napa Valley. *Great
fruit, luscious texture, lovely. Drink now and for
the next 10 years.*
☆☆☆  1983 CABERNET SAUVIGNON ($21.00) Alexander Valley.
*Soft, generous flavors of plum and spice, dark, rich.
Drink 1990.*
☆☆☆☆  1983 CABERNET SAUVIGNON ($21.00) Napa Valley. *Crisp,
clean, ripe and earthy, with lively fruit. Drink
1990.*

ॐ

## Silverado Vineyards            NAPA COUNTY
### WHITE
☆☆☆  1982 CHARDONNAY ($10.00) Estate, Napa Valley. *Complex
yet crisp and very attractive.*
☆☆☆  1983 CHARDONNAY ($10.00) Napa Valley. *Fat, fruity, rich
yet balanced, lovely.*
☆☆☆  1984 CHARDONNAY ($11.00) Napa Valley. *Balanced, fresh,
crisp, charming, with nice oak and fruit.*
☆☆☆  1986 SAUVIGNON BLANC ($8.00) Napa Valley. *Mouthfill-
ing, ripe, rich, clean and delicious.*

## RED

☆☆☆ 1981 CABERNET SAUVIGNON ($11.00) Napa Valley. *Herbal, fresh, and fruity, with lovely structure. Drink now.*

☆☆☆ 1982 CABERNET SAUVIGNON ($11.00) Napa Valley. *Fat, lush, smooth with lively acidity and good structure. Drink 1989.*

☆☆☆ 1983 CABERNET SAUVIGNON ($11.00) Napa Valley. *Crisp, snappy, fresh, softly textured, lovely finish.*

☆☆☆ 1984 CABERNET SAUVIGNON ($11.50) Napa Valley. *Soft, fresh, delicate, nicely balanced, charming. Drink 1989.*

☆☆☆ 1983 MERLOT ($12.00) Napa Valley. *Ripe and lush, earthy and complex; super.*

☆☆ 1984 MERLOT ($11.50) Napa Valley. *Big, soft, ripe and intense. Drink 1989.*

❧

# Simi Winery                              SONOMA COUNTY

## WHITE

☆☆☆ 1982 CHARDONNAY ($11.00) Sonoma. *Rich, clean, delightful.*

☆☆☆☆ 1982 CHARDONNAY ($20.00) Reserve, Sonoma. *Rich, smooth, oaky, complex, stunning. Barrel fermented; 90% new French oak used.*

☆☆☆ 1983 CHARDONNAY ($12.00) 59% Mendocino, 41% Sonoma. *Fresh, varietal, balanced, crisp, lovely.*

☆☆☆ 1983 CHARDONNAY ($23.50) Reserve, Sonoma. *Crisp, fruity, silky, lovely structure, varietally intense.*

☆☆☆ 1984 CHARDONNAY ($13.00) 57% Mendocino, 43% Sonoma. *Fresh, clean, crisp, balanced, with good fruit and lovely oak.*

☆☆☆ 1985 CHARDONNAY ($11.00) 51% Mendocino, 49% Sonoma. *Crisp fruit, rich varietal flavors, good balance.*

☆☆☆ 1986 CHENIN BLANC ($6.50) Mendocino. *A definitive Chenin Blanc. Crisp, lush, fruity, balanced.*

## ROSE

☆☆☆ 1986 ROSE OF CABERNET SAUVIGNON ($6.75) Sonoma. *Crisp, fresh, varietal, balanced, lovely. A serious wine that is fun and delicious.*

☆☆☆ 1985 ROSE OF CABERNET SAUVIGNON ($6.50) Sonoma. *Crisp, clean, tangy fruit; less varietal than the '84.*

## RED

☆☆ 1978 CABERNET SAUVIGNON ($8.00) Alexander Valley. *Soft, lush; lacks stuffing.*

☆☆☆ 1979 CABERNET SAUVIGNON ($9.00) Alexander Valley. *Varietal and meaty, with lean structure and good fruit. Ready to drink now and for several years.*

☆☆☆☆ 1979 CABERNET SAUVIGNON ($19.00) Reserve, Alexander Valley. *Rich, beautifully structured, with firm fruit and supple textures. Drink 1988 and beyond.*

☆☆☆ 1980 CABERNET SAUVIGNON ($10.00) Alexander Valley. *Herbal, lush, soft and concentrated. Ready to drink.*

☆☆☆ 1980 CABERNET SAUVIGNON ($19.00) Reserve, Alexander Valley. *Ripe, dense, lush, soft, complex. Drink 1989.*

☆☆ 1981 CABERNET SAUVIGNON ($11.00) Alexander Valley. *Herbal, lean, fruity and well structured. Drink now.*

☆☆☆ 1981 CABERNET SAUVIGNON ($20.00) Reserve, Alexander Valley. *Rich and complex, with firm structure and well-defined fruit. Long and lovely, with focus and breeding. Drink 1993.*

☆☆☆ 1982 CABERNET SAUVIGNON ($11.00) Sonoma. *5% Merlot. Aromatic, lush and very fruity. Firmly structured for long aging. Drink 1988.*

☆☆☆ 1983 CABERNET SAUVIGNON ($12.00) Sonoma. *Crisp, charming, clean, with lush, lively fruit. Drink 1989.*

☆☆☆ 1984 CABERNET SAUVIGNON ($11.00) Sonoma. *Snappy, crisp, spicy, lively and quite appealing. Drink 1989.*

☆☆ 1978 ZINFANDEL ($7.00) Alexander Valley. *Soft, herbal and appealing.*

☆☆ 1980 ZINFANDEL ($6.25) Alexander Valley. *Peppery, rich, clean, varietal.*

☆☆ 1981 ZINFANDEL ($7.00) Alexander Valley. *Lush, clean, fat, rich.*

1982 ZINFANDEL ($7.25) Sonoma. *Thin and vegetal.*

### Siskiyou Vineyards                              OREGON
#### RED

☆ 1982 CABERNET SAUVIGNON ($9.75) Oregon. *Big, rich, lacking varietal character.*

☆ 1981 PINOT NOIR ($9.00) Oregon. *Lush, fat, sweetish.*

☆ 1982 PINOT NOIR ($10.00) Oregon. *Simple, decent, not much.*

☆☆ 1983 PINOT NOIR ($9.00) Oregon. *Simple, clean, fresh, attractive.*

☆ 1982 ZINFANDEL ($7.00) Oregon. *Earthy, intense and fruity, with some muddiness.*

### Sky Vineyards                                   NAPA
#### RED

☆☆☆ 1982 ZINFANDEL ($8.00) Napa Valley. *Rich, deep, clean, fruity, lovely*

### Smith & Hook Vineyard            MONTEREY COUNTY
#### RED

1979 CABERNET SAUVIGNON ($9.00) Monterey. *Vegetal and atypical.*

1980 CABERNET SAUVIGNON ($9.50) Monterey. *Weedy; nice texture but not likable.*

☆☆ 1981 CABERNET SAUVIGNON ($13.50) Estate, Monterey. *Soft, lush, fruity, clean, very nice.*

☆☆ 1982 CABERNET SAUVIGNON ($13.50) Estate, Monterey. *Lush, earthy, deep. Drink 1988.*

☆☆ 1983 CABERNET SAUVIGNON ($13.50) Estate, Monterey. *Soft, lush, dense, clean, attractive.*

☆☆ 1985 DEER VALLEY CABERNET SAUVIGNON ($5.50) Monterey. *Tart, chalky, oniony, decent.*

### Smith-Madrone                               NAPA COUNTY
#### WHITE

☆☆ 1982 CHARDONNAY ($12.50) Napa Valley. *Toasty, rich, vinous. Nice but lacking freshness.*

☆☆ 1983 CHARDONNAY ($12.50) Estate, Napa Valley. *Clean, tart, apple flavors.*

☆☆ 1984 CHARDONNAY ($12.00) Estate, Napa Valley. *Crisp, lean, balanced, clean, austere.*

**RED**

☆☆☆☆ 1979 CABERNET SAUVIGNON ($14.00) Estate, Napa Valley. *Rich and intense; velvety and complex. Drink now.*

☆☆☆ 1980 CABERNET SAUVIGNON ($14.00) Estate, Napa Valley. *Soft, rich, balanced. More conventional than the '79. Drink 1988.*

☆☆☆ 1982 CABERNET SAUVIGNON ($13.00) Estate, Napa Valley. *3.5% Cabernet Franc. Fruity, tart, clean, complex. Drink 1988.*

☆☆☆ 1983 PINOT NOIR ($10.00) Napa Valley. *Crisp, clean, earthy, varietal, attractive.*

☆ 1984 PINOT NOIR ($10.00) Estate, Napa Valley. *Woody, earthy, musty, decent fruit.*

಄

## Smothers Brothers Wines          SONOMA COUNTY

**WHITE**

☆☆☆ 1982 CHARDONNAY ($12.50) Remick Ridge Ranch, Sonoma. *Classically balanced, richly fruited, nice oak.*

☆☆ 1983 CHARDONNAY ($10.00) Green Pastures, Sonoma. *Rich, deep, varietal, quite charming.*

☆☆ 1983 CHARDONNAY ($12.50) Remick Ridge Ranch, Sonoma Valley. *Rich oak and clean fruit; quite appealing.*

☆ 1984 VINE HILL WINES WHITE RIESLING ($12.00) Late Harvest, Sonoma. *375 ml. 10.4% residual sugar. Fat, lush, heavy, decent.*

**RED**

☆☆☆ 1979 CABERNET SAUVIGNON ($12.50) Alexander Valley. *Very fresh and crisp; ripe and structured; mellow and charming.*

☆☆☆ 1980 CABERNET SAUVIGNON ($12.50) Alexander Valley. *Fruity, clean, superbly balanced. Lovely now.*

☆☆☆ 1981 CABERNET SAUVIGNON ($10.00) Alexander Valley. *Rich, bright, intense, balanced. Drink 1989.*

☆☆ 1982 CABERNET SAUVIGNON ($12.50) Alexander Valley. *Tart, clean, complex, balanced, charming. Drink 1988.*

☆☆ 1980 ZINFANDEL ($7.50) Sonoma. *Earthy, crisp and fruity. Drink now.*

಄

## Snoqualmie Winery          WASHINGTON

**WHITE**

1983 SADDLE MOUNTAIN CHARDONNAY ($5.50) Washington. *Dull, decent.*

☆ 1983 F.W. LANGGUTH CHARDONNAY ($6.50) Columbia Valley. *Crisp, clean, fresh, elegant.*

☆ 1984 SADDLE MOUNTAIN CHARDONNAY ($5.50) Washington. *Simple and dull.*

☆ 1984 CHARDONNAY ($6.00) Early Release, Yakima Valley. *Crisp, decent.*

1984 CHARDONNAY ($8.00) Yakima Valley. *Muddy, odd.*

1984 F.W. LANGGUTH JOHANNISBERG RIESLING ($7.00) Late Harvest, Columbia Valley. *6.0% residual sugar. Flat, dull, uninteresting.*

☆☆ 1984 SADDLE MOUNTAIN JOHANNISBERG RIESLING ($7.00) Late Harvest, Washington. *6.3% residual sugar. Crisp, dense, decent.*

☆☆☆ 1984 F.W. LANGGUTH JOHANNISBERG RIESLING
($8.50) Special Reserve Late Harvest, Columbia
Valley. *8.5% residual sugar. Lush, fat, clean, crisp,
very nice.*

1984 JOHANNISBERG RIESLING ($13.00) Late Harvest-
Signature Reserve, Yakima Valley. *9% residual
sugar. Candied, botrytis, unattractive.*

☆☆ 1982 F.W. LANGGUTH WHITE RIESLING ($6.00) Late
Harvest, Washington. *4.1% residual sugar. Fruity,
simple, fresh and attractive.*

**RED**

☆☆☆ 1983 CABERNET SAUVIGNON ($10.00) Yakima Valley.
*Lush, deep, tangy fruit, charming balance. Drink
1989.*

☆☆ 1984 MERLOT ($9.00) Signature Reserve, Yakima Valley,
Washington. *Herbal, decent fruit, clean.*

෯

## Soda Rock Winery            SONOMA COUNTY

**RED**

NV CHARLES COUNTRY RED ($5.00) Sonoma. *Volatile
acidity, not much.*

☆ 1979 PINOT NOIR ($14.00) Sonoma. *Tannic, varietal, clean,
decent.*

෯

## Sokol Blosser Winery          OREGON

**WHITE**

☆☆ 1985 CHARDONNAY ($15.00) Oregon. *Buttery, toasty,
oaky, rich, but the finish is too sour.*

☆ 1986 WHITE RIESLING ($10.00) Select Harvest, Yamhill.
*Flat, decent, apples.*

**RED**

☆☆☆ 1979 PINOT NOIR ($9.00) Hyland, Yamhill. *Intense, rich
and toasty. Balanced and clean.*

☆☆ 1979 PINOT NOIR ($10.00) 83% Estate, 17% Durant,
Yamhill. *Toasty, clean and subtle. Quite elegant.*

☆ 1982 PINOT NOIR ($8.95) Yamhill. *Peppery, thin, underripe,
woody.*

☆☆☆ 1983 PINOT NOIR ($9.95) Hyland, Yamhill. *Varietal, bal-
anced, clean, lovely.*

☆☆ 1983 PINOT NOIR ($9.95) Red Hills, Yamhill. *Fat, rich,
clean.*

☆☆☆ 1985 PINOT NOIR ($15.00) Red Hills, Oregon. *Crisp,
snappy, fruity, good structure.*

෯

## Sonoma-Cutrer Vineyards       SONOMA COUNTY

**WHITE**

☆☆☆☆ 1981 CHARDONNAY ($14.50) Les Pierres, Sonoma Valley.
*Crisp and rich; complex and remarkably elegant.
Aging magnificently.*

☆☆ 1982 CHARDONNAY ($10.00) Russian River Ranches, Rus-
sian River Valley. *Crisp, fruit, decent.*

☆☆ 1982 CHARDONNAY ($13.00) Cutrer, Russian River Valley.
*Rich, balanced, clean and varietal.*

☆☆☆ 1982 CHARDONNAY ($15.50) Les Pierres, Sonoma Valley.
*Crisp and lovely at its best—but there is some bot-
tle variation. Aging nicely.*

☆☆☆ 1983 CHARDONNAY ($10.75) Russian River Ranches, Rus-
sian River Valley. *Rich, oaky, nicely balanced, with
good fruit and acidity.*

☆☆☆ 1983 CHARDONNAY ($13.50) Cutrer, Sonoma Valley. *Crisp, balanced, clean and elegant. Lovely fruit and oak.*

☆☆☆☆ 1983 CHARDONNAY ($15.50) Les Pierres, Sonoma Valley. *Elegant, balanced, lovely new oak and deep fruit. Stunning.*

☆☆☆ 1984 CHARDONNAY ($11.25) Russian River Ranches, Russian River Valley. *Balanced, clean, soft and delicious. Lovely oak and elegant fruit.*

☆☆ 1984 CHARDONNAY ($14.00) Cutrer, Sonoma. *Fruity, clean, decent, lacking charm.*

☆☆☆☆ 1984 CHARDONNAY ($16.75) Les Pierres, Sonoma Valley. *Fresh, clean, elegant structure, delicate oak, superb balance. Drink 1989.*

☆☆☆☆ 1985 CHARDONNAY ($11.75) Russian River Ranches, Russian River Valley. *Crisp, clean, varietal, balanced, elegant. Superbly understated; a classic.*

☆☆☆ 1985 CHARDONNAY ($14.75) Cutrer, Russian River Valley. *Smooth, rich, intensely varietal and nicely balanced.*

☆☆☆☆ 1985 CHARDONNAY ($17.50) Les Pierres, Sonoma Valley. *Elegant, lush, exquisitely structured and balanced. Lovely fruit and oak. Great now—even better in a year or two.*

☆☆☆ 1986 CHARDONNAY ($10.00) Russian River Ranches, Russian River Valley. *Crisp, fresh, lean, well structured, long snappy finish.*

❧

## Sonoma Hills Winery SONOMA COUNTY

### WHITE

☆☆ 1984 CHARDONNAY ($10.00) Sonoma Valley. *Decent, clean, slightly vegetal.*

☆☆☆ 1985 CHARDONNAY ($11.00) Sonoma Valley. *Crisp, fresh, fruity, juicy, delicious.*

❧

## Sotoyome Winery SONOMA COUNTY

### RED

☆☆☆ NV BURGUNDY ($2.75) Sonoma. *Spicy, clean, intense, ripe, complex, amazing.*

☆ 1978 CABERNET SAUVIGNON ($7.50) Sonoma. *Big, forward and pleasant but lacking grace or depth.*

☆☆☆ 1979 CABERNET SAUVIGNON ($5.75) Dry Creek Valley. *Warm, toasty, clean and intense, with some weeds. Drink now.*

☆☆ 1980 CABERNET SAUVIGNON ($5.75) Dry Creek Valley. *Lush, rich, intense, forward. Drink now.*

☆ 1980 PETITE SIRAH ($5.25) Russian River Valley. *Big, fat, rich.*

☆☆ 1979 ZINFANDEL ($4.75) Sonoma. *Big, deep, hearty.*

❧

## Spottswoode Winery NAPA COUNTY

### WHITE

☆☆☆ 1986 SAUVIGNON BLANC ($10.00) Napa Valley. *25% Semillon. Crisp, fresh, lively, good rounded fruit flavors.*

### RED

☆☆☆☆ 1982 CABERNET SAUVIGNON ($18.00) Estate, Napa Valley. *Beautifully structured, rich fruit and oak. Drink 1990.*

☆☆☆ 1983 CABERNET SAUVIGNON ($18.00) Napa Valley. *Ripe, rich, powerful, deep, fruity. Great, but not as great as the 1982. Drink 1996.*

☆☆☆☆ 1984 CABERNET SAUVIGNON ($25.00) Estate, Napa Valley. *4% 1985 Cabernet Franc. Crisp, intense fruit, lovely oak, great structure. A masterpiece. Drink 1992.*

🙦

## Spring Mountain Vineyards                NAPA COUNTY
### WHITE

☆☆☆ 1983 CHARDONNAY ($12.50) Napa Valley. *Rich, deep, round, intense, quite charming.*

☆ 1984 CHARDONNAY ($15.00) Napa Valley. *Earthy, complex, overdone, odd.*

☆☆☆ 1985 CHARDONNAY ($15.00) Napa Valley. *Toasty, fresh, clean, complex, quite charming.*

### RED

☆☆ 1979 CABERNET SAUVIGNON ($13.00) Napa Valley. *Tarry and rich, with good fruit and some elegance.*

☆ 1981 CABERNET SAUVIGNON ($15.00) Napa Valley. *Soft, smooth, vegetal.*

☆☆☆ 1982 CABERNET SAUVIGNON ($14.00) Napa Valley. *Spicy, good oak, lovely balance. Drink 1990.*

🙦

## Stag's Leap Wine Cellars                 NAPA COUNTY
### WHITE

☆☆ 1982 CHARDONNAY ($13.50) Napa Valley. *Angular, crisp, simple and clean, with excellent aging potential.*

☆☆ 1984 CHARDONNAY ($13.50) Napa Valley. *Lean, crisp, clean, well made but not especially likable.*

☆☆☆ 1985 CHARDONNAY ($20.00) Reserve, Napa Valley. *Soft, rich, oaky, intense, ripe. One of the best Chardonnays yet from Stag's Leap.*

☆☆☆ 1986 CHARDONNAY ($17.00) Napa Valley. *Crisp, clean, rich fruit and oak, great balance.*

☆☆☆ 1986 CHARDONNAY ($18.00) Beckstoffer, Napa Valley. *Intense fruit, long, rich flavors, excellent balance and finish.*

☆☆☆☆ 1986 CHARDONNAY ($20.00) Reserve, Napa Valley. *Exquisite new oak, long, elegant fruit flavors; stunning.*

☆ 1986 SAUVIGNON BLANC ($9.00) Rancho Chimiles, Napa Valley. *Heavy, with intense, composty aromas and flavors; resinous and not appealing.*

☆☆☆ 1986 WHITE RIESLING ($7.50) Napa Valley. *1% residual sugar. Crisp, clean, spicy, varietal, nicely balanced.*

### RED

☆☆☆ 1978 CABERNET SAUVIGNON ($15.00) Lot 2, Napa Valley. *Violets and oak; clean, bright, intense. Drink now through 1992.*

☆☆☆☆ 1978 CABERNET SAUVIGNON ($35.00) Cask 23, Napa Valley. *Bursting with flavor, intense yet well bred. Drink 1989.*

☆☆☆ 1979 CABERNET SAUVIGNON ($12.50) Estate, Napa Valley. *Lush, ripe, fresh and fruity—but not as impressive as the '78 Lot 2.*

☆ 1979 CABERNET SAUVIGNON ($35.00) Cask 23, Napa Valley. *Old, tired, lacking fruit, earthy, over the hill.*

☆☆☆☆ 1980 CABERNET SAUVIGNON ($11.00) Napa Valley. *Velvety, rich, complex, superb. Ready now and should last for many years.*

☆☆☆☆ 1981 CABERNET SAUVIGNON ($15.00) Stag's Leap, Napa Valley. *Lush, deep, beautifully structured. Ready now and should be lovely for the next decade.*

☆☆ 1982 HAWK CREST CABERNET SAUVIGNON ($6.00) North Coast. *Soft, earthy, clean, lush. Drink 1988.*

☆☆☆ 1983 CABERNET SAUVIGNON ($17.00) Stag's Leap, Napa Valley. *Crisp, varietal, clean and beautifully structured. Charming and very drinkable. Drink now.*

☆☆☆ 1983 CABERNET SAUVIGNON ($35.00) Cask 23, Napa Valley. *Big, cedar and coffee flavors, fat, lush, softly structured. Drink 1992.*

☆☆ 1984 HAWK CREST CABERNET SAUVIGNON ($7.00) North Coast. *Fresh, balanced, varietal, nicely structured. Drink now.*

☆☆☆ 1984 CABERNET SAUVIGNON ($14.25) Napa Valley. *Soft, crisp, earthy, very drinkable now; lacking structure for the long pull.*

☆☆☆ 1984 CABERNET SAUVIGNON ($21.00) Stag's Leap, Napa Valley. *Pruny, plummy, clean and oaky, with lots of vanilla and fresh fruit. Drink 1992.*

☆☆☆ 1984 CABERNET SAUVIGNON ($35.00) Cask 23, Stag's Leap, Napa Valley. *Toasty, rich, herbal, smooth, complex, elegant and beautifully structured. Drink 1991.*

☆☆☆ 1985 CABERNET SAUVIGNON ($15.00) Napa Valley. *Soft, lush, meaty, smooth, complex and fruity. A delicious and classic Stag's Leap District wine.*

☆☆☆ 1985 CABERNET SAUVIGNON ($25.00) Stag's Leap, Napa Valley. *Rich, smokey, concentrated fruit, deep, luscious, complex.*

☆☆☆ 1985 CABERNET SAUVIGNON ($35.00) Cask 23, Stag's Leap, Napa Valley. *Big and fleshy, ripe and intense. Drink 1994.*

☆☆☆ 1979 MERLOT ($7.50) Estate, Napa Valley. *Rich, balanced, supple, classic. Will continue to age well.*

☆☆ 1982 MERLOT ($13.50) Napa Valley. *Lush, herbal, clean and nicely structured. Drinking nicely now.*

☆☆☆ 1983 MERLOT ($14.50) Stag's Leap, Napa Valley. *Soft, lush, velvety, rich fruit, lovely.*

☆☆ 1984 MERLOT ($15.00) Napa Valley. *Soft, herbaceous, lush, clean, decent. Drink now.*

☆☆☆ 1978 PETITE SIRAH ($8.50) Napa Valley. *Ripe and full, with lovely, well-defined varietal character.*

☆☆ 1980 PETITE SIRAH ($8.50) North Coast. *Soft, clean, varietal, a bit short.*

☆☆ 1982 PETITE SIRAH ($7.00) Napa Valley. *Some odd aromas, jammy fruit, ripe, lush.*

❧

## Stags' Leap Winery                           NAPA COUNTY
### RED

☆☆ 1979 MERLOT ($12.00) Napa Valley. *Big, heavy and tannic, with good fruit. Mellowing nicely.*

☆☆ 1981 MERLOT ($13.50) Napa Valley. *Dense, rich, lacking structure. Drink now.*

☆ 1973 PETITE SIRAH ($37.50) Napa Valley. *Deep, intense, overripe.*

☆☆ 1974 PETITE SIRAH ($37.50) Napa Valley. *Intense, deep, low in fruit.*

☆☆ 1978 PETITE SIRAH ($12.00) Napa Valley. *Fruity, clean, nicely structured.*
☆☆☆ 1979 PETITE SIRAH ($8.75) Napa Valley. *Soft, varietal, clean, lush and superb. Drink now.*
☆☆ 1980 PETITE SIRAH ($10.00) Napa Valley. *Leathery, intense, clean and well made.*
☆☆ 1982 PETITE SIRAH ($10.00) Napa Valley. *Ripe, rich, velvety.*

🍂

## P and M Staiger                    SANTA CRUZ COUNTY
### WHITE
☆☆☆ 1982 CHARDONNAY ($10.00) Estate, Santa Cruz Mountains. *Lemony crisp, clean, rich, fruity, with lovely oak.*

🍂

DAVID S. STARE *see* Dry Creek Vineyard

## Staton Hills Vineyard & Winery        YAKIMA VALLEY
### RED
☆☆ 1985 MERLOT ($9.00) Washington. *Snappy, simple, decent.*

🍂

STEARNS WHARF *see* Copenhagen Cellars

STEINER *see* Fulton Valley Winery

## Steltzner Vineyards                    NAPA COUNTY
### RED
☆☆☆ 1978 CABERNET SAUVIGNON ($14.00) Stag's Leap District, Napa. *Lovely ripe fruit flavors and ideal balance. Drink 1988.*
☆☆☆ 1979 CABERNET SAUVIGNON ($14.00) Stag's Leap District, Napa. *Bright, rich and lush, with lovely oak and fruit. Ready to drink.*
☆☆☆ 1980 CABERNET SAUVIGNON ($14.00) Estate, Napa Valley. *Dense, rich, angular, with a scent of violets. Drink 1989.*
☆☆☆ 1981 CABERNET SAUVIGNON ($14.00) Napa Valley. *Fruity, rich, fat and velvety, with great complexity. Drink 1990.*
☆☆☆ 1982 CABERNET SAUVIGNON ($14.00) Napa Valley. *Lovely, rich, balanced, clean, delightful. Drink 1990.*
☆☆ 1983 CABERNET SAUVIGNON ($14.00) Napa Valley. *Plummy, chalky, intense, ripe, rich, less focused than previous vintages. Drink 1990.*

🍂

## Robert Stemmler Winery               SONOMA COUNTY
### WHITE
○ 1983 CHARDONNAY ($12.00) Sonoma. *Tanky, unpleasant.*
☆☆ 1985 CHARDONNAY ($10.00) Sonoma. *Dry, heavy, intense oak.*
### RED
☆☆☆ 1978 CABERNET SAUVIGNON ($12.50) Sonoma. *Intense, clean and supple.*
☆☆☆ 1979 CABERNET SAUVIGNON ($12.50) Sonoma. *Soft and balanced, with lovely fruit. Complex. Drink now.*
☆ 1982 CABERNET SAUVIGNON ($15.00) Sonoma. *Rich, decent, a bit short.*

☆☆☆ 1982 PINOT NOIR ($15.00) Forchini, Dry Creek Valley. *Clean, soft, rich, fruity, very lovely.*

☆☆ 1985 PINOT NOIR ($18.00) Sonoma. *Varietal, complex, thin and a bit green.*

❧

## Sterling Vineyards                                 NAPA COUNTY

### WHITE

☆☆☆ 1982 CHARDONNAY ($14.00) Estate, Napa Valley. *Crisp, fruity, elegant, balanced, clean.*

☆☆☆☆ 1983 CHARDONNAY ($15.00) Diamond Mountain Ranch, Napa Valley. *Lush, intense, complex, beautifully structured, with soft fruit and lovely oak. A remarkable wine.*

☆☆ 1984 CHARDONNAY ($14.00) Napa Valley. *Hard-edged, heavy oak, varietal, somewhat alcoholic.*

☆☆☆ 1984 CHARDONNAY ($15.00) Diamond Mountain Ranch, Napa Valley. *Lean and hard but nicely structured, with great power and depth. A wine built to last.*

☆☆☆ 1985 CHARDONNAY ($14.00) Estate, Napa Valley. *Soft, crisp, balanced, lovely.*

☆☆☆ 1986 CHARDONNAY ($14.50) Estate, Napa Valley. *Crisp, lean, bright fruit and good structure.*

☆☆☆ 1986 SAUVIGNON BLANC ($10.00) Napa Valley. *Lemony, crisp, clean, fresh, good varietal character.*

### BLANC DE NOIR

☆☆☆ 1986 CABERNET BLANC ($6.50) Napa Valley. *Crisp, fresh, varietal, lively fruit, exceptional.*

### RED

☆☆ 1978 CABERNET SAUVIGNON ($12.00) Estate, Napa Valley. *Tangy, fruity, rich and herbaceous. Ready now.*

☆☆☆ 1978 CABERNET SAUVIGNON ($20.00) Reserve, Estate, Napa Valley. *Meaty, tannic, great fruit. Will age for six years or more. Drink 1988.*

☆☆☆ 1979 CABERNET SAUVIGNON ($27.50) Reserve, Estate, Napa Valley. *Spicy, peppery, berried, tart, lush, superb. Ready now and for the next decade. Will peak around 1990.*

☆☆ 1980 CABERNET SAUVIGNON ($12.50) Estate, Napa Valley. *Classy, firm, ripe, smooth, some weediness.*

☆☆☆ 1980 CABERNET SAUVIGNON ($30.00) Reserve, Estate, Napa Valley. *23.9% Merlot. Soft, rich, oaky and deep. Ready to drink.*

☆☆☆ 1981 CABERNET SAUVIGNON ($30.00) Reserve, Napa Valley. *Lush, herbal, concentrated, lovely. Drink 1990.*

☆☆ 1982 CABERNET SAUVIGNON ($12.50) Estate, Napa Valley. *Soft, rich, deep, earthy, some vegetal notes. Drink 1988.*

☆☆☆☆ 1982 CABERNET SAUVIGNON ($15.00) Diamond Mountain Ranch, Napa Valley. *Intense, balanced, deep, complex, remarkable. Drink 1989.*

☆ 1982 CABERNET SAUVIGNON ($22.50) Reserve, Estate, Napa Valley. *Green olive and herbal flavors. Decent but lacking fruit and richness.*

☆☆☆ 1983 CABERNET SAUVIGNON ($12.50) Estate, Napa Valley. *14% Merlot. Crisp, fresh, great structure, lovely fruit. Drink 1989.*

☆ 1983 CABERNET SAUVIGNON ($15.00) Diamond Mountain Ranch, Napa Valley. *Dense, berried, alcoholic, lacking finesse. Drink 1990.*

☆☆☆ 1983 CABERNET SAUVIGNON ($22.50) Reserve, Napa Valley. *Lush cassis flavors, good structure, long finish. Drink 1991.*

☆☆☆ 1984 CABERNET SAUVIGNON ($12.50) Estate, Napa Valley. *Lively varietal fruit, good balance, very attractive. Drink now.*

☆☆☆ 1984 CABERNET SAUVIGNON ($15.00) Diamond Mountain Ranch, Napa Valley. *Lush, deep, varietal fruit, clean, crisply structured. Drink 1990.*

☆☆☆☆ 1979 MERLOT ($12.00) Estate, Napa Valley. *Rich, clean, supple, complex, lovely. Aging nicely.*

☆☆☆ 1980 MERLOT ($11.00) Napa Valley. *Lovely balance; nice fruit and oak. Drink now.*

☆☆☆ 1981 MERLOT ($11.00) Napa Valley. *Elegant, lush, complex and firmly structured.*

☆☆☆ 1982 MERLOT ($11.00) Napa Valley. *Rich, tangy, varietal and fresh. Drink now and for the next few years.*

☆☆☆ 1983 MERLOT ($11.00) Estate, Napa Valley. *20% Cabernet Sauvignon. Soft, rounded, richly fruited, nicely balanced. Drink now.*

☆☆☆ 1984 MERLOT ($11.50) Estate, Napa Valley. *Rich, lush, balanced, classically structured, lovely. Drink 1990.*

## Stevenot Vineyards                    CALAVERAS COUNTY

### WHITE

☆☆ 1982 CHARDONNAY ($8.50) Brutocao, Mendocino. *Fresh, crisp, clean, with lots of lovely fruit.*

☆☆ 1983 CHARDONNAY ($6.00) California. *Fresh, simple, clean. The grapes are from Lodi.*

☆☆☆ 1983 CHARDONNAY ($11.00) Estate, Calaveras. *The first "estate" Chardonnay. Delicate, soft, with nice oak.*

☆☆☆ 1984 CHARDONNAY ($9.00) Proprietor's Reserve, Calaveras. *Rich, clean, lush, lovely, long finish.*

☆☆ 1984 CHARDONNAY ($10.00) Estate, Calaveras. *Crisp, clean, attractive.*

1985 CHARDONNAY ($6.00) California. *Flat, earthy, too woody, not much fruit or varietal character.*

1985 CHARDONNAY ($9.00) Grand Reserve, Calaveras. *Sour, unattractive.*

☆ 1986 CHARDONNAY ($6.00) California. *Weedy, clean, unpleasant.*

☆☆ 1985 MUSCAT ($7.50) San Luis Obispo. *8% residual sugar. Spicy, spritzy, fresh.*

### RED

☆☆ 1980 CABERNET SAUVIGNON ($8.00) Calaveras. *Lush, smooth, herbal and complex. Ready to drink.*

1981 CABERNET SAUVIGNON ($8.00) Calaveras. *5% Merlot. Berried, heavy and overdone.*

☆☆ 1982 CABERNET SAUVIGNON ($10.00) Calaveras. *Chocolatey, thick, clean.*

1983 CABERNET SAUVIGNON ($8.50) Calaveras. *Flat, simple, lacking fruit.*

☆☆ 1984 CABERNET SAUVIGNON ($8.00) Calaveras. *Decent fruit and structure but a little dull.*

1984 CABERNET SAUVIGNON ($15.00) Grand Reserve, Calaveras. *Soft, flat, sweet, odd.*

1981 ZINFANDEL ($6.00) Calaveras. *Overdone, berried, not attractive.*

☆☆☆ 1983 ZINFANDEL ($6.00) Amador. *Lush, ripe, fresh, lovely, clean, deep.*

☆☆ 1984 ZINFANDEL ($6.00) Calaveras. *Decent fruit but a bit tired.*

ଚୈ

## Stewart Vineyards                    WASHINGTON
### WHITE
☆☆ 1986 WHITE RIESLING ($14.00) Select Late Harvest, Columbia Valley. *10% residual sugar. Crisp, lush, snappy acidity, decent.*

ଚୈ

## Stone Hill Winery                    MISSOURI
### RED
☆☆ 1981 NORTON ($25.00) Estate, Hermann. *Clean, good structure, ripe, balanced.*

ଚୈ

## Stonegate Winery                    NAPA COUNTY
### WHITE
☆ 1982 CHARDONNAY ($9.00) Alexander Valley. *Oily, thick, butterscotch, slightly sweet.*

☆☆ 1982 CHARDONNAY ($10.00) Napa Valley. *Decent fruit; simple, clean and lean—an attractive food wine.*

☆☆ 1983 CHARDONNAY ($14.00) Napa Valley. *Overripe, intense, tropical fruit flavors. Big but balanced.*

☆☆☆ 1984 CHARDONNAY ($11.00) Napa Valley. *Crisp, fresh, snappy, balanced, charming.*

### RED
☆☆ 1978 CABERNET SAUVIGNON ($8.50) Vail Vista, Alexander Valley. *Berried, intense, oaky; not appealing.*

☆☆☆ 1978 CABERNET SAUVIGNON ($12.00) Steiner, Sonoma. *Rich fruit and lovely balance. Drink now and beyond.*

☆☆☆ 1979 CABERNET SAUVIGNON ($12.00) Vail Vista, Alexander Valley. *Herbal, ripe, complex, forward, very attractive. Drink 1988.*

☆☆☆ 1979 CABERNET SAUVIGNON ($12.00) Napa Valley. *Full, ripe, good varietal character. Drink now.*

☆☆☆☆ 1980 CABERNET SAUVIGNON ($8.50) Vail Vista, Alexander Valley. *Eucalyptus and berries; complex and superb. Drink now or hold.*

☆☆ 1980 CABERNET SAUVIGNON ($12.00) Napa Valley. *Hard, structured, clean, attractive. Drink 1988.*

☆☆ 1981 CABERNET SAUVIGNON ($12.00) Napa. *Minty, spicy, soft, fleshy, cedary notes. Drink 1988.*

☆☆☆ 1982 CABERNET SAUVIGNON ($9.00) Napa Valley. *Clean and firm, with good fruit.*

☆☆ 1975 MERLOT ($12.00) Spaulding, Napa Valley. *Bordeaux-like, soft and elegant; a bit short.*

☆☆☆ 1977 MERLOT ($12.00) Spaulding, Napa Valley. *Dense, well balanced and clean, with nice violet tones.*

☆☆ 1978 MERLOT ($9.00) Spaulding, Napa Valley. *Minty, clean, rich, intense. Lovely balance, aging potential. Still lively.*

☆☆☆ 1979 MERLOT ($12.00) Spaulding, Napa Valley. *Rich, intense, classic, with lovely oak.*

☆☆☆ 1980 MERLOT ($12.00) Spaulding, Napa Valley. *Crisp and forward; clean and tannic. Needs some age. Drink 1988.*

☆☆☆ 1982 MERLOT ($12.00) Spaulding, Napa Valley. *Lush, clean, balanced. Drink now.*

ଚୈ

## Stoneridge                                   AMADOR COUNTY
### RED
○  1981 ZINFANDEL ($6.50) Twin Rivers, El Dorado. *Dirty, tanky, unpleasant.*

᠁

## Stony Hill Vineyards                          NAPA COUNTY
### WHITE
☆☆  1980 CHARDONNAY ($12.00) Estate, Napa Valley. *Pleasant, balanced. Gradually improving with age.*
☆☆  1982 CHARDONNAY ($12.00) Estate, Napa Valley. *Pleasant but withdrawn. Balanced, clean. Beginning to come around.*
☆☆☆  1983 CHARDONNAY ($13.00) Napa Valley. *Rich, round and full-bodied, with forward fruit and lush texture.*
☆☆☆  1984 CHARDONNAY ($12.00) Estate, Napa Valley. *Soft, round, lovely fruit. Delicious oak, excellent structure. Drink 1990.*
☆☆☆  1985 CHARDONNAY ($16.00) Napa Valley. *Big, lush and forward, with depth and complexity. Drink 1991.*

᠁

## Storybook Mountain Vineyards                  NAPA COUNTY
### RED
☆☆☆  1980 ZINFANDEL ($7.75) Sonoma. *Rich nose; crisp, high-acid wine. Atypical but nice.*
☆☆☆  1981 ZINFANDEL ($7.75) Napa Valley. *Big but balanced and very attractive.*
☆☆☆  1981 ZINFANDEL ($9.50) Estate Reserve, Napa Valley. *Rich, intense, fruity and lovely. Extremely Bordeaux-like.*
☆☆☆☆  1983 ZINFANDEL ($8.00) Napa Valley. *Strawberry fruit, rich, lovely texture, really gorgeous. Drink now.*
☆☆☆☆  1983 ZINFANDEL ($12.50) Estate Reserve, Napa Valley. *Rich, powerful yet elegant, wonderful fruit, great structure.*
☆☆☆  1984 ZINFANDEL ($9.50) Napa Valley. *Crisp, lean, berried, lovely structure and aging potential.*

᠁

## Stratford                                     NAPA COUNTY
### WHITE
☆☆☆  1985 CHARDONNAY ($9.00) California. *Fresh, snappy, lovely fruit, clean, balanced.*
☆☆☆  1986 CANTERBURY SAUVIGNON BLANC ($6.00) California. *Bright, fresh, balanced, charming.*
☆☆☆  1986 SAUVIGNON BLANC ($6.75) California. *Crisp, lush fruit and herbs, nice soft texture.*
### RED
☆☆  1982 CABERNET SAUVIGNON ($7.50) California. *Soft, crisp, earthy, clean, nicely made. Drink now.*
☆☆☆  1983 CABERNET SAUVIGNON ($8.50) California. *Rich, deep, lush, complex. Drink 1989.*
☆☆  1984 CABERNET SAUVIGNON ($9.00) California. *10% Merlot. Snappy, fresh, clean, balanced, attractive.*
☆☆☆  1983 MERLOT ($8.50) California. *Fresh, clean, nicely structured. Drink 1988.*

᠁

## Straus Vineyards                              SONOMA COUNTY
### RED
☆☆☆  1984 MERLOT ($9.00) 75% Napa Valley, 25% Sonoma. *Bright, fruity, clean and spicy, with good balance and intensity.*

᠁

## *Streblow Vineyards* NAPA COUNTY

### WHITE

☆☆ 1985 SAUVIGNON BLANC ($7.50) Rancho Otranto, Napa Valley. *Crisp, lean, fruity, varietal, decent.*

☆ 1986 SAUVIGNON BLANC ($7.50) Rancho Otranto, Napa Valley. *Lean, varietal, decent but with a touch of oxidation.*

### RED

☆☆☆ 1985 CABERNET SAUVIGNON ($14.00) Estate, Napa Valley. *Soft, fresh, berry fruit, clean, new oak, lovely structure. Drink 1990.*

🍂

## *Rodney Strong Vineyards* SONOMA COUNTY

### WHITE

1982 CHARDONNAY ($10.00) River West, Sonoma. *Earthy, bitter, vegetal, oily.*

☆ 1983 CHARDONNAY ($10.00) Chalk Hill, Sonoma. *Heavy, vegetal, overripe, pineapple flavors.*

1984 CHARDONNAY ($10.00) River West, Russian River Valley. *Tired, tart, no fruit.*

1984 WINDSOR VINEYARDS CHARDONNAY ($10.00) Steelhead Ranch, Russian River Valley. *Heavy, dull, not much.*

☆☆ 1984 WINDSOR VINEYARDS CHARDONNAY ($10.00) River East, Russian River Valley. *Tangy, ripe, rich fruit, oaky.*

☆☆ 1984 WINDSOR VINEYARDS CHARDONNAY ($13.50) Sayre Signature, Sonoma. *Soft, rich, crisp, attractive.*

☆☆ 1985 CHARDONNAY ($9.50) Chalk Hill, Sonoma. *Toasty, mature, not much fresh fruit but some nice honey on the finish.*

☆☆☆ 1986 CHARDONNAY ($8.25) Sonoma. *Crisp, spicy, balanced, lively, decent.*

☆☆ 1985 FUME BLANC ($7.25) Charlotte's Home, Alexander Valley. *Crisp, clean, fresh, good balance.*

1982 WINDSOR VINEYARDS JOHANNISBERG RIESLING ($6.75) Select Late Harvest, Estate, Russian River Valley. *14.9% residual sugar. Oxidized in the nose, soft, decent.*

☆☆☆ 1984 JOHANNISBERG RIESLING ($9.00) Late Harvest, LeBaron, Russian River Valley. *375 ml. 6.7% residual sugar. Candied, fresh, botrytis, clean, lush.*

☆☆☆ 1985 JOHANNISBERG RIESLING ($9.00) Late Harvest, LeBaron, Russian River Valley. *11.8% residual sugar. Soft, lush, botrytis and honeyed fruit.*

☆☆ 1985 WINDSOR MUSCAT ($10.00) Late Harvest, Alexander Valley. *6.7% residual sugar. Fresh, attractive, simple, soda pop flavors.*

### RED

☆☆ NV WINDSOR VINEYARDS BURGUNDY ($3.75) California. *Fruity, decent, clean.*

☆ 1978 CABERNET SAUVIGNON ($11.00) Alexander's Crown, Estate, Sonoma. *This once grand wine is beginning to show its age.*

☆☆ 1979 CABERNET SAUVIGNON ($12.00) Sonoma. *Soft and herbal, clean and elegant.*

☆☆☆ 1979 CABERNET SAUVIGNON ($12.95) Alexander's Crown, Alexander Valley. *Rich, earthy and dense, with good structure.*

☆☆  1980 WINDSOR VINEYARDS CABERNET SAUVIGNON
($9.00) Lot 1, North Coast. *Violets and rich vari-
etal flavors.*

1981 CABERNET SAUVIGNON ($7.00) Vintner Grown,
Sonoma. *Muddy, barnyard flavors.*

☆☆  1981 CABERNET SAUVIGNON ($12.00) Alexander Valley.
*Balanced, soft, clean, lush. Drink now.*

☆☆☆ 1982 CABERNET SAUVIGNON ($6.00) Mendocino. *1.11%
residual sugar. Good varietal character, clean.*

1982 CABERNET SAUVIGNON ($7.00) Sonoma. *Bell pep-
pers, intense vegetation, unappealing.*

☆☆  1982 WINDSOR VINEYARDS CABERNET SAUVIGNON
($12.00) Private Reserve, Vintner Grown, Alex-
ander Valley. *Herbal, varietal, decent.*

☆☆☆ 1982 WINDSOR VINEYARDS CABERNET SAUVIGNON
($12.00) River West, Russian River Valley. *Herbal,
clean, fruity, attractive. Drink now.*

☆☆☆ 1982 WINDSOR VINEYARDS CABERNET SAUVIGNON
($12.00) Signature Selection, Sonoma. *Fresh,
snappy, clean, varietal, super.*

☆☆  1984 CABERNET SAUVIGNON ($11.00) Alexander's
Crown, Alexander Valley. *Rich, ripe, complex,
nicely structured, earthy flavors. Drink 1990.*

1981 PINOT NOIR ($8.50) River East, Russian River Valley.
*Lacking fruit, dull, dried out.*

☆☆☆ 1984 PINOT NOIR ($8.50) River East, Russian River Valley.
*Fresh, crisp, lively, super.*

1979 ZINFANDEL ($5.00) Old Vines River West, Russian
River Valley. *Meaty, clean, not much.*

☆  1980 ZINFANDEL ($12.00) Old Vines River West, Russian
River Valley. *Earthy, meaty, spicy, with some dis-
turbing composty flavors.*

❧

## Stuermer Winery                              LAKE COUNTY
### RED

☆☆  1979 LOWER LAKE WINERY CABERNET SAUVIGNON
($7.50) 41% Stromberg, 40% Holdenreid, 19%
Lovisone, Lake. *Good oak and fruit; clean but not
likable.*

☆☆☆☆ 1979 LOWER LAKE WINERY CABERNET SAUVIGNON
($12.00) Devoto, Lake. *Lush, deep, balanced, su-
perb. Drink now.*

☆  1979 LOWER LAKE WINERY CABERNET SAUVIGNON
($12.00) Reserve, Devoto, Lake. *Raisiny, intense
and a trifle weedy.*

☆☆  1980 LOWER LAKE WINERY CABERNET SAUVIGNON
($8.50) 52% Holdenreid, 32% Devoto, 19%
Lovisone, Lake. *Good, open, rich, fresh, balanced.
Charming fruit.*

☆☆  1981 LOWER LAKE WINERY CABERNET SAUVIGNON
($8.50) Lake. *Herbal, nicely made, easygoing.
Drink now.*

☆☆  1982 ARCADIA CABERNET SAUVIGNON ($8.00) Lake.
*Tart and thin but with good varietal flavors.*

☆  1982 CABERNET SAUVIGNON ($15.00) Lake. *Lush, vel-
vety, vegetal, decent.*

❧

## Sullivan Vineyards Winery              NAPA COUNTY
### WHITE
1985 CHARDONNAY ($10.00) Napa Valley. *Dull, off flavors.*

**RED**

☆☆☆ 1981 CABERNET SAUVIGNON ($14.00) Napa Valley. *Big, meaty and intense, with good complexity. Aging well.*

☆ 1984 CABERNET SAUVIGNON ($16.00) Estate, Napa Valley. *Heavy, deep, earthy, decent. Drink 1992.*

ᴥ

## Summerhill Vineyards    SANTA CLARA COUNTY

**WHITE**

1985 CHARDONNAY ($7.50) California. *Tart, crisp, herbal, odd.*

ᴥ

## Summum    UTAH

**ROSE**

NV ROSE TABLE WINE Utah. *Odd, lacking depth. Not sold; the church accepts donations.*

ᴥ

SUN COUNTRY *see* Canandaigua Wine Company

SUNNY ST. HELENA *see* Merryvale Vineyards

## Sunrise Winery    SANTA CLARA COUNTY

**WHITE**

☆ 1982 CHARDONNAY ($10.00) North Coast. *Some off flavors but good acidity; decent.*

**RED**

☆☆☆ 1980 PINOT NOIR ($8.00) Glen Ellen, Sonoma. *Peppery, rich, rounded, superb.*

☆ 1980 PINOT NOIR ($8.00) Iron Horse, Sonoma. *Earthy, rich and overdone.*

ᴥ

## Susiné Cellars    SOLANO COUNTY

**WHITE**

1985 CHARDONNAY ($6.00) Napa Valley. *Oaky, heavy, unattractive.*

**RED**

☆☆☆ 1980 ZINFANDEL ($5.00) Amador. *Lush, clean and fruity.*

ᴥ

## Sutter Home Winery    NAPA COUNTY

**BLANC DE NOIR**

☆☆ 1986 WHITE ZINFANDEL ($4.75) California. *Decent, fruity, clean, varietal, sweet. America's most popular White Zinfandel in its best version yet.*

**RED**

☆☆ 1979 ZINFANDEL ($5.95) Deaver, Amador. *Rich, jammy, berried.*

☆ 1980 ZINFANDEL ($6.00) Deaver, Amador. *Dense and raisiny, with very little fruit; hot and powerful.*

☆☆ 1980 ZINFANDEL ($8.75) Reserve, Deaver, Amador. *Clean, complex, low fruit, nice.*

1981 ZINFANDEL ($5.95) Deaver, Amador. *Hard, bitter, lacking fruit.*

☆ 1981 ZINFANDEL ($8.75) Reserve, Deaver, Amador. *Rich, deep, raisiny, unattractive.*

☆ 1982 ZINFANDEL ($6.25) Amador. *Decent, dry, fruity, clean.*

ᴥ

## Joseph Swan Vineyards          SONOMA COUNTY
### WHITE
○ 1982 CHARDONNAY ($12.00) Northern Sonoma. *Harsh, off, unattractive.*
### RED
☆☆☆ 1978 PINOT NOIR ($20.00) Sonoma. *Nice fruit, good oak, complex. Ready to drink now.*

☆☆☆ 1983 PINOT NOIR ($15.75) Estate, Northern Sonoma. *Crisp, cherry fruit, lovely earthy flavors and varietal character.*

☆☆☆☆ 1980 ZINFANDEL ($9.00) Sonoma. *Lovely ripe fruit, crisp acidity and spicy, complex flavors.*

☆☆☆ 1983 ZINFANDEL ($8.00) Sonoma. *Crisp, clean, tangy, lovely varietal fruit; charming.*

≈∙

## Sycamore Creek Vineyards     SANTA CLARA COUNTY
### WHITE
☆ 1982 CHARDONNAY ($12.00) Estate, California. *Vinous, heavy, rich but lacking depth.*

☆☆ 1982 CHARDONNAY ($12.00) La Reina, Monterey. *European in style; decent, acidic, varietal.*

☆☆ 1983 CHARDONNAY ($15.00) Estate, California. *Rich, deep, clean, lacking fruit.*

1984 CHARDONNAY ($10.00) Sleepy Hollow, Monterey. *Tart, sour, oily, unappealing.*

☆ 1985 CHARDONNAY ($8.50) 10th Anniversary Vintage, Central Coast. *Soft, clean, flabby, decent.*

1985 JOHANNISBERG RIESLING ($7.50) Bien Nacido, Santa Barbara. *Sappy, simple, not much.*
### RED
☆☆ 1981 CABERNET SAUVIGNON ($18.00) Central Coast, California. *Big and intense, with good fruit. Overpriced. Ready to drink.*

☆ 1982 CABERNET SAUVIGNON ($20.00) Central Coast. *Decent, dull.*

☆☆ 1984 CARIGNANE ($6.50) Proprietor Grown, Santa Clara. *Tannic, grapey, berried, intense. Drink now.*

☆ 1981 PINOT NOIR ($7.50) Monterey. *Green, crisp, clean, decent.*

☆ 1980 ZINFANDEL ($9.00) Morgan Hill, California. *Big, late-harvest style. Intense, concentrated, overdone.*

☆☆ 1981 ZINFANDEL ($9.00) Morgan Hill, California. *A bit better than the '80—rich, spirited and attractive.*

☆☆☆ 1982 ZINFANDEL ($9.00) Estate, Morgan Hill, California. *Crisp, fruity, balanced, delicious. Drink now.*

☆☆☆ 1983 ZINFANDEL ($10.00) Proprietor Grown, California. *Crisp, fruity, balanced, lovely.*

☆☆ 1984 ZINFANDEL ($10.00) Proprietor Grown, Santa Clara. *Rich, dense, concentrated, clean, attractive.*

≈∙

## Tabor Hill Winery                      MICHIGAN
### WHITE
1983 CHARDONNAY ($13.00) Winemaster Selection, Estate, Lake Michigan Shore. *Simple, dull, unattractive.*

≈∙

# Taft Street Winery                    SONOMA COUNTY
## WHITE
☆☆ 1982 CHARDONNAY ($11.00) 77% Tepusquet, Santa Barbara; 23% Iron Horse, California. *Toasty, crisp and nicely made.*

☆☆ 1983 CHARDONNAY ($11.00) 58% Tepusquet, 42% Sonoma-Cutrer, Santa Barbara-Sonoma. *Crisp, complex.*

☆☆ 1984 CHARDONNAY ($6.00) Early Cuvée, California. *Simple, fresh and clean.*

☆☆ 1985 CHARDONNAY ($9.00) Russian River Valley. *Crisp, lemony, clean, decent.*

☆☆ 1986 CHARDONNAY ($1.75) Sonoma. *187 ml. Little bottle but a charming wine, with fruit, oak, spice and balance.*

☆☆ 1986 CHARDONNAY ($9.50) Russian River Valley. *Soft, decent, clean, simple.*

## RED
☆☆☆ 1982 MEDALLION ($9.75) 61% Sonoma Valley, 39% Napa. *61% Merlot, 26% Cabernet, 13% Cabernet Franc. Still lovely. Drink up.*

☆☆☆ 1983 CABERNET SAUVIGNON ($9.00) Napa Valley. *Crisp, clean, fruity, smooth, lean, good structure, long finish. Drink 1988.*

☆☆ 1984 CABERNET SAUVIGNON ($1.75) Napa. *187 ml. Little bottle but nice, soft herbs and varietal fruit. Drink now.*

1985 MERLOT ($10.00) Sonoma. *Bitter, tannic.*

1983 PINOT NOIR ($7.50) Monterey. *Vegetal, earthy, not attractive.*

☆☆ 1983 PINOT NOIR ($9.00) Tepusquet, Santa Maria Valley. *Earthy, crisp, decent.*

邝

# Robert Talbott Vineyards        MONTEREY COUNTY
## WHITE
☆☆☆ 1983 CHARDONNAY ($16.00) Monterey. *Rich, lush, oaky, charming and complex.*

☆☆☆☆ 1985 CHARDONNAY ($16.00) Monterey. *Rich, oaky, intense fruit, silky texture, superb.*

邝

# Ivan Tamas                    SANTA CLARA COUNTY
## WHITE
☆☆ 1984 CHARDONNAY ($6.00) 40% Tepusquet, 30% Santa Maria Hills, 30% Newhall, Central Coast. *Fresh, round, clean, ripe fruit, crisp acidity.*

☆☆ 1985 CHARDONNAY ($6.00) Central Coast. *Oak and ripe fruit, pleasant, smooth, clean.*

## RED
☆☆ 1982 CABERNET SAUVIGNON ($6.00) North Coast. *Soft, varietal, clean, attractive, lacking structure.*

☆☆ 1983 CABERNET SAUVIGNON ($6.00) McNab, Mendocino. *Lush, ripe, clean, good balance—better than the 1982.*

☆☆ 1984 CABERNET SAUVIGNON ($6.00) Mendocino. *Plummy, cassis flavors, meaty, American oak.*

☆☆ 1985 CABERNET SAUVIGNON ($6.00) North Coast. *Soft, decent, clean, balanced.*

邝

TANBARK HILL *see* Philip Togni Vineyard

## Tarula Farms Wine Growers                                OHIO
### WHITE
☆ 1985 SEYVAL BLANC ($7.50) Estate, Ohio. *Rich, earthy, complex, intense, heavy.*

🦢

## Taylor California Cellars              MONTEREY COUNTY
### WHITE
☆ NV CHABLIS ($2.50) California. *2% residual sugar. Dull, fat, neutral.*

☆☆ NV RHINE ($2.50) California. *2.5% residual sugar. Crisp, clean, decent, fresh.*

☆☆ 1985 GREAT WESTERN WINERY CHARDONNAY ($6.00) Special Selection, Estate, Finger Lakes. *Soft, fragrant, clean, ripe, attractive.*

☆ 1986 GEWURZTRAMINER ($6.00) Special Selection, Estate, Finger Lakes. *2.4% residual sugar. Spicy, balanced, ripe; heavy flavors.*

1984 GREAT WESTERN WINERY JOHANNISBERG RIESLING ($6.00) Special Selection, Estate, Finger Lakes. *Moldy, odd flavors.*

☆ 1984 GREAT WESTERN WINERY RAVAT ($6.00) Premium, Special Selection, Finger Lakes. *Clean, tart, volatile.*

☆ 1984 GREAT WESTERN WINERY VIDAL BLANC ($4.25) Special Selection, Late Harvest, Laursen Farm, Estate, Finger Lakes. *4.2% residual sugar. Crisp, clean, fresh, oily. Nice.*

☆☆ 1985 VIDAL BLANC ($10.00) Special Selection, Ice Wine, Estate, Finger Lakes. *375 ml. 26% residual sugar. Syrupy, intense, botrytis and honey flavors; rich and ripe, with some volatile acidity.*

### SPARKLING
NV BRUT ($5.90) California. *Charmat. Heavy, coarse.*

NV EXTRA DRY ($6.00) California. *Dull, clumsy.*

NV PINK CHAMPAGNE ($6.00) California. *Syrupy, dull, simple.*

### RED
☆☆ NV ZINFANDEL ($4.30) California. *Nice balance, clean flavors.*

🦢

## Taylor Wine Company                          NEW YORK
### SPARKLING
○ NV BRUT ($7.50) New York State. *Transfer. Sweet.*

NV BRUT NATUREL ($11.00) New York. *Oily, vegetal, heavy.*

☆☆ NV GREAT WESTERN BLANC DE BLANCS ($9.00) New York. *Crisp, clean, fresh, simple, attractive.*

NV GREAT WESTERN PINK CHAMPAGNE ($9.00) New York State. *Very sweet.*

NV GREAT WESTERN NATUREL ($9.90) New York State. *Foxy but clean.*

🦢

## Tedeschi Vineyard and Winery              HAWAII
### WHITE
☆☆ NV MAUI BLANC ($3.50) Maui, Hawaii. *Made from pineapple. Fresh, clean, lovely fruit.*

**SPARKLING**

NV ERDMAN-TEDESCHI BLANC DE NOIR ($12.00) Maui, Hawaii. *Made from Carnelian grapes. Decent, a bit heavy and dull.*

☆ 1981 BLANC DE NOIR ($15.00) Hawaii. *100% Carnelian. Lush, fruity, clean, some coarseness.*

☆ 1982 ERDMAN-TEDESHI BLANC DE NOIR ($15.00) Maui. *Made from Carnelian grapes. Heavy, rich, dull.*

**RED**

☆ 1986 MAUI NOUVEAU CARNELIAN ($7.75) Hawaii. *Spicy, grapey, astringent, decent.*

৯১

## Tepusquet                                    SANTA BARBARA COUNTY
**BLANC DE NOIR**

☆☆☆ 1986 WHITE CABERNET SAUVIGNON ($4.00) Paso Robles. *1.98% residual sugar. Soft, fresh, fruity, clean, varietal.*

**RED**

☆☆ 1982 CABERNET SAUVIGNON ($8.00) Vineyard Reserve, Santa Maria Valley. *35% Merlot. Soft, rich, weedy, pleasant. Drink now.*

৯১

## Tewksbury Wine Cellars                              NEW JERSEY
**WHITE**

☆ 1985 PROPRIETOR'S SELECT WHITE ($9.00) Hunterdon. *Crisp, clean, tangy, a bit vinous.*

☆☆ 1983 CHARDONNAY ($9.00) Hunterdon, New Jersey. *Elegant, fresh, with good fruit and complexity.*

○ 1984 CHARDONNAY ($9.00) Hunterdon. *Sour, stinky.*

NV VIDAL BLANC ($6.00) New Jersey. *Sour, vegetal, unpleasant.*

**RED**

☆ 1983 CHAMBOURCIN ($8.00) Hunterdon. *Smokey, tart, crisp, soft fruit, meaty.*

৯১

## Texas Vineyards                                      TEXAS
**WHITE**

○ 1985 IVAHNOE BLANC ($4.00) Texas. *1.9% residual sugar. Oily, heavy, awful.*

☆ 1984 CHARDONNAY ($8.00) Floyd. *Crisp, fresh fruit, a bit underripe.*

☆☆ 1985 CHARDONNAY ($9.00) Texas. *Crisp, clean, decent.*

☆☆ 1985 MUSCAT ($8.00) Pecos. *2.9% residual sugar. Fresh, spicy, attractive.*

**BLANC DE NOIR**

☆ 1986 IVANHOE BLUSH ($4.50) Texas. *Dry, vegetal.*

1986 WHITE ZINFANDEL ($6.00) Texas. *Chalky, odd.*

**RED**

☆ 1984 IVANHOE ROSE ($7.00) Texas. *Simple, clean, decent.*

৯১

## Paul Thomas Wines                               WASHINGTON
**WHITE**

☆☆☆ 1986 JOHANNISBERG RIESLING ($7.00) Washington. *Spicy, clean, balanced, lovely fruit.*

**RED**

☆ 1981 CABERNET SAUVIGNON ($13.50) 5th Anniversary, Washington. *Meaty; some vegetal qualities but rich and well made. Drink now.*

☆☆ 1982 CABERNET SAUVIGNON ($12.00) Bacchus, Washington. *Crisp and clean, with lovely varietal character and supple texture. Drink 1988.*

☆ 1983 CABERNET SAUVIGNON ($13.00) Washington. *Lush vegetation, ripe cherry fruit, a bit overdone.*

❧

## Tijsseling Vineyards  MENDOCINO COUNTY
### WHITE

☆☆ 1983 CHARDONNAY ($7.75) Mendocino. *Crisp, fruity, attractive.*

### SPARKLING

☆ 1982 BRUT ($12.00) Estate, Mendocino. *100% Chardonnay. Spicy, coarse, decent.*

1983 BLANC DE BLANC BRUT ($13.00) McNab Ranch, Mendocino. *100% Chardonnay. Heavy, oily, balanced, decent.*

### RED

☆☆ 1982 DRY RED TABLE WINE ($4.00) Estate, Mendocino. *Fresh and charming; a bit tannic.*

☆☆ 1981 CABERNET SAUVIGNON ($7.25) Mendocino. *Oaky, clean, attractive. Drink now.*

❧

## Tobias Vineyards  SAN LUIS OBISPO COUNTY
### RED

☆☆ 1981 ZINFANDEL ($8.25) Benito Dusi Ranch, Paso Robles. *Big, lush, ripe and forward.*

☆ 1982 ZINFANDEL ($8.25) Dusi Ranch, Paso Robles. *Lush, deep, rich but too earthy.*

❧

## Philip Togni Vineyard  NAPA COUNTY
### WHITE

☆☆☆☆ 1985 SAUVIGNON BLANC ($10.00) Napa Valley. *Crisp, lean, varietal, very French. Perhaps the best American Sauvignon Blanc ever made.*

☆☆☆ 1986 SAUVIGNON BLANC ($10.00) Napa Valley. *Crisp, lean, snappy fruit, lovely varietal character. Very French.*

### RED

☆ 1985 CA' TOGNI ($12.50) Estate, Napa Valley. *375 ml. A sweet wine made from Black Hamburg (Black Muscat). Soft, syrupy, simple, with some black currant fruit; lacking depth.*

☆☆☆☆ 1984 CABERNET SAUVIGNON ($18.00) Napa Valley. *Lush fruit, stunning structure, lovely cherry flavors, a great one. Drink 1989.*

☆☆☆ 1985 TANBARK HILL CABERNET SAUVIGNON ($15.00) Napa Valley. *Dark, rich and lush with cassis and plum flavors; rich oak and a long finish. Drink 1990.*

☆☆☆ 1985 CABERNET SAUVIGNON ($20.00) Estate, Napa Valley. *Tart, lean, elegant, with great depth and lively flavors. Drink 1993.*

❧

## Tomasello Winery  NEW JERSEY
### WHITE

☆ 1985 CHARDONNAY ($10.00) Oak Cask Reserve, Atlantic. *Crisp, snappy, tart, unusual but drinkable.*

☆ 1985 SEYVAL BLANC ($6.00) Atlantic. *Soft, dry, decent, too much sulfur.*

### SPARKLING
NV  BLANC DE BLANC ($5.25) American. *Sweet, bitter, heavy, ugly.*

○  NV  BLANC DE BLANC NATUREL ($7.50) American. *Oily, dull, ugly.*

&

TONIO CONTI *see* Adelaida Cellars

## Topolos at Russian River          SONOMA COUNTY
### WHITE
☆☆  1982 CHARDONNAY ($8.50) Sonoma. *Balanced, clean, oaky, subdued.*

○  1984 CHARDONNAY ($9.50) Russian River, Sonoma. *Dull, very unpleasant.*

### RED
☆☆☆  NV  RESERVE RED ($4.50) Sonoma. *Tart, crisp, ripe, fruity, delicious.*

☆☆  1980 CABERNET SAUVIGNON ($9.50) Sonoma. *Dark, earthy and intense.*

☆☆☆  1981 CABERNET SAUVIGNON ($9.50) Sonoma. *Clean, elegant, lovely fruit, delightful. Drink 1987.*

☆☆☆  1980 ZINFANDEL ($7.50) Sonoma. *Spicy, berried and oaky— a lovely wine. Drink now and beyond.*

☆☆  1982 ZINFANDEL ($10.50) Ultimo, Sonoma Mountain, Sonoma. *Big, berried, tart.*

&

## Toyon Vineyards          SONOMA COUNTY
### WHITE
☆☆☆  1982 CHARDONNAY ($10.00) Estate, Alexander Valley. *Lush, balanced, clean.*

☆☆☆  1983 CHARDONNAY ($8.50) Dry Creek Valley. *Crisp, earthy, lovely fruit.*

### RED
☆  1979 CABERNET SAUVIGNON ($7.00) Edna Valley. *Weedy but crisp and drinkable.*

☆☆☆  1982 CABERNET SAUVIGNON ($10.00) Estate, Alexander Valley. *Lush, balanced, clean. Ready to drink.*

☆☆☆  1983 CABERNET SAUVIGNON ($10.00) Alexander Valley. *Soft, velvety, lush, lovely fruit, clean. Drink 1988.*

&

## Traulsen Vineyards          NAPA COUNTY
### RED
☆☆☆  1980 ZINFANDEL ($8.50) Napa Valley. *Rich, snappy, clean and beautifully fruity.*

&

## Trefethen Vineyards Winery          NAPA COUNTY
### WHITE
☆☆☆  NV  ESCHOL WHITE ($5.50) Napa Valley. *77% Chardonnay, 20% White Riesling, 3% Pinot Noir Blanc. Round, fruity, clean and balanced, with charming spice.*

☆☆  1982 CHARDONNAY ($13.50) Napa Valley. *Clean, crisp, simple, decent.*

☆☆  1984 CHARDONNAY ($14.00) Napa Valley. *Rich, deep, ripe, oaky and attractive. A bit less focused than previous vintages.*

☆  1985 WHITE RIESLING ($7.00) Estate, Napa Valley. *0.5% residual sugar. Tart, decent, fresh, simple.*

## RED

☆☆☆ NV  ESCHOL RED ($5.25) Napa Valley. *43% Cabernet Sauvignon, 27% Pinot Noir, 17% Merlot, 13% Zindandel. Soft, lush, lovely berry fruit; completely delicious.*

☆  1978 CABERNET SAUVIGNON ($10.00) Estate, Napa Valley. *Pleasant but a rather minor effort.*

☆  1979 CABERNET SAUVIGNON ($11.00) Napa Valley. *Pleasant but vegetal; simple and lacking depth.*

1980 CABERNET SAUVIGNON ($12.50) Napa Valley. *Overwhelmed by vegetal qualities.*

☆  1981 CABERNET SAUVIGNON ($12.50) Estate, Napa Valley. *Still vegetal but less obnoxious than previous vintages.*

1982 CABERNET SAUVIGNON ($11.00) Napa Valley. *15.6% Merlot. Sour, earthy, unappealing.*

☆  1981 PINOT NOIR ($8.50) Napa Valley. *Tart, underripe, not much interest here.*

☆☆ 1984 PINOT NOIR ($10.75) Napa Valley. *Crisp, snappy, herbal, clean fruit, attractive.*

இ

## *Trentadue Winery*                    SONOMA COUNTY
### WHITE
1984 CHARDONNAY ($9.50) Alexander Valley. *Soft, dull, lacking character.*
### RED
☆☆☆ 1985 OLD PATCH RED ($4.75) Alexander Valley. *Dark, ripe, grapey; a delicious old-style, Italianate wine.*

1980 MERLOT ($7.50) Alexander Valley. *Jammy, rich, intense but not varietal.*

☆☆☆ 1985 MERLOT ($10.25) Napa Valley. *Soft, lush, ripe, berried, lovely fruit.*

☆  1980 ZINFANDEL ($7.50) Late Harvest, Alexander Valley. *3.2% residual sugar. Jammy and sweet, with good acid balance.*

இ

## *Michel Tribaut de Romery*          ALAMEDA COUNTY
### SPARKLING
☆☆ NV  BLANC DE NOIR ($12.00) Monterey. *Ripe, fresh, clean, complex flavors. Used to celebate the big bridge's 50th anniversary.*

☆  NV  BRUT ($16.00) Monterey. *Graceless, dull, lacking finesse.*

☆  1983 BLANC DE NOIR ROSE ($14.00) Monterey. *Simple, clean, dull, decent.*

☆☆☆ 1984 BRUT ($12.00) Monterey. *Snappy, crisp, rich, deep, with good yeast and fruit.*

☆  1984 ROSE ($14.50) Monterey. *Coarse, heavy, no finesse, vegetal, balanced, decent.*

இ

TRIONE *see* Geyser Peak Winery

TRILLIUM *see* Good Harbor Vineyards

## *Truluck Vineyards & Winery*          SOUTH CAROLINA
### RED
☆  1981 CHAMBOURCIN ($6.00) Estate, South Carolina. *Fruity, clean, quite respectable.*

இ

## *Tualatin Vineyards* OREGON
### WHITE
☆ 1983 CHARDONNAY ($9.50) Estate, Willamette Valley. *Odd, yeasty, overdone.*

☆ 1985 CHARDONNAY ($13.00) Private Reserve, Estate, Willamette Valley. *Varietal, fat, lush, a bit flabby.*
### RED
☆ 1980 PINOT NOIR ($9.75) Estate, Willamette Valley. *Soft, earthy, good varietal character.*

☆ 1983 PINOT NOIR ($9.75) Willamette Valley, Oregon. *Peppery, spicy, lacking fruit and complexity.*

☆☆☆ 1985 PINOT NOIR ($13.00) Private Reserve, Estate, Willamette Valley. *Soft, lovely cherry flavors, clean, balanced, charming.*

🙚

## *Tucker Cellars* WASHINGTON
### WHITE
1983 CHARDONNAY ($8.00) Yakima Valley. *Crisp but weird flavors.*

☆☆ 1985 MUSCAT ($6.50) Yakima Valley. *3.2% residual sugar. Crisp, fresh, spicy, nicely balanced.*

🙚

## *Tudal Winery* NAPA COUNTY
### WHITE
☆☆☆ 1982 CHARDONNAY ($9.00) Edna Valley. *Rich oak, ripe fruit, lovely varietal character.*
### RED
☆☆☆ 1979 CABERNET SAUVIGNON ($10.75) Napa Valley. *Deep, velvety, herbal and impressive.*

☆☆☆ 1980 CABERNET SAUVIGNON ($11.50) Napa Valley. *Dense, rich, ripe, nicely structured. Still lively and attractive.*

☆☆☆ 1981 CABERNET SAUVIGNON ($11.50) Napa Valley. *Herbal, soft, luxurious, chocolatey, lush.*

☆☆☆ 1982 CABERNET SAUVIGNON ($12.00) Estate, Napa Valley. *Clean, lush, herbs and ripe fruit, charming. Drink 1991.*

☆☆☆ 1983 CABERNET SAUVIGNON ($12.50) Estate, Napa Valley. *Fresh, lovely fruit, clean oak. Drink 1991.*

☆☆☆ 1984 CABERNET SAUVIGNON ($12.50) Estate, Napa Valley. *Fresh, rich flavors, lovely fruit, great structure, delicious. Drink 1988.*

🙚

## *Tulocay Winery* NAPA COUNTY
### WHITE
☆☆ 1982 CHARDONNAY ($10.00) Napa Valley. *Toasty, meaty, rich, complex; a bit heavy.*

☆☆☆ 1984 CHARDONNAY ($9.00) De Celles, Napa Valley. *Rich, round, clean, oaky, attractive.*
### RED
☆☆ 1981 CABERNET SAUVIGNON ($9.00) Napa Valley. *Big, ripe, attractive. Ready to drink.*

☆☆☆ 1984 CABERNET SAUVIGNON ($11.50) Egan, Napa Valley. *Deep, ripe, spicy, with lovely oak and rich fruit. Drink 1992.*

☆☆ 1979 PINOT NOIR ($7.50) Napa Valley. *Simple but very nice.*

☆☆ 1980 PINOT NOIR ($9.50) Napa Valley. *Pleasant, soft, varietal.*

☆☆ 1981 PINOT NOIR ($9.50) Napa Valley. *Simple, clean, attractive.*

○ 1982 PINOT NOIR ($12.50) Haynes, Napa Valley. *Strange, flowery, off flavors.*

☆☆☆ 1980 ZINFANDEL ($6.50) Napa Valley. *Charming and restrained. Balanced, clean, bright. Drink now.*

ได

## Tyland Vineyards                    MENDOCINO COUNTY
### WHITE
☆☆☆ 1982 CHARDONNAY ($8.75) Estate, Mendocino. *Wonderful fruit and acid; varietal and delightful.*

☆☆☆ 1985 MENDOCINO ESTATE CHARDONNAY ($5.00) Mendocino. *Elegant, crisp, fresh, lovely oak, very appealing.*

### SPARKLING
☆☆ NV BLANC DE BLANC ($9.00) Estate, Mendocino. *100% Chenin Blanc. Complex, rich, a bit coarse but attractive—and at a good price.*

☆☆ 1982 BRUT ($11.50) Estate, Mendocino. *100% Pinot Noir. Rich, fruity, clean, coarse, pleasant.*

### RED
☆ 1979 CABERNET SAUVIGNON ($7.75) Mendocino. *A minor effort—lacking balance. Decent flavors.*

☆☆☆☆ 1982 MENDOCINO ESTATE CABERNET SAUVIGNON ($4.25) Estate, Mendocino. *Delicate, toasty, lovely fruit, charming. Drink now.*

☆☆☆ 1981 PETITE SIRAH ($7.00) Estate, Mendocino. *Fresh, tart, charming fruit, medium weight.*

☆☆ 1980 ZINFANDEL ($6.00) Mendocino. *Clean and fresh, featuring lush fruitiness.*

☆☆ 1981 ZINFANDEL ($3.50) Estate, Mendocino. *Fresh, balanced.*

ได

ULTRAVINO *see* Artisan Wines

## Valley View Vineyard                    OREGON
### WHITE
☆☆☆ 1982 CHARDONNAY ($7.50) Oregon. *Fresh, clean, snappy, with some depth.*

☆☆☆ 1985 CHARDONNAY ($15.00) Estate, Oregon. *Rich, fruity, but tight and crisp. Attractive.*

☆☆☆ 1985 MUSCAT ($5.00) Oregon. *Dry, fresh, crisp, delicate, charming.*

### RED
☆ 1981 MERLOT ($8.50) Oregon. *Big, leathery, intense, powerful, massive, earthy. Drink 1989.*

☆☆ 1983 MERLOT ($9.00) Oregon. *Dry, tight, lean, decent, balanced.*

☆☆☆ 1980 PINOT NOIR Oregon. *Rich, soft, round, fruity, lovely.*

ได

## Valley Vineyards                    OHIO
### WHITE
☆☆ 1985 CHABLIS SEYVAL BLANC ($3.75) Ohio River Valley. *Crisp, fresh, somewhat neutral but balanced and attractive.*

ได

## Van der Kamp
## Champagne Cellars                     SONOMA COUNTY
### SPARKLING
☆☆ 1983 BRUT ($14.50) Sonoma. *82% Pinot Noir, 18% Chardonnay. Rich, deep, a bit weird, flat.*
☆ 1985 BLANC DE NOIR BRUT ROSE ($14.50) Midnight Cuvée, Sonoma. *Clean, crisp, decent.*

෨෨

## Vega Vineyards Winery      SANTA BARBARA COUNTY
### WHITE
1982 CHARDONNAY ($9.50) Caldwell, Santa Ynez Valley. *Bitter and vinous.*
○ 1983 CHARDONNAY ($6.25) Caldwell, Santa Ynez Valley. *Oaky, vegetal.*
1984 CHARDONNAY ($9.00) Santa Maria Hills, Santa Barbara. *Dull, off flavors.*
☆ 1985 JOHANNISBERG RIESLING ($8.00) Special Selection Late Harvest, Estate, Santa Ynez Valley. *10% residual sugar. Vegetal, heavy, with some crispness.*
### RED
1980 CABERNET SAUVIGNON ($7.50) Santa Barbara. *Weedy, earthy, unappealing.*
☆☆☆ 1984 PINOT NOIR ($11.00) Sierra Madre Vineyard, Santa Barbara. *Intense, ripe, great varietal character.*

෨෨

VENDANGE *see* Sebastiani Vineyards

## Ventana Vineyards Winery      MONTEREY COUNTY
### WHITE
☆☆ NV WHITE TABLE WINE ($4.00) Monterey. *Clean, fresh and quite decent.*
☆☆ 1982 CHARDONNAY ($12.00) Barrel Fermented, Monterey. *Crisp, clean and quite attractive.*
☆☆☆ 1984 CHARDONNAY ($7.50) Gold Stripe Selection, Monterey. *Crisp, fresh, lovely.*
☆☆☆ 1984 CHARDONNAY ($14.00) Estate, Monterey. *Crisp, fruity, clean, charming. Some bottle variation.*
☆☆☆ 1985 CHARDONNAY ($14.00) Monterey. *Soft, lush, ripe, smooth, good oak.*
☆☆☆ 1986 SWEET LULU MUSCAT ($6.00) Late Harvest, Central Coast. *6% residual sugar. Spicy, crisp, fresh, lively, delicious.*
### SPARKLING
☆☆☆ 1981 CUVEE JDM ($20.00) Monterey. *Clean, fresh, balanced, complex. Quite impressive.*
### ROSE
☆☆ 1985 ROSE OF PETITE SIRAH ($5.00) Estate, Monterey. *Rich, heavy, intense, herbaceous, decent.*
### RED
○ 1981 PETITE SIRAH ($5.50) Estate, Monterey. *Overwhelmed by vegetation.*
☆☆☆ 1982 PINOT NOIR ($6.25) Estate, Monterey. *Crisp and tangy like a Beaujolais. Charming, varietal character, with clean flavors. Drink now.*

෨෨

## Vichon Winery                          NAPA COUNTY
### WHITE
☆☆ 1985 CHEVRIGNON ($9.60) Napa Valley. *52% Sauvignon Blanc, 48% Semillon. Grass and coffee in the nose; herbal, crisp, smooth, pleasant.*

☆☆ 1982 CHARDONNAY ($15.00) Napa Valley. *Toasty, crisp and hard-edged. Improving nicely.*

☆☆☆ 1983 CHARDONNAY ($15.00) Napa Valley. *Ripe, rich, oaky, with lovely fruit and varietal character.*

☆☆ 1984 CHARDONNAY ($12.00) Napa Valley. *Fat, oily, overripe.*

☆☆☆☆ 1985 CHARDONNAY ($15.00) Napa Valley. *A stunning wine. Crisp, fresh, balanced, lovely oak. A great first Chardonnay for the Mondavi regime.*

### RED

☆☆☆ 1980 CABERNET SAUVIGNON ($16.00) Fay, Napa Valley. *Lean and elegant, with Bordeaux-like structure. Drink now.*

☆☆☆ 1980 CABERNET SAUVIGNON ($16.00) Volker Eisele, Napa Valley. *Tangy, well structured, complex. Ready to drink now and for the next few years.*

☆☆☆☆ 1981 CABERNET SAUVIGNON ($12.75) Fay and Eisle, Napa Valley. *Rich and deep, with super structure, finesse and elegance. Drink 1988 and beyond.*

☆☆☆ 1982 CABERNET SAUVIGNON ($11.25) Napa Valley. *Fresh, lean, nicely made, good acidity, excellent structure. Lovely. Drink 1990.*

☆☆☆ 1982 CABERNET SAUVIGNON ($15.00) Volker Eisele, Napa Valley. *Intense fruit, herbal, berried, nice structure. Drink 1989.*

☆☆☆ 1983 CABERNET SAUVIGNON ($11.25) Napa Valley. *1.6% Cabernet Franc, 0.3% Merlot. Crisp, snappy, fresh and loaded with fruit. Drink 1992.*

☆☆☆ 1985 MERLOT ($14.00) Napa Valley. *Soft, velvety, with crisp acidity and long, lovely fruit flavors. A great first effort with this variety. Drink now.*

🎗

## Villa Helena Winery                    NAPA COUNTY
### WHITE

☆☆☆ 1984 CHARDONNAY ($11.00) Lot 2, Napa Valley. *Rich, clean, balanced, complex, charming.*

☆☆☆ 1984 CHARDONNAY ($12.00) Lot 1, Napa Valley. *Toasty, clean, rich varietal character, very likable.*

1985 SAUVIGNON BLANC ($6.50) Napa Valley. *Heavy, dull, oxidized.*

🎗

## Villa Mt. Eden Winery                    NAPA COUNTY
### WHITE

☆ NV RANCH WHITE ($4.50) Napa Valley. *50% Chardonnay, 30% Chenin Blanc, 20% Gewürztraminer. Simple, clean, decent. 0.9% residual sugar.*

☆☆ 1983 CHARDONNAY ($10.00) Estate, Napa Valley. *A bit on the oaky, heavy side. Clean fruit in the finish.*

☆☆☆ 1984 CHARDONNAY ($9.00) Estate, Napa Valley. *Rich, lush, soft, lovely follow-through.*

### RED

NV RANCH RED ($3.00) Napa Valley. *73% Pinot Noir, 26% Napa Gamay. Thin, dried-out fruit, unappealing.*

☆☆☆☆ 1978 CABERNET SAUVIGNON ($12.00) Estate, Napa Valley. *Lovely, clean oak; rich, deep flavors.*

☆☆☆ 1978 CABERNET SAUVIGNON ($25.00) Reserve, Estate, Napa Valley. *Rich, intense, better than the '79 Reserve. Drink 1989 or later.*

&#9734;&#9734;&#9734; 1979 CABERNET SAUVIGNON ($13.00) Estate, Napa Valley. *Soft, round, very attractive. Drink now.*

&#9734;&#9734;&#9734; 1979 CABERNET SAUVIGNON ($25.00) Reserve, Estate, Napa Valley. *Big, hard and tannic, with firm fruit; realizing its potential.*

&#9734;&#9734; 1980 CABERNET SAUVIGNON ($11.00) Estate, Napa Valley. *Tannic, rich, clean, intense, quite lovely. Drink now.*

&#9734;&#9734; 1981 CABERNET SAUVIGNON ($9.50) Estate, Napa Valley. *Balanced, pleasant, a bit tired. Drink now.*

&#9734;&#9734;&#9734;&#9734; 1981 CABERNET SAUVIGNON ($20.00) Reserve, Estate, Napa Valley. *Rich, minty, intense, soft, cherry fruit, superb. Drink 1990.*

&#9734;&#9734;&#9734; 1982 CABERNET SAUVIGNON ($25.00) Reserve, Napa Valley. *Firm, clean, dense, rich. Drink 1990 and beyond.*

&#9734;&#9734; 1978 PINOT NOIR ($10.50) Tres Ninos, Napa Valley. *Crisp, clean, appealing.*

&#9734;&#9734; 1981 PINOT NOIR ($5.00) Estate, Tres Ninos, Napa Valley. *Varietal, with some complexity; clean, attractive.*

&#9734; 1982 PINOT NOIR ($9.00) Tres Ninos, Napa Valley. *Heavy, raisiny, lacking finesse.*

&#8278;

## Viña Madre                                      NEW MEXICO
### RED
○ NV ZINFANDEL ($6.25) Shaffer, New Mexico. *Sweet, unpleasant.*

&#8278;

## Viña Vista Winery                        SONOMA COUNTY
### RED
&#9734; 1981 CABERNET SAUVIGNON ($6.00) Napa Valley. *Lush, fat, deep, with some vegetal qualities. Drink now.*

&#9734; 1984 CABERNET SAUVIGNON ($6.75) Alexander Valley. *Leathery, with minimal fruit and decent flavors.*

&#9734;&#9734;&#9734; 1985 MERLOT ($8.00) Alexander Valley. *Snappy, rich, balanced, lovely.*

&#8278;

VINE HILL WINES *see* Smothers Brothers Wines

## Vose Vineyards                               NAPA COUNTY
### RED
&#9734;&#9734;&#9734; 1978 CABERNET SAUVIGNON ($10.00) Special Reserve, Napa Valley. *Big, tart, deep and delicious. Aging well.*

&#9734;&#9734;&#9734; 1979 CABERNET SAUVIGNON ($12.50) Mt. Veeder, Napa Valley. *Lean and angular structure, tart, lovely. Drink now.*

1980 CABERNET SAUVIGNON ($12.50) Estate, Mt. Veeder, Napa Valley. *Big, fat and overdone.*

&#9734;&#9734; 1981 ZINFANDEL ($7.50) Napa-Mt. Veeder. *Snappy, ripe, interesting.*

&#8278;

## Wagner Vineyards                               NEW YORK
### WHITE
&#9734; NV WHITE TABLE WINE ($4.00) Finger Lakes. *A blend of Aurora and Seyval. Fresh, crisp, vegetal, oily.*

&#9734;&#9734; 1984 AURORA ($4.50) Finger Lakes. *Snappy, clean, fresh, very appealing.*

☆☆ 1984 CAYUGA ($5.00) Finger Lakes. *Off-dry, clean, fruity, lush.*

☆☆ 1983 CHARDONNAY ($10.80) Estate, New York. *Spicy, lush, varietal, clean, some oak.*

☆☆ 1984 CHARDONNAY ($11.00) Estate, Finger Lakes. *Rich, tart, some heavy herbal qualities; varietal.*

☆☆☆ 1985 CHARDONNAY ($10.80) Barrel Fermented, Estate, Finger Lakes. *Earthy, rich, fat, lush, ripe, intense. Delicious, but not for the faint of heart.*

☆☆☆ 1985 JOHANNISBERG RIESLING ($6.25) Estate, Finger Lakes. *Smokey, spicy, complex fruit.*

☆☆ 1985 JOHANNISBERG RIESLING ($6.75) Fermented Dry, Finger Lakes. *Soft, balanced, decent.*

1986 JOHANNISBERG RIESLING ($7.00) Finger Lakes. *Oily, heavy, lacking fruit.*

☆☆ 1984 RAVAT ($4.50) Special Selection, Finger Lakes. *2% residual sugar. Sweet, crisp, balanced, fresh, tangy.*

☆ 1985 SEYVAL BLANC ($5.00) Barrel Fermented, Estate, Finger Lakes. *Creamy, intense, heavy handed.*

### SPARKLING

☆☆ NV CELEBRATION CUVEE ($9.00) Finger Lakes. *1.2% residual sugar. Charmat method. Crisp, fresh, attractive.*

### ROSE

☆ 1984 ROSE ($3.50) Finger Lakes. *Mainly DeChaunac. Decent, clean, balanced, snappy.*

### RED

☆☆ NV ALTA B ($4.00) Finger Lakes. *Syrupy, sweet, soft and attractive.*

☆ NV RED TABLE WINE ($4.00) Finger Lakes. *Clean and innocuous, light.*

☆ NV DECHAUNAC ($5.00) Octagon Cellars Reserve, Finger Lakes. *Thin, vegetal, decent fruit and texture.*

☆☆ 1980 DECHAUNAC ($5.00) Cask Reserve, Finger Lakes. *Rich, soft, clean, quite elegant.*

🙚

## Walker Wines                    SANTA CRUZ COUNTY
### RED
1980 CABERNET SAUVIGNON ($7.00) Santa Clara. *Burnt, unattractive.*

☆☆ 1979 PETITE SIRAH ($5.50) San Luis Obispo. *Heavy, deep, concentrated. Drink 1988.*

🙚

## Warnelius Vineyards                    SONOMA COUNTY
### RED
☆☆☆ 1982 PETITE SIRAH ($4.00) Sonoma. *Cherry-berry, lush, clean, lovely.*

🙚

## Warner Vineyards                    MICHIGAN
### WHITE
○ 1981 AURORA ($3.50) Michigan. *Mousy, sweet, candied.*

🙚

## Waterbrook Winery                    WASHINGTON
### WHITE
☆☆☆ 1985 CHARDONNAY ($10.50) Washington. *Crisp, lean, lovely new oak, charming.*

## RED

☆☆ NV WATERBROOK RED ($5.00) Washington. *60% Merlot, 40% Cabernet Sauvignon. Earthy, spicy, clean, good, balance.*

☆☆☆ 1984 MERLOT ($12.00) Washington. *Classically proportioned, lovely fruit, great structure. Drink 1988.*

ॐ

## Weibel Vineyards ALAMEDA/MENDOCINO COUNTY

### WHITE

☆ 1983 CHARDONNAY ($6.50) Mendocino. *Clean, simple, decent.*

1984 CHARDONNAY ($6.50) Proprietor's Reserve, Mendocino. *Sappy, dull, unappealing.*

☆☆ 1985 CHARDONNAY ($6.50) Mendocino. *Tart, clean, crisp, attractive.*

☆☆ 1985 CHARDONNAY ($8.00) Private Reserve, Mendocino. *Crisp, varietal, a bit thin.*

### SPARKLING

NV SPUMANTE ($6.00) California. *Bitter, oxidized.*

☆ NV WHITE ZINFANDEL CHAMPAGNE ($6.00) California. *Sweet, oily, heavy, decent.*

☆ NV EXTRA DRY ($7.50) California. *Bitter, deep, decent.*

☆☆☆ NV BRUT ($13.00) Mendocino. *Crisp, snappy, balanced, delicious.*

☆☆☆ 1982 BRUT ($13.00) Mendocino. *Clean, ripe, fresh, intense color, lovely rounded finish.*

☆☆ 1983 BLANC DE NOIR ($11.00) Mendocino. *Tart, crisp, clean, decent.*

### ROSE

☆ 1985 REFOSCO ROSE ($4.50) Mendocino. *Vegetal, spicy.*

### RED

☆☆ 1978 CABERNET SAUVIGNON ($7.00) Mendocino. *Clean, balanced, attractive. Drink now.*

☆ 1978 CABERNET SAUVIGNON ($9.50) Proprietor's Reserve, Mendocino. *Decent, clean, varietal.*

☆ 1979 CABERNET SAUVIGNON ($10.00) Proprietor's Reserve, Mendocino. *Varietal, clean but lacks fruit and definition.*

☆☆ 1980 CABERNET SAUVIGNON ($9.00) Proprietor's Reserve, Mendocino. *Tannic, fresh and varietal, with dense fruit. Ready to drink.*

1978 PETITE SIRAH ($4.50) Mendocino. *Thin, minty, lacking fruit.*

☆☆ 1972 PINOT NOIR ($10.00) Santa Clara Valley. *Earthy, complex; holding up nicely.*

☆ 1976 PINOT NOIR ($4.50) Monterey. *Varietal, mature, some life still left.*

☆☆☆ 1976 PINOT NOIR ($9.50) Santa Clara Valley. *Rich, round, balanced, very attractive.*

☆☆☆ 1978 PINOT NOIR ($8.00) Proprietor's Reserve, Mendocino. *Lush, deep, clean; nicely made.*

☆ 1980 PINOT NOIR ($8.50) Proprietor's Reserve, Mendocino. *Dull, simple.*

☆☆☆ 1981 PINOT NOIR ($8.00) Proprietor's Reserve, Mendocino. *Clean, lovely, somewhat simple but charming.*

☆ 1981 PINOT NOIR ($10.00) Fremont 25th Anniversary, Mendocino. *Pleasant, short, simple.*

1978 ZINFANDEL ($4.00) Mendocino. *Thin, clean, with very little varietal character or depth.*

☆☆ 1980 ZINFANDEL ($8.00) Proprietor's Reserve, Mendocino. *Tart, crisp, fruity; nice. Drink now.*

ॐ

## *Weinstock Cellars*                              SONOMA COUNTY

### WHITE

☆ 1984 CHARDONNAY ($7.50) Alexander Valley. *Kosher. Simple, clean, dull, not much fruit.*

☆☆☆ 1985 CHARDONNAY ($6.50) Alexander Valley. *Kosher. Clean, fresh, lush fruit, charming.*

### BLANC DE NOIR

☆☆☆ 1986 WHITE ZINFANDEL ($5.50) Dry Creek Valley. *Kosher. Lively, crisp, tangy, delicious.*

ॐ

## *Wente Brothers*                               ALAMEDA COUNTY

### WHITE

☆☆ 1982 CHARDONNAY ($7.00) California. *Clean, simple, subdued, mildly appealing.*

1982 CHARDONNAY ($7.75) 10th Anniversary, California. *Vegetal, tart.*

☆☆ 1983 CHARDONNAY ($7.50) California. *Tart, varietal, simple, no oak.*

☆☆ 1984 CHARDONNAY ($7.50) Arroyo Seco. *Lush, meaty, heavy.*

☆☆ 1984 CHARDONNAY ($7.50) California. *Clean, fresh, varietal, no oak.*

☆☆☆☆ 1984 CHARDONNAY ($10.00) Reserve, Arroyo Seco. *A lovely combination of new oak and crisp but rich varietal fruit. Wente's best Chardonnay ever.*

☆☆ 1985 CHARDONNAY ($5.50) Arroyo Seco. *Clean, simple, crisp, varietal.*

☆ 1985 CHARDONNAY ($7.50) California. *Varietal and clean but flat and uninteresting. No oak. Could age well.*

☆☆☆ 1986 GEWURZTRAMINER ($7.50) Dry, Vintner Grown, Arroyo Seco. *Crisp, clean, varietal complex.*

☆ 1986 GEWURZTRAMINER ($7.50) California. *Clean, simple, hardly any varietal character.*

☆☆☆ 1985 JOHANNISBERG RIESLING ($10.00) December Harvest, Vintner Grown, Arroyo Seco. 7.22% residual sugar. *Lush, deep, fruity, toasty, botrytis.*

☆☆ 1986 SAUVIGNON BLANC ($9.00) Special Selection, Fortney Stark, Chalk Hill. *Soft, sweet pea flavors, fresh, clean, assertively varietal.*

☆☆ 1986 SEMILLON ($7.00) Estate, Livermore. *Soft, ripe, clean, lightly herbal, appealing.*

☆☆ 1986 WHITE TABLE WINE ($5.00) Le Blanc de Blancs, California. *Fresh, soft, fruity, clean and charming.*

### SPARKLING

☆☆☆ 1981 BRUT ($8.95) Monterey. *Fresh, balanced, elegant, very good.*

☆☆ 1982 BRUT ($9.00) Arroyo Seco. 47% *Chardonnay,* 29% *Pinot Noir,* 24% *Pinot Blanc. Clean, crisp, complex, charming.*

### BLANC DE NOIR

☆ 1986 WHITE ZINFANDEL ($5.00) California. *Soft, clean, dull, watery.*

### RED

1979 CABERNET SAUVIGNON ($5.75) 100th Anniversary, California. *Soft and dull, lacking depth.*

1980 CABERNET SAUVIGNON ($6.00) California. *Dark, dank, muddy.*

☆☆ 1978 PETITE SIRAH ($6.25) Centennial Reserve, Estate, Livermore Valley. *Rich, deep, soft.*

☆☆ 1980 PETITE SIRAH ($5.00) Estate, Livermore Valley. *Jammy, big and tannic. Good fruit. Ready to drink.*

☆☆ 1983 ZINFANDEL ($7.00) Special Selection, Raboli, Livermore Valley. *Plummy, spicy, lacking character, attractive but unexciting.*

❧

## West Park Wine Cellars                    NEW YORK
### WHITE
☆☆☆ 1985 CHARDONNAY ($10.00) New York. *Lush, rich, good oak, lovely fruit.*

❧

## West-Whitehill Winery                    WEST VIRGINIA
### RED
☆☆ NV HIGHLAND RED ($4.50) West Virginia. *Clean, decent, snappy fruit.*

❧

## Weston Winery                    IDAHO
### WHITE
☆☆ 1985 CHARDONNAY ($7.50) Barrel Fermented, Idaho. *Rich, earthy, toasty, ripe, fat, lush.*

❧

WESTWOOD *see* Wolterbeek Westwood Winery

## Whaler Vineyards                    MENDOCINO COUNTY
### BLANC DE NOIR
☆☆ 1986 WHITE ZINFANDEL ($5.25) Estate, Mendocino. *Crisp, fresh, strawberry flavors, off-dry.*
### RED
☆☆ 1981 ZINFANDEL ($5.25) Mendocino. *Fruity, fresh and appealing. Drink now.*
☆☆ 1983 ZINFANDEL ($7.00) Estate, Mendocino. *Rich, deep, lush, decent.*
☆☆ 1985 ZINFANDEL ($7.50) Estate, Mendocino. *Crisp, spicy, tart, a bit thin.*

❧

## William Wheeler Winery                    SONOMA COUNTY
### WHITE
☆☆☆ 1982 CHARDONNAY ($10.00) Monterey. *Herbaceous, rich and lovely.*
☆☆☆ 1982 CHARDONNAY ($11.00) Sonoma. *Rich, vinous, oaky yet crisp and fruity.*
☆☆☆ 1983 CHARDONNAY ($10.00) Monterey. *Rich yet crisp and fruity.*
☆☆☆ 1983 CHARDONNAY ($11.00) Sonoma. *Lush, rich, balanced, deep, attractive.*
☆☆☆ 1984 CHARDONNAY ($11.00) Sonoma. *Crisp, clean, balanced, focused, charming.*
☆☆☆ 1985 CHARDONNAY ($13.50) Sonoma. *Crisp, round, fresh, charming and balanced fruit, delicious.*
☆☆☆ 1986 CHARDONNAY ($11.50) Sonoma. *Snappy, fresh, varietal fruit, with nice oak and good balance; lemony finish.*
☆ 1986 SAUVIGNON BLANC ($8.00) Sonoma. *Intense varietal fruit, some bitterness.*
### BLANC DE NOIR
☆☆☆ 1986 WHITE ZINFANDEL ($5.50) Young Vines, Sonoma. *Fresh, balanced, fruity, really lovely.*
☆☆☆ 1987 WHITE ZINFANDEL ($5.50) Young Vines, Sonoma. *Fresh, tangy, bright, varietal fruit, relatively dry.*

## RED

☆☆☆ 1979 CABERNET SAUVIGNON ($7.50) Dry Creek Valley. *40% Merlot. Snappy, balanced, intense, rich. Drink 1990.*

☆☆☆☆ 1980 CABERNET SAUVIGNON ($12.00) Special Reserve, Norse, Dry Creek Valley. *Richly varietal, supple, fruity, superbly structured.*

☆ 1981 CABERNET SAUVIGNON ($9.00) Dry Creek Valley. *Fat, weedy.*

☆☆ 1981 CABERNET SAUVIGNON ($13.50) Private Reserve, Norse, Dry Creek Valley. *Herbal, lush, dense, with good structure. Ready to drink.*

1982 CABERNET SAUVIGNON ($10.00) Dry Creek Valley. *Overwhelmed by vegetal flavors.*

☆ 1982 CABERNET SAUVIGNON ($10.00) Private Reserve, Norse, Dry Creek Valley. *Lush, rich, decent.*

☆☆ 1983 CABERNET SAUVIGNON ($9.00) Dry Creek Valley. *Woody, herbal, earthy, rich flavors, gentle finish. Clean, attractive. Drink 1992.*

☆☆☆ 1984 CABERNET SAUVIGNON ($9.00) Dry Creek Valley. *Lush, rich, herbal, varietal, good structure. Drink 1991.*

❧

## White Oak Vineyards                SONOMA COUNTY

### WHITE

☆☆☆ 1982 CHARDONNAY ($10.00) Sonoma. *Rich, vinous nose, heavy but well balanced; big but lovely.*

☆☆ 1983 CHARDONNAY ($10.00) Sonoma. *Oaky, austere, pleasant, clean.*

☆☆☆ 1984 CHARDONNAY ($10.00) Sonoma. *Soft and complex, with lovely fruit and attractive oak. Well made and nicely balanced.*

☆☆☆ 1985 CHARDONNAY ($10.00) Sonoma. *Big, buttery, brawny, lovely lush texture.*

☆☆☆☆ 1985 CHARDONNAY ($14.50) Meyers LTD Reserve, Alexander Valley. *Lush, sweet new oak, ripe fruit, complex, delicious flavors.*

☆☆ 1986 CHARDONNAY ($15.00) Meyers LTD Reserve, Sonoma. *Clean, crisp, fruity, decent.*

☆☆☆ 1986 SAUVIGNON BLANC ($7.50) Sonoma. *Soft, lush, deep, strong varietal character.*

### RED

☆☆☆ 1984 CABERNET SAUVIGNON ($11.00) Myers, Alexander Valley. *Spicy, crisp, tangy fruit, lovely, clean. Drink 1988.*

☆☆☆ 1982 ZINFANDEL ($6.00) Dry Creek Valley. *Fruity, crisp, tannic, balanced.*

☆☆ 1984 ZINFANDEL ($9.00) Saunders, Dry Creek Valley. *Crisp, lively, fresh, quite nice.*

❧

## Whitehall Lane Winery               NAPA COUNTY

### WHITE

☆☆ 1983 CHARDONNAY ($12.00) Cerro Vista, Napa Valley. *Oaky, decent, lacks focus.*

1984 CHARDONNAY ($12.00) Estate, Napa Valley. *Spicy, soft, flabby, oxidized.*

☆☆ 1986 SAUVIGNON BLANC ($8.00) Estate, Napa Valley. *Sweet pea, varietal flavors, crisp, clean and delightful.*

**RED**

☆☆ NV CABERNET SAUVIGNON ($6.00) Napa Valley. *Minty, clean, decent and simple.*

☆☆ 1980 CABERNET SAUVIGNON ($12.00) Napa Valley. *5% Merlot. Big, intense, tannic, oaky. Drink now.*

☆☆☆ 1981 CABERNET SAUVIGNON ($12.00) Napa Valley. *Big, ripe and overdone but great fruit saves it. Ready to drink.*

☆☆☆ 1982 CABERNET SAUVIGNON ($12.00) Napa Valley. *Lush, deep, clean, nicely structured and varietal. Drink now.*

☆☆☆ 1983 CABERNET SAUVIGNON ($14.00) Napa Valley. *Rich, dense, berried, lush, super. Drink 1989.*

☆☆ 1984 CABERNET SAUVIGNON ($14.00) Napa Valley. *Crisp, good, clean, fresh.*

☆☆☆ 1982 MERLOT ($10.00) Knights Valley. *Dark, rich, intense, with lovely fruit. Ready to drink.*

☆☆☆ 1983 MERLOT ($12.00) Knights Valley. *Lush, fat, fruity, clean, lovely. Drink now.*

☆☆☆ 1984 MERLOT ($14.00) Knights Valley. *Soft, fresh, supple, easy-going and charming.*

☆ 1984 PINOT NOIR ($7.50) Napa Valley. *Meaty, unfocused, decent.*

❧

## Whitford Cellars                          NAPA COUNTY

**WHITE**

☆☆ 1983 COOMBSVILLE VINEYARD CHARDONNAY ($5.50) Napa Valley. *Fruity, clean, some oiliness.*

☆☆☆ 1984 CHARDONNAY ($8.50) Haynes, Napa Valley. *Lush fruit, rich oak, barrel fermentation complexity.*

☆☆☆ 1985 CHARDONNAY ($12.00) Haynes, Napa Valley. *Crisp, balanced, good fruit, toasty oak.*

❧

## Wickham Vineyards                          NEW YORK

**WHITE**

☆ 1984 CAYUGA ($4.50) Finger Lakes. *Neutral, decent.*

1984 CHARDONNAY ($7.00) Finger Lakes. *Overripe, cidery, unpleasant.*

1984 RAVAT ($6.50) Select Late Harvest, Finger Lakes. *4.9% residual sugar. Heavy, vegetal.*

❧

## Widmer's Wine Cellars                          NEW YORK

**WHITE**

☆☆ 1985 SEYVAL BLANC ($6.25) Private Reserve, Finger Lakes. *Soft, off-dry, pleasant.*

**SPARKLING**

☆☆ NV LAKE NIAGARA SEMI-DRY ($4.50) New York. *Fresh, decent, unusual.*

❧

## Wiederkehr Wine Cellars                          ARKANSAS

**WHITE**

1985 MUSCAT DI TANTA ($7.00) Atlus. *5% residual sugar. Fat, unappealing, some spoilage.*

**RED**

☆☆ 1982 CABERNET SAUVIGNON ($6.00) Arkansas Mountain. *Soft, varietal, clean, crisp, quite elegant. Drink now.*

❧

## Hermann J. Wiemer Vineyard                    *NEW YORK*
### WHITE
☆ 1982 CHARDONNAY ($10.00) Estate, Finger Lakes. *Clean but lacking character.*

☆☆☆ 1984 CHARDONNAY ($10.00) Finger Lakes. *Good body, nice fruit, some delicate oak. Very appealing.*

☆☆☆ 1986 CHARDONNAY ($12.00) Finger Lakes. *Crisp, lean and nicely structured. Fresh and fruity, with lovely balance.*

☆☆ 1984 JOHANNISBERG RIESLING ($9.00) Late Harvest, Finger Lakes. *3.5% residual sugar. Sulfur, crisp, rich, deep, clean. Nice fruit, good balance.*

☆☆☆ 1986 JOHANNISBERG RIESLING ($12.00) Late Harvest, Finger Lakes. *3.7% residual sugar. Delicate, apple fruit flavors, fresh and balanced.*

☆☆ 1986 JOHANNISBERG RIESLING ($19.00) Individual Bunch Selected Late Harvest, Estate, Finger Lakes. *375 ml. 10.8% residual sugar. Spicy, apple fruit, rich, complex, slightly oily flavors.*

WILD HORSE *see* Santa Lucia Winery

## J. Wile & Sons                    *NAPA COUNTY*
### WHITE
☆☆☆ 1986 CHARDONNAY ($7.00) Estate, Napa Valley. *Crisp, elegant, complex, with rich oak and lovely fruit.*

☆☆☆ 1986 SAUVIGNON BLANC ($6.00) Estate, Napa Valley. *Spicy, crisp, lively, with good varietal fruit.*
### RED
☆☆ 1985 CABERNET SAUVIGNON ($7.00) Napa Valley. *15% Pinot Noir, 8% Merlot. Soft, clean, complex yet fresh.*

## Williams Selyem Winery                    *SONOMA COUNTY*
### RED
☆☆ 1983 PINOT NOIR ($7.00) Sonoma. *Great structure and varietal complexity; very good.*

## Wimberley Valley Wines                    *TEXAS*
### WHITE
1985 CHARDONNAY ($4.00) Lynn. *Oxidized, sweet, heavy.*

## Windemere                    *SONOMA COUNTY*
### WHITE
☆ 1985 CHARDONNAY ($12.00) MacGregor, Edna Valley. *Heavy, oily, clumsy, decent.*

☆☆☆ 1986 CHARDONNAY ($12.00) MacGregor, Edna Valley. *Crisp, focused, clean, fruity, lean and lively.*

WINDSOR VINEYARDS *see* Rodney Strong Vineyards

## The Wine Group                    *SAN FRANCISCO COUNTY*
### SPARKLING
☆☆ NV FRANZIA SPARKLING ROMAN RASPBERRY ($3.00) California. *Crisp, clean, luscious, lovely berry flavor.*

NV FRANZIA LIGHT CHAMPAGNE ($3.50) California. *Dull.*

☆ NV FRANZIA WHITE ZINFANDEL CHAMPAGNE ($3.50) California. *Fresh, clean, sweet, attractive.*

&

## Winery of the Little Hills — MISSOURI
### WHITE
☆ 1985 VIDAL BLANC ($5.50) Missouri. *Crisp, smokey, decent fruit.*
### SPARKLING
○ 1984 BRUT ($7.00) Missouri. *Bitter and ugly.*

&

## The Winery Rushing — MISSISSIPPI
### ROSE
1984 MUSCADINE ROSE ($5.00) Mississippi. *Bubble gum nose, sweet, heavy, difficult.*

&

## Winterbrook Vineyards — AMADOR COUNTY
### RED
☆☆☆ 1984 ZINFANDEL ($5.50) Amador. *Soft, fruity, clean, lovely.*

&

## Winters Winery — YOLO COUNTY
### RED
☆☆ 1981 PETITE SIRAH ($6.00) California. *Toasty, rich, velvety, clean, attractive.*
☆☆☆ 1979 PINOT NOIR ($6.00) Napa Valley. *Burgundian, rich, deep; very lovely. Beginning to show some age.*
1981 ZINFANDEL ($5.50) Shenandoah Valley, Amador. *Raisiny, dull.*

&

WOLFSPIERRE *see* Fulton Valley Winery

## Wollersheim Winery — WISCONSIN
### RED
1982 DOMAINE RESERVE ($9.00) Wisconsin. *Dull, not much.*

&

## Wolterbeek Westwood Winery — EL DORADO COUNTY
### WHITE
☆☆☆ 1984 WESTWOOD CHARDONNAY ($10.00) El Dorado. *Buttery, lush, toasty, rich, deep.*
☆ 1985 WESTWOOD CHARDONNAY ($10.00) El Dorado. *Earthy, overdone, some nice varietal fruit, but some dirty flavors.*
○ 1986 SAUVIGNON BLANC ($7.00) El Dorado. *Oily, bitter, heavy, no fruit.*
### RED
☆☆ 1984 WESTWOOD PINOT NOIR ($7.50) La Serenidad, Clear Lake. *Balanced, smooth, varietal, clean, charming.*
1985 WESTWOOD PINOT NOIR ($9.50) Haynes, Napa Valley. *Spicy, toasty, crisp, interesting fruit.*

&

WOODBURNE *see* Columbia Winery

## Woodbury Winery — MARIN COUNTY
### WHITE
☆☆☆ 1986 CHARDONNAY ($8.00) Estate, New York. *Crisp, lean, well structured, with toasty oak and some very Burgundian finesse.*

**SPARKLING**
NV   SPUMANTE ($8.00) New York. *Minty, unattractive.*
**RED**
1981 CABERNET SAUVIGNON ($3.00) Signature Selections, Mendocino. *Tannic, thin, drinkable.*
1980 MERLOT ($3.30) Signature Selections, Napa Valley. *Dull, odd flavors.*
**FORTIFIED**
☆ 1979 PORT ($8.00) Alexander Valley. *Pinot Noir. Lush, deep, a bit oily and vegetal.*

&

## Woodside Vineyards     SANTA CLARA COUNTY
**WHITE**
☆☆ 1982 CHARDONNAY ($11.00) Santa Cruz Mountains. *Fresh, clean, snappy.*
☆☆☆ 1982 CHARDONNAY ($11.50) Ventana, Monterey. *Lovely fruit, lush, deep; very attractive.*
☆☆ 1983 CHARDONNAY ($12.00) Santa Cruz Mountains. *Lush, rich, fruity, clean, appealing.*
**RED**
☆☆ 1978 CABERNET SAUVIGNON ($7.50) Fay, Stag's Leap Area, Napa Valley. *Fresh, clean, complex and surprising. Drink now.*
☆☆ 1978 CABERNET SAUVIGNON ($9.00) Santa Cruz Mountains. *Ripe, oaky, forward. Ready to drink.*
1982 CABERNET SAUVIGNON ($8.50) Estate, Santa Cruz Mountains. *Heavy, vegetal, oafish.*

&

## Yakima River Winery     WASHINGTON
**RED**
☆ 1980 CABERNET SAUVIGNON ($10.50) Special Selection, Washington State. *Tea-like, soft and fruity.*

&

## Yamhill Valley Vineyards     OREGON
**WHITE**
☆☆ 1985 CHARDONNAY ($13.00) Oregon. *Green, lean, tight, clean, attractive.*
**RED**
☆☆☆ 1983 PINOT NOIR ($17.00) Yamhill Valley. *Dark, rich, peppery, lovely cherry fruit, supple and lush.*

&

YORK CREEK *see* Belvedere Wine Company

## York Mountain Winery     SAN LUIS OBISPO COUNTY
**WHITE**
☆ 1982 CHARDONNAY ($7.50) MacBride, San Luis Obispo. *Snappy, lemony, lacking depth; decent.*
**RED**
☆☆☆ 1981 ZINFANDEL ($6.95) Estate, San Luis Obispo. *Tart and grapey; with some volatility and great fruit.*

&

ROBERT YOUNG VINEYARDS *see* Belvedere Wine Company

## Yverdon     NAPA COUNTY
**RED**
☆☆ 1978 CABERNET SAUVIGNON ($8.00) Napa Valley. *Earthy and fat, with nice fruit.*

&

## Zaca Mesa Winery            SANTA BARBARA COUNTY

### WHITE

☆☆☆ 1982 CHARDONNAY ($10.00) Santa Barbara. *Soft and oaky, with finesse.*

☆ 1982 CHARDONNAY ($12.00) American Reserve, Santa Barbara. *Heavy, with some vegetal notes, ripe, fruity.*

1983 CHARDONNAY ($9.75) Santa Barbara. *Oily, vegetal, heavy, unattractive.*

☆☆ 1984 CHARDONNAY ($9.75) Santa Barbara. *A bit oily and heavy but varietal and balanced. Quite nice.*

☆☆☆ 1984 CHARDONNAY ($12.75) American Reserve, Santa Barbara. *Ripe, crisp, lovely oak and fruit, good balance.*

☆☆☆ 1985 CHARDONNAY ($10.00) Santa Barbara. *Soft, fresh, with lovely varietal flavors and subtle oak.*

### BLANC DE NOIR

☆☆ 1984 BLANC DE NOIR ($4.50) Central Coast. *Clean, decent, herbaceous.*

### RED

☆☆☆ 1979 CABERNET SAUVIGNON ($8.00) Santa Ynez Valley. *12% Merlot. Lush, deep, intense. Ready now and for a few more years.*

☆ 1980 CABERNET SAUVIGNON ($12.50) Santa Ynez Valley. *Vegetal quality dominates.*

☆ 1981 CABERNET SAUVIGNON ($12.00) American Reserve, Santa Ynez Valley. *Herbal, fruity, concentrated, with some difficult flavors.*

☆ 1982 CABERNET SAUVIGNON ($12.75) American Reserve, Santa Barbara. *Fat, earthy, lush, decent.*

☆☆☆ 1983 CABERNET SAUVIGNON ($8.50) Central Coast. *Crisp, clean, rich fruit, soft, velvety.*

☆☆☆ 1983 CABERNET SAUVIGNON ($12.75) American Reserve, Santa Barbara. *Rich, deep, clean, complex, lovely texture and balance. Drink 1989.*

☆☆☆ 1978 PINOT NOIR ($10.00) Special Selection, Estate, Santa Ynez Valley. *Vinous, complex and rich, with good acid balance. Getting a bit tired.*

○ 1981 PINOT NOIR ($13.25) American Reserve, Santa Ynez Valley. *Smokey, vegetal, cooked.*

1983 PINOT NOIR ($12.75) American Reserve, Santa Barbara. *Grassy, barnyard, bitter, overripe.*

☆☆☆ 1984 PINOT NOIR ($12.75) American Reserve, Santa Barbara. *Clean, elegant, cherry flavors, lovely.*

❧

## ZD Wines                          NAPA COUNTY

### WHITE

☆☆ 1982 CHARDONNAY ($14.00) California. *Big, heavy, fat.*

☆☆☆ 1984 CHARDONNAY ($14.00) California. *Toasty, spicy, lovely texture, ripe, buttery and oaky.*

☆☆☆ 1985 CHARDONNAY ($16.00) California. *Fruity, rich, deep, lush, spicy.*

☆ 1986 CHARDONNAY ($18.00) California. *Big, rich, oily; lacking finesse and charm.*

☆☆☆ 1986 WHITE RIESLING ($10.00) Select Late Harvest, Los Carneros. *375 ml. 13.1% residual sugar. Apricot and honey, rich, silky, well balanced, crisp and delicious.*

## RED

☆ 1979 CABERNET SAUVIGNON ($15.00) California. *24% Merlot, grapes from Napa and Santa Maria. Fat and clumsy.*

☆☆ 1980 CABERNET SAUVIGNON ($12.00) California. *Dense and raisiny but appealing.*

☆☆ 1980 CABERNET SAUVIGNON ($14.00) Napa Valley. *Toasty nose, deep, with complex flavors.*

☆☆ 1981 CABERNET SAUVIGNON ($10.00) Napa Valley. *Intense, heavy, deep. Drink 1989 and beyond.*

1982 CABERNET SAUVIGNON ($12.00) California. *Oaky and vegetal, lush, overripe, dull, clumsy.*

☆☆ 1983 CABERNET SAUVIGNON ($14.00) Napa Valley. *Rich, assertive, herbal fruit, concentrated flavors, long intense finish. Drink 1991.*

☆☆ 1979 MERLOT ($9.50) California (75% Napa, 25% Santa Barbara). *Big berry taste; crude, tannic, appealing. Mellowing nicely.*

☆☆ 1980 PINOT NOIR ($12.50) 66% Madonna, 33% Toribeth, Carneros, Napa. *Deep and rich. Good fruit and complexity.*

☆ 1982 PINOT NOIR ($12.50) Napa Valley. *Earthy, fleshy, dense, tart.*

☆☆ 1983 PINOT NOIR ($12.00) Napa Valley. *Rich, meaty, lush, decent but lacking finesse.*

☆☆☆ 1984 PINOT NOIR ($12.50) Napa Valley. *Spicy, clean, crisp, lovely.*

☆☆ 1980 ZINFANDEL ($7.50) Estate, Napa. *Raisiny and intense.*

ॐ

STEPHEN ZELLERBACH VINEYARD *see* Estate William Baccala

## Ziem Vineyards                                    MARYLAND

## RED

☆☆ NV CHANCELLOR ($5.00) New York State. *Crisp, fresh, with good fruit and great color. Ready to drink.*

☆ NV LANDOT NOIR ($5.00) New York State. *Soft, rich, with good acidity but thin texture.*

ॐ

## ZMoore                                    SONOMA COUNTY

## WHITE

☆☆ 1985 CHARDONNAY ($11.00) California. *Tangy, crisp, balanced, lacking fruit.*

☆☆☆ 1986 GEWURZTRAMINER ($8.25) Sonoma. *Dry, spicy, soft, fresh, delicate, excellent.*

☆☆☆ 1987 QUAFF GEWURZTRAMINER ($5.50) Sonoma. *1.9% residual sugar. Spicy, bright, clean, crisp, delightful.*

ॐ

# *Four-Star Wines*

## WHITE

### Non Varietal

1986 Maurice Carrie Winery MOSCATO CANELLI ($7.00) Temecula.

1986 Robert Pecota Winery MUSCAT BLANC ($8.50) California.

### Chardonnay

1984 Acacia Winery ($14.00) Napa Valley-Carneros.

1983 Au Bon Climat ($20.00) Babcock, Santa Barbara.

1985 Au Bon Climat ($20.00) Reserve, Santa Barbara.

1983 Estate William Baccala ($11.00) Mendocino.

1984 Beringer Vineyards ($15.00) Private Reserve, Estate, Napa Valley.

1985 Beringer Vineyards ($14.50) Private Reserve, Estate, Napa Valley.

1984 The Brander Vineyard ($11.00) Santa Ynez Valley.

1982 Chalone Vineyard ($17.00) Estate, Monterey.

1981 Château St. Jean ($18.00) Robert Young, Alexander Valley.

1985 Château St. Jean ($18.00) Robert Young, Alexander Valley.

1986 Château St. Jean ($18.00) Robert Young, Alexander Valley.

1985 The Christian Brothers ($8.50) Napa Valley.

1984 Clos du Bois Winery ($15.00) Calcaire, Alexander Valley.

1984 Clos du Bois Winery ($18.00) Proprietor's Reserve, Alexander Valley.

1985 B.R. Cohn Winery ($20.75) Olive Hill, Sonoma Valley.

1985 Congress Springs Vineyard ($20.00) Estate, Santa Cruz Mountains.

1984 Cronin Vineyards ($13.50) Alexander Valley.

1984 Cronin Vineyards ($13.50) Ventana, Monterey.

1984 Cronin Vineyards ($14.00) Napa Valley.

1985 Cronin Vineyards ($12.00) Vanumanutagi, Santa Cruz Mountains.

1985 Cronin Vineyards ($14.00) Ventana, Monterey.

1986 Cuvaison Vineyard ($13.50) Napa Valley.

1984 De Loach Vineyards ($12.50) Russian River Valley.

1983 Far Niente Winery ($18.00) Napa Valley.

1985 Forman Vineyard ($18.00) Napa Valley.

1984 Grgich Hills Cellar ($18.00) Napa Valley.

1985 Grgich Hills Cellar ($18.00) Napa Valley.

1985 Groth Vineyards and Winery ($12.00) Napa Valley.

1984 Hacienda Winery ($10.00) Clair de Lune, Sonoma.

1983 Handley Cellars ($12.50) Dry Creek Valley.

1985 Jepson Vineyards ($12.00) Mendocino.

1985 Kalin Cellars ($17.50) Cuvée BL, Potter Valley.

1984 Kistler Vineyards ($15.00) Dutton Ranch, Sonoma.

1986 Kistler Vineyards ($18.00) Kistler, Sonoma Valley.

1985 La Crema ($11.00) California.

1985 La Crema ($18.00) Reserve, California.

1982 Matanzas Creek Winery ($18.00) Estate, Sonoma Valley.

1983 Matanzas Creek Winery ($18.00) Estate, Sonoma Valley.

1984 Matanzas Creek Winery ($15.00) Sonoma Valley.

1985 The Meeker Vineyard ($11.00) Dry Creek Valley.

1981 Robert Mondavi Winery ($20.00) Reserve, Napa Valley.

1985 Robert Mondavi Winery ($22.50) Reserve, Napa Valley.

1984 Monticello Cellars ($12.50) Corley, Napa.

1982 Morgan Winery ($12.00) Cobblestone, Hillside, Monterey.

1985 Morgan Winery ($13.00) Monterey.

1985 Mount Eden Vineyards ($25.00) Santa Cruz Mountains.

1984 Robert Pecota Winery ($13.50) Canepa, Alexander Valley.
1984 Qupé ($9.00) Sierra Madre, San Luis Obispo.
1982 Martin Ray Vineyards ($14.00) Dutton Ranch, Sonoma.
1985 Revere Winery ($15.00) Napa Valley.
1982 St. Francis Vineyards ($14.00) Jacobs, Carneros District, Napa.
1984 St. Francis Vineyards ($12.00) Barrel Select, Estate, Sonoma Valley.
1986 St. Francis Vineyards ($14.00) Barrel Select, Estate, Sonoma Valley.
1985 Sanford Winery ($19.00) Barrel Select, Santa Barbara.
1984 Sequoia Grove Vineyards ($14.00) Estate, Napa Valley.
1982 Simi Winery ($20.00) Reserve, Sonoma.
1981 Sonoma-Cutrer Vineyards ($14.50) Les Pierres, Sonoma Valley.
1983 Sonoma-Cutrer Vineyards ($15.50) Les Pierres, Sonoma Valley.
1984 Sonoma-Cutrer Vineyards ($16.75) Les Pierres, Sonoma Valley.
1985 Sonoma-Cutrer Vineyards ($11.75) Russian River Ranches, Russian River Valley.
1985 Sonoma-Cutrer Vineyards ($17.50) Les Pierres, Sonoma Valley.
1986 Stag's Leap Wine Cellars ($20.00) Reserve, Napa Valley.
1983 Sterling Vineyards ($15.00) Diamond Mountain Ranch, Napa Valley.
1985 Robert Talbott Vineyards ($16.00) Monterey.
1985 Vichon Winery ($15.00) Napa Valley.
1984 Wente Brothers ($10.00) Reserve, Arroyo Seco.
1985 White Oak Vineyards ($14.50) Meyers LTD Reserve, Alexander Valley.

### Fume Blanc
1986 Château St. Jean ($10.50) La Petite Etoile, Russian River Valley.

### Gewurztraminer
1984 Château St. Jean ($14.00) Select Late Harvest, Belle Terre, Anderson Valley.

### Johannisberg Riesling
1986 Freemark Abbey Winery EDELWEIN GOLD ($18.50) Napa Valley.
1985 Hafner Vineyard ($15.00) Special Selection Late Harvest, Estate, Alexander Valley.
1982 Hidden Cellars ($10.00) Late Harvest, Bailey J. Lovin, Mendocino.
1985 Kenwood Vineyards ($10.00) Late Harvest, Estate, Sonoma.
1982 Milano Winery ($25.00) Individual Bunch Select Late Harvet, Ordway's Valley Foothills, Mendocino.
1985 Joseph Phelps Vineyards ($11.75) Late Harvest, Napa Valley.

### Sauvignon Blanc
1986 Clos du Bois Winery ($7.50) Alexander Valley.
1986 Kendall-Jackson Vineyards & Winery ($11.00) Jackson, Lake.
1986 Kenwood Vineyards ($8.75) Sonoma Valley.
1985 Philip Togni Vineyard ($10.00) Napa Valley.

### Scheurebe
1982 Joseph Phelps Vineyards ($15.00) Special Select Late Harvest, Napa Valley.
1985 Joseph Phelps Vineyards ($15.00) Select Late Harvest, Napa Valley.

### Symphony
1986 Château DeBaun ($10.50) Theme, Sonoma.
1986 Château DeBaun ($12.00) Finale, Sonoma.

### White Riesling
1986 Château Morrisette Winery ($6.25) Virginia.

## SPARKLING
### Non Varietal
Domaine Mum BRUT ($14.50) Cuvée Napa, Napa Valley.
1982 Robert Hunter BRUT DE NOIRS ($13.50) Sonoma.

## RED
### Non Varietal

1985 Bonny Doon Vineyard LE CIGARE VOLANT ($12.50) California

1982 Carmenet Vineyard CARMENET RED ($16.00) Sonoma Valley.

1981 Clos du Bois Winery MARLSTONE ($16.00) Alexander Valley.

1985 Dominus DOMINUS ($35.00) Estate, Napa Valley.

1985 Flora Springs Wine Company TRILOGY ($20.00) Napa Valley.

1983 Freemark Abbey Winery CABERNET BOSCHE ($18.00) Napa Valley.

1983 Merryvale Vineyards RED TABLE WINE ($19.50) Napa Valley.

1983 Joseph Phelps Vineyards INSIGNIA ($25.00) Napa Valley.

1985 Preston Vineyards SIRAH SYRAH ($9.50) Estate, Dry Creek Valley.

### Cabernet Sauvignon

1984 Acacia Winery ($15.00) Napa Valley.

1980 Belvedere Wine Company ROBERT YOUNG VINEYARDS ($12.00) Sonoma.

1984 Belvedere Wine Company ROBERT YOUNG VINEYARDS ($12.00) Alexander Valley.

1978 Beringer Vineyards ($22.00) Private Reserve, Lemmon Ranch, Napa Valley.

1980 Beringer Vineyards ($20.00) Private Reserve, Lemmon-Chabot, Napa Valley.

1981 Beringer Vineyards ($25.00) Lemmon-Chabot, Napa Valley.

1982 Beringer Vineyards ($18.00) Private Reserve, Napa Valley.

1981 Buena Vista Winery ($18.00) Special Selection, Estate, Sonoma Valley-Carneros.

1978 Burgess Cellars ($16.00) Vintage Selection, Napa Valley.

1979 Caymus Vineyards ($30.00) Special Selection, Estate, Napa Valley.

1980 Caymus Vineyards ($12.50) Estate, Napa Valley.

1981 Caymus Vineyards ($12.50) Estate, Napa Valley.

1981 Caymus Vineyards ($35.00) Special Selection, Napa Valley.

1982 Caymus Vineyards ($35.00) Special Selection, Napa Valley.

1983 Caymus Vineyards ($15.00) Napa Valley.

1984 Caymus Vineyards ($12.00) Cuvée, Napa Valley.

1980 Chappellet Vineyard ($18.00) Napa Valley.

1983 Château Montelena Winery ($18.00) Estate, Napa Valley.

1979 Château St. Jean ($17.00) Wildwood, Sonoma Valley.

1981 Clos du Bois Winery ($9.00) Alexander Valley.

1980 Clos du Val ($12.50) Napa Valley.

1981 Clos du Val ($12.50) Napa Valley.

1984 Conn Creek Winery ($25.00) Private Reserve, Collins, Napa Valley.

1982 Cosentino Wine Company CRYSTAL VALLEY CELLARS ($9.50) Reserve Edition, North Coast.

1982 Diamond Creek Vineyards ($20.00) Volcanic Hill, Napa Valley.

1983 Diamond Creek Vineyards ($20.00) Red Rock Terrace, Napa Valley.

1983 Diamond Creek Vineyards ($20.00) Volcanic Hill, Napa Valley.

1984 Diamond Creek Vineyards ($25.00) Red Rock Terrace, Napa Valley.

1985 Diamond Creek Vineyards ($30.00) Red Rock Terrace, Napa Valley.

1982 Duckhorn Vineyards ($15.00) Napa Valley.

1983 Duckhorn Vineyards ($16.00) Napa Valley.

1979 Dunn Vineyards ($12.00) Napa Valley.

1980 Dunn Vineyards ($12.50) Napa Valley.

1981 Dunn Vineyards ($12.50) Howell Mountain-Napa Valley.

1982 Dunn Vineyards ($12.50) Napa Valley.

1982 Dunn Vineyards ($14.00) Howell Mountain.

1983 Dunn Vineyards ($18.00) Napa Valley.

1983 Far Niente Winery ($25.00) Estate, Napa Valley.

1984 Forman Vineyard ($16.50) Napa Valley.

1984 Frog's Leap Winery ($12.00) Napa Valley.

1984 Fulton Valley Winery STEINER ($15.00) Wolfspierre Vineyards, Steiner, Sonoma Mountain.

1982 Groth Vineyards and Winery ($13.00) Napa Valley.

1981 Gundlach-Bundschu Winery ($12.00) Batto Ranch, Sonoma Valley.

1978 Heitz Wine Cellars ($20.00) Bella Oaks, Napa Valley.

1979 Heitz Wine Cellars ($30.00) Martha's, Napa Valley.

1982 Heitz Wine Cellars ($35.00) Martha's, Napa Valley.

1980 William Hill Winery ($18.00) Napa Valley.

1982 William Hill Winery ($15.00) Gold Label, Napa Valley.

1982 Inglenook Napa Valley ($18.50) Reserve Cask, Estate, Napa Valley.

1981 Iron Horse Vineyards ($13.50) Estate, Green Valley, Sonoma.

1983 Kenwood Vineyards ($30.00) Artist Series, Sonoma Valley.

1984 Kenwood Vineyards ($16.00) Jack London, Sonoma Valley.

1984 Kenwood Vineyards ($30.00) Artist Series, Sonoma Valley.

1981 Lakespring Winery ($11.00) Napa Valley.

1982 Lakespring Winery ($14.00) Napa Valley.

1981 Laurel Glen Vineyard ($12.50) Estate, Sonoma Mountain.

1985 Laurel Glen Vineyard ($18.00) Estate, Sonoma Mountain.

1984 Livingston Vineyards ($18.00) Moffett, Napa Valley.

1978 Robert Mondavi Winery ($40.00) Reserve, Napa Valley.

1980 Robert Mondavi Winery OPUS ONE ($50.00) Napa Valley.

1981 Robert Mondavi Winery OPUS ONE ($50.00) Napa Valley.

1982 Robert Mondavi Winery ($35.00) Reserve, Napa Valley.

1982 Robert Mondavi Winery OPUS ONE ($50.00) Napa Valley.

1983 Robert Mondavi Winery ($11.75) Napa Valley.

1983 Robert Mondavi Winery ($30.00) Reserve, Napa Valley.

1983 Robert Mondavi Winery OPUS ONE ($50.00) Napa Valley.

1980 Monterey Peninsula Winery ($25.00) Monterey.

1980 Monticello Cellars ($9.75) Napa Valley.

1982 Monticello Cellars ($14.50) Corley Reserve, Cope, Napa Valley.

1984 Monticello Cellars ($10.75) Jefferson Cuvée, Napa Valley.

1984 Monticello Cellars ($18.50) Corley Reserve, Napa Valley.

1981 Newton Vineyard ($12.50) Estate, Napa Valley.

1983 Newton Vineyard ($9.00) Napa Valley.

1981 Robert Pepi Winery ($14.00) Vine Hill Ranch, Napa Valley.

1983 Joseph Phelps Vineyards ($25.00) Eisele, Napa Valley.

1985 Plam Vineyards & Winery ($12.00) Napa Valley.

1981 Martin Ray Vineyards ($16.50) Steltzner, Napa Valley.

1984 Ridge Vineyards ($40.00) Monte Bello, California.

1985 Ridge Vineyards ($30.00) Monte Bello, California.

1983 St. Andrews Winery ($7.50) Glendale Ranch, Napa Valley.

1980 St. Clement Vineyards ($12.50) Napa Valley.

1981 St. Clement Vineyards ($12.50) Napa Valley.

1982 Silver Mountain Vineyards ($19.00) Alexander Valley.

1982 Silver Mountain Vineyards ($19.00) Napa Valley.

1983 Silver Oak Wine Cellars ($21.00) Napa Valley.

1979 Simi Winery ($19.00) Reserve, Alexander Valley.

1979 Smith-Madrone ($14.00) Estate, Napa Valley.

1982 Spottswoode Winery ($18.00) Estate, Napa Valley.

1984 Spottswoode Winery ($25.00) Estate, Napa Valley.

1978 Stag's Leap Wine Cellars ($35.00) Cask 23, Napa Valley.

1980 Stag's Leap Wine Cellars ($11.00) Napa Valley.

1981 Stag's Leap Wine Cellars ($15.00) Stag's Leap, Napa Valley.

1982 Sterling Vineyards ($15.00) Diamond Mountain Ranch, Napa Valley.

1980 Stonegate Winery ($8.50) Vail Vista, Alexander Valley.

1979 Stuermer Winery LOWER LAKE WINERY ($12.00) Devoto, Lake.

1984 Philip Togni Vineyard ($18.00) Napa Valley.

1982 Tyland Vineyards MENDOCINO ESTATE ($4.25) Estate, Mendocino.

1981 Vichon Winery ($12.75) Fay and Eisle, Napa Valley.

1978 Villa Mt. Eden Winery ($12.00) Estate, Napa Valley.

1981 Villa Mt. Eden Winery ($20.00) Reserve, Estate, Napa Valley.

1980 William Wheeler Winery ($12.00) Special Reserve, Norse, Dry Creek Valley.

### Landot Noir

1982 Baldwin Vineyards ($6.00) New York.

### Merlot

1984 Buena Vista Winery ($14.50) Private Reserve, Carneros.

1983 Clos du Val ($14.00) Napa Valley.

1984 Cuvaison Vineyard ($13.50) Anniversary Reserve, Napa Valley.

1984 Dehlinger Winery ($12.00) Sonoma.

1981 Duckhorn Vineyards ($12.50) Three Palms, Napa Valley.

1981 Duckhorn Vineyards ($13.00) Napa Valley.

1982 Duckhorn Vineyards ($13.00) Napa Valley.

1983 Duckhorn Vineyards ($15.00) Napa Valley.

1983 Duckhorn Vineyards ($18.00) Three Palms, Napa Valley.

1984 Duckhorn Vineyards ($15.00) Napa Valley.

1984 Duckhorn Vineyards ($18.00) Three Palms, Napa Valley.

1985 Duckhorn Vineyards ($18.00) Three Palms, Napa Valley.

1983 Gundlach-Bundschu Winery ($12.00) Estate, Sonoma Valley.

1985 Gundlach-Bundschu Winery ($12.00) Rhinefarm, Estate, Sonoma Valley.

1982 Robert Keenan Winery ($12.50) Napa Valley.

1983 Robert Keenan Winery ($15.00) Napa Valley.

1984 Robert Keenan Winery ($16.00) Napa Valley.

1985 Matanzas Creek Winery ($12.50) Sonoma.

1985 Newton Vineyard ($12.00) Napa Valley.

1979 Rutherford Hill Winery ($9.25) Napa Valley.

1983 Shafer Vineyards ($10.00) Napa Valley.

1979 Sterling Vineyards ($12.00) Estate, Napa Valley.

### Pinot Noir

1980 Acacia Winery ($15.00) Madonna, Napa Valley-Carneros.

1980 Acacia Winery ($15.00) St. Clair, Napa Valley-Carneros.

1982 Acacia Winery ($15.00) St. Clair, Napa Valley-Carneros.

1982 Acacia Winery ($15.00) Winery Lake, Napa Valley-Carneros.

1983 Acacia Winery ($15.00) St. Clair, Napa Valley-Carneros.

1983 Acacia Winery ($15.50) Madonna, Napa Valley-Carneros.

1984 Acacia Winery ($11.00) Napa Valley.

1984 Acacia Winery ($16.00) St. Clair, Napa Valley.

1981 Belvedere Wine Company WINERY LAKE ($12.00) Estate, Los Carneros.

1984 Calera Wine Company ($25.00) Selleck, California.

1977 Carneros Creek Winery ($12.50) Napa Valley.
1983 Carneros Creek Winery ($16.00) Napa Valley.
1981 Chalone Vineyard ($28.00) Reserve, Estate, Chalone.
1984 Thomas Fogarty Winery ($15.00) Winery Lake, Napa Valley.
1982 La Crema ($10.00) Porter Creek, Russian River Valley.
1984 La Crema ($14.00) California.
1985 Robert Mondavi Winery ($18.00) Reserve, Napa Valley.

### Red Table Wine
1984 Merryvale Vineyards ($18.00) Napa Valley.

### Zinfandel
1985 Clos du Val ($12.00) Napa Valley.
1985 Fetzer Vineyards ($5.00) Lake.
1982 Grgich Hills Cellar ($10.00) Alexander Valley.
1984 Grgich Hills Cellar ($10.00) Alexander Valley.
1984 Kendall-Jackson Vineyards & Winery ($8.00) Mariah, Mendocino.
1984 Lytton Springs Winery ($8.00) Sonoma.
1985 Lytton Springs Winery ($8.00) Sonoma.
1984 Nalle ($8.00) Dry Creek Valley.
1985 Nalle ($8.00) Dry Creek Valley.
1985 Quivera ($7.00) Dry Creek Valley.
1985 Ravenswood ($10.00) Dickerson, Napa Valley.
1984 Rosenblum Cellars ($9.00) Reserve, Napa Valley.
1985 Shenandoah Vineyards ($7.50) Special Reserve, Amador.
1983 Storybook Mountain Vineyards ($8.00) Napa Valley.
1983 Storybook Mountain Vineyards ($12.50) Estate Reserve, Napa Valley.
1980 Joseph Swan Vineyards ($9.00) Sonoma.

### FORTIFIED
### Non Varietal
1984 Quady Winery ELYSIUM ($11.00) California.

ঽ

# Good-Value Wines

### WHITE
### Non Varietal
☆☆     Almaden Vineyards GOLDEN CHABLIS ($2.50) California.
☆☆     Almaden Vineyards MONTEREY CHABLIS ($2.50) Monterey.
☆☆ 1985 Buena Vista Winery CHAARBLANC ($4.75) Carneros.
☆☆☆ 1985 Buena Vista Winery SPICELING ($5.50) Carneros.
☆☆ 1985 Callaway Vineyard and Winery VIN BLANC ($4.75) California.
☆☆☆ 1986 Carmenet Vineyard COLOMBARD ($5.00) Old Vines, Barrel Fermented, Cyril Saviez, Napa Valley.
☆☆ 1985 Château Julien EMERALD BAY MONTONNAY ($3.50) Monterey.
☆☆☆ 1985 Château St. Jean VIN BLANC ($4.00) Sonoma.
☆☆     Château Ste. Michelle FARRON RIDGE CELLARS WHITE TABLE WINE ($3.10) Washington.
☆☆☆     The Christian Brothers PREMIUM WHITE ($4.00) California.
☆☆ 1986 Christophe Vineyards JOLIESSE ($4.75) California.
☆☆☆     Claiborne & Churchill Vintners EDELZWICKER ($4.75) Paragon, Edna Valley.
☆☆     Clos du Val WHITE TABLE WINE ($5.00) California.
☆☆☆ 1985 Ferrara Winery MUSCAT OF ALEXANDRIA ($6.35) San Diego.
☆☆     E. & J. Gallo Winery RHINE WINE ($1.75) California.

☆☆ E. & J. Gallo Winery CHABLIS BLANC ($2.00) California.

☆☆☆ E. & J. Gallo Winery RESERVE CHABLIS ($2.60) California.

☆☆ Gundlach-Bundschu Winery SONOMA WHITE WINE ($4.00) Sonoma Valley.

☆☆☆ Haywood Winery LINGUINI WHITE ($4.50) Sonoma.

☆☆ 1985 Hidden Cellars BON FUME ($5.00) Mendocino.

☆☆ 1985 Husch Vineyards LA RIBERA BLANC ($5.00) Estate, Mendocino.

☆☆ 1984 Jekel Vineyard ARROYO BLANC ($6.50) Monterey.

☆☆ Knapp Farms WINDMILL CHABLIS ($4.00) Finger Lakes.

☆☆ 1985 Mirassou Vineyards MONTEREY RIESLING ($5.50) Monterey.

☆☆ 1986 Robert Mondavi Winery ROBERT MONDAVI WHITE ($4.00) California.

☆☆ 1985 The Monterey Vineyards CLASSIC WHITE ($4.00) Monterey.

☆☆ 1986 The Monterey Vineyards CLASSIC WHITE ($4.00) Monterey.

☆☆ 1985 Oak Ridge Vineyards WHITE BURGUNDY ($5.00) California.

☆☆ 1985 Olson Vineyards Winery GLACIER WHITE ($4.50) California.

☆☆ Orleans Hill Vinicultural Corporation CAJUN WHITE ($4.50) California.

☆☆ 1985 Pat Paulsen Vineyards REFRIGERATOR WHITE ($4.25) Sonoma.

☆☆☆ 1986 Pat Paulsen Vineyards REFRIGERATOR WHITE ($4.00) Sonoma.

☆☆ 1985 The R. H. Phillips Vineyards NIGHT HARVEST CUVEE ($3.75) Dunnigan Hills, Yolo.

☆☆ Pindar Vineyards PROPRIETOR'S BLEND ($6.00) Long Island.

☆☆ 1986 Prince Michel Vineyards WHITE BURGUNDY ($6.00) Virgina.

☆☆ 1986 Raymond Vineyard & Cellar VINTAGE SELECT WHITE ($5.00) California.

☆☆ Taylor California Cellars RHINE ($2.50) California.

☆☆☆ Trefethen Vineyards Winery ESCHOL WHITE ($5.50) Napa Valley.

☆☆ Ventana Vineyards Winery WHITE TABLE WINE ($4.00) Monterey.

### Aurora
☆☆ 1984 Wagner Vineyards ($4.50) Finger Lakes.

### Cayuga
☆☆ 1984 Glenora Wine Cellars ($5.25) Spring Ledge Farms, Finger Lakes.

☆☆ 1985 Glenora Wine Cellars ($4.75) Spring Ledge Farms, Finger Lakes.

### Chardonnay
☆☆☆ 1985 Alexander Valley Fruit & Trading Company ($8.00) Alexander Valley.

☆ 1985 Almaden Vineyards ($5.00) Monterey

☆☆☆ 1984 Artisan Wines ($8.75) Napa Valley.

☆☆ 1982 Estate William Baccala STEPHEN ZELLERBACH VINEYARD ($6.00) Alexander Valley.

☆☆☆ 1986 Estate William Baccala STEPHEN ZELLERBACH VINEYARD ($6.00) California.

☆☆☆ 1984 Bandiera Winery ($6.25) Sonoma.

☆☆ 1985 Belvedere Wine Company ($4.75) Discovery Series, Napa Valley.

☆☆☆ 1985 Beringer Vineyards NAPA RIDGE ($5.75) California.

☆☆ 1986 Beringer Vineyards NAPA RIDGE ($5.75) North Coast.

☆☆ 1983 Byrd Vineyards ($7.50) Estate, Catoctin.

☆☆☆ 1984 Castoro Cellars ($6.75) San Luis Obispo.

☆☆ 1985 Caymus Vineyards LIBERTY SCHOOL ($6.00) Lot 7, California.

☆☆ 1986 Caymus Vineyards LIBERTY SCHOOL ($6.00) Lot 10, California.

☆☆ 1983 Chalk Hill Winery ($7.00) Sonoma.

☆☆ 1984 Chalk Hill Winery ($8.00) Sonoma.

☆☆☆ 1985 Chalk Hill Winery ($8.00) Sonoma.

☆☆☆ 1985 Château Diana ($6.50) Napa Valley.

☆☆☆ 1986 Château Ste. Michelle COLUMBIA CREST ($8.00) Columbia Valley.

☆☆☆ 1984 Christophe Vineyards ($5.50) California.

☆☆ 1983 Clos du Bois Winery RIVER OAKS VINEYARDS ($6.00) Sonoma.

☆☆ 1984 Clos du Bois Winery ($6.00) Alexander Valley.

☆☆ 1984 Clos du Bois Winery RIVER OAKS VINEYARDS ($6.00) Alexander Valley.

☆☆☆ 1985 Clos du Bois Winery RIVER OAKS VINEYARDS ($6.25) Sonoma.

☆☆☆ 1983 Colony ($6.00) Sonoma.

☆☆☆ 1984 Colony ($6.00) Gauer Ranch, Alexander Valley.

☆☆ 1986 Colony NORTH COAST CELLARS ($6.00) North Coast.

☆☆☆ 1983 Concannon Vineyard ($8.00) Selected Vineyards, 38% Mistral, 62% Tepusquet, California.

☆☆ 1984 Corbett Canyon Vineyards ($6.00) Coastal Classic, Central Coast.

☆☆ 1985 Corbett Canyon Vineyards ($6.00) Coastal Classic, California.

☆☆ 1986 Domaine St. Georges ($4.50) Sonoma.

☆ 1983 J. Patrick Doré ($4.75) California.

☆☆ 1984 J. Patrick Doré ($4.00) Santa Maria Valley.

☆☆☆ 1984 J. Patrick Doré ($5.50) Signature Selection, Santa Maria Valley.

☆☆☆ 1984 Ehlers Lane Winery ($13.00) Napa Valley.

☆☆ 1983 Fetzer Vineyards ($6.50) Sundial, Mendocino.

☆☆ 1984 Fetzer Vineyards ($6.50) Sundial, Mendocino.

☆☆☆ 1984 Fetzer Vineyards ($8.00) Barrel Select, California.

☆☆ 1985 Fetzer Vineyards ($6.50) Sundial, Mendocino.

☆☆ 1986 Fetzer Vineyards ($6.50) Sundial, Mendocino.

☆☆ 1983 Fisher Vineyards EVERYDAY ($8.50) Sonoma.

☆☆☆ 1984 Fisher Vineyards EVERYDAY ($8.50) Sonoma.

☆☆☆ 1985 Five Palms Winery ($8.00) Napa Valley.

☆☆ 1985 Franciscan Vineyards ESTANCIA ($6.00) Alexander Valley.

☆☆☆ 1986 Gan Eden Winery ($7.50) Alexander Valley.

☆☆☆ 1984 Geyser Peak Winery ($7.00) Sonoma Valley-Carneros.

☆☆☆ 1985 Geyser Peak Winery ($7.00) Sonoma Valley-Carneros.

☆☆☆ 1984 Glen Ellen Winery ($7.00) Lot II, Sonoma Valley.

☆☆ 1985 Glen Ellen Winery ($5.00) Proprietor's Reserve, California.

☆☆ 1984 William Hill Winery ($6.00) Silver Label, Napa Valley.

☆☆ 1985 Inglenook Napa Valley ($5.00) Napa Valley.

☆☆ 1985 Jaeger Family Wine Company HUNTER ASHBY ($6.00) Napa Valley.

☆☆ 1985 Kenworthy Vineyards ($7.00) Stonebarn, El Dorado.

☆☆ 1985 Konocti Winery ($6.50) Lake.

☆☆☆ 1986 Konocti Winery ($6.50) Lake.

☆☆ 1985 Landmark Vineyards CYPRESS LANE VINEYARDS ($6.00) California.

☆☆☆ 1985 Lazy Creek Winery ($8.75) Estate, Anderson Valley.

☆☆ 1985 Long Vineyards ($4.50) California.

☆☆ 1986 M. Marion & Company ($6.00) California.

☆☆ 1985 Meier's Wine Cellars ($5.00) Isle St. George.

☆☆ 1983 Michtom Vineyards ($7.00) Alexander Valley.

☆☆☆ 1984 Moceri Winery ($5.00) San Bernabe, Monterey.

☆☆ 1985 Moceri Winery ($5.00) Monterey.

☆☆☆ 1984 The Monterey Vineyards ($7.00) Monterey.

☆☆☆ 1985 The Monterey Vineyards ($7.00) Monterey.

☆☆☆ 1984 Monticello Cellars LLORDS AND ELWOOD WINE CELLARS ($8.00) The Rare, Napa Valley.

☆☆ 1984 Navarro Vineyards and Winery ($5.50) Vin Blanc, Mendocino.

☆☆ 1984 Orleans Hill Vinicultural Corporation ($6.75) Clarksburg.

☆☆☆ 1984 J. Pedroncelli Winery ($7.75) Dry Creek Valley.

☆☆ 1986 The R. H. Phillips Vineyards ($6.00) California.

☆☆ 1984 Raymond Vineyard & Cellar LA BELLE ($6.00) California.

☆☆ 1985 Raymond Vineyard & Cellar LA BELLE ($5.00) California.

☆☆ 1984 Round Hill Cellars ($4.75) California.

☆☆☆ 1984 Round Hill Cellars HOUSE ($5.00) California

☆☆ 1984 Round Hill Cellars ($7.50) Napa Valley Reserve, Napa Valley.

☆☆ 1985 Round Hill Cellars HOUSE ($5.00) California.

☆☆☆ 1985 St. Andrews Winery ($7.50) Napa Valley.

☆☆ 1984 San Martín Winery ($7.00) Central Coast.

☆☆ 1986 San Martín Winery CRYSTAL CREEK ($4.00) Monterey.

☆☆ 1985 Seghesio Winery ($5.50) California.

☆☆☆ 1985 Shafer Vineyards CHASE CREEK ($7.00) Napa Valley.

☆☆ 1986 Taft Street Winery ($1.75) Sonoma.

☆☆ 1984 Ivan Tamas ($6.00) 40% Tepusquet, 30% Santa Maria Hills, 30% Newhall, Central Coast.

☆☆ 1985 Taylor California Cellars GREAT WESTERN WINERY ($6.00) Special Selection, Estate, Finger Lakes.

☆☆☆ 1985 Tyland Vineyards MENDOCINO ESTATE ($5.00) Mendocino.

☆☆☆ 1984 Ventana Vineyards Winery ($7.50) Gold Stripe Selection, Monterey.

☆☆☆ 1985 Weinstock Cellars ($6.50) Alexander Valley.

☆☆ 1985 Wente Brothers ($5.50) Arroyo Seco.

☆☆ 1983 Whitford Cellars COOMBSVILLE VINEYARD ($5.50) Napa Valley.

☆☆☆ 1984 Whitford Cellars ($8.50) Haynes, Napa Valley.

☆☆☆ 1986 J. Wile & Sons ($7.00) Estate, Napa Valley.

### Chenin Blanc

☆☆☆ 1986 Granite Springs Winery ($5.00) El Dorado.

☆☆ 1985 Raymond Vineyard & Cellar LA BELLE ($3.00) Napa Valley.

### French Colombard

☆☆ 1984 Chalone Vineyard GAVILAN ($4.00) Cyril Saviez, Monterey.

☆☆ E. & J. Gallo Winery ($2.30) California.

### Fume Blanc

☆☆☆ 1986 Château St. Jean ($6.00) Sonoma.

☆☆ 1985 Jaeger Family Wine Company HUNTER ASHBY ($4.00) Napa.

☆☆☆ 1986 Konocti Winery ($5.50) Lake.

☆☆ 1986 Round Hill Cellars HOUSE ($5.00) Napa Valley.

### Gewurztraminer
☆☆ 1986 Ste. Chapelle Winery ($4.50) Idaho.
☆☆☆ 1987 ZMoore QUAFF ($5.50) Sonoma.

### Johannisberg Riesling
☆☆☆ 1986 Château Ste. Michelle ($5.50) Washington.

### Muller-Thurgau
☆☆☆ 1985 Château Benoit Winery ($6.00) Oregon.

### Ravat
☆☆ 1984 Wagner Vineyards ($4.50) Special Selection, Finger Lakes.

### Sauvignon Blanc
☆☆ 1986 Artisan Wines CRUVINET ($5.00) 51% Russian River Valley, 49% Alexander Valley.
☆☆ 1986 Belvedere Wine Company ($4.00) Discovery Series, Sonoma.
☆☆☆ 1986 Bergfeld Wine Cellars ($5.00) Reserve, Estate, Napa Valley.
☆☆☆ 1986 Christophe Vineyards ($5.75) California.
☆☆ 1985 Colony NORTH COAST CELLARS ($5.00) North Coast.
☆☆ 1986 Corbett Canyon Vineyards ($6.00) Coastal Classic, California.
☆☆ 1985 J. Patrick Doré ($4.00) California Florals, California.
☆☆ 1984 E. & J. Gallo Winery ($3.50) California.
☆☆ 1985 Herbert Vineyards ($5.00) El Dorado.
☆☆ 1986 Landmark Vineyards CYPRESS LANE VINEYARDS ($4.50) California.
☆☆☆ 1986 Mariposa Wines ($5.00) Lake.
☆☆☆ 1986 The Mountain View Winery ($5.00) Mendocino.
☆☆☆ 1986 The R. H. Phillips Vineyards ($4.25) Night Harvest, Dunnigan Hills, Yolo.
☆☆☆ 1986 Preston Vineyards ($6.75) Cuvée de Fumé, Dry Creek Valley.
☆☆ 1985 Raymond Vineyard & Cellar LA BELLE ($4.75) California.
☆☆☆ 1986 San Martín Winery CRYSTAL CREEK ($3.50) Mendocino.

### Semillon
☆☆ 1985 Château Ste. Michelle ($5.50) Washington.
☆☆ 1986 Château Ste. Michelle COLUMBIA CREST ($5.00) Columbia Valley.

### Seyval Blanc
☆☆☆ 1985 Heron Hill Vineyards ($5.00) Ingle, Finger Lakes.
☆☆ 1985 Lucas Vineyards ($4.75) Finger Lakes.
☆☆☆ 1986 Oakencroft Vineyard and Winery ($6.00) Virginia.
☆☆ 1985 Valley Vineyards CHABLIS ($3.75) Ohio River Valley.

### White Riesling
☆☆☆☆ 1986 Château Morrisette Winery ($6.25) Virginia.
☆☆☆ 1986 Konocti Winery ($5.50) Lake.
☆☆☆ 1984 Preston Wine Cellars ($5.75) Late Harvest, Collector Series, Preston, Washington.

### White Table Wine
☆☆ 1984 Almaden Vineyards CHARLES LEFRANC CELLARS ($3.40) California.
☆☆ 1986 Arciero Winery ($3.50) La Venera, Central Coast.
☆☆☆ 1986 Château St. Jean ($4.00) Sonoma.
☆☆ 1986 Wente Brothers ($5.00) Le Blanc de Blancs, California.

### SPARKLING
#### Non Varietal
☆☆ Almaden Vineyards GOLDEN CHAMPAGNE ($4.00) California.

☆☆ Almaden Vineyards BLUSH CHAMPAGNE ($5.25) California.

☆☆ Cosentino Wine Company CRYSTAL VALLEY CELLARS EXTRA DRY ($6.50) California.

☆☆☆ E. & J. Gallo Winery ANDRE PINK CHAMPAGNE ($4.00) California.

☆☆ E. & J. Gallo Winery ANDRE BRUT ($4.20) California.

☆☆☆ E. & J. Gallo Winery BALLATORE SPUMANTE ($4.50) California.

☆☆ Guild Wineries COOK'S CHAMPAGNE CELLARS AMERICAN CHAMPAGNE, IMPERIAL ($5.00) California.

☆☆ Guild Wineries COOK'S CHAMPAGNE CELLAR AMERICAN WHITE ZINFANDEL ($5.75) California.

☆☆ The Wine Group FRANZIA SPARKLING ROMAN RASPBERRY ($3.00) California.

## BLANC DE NOIR
### Non Varietal

☆☆☆ 1986 Baily Vineyard and Winery CABERNET BLANC ($5.00) Temecula.

☆☆☆ 1986 Buena Vista Winery STEELHEAD RUN ($4.75) Blanc de Pinot Noir, Carneros.

☆☆☆ 1986 J. Carey Cellars CABERNET BLANC ($5.50) Estate, Santa Ynez Valley.

☆☆☆ 1986 Fetzer Vineyards BEL ARBRES WHITE MERLOT ($5.00) California.

☆☆☆ 1986 Fetzer Vineyards BEL ARBRES WHITE PINOT NOIR ($5.00) Mendocino.

☆☆☆ 1986 Fritz Cellars PINOT NOIR BLANC ($4.75) Russian River Valley.

☆☆ 1986 La Buena Vida Vineyards SPRINGTOWN MIST ($4.00) Parker.

☆☆☆ 1986 Mirassou Vineyards PASTEL ($5.00) California.

### Gamay Beaujolais

☆☆ 1986 Almaden Vineyards CHARLES LEFRANC CELLARS ($4.00) Nouveau Blanc, Sage Ranch, Paicines.

### White Cabernet Sauvignon

☆☆☆ 1986 Tepusquet ($4.00) Paso Robles.

### White Riesling

☆☆ 1987 Shenandoah Vineyards ($5.00) Amador Tountyey.

### White Zinfandel

☆☆☆ 1986 Buehler Vineyards ($5.00) Napa Valley.

☆☆☆ 1987 Fetzer Vineyards ($5.00) California.

☆☆☆ 1986 Karly ($5.25) Amador.

☆☆☆ 1986 J. Lohr Winery ($4.50) California.

☆☆☆ 1986 Martin Brothers Winery ($5.50) Paso Robles.

☆☆☆ 1986 J. Pedroncelli Winery ($4.50) Sonoma.

☆☆ 1986 San Martin Winery CRYSTAL CREEK ($3.00) Central Coast.

☆☆☆ 1987 Santa Barbara Winery ($6.00) Central Coast.

☆☆☆ 1986 Shenandoah Vineyards ($5.00) Amador.

☆☆☆ 1986 William Wheeler Winery ($5.50) Young Vines, Sonoma.

☆☆☆ 1987 William Wheeler Winery ($5.50) Young Vines, Sonoma.

## ROSE
### Non Varietal

☆☆ Crown Regal Wine Cellars KESSER KOSHER CONCORD ($3.00) New York.

☆☆ E. & J. Gallo Winery CARLO ROSSI VIN ROSE ($2.30) California.

☆☆☆ 1985 Mirassou Vineyards PETITE ROSE ($4.00) California.

☆☆ 1986 Robert Mondavi Winery ZINFANDEL ROSE ($5.00) California.

## RED
### Non Varietal

☆☆ Almaden Vineyards MONTEREY BURGUNDY ($2.50) Monterey.

☆☆ 1982 Almaden Vineyards CALIFORNIA PREMIUM RED ($7.00) California.

☆☆ 1983 Boeger Winery HANGTOWN RED ($4.00) California.

☆☆☆ 1985 Bonny Doon Vineyard GRAHM CREW VIN ROUGE ($6.50) California.

☆☆ Calera Wine Company ROUGE DE ROUGE ($4.00) California.

☆☆ 1985 Chaddsford Winery COUNTRY ROUGE ($4.50) Pennsylvania.

☆☆ 1983 Clos du Bois Winery VIN ROUGE ($4.50) Alexander Valley.

☆☆ Delicato Vineyards BURGUNDY ($2.40) Northern California.

☆☆ Frick Winery CAFE RED ($4.00) California.

☆☆ E. & J. Gallo Winery HEARTY BURGUNDY ($1.75) California.

☆☆☆ Glen Ellen Winery PROPRIETOR'S RESERVE RED ($3.00) California.

☆☆☆ Golden Creek Vineyard CABERLOT ($4.50) Sonoma.

☆☆☆ Gundlach-Bundschu Winery SONOMA RED WINE ($3.50) Sonoma Valley.

☆☆☆ Heitz Wine Cellars RYAN'S RED ($5.75) Napa Valley.

☆☆☆ Hop Kiln Winery BIG RED ($6.50) Russian River Valley.

☆☆ Hopkins Vineyard SACHEM'S PICNIC RED ($5.00) American.

☆☆☆ 1982 Inglenook Napa Valley NAPA VALLEY RED ($4.00) Napa Valley.

☆☆ 1983 Kenwood Vineyards VINTAGE TABLE RED ($4.50) California.

☆☆ 1981 Louis M. Martini BARBERA ($4.50) California.

☆☆ 1984 Robert Mondavi Winery ROBERT MONDAVI RED ($5.00) California.

☆☆ 1985 Robert Mondavi Winery ROBERT MONDAVI RED ($3.75) California.

☆☆ 1982 The Monterey Vineyards CLASSIC RED ($4.25) California.

☆☆ 1983 The Monterey Vineyards CLASSIC RED ($4.00) Monterey.

☆☆☆ Navarro Vineyards and Winery CABERNET SAUVIG-NON TABLE WINE ($7.00) Mendocino.

☆☆☆ 1984 Olson Vineyards Winery VIKING RED ($6.00) Mendocino.

☆☆ 1984 Pat Paulsen Vineyards AMERICAN GOTHIC RED ($6.50) Sonoma.

☆☆☆☆ 1985 Preston Vineyards SIRAH SYRAH ($9.50) Estate, Dry Creek Valley.

☆☆ 1983 Raymond Vineyard & Cellar VINTAGE SELECT RED ($5.00) California.

☆☆ 1986 Charles F. Shaw Vineyard GAMAY NOUVEAU ($5.50) Napa Valley.

☆☆☆ 1986 Charles F. Shaw Vineyard NAPA GAMAY ($6.00) Napa Valley.

☆☆☆ Sotoyome Winery BURGUNDY ($2.75) Sonoma.

☆☆ Rodney Strong Vineyards WINDSOR VINEYARDS BURGUNDY ($3.75) California.

☆☆☆      Topolos at Russian River RESERVE RED ($4.50) Sonoma.

☆☆☆      Trefethen Vineyards Winery ESCHOL RED ($5.25) Blend 184, Napa Valley.

☆☆☆  1985 Trentadue Winery OLD PATCH RED ($4.75) Alexander Valley.

☆☆      Waterbrook Winery WATERBROOK RED ($5.00) Washington.

## Cabernet Sauvignon

☆☆☆  1985 Alba Vineyard ($8.00) New Jersey.

☆☆☆  1981 Almaden Vineyards ($4.00) Monterey.

☆☆☆  1981 Almaden Vineyards CHARLES LEFRANC CELLARS ($8.50) Monterey.

☆☆☆  1982 Almaden Vineyards ($5.00) Monterey.

☆☆☆  1979 Baldinelli Vineyards ($7.00) Estate, Amador.

☆☆☆  1981 Bandiera Winery JOHN B. MERRITT ($8.00) Sonoma.

☆☆   1982 Bandiera Winery ($4.00) North Coast.

☆☆☆  1982 Bandiera Winery JOHN B. MERRITT ($6.50) Dry Creek Valley.

☆☆☆  1983 Bandiera Winery ($4.50) North Coast.

☆☆   1981 Beringer Vineyards ($7.00) Napa Valley.

☆☆   1982 Beringer Vineyards NAPA RIDGE ($5.50) North Coast.

☆☆   1983 Castoro Cellars ($6.75) San Luis Obispo.

☆☆      Caymus Vineyards LIBERTY SCHOOL ($6.00) Lot 16, California.

☆☆   1982 Caymus Vineyards LIBERTY SCHOOL ($6.00) Lot 11, Alexander Valley.

☆☆☆  1982 Caymus Vineyards LIBERTY SCHOOL ($6.00) Lot 12, Alexander Valley.

☆☆☆  1984 The Christian Brothers ($7.50) Napa Valley.

☆☆   1982 Christophe Vineyards ($4.50) California.

☆☆☆  1982 Christophe Vineyards ($5.50) Napa Valley.

☆☆☆  1979 Clos du Bois Winery RIVER OAKS VINEYARDS ($5.95) Alexander Valley.

☆☆☆  1981 Clos du Bois Winery RIVER OAKS VINEYARDS ($6.25) Healdsburg, Sonoma.

☆☆☆☆  1981 Clos du Bois Winery ($9.00) Alexander Valley.

☆☆   1984 Clos du Bois Winery RIVER OAKS VINEYARDS ($6.00) North Coast.

☆☆☆  1984 Clos du Val GRAN VAL ($8.50) Napa Valley.

☆☆☆  1982 Colony ($7.00) Sonoma.

☆☆   1983 Corbett Canyon Vineyards ($7.00) Central Coast.

☆☆☆  1984 Corbett Canyon Vineyards ($8.00) Select, Central Coast.

☆☆☆  1982 Cosentino Wine Company CRYSTAL VALLEY CELLARS ($8.00) North Coast.

☆☆   1980 Devlin Wine Cellars ($6.00) Sonoma.

☆☆   1981 Domaine St. Georges CAMBIASO VINEYARDS ($4.75) Dry Creek Valley.

☆☆☆  1981 J. Patrick Doré ($4.25) Signature Selections, Napa Valley.

☆☆   1982 J. Patrick Doré ($4.00) Signature Selections, Sonoma.

☆    1982 Fetzer Vineyards ($5.50) Lake.

☆☆   1983 Fetzer Vineyards ($5.50) Lake.

☆☆☆  1984 Fetzer Vineyards ($6.50) Lake.

☆☆☆  1985 Fetzer Vineyards ($6.50) California.

☆☆   1983 Fitch Mountain Cellars ($5.00) Mendocino.

☆☆☆  1984 Five Palms Winery ($6.00) Napa Valley.

☆☆   1985 Five Palms Winery ($6.00) Napa Valley.

☆☆   1980 Louis Foppiano Wine Company ($6.50) Sonoma.

☆☆☆  1981 Louis Foppiano Wine Company ($7.75) Russian River Valley.

☆☆ 1983 Louis Foppiano Wine Company RIVERSIDE FARM ($4.00) North Coast.

☆☆☆ 1984 Louis Foppiano Wine Company ($8.00) Sonoma.

☆☆☆ 1980 Franciscan Vineyards ($7.50) Alexander Valley.

☆☆☆ 1983 Franciscan Vineyards ESTANCIA ($6.00) Alexander Valley.

☆☆☆ 1981 Fritz Cellars ($7.00) North Coast.

☆☆ 1980 E. & J. Gallo Winery ($4.50) Limited Release, California.

☆☆☆ 1983 Geyser Peak Winery ($7.00) Sonoma.

☆☆ 1982 Glen Ellen Winery ($4.00) Proprietor's Reserve, Sonoma.

☆☆ 1986 Golden Creek Vineyard ($6.00) California.

☆☆ 1983 Grand Cru Vineyards ($4.50) Vin Maison, California.

☆☆☆ 1980 Guenoc Winery ($8.00) 70% Lake, 30% Napa.

☆☆☆ 1981 Guenoc Winery ($8.00) Lake.

☆☆ 1978 Guild Wineries CRESTA BLANCA ($5.00) Mendocino.

☆☆ 1978 Inglenook Napa Valley ($6.00) Napa Valley.

☆☆☆ 1979 Inglenook Napa Valley ($7.00) Centennial, Napa.

☆☆☆ 1983 Inglenook Napa Valley ($5.00) Cabinet Selection, Napa Valley.

☆☆☆ 1984 Kendall-Jackson Vineyards & Winery ($7.50) Lake.

☆☆ 1982 Kenworthy Vineyards ($6.00) Stonebarn, El Dorado.

☆☆ 1983 Konocti Winery ($5.75) Lake.

☆☆☆ 1984 J. Lohr Winery ($5.00) California.

☆☆☆ 1984 M. Marion & Company ($4.50) Napa Valley, Sonoma Valley.

☆☆ 1984 Mariposa Wines ($7.00) Napa.

☆☆ 1982 Louis M. Martini ($7.00) North Coast.

☆☆☆ 1983 Paul Masson Vineyards ($6.25) Sonoma.

☆☆☆ 1983 Mill Creek Vineyards FELTA SPRINGS ($5.00) Sonoma.

☆☆☆ 1983 Monteviña Wines ($7.50) Shenandoah Valley, California.

☆☆☆ 1983 Mount Palomar Winery ($7.50) Napa Valley.

☆☆☆ 1983 The R. H. Phillips Vineyards ($6.00) California.

☆☆ 1982 Raymond Vineyard & Cellar LA BELLE ($6.00) California.

☆☆ 1983 Raymond Vineyard & Cellar LA BELLE ($5.00) California.

☆☆☆☆ 1983 St. Andrews Winery ($7.50) Glendale Ranch, Napa Valley.

☆☆ 1983 San Antonio Winery MADDALENA ($5.00) Sonoma.

☆☆ 1984 San Martín Winery CRYSTAL CREEK ($4.00) Santa Barbara.

☆☆ 1985 Sebastiani Vineyards VENDANGE ($4.00) Reserve, California.

☆☆ 1982 Stag's Leap Wine Cellars HAWK CREST ($6.00) North Coast.

☆☆ 1984 Stag's Leap Wine Cellars HAWK CREST ($7.00) North Coast.

☆☆ 1984 Taft Street Winery ($1.75) Napa.

☆☆ 1984 Ivan Tamas ($6.00) Mendocino.

☆☆☆☆ 1982 Tyland Vineyards MENDOCINO ESTATE ($4.25) Estate, Mendocino.

☆☆ 1978 Weibel Vineyards ($7.00) Mendocino.

☆☆ Whitehall Lane Winery ($6.00) Napa Valley.

### Chancellor
☆☆☆ 1983 Plane's Cayuga Vineyard ($5.00) Finger Lakes.

### Charbono
☆☆☆ 1981 Inglenook Napa Valley ($7.00) Napa Valley.

### Gamay
☆☆☆ 1986 J. Lohr Winery ($4.50) Monterey Gamay, Greenfield, Monterey.

## Gamay Beaujolais
☆☆ 1985 Robert Pecota Winery ($5.00) Napa Valley.

## Landot Noir
☆☆☆☆ 1982 Baldwin Vineyards ($6.00) New York.

## Merlot
☆☆☆ 1984 Château Souverain ($8.00) Sonoma.
☆☆☆ 1981 Clos du Bois Winery ($8.50) Alexander Valley.
☆☆ 1981 Crescini Wines ($6.50) Napa Valley.
☆☆☆ 1981 Franciscan Vineyards ($8.50) Napa Valley.
☆☆☆ 1982 Geyser Peak Winery ($5.50) Trione Family, Alexander Valley.
☆☆ 1982 Haviland Vinyards ($6.00) Manor Reserve, Washington.
☆☆☆ 1983 Round Hill Cellars ($7.50) Napa Valley.
☆☆☆ 1983 Stratford ($8.50) California.

## Petite Sirah
☆☆ 1983 Bogle Vineyards ($5.00) Clarksburg.
☆☆ 1982 Fetzer Vineyards ($5.50) Mendocino.
☆☆ 1979 Louis Foppiano Wine Company ($5.50) Sonoma.
☆☆☆ 1981 Inglenook Napa Valley ($6.00) Napa Valley.
☆☆☆ 1982 Inglenook Napa Valley ($5.50) Napa Valley.
☆☆ 1982 Louis M. Martini ($5.00) Napa Valley.
☆☆ 1983 Louis M. Martini ($5.00) Napa Valley.

## Pinot Noir
☆☆ 1982 Almaden Vineyards ($5.00) San Benito.
☆☆ 1980 Burgess Cellars ($6.00) Napa Valley.
☆☆☆ 1981 Caymus Vineyards ($7.50) Estate, Napa Valley.
☆☆ 1980 Clos du Bois Winery ($6.50) Alexander Valley.
☆☆☆ 1979 Felton Empire Vineyards ($7.50) Maritime Series, Reserve, Chaparral, San Luis Obispo.
☆☆ 1981 Felton Empire Vineyards ($7.50) Fort Ross, Sonoma.
☆☆☆ 1979 Fritz Cellars ($6.50) Sonoma.
☆☆ 1980 Inglenook Napa Valley ($6.00) Napa Valley.
☆☆ 1984 Jaeger Family Wine Company HUNTER ASHBY ($7.00) Napa Valley.
☆☆☆ 1983 Knudsen-Erath Winery ($12.50) Vintage Select, Yamhill.
☆☆☆ 1978 Louis M. Martini ($8.00) Special Selection, California.
☆☆ 1982 Louis M. Martini ($6.00) Napa Valley.
☆☆ 1983 Louis M. Martini ($5.85) Napa Valley.
☆☆☆ 1983 McHenry Vineyard ($14.50) Estate, Santa Cruz Mountains.
☆☆ 1981 Mill Creek Vineyards ($7.00) Dry Creek Valley, Sonoma.
☆☆☆ 1985 Parducci Wine Cellars ($5.50) Mendocino.
☆☆☆ 1984 Saintsbury Winery ($8.00) Garnet, Carneros.
☆☆☆ 1986 Saintsbury Winery ($8.00) Garnet, Santa Barbara.
☆☆ Sebastiani Vineyards AUGUST SEBASTIANI ($5.75) Country, California.

## Red Table Wine
☆☆ 1986 Chaddsford Winery ($5.00) Pennsylvania.
☆☆☆ 1984 J. W. Morris Wineries ($3.00) California.
☆☆ 1984 Orleans Hill Vinicultural Corporation ($4.00) California.

## Zinfandel
☆☆ Almaden Vineyards ($2.50) California.
☆☆☆ 1980 Bandiera Winery ($4.25) North Coast.
☆☆ 1982 Buehler Vineyards ($6.00) Estate, Napa Valley.
☆☆☆ 1983 Buehler Vineyards ($6.00) Napa Valley.
☆☆ 1981 Buena Vista Winery ($6.00) Sonoma.
☆☆☆ 1979 Carmel Bay Winery ($5.00) Shandon Valley, San Luis Obispo.
☆☆☆ 1982 Caymus Vineyards ($7.50) Napa Valley.
☆☆ 1982 Colony ($5.00) Sonoma.

☆☆☆ 1983 Colony ($2.50) Sonoma Valley.
☆☆☆ 1981 Deer Park Winery ($6.50) Napa Valley.
☆☆ 1985 Delicato Vineyards ($5.30) California.
☆☆ 1983 J. Patrick Doré ($4.00) Signature Selection, Mendocino.
☆☆☆ 1979 Fetzer Vineyards ($7.50) Lolonis, Mendocino.
☆☆ 1982 Fetzer Vineyards ($5.50) Mendocino.
☆☆ 1983 Fetzer Vineyards ($4.50) Lake.
☆☆ 1984 Fetzer Vineyards ($5.00) Lake.
☆☆☆☆ 1985 Fetzer Vineyards ($5.00) Lake.
☆☆ 1986 Fetzer Vineyards ($5.00) Lake.
☆☆ 1984 Fitch Mountain Cellars ($5.00) 76% Sonoma, 24% Napa Valley.
☆☆ 1982 Louis Foppiano Wine Company RIVERSIDE FARM ($4.00) Sonoma.
☆☆☆ 1981 Frog's Leap Winery ($6.50) Spottswoode, Napa Valley.
☆☆☆ 1982 Glen Ellen Winery BENZIGER FAMILY WINERY & VINEYARDS ($4.50) Geyserville, Sonoma.
☆☆☆ 1981 Green and Red Vineyards ($5.75) Estate, Napa Valley.
☆☆☆ 1978 Grgich Hills Cellar ($9.00) Alexander Valley.
☆☆☆ 1983 Guenoc Winery ($5.00) Lake.
☆☆☆ 1984 Guenoc Winery ($5.00) Guenoc Valley.
☆ 1980 Guild Wineries CRESTA BLANCA ($4.00) Mendocino.
☆☆☆ 1983 Herbert Vineyards ($5.75) El Dorado.
☆☆☆      Marietta Cellars ($5.00) Old Vine Red, Lot Number 4, Sonoma.
☆☆☆ 1984 Louis M. Martini ($5.85) Napa.
☆☆ 1984 Paul Masson Vineyards ($3.35) California.
☆☆☆ 1981 Monteviña Wines ($6.50) Estate, Shenandoah Valley, California.
☆☆ 1983 Monteviña Wines ($5.00) Montino, Estate, Shenandoah Valley.
☆☆      Nevada City Winery SIERRA MOUNTAIN ($3.75) Nevada County.
☆☆ 1983 J. Pedroncelli Winery ($4.50) Sonoma.
☆☆ 1984 Joseph Phelps Vineyards ($5.75) Napa Valley.
☆☆ 1985 Joseph Phelps Vineyards ($6.00) Napa Valley.
☆☆☆ 1982 Round Hill Cellars ($5.00) Napa Valley.
☆☆ 1986 Santa Barbara Winery ($5.50) Nouveau, Santa Ynez Valley.
☆☆ 1987 Santa Barbara Winery ($6.00) Beaujour, Santa Ynez Valley.
☆☆☆ 1982 Sausal Winery ($5.60) Alexander Valley.
☆☆      Sebastiani Vineyards AUGUST SEBASTIANI ($5.75) California.
☆☆ 1982 Sebastiani Vineyards ($5.00) Sonoma Valley.
☆☆ 1983 Seghesio Winery ($4.00) Sonoma.
☆☆☆ 1984 Winterbrook Vineyards ($5.50) Amador.


## FLAVORED
### Non Varietal

☆☆      California Cooler CALIFORNIA COOLER CITRUS ($0.75) California.
☆☆      California Cooler CALIFORNIA COOLER ORANGE ($0.75) California.
☆☆      Canandaigua Wine Company SUN COUNTRY COOLER ORANGE ($0.75) American.
☆☆      Canandaigua Wine Company SUN COUNTRY COOLER TROPICAL FRUIT ($0.75) American.
☆☆      E. & J. Gallo Winery TYROLIA ($1.50) California.

# Tasting Notes

# Tasting Notes

# Tasting Notes

# Tasting Notes

# Tasting Notes

# Tasting Notes

# Tasting Notes

# Tasting Notes